THE STUDENT EDITION OF

MINITAB® Release 8

Statistical software...*adapted for education*

Limited Warranty

Addison-Wesley warrants that The Student Edition of Minitab ("the program") will substantially conform to the published specifications and to the documentation during the period of 90 days from the date of original purchase, provided that it is used on the computer hardware and with the operating system for which it was designed. Addison-Wesley also warrants that the magnetic media on which the program is distributed and the documentation are free from defects in materials and workmanship during the period of 90 days from the date of original purchase. Addison-Wesley will replace defective media or documentation or correct substantial program errors at no charge, provided you return the item with dated proof of purchase to Addison-Wesley within 90 days of the date of original purchase. If Addison-Wesley is unable to replace defective media or documentation or correct substantial program errors, your license fee will be refunded. These are your sole remedies for any breach of warranty.

Except as specifically provided above, Addison-Wesley makes no warranty or representation, either express or implied, with respect to this program, documentation, or media, including their quality, performance, merchantability, or fitness for a particular purpose.

Because programs are inherently complex and may not be completely free of errors, you are advised to verify your work. **In no event will Addison-Wesley or Minitab be liable for direct, indirect, special, incidental, or consequential damages arising out of the use of or inability to use the program, documentation, or media,** even if advised of the possibility of such damages. Specifically, neither Addison-Wesley nor Minitab is responsible for any costs including, but not limited to, those incurred as a result of lost profits or revenue (in any case, the program must be used only for educational purposes, as required by your license), loss of use of the computer program, loss of data, the costs of recovering such programs or data, the cost of any substitute program, claims by third parties, or for other similar costs. In no case shall the liability of Addison-Wesley or Minitab exceed the amount of the license fee.

The warranty and remedies set forth above are exclusive and in lieu of all others, oral or written, express or implied. No Addison-Wesley dealer, distributor, agent, or employee is authorized to make any modification or addition to this warranty.

Some states do not allow the exclusion of implied warranties; if any implied warranties are found to exist, they are hereby limited in duration to the 90-day life of the express warranties given above. Some states do not allow the exclusion or limitation of incidental or consequential damages, nor any limitation on how long implied warranties last, so these limitations may not apply to you. This warranty gives you specific legal rights and you may also have other rights which vary from state to state.

To obtain performance of this warranty, return the item with dated proof of purchase within 90 days of the purchase date to: Addison-Wesley Publishing Company, Inc., Educational Software Division, Jacob Way, Reading, MA 01867.

THE STUDENT EDITION OF
MINITAB® Release 8
Statistical software...*adapted for education*

Robert L. Schaefer Miami University at Oxford
Elizabeth Farber Bucks County Community College

Addison-Wesley Publishing Company, Inc.
Benjamin/Cummings Publishing Company, Inc.

Reading, Massachusetts · Redwood City, California · New York
Don Mills, Ontario · Wokingham, England · Amsterdam · Bonn
Sydney · Singapore · Tokyo · Madrid · San Juan · Milan · Paris

The Student Edition of MINITAB is published by Addison-Wesley Publishing Company, Inc. and Benjamin/Cummings Publishing Company, Inc. Contributors included:

Betsy Burr, Sponsoring Editor
Kristen Duerr, Project Coordinator
Barbara Clemens, Project Manager
Joan Carey, Developmental Editor
Mary Coffey, Production Manager
Nancy Benjamin, Production Supervisor
Susan Marsh, Text Designer
Linda Enrico, Cover and Package Designer
Joeth Barlas, Copy Editor
Patricia Gordon, Manufacturing Media Supervisor
TSI Graphics, Inc., Compositor

Photo and Minitab at Work credits appear on p. 604, which constitutes an extension of the copyright page.

Reprinted July, 1994.
ISBN 0-201-50649-1 (DOS 5 1/4" format)
ISBN 0-201-50650-5 (DOS 3 1/2" format)
ISBN 0-201-82048-X (User's Manual)
Note: This product is also available in Macintosh format.

2 3 4 5 6 7 8 9 10–MU–9897969594

PREFACE

Welcome to The Student Edition of Minitab.

Minitab is a powerful tool originally developed at The Pennsylvania State University as a teaching aid for introductory statistics courses. Minitab is one of the most widely accepted statistical analysis packages for college instruction, and is currently used at over 2,000 schools. Minitab has also proven itself as an established research tool and is installed on mainframe, mini-, and microcomputers at over 3,000 sites in 51 countries worldwide, and is used by three-quarters of the companies listed in *Fortune* magazine's listing of the top 50 companies. Except for a few features, The Student Edition of Minitab is an identical version of this program and is designed to provide students with a tool for describing, analyzing, and displaying data.

The Student Edition of Minitab includes the following:

- a menu-driven interface providing easy access to all Minitab's statistical, graphical, and data management capabilities
- a data window permitting data entry, editing, and browsing in a spreadsheet-like display
- an on-screen help window that displays information on Minitab menus, commands, and options
- the ability to import and export data
- Lotus® 1-2-3® compatibility

- statistical process control charts
- similar interface, commands, and output across Macintosh and DOS platforms

Objectives

The Student Edition of Minitab is designed to introduce students to a powerful statistical analysis program they can use to analyze and describe data. The primary objectives of the package are:

- to provide a complete educational environment for learning Minitab
- to provide students with a powerful and versatile tool that will enhance their learning experience
- to teach students the basics of Minitab in the context of case studies and data from business, life sciences, engineering, and the social sciences
- to provide teachers with a flexible means of integrating technology into their classrooms

What's in This Edition?

The Student Edition of Minitab for the IBM features the same functionality as the previous IBM PC Student Edition, with the following new or enhanced features.

Software

- larger worksheets that allow up to 3,500 data points and up to 100 columns
- new menu-driven interface with menus, dialog boxes, and improved access to help information
- the Minitab command language is still available
- the ability to scroll and to copy and paste in the Session window
- data editor that allows data entry and editing in a spreadsheet format
- high-resolution graphics for histograms, boxplots, scatter plots, multiple scatter plots, and control charts

- titles, footnotes, axis labels on both low- and high-resolution plots
- multiple comparison procedures including Tukey, Fisher, Dunnet, and MCB with one-way analysis of variance
- SORT of multiple columns with BY and DESCENDING
- alpha data up to 80 characters long supported in COPY, DELETE, INFO, READ, INSERT, SORT, STACK, UNSTACK, and WRITE
- various additional commands, i.e., INDICATOR, YESNO, SAMPLE, MTSPLOT, COVARIANCE, CENTER, ONEWAY, ANOVA
- eleven statistical process control charts, including XBARCHART, RCHART, PCHART, and ICHART

Manual

- new tutorials, including a tutorial on statistical process control charts, and an expanded tutorial on macros
- completely new examples, case studies, and exercises
- new data sets throughout with an emphasis on real-world data
- "Minitab at Work" boxes that show how Minitab is used in organizations throughout the United States
- Exploring Data section that describes all data sets, including five larger data sets with suggestions for analysis

Organization of This Manual

The manual is organized into four sections. Part I, Getting Started, begins by detailing the contents of the Student Edition package. Chapter 1 includes a concise explanation of the conventions used throughout the manual, an introduction to the fundamentals of DOS, and information regarding technical support. Chapters 2 and 3 include complete, easy-to-follow instructions for installing, starting, and exiting Minitab. Chapter 4 consists of a comprehensive sample session, designed to give students an overview of the program and to interest them in its capabilities.

Part II, Tutorials, is the heart of the manual. It contains fourteen interactive tutorials that teach students how to use Minitab by working with case studies from business, engineering, life sciences, and the social sciences.

Each tutorial begins with a list of objectives, and includes case studies that introduce students to Minitab commands. As students perform steps in the tutorial, screen views are shown in the manual to keep students on track and illustrate Minitab concepts and features. Each tutorial requires approximately 45 minutes to complete (not including practice problems).

Each tutorial ends with a summary and review section that includes a list of menu items that were introduced in or related to that tutorial. A set of practice problems follows, using the data sets from the tutorials as well as introducing new data sets. In selected tutorials, a "Minitab at Work" section illustrates how Minitab is used in organizations throughout the United States.

For those students unfamiliar with Minitab, the first four tutorials, dealing with data entry, manipulation, description, and summary, should be completed in order. The remaining tutorials can be completed in any sequence; however, the student should note that some tutorials are based on case studies introduced in earlier tutorials. The experienced Minitab user could proceed with any tutorial.

Part III, Exploring Data, contains descriptions of all the data sets used in the tutorials and practice problems. It also includes additional data sets, as well as larger data sets with suggestions for analysis.

Part IV, Reference, describes all of Minitab's features. It contains comprehensive descriptions of the Minitab commands, menus, functions, and Minitab basics. It also contains a discussion of selected Minitab topics, such as file types, importing and exporting data, and working with menus, dialog boxes, and the keyboard. In addition, it features chapters on more advanced topics: the data editor, the Minitab command language, and macros. Menu commands are cross-referenced to their corresponding Session window commands and the tutorials.

The Differences Between the Student Edition and the Standard Version

The Student Edition is completely compatible with the commercial program but has the following limitations:

- the worksheet is limited to 3,500 data points and 100 columns
- matrix functions are not included
- selected commands have not been included (see Appendix E for a complete listing)

Acknowledgments

The completion of this revision of The Student Edition of Minitab took over seven months and demanded a diverse team. At this time, we could not possibly list the complete team, since we had limited, if any, interaction with most of its members. Long before we wrote our first sentence, there were those who outlined what this manual would look like. Long after we wrote our last word, others took over to edit, produce, distribute, and market the final product. Everyone on the team, and their contributions, was crucial to the success of the revision. In particular, we would like to recognize those individuals with whom we worked on a regular basis.

Betsy Burr was instrumental in getting this project started. From her preliminary contact meeting to recruiting the final team, her organizational skill is attested to by the fact that this manuscript was completed well within schedule and incorporates her vision of what The Student Edition of Minitab would be. Many of the innovative features of this edition are due to her.

On a day-to-day basis we operated most closely and most frequently with Barbara Clemens and Kristen Duerr. The ambitious schedule, which seemed impossible at times, was easily met through their efforts. To successfully coordinate activities spanning three seasons of the year, four states, two time zones, and three word processing systems on two different computer platforms demanded extraordinary patience, a never-ending sense of humor, and exceptional managerial skills. We could not have done it without both of them.

Joan Carey's developmental editing improved the manuscript with each reading. Her merger of the new user interface and the Minitab command language in the reference section was a stroke of genius. To do all of this so professionally and competently and on schedule, while caring for twin one-year-olds, still amazes us.

Our thanks to the staff and programmers of Minitab, Inc., especially to Mike McCormick, Gwen Stimely, Bob Graf, Denny Huber, and Emil Hrivnak, who provided us with their technical expertise and created the software for this package.

Alan Jacobs provided valuable, and much appreciated, insight and solutions to particularly annoying problems.

Finally, we are grateful to the many reviewers who took time to find many of the typos, misspellings, and non sequiturs that somehow find their way into every manuscript. Your questions, comments, and suggestions have significantly improved this manual.

We would also like to thank the many reviewers and class testers whose diligent reading and thoughtful comments strengthened this work immeasurably.

Reviewers

William Hannum, Syracuse University, New York
Richard S. Lehman, Franklin and Marshall, Pennsylvania
Don Myers, University of Arizona, Arizona
Alex Olsen, University of Lowell, Massachusetts
Calvin Williams, Clemson University, South Carolina

Class Testers

University of Lowell, Massachusetts
Coordinator: Alex Olsen
Student Testers: Joyce Elder, David Hedison, Joseph Misserville, Lyn Ann Misserville, Danielle White

Clemson University, South Carolina
Coordinator: Calvin Williams
Student Testers: Juliette Atkins, Wendy Cullen, Christopher Custodio, Amy Dickerson, Raymond Griffith

Robert L. Schaefer
Elizabeth Farber

CONTENTS

Part I
Getting Started

Part II
Tutorials

Part III
Exploring Data

Part IV
Reference

To my wife Alayne and my dad —R.L.S.

To my husband Richard and sons Douglas and Michael —E.F.

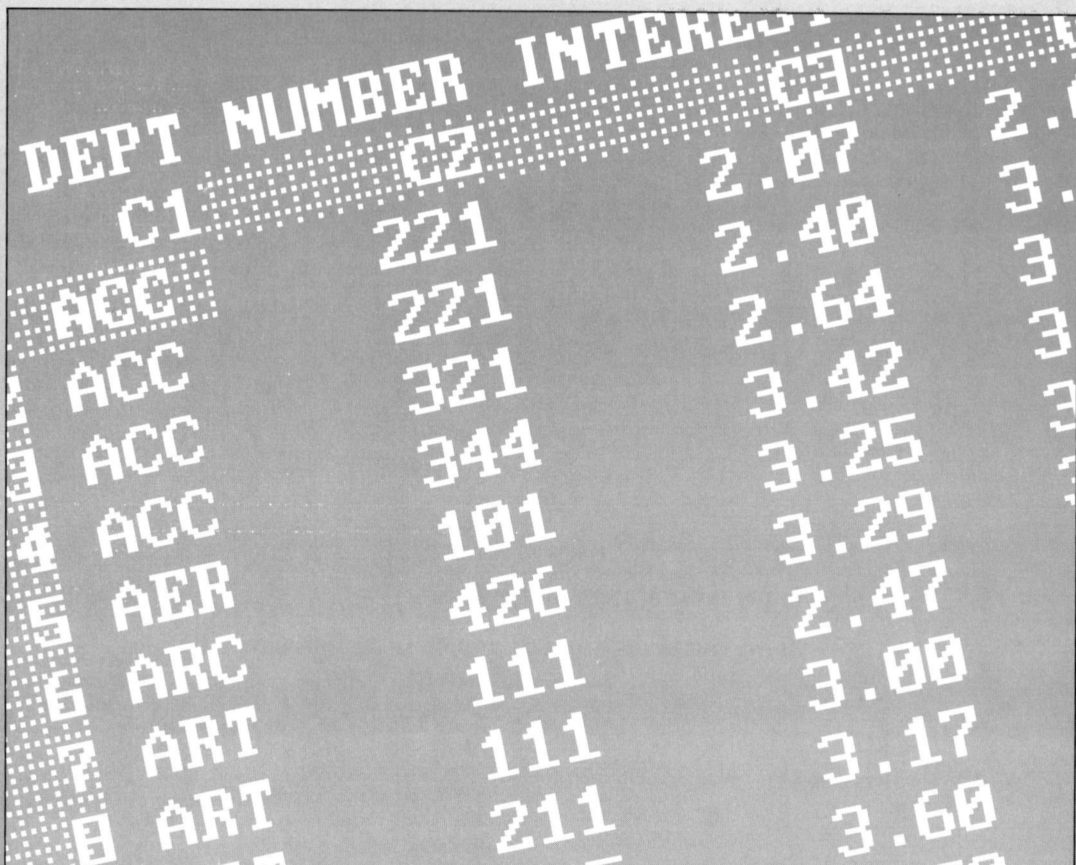
DEPT NUMBER INTEREST
C1 C2 C3
ACC 221 2.07
ACC 221 2.40
ACC 321 2.64
ACC 344 3.42
ACC 101 3.25
AER 426 3.29
ARC 111 2.47
ART 111 3.00
ART 211 3.17
ART 485 3.60
ART 155 2.50
ATH 212 2.92
ATH 111 1.44
CHM 141 2.17
CHM 142 1.38
CHM 193

PART I

Getting Started

CHAPTER 1

Before You Begin

Checking Your Package

The Student Edition of Minitab contains the following items:

- The User's Manual for *The Student Edition of Minitab* (this book).
- A Warranty Registration Card. Fill out this card and mail it back to Addison-Wesley Publishing Company right away. This registers you as a licensee of the package, and it makes you eligible to receive all further product information.
- A set of program disks, six if you are using 5¼″ disks, or three if you are using 3½″ disks.

3½″ disks:	or	5¼″ disks:
MINITAB 1/2		MINITAB 1
MINITAB 3/4		MINITAB 2
MINITAB 5/6		MINITAB 3
		MINITAB 4
		MINITAB 5
		MINITAB 6

  These disks contain the Minitab program.

- The Sample Files disk, containing all the sample files you will need to complete the tutorials and exercises in this book.
- A Quick Reference Card. This card summarizes all the menu and session commands in *The Student Edition of Minitab*. This will be

most useful after you have completed the tutorials and want to work on your own. Instead of looking back through the tutorials to find a command, you can consult the Quick Reference Card.

What's in This Book?

Part I, Getting Started, contains four chapters. Chapter 1 familiarizes you with Minitab and the basics of using DOS, and explains the typographical conventions used in this book.

Note: In this manual the term "Minitab" refers only to the version of the software you received in *The Student Edition of Minitab* package.

Chapter 2 shows you how to install the Minitab software. Chapter 3 describes how to start and stop Minitab and explains some of its basic features. Chapter 4 guides you through an actual Minitab session so you can sample Minitab's capabilities before you begin the tutorials.

Part II, Tutorials, is the heart of this book. Beginning with the simplest features of Minitab, the fourteen tutorials introduce the major features of the software in a step-by-step, hands-on format. The exercises and practice problems at the end of each tutorial reinforce the concepts you've learned. Most of the tutorials and the practice problems use many of the data sets on the Sample Files disk. The contents of the sample files are explained in Part III, Exploring Data. Because each tutorial builds on the preceding one, it is best that you go through them in order.

Part III, Exploring Data, contains descriptions of all the data sets in this package. They are intended for use by students who have completed the tutorials and have an understanding of most Minitab features. The topics of these data sets cover a variety of fields, including economics, education, linguistics, and marketing. The descriptions include a summary of each data set and questions to help direct data exploration for the larger data sets. The data sets are on the Sample Files disk.

Part IV, Reference, describes all Minitab menu commands and gives you more information on special topics. As you work through the tutorials and exercises, use the Reference section to look up commands by menu. The Reference section also contains chapters on the Minitab command language and Minitab macros. It will be especially helpful after you have completed the tutorials and begin to use Minitab to analyze your own data.

Required Computer System

You will need the following computer equipment to run Minitab:

- An IBM or compatible microcomputer with the Intel 80286 processor or higher (that is, at least an IBM PC/AT-type computer); 8086 and 8088 models are not recommended
- DOS version 3.0 or later
- A hard disk drive with at least 3.2 megabytes (3.2Mb) of available hard disk storage and one floppy disk drive
- For high-resolution graphics, you need an additional 600Kb of hard disk space and a graphics board
- At least 1 megabyte (1Mb) of random access memory (RAM), including at least 465Kb of available conventional memory and 150Kb of available extended or expanded memory
- For optimum performance, a math coprocessor is strongly recommended

Minitab runs as a non-Windows™ application under Windows 3.0. It also runs on networks. For additional information on optimizing performance, see Appendix B, Additional Installation and System Notes. This appendix explains other advanced features, including options for starting Minitab, and tips on running Minitab under Windows version 3.0.

Typographical Conventions

A number of typographical conventions and symbols are used throughout this manual to make the material easier to use.

Any action that you take appears on a line by itself, indented and preceded by this symbol: ■. For example:

- Choose Edit **L**ast Command Dialog from the **E**dit menu

Bold type indicates letters, numbers, or symbols you type from the keyboard; bold type is also used to represent letters that are highlighted or colored on the screen (depending on your monitor type), usually indicating letters you can use with Alt as a keyboard shortcut for a command. New terms and concepts appear in italic type.

Choose means to make a menu selection using either the keyboard or the mouse. Specific mouse techniques are described in Chapter 3 (see the section Using the Mouse).

Type means to type a key or keys as shown in the order they appear. It is important to type them in sequence exactly as they are shown, including any punctuation or spaces.

Press means to strike or press a key (for instance, Tab or ↵). It can also mean to push down the mouse button. The Alt key is always used with another key. You press and hold down Alt and then press another key, much as you use the Shift key with another key. Alt key combinations are used as shortcuts. For example, the instruction Alt-**C** means that you hold down Alt and, while still holding it down, press the C key.

Keyboard shortcuts appear throughout this manual in a tinted box for easy reference. Cautions are preceded by the symbol.

Mouse instructions appear in shaded boxes at selected locations in the margin throughout the text. If you are using a mouse with your computer, you may use these instructions instead of the comparable keyboard instructions. Once mouse instructions have been given for a particular dialog box, however, they will not be repeated in that tutorial.

In later tutorials, as you become more familiar with Minitab, instructions are shortened using the symbol ▶. For example, the instructions to pull down the Stat menu, choose Basic Statistics, and then choose Descriptive Statistics will be shortened to:

- Choose **S**tat ▶ **B**asic Statistics ▶ **D**escriptive Statistics

Technical Support

Neither Addison-Wesley Publishing Company, Inc. nor Minitab, Inc. provides telephone assistance to users of *The Student Edition of Minitab*. However, registered instructors who have adopted this product for their students do receive telephone support, so you should report any software problems to your professor. Be sure to note what you were doing when the problem occurred, as well as the exact error message.

Instructors can register by completing the Warranty Registration Card included with the package.

If you would like to receive newsletters and product announcements from Minitab, Inc., write a note requesting to be put on the Minitab mailing list, and include your name, address, and telephone number. Mail it to Minitab, Inc., 3081 Enterprise Drive, State College, PA 16801-3008.

Using DOS

DOS is an acronym for disk operating system. A comp
system is a program that controls the operation of cor
and data; it enables programs to communicate with input and output
devices such as keyboards, monitors, and printers.

DOS designates a computer's disk drives, whether they are floppy disk drives or hard disks, with successive letters (A, B, C, and so on). The first floppy disk drive that lights up after you turn on the computer is the "A" drive. If you have a second floppy drive, it is called the "B" drive; the hard drive is usually called the "C" drive.

When you turn on your computer, the first screen you see depends on what version of DOS you are running and whether you have a menu program. You will need to access the DOS *command prompt,* usually seen as C:\>. The DOS command prompt is broken into two parts. The first, "C:", indicates the active drive. The second part of the DOS prompt identifies the active *directory.* A directory is like a file folder in which you store information. For example, the DOS prompt you will see later, "C:\MINITAB>", indicates that drive C is active and that you are in the MINITAB directory of the disk in that drive. The command prompt "C:\>", shown in Figure GS-1, indicates that you are in the home or "root" directory on the hard drive C.

FIGURE GS-1
The DOS prompt

```
Microsoft(R) MS-DOS(R) Version 5.00
             (C)Copyright Microsoft Corp 1981-1991.

C:\>
```

Note: Your version of DOS may be different from that shown in these figures.

DOS uses this prompt to ask you for input; when the prompt appears, you type commands after it.

Formatting Disks

The Student Edition of Minitab includes disks that contain the Minitab program and sample files. You will need to make a backup copy of the Sample Files disk. (You may use the original program disks for installing Minitab, but you will use the Sample Files disk whenever the tutorials ask you to open a sample file; furthermore, you may want to save your modified sample files on the Sample Files disk as disk space permits. Since you will be working regularly with the Sample Files disk, you should use your backup copy instead of the original. Put the original disk away in a safe place and keep the backup copy for everyday use.

You will need either 3½″ or 5¼″ blank disks, depending on the size of your disk drive. If you purchase disks to use as backups, you will need to *format* them before you can copy anything onto them. When you format a disk, you are setting it up so that DOS can store and read information on it. Make sure you know the name of the drive you will use (usually "A" or "B"). To format a new disk using DOS:

- Make sure the DOS prompt (C:\> or just C>) appears on your screen; this indicates that you are operating DOS from the hard drive

If you aren't sure how to do this, see your instructor or the user's manual for your computer.

To tell DOS to format a disk inserted in the A drive (you may use upper- or lowercase letters when typing commands into DOS):

- Type **FORMAT A:**

Whenever you designate a drive, you must insert a colon (:) after it. The screen should resemble Figure GS-2.

FIGURE GS-2
The DOS FORMAT command

```
Microsoft(R) MS-DOS(R) Version 5.00
             (C)Copyright Microsoft Corp 1981-1991.

C:\>FORMAT A:
```

- Press [↵]

The message that appears depends on the version of DOS you have. In any case, you will be told to insert the disk to format.

- Make sure the disk you want to format is not write-protected (make sure the tab in the disk's corner is closed or, if you are using 5¼″ disks, make sure there is no *write-protect tab* sticker that wraps around the notch on the right edge of the disk)

- Insert the disk into drive A:
- Press [↵]

The computer formats the disk (if DOS asks for a name, you don't need to enter one; just press [↵]). When the disk is formatted, DOS reports that the format is complete and asks if you want to format another.

- Type **N** for No and press [↵]
- Remove the formatted disk from the disk drive

The disk is now ready to receive information.

Copying the Sample Files Disk

To make a copy of your Sample Files disk:

- Before you begin, make sure the original Sample Files disk is write-protected so you cannot accidentally alter or erase any information on it. If necessary, attach a write-protect tab or open the write-protect window on the original disk. Also check that the disk you will use for the backup copy is *not* write-protected.
- Insert the original Sample Files disk in the A drive

If the A:> prompt is not on the screen, make the A drive current:

- Type **A:** and press [↵]

To copy the contents of the original Sample Files disk to the backup disk:

- If you have two disk drives, insert the formatted, blank disk in drive B
- Type **XCOPY A:*.* B: /S** and press [↵]

The asterisks tell DOS to copy every file on the disk in drive A to the disk in drive B and to use the same names for the disk files and the disk itself.

The lights next to the drive doors go on and DOS lists the files it is copying.

Then, when the copying is finished:

- Remove the backup disk from the drive.
- Label it "Backup Sample Files." If you are using 5¼" disks, use a felt-tip pen to write on the label.

Note: You can also use the DISKCOPY program to make a backup copy.

Once you have a backup copy of the Minitab Sample Files disk, you should put the original Minitab disk in a safe place and use the backup copy for your work.

Checking Disk Space

You will be ready to install Minitab once you have checked whether your hard disk has sufficient space. You need at least 3.2Mb (equivalent to 3,200,000 bytes) of available memory to install Minitab. To check your hard disk for space:

- Go to the DOS prompt (C:\>)
- Type **DIR**
- Press [↵]

This command displays a variety of information, including a report on the amount of available space on the hard disk. Figure GS-3 shows a typical DIR report.

FIGURE GS-3
The DIR report

```
C:\PRINTER>dir

 Volume in drive C is C_DRIVE
 Volume Serial Number is 4339-17D2
 Directory of C:\PRINTER

.            <DIR>      09-28-91   4:24p
..           <DIR>      09-28-91   4:24p
FEEDBACK DOC        1115 07-17-88   2:35p
GIFDOT   EXE       81851 01-08-89   1:42a
GIFDOT13 DOC       24746 01-06-89   7:09p
GIFDOT13 ZIP       88192 06-19-90  11:17p
README   1ST        1334 01-05-89   1:17a
REGISTER DOC        1748 01-04-89  11:32p
TEST     GIF        6873 12-11-88   4:49a
VGACAP   COM        1208 09-23-88   2:34a
VGAFIX   ASM        2702 07-15-88   1:35a
VGAFIX   COM         269 07-15-88   1:36a
VGAFIX   DOC        5331 07-17-88   2:31p
       13 file(s)     215369 bytes
                    23367680 bytes free
```

The amount of free space on this hard disk, about 23 Megabytes (23 Mb)

If you do not have 3.2Mb of available space, you can remove unnecessary files to free up disk space.

CAUTION: If you are on a network and need additional disk space in the volume or disk you are working with, consult your teacher or lab instructor before removing any files that aren't yours.

You are now ready to install Minitab.

CHAPTER 2

Installing Minitab

To use *The Student Edition of Minitab* software, you must first install it on your hard disk and then follow the steps to set up drivers and extended memory.

Note: Network Administrators should consult Appendix B, Additional Installation and System Notes, for details on running Minitab in a network environment.

Before Installation

Before installing Minitab on your hard disk, you should:

- Refer to the section entitled Checking Your Package in Chapter 1 for a list of the disks in your Minitab package.
- If your computer is on a network, check with your instructor or lab manager before installing Minitab.
- Make sure you have the current version of DOS (3.0 or later) and that your system and hardware meet the requirements listed in the previous chapter.

CAUTION: Because the Minitab disks contain compressed files, you must use the Install program to install files to your hard disk. You will not be able to use these files if you copy them directly from the original disks to your hard disk.

Installing Minitab

The Minitab Install program automatically installs Minitab into a directory named MINITAB on your hard disk.

Note: If you have an older version of Minitab in a directory with that name, erase all Minitab files before you install. Alternatively, you can install the new version in a new directory.

To install *The Student Edition of Minitab*:

- Make sure your Minitab disks are *not* write-protected. For 3½″ disks, the small window in the upper right corner of the disk should be closed; for 5¼″ disks, make sure the notch on the right edge of the disk is visible
- If necessary, turn on the computer
- Go to the DOS prompt (C:\>)

Note: If your computer is on a network, your DOS prompt may display a letter other than C:.

If you are running DOS from a shell or menu program, and you don't know how to reach the DOS prompt, ask your instructor for the command you need.

- Insert the first Minitab disk (MINITAB 1 if you have 5¼″ disks or MINITAB 1/2 if you have 3½″ disks) in your computer's floppy drive (referred to in this section as drive A; substitute the appropriate letter if you are using a different drive)
- Type **A:** after the C:\> prompt to make drive A the default and press [↵]
- Type **INSTALL** and press [↵] to begin installation
- Personalize your Minitab program by entering your name and school, following the instructions on the screen; personalization occurs only the first time you install Minitab
- Continue until you see the INSTALL main menu on the screen
- Press [↵] to choose the first option, Install the Student Edition of MINITAB Release 8 onto Hard Disk

- Follow the directions on the screen until Minitab is installed

The installation takes about 20 minutes.

The Minitab directory includes the file READ.ME, a text (ASCII) file that lists features new to Release 8, known problems, and workarounds. The text file PACKING.LST lists the names of all files distributed with *The Student Edition of Minitab Release 8.* After installation, you may want to use the DOS command PRINT to print the file READ.ME for your reference.

Setting Up Drivers

After installing Minitab, you need to set up the program so it can produce high-resolution graphics on your particular monitor and print on your printer. If you have just completed the installation, the MSETUP menu is already on your screen, and you can skip to the third bulleted instruction below. If the MSETUP menu is not on your screen, and you want to modify your drivers, you need to open the MINITAB directory. If the prompt is not C:\MINITAB, at the DOS prompt:

- Type **CD \MINITAB** (CD stands for "change directory")

From this directory, you can run the *MSETUP program,* a program that allows you to set up or configure Minitab for your computer, monitor, and printer. To set up Minitab according to your hardware capabilities, run the MSETUP program after the MINITAB> prompt:

- Type **MSETUP**

The MSETUP main menu appears.

- Make sure the first option, Select Screen Driver for Hi-Res Graphics, is highlighted (if it is not, press [↑] or [↓] until it is)
- Press [↵] to see the list of available drivers
- Use the arrow keys to select the correct screen driver for your computer's graphics board, and then press [↵] (if you are not sure what driver your computer uses, check the computer manual or check with your professor or lab instructor)

The MSETUP main menu reappears.

- Press [↓] to highlight Select Printer Driver for High-Res Graphics

- Press [↵]
- When you see the list of available printer drivers, use the directional arrow keys to highlight the printer you will use
- Press [↵]

If you want to erase unselected driver files from your hard disk to free hard disk space:

- Choose Delete Unnecessary Graphics Drivers from the MSETUP main menu and press [↵]
- Press [↓] to select Delete drivers NOT named above, and press [↵]

If you need any of those files later, you can install them from your original Minitab disks.

- Press [Esc] to exit from the MSETUP menu

Setting Up Extended Memory

There are three types of memory used by personal computers. Typically, computers run programs in what is called "conventional memory." The two other kinds of memory are "extended memory" or "expanded memory." Your computer should have 465Kb of conventional memory to run Minitab. Minitab also requires that your computer have 150Kb of either extended or expanded memory:

Your computer *must* be set up properly to use this extended memory. Otherwise, Minitab will be slow and mouse operations will not always work correctly.

To make sure your computer is set up properly for extended memory, you will need to go to the root directory and display a file called CONFIG.SYS, which should already be on your system.

Make sure you are already at the root directory, usually C:. If not,

- Type **C:** and press [↵]
- Type **CD** and press [↵]
- Type **TYPE CONFIG.SYS** press [↵]

The contents of your CONFIG.SYS file should appear on the screen. You will need to determine if the file uses any extended memory managers. Look for a line in the file such as DEVICE = HIMEM.SYS or DEVICE = QEMM386.SYS.

There are other memory manager device drivers. If you are unsure whether your CONFIG.SYS file contains such a device driver, check with your instructor.

If your CONFIG.SYS file does not contain a memory manager device driver, you will need to add one that specifies HIMEM.SYS as the device driver:

- Use a text editor or a word processor (such as WordPerfect) to add the following line to the beginning of your CONFIG.SYS file:

  DEVICE = C:\MINITAB\HIMEM.SYS

Note: If you are not familiar with text editors or have never modified a CONFIG.SYS file, see your instructor or lab assistant for help.

If your Minitab directory is not C:\MINITAB, substitute your Minitab directory in the line you type. Minitab installation includes the file HIMEM.SYS.

- Be sure to save the saved CONFIG.SYS file in a text (ASCII) file format
- Reboot your computer, so your changes will take effect

Note: The file PACKING.LST in the Minitab directory lists which version of HIMEM.SYS was supplied with your copy of Minitab. If you have a more current version of HIMEM.SYS, use that newer version instead.

For more information on Minitab's performance and memory usage, see Appendix B, Additional Installation and System Notes.

You are now ready to begin working with the program. Chapter 3 shows you how to open and close Minitab, and Chapter 4 takes you through a sample session. If you've never used Minitab before, you should go through these chapters before beginning the tutorials.

CHAPTER 3

Starting and Stopping Minitab

If you have not installed *The Student Edition of Minitab* Release 8 on your computer's hard disk, you should do so now. Refer to the previous chapter for instructions.

Starting Minitab

To start *The Student Edition of Minitab* Release 8:

- If it is not already turned on, turn on your computer
- Go to the DOS prompt (C:\>) (see your instructor or check your computer manual if you are not sure how)

Note: If the Minitab directory is not on your path, you may need to type **CD \MINITAB** before you type **MINITAB** to start the program.

- Type **MINITAB** at the DOS prompt
- Press [↵]

After a moment, the Minitab startup screen appears. You may press [↵] to continue or wait a few seconds until the screen disappears.

Minitab's *Session window* then appears. It displays the main menu bar and the Minitab prompt, MTB > (Figure GS-4).

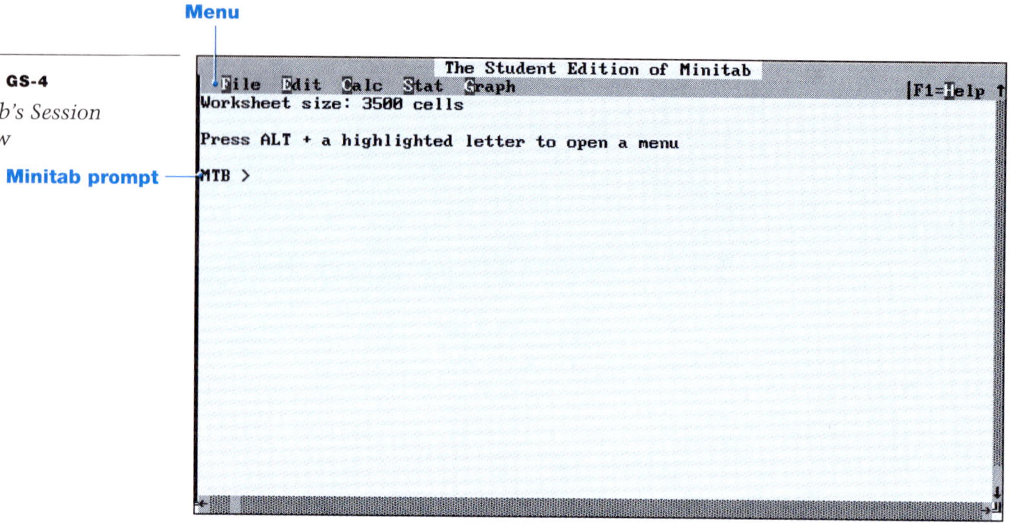

FIGURE GS-4
Minitab's Session window

Windows and Screens

Minitab has both windows and screens; windows have scroll bars but screens do not. Minitab has two types of windows: the Session window and the Help window. When you start Minitab, it automatically opens the Session window. This is the "home base" from which you issue most Minitab commands and see the results of those commands. The Help window is available whenever you need information on any Minitab function.

Minitab includes two types of screen: the Data screen and graphics screens. You can use the Session window to issue commands, then move to the Data screen to work directly with the data. You can create graphics screens by telling Minitab to produce a high-resolution graph.

The Session Window

The Session window displays a record of Minitab commands and functions, as well as the results or output you have used in a work session. Minitab also displays notes and error messages in the Session window. You look here to see numerical summaries and statistical analyses, as well as some Minitab graphics. You can also type session commands directly into this window. (See Appendix B, Additional System and

Installation Notes, for information on the amount of information the Session window can hold.)

Session Window Menus

Glance back at Figure GS-4. The *menu bar* across the top of the screen lists the Minitab Session window menus. Each menu lists groups of related commands that operate the program.

To view the Stat menu, for example, first move to the menu bar:

- Press [F10]

The word File is now highlighted.

- Press [→] three times to highlight the word Stat
- Press [↵]

You can now see the commands available on the Stat menu. The following paragraphs describe the uses of each pull-down menu. As you read about each menu, use [→] and [←] to look at its commands. Do not select any commands at this time.

Note: Mouse users can refer to the sections later in this chapter for information on using a mouse in Minitab.

File menu. Lets you open and save worksheets. Lets you import and export text, start or stop recording commands into either a data file or a macro. Lets you restart Minitab or quit the program.

Edit menu. Allows you to move to the Data screen. Lets you cut, copy, paste, or clear items on the screen. Allows you to get information on the current worksheet, display worksheet data in the Session window, and place repetitive data into a column. Lets you return to the last command dialog that you edited. Allows you to save preferences for the colors of various elements on the screen.

Calc menu. Allows you to generate random data and work with various probability distributions. Lets you apply various functions to data, create indicator (dummy) variables, center and scale data, and sort and rank columns of data. Allows you to delete rows of data, erase variables, copy columns, code data values, stack and unstack blocks of columns, convert alpha data to numbers and vice versa, and concatenate several alpha columns into one.

Stat menu. Allows you to do basic descriptive statistics, simple, multiple, and stepwise regressions, and multifactor analysis of variance. Lets you display control charts. Lets you check for autocorrelation, fit a Box-Jenkins ARIMA model, do cross-tabulation and a chi-square analysis, and do various nonparametrics tests.

Graph menu. Allows you to display various graphs, including histograms, boxplots, stem-and-leaf plots, scatter plots, time series plots, and pseudo three-dimensional plots.

When you finish looking over the menus, exit from the menu bar:

- Press [Esc]

Choosing Commands: Using the Help Menu

Minitab menus make available the commands and functions of the software. By listing the commands rather than asking you to remember them, the menu makes it easier for you to get your work done.

You also access the Help menu through the Session window. At the far right of the menu bar, you see the note, F1=Help. (The [F1] key is one of ten—or, sometimes, twelve—*function keys* located along the top or the left side of the keyboard.) If you press [F1], the Help menu opens. Try it:

- Press [F1]

Minitab displays a list of all available Help overview topics. If you want to learn more about the Help menu:

- Press [↓] once to highlight Introduction to Minitab...
- Press [↵]

The Help window appears. The window is not large enough to display all the information at once, so you need to scroll to read all of it.

Most documents, and many directories, are larger than the window through which they are viewed. To see the hidden parts of a document or directory, you have to scroll through the window, using the *scroll bars* (Figure GS-5) if you have a mouse, or use PgUp or PgDn.

FIGURE GS-5

The Help window, showing scroll bar

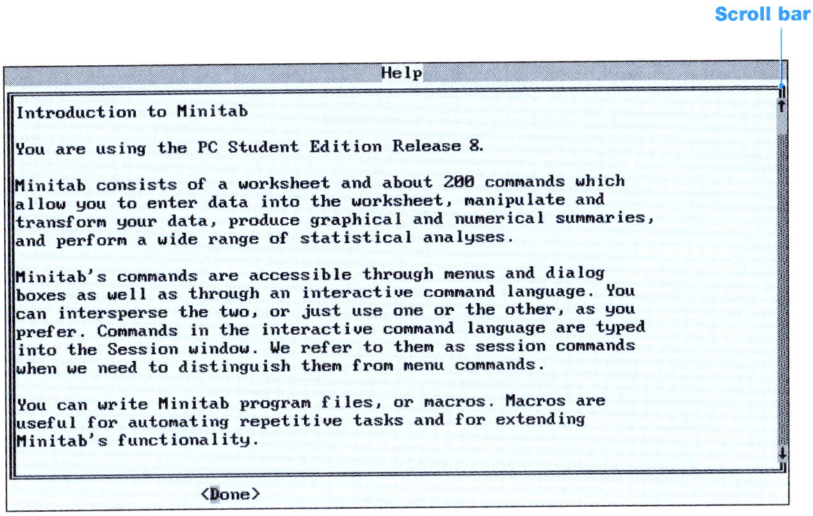

Scroll bars are useful if you have a mouse. Windows can have either a horizontal scroll bar along the bottom of the window, a vertical scroll bar along the right side, or both. Horizontal scroll bars move the contents of a window or document from side to side, and vertical scroll bars move them up and down. The Help window in Figure GS-5 has only a vertical scroll bar.

- Read the information in the Help window
- When you are ready for more, press ↓ to scroll down line by line; the contents of the window scroll past until you release the key or reach the bottom

When you reach the bottom and finish reading the entry:

- Press PgUp

This moves you back to the top of the window.

Key Combinations

Minitab has many keyboard shortcuts that you can use to get around windows and screens. Some of them involve single keys, such as [PgUp], while others involve *key combinations* (that is, holding down one key while pressing another).

Note: In this book, whenever you see two keys joined with a hyphen, this means you are to use these keys in combination, holding down the first key while you press the second key.

You will use a key combination to exit from the Help window. At the bottom of the window you see the word **D**one, with the D highlighted or colored (depending on your monitor type). You can press the D key in combination with [Alt] to tell Minitab you are done with the Help window. To exit:

- Press [Alt]-D for **D**one

Minitab returns you to the Session window.

As you work with Minitab, you will find that the Session window fills up quickly. You will often need to scroll up and down to find the information you need. You can use any of these techniques to move around the Session window.

The Data Screen

The Data screen is the worksheet where you can enter and edit data. To reach it, use the Data Screen command on the Edit menu:

- Press [F10] to highlight the menu bar
- Press [→] once to highlight the word Edit
- Press [↵]

The Data Screen command is the first command on the Edit menu and is automatically highlighted. To execute that command:

- Press [↵]

The screen you see (Figure GS-6) presents a worksheet consisting of vertical columns and horizontal rows. In general, each column contains data for one variable and each row contains the information for one case. This screen provides a convenient way to enter data, name columns, browse through data, and edit individual cells (a cell is the intersection of a row and a column).

FIGURE GS-6
The Data screen

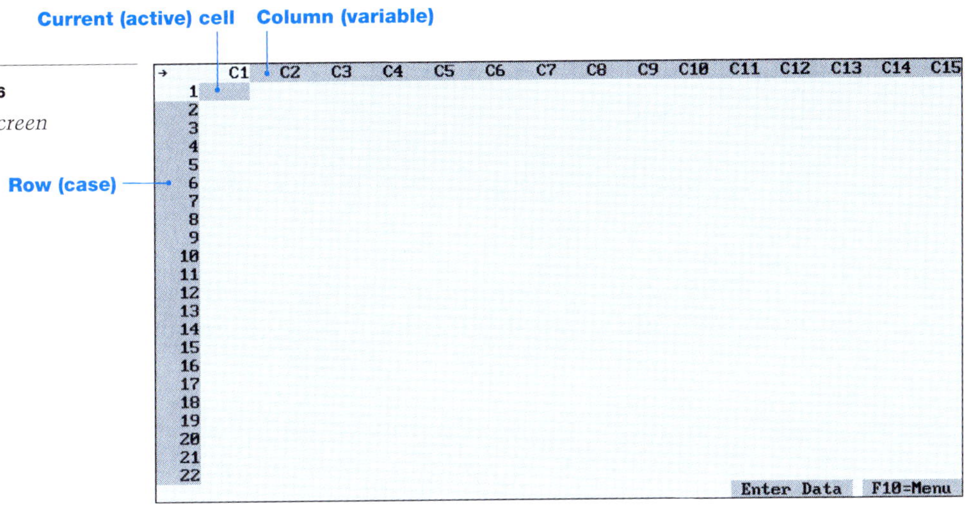

Minitab updates the Data worksheet automatically whenever you make any changes to it. The worksheet has 100 columns and as many rows as available memory will allow (the number of rows times the number of columns must be less than 3500). Columns are referred to by column number (C1, C2, ..., C100) or by name. Currently, the columns (which are also called variables) in this worksheet are unnamed. Rows are referred to by their numerical designations: 1, 2, and so on.

Notice that the cell in column C1, row 1 is highlighted. This is the *current* (or *active*) cell. You can activate any cell in the worksheet by using the arrow keys to move to that cell.

The Data Screen Menu

The Data worksheet screen has its own menu that lists commands commonly used to enter or edit data. To open the Data screen menu:

- Press F10

This menu allows you to get Help, edit within a cell, change entry direction, compress the display, go to any cell or to the active cell, go to the next row or column, insert and delete cells and rows, format a column, name columns, or display the Session window. You'll practice using this menu in the following chapter. To return to the Session window:

- Use [↓] to highlight the last command on the menu, Go to Minitab Session
- Press [↵]

Note: You can also type the highlighted letter of the command—in this case, M.

If you have a mouse, read the following sections. If you don't, skip to the last section in this chapter, Exiting from Minitab.

Using the Mouse

It is becoming more common for computers to be equipped with a mouse; if you have one, you can use it to simplify many procedures in Minitab. Your physical actions in moving the mouse have corresponding results on the screen: if you move the mouse, the *mouse pointer* (small box) moves. (There is a similar cursor blinking after the MTB > prompt.)

For example, with the Session window open, watch the screen as you:

- Move the mouse in a circle on your table; the cursor mirrors your actions on the screen
- Move the mouse up and to the right, until the cursor reaches the upper right corner of the screen (though you move the mouse farther, the cursor doesn't move: it has reached the boundaries of the screen)
- Pick up the mouse, circle it around in the air, and put it down: nothing happens

For the mouse to work, the mechanism on the bottom has to be in contact with a real surface—preferably the table or a mouse pad. If you do not have enough room to move the mouse on your table, or if it runs into something, just lift it, put it back down where there's space, and continue.

Mouse Techniques

To select an object on the screen, place your mouse pointer on that object and click—that is, press and release the mouse button. Try opening the Edit menu using the mouse:

- Move the mouse until the pointer is on top of the word Edit
- Hold the mouse still as you press and release the mouse button

This action is called *clicking*. The Edit menu opens. You can use the mouse to choose the first command and go to the Data screen:

- Move the pointer to the first Edit menu command, Data Screen
- Click anywhere on the line that contains the Data Screen command

The Data screen appears. It is easy to navigate through the Data worksheet using the mouse. To activate the cell corresponding to C2 row 2:

- Move the mouse pointer to C2 row 2 and click

C2 row 2 is now active. To open the Data screen menu:

- Move the mouse pointer to the note at the bottom right of the screen that says F10=Menu and click

The Data screen Help menu opens. In the tutorials, the instruction to click with the mouse will be indicated like this: Click the first line on the menu, Help.

- Click the first line on the menu, About the Data Screen

The Help window describing the Data screen opens. As you read the information it contains:

- Press the down arrow on the vertical scroll bar at the right of the window; hold down the mouse button until the text has scrolled to the end

This technique is called *pressing*. It is similar to holding down [↓] on the keyboard to scroll through the Data screen, as you did earlier. The text of the Help window tells you how to navigate the Data screen. When you finish reading it:

- Click the Done button (a screen *button* is anything within pointed arrows (< >); clicking anywhere within the arrows operates the button)

- Click the F10=Menu box in the lower right corner of the screen
- Click the last option, Go to Minitab Session

Another mouse technique is called *dragging.* When you are back in the Session window:

- Move the mouse to the F1=Help box; press and hold down the mouse button
- Without releasing the button, drag the pointer down the Help menu until the second option, Introduction to Minitab, is highlighted
- When the second option is highlighted, release the mouse button

You have reduced the action of clicking twice to just dragging once; the result is the same, but dragging is faster. Dragging is one of the principal ways to execute an action with a mouse. You'll use this technique often in Minitab to choose items from a menu.

- Read the introductory material, then click Done

You can cancel a menu selection by moving the pointer off the menu *before you release the mouse button,* then releasing the mouse button. Try canceling a menu selection:

- Use the drag technique to highlight the Edit menu's Set Colors selection, but do not release the mouse button
- Drag the pointer off the Edit menu, then release the mouse button

The Edit menu disappears. Because you didn't release the mouse button while the mouse pointer was over the highlighted Set Colors command, it was not chosen.

The Student Edition of Minitab is designed to accommodate both mouse and keyboard users. In the tutorials, directions are for keyboard users. If you are using a mouse, you can refer to the Mouse User boxes that appear in the margins at selected locations throughout the text.

Exiting from Minitab

There are two ways to exit from Minitab if you are using the keyboard:

- Press [F10] and then [↵] to open the File menu

You could use [↓] to highlight the Exit option and then press [↵]. However, the Alt + X following the Exit option on the menu indicates that the command can also be executed using the [Alt]-X key combination. Try it:

- Press [Esc] to close the File menu
- Press [Alt]-X

You have executed the Exit command without using the menu.

- Press [↵] to exit without saving the worksheet

Minitab returns you to the DOS prompt or your computer's menu.

To exit from Minitab if you are using a mouse:

- Drag the mouse cursor to the Exit line on the File menu and release the mouse button. Click for exiting without saving the worksheet. This will stop the Minitab program and return you to DOS.

Chapter 4 takes you through a sample Minitab session, and gives you an opportunity to work with data and graphs.

CHAPTER 4

Sample Session

Objectives

In this sample session you will learn to:

- open and explore an existing worksheet
- create a new variable using basic arithmetic functions that operate on existing variables within a worksheet
- describe the characteristics of a variable using basic statistics
- create two high-resolution graphs based on the data in a worksheet
- correlate two variables in a worksheet

Before beginning this session, make sure that:

- You have installed Minitab on your computer's hard disk. Refer to Chapter 2 of Getting Started for instructions.
- You have a backup copy of *The Student Edition of Minitab* Sample Files disk from your package. This disk contains the PROF.MTW file that you will work with in this session.

Note: Do not use the original Sample Files disk. Use the backup disk you made earlier.

Case Study: Faculty Survey

As president of the student government at your school, you have just received the results of a faculty survey made by the student government. You want to prepare an article for the student government newsletter that describes some high points of the survey results. You decide to use Minitab to do some preliminary analysis. (The sample file contains actual data from a recent survey at a university in the United States.)

Exploring an Existing Worksheet

To open the file that contains the survey data:

- Type **MINITAB** after the DOS prompt (C:\>) and press [↵]

After a moment the Minitab startup screen appears. Press any key or wait 5 seconds for Minitab to continue automatically. When the Session window appears, open the PROF.MTW worksheet:

- Insert your backup Sample Files disk into the A drive
- Press [F10] and then [↵] (since the File menu is highlighted)
- Press [↵] to choose **O**pen Worksheet...

The Open dialog box appears, allowing you to specify the type of worksheet you want to open. Minitab worksheet is the default (preselected) option.

- Press [↵] to open a Minitab worksheet

The Open File dialog box appears. You will open the PROF.MTW file, which is in the GETSTART directory of the A drive.

- Press [Tab] to move to the Files list box
- Use [↓] to highlight the A drive and press [↵]
- Use [↓] to highlight the GETSTART directory
- Press [↵]

- Highlight PROF.MTW and press [↵]

The PROF.MTW worksheet is now open. To see it you need to go to the Data worksheet.

- Press [F10], use [→] to highlight the Edit menu, and press [↵]
- The first option, Data Screen, is highlighted
- Press [↵]

Note: Notice the keyboard shortcut [Alt]-D next to the Data Screen command. From now on you will move to the Data worksheet using that shortcut.

Note: From now on, instructions to select menu commands will be condensed to: Choose **D**ata Screen from the **E**dit menu

The Data worksheet should look like Figure GS-7.

FIGURE GS-7
The PROF.MTW worksheet

	DEPT	NUMBER	INTEREST	MANNER	COURSE	INSTRUCR	RESPONDS	SIZE	YEAR		
→	C1	C2	C3	C4	C5	C6	C7	C8	C9	C10	C11
1	ACC	221	2.07	2.67	2.27	2.73	15	41	2		
2	ACC	221	2.40	3.07	2.75	3.38	15	41	2		
3	ACC	321	2.64	3.36	3.00	3.45	11	31	3		
4	ACC	344	3.42	3.67	3.42	3.67	12	36	3		
5	AER	101	3.25	3.50	3.13	3.13	8	52	1		
6	ARC	426	3.29	3.12	3.35	3.41	15	15	4		
7	ART	111	2.47	1.73	2.33	2.00	15	22	1		
8	ART	111	3.00	3.42	3.08	3.17	12	21	1		
9	ART	211	3.17	2.00	2.67	2.33	6	15	2		
10	ART	485	3.60	3.90	3.50	3.70	10	15	4		
11	ATH	155	2.50	2.64	2.79	3.00	14	49	1		
12	ATH	212	2.92	3.09	2.83	3.17	12	46	2		
13	CHM	111	1.44	2.78	2.00	2.78	9	68	1		
14	CHM	141	2.17	3.42	2.75	3.17	12	114	1		
15	CHM	142	1.38	0.92	1.46	1.46	13	64	1		
16	COM	193	3.71	3.64	3.36	3.64	14	44	1		
17	COM	205	3.83	3.83	3.83	3.83	6	16	2		
18	COM	231	3.13	3.73	3.20	3.67	15	27	2		
19	COM	359	3.30	3.00	3.00	3.20	10	29	3		
20	COM	431	3.00	3.44	2.78	3.33	10	72	4		
21	COM	437	3.11	3.33	3.11	3.44	9	15	4		
22	DSC	205	2.00	2.21	2.07	2.46	14	*	2		

Enter Data F10=Menu

The data in this worksheet are the results of the student government survey.

The student government randomly distributed surveys to 15 students in each of 146 classes in a variety of disciplines. The survey asked students to evaluate the course and its instructor. Each participating class received 15 surveys. Some classes returned all 15 surveys, while others returned fewer. The results for each class were averaged for use in this worksheet (Figure GS-7). There are 9 columns and 146 rows. Each row presents a summary of the information taken from the 1–15 surveys returned from a particular class.

The nine columns present the following information:

Number	**Name**	**Description**
C1	DEPT	The academic department of the course to which the 15 surveys were distributed
C2	NUMBER	The course number
C3	INTEREST	The class average of the surveyed students' responses to the statement: *The course stimulated your interest in this area.* The scale for this statement was 0 = strongly disagree, 1 = disagree, 2 = neutral, 3 = agree, and 4 = strongly agree
C4	MANNER	The class average of the surveyed students' responses to the statement: *The instructor presented course material in an effective manner.* The scale for this statement was 0 = strongly disagree, 1 = disagree, 2 = neutral, 3 = agree, and 4 = strongly agree
C5	COURSE	The class average of the surveyed students' responses to the statement: *Overall, I would rate this course as.* The scale for this statement was 0 = poor, 1 = below average, 2 = average, 3 = above average, and 4 = excellent
C6	INSTRUCR	The class average of the surveyed students' responses to the statement: *Overall, I would rate this instructor as.* The scale for this statement was 0 = poor, 1 = below average, 2 = average, 3 = above average, and 4 = excellent
C7	RESPONDS	The number of completed surveys returned out of the 15 surveys distributed

C8	SIZE	The number of students in the class
C9	YEAR	The level of the course. The number 1 = first year, 2 = sophomore, 3 = junior, and 4 = senior

To return to the Session window:

- Press F10 to see the Data screen menu

Notice that the Go to Minitab Session command has a keyboard equivalent after it, Alt + M. This means that you can use the key combination Alt-M to return you to the Session window

- Press Alt-M to return to the Session window

To see a summary of the contents of the PROF.MTW worksheet:

- Choose Get **W**orksheet Info... from the **E**dit menu

SHORTCUT

You can also use the Alt-E key combination and then press the letter W.

The Get Worksheet Info *dialog box* (Figure GS-8) appears.

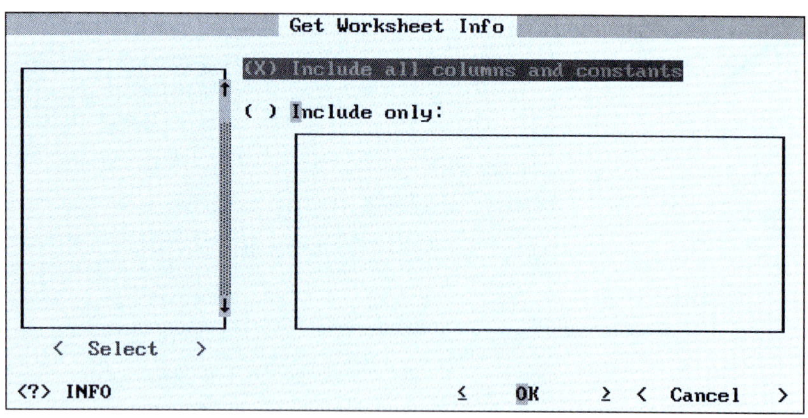

FIGURE GS-8
The Get Worksheet Info dialog box from the Edit menu

A dialog box tells you what information you need to supply to Minitab and asks for your response.

- Press [↵] to get information on all columns and constants

The Get Worksheet Info command summarizes the worksheet contents in the Session window. The display for this worksheet lists the nine variables in the worksheet, the number of cells in each column (146) and the number of missing cells in each column. The 16 in the MISSING column for variable C8 means that the class size for 16 of the courses was unavailable or missing.

Creating a New Variable

In your article about the survey, you want to report the percentage of students within a class that completed surveys. To determine this percentage, you would use the following equation:

$$\text{\% of responses in the class} = \frac{\text{number of responses in the class}}{\text{number of students in the class}} \times 100$$

The numerator in the above fraction corresponds to variable C7 RESPONDS in the worksheet, and the denominator to variable C8 SIZE. You will store the results in C10 PERCENT. Using the variables in the worksheet, the equation becomes:

$$C10 = \frac{C7}{C8} \times 100 \quad \text{(or C7/C8 * 100, in Minitab's language)}$$

To perform these calculations using the menu, use the following keyboard shortcuts:

- Open the **C**alc menu by pressing [Alt]-C; C is highlighted to indicate that it is the operative letter

You can choose Functions and Statistics by pressing the highlighted letter:

- Press F for **F**unctions and Statistics

The Functions and Statistics submenu appears.

- Press G for **G**eneral Expressions

The General Expressions dialog box (Figure GS-9) appears.

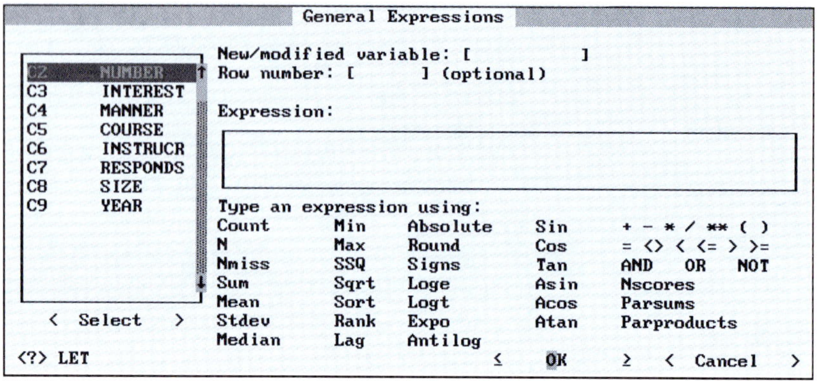

FIGURE GS-9

The General Expressions dialog box from the Calc menu

The cursor is blinking in the text box labeled New/modified variable, indicating it is active; it is here that you tell Minitab where to store the new information.

- Type **C10** in the New/modified variable text box
- Press Tab twice

You will use Tab and the arrow keys to move the cursor around dialog boxes. The cursor moves to the Expression text box. Now you'll type the formula, or expression, that creates the new variable:

- Type **C7/C8*100**
- Press Tab to highlight OK, and press ↵
- Go to the Data worksheet by pressing Alt-D
- Scroll, if necessary, to see C10

Column C10 of the worksheet shows the percentage of students within each class who completed surveys. To add a name to this tenth column:

- Press → to move to C10
- Press ↑ until the name cell above C10 is highlighted
- Type **PERCENT**
- Press ↵

Column C10 in the Data worksheet (Figure GS-10) now has a name to remind you that its contents are the percentage of the class that participated in the survey.

FIGURE GS-10
The Data worksheet with C10 PERCENT

→	NUMBER C2	INTEREST C3	MANNER C4	COURSE C5	INSTRUCR C6	RESPONDS C7	SIZE C8	YEAR C9	PERCENT C10	C11
1	221	2.07	2.67	2.27	2.73	15	41	2	36.585	
2	221	2.40	3.07	2.75	3.38	15	41	2	36.585	
3	321	2.64	3.36	3.00	3.45	11	31	3	35.484	
4	344	3.42	3.67	3.42	3.67	12	36	3	33.333	
5	101	3.25	3.50	3.13	3.13	8	52	1	15.385	
6	426	3.29	3.12	3.35	3.41	15	15	4	100.000	
7	111	2.47	1.73	2.33	2.00	15	22	1	68.182	
8	111	3.00	3.42	3.08	3.17	12	21	1	57.143	
9	211	3.17	2.00	2.67	2.33	6	15	2	40.000	
10	485	3.60	3.90	3.50	3.70	10	15	4	66.667	
11	155	2.50	2.64	2.79	3.00	14	49	1	28.571	
12	212	2.92	3.09	2.83	3.17	12	46	2	26.087	
13	111	1.44	2.78	2.00	2.78	9	68	1	13.235	
14	141	2.17	3.42	2.75	3.17	12	114	1	10.526	
15	142	1.38	0.92	1.46	1.46	13	64	1	20.313	
16	193	3.71	3.64	3.36	3.64	14	44	1	31.818	
17	205	3.83	3.83	3.83	3.83	6	16	2	37.500	
18	231	3.13	3.73	3.20	3.67	15	27	2	55.556	
19	359	3.30	3.00	3.00	3.20	10	29	3	34.483	
20	431	3.00	3.44	2.78	3.33	10	72	4	13.889	
21	437	3.11	3.33	3.11	3.44	9	15	4	60.000	
22	205	2.00	2.21	2.07	2.46	14	*	2	*	

Enter Data   F10=Menu

As you scroll through the data in C10, you see that in some classes as many as 100.00% of the students were surveyed, but in other classes the percentage was as low as 10.526%. Is this the maximum and minimum? What is the average percent surveyed? Can you summarize the results? Continue to investigate the PERCENT variable to learn more about its characteristics.

- Return to the Session window by pressing [Alt]-M

Describing a Variable Using Basic Statistics

To get a bit more detail about the average percentage of the class that filled out questionnaires, you decide to obtain some basic statistics related to the C10 variable you just created.

- Press [Alt]-S for Stat
- Press B for **B**asic Statistics
- Press [↵] (since **D**escriptive Statistics... is already highlighted)

The Descriptive Statistics dialog box (Figure GS-11) appears.

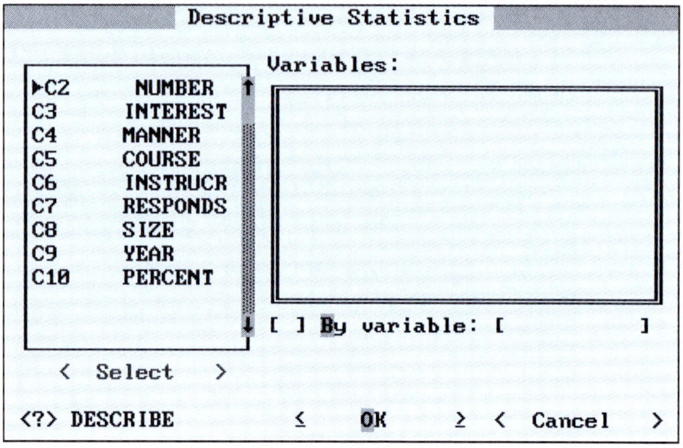

FIGURE GS-11

The Descriptive Statistics dialog box from the Stat menu

- Press [F2] to move the cursor to the list box on the left
- Use [↓] to move the cursor to C10 PERCENT
- Press the Space bar to highlight C10 PERCENT
- Press [F2] again

  The variable name PERCENT now appears in the Variables text box.

- Press [Alt]-O for **O**K

The Session window (Figure GS-12) displays the statistics.

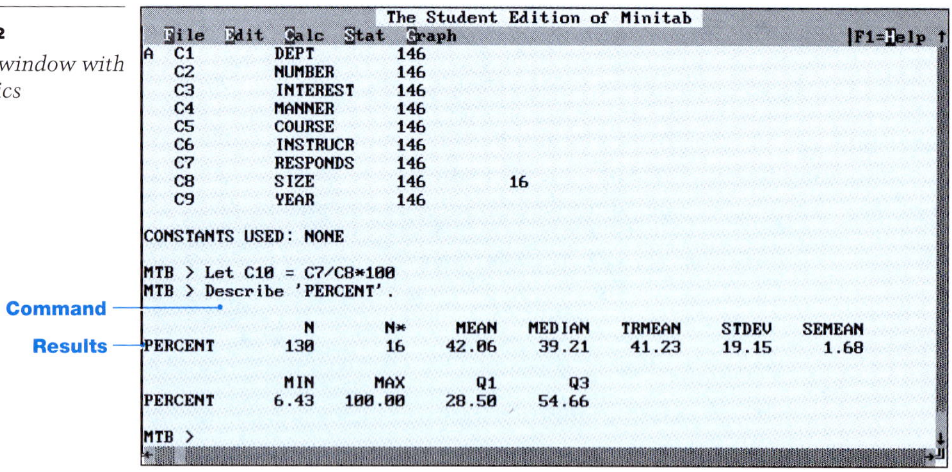

FIGURE GS-12

The Session window with basic statistics

The upper part of Figure GS-12 displays the commands and results of previous menu actions. The lower part contains eleven statistics related to the C10 variable, including the mean, standard deviation, and median.

The output shown in the Session window tells you that an average of approximately 42% (MEAN = 42.06) of the students were surveyed in each class. There was a fair amount of variability (STDEV = 19.15). For example, in some classes only 6.4% (MIN = 6.43) of the class returned the survey, while in others 100% (MAX = 100.00) of the class provided information. You will learn more about these and other statistics in the tutorials.

Creating High-Resolution Graphs

As a senior looking back over your college career, you believe that your classes this year seem much more interesting than they did your first year. You wonder if this is true for other students. To find out, you decide to see if there's any relationship between course level and interest in the class. To do this, you create a boxplot display.

- Choose **B**oxplot... from the **G**raph menu

The Boxplot dialog box (Figure GS-13) appears.

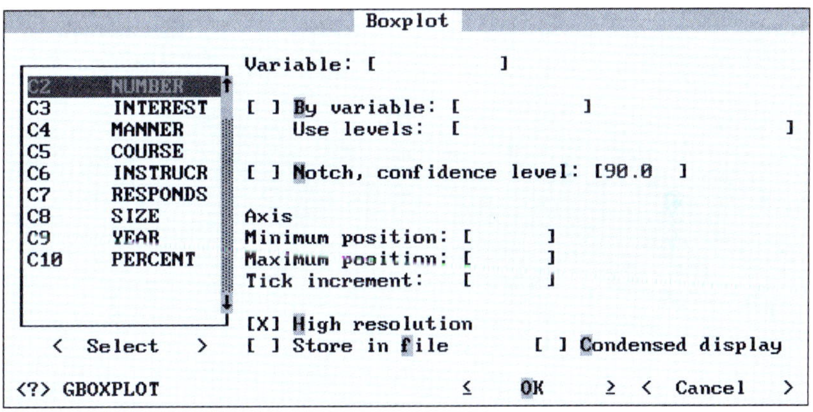

FIGURE GS-13

The Boxplot dialog box from the Graph menu

To activate the list box:

- Press [F2]
- Use [↓] to highlight C3 INTEREST
- Press [F2] again
- Press the Space bar to select (place an X in) the By variable checkbox
- Press [Tab]
- Press [F2], highlight C9 YEAR, and press [F2] again
- Press [↵]

Note: For the remainder of this chapter, the first three commands above will be abbreviated as: Select C3 INTEREST for the Variable text box.

Minitab displays four boxplots (Figure GS-14) that show the trend in students' levels of interest as they progress through college.

FIGURE GS-14

Boxplots showing interest by year

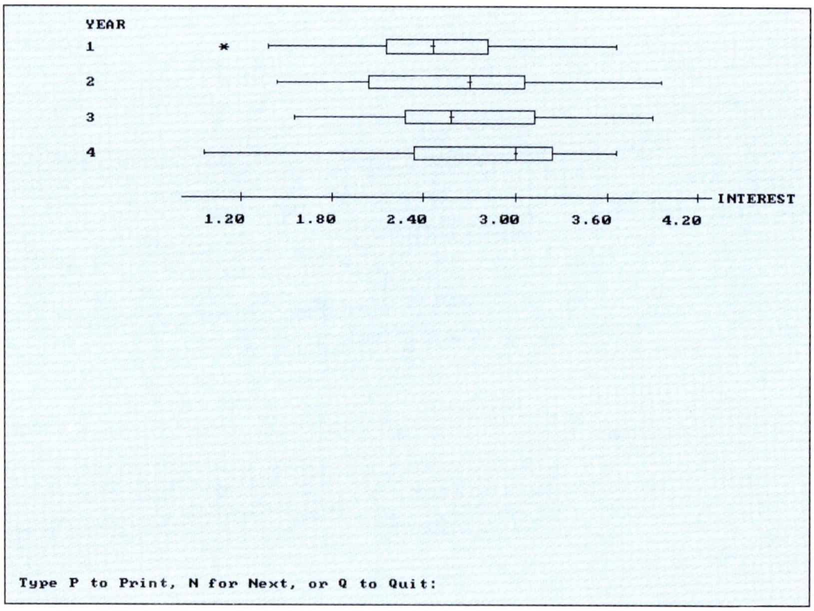

The plus sign (+) in each box represents the median interest level for each rating. This graph appears to show that senior and sophomore classes are more interesting than freshman and junior classes. However, the ends of the "whiskers" that extend from either side of the boxes indicate the largest and smallest values for each year's class interest. Note the large range of interest rating for each year. Because of this large variability in interest, you would not want to claim that seniors are more interested in their classes than are first-year students.

To return to the Session window:

- Press Q for Quit

You also wonder whether students who do not like the subject of a course rate their instructor lower. A scatter plot will show the relationship between course rating and instructor rating.

- Choose Scatter **P**lot... from the **G**raph menu

The Scatter Plot dialog box (Figure GS-15) appears.

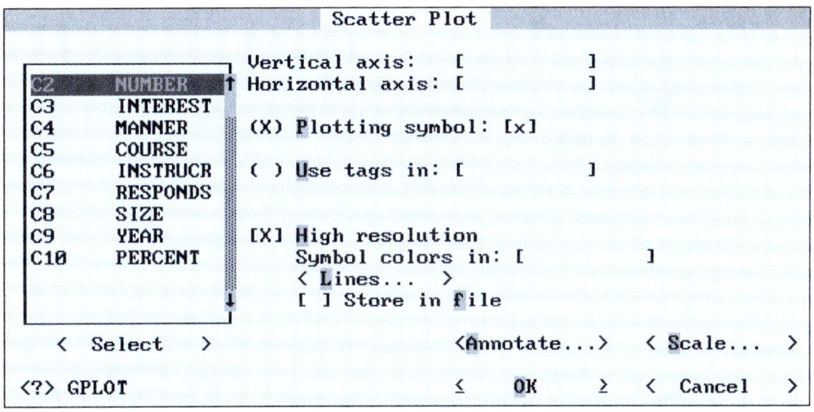

FIGURE GS-15

The Scatter Plot dialog box from the Graph menu

- Select C6 INSTRUCR for the Vertical axis text box
- Select C5 COURSE for the Horizontal axis text box
- Make sure that the box labeled High resolution has an X in it
- Press ↵

Minitab displays a scatter plot (Figure GS-16) that shows the relationship between course ratings and instructor ratings.

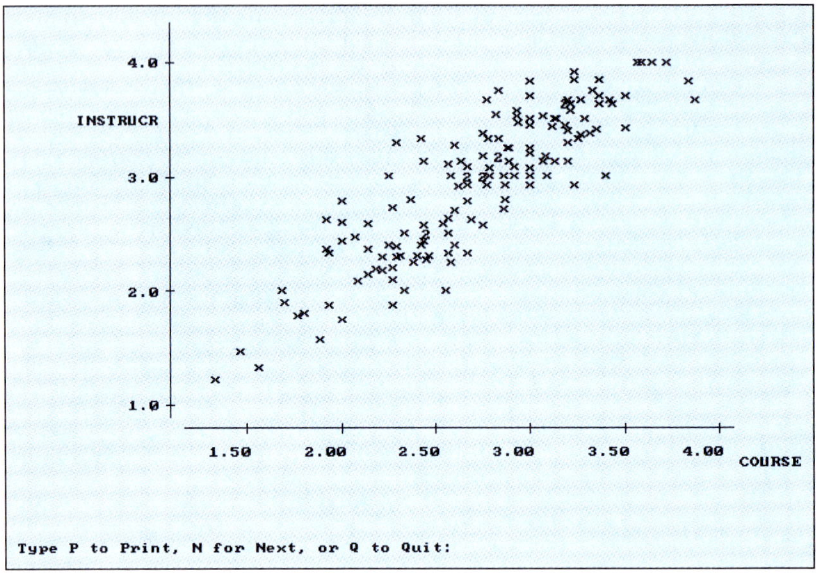

FIGURE GS-16

Scatter plot showing instructor ratings plotted versus course ratings

Your suspicions are confirmed. In general, students rate instructors relatively lower in courses they do not like than in those they do. But note that regardless of course rating, there is quite a bit of variation in professor ratings. Students who rated the course 3.00 (a high rating) rated the instructor anywhere from approximately 2.8 to 3.8. Again, the data are highly variable. You decide to include the scatter plot in your article. To print it onto a piece of paper:

- Make sure your printer is turned on and correctly hooked up to your computer
- Press P for Print
- Press Q for Quit

You now have a copy of the scatter plot that you can insert in your article.

Note: If you are using a shared printer on a network and have difficulty printing, consult your network administrator or lab instructor.

Correlating Two Variables

To verify the apparent relationship between course and instructor ratings, you decide to correlate the course ratings and instructor ratings you used to create the scatter plot.

- Choose **B**asic Statistics and then **C**orrelation... from the **S**tat menu

The Correlation dialog box (Figure GS-17) appears.

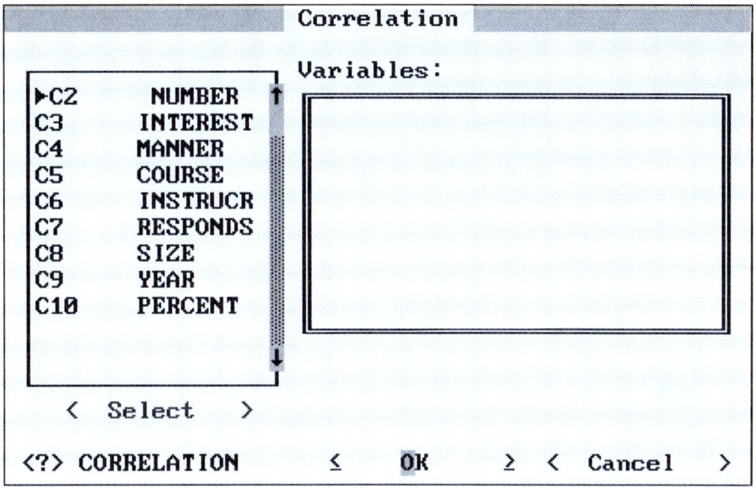

FIGURE GS-17
The Correlation dialog box from the Stat menu

To select C5 COURSE and C6 INSTRUCR:

- Select C5 COURSE and C6 INSTRUCR for the Variables text box
- Press Alt-O

The Session window (Figure GS-18) now displays the correlation between the COURSE variable and the INSTRUCR variable.

FIGURE GS-18

The Session window with correlation results

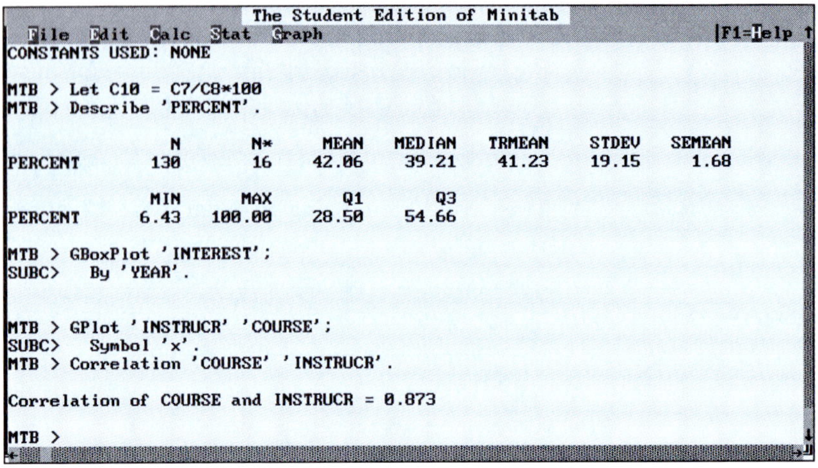

The correlation value of 0.873 indicates that there is indeed a strong positive and linear relationship between course and instructor ratings. This will be an interesting point to make in your article.

Exiting from Minitab

To exit from the Minitab program:

- Choose **Exit** from the **File** menu

A dialog box (Figure GS-19) appears, asking if you want to save the changes made to this worksheet.

FIGURE GS-19

The Exit dialog box from the File menu

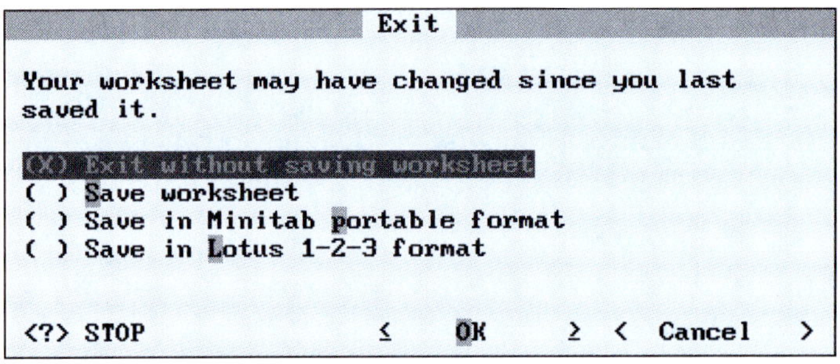

For now, leave the sample file unchanged in case someone else wants to use it.

- Press [↵] to exit from Minitab without saving the worksheet

You have seen some of Minitab's potential. Now proceed to the tutorials, where you'll get hands-on experience using Minitab to create your own worksheets and graphs. The Reference section of this manual (Part IV) documents all of Minitab's capabilities.

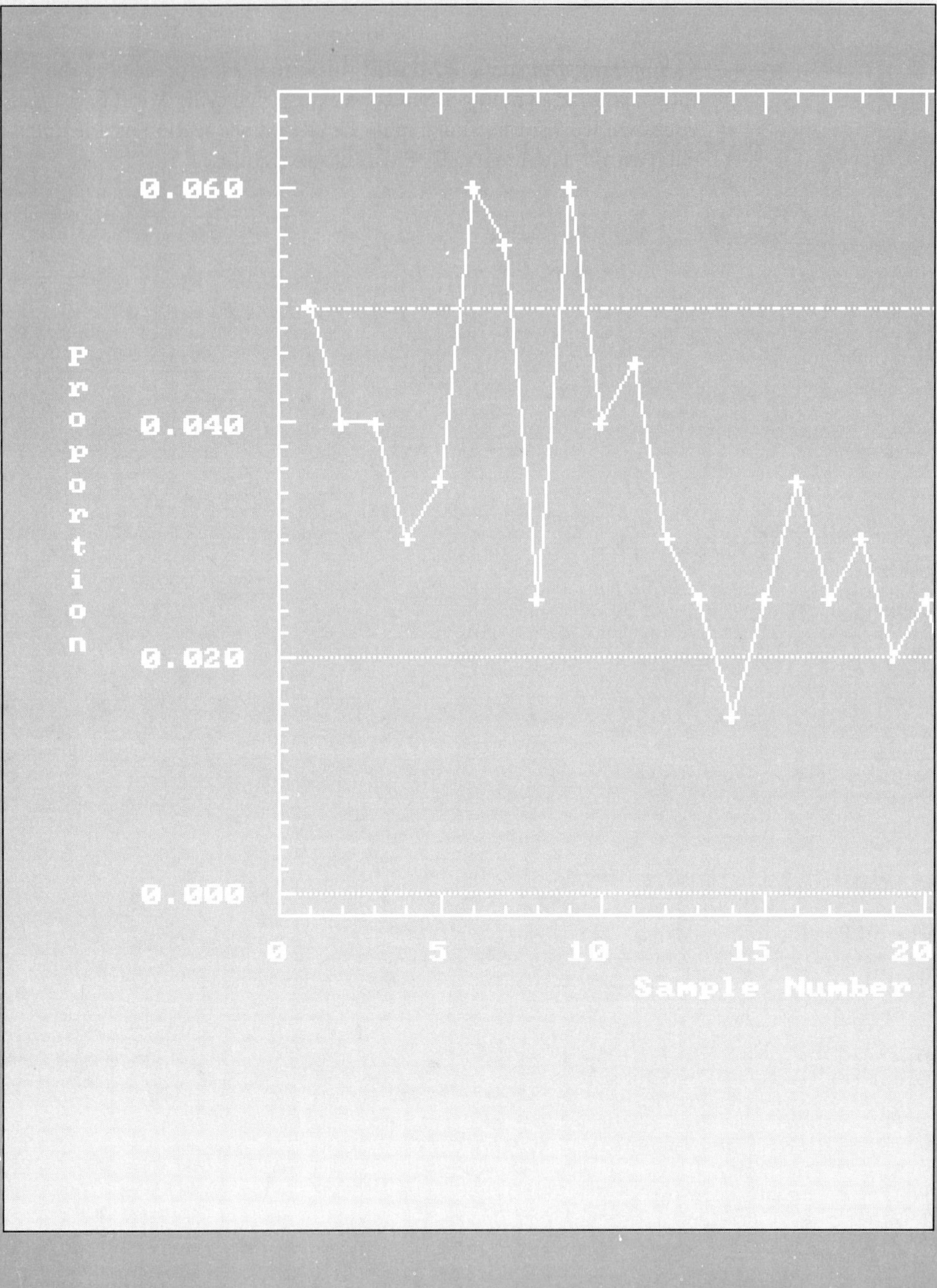

0.060
0.040
0.020
0.000
Proportion
0
5
10
15
20
Sample Number

Part II

Tutorials

TUTORIAL 1

Working with Data

In each of the fourteen tutorials in *The Student Edition of Minitab,* you solve various statistical problems found in diverse fields such as business, psychology, education, health care, and science. In Tutorial 1 you learn the fundamentals of working with Minitab as you are introduced to various ways of collecting and organizing data—the initial step in solving any statistical problem. By participating in three different scenarios you learn how to work with data and navigate about Minitab.

Objectives

In this tutorial you will learn to:

- enter and manipulate data within the Data worksheet
- save and open Minitab data files
- use Minitab's Help function to find on-line information about a topic
- import data created in a word processor
- begin working with data in the Session window

Case Study: Nutrition

You have just been hired as a nutritionist for a major hospital. Your responsibilities include the planning of healthy, economical meals that are also appealing in taste. The first day your supervisor, Patricia Johnson, assigns you the task of planning a pasta meal. She furnishes you with data collected by a research company that tested fifteen different brands of pasta (the only brands that the hospital's food supplier can obtain). The tests evaluated overall sensory quality, cost per serving size (10 oz. cooked pasta for a main serving), and number of calories per serving. In the past there have been many complaints about the hospital's food. By statistically analyzing the various brands, you'll be able to improve the food service while staying within a tight budget.

In this tutorial, you begin the statistical analysis by entering the data "found" in Figure 1-1 into Minitab and computing other factors using cost and calories variables. In later tutorials, when you are more comfortable with the operation of Minitab, you perform more sophisticated analyses that will help you determine which brand of pasta to recommend to Ms. Johnson.

FIGURE 1-1
Pasta study data

Row	Rating	Cost per Serving (cents)	Calories per Serving
1	very good	44	335
2	fair	22	350
3	very good	16	350
4	good	16	355
5	good	18	375
6	fair	22	390
7	excellent	16	340
8	poor	80	445
9	good	25	380
10	very good	20	365
11	good	23	405
12	good	13	335
13	very good	27	355
14	good	47	480
15	good	23	350

Using Minitab Menus

Minitab interacts with the user in two different ways: through the main screen (the Session window) where you do all your statistical analysis, and through another screen (the Data worksheet) specifically provided for easy data entry.

To start Minitab:

- Type **MINITAB** at the DOS prompt and press [↵] (see Chapter 2 of Getting Started if you need to review)

Note: To start Minitab from the DOS prompt, you may need to change to the Minitab directory by typing, for example, **CD \MINITAB** before you type **MINITAB** to start the program.

When you start Minitab, the first thing you see is the main screen, called the *Session window*, shown in Figure 1-2.

FIGURE 1-2
The Session window

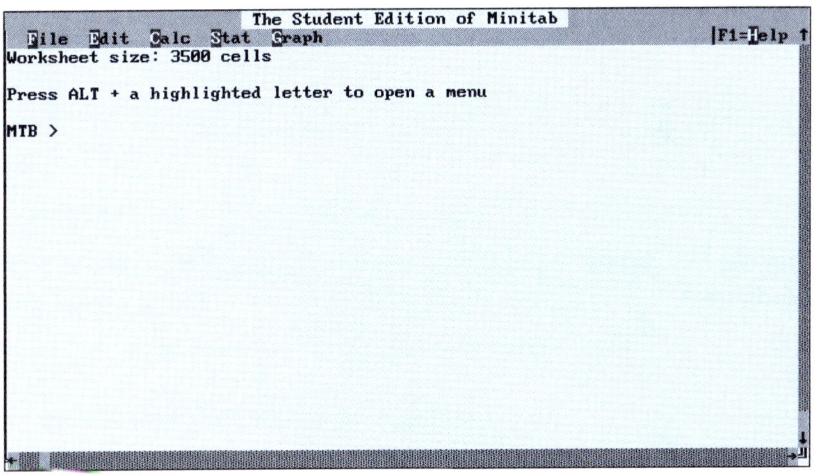

The horizontal bar across the top of the screen is called the *menu bar*. Minitab has five main menus (File, Edit, Calc, Stat, and Graph) from which you can issue commands. On the right is the Help menu; later in this tutorial you will learn to use this menu to get help quickly.

At the top of the Session window, Minitab reports the worksheet size and explains how to open a menu. The bottom line is the MTB > prompt, which provides an alternative way to enter commands. (You will learn more about the MTB > prompt later in this tutorial.) Minitab uses the rest of the Session window to display the results of the commands you issue.

For entering and editing data, Minitab provides a worksheet, called the *Data worksheet*, which you use to enter the pasta data. The command to reach the Data worksheet is located on the Edit menu. To go to the Data worksheet, you first have to access the menu bar:

- Press [F10]

Mouse Users:

To open the Edit Menu and Select Data Screen, click Edit then click Data Screen

The cursor is now in the menu bar. To view the Edit menu:

- Press [→] to highlight **E**dit
- Press [↵] to open the Edit menu

Note: If the directional arrows on your keyboard don't seem to be working and you are using the keypad, check to see that the Num Lock key is not engaged. To unlock, just press the Num Lock key.

The Edit menu contains commands you use to display and work with your data. Minitab automatically highlights the first choice, Data screen. Pressing [↵] executes whatever command is highlighted. Because you want to go to the Data screen:

- Press [↵]

Viewing the Data Worksheet

You should now see a grid similar to the one shown in Figure 1-3. This is the Data worksheet.

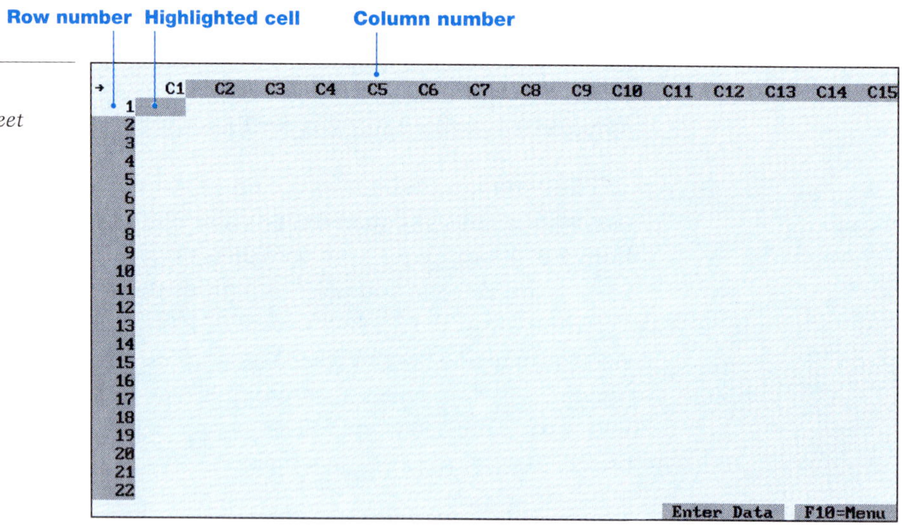

FIGURE 1-3
The Data worksheet

The worksheet consists of rows and columns. The intersection of a row and a column is known as a *cell*. The highlighted cell in the upper left corner corresponds to row 1, column 1. Each cell is identified by its column (C1, C2, C3...) and its row (1, 2, 3...).

Each column records a different variable. In the following steps, you record the rating for each brand in C1, the cost per serving in C2, and the calories per serving in C3. Each row contains all data from one individual case—in this example, a certain brand of pasta.

Only one cell in the data worksheet is *active* at a given time; in this case, the active cell is C1 row 1. Any information typed from the keyboard goes into the active cell.

Moving Around the Data Worksheet

You can easily change the active cell when you want to work on different parts of the Data worksheet.

- Press [→]

This action highlights C2 row 1. Now change the active cell:

- Press [↓] and hold it down until you reach row 10

Mouse Users:

To activate any cell in the worksheet, click it once.

The active cell is now C2 row 10. In Minitab, you can only see a certain number of columns and rows at one time; the number you see depends on the size of your screen. The Data worksheet in *The Student Edition of Minitab* actually has 100 columns. To see more of them:

- Press [→] and hold it down

The window scrolls horizontally to reveal additional columns; it continues until you release the arrow key. To scroll down the worksheet:

- Press [↓] and hold it down

Now the window scrolls down to show additional rows. To go directly to the beginning of the worksheet:

- Press and hold down [Ctrl] as you press [Home]

You go directly to C1 row 1, and Minitab highlights that cell.

Using the Data Screen Menu

You can also move around the worksheet using the Go to Cell command. Notice that in the lower right corner of the Data worksheet, Minitab tells you that F10=Menu.

- Press [F10]

The menu that appears is called the *Data screen menu*. To activate the Go to Cell command:

- Press [↓] four times to highlight **G**o to Cell...

Your screen should resemble Figure 1-4.

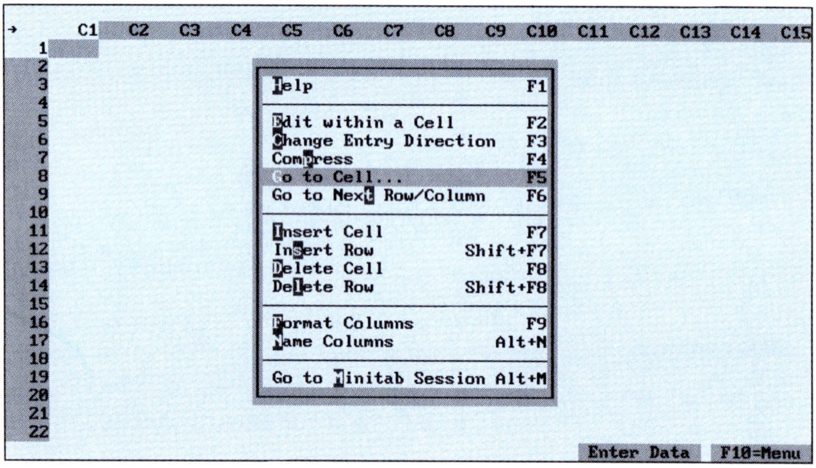

FIGURE 1-4
The Data screen menu with Go to Cell selected

Whenever Minitab requires information from you, a *dialog box* appears on the screen to request it. To access the Go To a Cell dialog box:

- Press [↵]

The Go To a Cell dialog box appears, as shown in Figure 1-5.

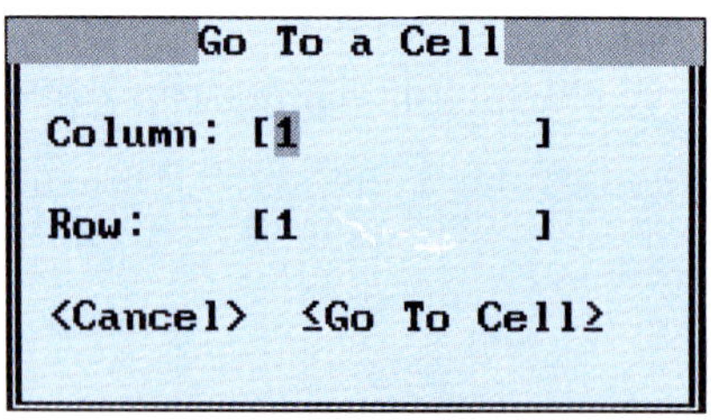

FIGURE 1-5
The Go To a Cell dialog box

The dialog box displays the column and row numbers of the active cell, in this case, C1 row 1. The 1 in the Column text box is highlighted; as in the worksheet, anything you type will be entered in this box. To go to C30 row 40:

- Type **30**

In the tutorials, any text that you should type will be printed in bold letters. To highlight the Row box:

Mouse Users:

To activate the Row box, click it once. Then type the row number.

- Press [Tab]
- Type **40** in the Row text box
- Press [Tab] twice to highlight the Go To Cell button
- Press [↵]

Now the active cell is C30 row 40. To practice this method of moving about, you can use a shortcut:

- Press [F10] to open the Data screen menu

Notice that certain letters, usually the first letter of a command, stand out from the others (either because they are a different color or are highlighted, depending on your monitor). You can press the highlighted letter to execute the command. Notice that the letter **G** is highlighted in the Go to Cell command. To open the Go To a Cell dialog box:

- Type **G**

The Go To a Cell dialog box appears as before. To go to the beginning of the worksheet:

- Type **1** and press [Tab]
- Type **1**
- Press [↵]

To execute the Go To Cell command at the bottom of the dialog box, you do not have to tab to the command button. You can simply press [↵] to execute the command. You are now back at the beginning of the worksheet.

Entering Data

You are now ready to enter the pasta data from Figure 1-1 into the worksheet.

- Press the Caps Lock key
- Type the first rating, **VERY GOOD,** in C1 row 1

If you make a mistake, press the Backspace key to delete a character. When you finish entering the data for the first cell, you will press [↵] (but don't press it yet). This tells Minitab to accept the data in the current cell; it also moves you either across or down, depending on the direction of the data-entry arrow in the upper left corner. To change the direction of the data-entry arrow:

- Press [F10]
- Type **C** for **C**hange Entry Direction, the third option

Notice that the direction of the data-entry arrow has changed. To change it back:

- Press [F10]

Notice also that the Change Entry Direction command on the Data screen menu is followed by F3. This indicates that pressing [F3] has the same effect as opening the menu and typing the command letter. Try it:

- Press [F3]

The direction of the data-entry arrow changes.

- Press [F3] again

This time you changed the direction of the arrow without opening the menu. All the Data screen menu commands have similar keyboard shortcuts. Once you learn them, you can bypass the menu and speed your data entry.

Since you will enter the pasta data row by row:

- Make sure the data-entry arrow is pointing to the right; press [F3] if it is not
- Press [↵]

Mouse Users:

You can click on the data-entry arrow to change its direction.

Notice that column C1 widens automatically to accommodate the entire entry.

- Type **44** and press [↵]
- Type **335**

You have entered the first row of data. Now you are ready to enter the second. To see how to get to the second row:

- Press [F10]

Notice that the Data screen menu command Go to Next Row/ Column includes the keyboard shortcut F6. Pressing [F6] moves you to the beginning of the next row (if the arrow points to the right) or the top of the next column (if the arrow points down).

- Press [F6] to go to the beginning of the next row
- Type **FAIR** and press [↵]
- Continue in this manner ([↵] for next column, [F6] for the first column in the next row) until you have entered all the data in Figure 1-1

Mouse Users:

To change a column name, double click it to highlight it, then type the correct name.

Here is a summary of keystrokes you can use when entering your data. With the data-entry arrow pointing to the right, to enter by rows:

- Pressing [↵] accepts any data you have entered and moves the active cell one column to the right
- Pressing [F6] accepts any data you have entered and moves the active cell to the beginning of the next row

With the data-entry arrow pointing down, to enter by columns:

- Pressing [↵] accepts any data you have entered and moves the active cell one row down
- Pressing [F6] accepts the data you have entered and moves the active cell to the top of the next column

Note: If the operations in the Data worksheet don't seem to be working, the problem may be that you have not pressed [↵] to tell Minitab to accept the data in the active cell. You can also press [Esc] to exit from the active cell without recording an entry in that cell.

Check your data. If you find a typographical error after you leave a cell, you can fix it easily. Notice the box in the lower right corner of the screen that says "Enter Data." This means that Minitab's Data worksheet is currently in the enter mode.

The Data worksheet also has an edit mode that you can use when you need to edit the data in your worksheet. To access the edit mode:

- Highlight the cell you want to correct
- Press [F10] to open the Data screen menu

To edit data you can use the Edit within a Cell command or [F2]. Try the shortcut:

- Press [F2] to edit within the cell you have highlighted

Notice that the Enter Data box changes to Edit Cell, indicating that Minitab is now in the edit mode. Notice the new box, Insert, to the left of the Edit Cell box. This means that Minitab is in the *insert* entry mode, in which any data you type pushes the contents of the cell to the right. In this mode, Minitab does not delete any characters unless you backspace over them. To delete characters:

- Use [→] to move the cursor to the right of the mistake, then backspace over it and type the correct entry
- Press [↵]

You can change from the insert mode to the overwrite mode by pressing [Ins]. Try it:

- Highlight another cell using any of the four arrow keys
- Press [F2] and then [Ins]

The Insert box changes to Overwrite. Any character you type now replaces the character under the cursor rather than displacing it to the right.

- Press [Esc] to exit from the cell (without changing the cell contents) when you finish trying Overwrite

Note: At any time you can replace the value in a cell with a new value. Just highlight the cell, type the new value, and press [↵].

Alpha Data

Notice that C1 contains words, called *alpha data*, while C2 and C3 contain numbers. When you start typing in a column, Minitab classifies a column as alpha if it finds alphabetic characters there.

Note: Once a column is designated as numeric, you cannot enter alpha data in the column unless you erase the variable. (You will learn how to do that later in this tutorial.)

Naming Columns

It is easier to work with data if you give each column in your worksheet a meaningful name. Column or variable names may contain up to 8 characters. When you name a column, do not use the special characters ' or #. For now, do not include spaces in variable names. Minitab displays column names above the column label row that contains the designations C1, C2, C3, and so on. To name C1:

- Highlight any cell in C1
- Press [F10]
- Press the N key to issue the **N**ame Columns command

Note: With the menu open you press the N key to issue the Name Columns command. You could issue the command without opening the menu by pressing [Alt]-N, as the note to the right of the command indicates.

The cell above C1 is now highlighted.

- Type **RATING**
- Press [↵]
- Type **CENTS** for C2 and **CALS** for C3
- Press [↓] to move back into the worksheet

In *The Student Edition of Minitab* you type variable names, alpha data, and data set names in uppercase. In your own work, however, you can use any mixture of upper- or lowercase letters.

Your worksheet should now look like Figure 1-6.

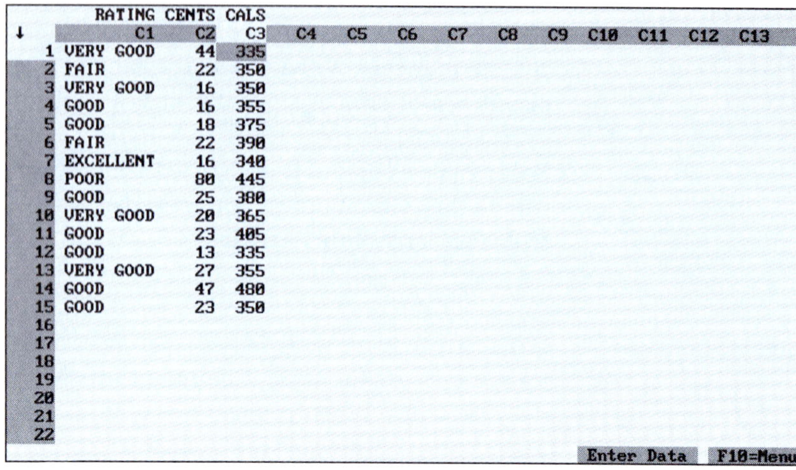

FIGURE 1-6
Pasta data with columns named

Saving Data

Unsaved work exists only in the computer's temporary memory until you save it to disk. It is good practice to save your work frequently to ensure that it will not be lost in the event of a power failure. You have the option of saving to the hard disk or floppy disk, depending on your hardware and your laboratory's policies. In this manual you may save all files to your backup Sample Files floppy disk as space permits. If you want to save your files to a different disk, see your instructor or laboratory director for details.

The Data worksheet is used only for entering and editing data. To save the pasta data into a file, you must return to the Session window that you saw earlier in this tutorial. To return to the Session window:

- Press [F10] to open the Data screen menu
- Press the M key to select the Go to **M**initab Session command

Note: You can use the key combination [Alt]-M without opening the menu, as indicated by the note to the right of the command.

The main menu bar is at the top of the Session window. The File menu contains the command used to save the Minitab worksheet as a file. To highlight the File menu:

- Press [F10]

- Press [↵] to open the **F**ile menu
- Press the A key to select Save Worksheet **A**s...

The Save As dialog box that appears gives you the option to save the worksheet in several formats. To save the pasta data as a Minitab worksheet, use the default selection:

- Press [Tab] to highlight **S**elect File (this option allows you to name the worksheet)
- Press [↵]

A second Save As dialog box appears as in Figure 1-6a.

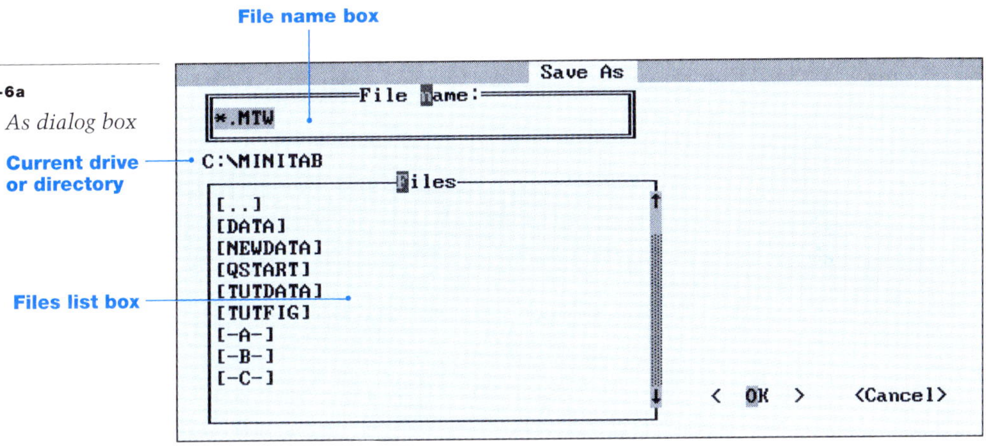

FIGURE 1-6a
The Save As dialog box

This dialog box contains three parts: the File name box at the top, a line of text displaying the current drive or directory, and the Files list box at the bottom. (Buttons for the OK and Cancel options are on the bottom right.)

You use the File name box at the top to give your pasta file a name. The Files list box at the bottom lists all directory files, or subdirectories in the current drive or directory; it also lists other drives on your computer, [-A-], [-B-], [-C-], and so on. The option [..] may be present; select it to exit from the current directory. You may have to scroll down to see these options if your computer contains a large number of directories. To select the drive containing the Sample Files disk:

- Press [Tab] to highlight the **F**iles list box

Note: In all dialog boxes, Minitab highlights the *active field* (this includes text boxes and list boxes) with double borders. The Files list box should now have a double border to indicate that it is the active field.

- Insert the Sample Files disk into the A drive (if that is the drive you plan to use)
- Press [↓] to highlight the A drive (you may have to scroll down to reach it)
- Press [↵]

The Files list box now lists the directories for each tutorial on the Sample Files disk. You will store the pasta data in the TUT1 directory:

- If necessary, press [↓] to highlight the TUT1 directory
- Press [↵]

> **Mouse Users:**
>
> Double click the TUT1 directory

The Files list box now lists any files in the TUT1 directory of the Sample Files disk. Notice that the current directory name displayed between the two boxes is A:\TUT1. To give the pasta data file a name:

- Press [Shift] and [Tab] simultaneously to activate the File **n**ame box
- Type **PASTA**

The screen should look like Figure 1-7.

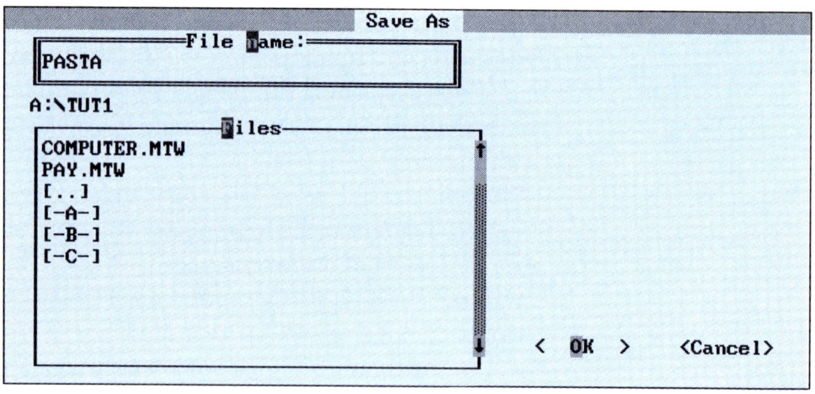

FIGURE 1-7
The completed Save As dialog box

- Press [↵]

Note: If you see a "WRITE PROTECT ERROR" message, remove the disk. For 3½" disks, move the small tab in the disk's upper right corner so you can no longer see through the square hole. For 5¼" disks, remove the write-protect tab covering the notch in the upper right corner of the disk. This unlocks the disk and allows you to save files there.

As you change your data, use this same procedure to save the updated file. The updated file always replaces the previous version, unless you rename the new file.

CAUTION: After you finish the tutorials and start work on your own data always save your data before you restart or exit from Minitab, or before you open a new worksheet.

Take a break now:

- Press F10 and then ↵ to open the File menu
- Type **x** for **Exit**
- Press ↵ to exit from Minitab without saving the worksheet

Retrieving Data

To retrieve your data:

- Restart Minitab

Your pasta data are stored on the backup Sample Files disk in the TUT1 directory.

- Make sure the backup Sample Files disk is in your computer

To select the Open Worksheet command from the File menu, you could press F10 and then ↵. However, there is a quicker way. Notice that one letter in each menu command is colored or highlighted. By combining the Alt key with one of the highlighted letters in the menu bar (**F** for **F**ile, **E** for **E**dit, and so on) you can open the corresponding menu.

Note: You may not always be able to use Alt plus a letter as a shortcut if other software uses the same key combination as Minitab. Note that Minitab never requires the use of [Alt]; there is always an alternative way to perform the same action. In this case, you would use the [Alt] method.

- Press and hold down [Alt] while you type the letter **F**

The [Alt] key combinations make it easy to issue commands both from the menus and in the dialog boxes. Because the Open Worksheet command is already highlighted, you need only:

- Press [Alt]

To confirm that you want to open a Minitab worksheet:

- Press [Alt]

The Open File dialog box appears.

- Press [Alt] to highlight the Files list box

Mouse Users:

Double click the backup Sample Files disk, TUT1, and PASTA.MTW

- If necessary, scroll to and highlight the drive containing the backup Sample Files disk (for example, [-A-]) and press [Alt]
- Scroll to and highlight the TUT1 directory and press [Alt]
- Scroll to and highlight PASTA.MTW

Note that the worksheet name in the Files list box is now PASTA.MTW. When you saved the PASTA file, Minitab automatically added the file extension .MTW after the filename. As you will see, Minitab can create a variety of files for different purposes. Files with the .MTW extension can be read quickly by Minitab, but other software such as text editors cannot read the files in this format.

To retrieve the file:

- Press [Alt]

You will now learn an important shortcut—one that enables you to switch quickly between the Session window and the Data screen.

- Press [Alt]-E to open the **E**dit menu

You could type **D** to issue the first command and go to the **D**ata screen. But notice the shortcut [Alt]-D to the right of the first command. Pressing [Alt] and the letter D has the same effect. Furthermore, you do not have to open the menu to use this shortcut. Try it:

- Press [Esc] to close the Edit menu
- Press [Alt]-D

Note: Pressing [Esc] cancels any menu, dialog box, or active cell.

The Data screen now displays the pasta data you saved. Once you begin using the Session window commands, you will regularly move back and forth between the Data worksheet and the Session window. The [Alt]-D key combination is an easy way to do it. Pressing [Alt]-M (for the **M**initab Session command from the Data screen menu) sends you the other way:

- Press [Alt]-M

You are back in the Session window.

You can issue many Minitab commands using keyboard shortcuts instead of the menu bar. Keyboard shortcuts are indicated in a separate box like this:

SHORTCUT

[Alt]-D = **Data Screen**

Any time you see a keyboard shortcut to the right of a menu selection, you can issue the command from the keyboard.

Manipulating Data with the General Expressions Command

In developing your pasta budget, you will compute the total cost for feeding 200 patients. The General Expressions command lets you perform many mathematical operations on columns. Minitab uses the symbols +, –, *, /, and ** to add, subtract, multiply, divide, and raise to a power, respectively.

Note: In later tutorials you will use the General Expressions command to perform various algebraic and statistical operations.

The following steps show you how Minitab can simply multiply the cost per serving by 200.

- Press [Alt]-C to open the **C**alc menu

An arrow [>>] to the right of a menu selection indicates a submenu with additional choices. The General Expressions command is located on the Functions and Statistics submenu.

- Type **F** to open the **F**unctions and Statistics submenu

The screen should look similar to Figure 1-8, which shows the Functions and Statistics submenu to the right of the Calc menu.

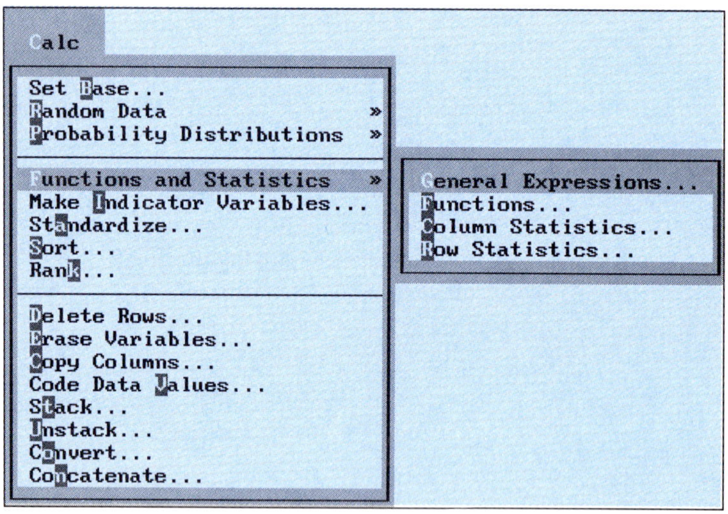

FIGURE 1-8
The Functions and Statistics submenu from the Calc menu

Because the General Expressions command is already highlighted:

- Press [↵] (pressing G would have the same effect)

Note: For the remainder of this tutorial, these actions will be abbreviated as: "Choose **F**unctions and Statistics and then **G**eneral Expressions... from the **C**alc menu."

The General Expressions dialog box appears. The screen should be similar to Figure 1-9.

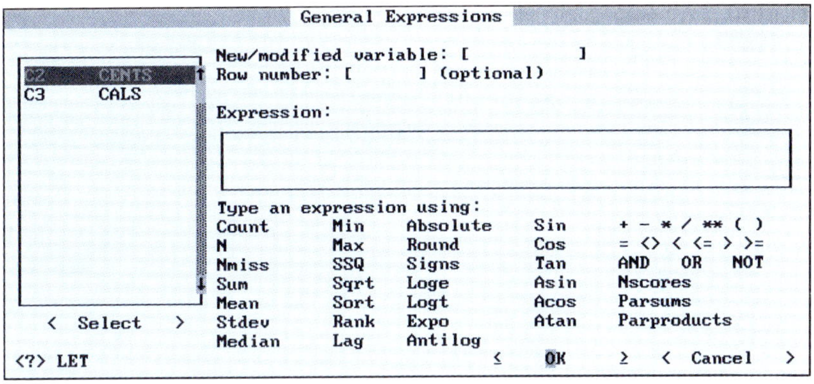

FIGURE 1-9
The General Expressions dialog box from the Functions and Statistics submenu of the Calc menu

You will compute the daily cost for each brand of pasta for 200 patients and store the results in C4. First, name the new variable in the New/modified variable text box:

- Type **COST200**

When you type in a name for the New/modified variable, Minitab uses the next available column (C4 in this example) and automatically names that column with what you have typed. If you include spaces or other special characters in a name, use single quotes around the column name. For example, if you name the variable COST 200 (with a space), you would type 'COST 200'. Remember that you cannot use the characters | or # in a variable name.

To move the cursor to the Expression text box:

- Press [Tab] twice

Note: [Tab] moves the cursor to different areas in a dialog box. If you are using a mouse, you can move the cursor by clicking the box or button you need. If you want to return to a text box above your present location, you can continue to press [Tab] until you return to the text box you want. You can also press [Shift]-[Tab] to go backward.

Now enter the formula in the Expression text box:

- Type **C2*200**
- Press [Tab] to exit from the Expression text box and highlight **OK**
- Press [↵]

With this formula, you are telling Minitab to multiply each of the values in C2 by 200.

- Press [Alt]-D to return to the Data worksheet

The worksheet reappears with the calculations completed and the results listed in C4. Your original cost per serving data was in cents, so the cost to feed 200 patients is also in cents. To change to dollars, divide each entry in C4 by 100:

- Press [Alt]-M to return to the Session window
- Choose **F**unctions and Statistics and then **G**eneral Expressions... from the **C**alc menu (press [Alt]-C, F, and [↵])

In the New/modified variable text box:

- Type **DOL200**
- Press [Tab] twice

In the Expression text box:

- Type **C4/100,** press [Tab], and press [↵]

You have instructed Minitab to divide all the values in C4 by 100 and place the results in C5. To view this new column:

- Press [Alt]-D to go to the Data worksheet

C5 DOL200 contains the new data.

- Press [Alt]-M to return to the Session window

Next you'll practice creating new variables by calculating the cost (in dollars) of feeding 250 patients and 300 patients in C6 and C7, respectively. But this time you will multiply the quantity and convert the amount to dollars in a single step.

- Choose **F**unctions and Statistics and then **G**eneral Expressions... from the **C**alc menu

In the New/modified variable text box:

- Type **DOL250** and press [Tab] twice
- Type **C2*250/100** in the Expression text box

To execute the commands in the dialog box, you could press [Tab] to highlight **O**K, as you have been doing. But notice that the "O" of **O**K is highlighted. This means you can use a key combination to issue the OK command.

- Press [Alt]-O

To calculate the cost of feeding 300 patients, you will have to change the 250 in the formula to 300. There is a way to do this without retyping the entire expression:

- Choose Edit **L**ast Command Dialog... from the **E**dit menu (press [Alt]-E and L)

SHORTCUT

[Alt]-L = Edit **L**ast Command Dialog

The last dialog box you worked on reappears. In the New/modified variable text box:

- Press [→] once
- Press the backspace key three times to delete the 250
- Type **300** in its place
- Press [Tab] twice

In the Expression text box:

- Use [←] to move just right of the 250
- Press the backspace key three times to delete the 250
- Type **300** in its place
- Press [Alt]-O (the letter "Oh") to execute the commands
- Go to the Data worksheet ([Alt]-D) to view the new columns

For each pasta brand, you now have the costs to feed 200, 250, and 300 patients.

- Return to the Session window ([Alt]-M)

Many of the patients are on an 1800-calorie-a-day diet. For each brand of pasta, calculate how many calories for the day would remain once a patient has eaten a meal made from that particular brand. Store the result in C8:

- Choose Edit **L**ast Command Dialog... from the **E**dit menu ([Alt]-L)

In the General Expressions dialog box:

- Type **CALLEFT** in the New/modified variable text box and press [Tab] twice
- Type **1800-C3** in the Expression text box and press [Alt]-O
- Go to the Data worksheet ([Alt]-D)

C8 now lists the calories remaining after a patient has eaten a 10 oz. serving of the various brands of pasta. You can use this information to determine which brand gives you the most flexibility in patient diets.

Copying a Column

Although you initially recorded the rating for each brand in C1, it would be convenient to repeat this information in C9 so it will be visible when you use columns farther to the right in the worksheet. Minitab's Copy Columns command can duplicate data from one column to another. To copy the data from C1 RATING into C9:

- Return to the Session window ([Alt]-M)
- Choose **C**opy Columns... from the **C**alc menu

The Copy dialog box shown in Figure 1-10 appears.

FIGURE 1-10

The Copy dialog box from the Calc menu

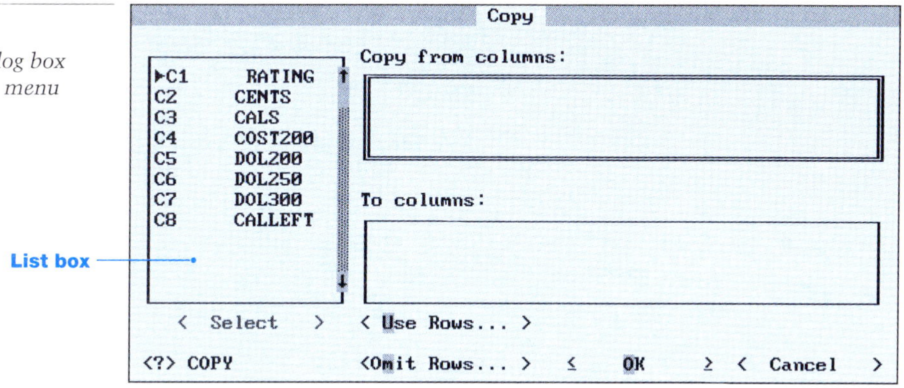

The list box on the left contains your column numbers and names.

- Press F2 to activate the list box

Notice the arrow to the left of C1 RATING. This arrow appears whenever you are in a text box that can accommodate more than one column at a time. In the Copy from columns text box, you can select more than one column to copy. When you are selecting a column for a text box that can only accommodate one entry, the arrow does not appear in the list box. To select C1:

> **Mouse Users:**
> Double click C1 RATING

- Press the Space bar to highlight C1 RATING
- Press F2 again

This records the variable C1 RATING in the Copy from columns text box, indicating that this is the column you want to copy. Pressing F2 from a text box moves you in and out of the list box; pressing the Space bar highlights the column you want to use.

- Press Tab

In the To columns text box:

- Type '**RATING A**' (be sure to include the single quotation marks, since this name has a space)
- Press Alt-O

Note: Each Minitab column must have a unique name, or no name at all.

- Go to the Data worksheet ([Alt]-D)

The data values now appear in C9 as well as in C1.

- Return to the Session window ([Alt]-M)

Getting Help

If you forget any of the specifics about a command, you can get help easily from the dialog box. Try getting help with the Copy Columns command:

- Press [Alt]-L to open the last dialog box

Notice the question mark <?> in the lower left corner of the Copy dialog box. You can access Minitab's Help command from there:

Mouse Users:

Double click the <?> button

- Press [Tab] six times to highlight the <?> button
- Press [↵]

An explanation of the Copy Columns command appears in a separate window, as shown in Figure 1-11. You can use [↑], [↓], [PgUp], and [PgDn] to scroll through the Help window.

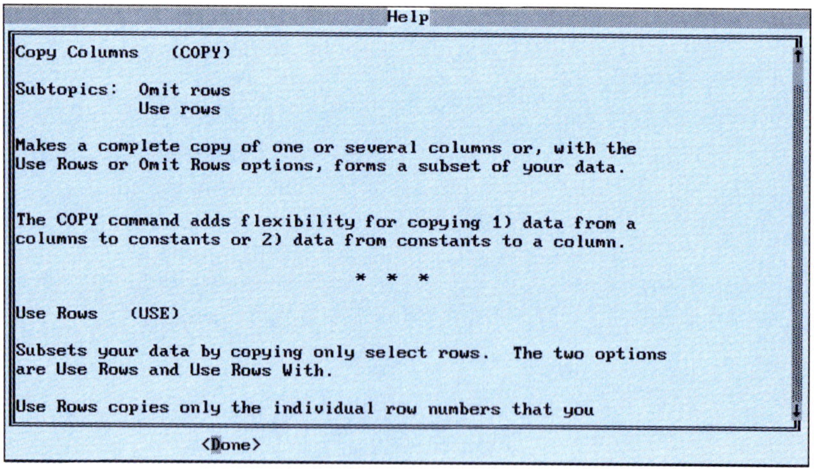
Help

Copy Columns (COPY)

Subtopics: Omit rows
Use rows

Makes a complete copy of one or several columns or, with the Use Rows or Omit Rows options, forms a subset of your data.

The COPY command adds flexibility for copying 1) data from a columns to constants or 2) data from constants to a column.

* * *

Use Rows (USE)

Subsets your data by copying only select rows. The two options are Use Rows and Use Rows With.

Use Rows copies only the individual row numbers that you

<Done>

FIGURE 1-11
The Copy Columns Help window

When you finish reading the information:

- Press [Alt]-D for **D**one
- Press [Esc] to exit from the Copy Columns dialog box

There are other ways to get help in Minitab. Notice in the upper right corner of the Session window the note, F1=Help. Pressing [F1] opens a special Help menu that lists a number of different topics for which you can get help. To open the Help menu:

- Press [F1]

To read about the first option, How to Use Help (which is automatically highlighted):

- Press [↵]

The Help window displays information on using Minitab's Help function. When you have read as much of it as you want (you can scroll down to read it all):

- Press [Alt]-D for **D**one

Mouse Users:

Click Done

You have seen two ways of getting help—from inside the dialog boxes or from the Help menu. The Data screen has its own Help menu that you can open by pressing [F1] from the Data worksheet.

By now you have practiced entering and manipulating data; in the process you have performed some simple analysis. You've probably had your fill of pasta by now, so take a brief break. When you come back you will be working on an entirely different case study.

If you plan to begin the next case study within a few minutes:

- Choose Restart **M**initab from the **F**ile menu

If you will be taking a long break:

- Choose E**x**it from the **F**ile menu

SHORTCUT

[Alt]-X = Exit

You do not need to save the current version of the pasta data because you will use a fresh data set to perform more statistical analyses later.

- Press [↵] to exit without saving this version of the worksheet

Case Study: Consultant

Technitron, a mid-sized corporation, recently hired you as a managerial consultant and asked you to analyze the salary structure of the sales department. Brett Reid, one of your co-workers, has gathered data on the sales department personnel and entered it in a Minitab file named PAY.MTW. This file is included on the Sample Files disk. You hope that you can eliminate any salary inequities by analyzing this data. Brett informs you that some employees on his list have left Technitron; there are also some new employees whose records must be added. Start by updating information contained in this file.

- Insert your backup Sample Files disk into the disk drive

If you did not exit from Minitab at the end of the last section, you can skip the restart command. If you exited from Minitab in the last section, you will need to restart Minitab before opening the PAY.MTW data:

- Restart Minitab
- Choose **O**pen Worksheet... from the **F**ile menu

> **SHORTCUT**
>
> [Alt]-O = **O**pen Worksheet

- Press [↵] to confirm opening a Minitab worksheet
- Press [Tab]
- Scroll to the correct drive using [↓] and press [↵]
- If necessary, highlight the TUT1 directory and press [↵]
- Open PAY.MTW by highlighting it and pressing [↵]

Note: From now on, these instructions will be condensed to: Open PAY.MTW from the TUT1 directory.

To see the worksheet:

- Go to the Data screen ([Alt]-D)

The worksheet should resemble Figure 1-12.

FIGURE 1-12

The sales department Data worksheet

	SALARY	YRS EM	PRIOR YR	EDUC	AGE	ID	GENDER	GENDER N				
↓	C1	C2	C3	C4	C5	C6	C7	C8	C9	C10	C11	C12
1	38985	18	7	9	52	412	M	0				
2	28938	12	5	4	39	517	F	1				
3	32920	15	3	9	45	458	F	1				
4	29548	5	6	1	30	604	M	0				
5	31138	11	11	6	46	562	F	1				
6	24749	6	2	0	26	598	F	1				
7	41889	22	16	7	63	351	M	0				
8	31528	3	11	3	35	674	M	0				
9	38791	21	4	5	48	356	M	0				
10	39828	18	6	5	47	415	F	1				
11												
12												
13												
14												
15												
16												
17												
18												
19												
20												
21												
22												

Enter Data F10=Menu

Brett measured seven variables for each employee. C1 contains the individual's annual salary, C2 the number of years at Technitron, C3 the years of experience prior to coming to Technitron, C4 the years of education after high school, C5 the age at last birthday, C6 the employee identification number, C7 the gender (note that, because it is an alpha variable, it is left-justified), and C8 the gender in numeric format (1 for female and 0 for male).

Deleting and Inserting Rows

Now start to update Brett's data. Employee number 562 (row 5) has left Technitron, so you need to remove her data from the worksheet.

- Press [↓] to highlight the first column in row 5
- Choose Delete Row from the Data screen menu

SHORTCUT

[Shift]-[F8] = Delete Row

The worksheet moves the lower rows up to fill in the space. There are now only nine employees on the data worksheet.

If you were to hire a replacement, you might want to insert the new employee's data into the worksheet at a particular location. Try inserting a row above what is now row 8.

- Highlight any cell in row 8
- Choose Insert Row from the Data screen menu

SHORTCUT

[Shift]-[F7] = Insert Row

Minitab inserts a blank row in this position and moves all the other rows down. You will see an asterisk in each cell of columns C1 through C8 in row 8, indicating that the information for the cell is *missing*.

- Delete the empty row by highlighting any cell in row 8, and then selecting Delete Row from the Data screen menu ([Shift]-[F8])

Your worksheet should now look like Figure 1-13.

FIGURE 1-13

The Data worksheet with one row deleted

↓	SALARY C1	YRS EM C2	PRIOR YR C3	EDUC C4	AGE C5	ID C6	GENDER C7	GENDER N C8	C9	C10	C11	C12
1	38985	18	7	9	52	412	M	0				
2	28938	12	5	4	39	517	F	1				
3	32920	15	3	9	45	458	F	1				
4	29548	5	6	1	30	604	M	0				
5	24749	6	2	0	26	598	F	1				
6	41889	22	16	7	63	351	M	0				
7	31528	3	11	3	35	674	M	0				
8	38791	21	4	5	48	356	M	0				
9	39828	18	6	5	47	415	F	1				
10												
11												
12												
13												
14												
15												
16												
17												
18												
19												
20												
21												
22												

Enter Data F10=Menu

Now Brett tells you that two new employees are being added to the department. You will put the data for these employees in rows 10 and 11. When you enter the new data, remember that [↵] moves you across the row if the data-entry arrow (in the upper left corner of the screen) points to the right.

- Press [F3] to change the direction of the data-entry arrow so that it points to the right if necessary

The new employee in row 10, a 23-year-old female, will earn a salary of $28,985. She has one year of prior experience and four years of post–high school education. Her employee number is 693. As a new employee, she will have 0 as the entry in C2 'YRS EM'.

- Type her data in row 10 (starting in C1 and pressing [↵] between each value): **28985 0 1 4 23 693 F 1**
- Press [F6] to move to the beginning of row 11

Note: If you notice a mistake after you have pressed [↵], return to that cell and press [F2]. That puts you in the Edit mode; you can backspace over the mistake and correct it.

You have much less information about the second new employee. He is male, his employee number is 694, and he has a salary of $32,782. Place an asterisk in each cell where the information is missing.

- Type his data in row 11: **32782 0 * * * 694 M 0**
- Press [F6]

The Data worksheet should now resemble Figure 1-14. Notice that an entry of 0 (zero) is different from the entry *, which indicates a missing value.

FIGURE 1-14

The Data worksheet with new employee information

	SALARY	YRS EM	PRIOR YR	EDUC	AGE	ID	GENDER	GENDER N				
→	C1	C2	C3	C4	C5	C6	C7	C8	C9	C10	C11	C12
1	38985	18	7	9	52	412	M	0				
2	28938	12	5	4	39	517	F	1				
3	32920	15	3	9	45	458	F	1				
4	29548	5	6	1	30	604	M	0				
5	24749	6	2	0	26	598	F	1				
6	41889	22	16	7	63	351	M	0				
7	31528	3	11	3	35	674	M	0				
8	38791	21	4	5	48	356	M	0				
9	39828	18	6	5	47	415	F	1				
10	28985	0	1	4	23	693	F	1				
11	32782	0	*	*	*	694	M	0				
12												
13												
14												
15												
16												
17												
18												
19												
20												
21												
22												

Enter Data F10=Menu

- Return to the Session window ([Alt]-M)

Deleting Columns

You have just learned that Technitron has a policy against recording age, so you need to delete the age variable.

- Choose **E**rase Variables... from the **C**alc menu
- Press [F2] and use [↓] to move the indicator arrow (currently to the left of C1 in the list box) to the C5 AGE line
- Press the Space bar to highlight C5 AGE
- Press [F2] to select it
- Press [Alt]-O for **O**K
- Return to the Data worksheet ([Alt]-D)

Mouse Users:

Double click C5 AGE

C5 is now blank. Check to see that your data worksheet contains only the information shown in Figure 1-15.

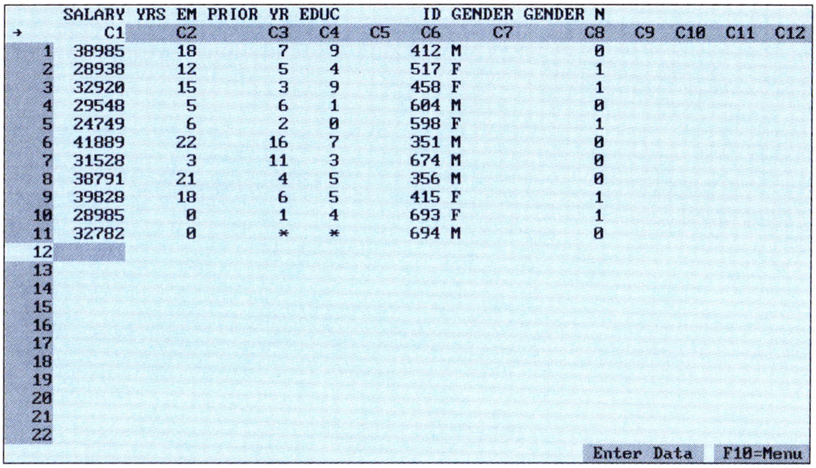

→	SALARY C1	YRS EM C2	PRIOR YR C3	EDUC C4	C5	ID C6	GENDER C7	GENDER N C8	C9	C10	C11	C12
1	38985	18	7	9		412	M	0				
2	28938	12	5	4		517	F	1				
3	32920	15	3	9		458	F	1				
4	29548	5	6	1		604	M	0				
5	24749	6	2	0		598	F	1				
6	41889	22	16	7		351	M	0				
7	31528	3	11	3		674	M	0				
8	38791	21	4	5		356	M	0				
9	39828	18	6	5		415	F	1				
10	28985	0	1	4		693	F	1				
11	32782	0	*	*		694	M	0				
12												
13												
14												
15												
16												
17												
18												
19												
20												
21												
22												

Enter Data F10=Menu

FIGURE 1-15
The Data worksheet without the AGE variable

Copying Parts of a Column

Earlier in this tutorial you copied a column in the PASTA worksheet. Now you will learn to copy *part* of a column.

Part of your investigation of the salary structure is to look at the relation between different variables and salaries. To do this, you need to put the male and female salaries in separate columns. To produce a column that contains only the salaries of the male employees, you want to copy only the male salaries from C1 into C9.

- Return to the Session window (Alt-M)
- Choose **C**opy Columns from the **C**alc menu (Alt-C, C)

First indicate the column you want to copy from:

- Press F2
- Press the Space bar to select C1 SALARY
- Press F2
- Press Tab

Then tell Minitab where to put the data.

- Type '**SAL MALE**' (include the quotes)

Mouse Users:

Click the Copy - Use Rows dialog box

To select only the salaries of male employees:

- Press Tab and ↵ (or just Alt-U) to open the Copy - **U**se Rows subdialog box

The Copy - Use Rows subdialog box appears (Figure 1-16).

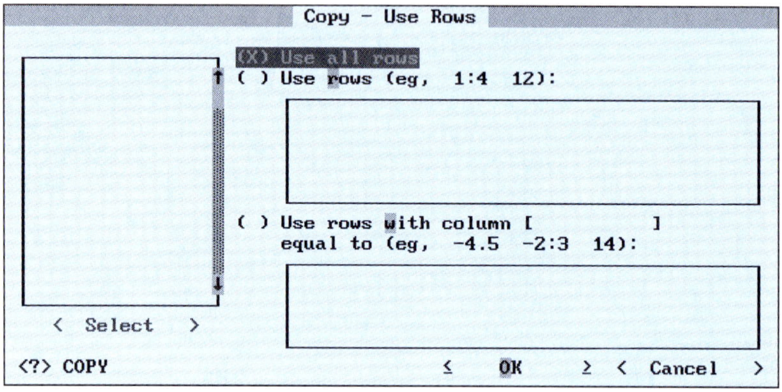

FIGURE 1-16
The Copy - Use Rows subdialog box

- Press ↓ twice to select the Use rows **w**ith column subcommand (or press Alt-W)
- Press Tab

The list box on the left lists the column names of all the numeric variables. C7 GENDER does not appear, because you cannot use alpha data to designate which rows to use.

- Press F2
- Press ↓ to select C8 GENDER N from the list box
- Press F2

Now you will tell Minitab to copy only the salaries of males from C1. (Remember that a value of 0 corresponds to a male.) In the box requesting the values to use:

- Type **0**
- Press Alt-O for **O**K twice

The Data worksheet now includes a list of male salaries in C9.

- Repeat the procedure to place all the female salaries in C10, naming this column 'SAL FEM' and typing **1** in the box requesting the values to use
- Return to the Data worksheet (Alt-D) and scroll to the right to view columns C9 and C10

You can now see the two subsets of the salary variable side by side (Figure 1-17).

FIGURE 1-17
The Data worksheet, showing male and female salaries

	SALARY	YRS EM	PRIOR YR	EDUC		ID	GENDER	GENDER N	SAL MALE	SAL FEM
→	C1	C2	C3	C4	C5	C6	C7	C8	C9	C10
1	38985	18	7	9		412	M	0	38985	28938
2	28938	12	5	4		517	F	1	29548	32920
3	32920	15	3	9		458	F	1	41889	24749
4	29548	5	6	1		604	M	0	31528	39828
5	24749	6	2	0		598	F	1	38791	28985
6	41889	22	16	7		351	M	0	32782	
7	31528	3	11	3		674	M	0		
8	38791	21	4	5		356	M	0		
9	39828	18	6	5		415	F	1		
10	28985	0	1	4		693	F	1		
11	32782	0	*	*		694	M	0		
12										
13										
14										
15										
16										
17										
18										
19										
20										
21										
22										

Enter Data F10=Menu

It appears that salaries of males and females are similar. In a later tutorial, you will examine the salary structure in more depth.

- Return to the Session window (Alt-M)
- Choose Restart **M**initab from the **F**ile menu (Alt-F, M)

You can save your worksheet if you want. When you return to this data you will open a new copy of the file.

- Press ↵ to restart Minitab without saving the worksheet

In the next section you will learn how to enter data from a file created in a word processor.

Case Study: Teaching

You have just completed your first marking period as a social studies teacher. You have submitted a progress report, written in a popular word processing program, to your principal, Ms. Taylor. The report contains your students' grades from the first three tests. One of your colleagues informs you that your school's computer lab has the Minitab program and explains that it could help you compute and analyze the grades. You can import the grades from your word processor directly into Minitab if you save them in an ASCII (an acronym for American Standard Code for Information Interchange) file. ASCII files are also called *text files*.

Importing a Data File Created with a Word Processor

For the purposes of this tutorial, the text-format data file has already been saved for you. The file, GRADES.DAT, is on your backup Sample Files disk, ready to be imported into Minitab. Each row contains all the information about a certain student: last name, first name, score on test 1, score on test 2, and score on test 3.

- Choose **I**mport ASCII Data... from the **F**ile menu

The Import ASCII Data dialog box (Figure 1-18) appears.

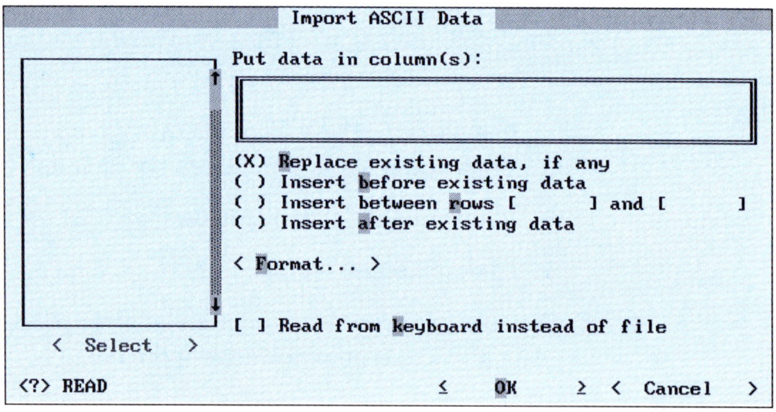

FIGURE 1-18
The Import ASCII Data dialog box from the File menu

Since each row of your data contains five entries, you need five columns to enter the data. In the Put data in column(s) text box:

- Type **C1-C5**

Note: A hyphen between columns designates a series of consecutive column numbers.

Because ASCII files are not spreadsheets, there is no convenient way to distinguish one column from another. The data are simply entered in rows, with the information for each variable separated by spaces. Minitab needs to know where the first column should end and the second should begin. When the data consist of numbers, you can just separate the numbers with spaces, and Minitab can read the data effortlessly. But when alpha data (like the names of your students) are involved, Minitab needs more information.

If you assign a certain number of spaces to each variable and use a certain number of spaces to separate one variable from another, Minitab can read along each row according to those specifications. The spaces can contain either characters or blanks. The GRADES.DAT file was created this way. To tell Minitab how many spaces have been assigned for each variable and between each variable:

Mouse Users:

Click the Format button

- Press [Alt]-F for Format

The Import ASCII Data - Format subdialog box appears (Figure 1-19.)

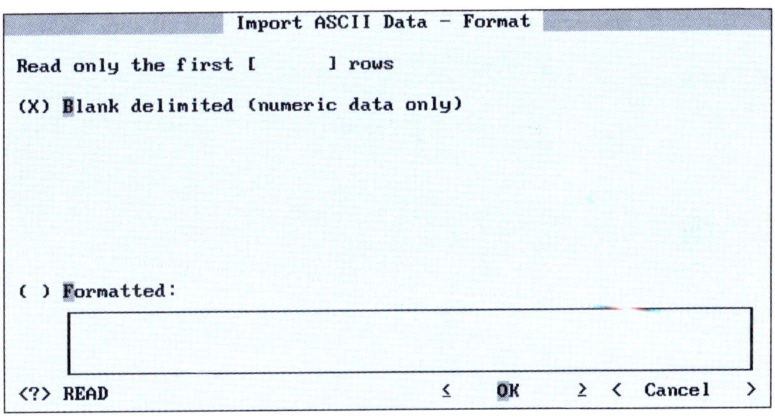

FIGURE 1-19
The Import ASCII Data - Format subdialog box

Minitab has a special text box where you can explain how the GRADES.DAT file was formatted:

- Press [Alt]-F to select Formatted

Minitab reads the ASCII text file according to the description you type here. You must supply Minitab with formatting codes in a computer language called *Fortran*. These codes tell Minitab the size (or width) of the columns, the kind of data in each column (alpha or numeric), and the number of spaces between columns. (See the Reference section for more information on Fortran codes.) For now, type the codes exactly as they are shown here:

- Press [Tab]
- Type **A9, 6X, A9, 7X, F3, 4X, F3, 5X, F3** (include commas and spaces)

"A" designates alpha data, "F" designates floating-point (numeric) data, and "X" designates the number of spaces between columns. Each row contains a last name, 9 characters long (A9), followed by 6 spaces (6X), followed by another alpha entry (A9) for the first name, followed by 7 spaces (7X), followed by three test grades (F3) separated by 4 spaces (4X) and 5 spaces (5X).

- Press [Alt]-O for **O**K twice

Now select the text file from your backup Sample Files disk:

- Press [Tab]
- Select GRADES.DAT from the TUT1 directory
- Press [↵]

Minitab imports your grades and displays the screen shown in Figure 1-20.

FIGURE 1-20
The Session window, showing test grades and commands

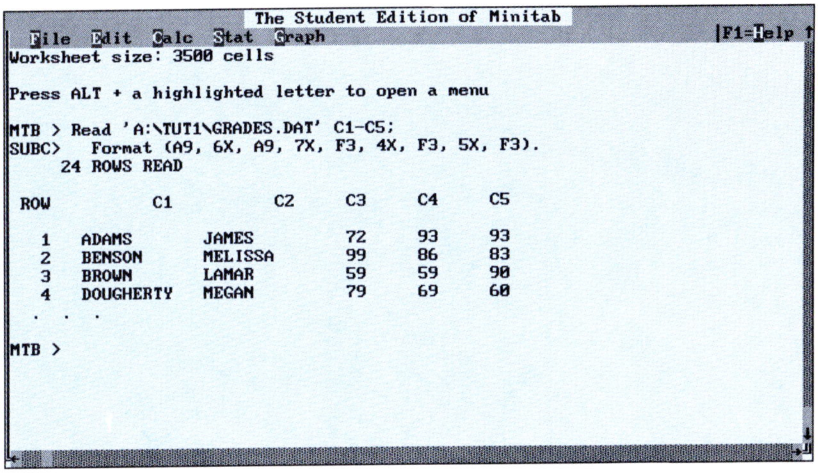

Using the Session Window

Until now you have been working primarily with the Data worksheet and issuing commands by selecting various menu options through the Session window. Another way to issue commands is by typing them directly into the Session window. To do this you need to know Minitab's command language. As you have issued commands from the menus, you have probably noticed that Minitab types these commands on the screen after the MTB > prompt. For example, in the Session window the first MTB > prompt is followed by the Minitab command, "Read," followed by the name of the file and the columns to be read. Minitab executed this command when you chose the Import ASCII Data command from the menu, following the steps outlined in the previous section. The semicolon at the end of the first line tells Minitab that a *subcommand* providing more information follows. The second line begins with "SUBC> Format" to indicate that the text file data are separated into columns as you specified in the Fortran format statement.

Minitab has read 24 rows; Minitab displays the first four. Your next command tells Minitab to display the entire data set. After the MTB > prompt at the bottom of the Session window:

Type **PRINT C1-C5**

For the remainder of the tutorials, you will type using uppercase letters; however, in your own work, you can use upper- or lowercase.

- Press [↵]

Minitab lists the data in C1 through C5, along with corresponding row numbers (Figure 1-21).

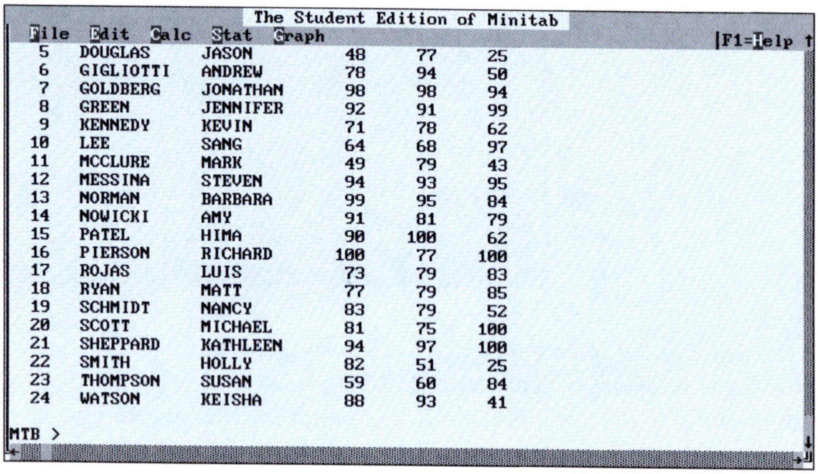
The Student Edition of Minitab

File Edit Calc Stat Graph | F1=Help

5	DOUGLAS	JASON	48	77	25
6	GIGLIOTTI	ANDREW	78	94	50
7	GOLDBERG	JONATHAN	98	98	94
8	GREEN	JENNIFER	92	91	99
9	KENNEDY	KEVIN	71	78	62
10	LEE	SANG	64	68	97
11	MCCLURE	MARK	49	79	43
12	MESSINA	STEVEN	94	93	95
13	NORMAN	BARBARA	99	95	84
14	NOWICKI	AMY	91	81	79
15	PATEL	HIMA	90	100	62
16	PIERSON	RICHARD	100	77	100
17	ROJAS	LUIS	73	79	83
18	RYAN	MATT	77	79	85
19	SCHMIDT	NANCY	83	79	52
20	SCOTT	MICHAEL	81	75	100
21	SHEPPARD	KATHLEEN	94	97	100
22	SMITH	HOLLY	82	51	25
23	THOMPSON	SUSAN	59	60	84
24	WATSON	KEISHA	88	93	41

MTB >

FIGURE 1-21
The Session window with test grades

The Session window automatically scrolls to keep the last line of output and the current MTB > prompt visible. If you want to see other parts of the data, you can scroll up and down or right and left in the Session window.

- Press [PgUp] to move up one screen
- Press [PgDn] to move down one screen
- Press [Ctrl]-[Home] to move to the beginning of the Session window
- Press [Ctrl]-[End] to return to the MTB > prompt

These key combinations also work in the Data worksheet. To see your grade records in the Data worksheet:

- Go to the Data worksheet ([Alt]-D)

Your data now appear in the familiar row-column configuration (Figure 1-22).

→	C1	C2	C3	C4	C5	C6	C7	C8	C9	C10	C11	C12	C13
1	ADAMS	JAMES	72	93	93								
2	BENSON	MELISSA	99	86	83								
3	BROWN	LAMAR	59	59	90								
4	DOUGHERTY	MEGAN	79	69	60								
5	DOUGLAS	JASON	48	77	25								
6	GIGLIOTTI	ANDREW	78	94	50								
7	GOLDBERG	JONATHAN	98	98	94								
8	GREEN	JENNIFER	92	91	99								
9	KENNEDY	KEVIN	71	78	62								
10	LEE	SANG	64	68	97								
11	MCCLURE	MARK	49	79	43								
12	MESSINA	STEVEN	94	93	95								
13	NORMAN	BARBARA	99	95	84								
14	NOWICKI	AMY	91	81	79								
15	PATEL	HIMA	90	100	62								
16	PIERSON	RICHARD	100	77	100								
17	ROJAS	LUIS	73	79	83								
18	RYAN	MATT	77	79	85								
19	SCHMIDT	NANCY	83	79	52								
20	SCOTT	MICHAEL	81	75	100								
21	SHEPPARD	KATHLEEN	94	97	100								
22	SMITH	HOLLY	82	51	25								

Enter Data F10=Menu

FIGURE 1-22
The Data worksheet with imported test grades

- Return to the Session window (Alt-M)

Your grade data have been imported into Minitab and are ready for analysis. You'll work more with these data later, using a fresh copy of the file.

- Choose E**x**it from the **F**ile menu (Alt-X)

Note: If you chose to save your worksheet and assign it a name, say GRADES, your grades are now stored in two different files: GRADES.DAT, the text file that can be read by your word processor, and GRADES.MTW, the file format that only Minitab can read.

- Press ↵ to exit from Minitab without saving the worksheet

Congratulations. You have just finished the first tutorial. Now that you have mastered the skills to prepare your data for analysis, you are ready to take a closer look at how Minitab operates. In the next tutorial you will learn more ways of altering or transforming your data.

Minitab Command Summary

The menus and commands introduced in or related to this tutorial are described in this section. You will find a complete explanation of all menus and commands in the Reference section of this manual.

Menu	Command	Function
File		
	Open Worksheet	Retrieves a previously saved worksheet
	Save Worksheet As	Saves a copy of the current worksheet and allows you to provide a name for the file
	Import ASCII Data	Reads an ASCII file into Minitab
	Export ASCII Data	Writes data from the current worksheet into an ASCII file
	Restart Minitab	Closes the current worksheet, erases all output in the Session window, and opens a blank worksheet in the Data screen
	Exit	Exits from the Minitab application
Edit		
	Data Screen	Opens the Data worksheet
	Edit Last Command Dialog	Recalls the last command dialog box that was opened, retaining the previous information
Calc		
	Function and Statistics General Expressions	Creates, transforms, and manipulates columns of data
	Delete Rows	Deletes any number of rows in the worksheet for specified columns
	Erase Variables	Erases or deletes a column(s) of the worksheet

	Copy Columns	Creates duplicate columns or parts of columns of one or many columns
Data Screen Menu		
	Help	Accesses Minitab's Help function
	Change Entry Direction	Changes the entry direction from across to down in the worksheet and vice versa
	Go to Cell	Activates a given cell in a worksheet
	Go to Next Row/Column	Depending on the direction of the data-entry arrow, highlights the first cell of the next row or column
	Insert Cell	Inserts a cell at the active cell and moves all cells in the column down
	Insert Row	Inserts a row in the worksheet above the current row of the worksheet
	Delete Cell	Deletes the active cell and moves all cells in the column up
	Delete Row	Deletes the entire row that contains the current active cell
	Name Columns	Highlights the name cell above the column containing the currently active cell
	Go to Minitab Session	Opens the Session window

Review and Practice

Matching

Match the following terms to their definitions by placing the correct letter next to the term it explains.

___ Session window

___ alpha data

___ *

___ Alt-D

___ Data worksheet

___ .MTW

___ Open Worksheet

___ variable

___ cell

a. A series of rows and columns in which Minitab displays data and information

b. Key combination to access the Data worksheet

c. Minitab commands and output are displayed in this window

d. Minitab designation for a missing value or information

e. The intersection of a row and column in a worksheet

f. Minitab command to retrieve a previously saved worksheet

g. File extension given to Minitab files created by the Save Worksheet As command

h. Type of data that contains characters other than numbers

i. Another name Minitab uses for a column of information or data in a worksheet

True/False

Mark the following statements T or F.

___ 1. Names can be assigned to a column by typing the name in the Data worksheet.

___ 2. The Insert Row command inserts an empty row immediately below the current row.

___ 3. Only a single row can be deleted from the worksheet using the Data screen menu Delete Row command.

___ 4. The Copy command can copy any part of a row to another row.

____ 5. Minitab worksheet files saved with the .MTW extension can be edited in any popular word processing package.

____ 6. Only Lotus 1-2-3 files can be imported into a Minitab worksheet.

____ 7. The Session window can be opened by pressing [Alt]-S.

____ 8. The Minitab Help command is available on the File menu.

____ 9. Column or variable names must be 8 characters or less.

____ 10. When entering data into the worksheet, pressing [↵] always moves you to the next cell to the right in the same row.

Practice Problems

1. The total snowfall amounts (in inches) for a small town in the upper Midwest for the past fifteen winters are:

   45.6 34.7 67.2 44.9 23.0 37.1 39.0 29.0 51.9 35.2 10.6
   38.6 40.2 55.1 49.3

   a. Enter this data into C1 and name the column SNOWFALL.

   b. Create a new column that represents the equivalent rainfall. (1″ of rain equals approximately 10″ of snow.) Name the column RAIN.

   c. Save your worksheet as SNOWFALL in the TUT1 directory.

2. The TV viewing times (in hours) of ten married couples who volunteered to monitor their television viewing habits for several months are:

Household	Husband	Wife
1	21	24
2	56	55
3	34	34
4	30	34
5	38	45
6	27	29
7	30	41
8	36	35
9	20	34
10	43	32

   a. Enter this data into C1 and C2 in a new worksheet. Name the two columns HUSBAND and WIFE.

   b. Compute the total viewing times for husbands and wives combined for the ten households and store these values in C3. Name this column TOTAL.

   c. Compute the difference in viewing times, C1 – C2, for husbands and wives, store your results in C4, and name the column DIFF.

   d. Save your worksheet in the TUT1 directory as 'TV VIEW'.

3. Open the COMPUTER.MTW data set from the TUT1 directory.

   a. Scroll through the worksheet to see what information the file contains.

   b. Use the Go to Cell command to activate the last cell in the last named column.

c. Add the following information about a Macintosh computer to the worksheet in C1 through C9:

68030 8 20 1 2 mono yes yes 1800

d. Save the worksheet in the TUT1 directory. Call it COMPUTE1.

TUTORIAL 2

Summarizing, Transforming, and Manipulating Data

Now that you are able to put data into a form that Minitab can read, you are ready to begin organizing and manipulating the data to perform various statistical analyses. You will continue the case study from Tutorial 1 where, as a new teacher, you learned to prepare your grades for Minitab analysis.

Objectives

In this tutorial you will learn to:

- summarize rows (individual cases) and columns (variables)
- combine or break down columns of data
- manipulate data by coding, ranking, and sorting
- standardize data from different variables in order to compare them
- view and print data

In Tutorial 1 you imported your grades from a word processor file. A copy of the grades worksheet, as it existed at the end of Tutorial 1, is on your backup Sample Files disk in the TUT2 directory.

- Start Minitab
- Open GRADEST2.MTW from the TUT2 directory on your backup Sample Files disk

Mean, Median, and Round

You would like to compute an average grade based on the three exams for each of your students. You could, of course, add each student's test grades from the third, fourth, and fifth columns of the appropriate row and divide by three using a calculator and enter the results in a column. But Minitab can compute each student's average with a single command:

- Choose **F**unctions and Statistics and then **G**eneral Expressions from the **C**alc menu (remember that you press [Alt]-C, then press F and G)

Note: The rest of this manual adopts the following shorthand to indicate commands you select from submenus: Choose **C**alc ▶ **F**unctions and Statistics ▶ **G**eneral Expressions...

In the General Expressions dialog box:

- Type **AVERG** in the New/modified variable text box and press [Tab] twice

Recall that Minitab assigns this name to the next available column—in this case, C6. To tell Minitab how to create the average:

- Type **(C3+C4+C5)/3** in the Expression text box and press [Alt]-O (be sure to include the parentheses in this expression; otherwise, you'll get the wrong result)

Note: You have probably noticed that the instructions tell you sometimes to press [Alt]-O and sometimes to press [↵] to execute a dialog box. When the text box can accommodate more than one line of text (as the Expression text box can), you cannot use [↵] to execute commands: you must use [Alt]-O instead.

Minitab stores the results in C6

- Go to the Data worksheet to see the new column, then return to the Session window

Minitab has an even simpler way for you to calculate the *mean* (or other statistic) of some or all of the data in a particular row and save the result in a column.

- Choose **C**alc ▶ **F**unctions and Statistics ▶ **R**ow Statistics...

The Row Statistics dialog box, shown in Figure 2-1, appears.

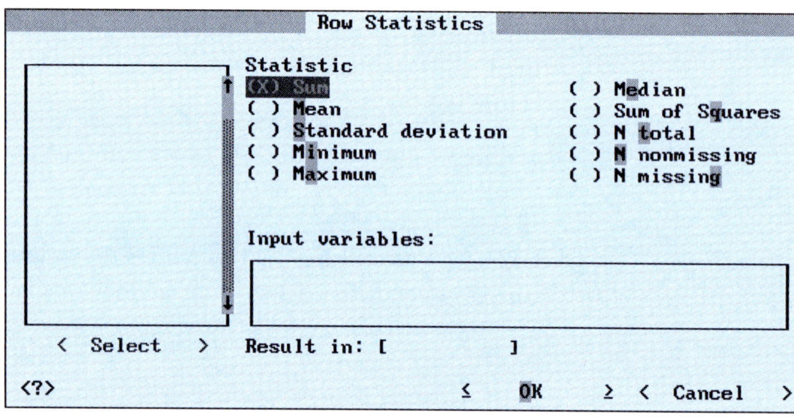

FIGURE 2-1
The Row Statistics dialog box from the Functions and Statistics submenu

Minitab can calculate several row statistics. To compute the mean of the three grades for each student recorded in C3, C4, and C5:

- Press Alt-M to select the **M**ean checkbox
- Press Tab

To enter the Input variables:

- Press F2 to highlight the list box
- Press the Space bar to highlight C3; press ↓ and then the Space bar, in sequence two more times to highlight C4 and C5
- Press F2

Mouse Users:

Click C3, C4, and C5 in the list box and click Select

TEST1-TEST3 now appears in the Input variables text box. To tell Minitab where to place the resulting means:

- Press Tab
- Type **RMEAN** in the Result in text box and press ↵
- Go to the Data worksheet

If you compare the entries in C6 and C7 (Figure 2-2), you see that the two methods produce the same results.

FIGURE 2-2
The Data worksheet, showing the mean calculated two ways

	LAST NAM	FIRST	TEST1	TEST2	TEST3	AVERG	RMEAN			
→	C1	C2	C3	C4	C5	C6	C7	C8	C9	C10
1	ADAMS,	JAMES	72	93	93	86.0000	86.0000			
2	BENSON,	MELISSA	99	86	83	89.3333	89.3333			
3	BROWN,	LAMAR	59	59	90	69.3333	69.3333			
4	DOUGHERTY,	MEGAN	79	69	60	69.3333	69.3333			
5	DOUGLAS,	JASON	48	77	25	50.0000	50.0000			
6	GIGLIOTTI,	ANDREW	78	94	50	74.0000	74.0000			
7	GOLDBERG,	JONATHAN	98	98	94	96.6667	96.6667			
8	GREEN,	JENNIFER	92	91	99	94.0000	94.0000			
9	KENNEDY,	KEVIN	71	78	62	70.3333	70.3333			
10	LEE,	SANG	64	68	97	76.3333	76.3333			
11	MCCLURE,	MARK	49	79	43	57.0000	57.0000			
12	MESSINA,	STEVEN	94	93	95	94.0000	94.0000			
13	NORMAN,	BARBARA	99	95	84	92.6667	92.6667			
14	NOWICKI,	AMY	91	81	79	83.6667	83.6667			
15	PATEL,	HIMA	90	100	62	84.0000	84.0000			
16	PIERSON,	RICHARD	100	77	100	92.3333	92.3333			
17	ROJAS,	LUIS	73	79	83	78.3333	78.3333			
18	RYAN,	MATT	77	79	85	80.3333	80.3333			
19	SCHMIDT,	NANCY	83	79	52	71.3333	71.3333			
20	SCOTT,	MICHAEL	81	75	100	85.3333	85.3333			
21	SHEPPARD,	KATHLEEN	94	97	100	97.0000	97.0000			
22	SMITH,	HOLLY	82	51	25	52.6667	52.6667			

Enter Data F10=Menu

- Return to the Session window

For more practice, use the Row Statistics function to compute the median of each row:

- Choose **E**dit ▶ Edit **L**ast Command Dialog... (Alt-L)
- Press Alt-E to select the Median checkbox

You will use the same Input variables, so:

- Press Tab twice
- Type **RMEDIAN** in the Result in text box and press ↵
- Go to the Data worksheet

Column C8, shown in Figure 2-3, now contains the medians of each student's test scores.

FIGURE 2-3

The Data worksheet with median test scores

	LAST NAM	FIRST	TEST1	TEST2	TEST3	AVERG	RMEAN	RMEDIAN		
→	C1	C2	C3	C4	C5	C6	C7	C8	C9	C10
1	ADAMS,	JAMES	72	93	93	86.0000	86.0000	93		
2	BENSON,	MELISSA	99	86	83	89.3333	89.3333	86		
3	BROWN,	LAMAR	59	59	90	69.3333	69.3333	59		
4	DOUGHERTY,	MEGAN	79	69	60	69.3333	69.3333	69		
5	DOUGLAS,	JASON	48	77	25	50.0000	50.0000	48		
6	GIGLIOTTI,	ANDREW	78	94	50	74.0000	74.0000	78		
7	GOLDBERG,	JONATHAN	98	98	94	96.6667	96.6667	98		
8	GREEN,	JENNIFER	92	91	99	94.0000	94.0000	92		
9	KENNEDY,	KEVIN	71	78	62	70.3333	70.3333	71		
10	LEE,	SANG	64	68	97	76.3333	76.3333	68		
11	MCCLURE,	MARK	49	79	43	57.0000	57.0000	49		
12	MESSINA,	STEVEN	94	93	95	94.0000	94.0000	94		
13	NORMAN,	BARBARA	99	95	84	92.6667	92.6667	95		
14	NOWICKI,	AMY	91	81	79	83.6667	83.6667	81		
15	PATEL,	HIMA	90	100	62	84.0000	84.0000	90		
16	PIERSON,	RICHARD	100	77	100	92.3333	92.3333	100		
17	ROJAS,	LUIS	73	79	83	78.3333	78.3333	79		
18	RYAN,	MATT	77	79	85	80.3333	80.3333	79		
19	SCHMIDT,	NANCY	83	79	52	71.3333	71.3333	79		
20	SCOTT,	MICHAEL	81	75	100	85.3333	85.3333	81		
21	SHEPPARD,	KATHLEEN	94	97	100	97.0000	97.0000	97		
22	SMITH,	HOLLY	82	51	25	52.6667	52.6667	51		

Enter Data F10=Menu

For your final grade report, you would like the average grades reported to the nearest integer. To do that, you have Minitab round the scores.

- Return to the Session window
- Choose **Calc** ▶ **Functions and Statistics** ▶ **Functions...**

To tell Minitab which column to round:

- Press [Tab]
- Press [F2] to activate the list box
- Press [↓] to highlight C7 RMEAN
- Press [F2]

Note: From now on, instructions to select a column for a text box will be condensed to: Select C7 RMEAN for the Input Column text box

To name the column that will contain the rounded mean:

- Type **AVERAGE** in the Result in text box
- Press [Alt]-D for Roun**d**

- Press [↵]
- Go to the Data worksheet

Each student's average of the three exams, rounded to the nearest integer, appears in column C9.

Summarizing Columns

Each row represents an individual case, such as one particular student's three test scores. When you perform row *functions,* you calculate a statistic (for example, the mean for each case) and place the results in a designated column.

Minitab's columns contain values of the same variable; for example, C3 contains all scores for Test 1. When you want statistics for a particular variable, or column, you use *column functions.* They produce single numbers that appear in the Session window, not in the Data worksheet. Minitab can store such values in specific *constant* locations that you assign: K1, K2, K3, and so on. It is useful to store a result as a constant if you plan to use it later.

Explore how Minitab handles operations on columns (variables) by finding the mean score of Test 1. Remember, this is not the mean of a single student's performance but of the whole class' performance on the first test.

- Go to the Session window
- Choose **Calc ▸ Functions and Statistics ▸ Column Statistics...**

The Column Statistics dialog box (Figure 2-4) appears.

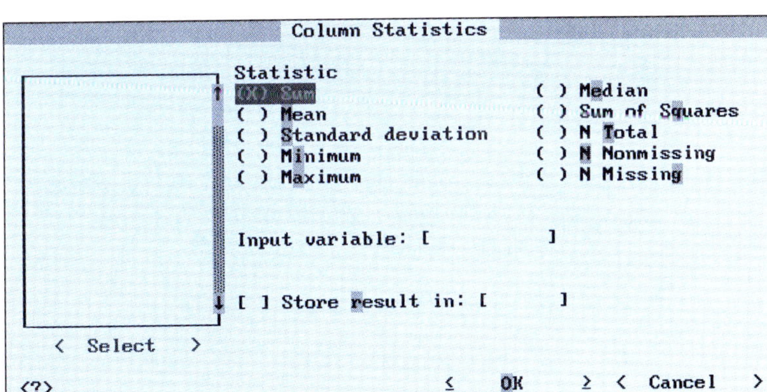

FIGURE 2-4
The Column Statistics dialog box from the Functions and Statistics submenu

- Press [Alt]-M for **M**ean
- Press [Tab]

To indicate the Input variable:

- Select C3 TEST1 as the Input variable
- Press [Alt]-R to select the Store **r**esult in checkbox and press [Tab]
- Type **K1** to store the result in constant K1 and press [↵]

> **Mouse Users:**
>
> Click the Store result in check-box to place an X in it

When you have completed this procedure, the Session window displays the results of the computation.

Your screen should look similar to Figure 2-5.

FIGURE 2-5

The Session window, showing the mean of Test 1

The last line shows that the mean of the Test 1 scores is 80.000.

Listing Columns in the Session Window

There are occasions when you would like to see only certain columns. To view these columns you can list them, in any order, in the Session window:

- Choose **E**dit ▶ Di**s**play Data...

The Display Data dialog box (Figure 2-6) appears.

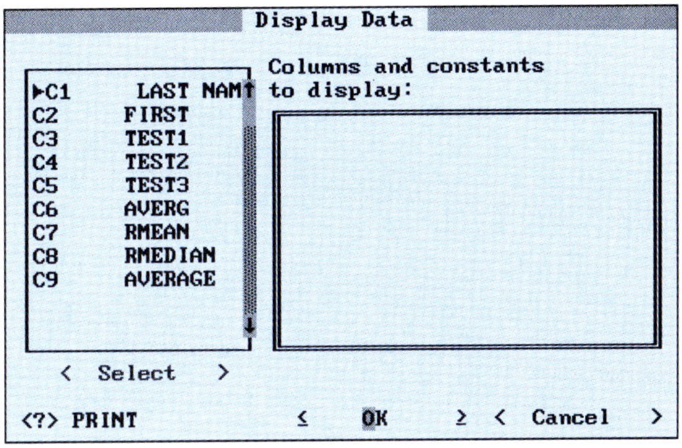

FIGURE 2-6

The Display Data dialog box from the Edit menu

- Select C1, C2, C3, C4, and C5 for the Columns and constants to display text box

> **Mouse Users:**
>
> Click OK

- Press Alt-O

The Session window lists your original data. Scroll up to the top of the list; note that Minitab has recorded the Print command, along with the columns you specified. Choosing the Display Data command from the menus is the same as typing **PRINT** in the Session window.

Combining Data with the Stack Command

Your principal, Ms. Taylor, has asked you to include in your report statistical information about all three tests combined. Minitab lets you combine all the data from several columns into a single column by stacking the columns on top of each other. This forms a new variable consisting of data from all the selected columns.

- Choose Calc ▶ Stack...

The Stack dialog box (Figure 2-7) appears.

FIGURE 2-7
The Stack dialog box from the Calc menu

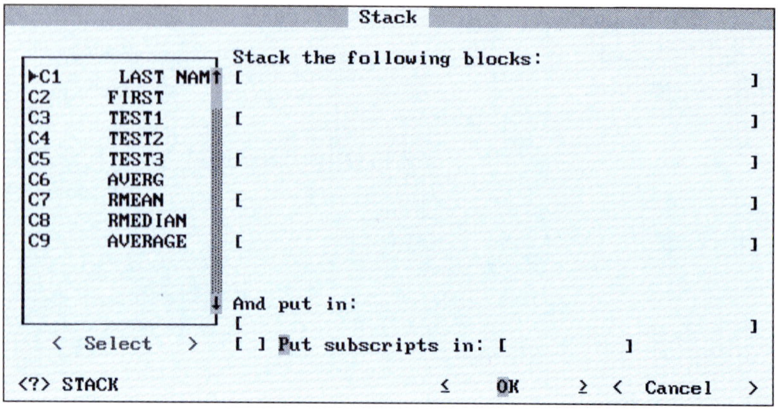

To indicate the three columns you want to stack:

- Select C3 TEST1 and press Tab
- Select C4 TEST2 and press Tab
- Select C5 TEST3 and press Tab three times
- Type **TOTAL** in the And put in text box

When you stack data, you can also have Minitab store a subscript variable that indicates the column from which the data originated:

- Press Alt-P for **P**ut subscripts in and press Tab
- Type **TEST**

Your screen should resemble Figure 2-8.

FIGURE 2-8
The completed Stack dialog box from the Calc menu

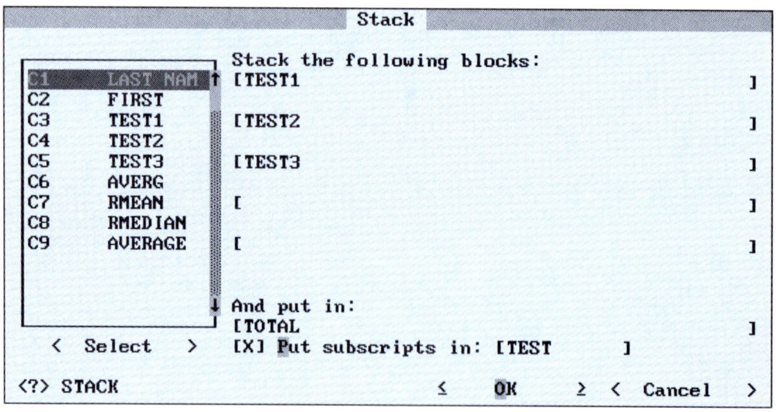

- Press [↵]

The commands you just issued are shown in the Session window. To see the actual stacked data:

- Go to the Data worksheet
- Scroll to the right so that C10 and C11 are visible
- Scroll down to view the lower part of C10

Notice how all the grades are "stacked" on top of one another (i.e., all three columns are listed in a single vertical column, which is three times as long as the original column). Note, too, that C11 (the subscript) identifies the test from which each grade originated.

Now have Minitab calculate the mean of C10 and view it in the Session window:

- Return to the Session window
- Choose **C**alc ▶ **F**unctions and Statistics ▶ **C**olumn Statistics...
- Press [Alt]-M for **M**ean and press [Tab]
- Select C10 TOTAL as the Input variable
- Press [Alt]-O

The last line of the Session window shows the mean for all the test scores you stacked in C10. You can report to Ms. Taylor that the average for all of your tests is a respectable 78.569.

Coding Data

The school district where you work uses the letter grades A, B, C, D, and F, based on a 4-point scale where 4 = A and 0 = F. To compute the students' grades, you need a new variable based on grade intervals. You will translate the grades into a four-point scale so grades falling in the interval of 90 to 100 are coded as a 4 (A), grades of 80-89 are coded as a 3 (B), grades of 70-79 as a 2 (C), 60-69 as a 1 (D), and grades 59 and below as a 0 (F). To code the students' average:

- Choose **C**alc ▶ Code Data **V**alues...

The Code Data Values dialog box appears. To indicate the location of the data you want to code:

- Select C9 AVERAGE and press Tab
- Type **GRADE** in the Into columns text box and press Tab

To specify the intervals, you can either list each value in the interval (separated by commas) or specify the first and last value in the range (with a colon between the two values).

- Type **90:100** and press Tab

Minitab interprets 90:100 as all grades between 90 and 100 inclusive. To indicate the new values that you want Minitab to assign:

- Type **4** and press Tab
- Type **80:89**, press Tab, type **3**, and press Tab
- Type **70:79**, press Tab, type **2**, and press Tab
- Type **60:69**, press Tab, type **1**, and press Tab
- Type **0:59**, press Tab, and type **0**

Your screen should look like Figure 2-9.

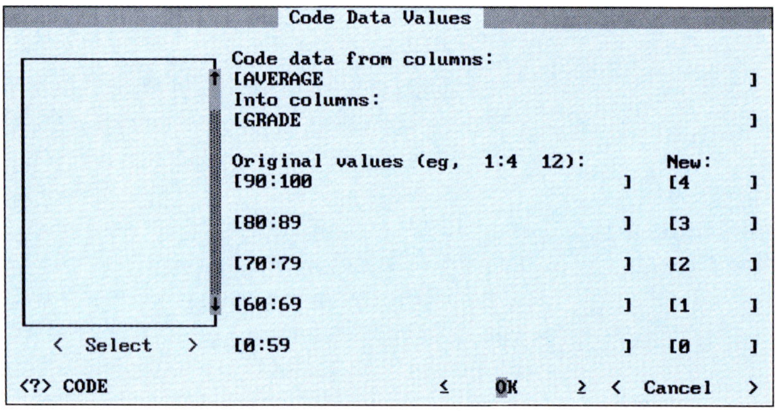

FIGURE 2-9
The completed Code Data Values dialog box from the Calc menu

- Press ↵
- Go to the Data worksheet
- Press Ctrl-Home to move to the beginning of the worksheet
- Scroll right to view C12

Compare columns C9 and C12 and notice that all students with a rounded mean between 90 and 100 are coded 4, those whose rounded means fell between 80 and 89 are coded 3, and so on. By scanning this column you can quickly determine which students are doing well and which need help.

Ranking Data

Ms. Taylor has asked you to rank your students' average exam scores in numerical order so she can see where each student falls in comparison with his or her classmates. Minitab ranks the data listed in any column by assigning a value of 1 to the lowest score, 2 to the second lowest, and so on. The top student is ranked number 24. To rank the average exam scores:

- Return to the Session window
- Choose **C**alc ▶ Ran**k**...

Specify the data you want to rank:

- Select C9 AVERAGE and press Tab
- Type **RANK** in the Put ranks in text box

The completed Rank dialog box should resemble Figure 2-10.

FIGURE 2-10

The completed Rank dialog box from the Calc menu

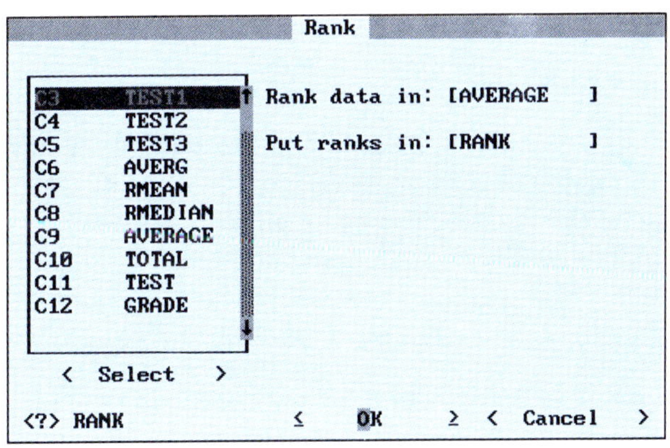

- Press ↵
- Go to the Data worksheet

If two or more scores are tied, Minitab assigns them a rank equal to the average of their separate ranks. Glance down C13 to see that the scores in twenty-first and twenty-second place (Steven Messina and Jennifer Green in rows 8 and 12) were each ranked 21.5, the average of 21 and 22. Verify that two students are tied for the top place in your class (remember that rank 1 is the lowest, not the highest). What are their names?

Sorting Data

Ms. Taylor has now asked you to print a list where the student who had the highest mean is listed first, the second highest next, and so on. Minitab can use up to four columns as the criteria for sorting.

If you simply sort C7 RMEAN, Minitab will rearrange the entries in that column but leave the others intact. You need to "carry along" (i.e., include) all of the columns in a worksheet that correspond to the data for an individual case (in this case study a single student).

- Go to the Session window
- Choose **Calc ▶ Sort...**

To indicate all the variables you want to sort:

- Press [F2]
- Highlight all the columns in the list box *except* C10 TOTAL and C11 TEST
- Press [F2] and press [Tab]

Do not sort C10 and C11 because they do not correspond to information about a particular row or student. They contain information about all of the exams for all students (with the test score in C10 and the indicator variable in C11).

You need to specify where you want Minitab to place the sorted data. In this case, you'll put it in the same location it now occupies.

- Again select all columns except C10 and C11 for the Put into text box and press [Tab] (make sure that the column order is identical to that in the Sort column(s) text box)

Now you will indicate which variable you want to use as your sort criterion. To use the student's average on the three exams, C7 RMEAN:

- Select C7 RMEAN for the Sort by column text box
- Press [Alt]-D to select the Descending checkbox

Your completed screen should look like Figure 2-11.

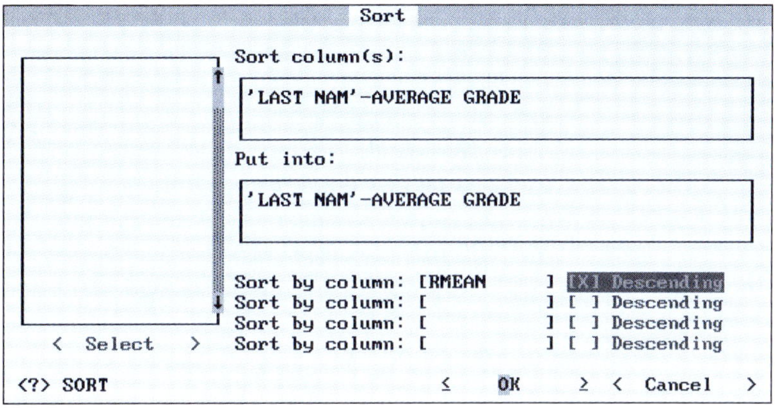

FIGURE 2-11

The completed Sort dialog box from the Calc menu

- Press [↵]
- Go to the Data worksheet

The students have been sorted according to their mean scores (Figure 2-12). Had you forgotten to "carry along" a column, its contents would not have been included in the sort. The wrong grade would then go with the wrong student.

FIGURE 2-12

The Data worksheet after sorting

	LAST NAM	FIRST	TEST1	TEST2	TEST3	AVERG	RMEAN	RMEDIAN	AVERAGE
→	C1	C2	C3	C4	C5	C6	C7	C8	C9
1	SHEPPARD,	KATHLEEN	94	97	100	97.0000	97.0000	97	97
2	GOLDBERG,	JONATHAN	98	98	94	96.6667	96.6667	98	97
3	GREEN,	JENNIFER	92	91	99	94.0000	94.0000	92	94
4	MESSINA,	STEVEN	94	93	95	94.0000	94.0000	94	94
5	NORMAN,	BARBARA	99	95	84	92.6667	92.6667	95	93
6	PIERSON,	RICHARD	100	77	100	92.3333	92.3333	100	92
7	BENSON,	MELISSA	99	86	83	89.3333	89.3333	86	09
8	ADAMS,	JAMES	72	93	93	86.0000	86.0000	93	86
9	SCOTT,	MICHAEL	81	75	100	85.3333	85.3333	81	85
10	PATEL,	HIMA	90	100	62	84.0000	84.0000	90	84
11	NOWICKI,	AMY	91	81	79	83.6667	83.6667	81	84
12	RYAN,	MATT	77	79	85	80.3333	80.3333	79	80
13	ROJAS,	LUIS	73	79	83	78.3333	78.3333	79	78
14	LEE,	SANG	64	68	97	76.3333	76.3333	68	76
15	GIGLIOTTI,	ANDREW	78	94	50	74.0000	74.0000	78	74
16	WATSON,	KEISHA	88	93	41	74.0000	74.0000	88	74
17	SCHMIDT,	NANCY	83	79	52	71.3333	71.3333	79	71
18	KENNEDY,	KEVIN	71	78	62	70.3333	70.3333	71	70
19	BROWN,	LAMAR	59	59	90	69.3333	69.3333	59	69
20	DOUGHERTY,	MEGAN	79	69	60	69.3333	69.3333	69	69
21	THOMPSON,	SUSAN	59	60	84	67.6667	67.6667	60	68
22	MCCLURE,	MARK	49	79	43	57.0000	57.0000	49	57

Enter Data F10=Menu

You now have a summary of your class' performance. Since your worksheet is sorted, you can quickly check to see which students are not doing well (those at the bottom of the list) and help them improve their grades.

Separating Data with Unstack

Ms. Taylor would like a separate listing for all grades within each of the ranges specified in the Code Data Values command. Just as you were able to combine several columns into a single column with the Stack command, Minitab lets you take a single column and break it into several new columns, according to the criteria you specify. In this section you will unstack C9 AVERAGE into five columns, C14 to C18. You will put all grades in the range of 0 to 59 in the first column (C14), all grades from 60 to 69 in the second (C15), and so on, using the grade data in C12:

- Return to the Session window
- Choose **Calc ▶ Unstack...**

The Unstack dialog box appears. To indicate which column you want to unstack:

- Select C9 AVERAGE and press [Tab]

To tell Minitab which subscripts to use to unstack:

- Select C12 GRADE and press [Tab]

Starting with the lowest category, specify the blocks of data you want to unstack:

- Type **F**, press [Tab], type **D**, press [Tab], type **C**, press [Tab], type **B**, press [Tab], type **A**

The completed Unstack dialog box should resemble Figure 2-13.

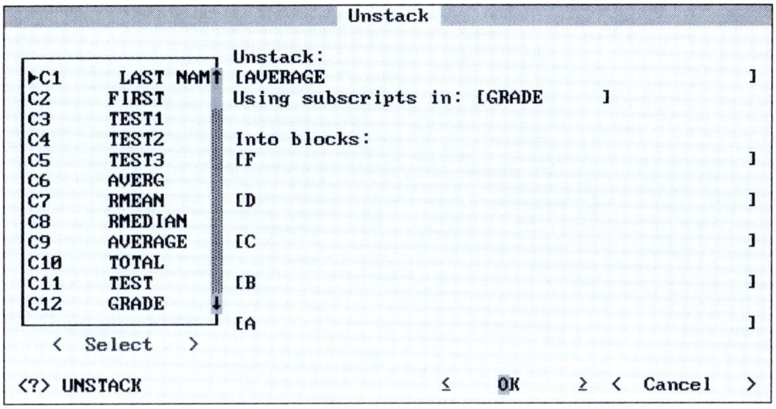

FIGURE 2-13

The completed Unstack dialog box from the Calc menu

- Press [↵]
- Go to the Data worksheet
- Scroll to the right

The Data worksheet (Figure 2-14) now shows the grades divided into categories.

FIGURE 2-14

The Data worksheet, with grades unstacked into intervals

	RMEAN	RMEDIAN	AVERAGE	TOTAL	TEST	GRADE	RANK	F	D	C	B	A
→	C7	C8	C9	C10	C11	C12	C13	C14	C15	C16	C17	C18
1	97.0000	97	97	72	1	4	17.0	57	69	78	89	97
2	96.6667	98	97	99	1	4	18.0	53	69	76	86	97
3	94.0000	92	94	59	1	4	5.5	50	68	74	85	94
4	94.0000	94	94	79	1	4	5.5			74	84	94
5	92.6667	95	93	48	1	4	1.0			71	84	93
6	92.3333	100	92	78	1	4	9.5			70	80	92
7	89.3333	86	89	98	1	3	23.5					
8	86.0000	93	86	92	1	3	21.5					
9	85.3333	81	85	71	1	3	7.0					
10	84.0000	90	84	64	1	3	11.0					
11	83.6667	81	84	49	1	3	3.0					
12	80.3333	79	80	94	1	3	21.5					
13	78.3333	79	78	99	1	2	20.0					
14	76.3333	68	76	91	1	2	14.5					
15	74.0000	78	74	90	1	2	14.5					
16	74.0000	88	74	100	1	2	19.0					
17	71.3333	79	71	73	1	2	12.0					
18	70.3333	71	70	77	1	2	13.0					
19	69.3333	59	69	83	1	1	8.0					
20	69.3333	69	69	81	1	1	16.0					
21	67.6667	60	68	94	1	1	23.5					
22	57.0000	49	57	82	1	0	2.0					

Enter Data F10=Menu

At this point you have eighteen students earning grades of A, B, or C and only six earning D's and F's. Also, your three students with D's are close to C's; you could speak with them and motivate them to work just a bit harder. All in all, it appears that your class is doing fairly well. Ms. Taylor should be pleased.

Standardizing Data

In addition to submitting the grades, you would like to report each student's progress during the marking period by comparing the grades from various tests. Each test reflects a score out of 100 possible points, but an 87 on an easy test might actually show less knowledge than a 75 on a more difficult test. If two scores come from two different populations, each with its own mean and standard deviation, you cannot compare them unless you *standardize* them. To compute standard z-scores for the various test grades:

- Return to the Session window
- Choose **Calc** ▶ **Standardize...**

The Standardize dialog box appears.

- Select C3 TEST1, C4 TEST2, and C5 TEST3 for the Input column(s)
- Press Tab
- Type **STD1 STD2 STD3**

The completed Standardize dialog box should look like Figure 2-15.

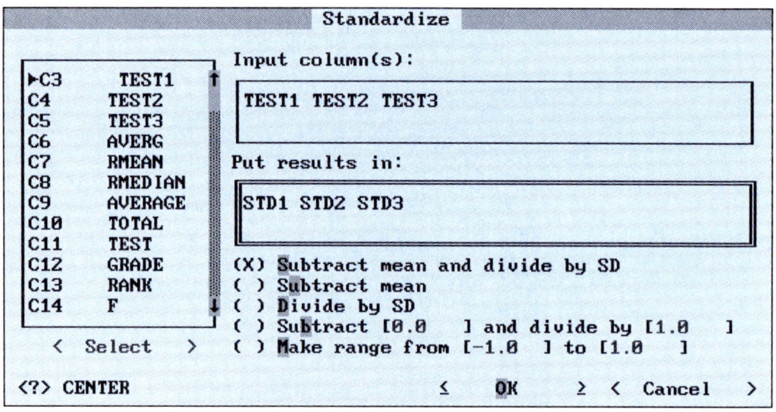

FIGURE 2-15
The completed Standardize dialog box from the Calc menu

- Press Alt-O
- Go to the Data worksheet

The standardized scores in Figure 2-16 allow you to easily determine how each student performed on each test, relative to the class.

FIGURE 2-16

The Data worksheet, showing standardized grades

	F	D	C	B	A	STD1	STD2	STD3				
→	C14	C15	C16	C17	C18	C19	C20	C21	C22	C23	C24	C25
1	57	69	78	89	97	0.89626	1.18275	1.05442				
2	53	69	76	86	97	1.15233	1.25805	0.80713				
3	50	68	74	85	94	0.76822	0.73098	1.01321				
4			74	84	94	0.89626	0.88157	0.84835				
5			71	84	93	1.21635	1.03216	0.39498				
6			70	80	92	1.28037	-0.32314	1.05442				
7						1.21635	0.35451	0.35376				
8						-0.51215	0.88157	0.76592				
9						0.06402	-0.47373	1.05442				
10						0.64018	1.40864	-0.51176				
11						0.70420	-0.02196	0.18890				
12						-0.19206	-0.17255	0.43619				
13						-0.44813	-0.17255	0.35376				
14						-1.02429	-1.00079	0.93078				
15						-0.12804	0.95687	-1.00634				
16						0.51215	0.88157	-1.37727				
17						0.19206	-0.17255	-0.92391				
18						-0.57617	-0.24784	-0.51176				
19						-1.34439	-1.67844	0.64227				
20						-0.06402	-0.92550	-0.59419				
21						-1.34439	-1.60315	0.39498				
22						-1.98457	-0.17255	-1.29484				

Enter Data   F10=Menu

You can quickly spot trends in a student's performance. For example, Jason Douglas's (row 5) performance dropped off on the last exam, while Lamar Brown's (row 19) improved.

- Return to the Session window

Getting Worksheet Information

When you work with a data set over the course of several days, it's easy to forget what you have done so far, especially if you have many variables and have performed many manipulations. Minitab's Get Worksheet Info command on the Edit menu provides a record of columns and their names in the worksheet. It also lists any constants you have used.

- Choose **E**dit ▶ Get **W**orksheet Info...

The Get Worksheet Info dialog box appears.

- Press [↵] to include all columns and constants

The Session window (Figure 2-17) displays information on every aspect of the worksheet.

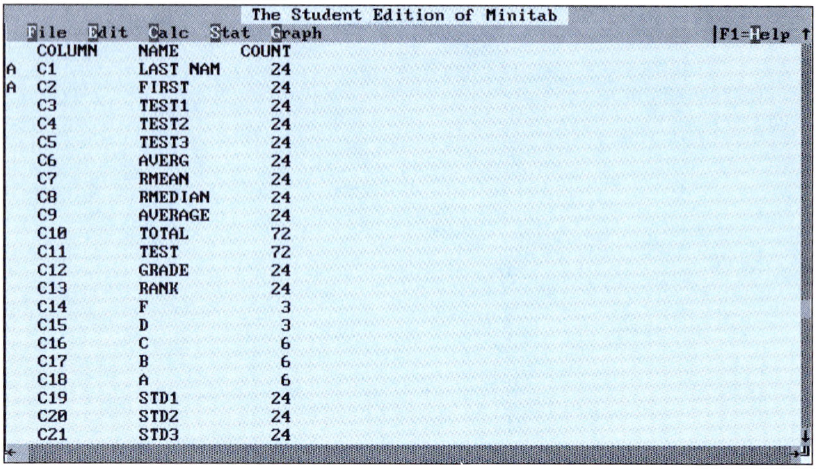

FIGURE 2-17
The Session window, showing worksheet information

You can see why it's important to give your columns meaningful names; they help you remember where you have stored information. The Get Worksheet Info command shows you the columns, names, and amount of data ("COUNT") in each column.

For example, you can use this information to see that columns C10 and C11 are 72 rows long, whereas most of the other columns are 24 rows long. (Recall that these were the two columns where you stacked the results from tests 1 through 3.) The Get Worksheet Info command can provide you with information about your worksheet in a compact form.

Printing the Record of Your Session

Now that you have summarized your class' performance, you will want to print your worksheet on paper (obtain a "hard copy" in computer language) to submit to Ms. Taylor. First, sort your grades data back into alphabetical order. Use the Sort command, selecting all columns that contain 24 entries (this excludes any columns that resulted from the Stack and Unstack commands):

- Choose **Calc ▶ Sort...**
- Select C1-C9, C12-C13, and C19-21 for the Sort Columns text box, and press [Tab]

- Repeat to put the same columns in the Put into text box, and press [Tab]; (make sure that the column order is identical to that in the Sort column(s) text box)
- Select C1 LAST NAM for the Sort by column text box and press [Tab] twice
- Select C2 FIRST for the second Sort by column text box, in case you have two students with the same last name
- Press [↵]
- Go to the Data worksheet and scroll back if necessary to view C1

Your worksheet is again in alphabetical order and you are ready to print it.

- Return to the Session window

You have already seen how to send your data to the Session window by using Minitab's Display Data command from the Edit menu (equivalent to typing PRINT after the MTB > prompt). Minitab's PAPER command sends the Session window output to the printer connected to your computer. Because there is no equivalent menu command for the PAPER command, you will type it directly after the MTB > prompt. To obtain a printed copy of the students' names, grades, and grade averages:

- Prepare your printer: check the cables and make sure the printer is on
- Type **PAPER** after the MTB > prompt and press [↵]

This command tells Minitab to send all future output and commands that are displayed in the Session window to the printer. To display the data in the Session window:

- Choose **E**dit ▶ D**i**splay Data...
- Select C1 LAST NAM, C2 FIRST, C9 AVERAGE, and C12 GRADE
- Press [Alt]-O

Minitab prints the columns (in the order listed) to both the screen and the printer. Figure 2-18 shows the printed grade list.

FIGURE 2-18

Printout of alphabetical grade list

```
MTB > Print 'LAST NAM' 'FIRST' 'AVERAGE' 'GRADE'.

 ROW        LAST NAM       FIRST   AVERAGE  GRADE

   1   SHEPPARD,      KATHLEEN        97      4
   2   GOLDBERG,      JONATHAN        97      4
   3   GREEN,         JENNIFER        94      4
   4   MESSINA,       STEVEN          94      4
   5   NORMAN,        BARBARA         93      4
   6   PIERSON,       RICHARD         92      4
   7   BENSON,        MELISSA         89      3
   8   ADAMS,         JAMES           86      3
   9   SCOTT,         MICHAEL         85      3
  10   PATEL,         HIMA            84      3
  11   NOWICKI,       AMY             84      3
  12   RYAN,          MATT            80      3
  13   ROJAS,         LUIS            78      2
  14   LEE,           SANG            76      2
  15   GIGLIOTTI,     ANDREW          74      2
  16   WATSON,        KEISHA          74      2
  17   SCHMIDT,       NANCY           71      2
  18   KENNEDY,       KEVIN           70      2
  19   BROWN,         LAMAR           69      1
  20   DOUGHERTY,     MEGAN           69      1
  21   THOMPSON,      SUSAN           68      1
  22   MCCLURE,       MARK            57      0
  23   SMITH,         HOLLY           53      0
  24   DOUGLAS,       JASON           50      0
```

To tell Minitab to stop sending Session window commands and output to your printer:

- Type **NOPAPER** and press ↵

Note: The PAPER command is designed for a stand-alone PC with a printer connected directly to it. It may not work on a network with shared printers. If this is the case on your network, you can use the Outfile command to store a record of the Minitab session to an ASCII file that you can print later from the DOS prompt.

Creating an Outfile

To control the amount of output you print, you can create and print an *outfile,* a file where Minitab stores the results from commands. The outfile is in text format, so you can import it into a word processing program and then incorporate it into your work, or you can print it from DOS.

To have Minitab create this outfile:

- Choose **File ▶ Other Files ▶ Start Recording Session...**

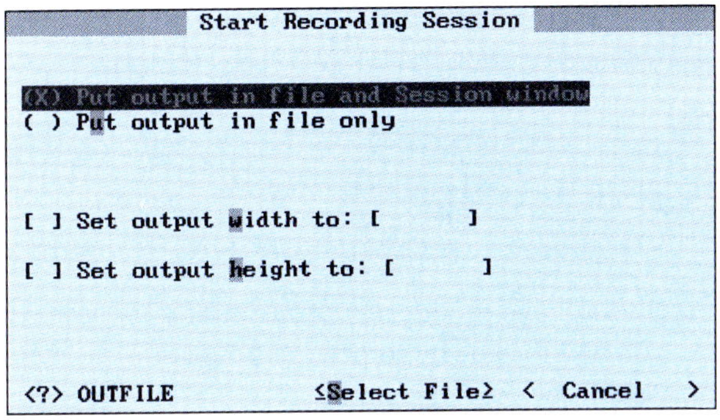

FIGURE 2-19

The Start Recording Session dialog box from the Other Files submenu

This tells Minitab to place all Session window commands and output into a new file until you tell it to stop. The Start Recording Session dialog box (Figure 2-19) appears.

The default setting in the dialog box sends output to both an outfile and the Session window.

- Press ↵

You are asked to name your outfile. Minitab automatically gives outfiles the extension .LIS; this makes them easy to distinguish from Minitab worksheet files, which have the extension .MTW.

- Press Tab and select the TUT2 directory from your backup Sample Files disk
- Press Shift-Tab to name your file
- Type **GRSORT**
- Press ↵

Most word processors can read .LIS files. You can edit GRSORT.LIS from your word processing program to prepare a report for Ms. Taylor, formatted any way you want.

Now select the variables you want to include in the outfile:

- Choose **E**dit ► Di**s**play Data...
- Select C1 LAST NAM, C2 FIRST, C9 AVERAGE, and C12 GRADE

Press Alt-O

This time Minitab displays the data from the columns you selected in the Session window and sends them to the GRSORT.LIS file. The outfile contains the Minitab commands and output for all commands given after the Start Recording Session command. To stop recording the output and end the outfile:

- Choose **F**ile ▶ Other **F**iles ▶ Stop Recording **S**ession...

You have produced a printout of your grade report and a file that you can format in your word processor to produce a clean copy for Ms. Taylor. In the next marking period, it will be much easier for you to organize your grades.

In the next tutorial you will learn how to produce graphical displays of your data.

If you plan to continue directly to the next tutorial:

- Choose **F**ile ▶ Restart **M**initab and press [↵] to exit without saving the worksheet

If you want to take a longer break:

- Choose **F**ile ▶ E**x**it

Minitab Command Summary

The menus and commands introduced in or related to this tutorial are described in this section. You will find a complete explanation of all menus and commands in the Reference section of this manual.

Menu	Command	Function
File		
	Other Files	
	Start Recording Session	Writes all commands and output to an outfile
	Stop Recording Session	Stops writing to the outfile
	Start Recording History	Writes all Minitab commands issued to a file
	Stop Recording History	Stops writing Minitab commands to the file

Edit		
	Display Data	Prints one or many columns in the Session window
	Get Worksheet Info	Prints a record (in the Session window) and constants used in a worksheet
Calc		
	Function and Statistics	
	General Expressions	Creates, transforms, and manipulates columns of data
	Functions	Creates, transforms, and manipulates columns of data using functions such as square root, logarithms, etc.
	Column Statistics	Computes summary statistics, such as mean, variance, etc., on all values in a column
	Row Statistics	Computes summary statistics for values in a row
	Sort	Sorts selected columns of the worksheet using up to four columns as the sorting criterion
	Rank	Ranks the data in one or many columns using the values in up to four columns
	Code Data Values	Changes numeric values or ranges of numeric values in a column to a specified coding scheme
	Stack	Takes the contents of two or more columns and forms a new column by stacking the columns, one on top of another; the number of cells in stacked columns is equivalent to the number of cells in the columns selected for stacking
	Unstack	Creates several columns of data by splitting a given column

Review and Practice

Matching

Match the following terms to their definitions by placing the correct letter next to the term it explains.

____ column operation

____ .LIS

____ Functions

____ row operation

____ Stack

____ N Missing

____ outfile

____ subscripts

____ Get Worksheet Info

a. A text file that optionally stores commands and output from a Minitab session

b. Minitab command that takes several columns of data and creates one column by placing each column on top of each other

c. An optional indicator variable created when Minitab stacks several columns into one column

d. Displays nonempty column numbers and corresponding names in the worksheet

e. An arithmetic operation on the entries in a given set of columns, done for every row of the worksheet

f. File extension name given to files created by the Outfile command

g. An operation using only the values in a given column

h. A summary statistic that determines how many observations in a row or column have missing values

i. Standard numeric operations that Minitab has preprogrammed and stored

True/False

Mark the following statements T or F.

____ 1. Row operation results must always be stored in a column.

____ 2. The results of column operations can be stored in a column or not at all.

____ 3. The Get Worksheet Info command displays all columns containing data in the current worksheet, the column names (if named), and the number of observations in the column.

____ 4. The Sort command automatically sorts all columns in the worksheet.

____ 5. The PRINT command can be used to obtain a printout on a piece of paper.

____ 6. The inter-quartile range is one of the statistics available in the Row Statistics and Column Statistics commands.

____ 7. Minitab always assigns the .LIS extension to files produced by the Outfile command.

____ 8. The Sort command sorts only numeric variables or columns.

____ 9. Many of the statistics in the Row Statistics command are also available in the Column Statistics command.

____ 10. Using Minitab's PAPER command sends only data, not Minitab commands, to the printer.

Practice Problems

1. Print out a copy of the SNOWFALL.MTW worksheet from the TUT2 directory. (You will need to open the worksheet and then print the data.)

2. Open TVVIEW.MTW from the TUT2 directory.

   a. Compute the mean, median, and sample standard deviation of TV viewing time for husbands, wives, and households.

   b. Compute the mean, median, and sample standard deviation of the difference between the husbands and wives, using the difference variable you created in Tutorial 1.

   c. Stack the times for both husbands and wives into C5; save the subscripts in C6.

   d. Print out the worksheet.

3. Open RADON.MTW from the TUT2 directory.

   a. Use the Get Worksheet Info command to determine what information has been saved in this data set. Which columns are used? What names have been assigned to them? How many observations does the data set contain?

   b. Code the age variable so that new homes are those that are less than 2 years old. Assign newer homes a code value of 0 and older homes a code of 1.

   c. Save the worksheet into the TUT2 directory and name the file RADON1.

   d. Sort the data set using the coded age variable. Delete the rows that correspond to older homes.

4. Open COMPUTER.MTW from the TUT2 directory.

   a. Use the Get Worksheet Info to determine what information has been saved in this data set. Which columns are used? What names have been assigned to these columns? How many observations does the data set contain?

   b. Sort the complete worksheet using the price, CPU, and speed columns as the sorting criteria.

   c. Print out the worksheet. Which 386 computer is the cheapest? Most expensive? Which 25-megahertz 486 computer is the cheapest? Does it come with software? A mouse?

TUTORIAL 3

Graphical Methods for Describing Data

The pictorial description of data is an essential aspect of statistical analysis. In this tutorial you will return to the role of the managerial consultant at Technitron. The company wants you to present a report of your preliminary findings about the sales department salary structure at the next staff meeting. For your presentation, you will use Minitab's graphical capabilities to summarize data values, investigate relationships, and finally, to produce printed versions of your graphs.

Objectives

In this tutorial you will learn to:

- graphically display any variable from a worksheet using character-based and high-resolution displays
- graph single variables using histograms, dotplots, stem-and-leaf plots, and box-and-whisker plots
- plot variables against each other using scatter plots and multiple scatter plots
- print or save your graphs for printing later

Graphics Modes

Minitab displays graphics in two modes, *regular* and *high-resolution (hi-res)*. Regular (character-based) graphs consist of keyboard characters such as * * *, +, --- or letters such as x. Hi-res graphs use more *pixels* (short for picture elements) per inch and produce clearer graphs. Although a hi-res graph looks more professional, a regular graph gives you the same kinds of information. Furthermore, not all graph types can be produced in a hi-res format.

Minitab places regular graphs in the Session window, but it displays each hi-res graph in the graph screen. Each hi-res graphic is a separate display; you can print it directly or save it to a file and print it later. In some cases, you can add descriptive text to the graph.

Graphing Single Variables

Minitab produces four types of graphics that summarize information in a single column: histograms, dotplots, stem-and-leaf plots, and box-and-whisker plots. When you decide which graphs to include in your presentation, consider the benefits and limitations of each type.

- A *histogram* is a clean, easy-to-read graph that groups data into classes and represents frequencies within classes by means of horizontal bars. The distribution of data is easy to see from this type of graph. Hi-res is the default setting for histograms, but you can choose regular graphics if you like.
- A *dotplot* displays each data value as a dot stacked above a horizontal axis. Like the histogram, it shows distribution characteristics for the data it describes. It is not available in hi-res format.
- A *stem-and-leaf* plot displays each data value and shows distribution characteristics of the data. It is available only in regular format.
- A *box-and-whisker* plot (or boxplot) lets you see the distributional characteristics of the data. You can display several different boxplots on the same graph screen to make comparisons among subgroups. By default, boxplots in Minitab are displayed in hi-res format.

To begin examining Technitron salaries, use Minitab to produce various graphs of the data in PAYT3.MTW.

- Start Minitab and insert your backup Sample Files disk
- Open PAYT3.MTW from the TUT3 directory

Creating Histograms

For the staff presentation, you want to represent the salary distribution among employees. The first graph you will produce is a histogram describing the data in C1 SALARY.

- Choose **Graph ▶ Histogram...**

The Histogram dialog box appears.

- Select C1 SALARY

> **SHORTCUT**
>
> Type **C1** directly into the text box to select C1.

> **Mouse Users:**
>
> Click the checkbox to remove the X

To create a regular (character-based) histogram:

- Press [Alt]-H to remove the X from the **H**igh resolution checkbox

The completed Histogram dialog box should resemble Figure 3-1.

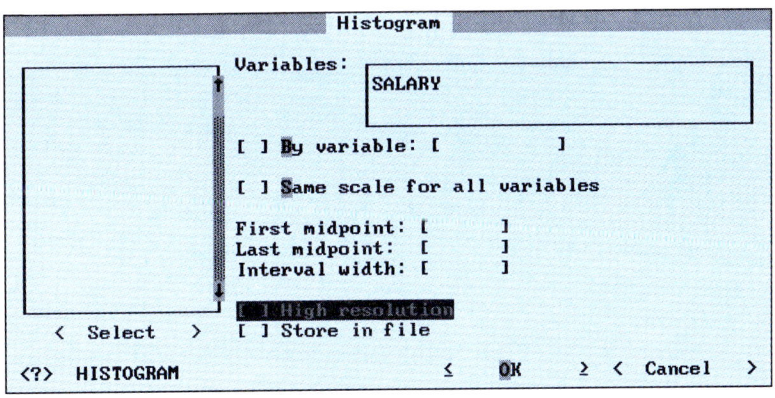

FIGURE 3-1
The completed Histogram dialog box from the Graph menu

- Press [↵]

The Session window displays the histogram, as shown in Figure 3-2.

FIGURE 3-2
The character-based salary histogram, displayed in the Session window

```
MTB > Histogram 'SALARY'.

Histogram of SALARY   N = 11

Midpoint   Count
   24000       1  *
   26000       0
   28000       2  **
   30000       1  *
   32000       3  ***
   34000       0
   36000       0
   38000       2  **
   40000       1  *
   42000       1  *
```

To see this same display in hi-res graphics:

- Choose **E**dit ▶ Edit **L**ast Command Dialog...
- Press [Alt]-H to select **H**igh resolution, then press [↵]

The hi-res histogram appears in its own graph screen (Figure 3-3).

FIGURE 3-3
The salary histogram in high-resolution format

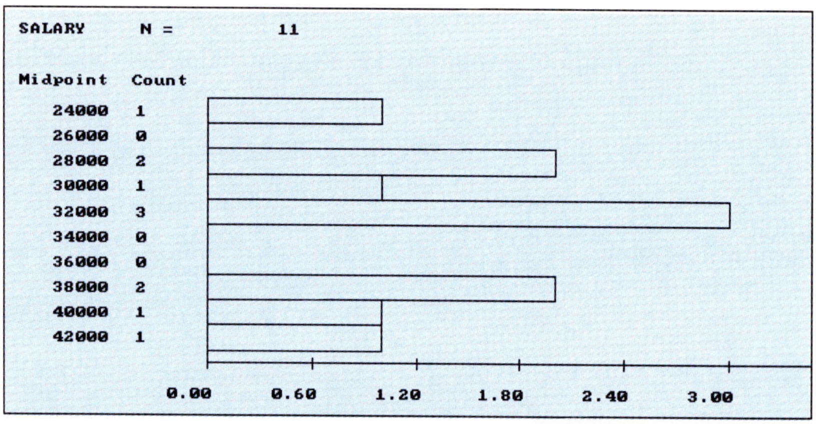

The histogram quickly shows which salary classes in your sample contain the most data values. Minitab constructs histograms with horizontal bars in the hi-res mode and asterisks in the regular mode. In both cases, the midpoint for each salary class (bar) is shown. The horizontal length of each bar (in high-resolution displays) or the number of asterisks (in regular displays) indicates the frequency of occurrence of the variable within that particular class. For example, there were three employees whose salaries fell between $31000 and $32999.

After looking at the first two histograms, you feel that the default selection of ten salary classes "chops" the data too much; you believe a histogram with only five classes might provide a clearer picture of your data. Generally speaking, the more bars in your histogram, the more finely "chopped up" your data will be.

Minitab used ten salary classes, each with a width of 2000 (you can determine the class width by subtracting any two adjacent midpoints, for example, 2000 = 26000 – 24000). To create a histogram with only five salary classes, try setting the class width to 4000.

At the bottom of the graphics screen Minitab explains the three options: P for Print, N for Next, or Q for Quit. To return to the Session window and create a new graphic with a class width of 4000:

- Press Q for Quit
- Choose **E**dit ▶ Edit **L**ast Command Dialog...
- Press [Tab] until you reach the Interval width text box
- Type **4000** and press [↵]

Mouse Users:

Click the Interval width text box

Since you did not turn off the hi-res option, your new histogram is displayed in its own graph screen. The resulting histogram has five classes, each with a width of 4000 (Figure 3-4).

If you want Minitab to create more classes, make the Interval width smaller.

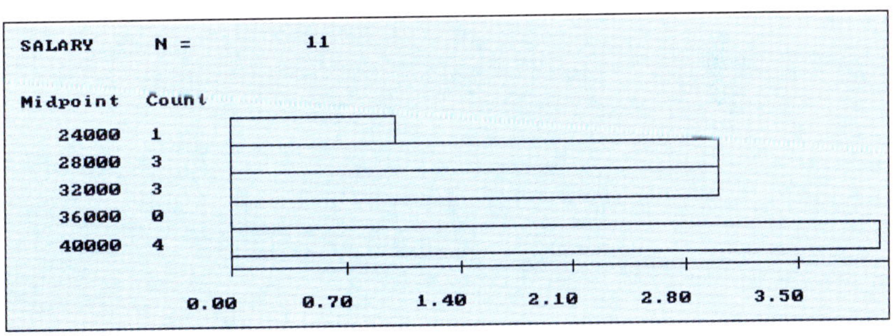

FIGURE 3-4
The Salary histogram with five salary classes

You can see that most of the employees in the sales department are in the highest salary class. Perhaps these are employees who have been working at Technitron a long time. It might be cost-effective to suggest a retirement incentive to reduce salary costs. The histogram also indicates a gap between the highest level of salary and the lower levels. Is this bad for employee morale?

To help investigate whether there is any sex discrimination at Technitron, you also want to compare male salaries to female salaries. To do that, you produce two histograms, one displaying male salaries and the other displaying female salaries.

- Press Q for Quit to return to the Session window
- Choose **E**dit ▶ Edit **L**ast Command Dialog...

When you select the By variable checkbox, you can produce separate histograms for each value of the second variable (also known as the *by variable*). For your report use C8 GENDER N as your by variable:

- Press [Alt]-B and press [Tab]
- Select C8 GENDER N
- Press [↵]

Note: By variables can contain only integer values.

Minitab generates two separate histograms (Figures 3-5 and 3-6), showing the salary of men (GENDER N = 0) and that of women (GENDER N = 1). Each of these two graphs appears in a separate screen; however, only the first case (GENDER N = 0) is currently visible.

FIGURE 3-5 *Histogram of male salaries*

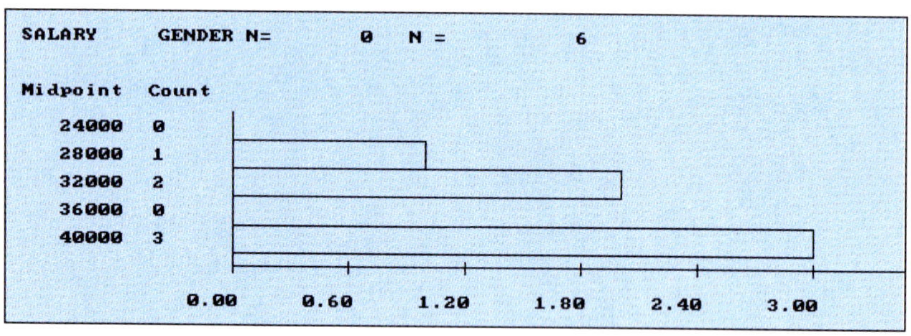

To see the other histogram (GENDER N = 1):

- Press N for Next

Figure 3-6, which has the same interval width as Figure 3-5, appears.

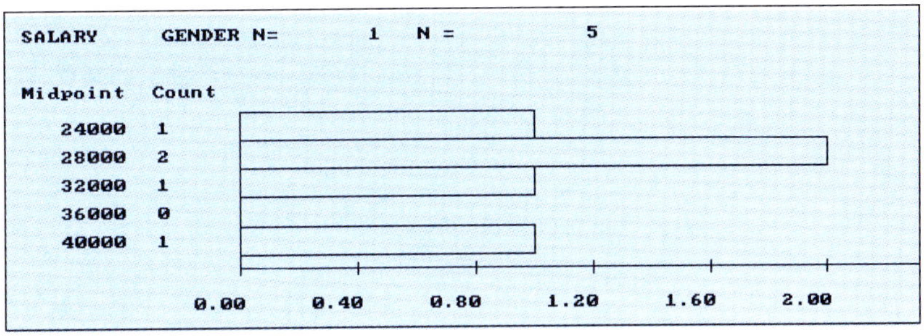

FIGURE 3-6
Histogram of female salaries

When you compare the two histograms, you see that female salaries are more equally distributed, while male salaries are concentrated toward the upper range of salaries. It would appear that Technitron is discriminatory in its salary structure; however, such a conclusion is premature because male employees might have been at the company longer. Further analysis will clear up the issue.

- Press Q for Quit

Creating a Dotplot

Now you will look at a dotplot representation of the data in C1 SALARY. As you do, you can compare the advantages of a dotplot over a histogram and decide which graphs you would like to include in your presentation.

- Choose **G**raph ▶ **D**otplot...

The Dotplot dialog box appears.

- Select C1 SALARY

The completed Dotplot dialog box should be similar to Figure 3-7.

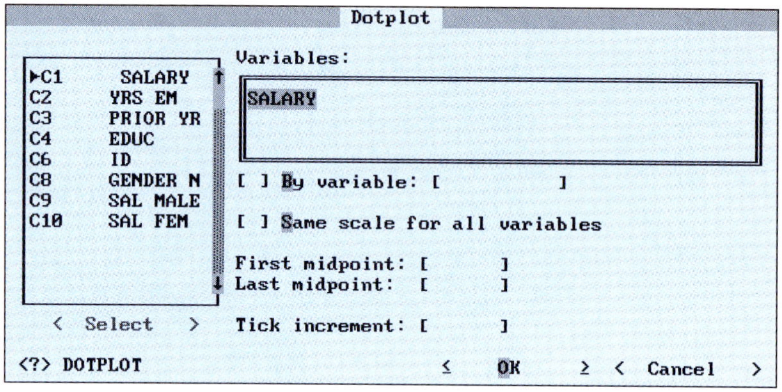

FIGURE 3-7
The completed Dotplot dialog box from the Graph menu

- Press [Alt]-O

Since Minitab uses regular graphics for dotplots, all dotplots are displayed in the Session window (Figure 3-8).

FIGURE 3-8
A dotplot of the salary data

```
MTB > DotPlot 'SALARY'.


                 .                 : .        .    :                          :    .          .
         ---+---------+---------+---------+---------+---------+---SALARY
         24500     28000     31500     35000     38500     42000
```

The dotplot of the salary data tells the same story as the histogram. Salaries range from approximately \$24000 to \$42000, with a fairly large gap in the middle.

To change the dotplot scale so that it is comparable to the scale shown in the histogram in Figure 3-4:

- Choose **E**dit ▶ Edit **L**ast Command Dialog...
- Tab to the First midpoint text box and type **20000**
- Tab to the Tick increment text box and type **4000**
- Press [↵]

As usual, Minitab records all commands (and in this case the output) in the Session window, as shown in Figure 3-9.

FIGURE 3-9
The salary dotplot with an increment of 4000

```
MTB > DotPlot 'SALARY';
SUBC>   Start 20000;
SUBC>   Increment 4000.

                      .         : .    .  :              :  .    .
          +----------+----------+----------+----------+----------+-------SALARY
      20000      24000      28000      32000      36000      40000
```

Each time you make a menu selection, you are actually issuing a Minitab command. When you use the menus, Minitab displays the corresponding commands in the Session window. Now look at the last three commands before the dotplot in Figure 3-9. The following table explains the meaning of each entry in the Session window:

Entry	Represents
MTB >	This is the Minitab prompt, displayed after Minitab finishes with the previous command. It indicates that Minitab is waiting for your next command.
DotPlot 'SALARY';	This command indicates that you chose Dotplot from the Graph menu and selected C1 SALARY as the variable to be plotted. If you had executed the dialog box without selecting any other options, this would be the only command shown in the Session window. The semicolon indicates that Minitab will next prompt you for a subcommand, which gives more information about the preceding command.
SUBC>	This is the Minitab subcommand prompt, indicating that a subcommand follows.
Start 20000;	You chose 20000 for the First midpoint; Minitab interprets this as the Start subcommand. The semicolon indicates that another subcommand follows.
Increment 4000.	This subcommand indicates that you specified 4000 as the tick increment. The period indicates that it was the last subcommand issued for the DotPlot 'SALARY'; command.

For many users, using the Minitab menus is the quickest way to issue commands. But those who use Minitab frequently and are proficient typists may find if more efficient to type the Minitab command language directly after the Session window MTB > prompt. However, these tutorials will continue to use menu commands. The Reference section contains more information about Minitab's command language.

Creating a Stem-and-Leaf Plot

A stem-and-leaf display is similar to a histogram, except that each data value is shown. Like dotplots, these displays are regular (not hi-res) graphs, and always appear in the Session window.

One important aspect of your report will concern the length of time the employees have been at Technitron. Construct a stem-and-leaf display for C2 YRS EM using Minitab's default scaling.

- Choose **G**raph ► **S**tem-and-Leaf...
- Select C2 YRS EM

The completed Stem-and-Leaf dialog box should resemble Figure 3-10.

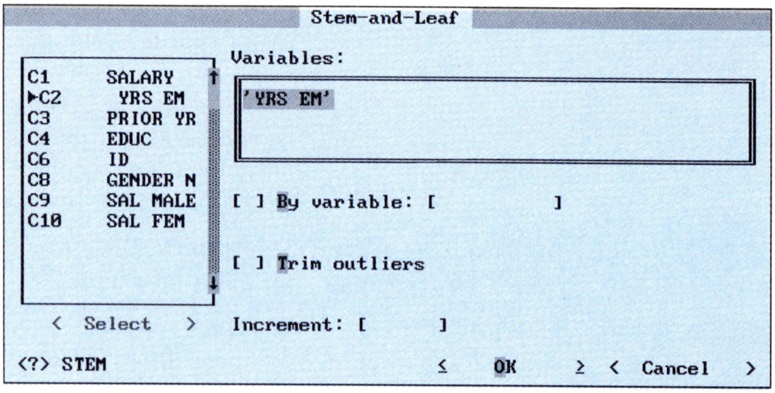

FIGURE 3-10
The completed Stem-and-Leaf dialog box from the Graph menu

- Press Alt-O

The stem-and-leaf display appears in the Session window (Figure 3-11).

FIGURE 3-11

Stem-and-leaf display of years employed

```
MTB > Stem-and-Leaf 'YRS EM'.

Stem-and-leaf of YRS EM    N  = 11
Leaf Unit = 1.0

   3    0 003
   5    0 56
  (1)   1 2
   5    1 588
   2    2 12
```

Depths — Stems — Leaves

For now, ignore the numbers in the far left column and look at the rest of the display. The numbers in the center column represent the stems (leftmost digits) of the data values. The column on the right contains the leaves (rightmost digits). Minitab reports a leaf unit of 1, so each leaf represents the one's digit of a data value. Each stem represents the ten's digit of the data value.

To reconstruct the data values from the stem-and-leaf plot, in the bottom line of Figure 3-11, the stem of 2 followed by leaves of 1 and 2 represents the values 21 and 22.

Many stem-and-leaf displays use one line per stem, but in this case Minitab chose two lines per stem. When two lines per stem are used, the first line of a stem contains leaves with the first five digits (0, 1, 2, 3, 4) and the second line of a stem the last five digits (5, 6, 7, 8, 9). To break up the data even more finely, you could use five lines per stem corresponding to leaf digits of (0,1), (2,3), (4,5), (6,7), and (8,9).

The first column in Minitab's stem-and-leaf display gives the *depths*, which are used to display cumulative frequencies. Starting from the top, the depths indicate the number of leaves that lie in the given row (or stem) and previous rows. The 5 in the second line from the top indicates that there are 5 leaves (0, 0, 3, 5, and 6) in the first two rows (or stems). If the line containing the median has any entries, the number in the left column represents the number of leaves on that line and is placed in parentheses. The median for this data set is 12.

Now change the increment from the default of 5 (where each stem value of 10 is divided between two lines) to 10.

- Choose **E**dit ▶ Edit **L**ast Command Dialog...
- Tab to the Increment text box and type **10**
- Press ↵

Now Minitab will record all values from the same stem on one line. The new display should resemble Figure 3-12.

FIGURE 3-12
Stem-and-leaf display with an increment of 10

```
MTB > Stem-and-Leaf 'YRS EM';
SUBC>   Increment 10.

Stem-and-leaf of YRS EM     N  = 11
Leaf Unit = 1.0

    5    0 00356
   (4)   1 2588
    2    2 12
```

This time there is only one line per stem. Compare the displays in Figures 3-11 and 3-12. Minitab's default graph with two lines per stem gives a more descriptive picture of the data, because it breaks up the data more finely.

Next, you will look at a stem-and-leaf display of the data values in C1 SALARY. Use Minitab's default settings to construct a stem-and-leaf display.

- Choose **G**raph ▶ **S**tem-and-Leaf...
- Select C1 SALARY
- Press [Alt]-O

The display appears in the Session window (Figure 3-13).

FIGURE 3-13
Stem-and-leaf display of SALARY

```
MTB > Stem-and-Leaf 'SALARY'.

Stem-and-leaf of SALARY     N  = 11
Leaf Unit = 1000

    1    2 4
    1    2
    4    2 889
    5    3 1
   (2)   3 22
    4    3
    4    3
    4    3 889
    1    4 1
```

In the stem-and-leaf displayed in the Session window, each leaf represents the thousands digit of your data value (because the leaf unit is 1000). Each stem represents the ten thousands digit. For example, the first entry of 2 4 translates to a data value of 24000 (20000 for the stem and 4000 for the leaf). This entry represents the actual salary value of 24749. To simplify the stem-and-leaf plot, Minitab uses only the first two digits of a salary.

For each stem in this particular display, there are five lines. To condense the salary stem-and-leaf display to two lines per stem, use an increment of 5000. (Recall that the leaf unit is 1000, so 10/2*1000 = 5000.)

- Choose **E**dit ▸ Edit **L**ast Command Dialog...
- Tab to the Increment text box and type **5000**
- Press [↵]

Minitab condenses the display to two lines per stem. In deciding whether to use any of these stem-and-leaf displays, you should consider how much opportunity you will have to interpret them. As you can see, they require some careful explanation. If the staff is familiar with these plots, they could provide an excellent picture of your information.

Creating a Boxplot

Of the four methods for displaying a single variable, the boxplot contains the most statistical information. Minitab can produce a boxplot using either regular graphics (output in the Session window) or hi-res graphics (output in its own graphics screen).

- Choose **G**raph ▸ **B**oxplot...
- Select C1 SALARY

The completed Boxplot dialog box (Figure 3-14) appears.

FIGURE 3-14
The completed Boxplot dialog box from the Graph menu

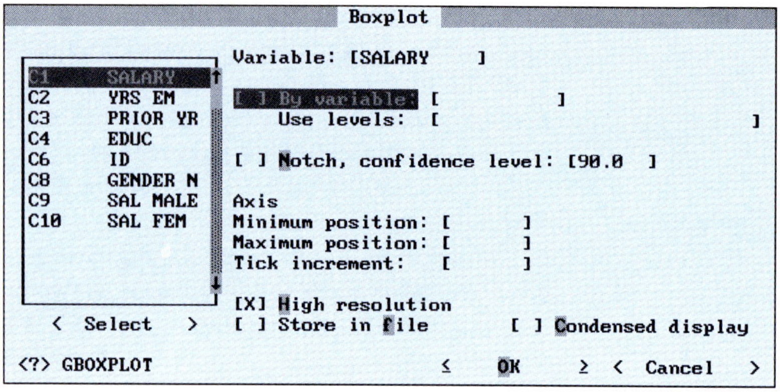

- Press ↵

The salary boxplot (Figure 3-15) appears.

FIGURE 3-15
Boxplot of salary data

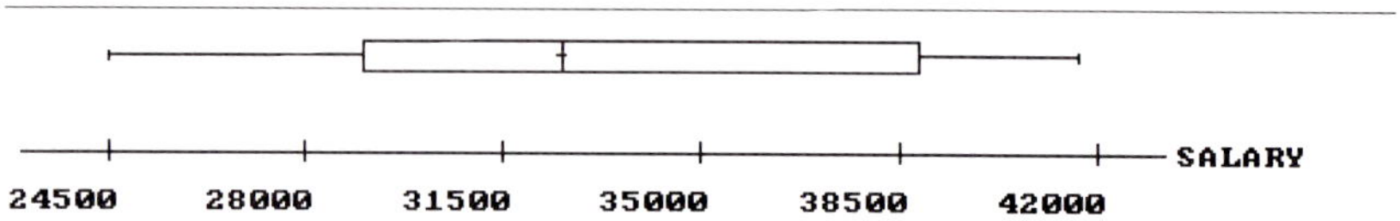

A boxplot uses five numbers to describe a set of data:

- the maximum value
- the upper hinge (roughly equivalent to the 75th percentile)
- the median (50th percentile)
- the lower hinge (roughly equivalent to the 25th percentile)
- the minimum value

A rectangle is constructed between the lower hinge and the upper hinge, with a + sign indicating the location of the median. The box encloses the *middle half* of the data. The whiskers extend in either direction to indicate the maximum and minimum values. If you decide to use this graph for your presentation, you can quickly show that the middle half of the salaries in the sales department fall between about 29000 and 39000, with half of all salaries below 32000 (the median) and half above.

Minitab can also display multiple boxplots for different groups of data on the same graphic screen. Recall that you had Minitab construct two histograms for salary using C8 GENDER N as the By variable. Compare that to how the boxplot handles that assignment.

- Press Q for Quit
- Choose **E**dit ▶ Edit **L**ast Command Dialog...
- Press [Alt]-B to select the **B**y variable checkbox and press [Tab]
- Select C8 GENDER N
- Press [↵]

The display of the two boxplots (one for 0 = male and the other for 1 = female) should resemble Figure 3-16.

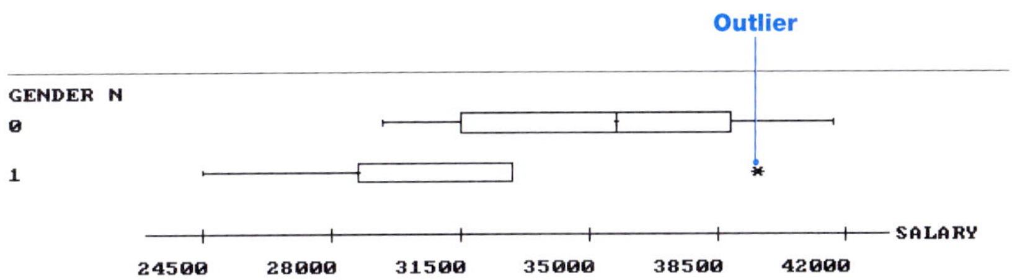

FIGURE 3-16
Boxplot of male and female salaries

The boxplot is the only type of graph that can display data by more than one subset on the same graph. Using these multiple boxplots, you can see that male salaries have a wider range and a higher median salary than female salaries. Referring to Figures 3-5 and 3-6, you reach the same conclusions: Men earn more than women at Technitron.

The * in the boxplot for female salaries represents an *outlier*—a data value that is far removed from the rest of the data. This value is inconsistent with the other female salaries.

- Press Q for Quit

Plotting One Variable Against Another

Although some types of graphics are appropriate for displaying single variables, both scatter plots and multiple scatter plots are designed to show the relationship between two variables.

MINITAB AT WORK

FORESTRY: Foresters rely on easily obtained measurements to estimate how much timber a given forest contains. Researchers at Allegheny National Forest hoped to find a way to predict the volume of an individual tree by measuring only its base diameter.

The Allegheny team cut down 31 black cherry trees and measured the diameter and timber volume of each tree. They entered the resulting data into Minitab and created scatter plots of various combinations of the two variables. They found that plotting volume against the square of the diameter produced a strong linear relationship: if they wanted to estimate the volume of a tree with, say, a 1-foot diameter, they would mark 12^2, or 144 inches, on the x-axis, and find the corresponding volume on the y-axis—approximately 23 cubic feet of timber.

The foresters now had a tool that allowed them to estimate timber volume without having to cut down trees. Although they used other Minitab procedures that gave a more accurate estimate of volume, the plotting phase helped them single out the best variable transformation to use as a predictor.

Creating a Scatter Plot

Up to this point, each of the graphs you constructed described a single variable such as C1 SALARY. Scatter plots show the relationship between two variables. Since Technitron wanted you to concentrate on salary structure, you began with four different single-variable graphs of salary. In examining the question of possible sex discrimination, you produced two histograms, one for male and one for female salaries. This made it easy to compare.

The question arose whether you should attribute the higher male salaries to discrimination or to longer tenure with Technitron. A scatter plot of the two variables, C1 SALARY and C2 YRS EM, lets you visualize the relationship between the two variables to determine which explanation is correct.

- Choose **G**raph ► Scatter **P**lot...
- Select C1 SALARY for the Vertical axis
- Select C2 YRS EM for the Horizontal axis and press [Tab]
- Type $ as the **P**lotting symbol

The completed Scatter Plot dialog box should resemble Figure 3-17.

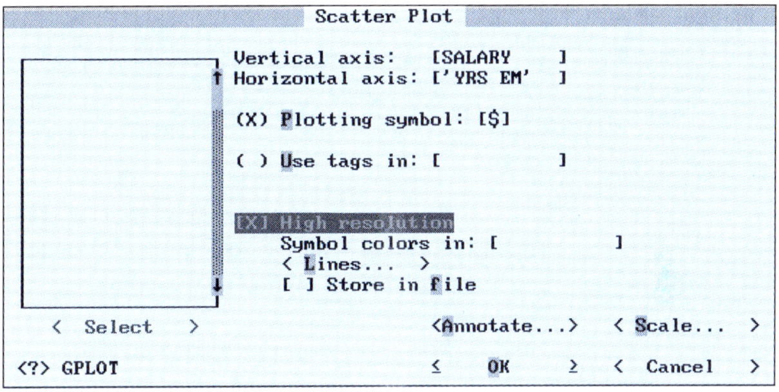

FIGURE 3-17
The completed Scatter Plot dialog box from the Graph menu

- Press [↵]

The graphics screen (using hi-res graphics) should look like Figure 3-18.

FIGURE 3-18
Scatter plot of salary versus years employed

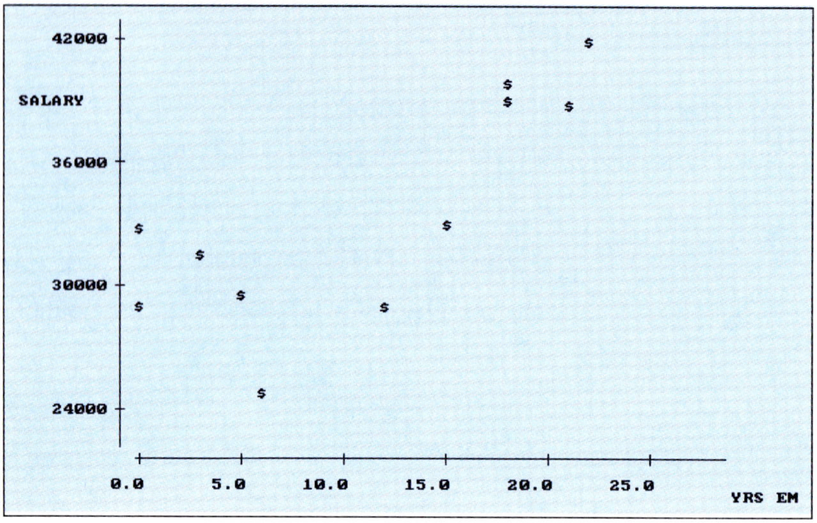

From this scatter plot it appears that, in general, people working at Technitron longer tend to have higher salaries. However, some of the new personnel have higher salaries than those who have worked there for six years.

This information will be useful for your report. You decide to add titles, footnotes, and axis labels to the scatter plot so that readers can readily understand it. To do so, use the Annotate option in the Scatter Plot dialog box (refer to Figure 3-17).

- Press Q for Quit
- Choose **E**dit ▶ Edit **L**ast Command Dialog...
- Press [Alt]-A for **A**nnotate
- Type **SALARY AT TECHNITRON CO.** in the Titles text box and press [Tab] three times
- Type **INFORMATION OBTAINED 1/9/92.** in the Footnotes text box and press [Tab] twice
- Type **YEARS AT TECHNITRON** in the Horizontal Axis Label text box and press [Tab]
- Type **SALARY IN $** in the Vertical Axis Label text box

The completed Annotate subdialog box should resemble Figure 3-19.

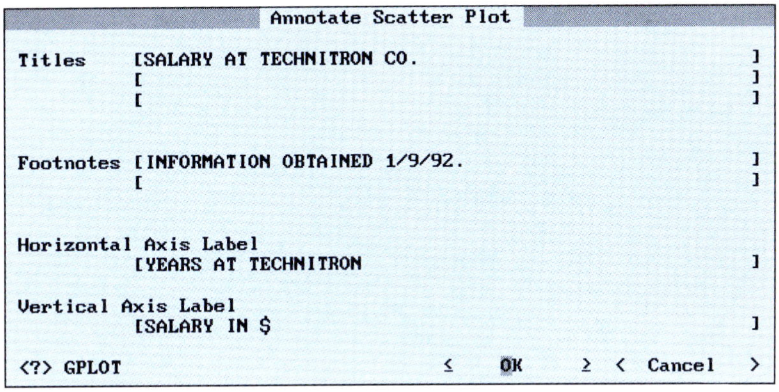

FIGURE 3-19
The completed Annotate subdialog box

- Press [↵]
- Press [Alt]-O (if you press [↵] Minitab will open the Scale subdialog box because it is highlighted)

Note: If more than two points occur at the same point on any scatter plot, Minitab will use the number of points as the plot symbol.

The graph on the screen (Figure 3-20) contains the same points as in Figure 3-18; however, the labels allow anyone viewing the plot to know exactly what you are presenting, when the information was obtained, and what it refers to.

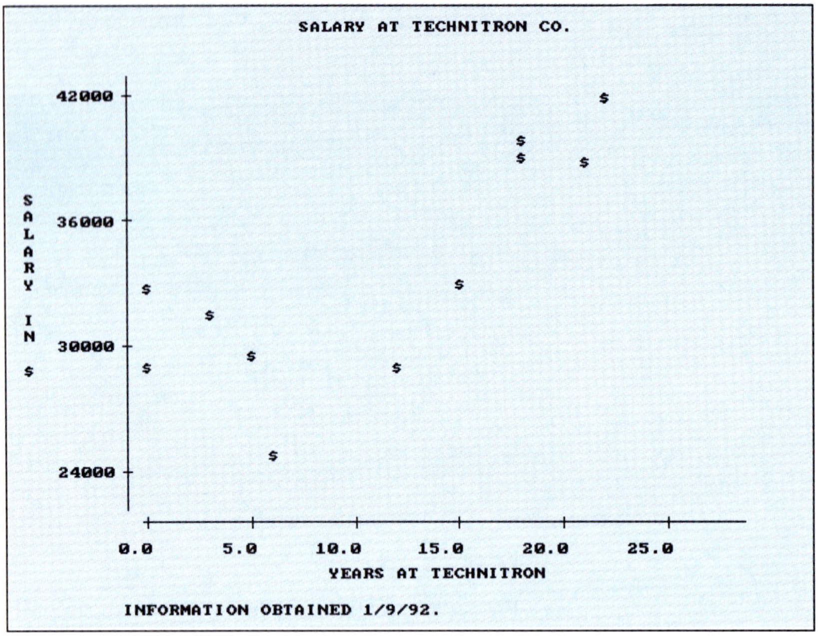

FIGURE 3-20
Annotated scatter plot of salary versus years employed

- Press Q for Quit

Using Tags in Scatter Plots

You can refine the scatter plot of C1 SALARY against C2 YRS EM by differentiating among the points according to a third variable. To get more information about possible sex discrimination, you will "tag" the points on the scatter plot using C8 GENDER N as your tag variable.

Note: Variables used as tag variables can contain only integer values.

Minitab plots all female salaries with the letter A and all male salaries with the letter Z. (See the Scatter Plot command in the Reference section or on-line help for information on why Minitab uses these two letters.)

- Choose **E**dit ▶ Edit **L**ast Command Dialog...
- Press Alt-U for **U**se tags in and press Tab
- Select C8 GENDER N as the tag variable
- Press Alt-A for **A**nnotate

- Tab to the second Footnotes text box
- Type **A = FEMALE and Z = MALE**
- Press [↵]
- Press [Alt]-O

The tagged scatter plot should look like Figure 3-21.

FIGURE 3-21

Scatter plot of salary versus years employed, tagged by gender

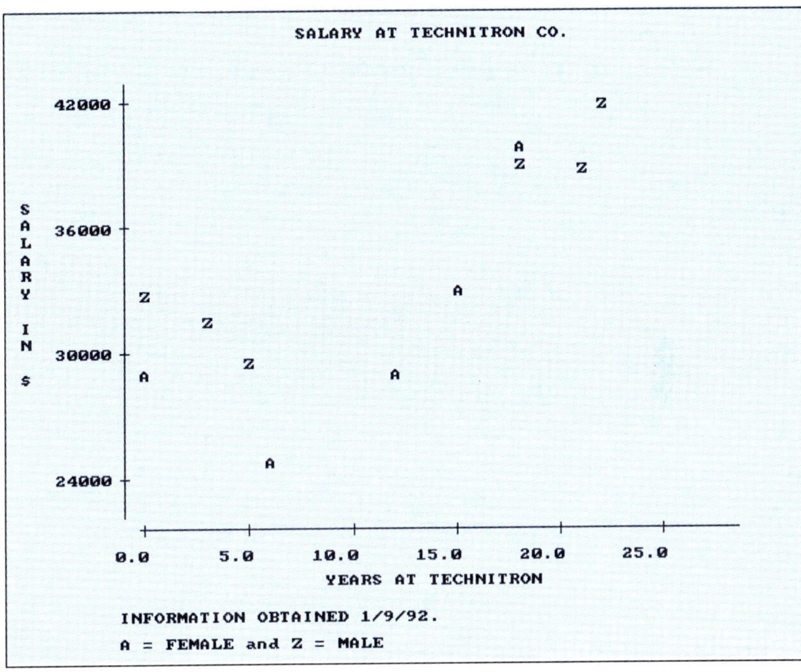

The points in the upper right corner of the graph show that men with higher salaries also have the most experience with Technitron. One woman with six years at Technitron has a lower salary than her more recently hired co-workers. Also, for the two most recent hires, the female's salary is lower than the male's. Perhaps it would be wise to look into the reason for this.

- Press Q for Quit

Creating a Multiple Scatter Plot

Minitab also lets you display several scatter plots on one set of axes. Suppose you wanted to compare the variable C1 SALARY with C2 YRS EM as well as with C3 PRIOR YR and C4 EDUC—all at the same time.

- Choose **G**raph ▶ **M**ultiple Scatter Plot...
- Select C1 SALARY for the first Vertical axis
- Select C2 YRS EM for the first Horizontal axis
- Select C1 SALARY for the second Vertical axis and C3 PRIOR YR for the second Horizontal axis
- Select C1 SALARY for the third Vertical axis and C4 EDUC for the third Horizontal axis

> **SHORTCUT**
>
> It may be quicker to type the column number in the text box, rather than using [F2] to select it from the list box.

The completed Multiple Scatter Plot dialog box should look like Figure 3-22.

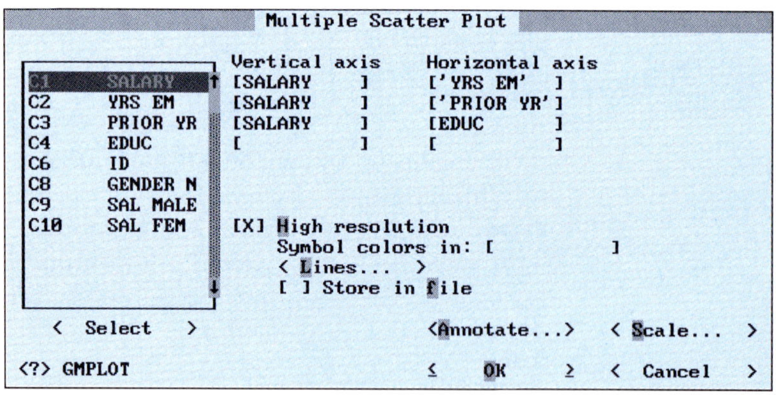

FIGURE 3-22
The completed Multiple Scatter Plot dialog box from the Graph menu

- Press [↵]

Minitab produces the multiple scatter plot shown in Figure 3-23.

FIGURE 3-23
Multiple scatter plot

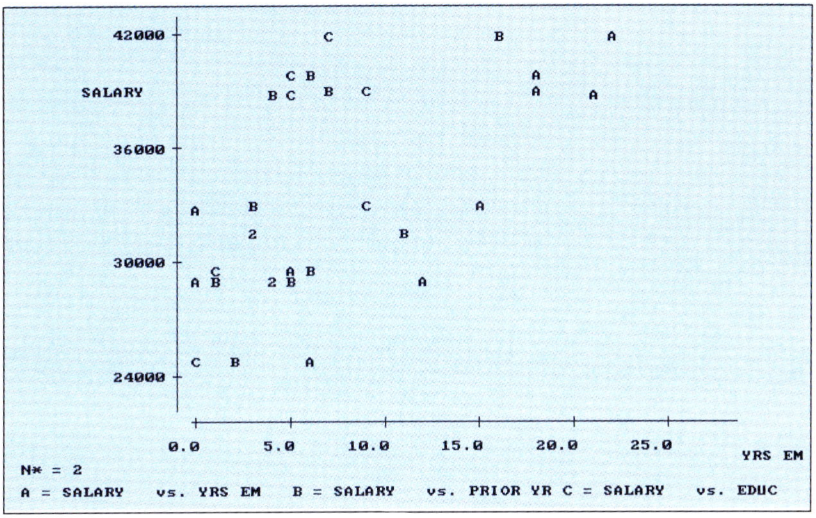

In the multiple scatter plot, Minitab uses a different symbol for each set of paired values. The symbol A is used for the plot of salary versus years employed, while the symbol B is used for salary versus prior years, and C for salary versus education. All three variables on the horizontal axis seem to have a positive relationship with salary.

Printing Graphs

Since your deadline is fast approaching, you may decide that you now have enough information for your preliminary presentation on the Technitron salary structure. A selection of the Minitab graphs will be a valuable supplement to your written report.

The method used to print your graphs depends on whether they are hi-res or character-based. You decide the high-resolution multiple scatter plot you just created could be useful. To print it:

- Make sure your printer is connected and the power is on
- Press P for Print

When your printer has finished printing the multiple scatter plot:

- Press Q for Quit

Note: If you are on a networked printer, the P command or the PAPER command described next may not work. If this is the case on your network, store the graph in a file using the FILE subcommand or by checking Store in file in the graph dialog box.

You also decide to include the stem-and-leaf display (Figure 3-11) because it gives a quick summary of the number of years each employee has served Technitron. Since this is a character-based graph displayed in the Session window, you use the PAPER command described in Tutorial 2 to print it:

- Prepare your printer
- Type **PAPER** after the MTB > prompt and press ↵
- Choose **G**raph ▶ **S**tem-and-Leaf...
- Select C2 YRS EM
- Press Alt-O

Minitab sends the graph to the screen and to your printer. Your printout should resemble Figure 3-24.

FIGURE 3-24
Printout of stem-and-leaf display

```
Stem-and-leaf of YRS EM     N  = 11
Leaf Unit = 1.0

    3     0 003
    5     0 56
   (1)    1 2
    5     1 588
    2     2 12
```

To continue working with Minitab after you print:

- Type **NOPAPER** after the MTB > prompt and press ↵

Saving Graphs

You may not always be able to print the graphs you want from the computer where you are working. In that case, you can save the graph to a separate file and print it later. To save the salary boxplot:

- Choose **G**raph ▶ **B**oxplot
- Select C1 SALARY
- Press [Alt]-F for the Store in **f**ile text box
- Press [↵]

Now name the file that will store the salary boxplot:

- Press [Tab] and select the TUT3 directory of your backup Sample Files disk
- Press [Shift]-[Tab]
- Type **BOX** as the filename
- Press [↵]

Minitab produces the boxplot as a new screen and also sends it to the file BOX.PRI. Notice that Minitab adds the .PRI extension to indicate that the file is configured for the printer. See Appendix C for more information on printing or plotting high-resolution graphs.

- Press Q for Quit

Now you are familiar with the tools necessary to display your data in attractive and easily comprehended pictorial form. In addition, you have prepared the graphs you need to present your preliminary findings on the salary structure at Technitron. You will find that the ability to graph your data will be helpful in analyzing it and eventually presenting it to others at the company. In the next tutorial, you will do more numerical analysis of data.

If you plan to continue directly to the next tutorial:

- Choose **F**ile ▶ Restart **M**initab and press [↵] to restart without saving the worksheet

If you want to take a longer break:

- Choose **F**ile ▶ E**x**it and press [↵] to exit without saving the worksheet

Minitab Command Summary

The menus and commands introduced in or related to this tutorial are described in this section. You will find a complete explanation of all menus and commands in the Reference section of this manual.

Menu	Command	Function
Graph		
	Histogram	Produces a histogram for each column of data requested
	Boxplot	Produces a boxplot display of a single column of data
	Dotplot	Produces a dotplot for each column requested
	Stem-and-Leaf	Produces a stem-and-leaf diagram for each column requested
	Scatter Plot	Displays a plot of two variables
	Multiple Scatter Plot	Plots several pairs of variables on the same axes, simultaneously

Review and Practice

Matching

Match the following terms to their definitions by placing the correct letter next to the term it explains.

____ multiple scatter plot

____ stem-and-leaf plot

____ graph screen

____ By variable

____ character-based display

____ scatter plot

____ Annotate

____ tag variable

____ histogram

____ high-resolution display

____ dotplot

a. An integer variable used to define groups

b. Location where high-resolution graphs and plots are displayed

c. A plot in which several pairs of variables are plotted on one graph

d. An integer variable used to define plot characters

e. Adds more detailed descriptions of axes and titles to plots

f. The result of selecting the high-resolution option

g. A graphical display that uses ordinary characters to create the display

h. Plot of one variable on the vertical axis and another on the horizontal axis

i. A histogram that uses dots to represent frequency

j. A graphical description of the frequency of a variable

k. A graphical description of the data in which the original data are evident

True/False

Mark the following statements T or F.

____ 1. All graphical displays in Minitab can be either character-based or high-resolution.

____ 2. High-resolution displays in Minitab are displayed in the Session window.

___ 3. For most displays (either high-resolution or character-based), you can change the scale, starting points, and increment values.

___ 4. All displays can be done separately for each value of another variable.

___ 5. You can attach labels of your own choosing to the axes of high-resolution histograms.

___ 6. Minitab allows you to annotate some graphical displays with titles and footnotes.

___ 7. Dotplots, histograms, and stem-and-leaf plots provide the same picture of a variable, only in different forms.

___ 8. By variables must have integer values only.

___ 9. Multiple boxplots can be displayed on the same screen.

___ 10. The only way to print a high-resolution graph is to use the PAPER command.

Practice Problems

1. Open FISH.MTW from the TUT3 directory.
   a. Plot the guarding time versus day. What happens to the percent guarding time over the days?
   b. Plot the guarding time versus day separately for each pH group. Is the relationship the same for the four pH groups?
   c. Plot the guarding time versus day separately for each pH group, using gender as a tag variable. How does gender of the fish affect the relationship?
2. Open GRADES.MTW from the TUT3 directory.
   a. Obtain the histogram, stem-and-leaf diagram, and dotplot of the first exam data. Compare the three displays. Do all three provide the same information about the class' performance on the first exam?
   b. Compare the histogram to the stem-and-leaf and dotplot displays. How many students scored more than 75% on the first exam? What were their scores?

c. Plot the second exam score against the first exam score. Does there appear to be a relationship?

3. Open KRUNCHY.MTW from the TUT3 directory.

   a. Produce a histogram of the sales increase data in C1. Do the data appear symmetric? If not, in which direction is the sales increase skewed?

   b. Produce a boxplot of the sales increase data in C1 separately for each ad medium in C2. How does the advertising medium affect sales?

   c. Produce a boxplot of the sales increase data in C1 separately for each ad agency in C3. How does the advertising agency affect sales?

TUTORIAL 4

Numerical Methods for Describing Data

In this tutorial, you will return to the nutrition case study from Tutorial 1 and continue to analyze the various brands of pasta. Your supervisor believes that you are familiar enough with Minitab to produce a report including basic statistics that describe the data. Your aim will be to recommend a brand of pasta.

Objectives

In this tutorial you will learn to:

- produce descriptive statistics
- convert alpha data to numeric data
- describe data separately for each value of a variable
- calculate frequencies for classes of data
- compute the covariance and correlation between variables

Describing Data

To determine which pasta brand to recommend in your report, you will need to produce various descriptive statistics summarizing the data you have been given. In class you have learned about many of the measures of central tendency and variation—the foundation of descriptive statistics. Most of these formulas are quite tedious to compute, even with a hand-held calculator. Minitab lets you generate ten commonly used descriptive statistics for as many columns as you designate, using a single command.

- If necessary, start Minitab
- Insert the backup Sample Files disk
- Open PASTAT4.MTW from the TUT4 directory

PASTAT4.MTW contains only the data from Figure 1-1 in Tutorial 1. In this tutorial you will need only these three columns of information.

You are most interested in describing the cost and the number of calories per serving, since it is these variables, in addition to the taste rating, that will determine which brand of pasta you will ultimately recommend. To generate the basic descriptive statistics:

- Choose **S**tat ▶ **B**asic Statistics ▶ **D**escriptive Statistics...
- Select C2 CENT/SER and C3 CAL/SER

The completed Descriptive Statistics dialog box should look like Figure 4-1.

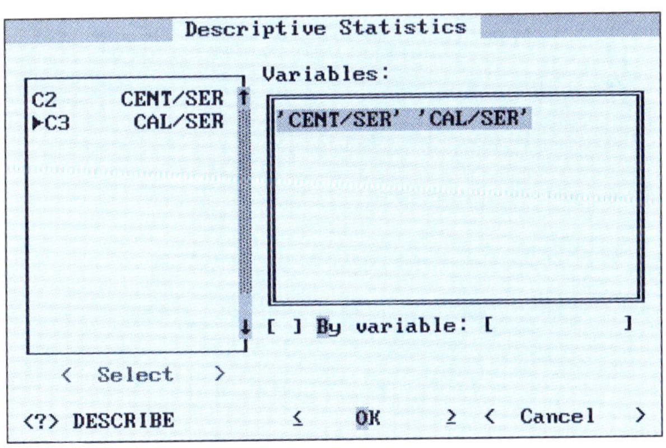

FIGURE 4-1
The completed Descriptive Statistics dialog box from the Basic Statistics submenu

- Press [Alt]-O

Minitab displays the requested statistics in the Session window (Figure 4-2).

FIGURE 4-2

Basic statistics for cents and calories per serving

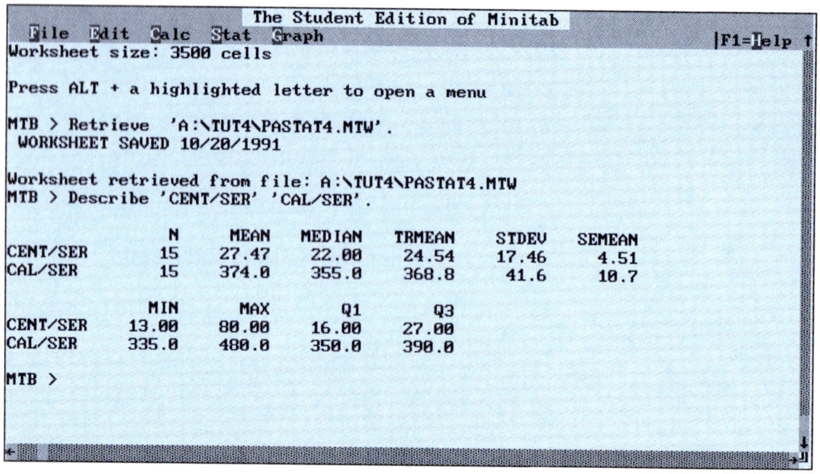

For each variable you selected, Minitab produces a row containing the following statistics:

- N, the number of cases
- MEAN, the mean
- MEDIAN, the median
- TRMEAN, the trimmed mean
- STDEV, the sample standard deviation
- SEMEAN, the standard error of the mean
- MIN, the variable's lowest value
- MAX, the variable's highest value
- Q_1, the first quartile
- Q_3, the third quartile

You have probably studied most of these terms in class, but some may not be familiar to you. For example, as you probably know, the sample mean can be distorted by extreme values (such as the 80 cents per serving for brand #8). In such cases it is often desirable to obtain a trimmed mean, TRMEAN, to give a more representative measure of central tendency. Minitab calculates the *trimmed mean* by discarding the top 5% of the data and the bottom 5%, then computing the mean of the central 90%. When no extreme values are present, the mean and the trimmed mean are relatively close in value.

As you scan the basic statistics Minitab has just produced, you notice that the mean cost per serving of 27.47 cents is larger than 24.54 cents, the trimmed mean. You suspect outliers. To construct a boxplot for the cost per serving data:

- Choose **Graph** ▶ **Boxplot...**
- Select C2 CENT/SER
- Press ↵

The boxplot appears on a separate screen, as shown in Figure 4-3.

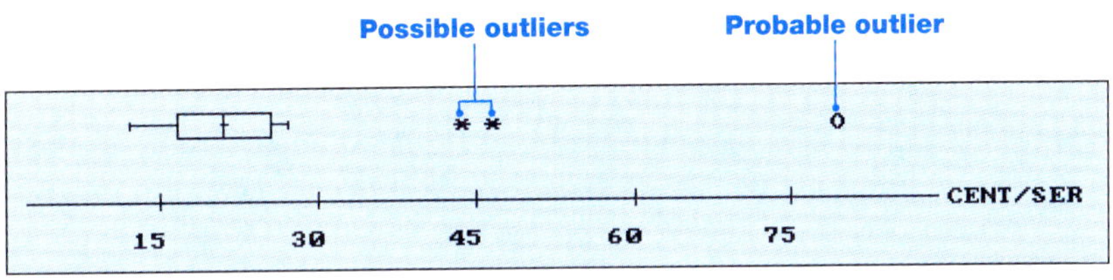

FIGURE 4-3
Boxplot of cents per serving

The + marks the median, 22 cents. The *'s indicate possible outliers and the 0 marks a probable outlier. The two *'s in this plot mark 44 and 47 cents, while the 0 marks the 80 cents. Q1 and Q3 (the 25th and 75th percentiles, respectively), 16 and 27 cents, approximate the vertical edges of the box. You were right. There are some unusually large cost values. You can note this in your report.

- Press Q for Quit

Other Descriptive Statistics

A measure of dispersion commonly used in business is the mean absolute deviation (MAD), the average of the absolute values of the deviations of the data from the mean. The MAD is not available in Minitab, but it can readily be obtained using Minitab functions. You will create a new variable representing the absolute values of the differences between the cost per serving and the mean (27.47):

- Choose **Calc** ▶ **Functions and Statistics** ▶ **General Expressions...**
- Type **'ABS DEVS'** (be sure to include the single quotes) and press [Tab] twice
- Type **ABSOLUTE(C2-27.47)** and press [Alt]-O
- Go to the Data worksheet

Column C4 now displays the absolute values of the difference between cost per serving and the average cost per serving. To obtain the mean of these absolute deviations:

- Return to the Session window
- Choose **Calc** ▶ **Functions and Statistics** ▶ **Column Statistics...**
- Press [Alt]-M and press [Tab]
- Select C4 ABS DEVS
- Press [↵]

The Session window displays the value of the MAD statistic (Figure 4-4). The value of 11.815 indicates that, on the average, costs per serving are approximately 12 cents from the mean.

FIGURE 4-4
The MAD statistic

```
MTB > Name c4 = 'ABS DEVS'
MTB > Let 'ABS DEVS' = ABSOLUTE(C2-27.47)
MTB > Mean 'ABS DEVS'.
   MEAN    =      11.815
```

As a nutritionist you want to provide a healthy, delicious dinner. But you also need to stay within your budget. The statistics you have computed so far represent summaries of all the brands you are considering. Since taste is an important concern, your supervisor has asked you to analyze the information further, investigating whether the more highly rated brands are also the most expensive with the fewest calories.

You will next describe the cost and calorie per serving data separately for each rating value. However, recall from Tutorial 3 that By variables must be integer values. Alpha variables cannot be used as By variables. Before you continue you must change (or *convert*) the ratings variable, which is currently an alpha variable, into a numeric variable with corresponding integer values.

Converting Alpha Data to Numeric

To convert alpha data to numeric, you must first enter a *conversion table* into the worksheet. The conversion table is a pair of columns; one contains the various alpha values and the other the corresponding numeric values.

Note: In this section you will convert an alpha variable to a numeric variable. You can also convert a numeric variable to an alpha variable.

In each row of this pair of columns, the alpha column entries contain the possible alpha variable values, and the numeric column contains the numbers to assign these alpha values. You will convert the alpha ratings data in C1 RATINGS using the following assignment:

Alpha Rating Value	Numeric Rating Value
EXCELLENT	1
VERY GOOD	2
GOOD	3
FAIR	4
POOR	5

For convenience, use adjacent columns and enter the data above exactly as it appears:

- Go to the Data worksheet

Make sure that the data-entry direction arrow points down:

- If necessary, press [F3] (the keyboard shortcut for the Change Entry Direction command)
- Highlight C5 row 1
- Type **EXCELLENT** and press [↵]
- Type **VERY GOOD** and press [↵]
- Type **GOOD** and press [↵]

- Type **FAIR** and press [↵]
- Type **POOR** and press [F6], the keyboard shortcut for moving to the top of the next column
- Type **1** and press [↵]
- Type **2** and press [↵]
- Type **3** and press [↵]
- Type **4** and press [↵]
- Type **5** and press [↵]

> **Mouse Users:**
>
> Click in the C5 name cell

To name C5 and C6:

- Highlight any cell in C5
- Press [Alt]-N
- Type **CONV A** and press [↵] to highlight the label cell above C6
- Type **CONV N** and press [↵]

Be sure to type the values exactly as given. Upper- and lowercase letters are considered different characters when Minitab converts data. The conversion columns in the Data worksheet should resemble Figure 4-5.

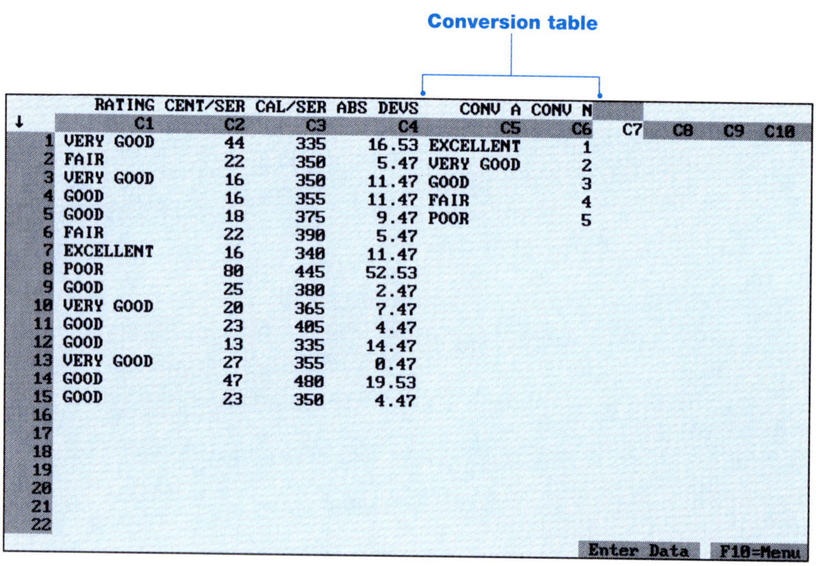

↓	RATING C1	CENT/SER C2	CAL/SER C3	ABS DEVS C4	CONV A C5	CONV N C6	C7	C8	C9	C10
1	VERY GOOD	44	335	16.53	EXCELLENT	1				
2	FAIR	22	350	5.47	VERY GOOD	2				
3	VERY GOOD	16	350	11.47	GOOD	3				
4	GOOD	16	355	11.47	FAIR	4				
5	GOOD	18	375	9.47	POOR	5				
6	FAIR	22	390	5.47						
7	EXCELLENT	16	340	11.47						
8	POOR	80	445	52.53						
9	GOOD	25	380	2.47						
10	VERY GOOD	20	365	7.47						
11	GOOD	23	405	4.47						
12	GOOD	13	335	14.47						
13	VERY GOOD	27	355	0.47						
14	GOOD	47	480	19.53						
15	GOOD	23	350	4.47						
16										
17										
18										
19										
20										
21										
22										

Enter Data F10=Menu

FIGURE 4-5
Conversion table in the Data worksheet

To convert the alpha data in C1 RATING:

- Return to the Session window
- Choose **C**alc ▶ C**o**nvert...
- Select C1 RATING for the Original data text box

To assign a name for the column containing the converted data:

- Type '**RATING N**' in the Converted data text box and press Tab

To tell Minitab where to find the appropriate conversion table:

- Select C5 CONV A for the Original Conversion Table column
- Select C6 CONV N for the Converted Conversion Table column

The completed Convert dialog box should resemble Figure 4-6.

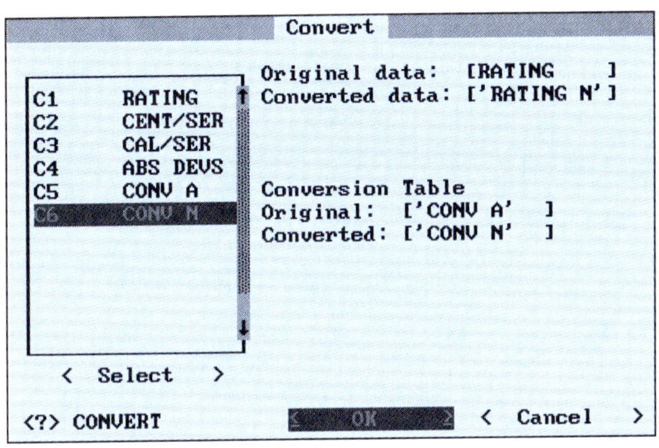

FIGURE 4-6
The completed Convert dialog box from the Calc menu

- Press ↵
- Go to the Data worksheet to see the result

Compare the pasta rating alpha data in C1 RATING to the numeric rating data in C7 RATING N in Figure 4-7. Minitab has converted the ratings using the conversion table in C5 and C6.

FIGURE 4-7

The Data worksheet with converted data

Alpha rating — Numeric rating

↓	RATING C1	CENT/SER C2	CAL/SER C3	ABS DEVS C4	CONV A C5	CONV N C6	RATING N C7	C8	C9
1	VERY GOOD	44	335	16.53	EXCELLENT	1	2		
2	FAIR	22	350	5.47	VERY GOOD	2	4		
3	VERY GOOD	16	350	11.47	GOOD	3	2		
4	GOOD	16	355	11.47	FAIR	4	3		
5	GOOD	18	375	9.47	POOR	5	3		
6	FAIR	22	390	5.47			4		
7	EXCELLENT	16	340	11.47			1		
8	POOR	80	445	52.53			5		
9	GOOD	25	380	2.47			3		
10	VERY GOOD	20	365	7.47			2		
11	GOOD	23	405	4.47			3		
12	GOOD	13	335	14.47			3		
13	VERY GOOD	27	355	0.47			2		
14	GOOD	47	480	19.53			3		
15	GOOD	23	350	4.47			3		
16									
17									
18									
19									
20									
21									
22									

Enter Data F10=Menu

Describing Data Separately for Each Value of a By Variable

Once you have converted the alpha ratings to numeric ratings you can use the numeric rating data to summarize separate cost and calorie per serving information:

- Return to the Session window
- Choose Stat ▶ **B**asic Statistics ▶ **D**escriptive Statistics
- Select C2 CENT/SER and C3 CAL/SERV as the Variables
- Press [Alt]-B and press [Tab]
- Select C7 RATING N for the By variable
- Press [↵]

The Session window displays the statistics shown in Figure 4-8.

FIGURE 4-8

Descriptive statistics of cents and calories per serving by rating

The Student Edition of Minitab

File Edit Calc Stat Graph |F1=Help

	RATING N	N	MEAN	MEDIAN	TRMEAN	STDEV	SEMEAN
CENT/SER	1	1	16.000	16.000	16.000	*	*
	2	4	26.75	23.50	26.75	12.37	6.18
	3	7	23.57	23.00	23.57	11.19	4.23
	4	2	22.000	22.000	22.000	0.000	0.000
	5	1	80.000	80.000	80.000	*	*
CAL/SER	1	1	340.00	340.00	340.00	*	*
	2	4	351.25	352.50	351.25	12.50	6.25
	3	7	382.9	375.0	382.9	48.6	18.4
	4	2	370.0	370.0	370.0	28.3	20.0
	5	1	445.00	445.00	445.00	*	*

	RATING N	MIN	MAX	Q1	Q3
CENT/SER	1	16.000	16.000	*	*
	2	16.00	44.00	17.00	39.75
	3	13.00	47.00	16.00	25.00
	4	22.000	22.000	*	*
	5	80.000	80.000	*	*
CAL/SER	1	340.00	340.00	*	*
	2	335.00	365.00	338.75	362.50
	3	335.0	480.0	350.0	405.0
	4	350.0	390.0	*	*

For each of the five ratings, Minitab has provided a summary of each of the two variables (cost and number of calories per serving). If N = 1 (as in the first row), then the standard deviation, the standard error of the mean, Q_1, and Q_3 are all undefined. Minitab uses asterisks to indicate that those values are missing.

The mean cost of the "excellent" (RATING N = 1) rated brands is 16 cents, which is the least expensive; the brand with the "poor" rating (RATING N = 5) has a mean of 80 cents per serving, which is the most costly. The mean costs per serving for the middle three ratings (2, 3, and 4) fall between these two values.

The mean calories-per-serving variable is highest for the poorly rated pasta, but low for the highly rated brand. It seems that the best-tasting pasta is the least expensive and also has low calories per serving. You seem to have the best of many worlds.

Calculating Frequencies

In your report, you would like to include information on *how many* brands from each of the five ratings (excellent to poor) were considered. The Tally command determines a count or frequency for each category of a variable or column, but only for discrete integer data. To get a count of how many brands are in each rating category:

- Choose Stat ▶ Tables ▶ Tally...
- Select C7 RATING N

The Tally command also gives you the option of displaying Percents (the number in each category divided by the total number), Cumulative counts, and Cumulative percents (the number and the percent of data values at or below the given value). In addition to Counts (the default option), select the remaining three options:

- Press [Tab] to highlight the first display option, Counts
- Press [↓] and the Space bar three times to select the other three options

The completed Tally dialog box should look like Figure 4-9.

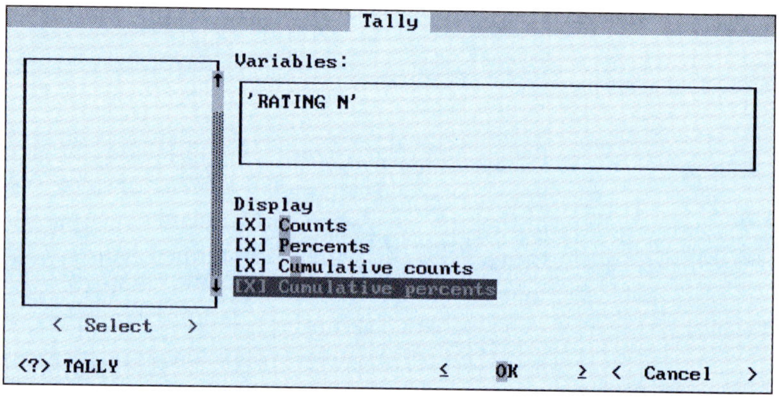

FIGURE 4-9
The completed Tally dialog box from the Tables submenu

Note: Variables used in the Tally command must contain integer values only.

- Press [↵]

Figure 4-10 shows the Session window with the tallied ratings.

FIGURE 4-10
Tally results for taste ratings

```
MTB > Tally 'RATING N';
SUBC>   Counts;
SUBC>   Percents;
SUBC>   CumCounts;
SUBC>   CumPercents.

RATING N  COUNT PERCENT CUMCNT  CUMPCT
       1      1    6.67      1    6.67
       2      4   26.67      5   33.33
       3      7   46.67     12   80.00
       4      2   13.33     14   93.33
       5      1    6.67     15  100.00
      N=     15
```

Minitab produces a table containing the values for all the options selected. The five numeric categories (1 for excellent, 2 for very good, and so on) are listed in the leftmost column under the column name RATING N. The next column contains a COUNT (or frequency) of each category. The PERCENT column shows the percent of the total that are in each rating class. Most of the brands available through your supplier are in the 3 or "good" category (7, or 46.67%). The CUMCNT column reveals that 12 of the 15 brands were at the "good" level or better, corresponding to a cumulative percent CUMPCT of 80. It's good to know that 80% of the brands available to you are rated at least "good." Make a mental note to include this fact in your report.

You now decide to tally the data on cost per serving. If the data contain too many categories, the Tally results will be too large to interpret effectively. Right now cost data have too many categories, because each category contains only one value. However, you can collapse the data into these classes:

Original Cost per Serving	Coded Cost
10 to 24	1
25 to 39	2
40 to 54	3
55 to 69	4
70 to 84	5

To regroup the data:

- Choose **C**alc ▶ Code Data **V**alues...
- Select C2 CENT/SER and press [Tab]
- Type **COSTCODE** and press [Tab]
- Type **10:24,** press [Tab], type **1** and press [Tab]
- Type **25:39,** press [Tab], type **2** and press [Tab]
- Type **40:54,** press [Tab], type **3** and press [Tab]

- Type **55:69,** press [Tab], type **4** and press [Tab]
- Type **70:84,** press [Tab], type **5**

The completed Code Data Values dialog box should look like Figure 4-11.

FIGURE 4-11
The completed Code Data Values dialog box from the Calc menu

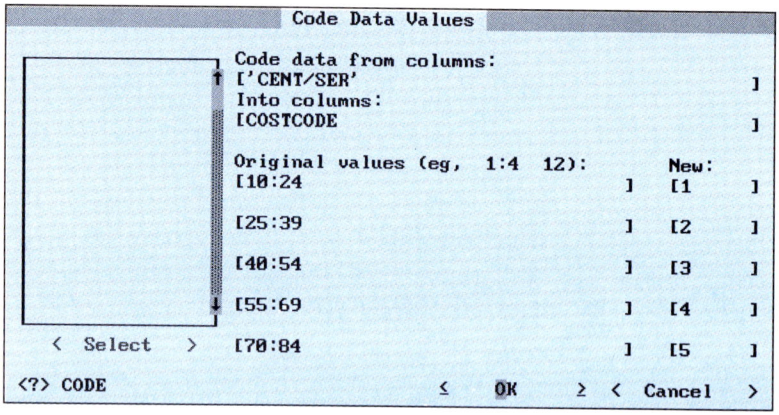

- Press [↵]

Minitab has coded or collapsed the cost per serving data into five categories. To obtain a frequency distribution table for C8 COSTCODE:

- Choose Stat ▶ Tables ▶ Tally...
- Select C8 COSTCODE
- In addition to Counts (the default selection) select Percents, Cumulative counts, and Cumulative percents
- Press [↵]

It would appear that you have quite a selection (10, or 66.67% of the available brands) of inexpensive pastas (COSTCODE = 1). If one of these has other desirable characteristics, your job of finding the best pasta is done.

Covariance

So far in this tutorial, you have characterized the behavior of individual variables, such as the cost per serving or the number of calories per serving. You now will change direction slightly and look at a measure of relationship between cost and calories per serving. To produce a pictorial display, in the form of a scatter plot, of the relationship between these two variables:

- Choose **G**raph ▶ Scatter **P**lot...
- Select C2 CENT/SER for the Vertical axis
- Select C3 CAL/SER for the Horizontal axis
- Press [↵]

The scatter plot should look like Figure 4-12.

FIGURE 4-12
Scatter plot of calories and cost per serving

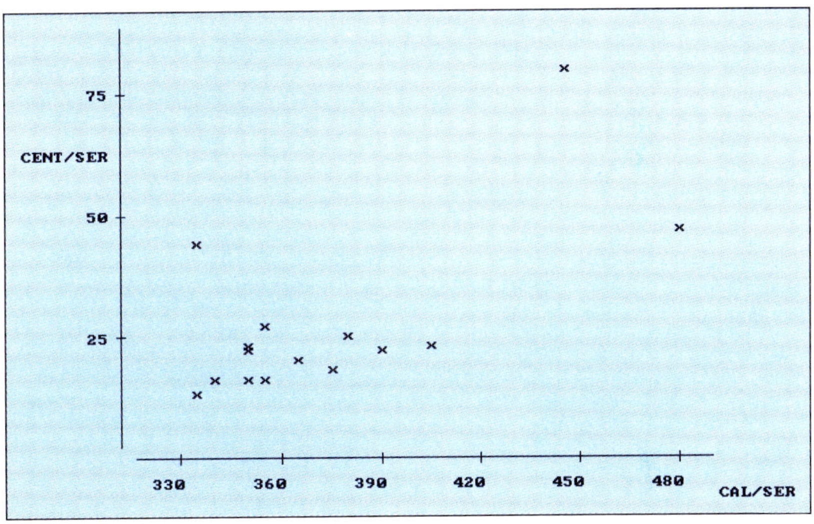

The scatter plot seems to indicate that more expensive brands have more calories. To quantify this relationship, find the *covariance,* a numerical summary of the relationship between two variables. Additionally, find the covariance of the numerical rating with each of the variables of cost per serving and number of calories per serving.

- Press Q for Quit

- Choose **Stat** ▶ **Basic Statistics** ▶ **Covariance...**
- Select C2 CENT/SER, C3 CAL/SER, and C7 RATING N as the Variables

The completed Covariance dialog box should look like Figure 4-13.

FIGURE 4-13
The completed Covariance dialog box from the Basic Statistics submenu

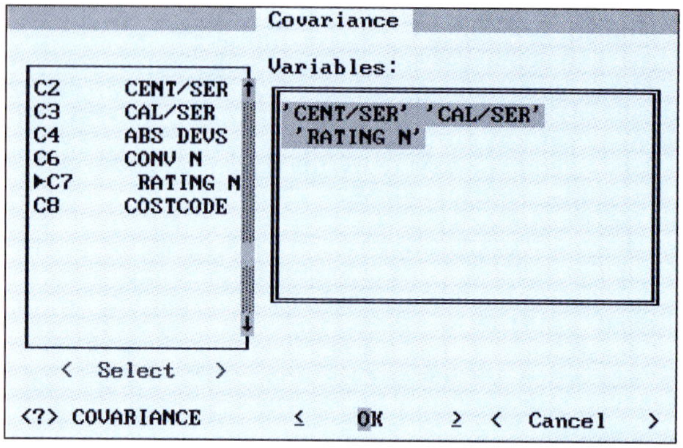

- Press Alt-O

The Session window should resemble Figure 4-14.

FIGURE 4-14
The covariance matrix

```
MTB > Covariance 'CENT/SER' 'CAL/SER'  'RATING N'.

            CENT/SER    CAL/SER   RATING N
CENT/SER    304.9810
CAL/SER     476.2143  1732.8572
RATING N      8.5667    20.9286     0.9810
```

Entries along the diagonal of the covariance matrix represent the covariance of each variable with itself. This is the variance of that variable. The other three values in the matrix are the covariance between the variables identified in the row and column.

The covariances are positive, indicating that high values of one variable in the pair are generally associated with high values in the other. Higher costs per serving tend to be associated with more calories, as the scatter plot in Figure 4-12 indicated. Since the numerical ratings ranged from 1 for "excellent" to 5 for "poor," the higher (worse) the rating of a brand, the higher its price and caloric content.

Correlation

Determine the correlation to provide numerical information about the direction and the strength of the pairwise linear relationship of these same three variables:

- Choose **Stat** ▶ **Basic Statistics** ▶ **Correlation...**
- Select C2 CENT/SER, C3 CAL/SER, and C7 RATING N as the Variables

The completed Correlation dialog box should look like Figure 4-15.

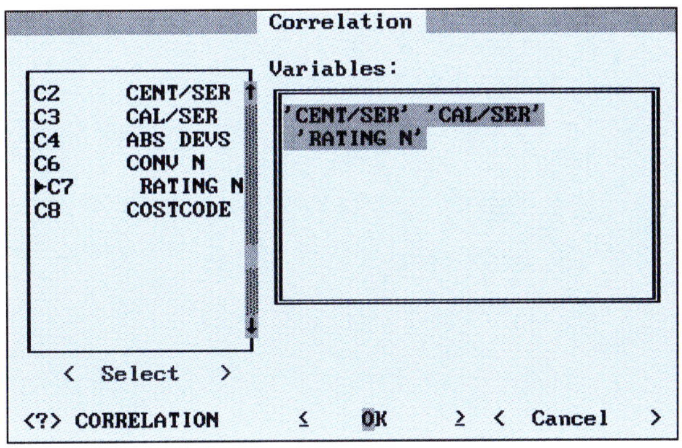

FIGURE 4-15
The completed Correlation dialog box from the Basic Statistics submenu

- Press [Alt]-O

The correlation matrix should appear as in Figure 4-16.

FIGURE 4-16
The correlation matrix

```
MTB > Correlation 'CENT/SER' 'CAL/SER'   'RATING N'.

          CENT/SER  CAL/SER
CAL/SER     0.655
RATING N    0.495     0.508
```

The correlation between cost and calories is 0.655, indicating a positive linear relationship between these two variables. The correlations between numerical rating and cost and calories per serving are both positive. Although higher numbers in the value rating variable (less desirable pasta, because 1 is excellent and 5 is poor) are associated with higher costs and more calories, the associations are not as strong as the cost and calorie relationship.

You have taken the first steps toward the ultimate goal of providing nutritious, low-cost meals that are also tasty. You have found that the cost for an individual portion of pasta can range from 16 cents to 80 cents, but half the brands will cost less than 22 cents a serving. You will report the trimmed mean of 24.54 cents as the measure of the average cost of an individual portion. You will be sure to include in your report that higher-cost pastas tended to have more calories. The one pasta (brand number 7) that received an excellent rating is both the cheapest and the lowest in calories. Not bad for your first day on the job—you found an excellent, inexpensive, low-calorie pasta to recommend in your report to your supervisor. Could a promotion be forthcoming?

If you plan to continue directly to the next tutorial:

- Choose **F**ile ▶ Restart **M**initab

If you want to take a longer break:

- Choose **F**ile ▶ E**x**it

Minitab Command Summary

The menus and commands introduced in or related to this tutorial are described in this section. You will find a complete explanation of all menus and commands in the Reference section of this manual.

Menu	Command	Function
Calc		
	Convert	Converts alpha data to numeric and vice versa
Stat		
	Basic Statistics	
	Descriptive Statistics	Provides numeric summary of central tendency and variability for one or several columns; can be used with a By variable to obtain summaries for each level of the By variable

Correlation	Provides the correlation between pairs of variables
Covariance	Provides the covariance between pairs of variables
Tables	
Tally	Provides a count or frequency of each value of an integer variable

Review and Practice

Matching

Match the following terms to their definitions by placing the correct letter next to the term it explains.

____ SEMEAN

____ trimmed mean

____ Correlation

____ CUMPCT

____ Descriptive Statistics

____ second quartile

____ Tally

____ STDEV

a. A sample mean after the smallest 5% and largest 5% of the data are deleted

b. Another name for the median

c. Minitab notation for the sample standard deviation

d. Minitab notation for the standard deviation of a sample mean

e. Minitab notation for the cumulative percent less than or equal to a given category

f. The Minitab command used to count frequencies for discrete data

g. The Minitab command used to compute ten statistical measures

h. A Minitab command used to summarize the linear relationship between two variables

True/False

Mark the following statements T or F.

____ 1. Conversion tables are created in the Data worksheet.

____ 2. The Tally command can only be used with integer data.

____ 3. The output from the Descriptive Statistics command is displayed in the Session window.

____ 4. The sample standard deviation is given in the Descriptive Statistics output.

____ 5. The mean absolute deviation is part of the Descriptive Statistics output.

____ 6. By variables must be integer valued.

____ 7. When Minitab prints a * for a summary statistic in the Descriptive Statistics output, it means that the number was too large to fit in the space provided.

____ 8. Both Tally and Correlate can be done using a By variable.

____ 9. CUMCNT is the way Minitab designates the cumulative number of values greater than the given category.

____ 10. The maximum and minimum values of a column are not part of the output of the Descriptive Statistics command.

Practice Problems

1. Open HORSE.MTW from the TUT4 directory. It contains information on a study of seed distribution by horses at a national park.

   a. Summarize the number of species at each of the sample sites along the trails. Use the EDGE1, EDGE2, and INT variables. Does there appear to be any difference in the number of species among samples taken farther away from the trail edge?

   b. Repeat part a) separately for each of the six trails. Do you reach the same conclusion as you did in part a)?

   c. Summarize the distance variable separately for each of the six trails. Are all of the trails the same length?

2. Open SALES.MTW from the TUT4 directory, describing sales trends.

   a. Describe the sales data for 1988 through 1991. Have sales increased over the years? Consistently? What percent increase has occurred in the past? What happened in 1991?

   b. Obtain the correlation matrix for the yearly sales data. Are the sales for each year correlated with one another? To what extent are they correlated?

   c. Obtain the covariances between each year's data. What value is on the diagonal of the resulting matrix? Verify your answer using the results from part a). Is the covariance matrix as informative as the correlation matrix in part b)?

3. Open TV VIEW.MTW from the TUT4 directory.

   a. Describe the TV viewing habits of husbands, wives, and households. Do your numbers indicate that husbands or wives watch more TV?

   b. Describe the difference in the TV viewing times of husbands and wives. Do your numbers indicate that this difference is different from zero?

4. Open PROF.MTW from the TUT4 directory.

   a. Use the Tally command to summarize the frequency of the different levels or years of courses surveyed (i.e., C9).

   b. How many questionnaires were filled out, on the average, in all the surveyed courses? Is the median much different from the mean?

   c. Correlate the INSTRUCT and COURSE ratings. Are the two correlated? Interpret your findings.

TUTORIAL 5

Distributions and Random Data

Probability distributions are the foundation for inferential statistics. In this tutorial you will examine several frequently used probability functions and probability density functions, then learn how to generate random samples from these distributions. First, you will act as a Red Cross volunteer trying to ascertain various probabilities of obtaining Type O blood donors from a given sample. Then you will generate a random sample for a genetics term paper. Finally you will work with your physiology professor on a study of the height of college students in the United States.

Objectives

In this tutorial you will learn to:

- compute probabilities, using both discrete probability functions and continuous probability density functions
- compute cumulative probabilities for various probability distribution functions

- generate random samples from populations that have given probability distributions
- use the inverse cumulative probability function to look up percentiles of various distributions
- generate normal scores and produce normal probability plots
- sample from a column, with and without replacement

Case Study: Blood Types

You have been a Red Cross volunteer for the last few years. The volunteer coordinator, Paul Van Vleck, just learned that you are gaining familiarity with Minitab. Eager to put your skills to work, he tells you that the supply of Type O blood is running dangerously low and that he anticipates needing from ten to twelve additional pints for surgeries scheduled in the upcoming week. Paul has recruited 25 unrelated potential donors. He wants to know if it is likely that next week's need for Type O blood can be met using these 25 donors or if he will have to recruit more donors.

Discrete Probability Functions

Your reference books tell you that 45 out of 100 people have Type O blood, so the probability of a randomly selected individual having Type O blood is 0.45. To help Paul you will need to compute P(X=K), the probability of K people having Type O blood, for values of K = 0, 1, 2,..., 25. In this case P(X=K) is a binomial probability function with n = 25 trials and p = 0.45. You could compute these probabilities using a calculator, but this would be tedious. Instead, you will have Minitab compute them.

You first create a column with the integers 0 to 25 stored in it. You could enter these numbers directly into the Data worksheet, but there is a much easier way:

- If necessary, start Minitab
- Choose **E**dit ▸ Set Patterned Data...

- Type **K** in the Put data into column text box and press [Tab] twice
- Type **0** (zero) in the Start at text box and press [Tab]
- Type **25** in the End at text box

The completed Set Patterned Data dialog box should look like Figure 5-1.

FIGURE 5-1

The completed Set Patterned Data dialog box from the Edit menu

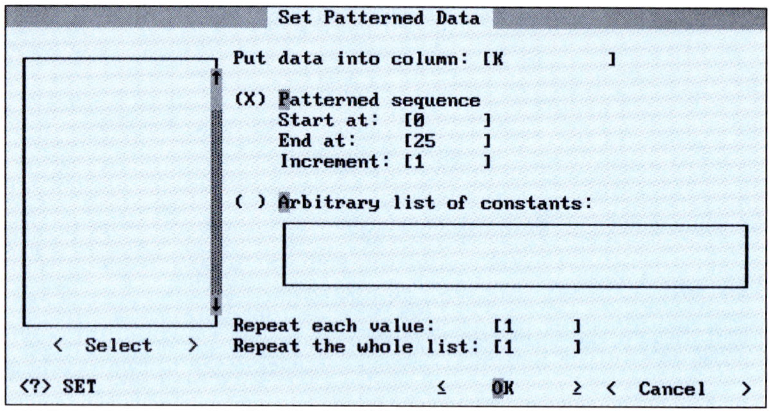

- Press [↵]
- Go to the Data worksheet

Minitab has entered the integers from 0 to 25 into the first column much more quickly than you could type them into the Data worksheet.

- Return to the Session window

  Now obtain the binomial probabilities for each value of K in C1:

- Choose **C**alc ▶ **P**robability Distributions ▶ **B**inomial...
- Press [Tab]
- Type **25** for Number of trials and press [Tab]
- Type **.45** for Probability of success and press [Tab] twice
- Select C1 K as the Input column

The completed Binomial Distribution dialog box should look like Figure 5-2.

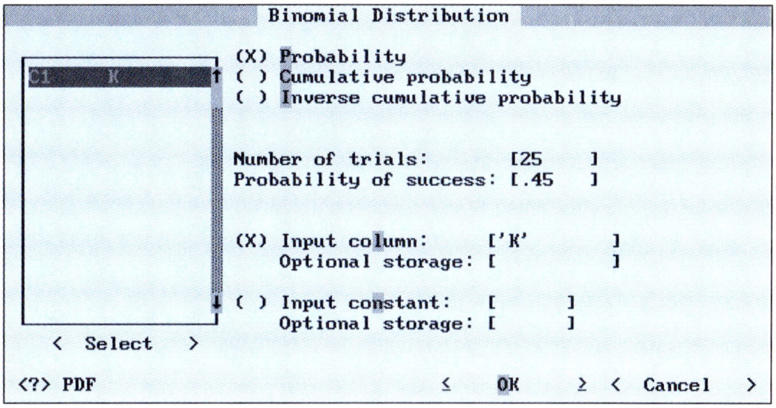

FIGURE 5-2
The completed Binomial Distribution dialog box from the Probability Distributions submenu

- Press ↵

Minitab lists the complete binomial probability distribution for n = 25 and p = 0.45 in the Session window, as shown in Figure 5-3.

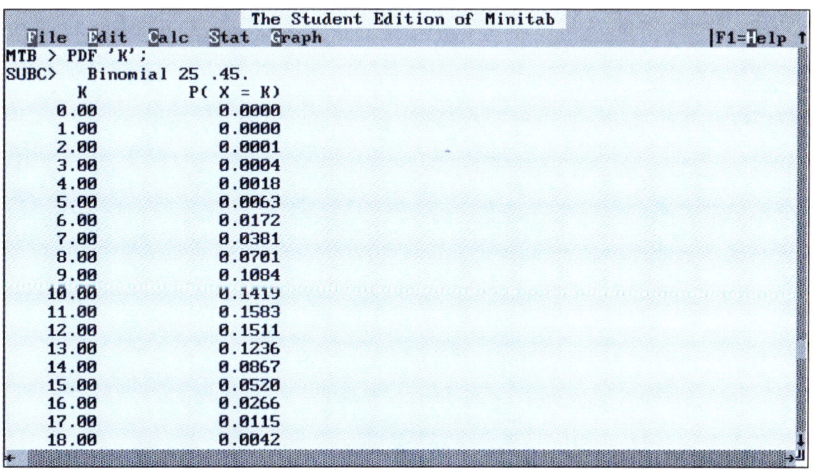

FIGURE 5-3
Binomial probability distribution in the Session window

Minitab displays the probability distribution in two columns. The first column contains the values representing the possible number of successes (people with Type O blood) and the second lists the corresponding probability of obtaining that number of successes. For example, the probability of having exactly 11 people in this sample with Type 0 blood is 0.1583.

The probability values in the Session window are rounded to the nearest ten thousandth. Probabilities below 0.00005 are listed as 0.0000. So the probability of obtaining 22 Type O individuals in your sample is not really 0.0000, but it is less than 0.00005.

You can also have Minitab save the probabilities into a column in the worksheet:

- Choose **E**dit ▶ Edit **L**ast Command Dialog...
- Press [Alt]-L for Input Co**l**umn and press [Tab] twice
- In the upper Optional storage text box, type **'P(X=K)'** (be sure to type the single quotation marks)
- Press [↵]
- Go to the Data worksheet

The binomial probabilities are now in C2 P(X=K) of the worksheet as in Figure 5-4.

FIGURE 5-4
Binomial distribution in the Data worksheet

	K	P(X=K)
→	C1	C2
1	0	0.000000
2	1	0.000007
3	2	0.000065
4	3	0.000407
5	4	0.001830
6	5	0.006290
7	6	0.017155
8	7	0.038097
9	8	0.070133
10	9	0.108387
11	10	0.141889
12	11	0.158306
13	12	0.151110
14	13	0.123636
15	14	0.086705
16	15	0.052023
17	16	0.026603
18	17	0.011523
19	18	0.004190
20	19	0.001263
21	20	0.000310
22	21	0.000060

Recall that Minitab rounded probabilities to the nearest thousandth in the Session window. In the Data worksheet, by default, results are displayed to the nearest one-millionth. Row 12 shows that P(X=11) has been rounded to the nearest one-millionth and the value of 0.158306 is displayed. You can display more or fewer places by using the Format column command from the Data worksheet menu, as described in Tutorial 1.

You note that you are most likely to obtain 10, 11, or 12 people with Type O blood in your sample of 25. However, these values will occur only 14.2%, 15.8%, and 15.1% of the time, respectively. Collectively, though, there is roughly a 50% chance that the 25 donors will yield 10, 11, or 12 people with Type O blood (14.2 + 15.8 + 15.1 = 45.1%).

When you do not need all values of the probability distribution, Minitab can compute the probability for a single value:

- Return to the Session window
- Choose **E**dit ▶ Edit **L**ast Command Dialog...
- Press [Alt]-N for Input co**n**stant and press [Tab]
- Type **10** and press [↵]

The Session window shows that the probability that X=10 is 0.1419. Verify that you obtained equivalent results in Figures 5-3 and 5-4.

To verify that the most likely values (highest probabilities) are 10, 11, and 12, produce a scatter plot of this binomial distribution:

- Choose **G**raph ▶ Scatter **P**lot...
- Select C2 P(X=K) for the Vertical axis
- Select C1 K for the Horizontal axis and press [Tab]
- Type **.** (a period) in the Plotting symbol text box and press [↵]

The scatter plot appears (Figure 5-5).

FIGURE 5-5
Scatter plot of probability versus number of successes

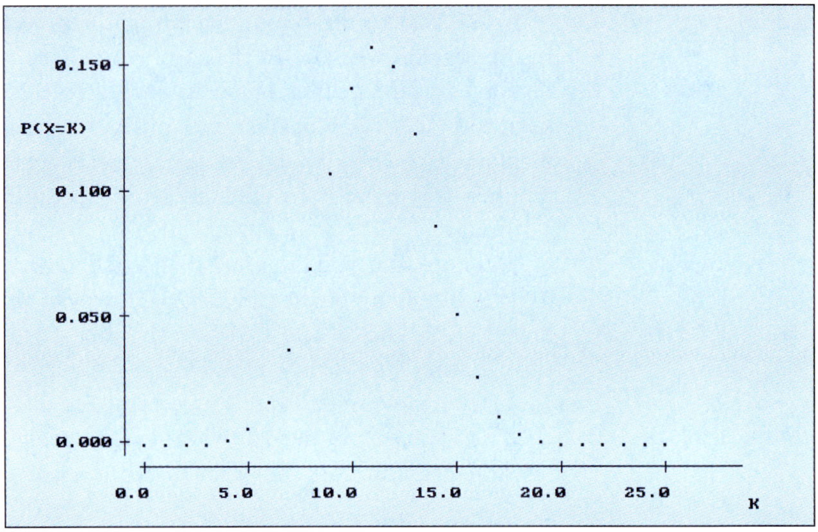

The dots are centered over each value of K=number of successes, K=0, 1, 2, ..., 25. The position of each dot corresponds to the probability that K Type O blood donors will be found in the sample of 25.

The peak of the plot occurs at K=11 and the next two tallest heights are at K=10 and 12. Indeed, the most likely number of Type O donors are 10, 11, and 12. Also note the shape of your plot; it is approximately bell-shaped. You will see more of the *bell-shaped* distribution later in this tutorial.

- Press Q for Quit

Cumulative Probability Distributions for Discrete Variables

In addition to computing individual probabilities, Minitab can compute cumulative probabilities for either an entire column or an individual value. After talking with the surgeons who will be performing next week's surgery, Paul informs you that he will need at least 13 pints of Type O blood; he needs to know the probability of getting 13 or more Type O donors in his sample of 25.

Compute the probability of obtaining 12 or fewer individuals with Type O blood from the sample of 25:

- Choose **C**alc ▶ **P**robability Distributions ▶ **B**inomial...
- Press [Alt]-C for **C**umulative probability and press [Tab]

- Type **25** and press [Tab]
- Type **0.45**
- Press [Alt]-N for Input constant and press [Tab]
- Type **12** in the Input constant text box and press [↵]

The Session window (Figure 5-6) shows the results.

FIGURE 5-6
Cumulative probability of obtaining 12 or fewer Type O donors

```
MTB > CDF 12;
SUBC>   Binomial 25 .45.
       K  P( X LESS OR = K)
    12.00           0.6937
```

You tell Paul that there is a probability of 69.37% that 12 or fewer people in this group of 25 will have Type O blood. In other words, there is less than a one-third (30.63%) chance of getting the 13 (or more) pints he needs.

Paul is concerned. The odds are pretty good that he will not be able to provide enough Type O blood. He asks you how many donors will be needed to be reasonably sure (probability ≥ 75%) of getting at least 13 Type O donors. You need to find the value of n so that $P(X \leq 12)$ is smaller than 25%.

You need to repeat the actions above, trying different values of n. To save you some time, try a value of n = 33 first:

- Choose **E**dit ▶ Edit **L**ast Command Dialog...
- Press [Tab]
- Type **33** in the Number of trials text box and press [↵]

Minitab reports that if 33 donors are selected, there is a 20.62% chance of getting 12 or fewer Type O donors (and hence a 79.38% probability of getting 13 or more). You are close. To determine if you can get by with fewer donors, try n = 32:

- Choose **E**dit ▶ Edit **L**ast Command Dialog...
- Press [Tab]
- Type **32** in the Number of trials text box and press [↵]

Using 32 donors, the probability of 12 or fewer is 25.12% (and only a 74.88% chance of getting 13 or more). This does not meet Paul's requirements, although it is very close. You tell Paul that he will need at least 33 donors to obtain at least 13 pints of Type O blood with a probability of at least 75%. Minitab saved you quite a bit of calculation time.

You have completed your volunteer research on blood type samples and must now turn your attention back to your course work.

- Choose **F**ile ▶ Restart **M**initab

Case Study: Genetics

In Mendel's classic genetics experiment, he theorized that a garden pea would be produced in the four phenotypes: smooth-yellow, smooth-green, wrinkled-yellow, and wrinkled-green. He also predicted these phenotypes would be produced in a 9:3:3:1 ratio. In other words, he predicted a 9/16 (.5625) probability of producing a smooth-yellow pea, a 3/16 (.1875) probability of producing a smooth-green pea, and so on. Your genetics professor, Dr. Michaels, has asked you to write a term paper about Mendel's pea experiments. As part of your paper, you will generate a random sample of peas and do various experiments of your own; this is called a *simulation.* You will simulate the results of a hypothetical experiment.

Generating Random Data from Discrete Distributions

Minitab offers you the ability of obtaining a random sample of data and simulating an experiment without leaving the computer. This saves time and money.

In the worksheet, you will enter two columns: one containing the four different phenotypes of peas, the other containing the theoretical probabilities of each phenotype. The Minitab command you will use to simulate the experiment requires that the phenotypes be described by numbers, so you will use the following numeric code:

Phenotype	Code	Probability
Smooth-yellow	1	0.5625
Smooth-green	2	0.1875
Wrinkled-yellow	3	0.1875
Wrinkled-green	4	0.0625

Enter this information into the worksheet:

- Go to the Data worksheet
- Assign the names TYPE and PROB to columns C1 and C2, respectively
- Enter the values **1**, **2**, **3**, and **4** in C1 TYPE to represent the four pea types
- Enter the values **0.5625**, **0.1875**, **0.1875**, and **0.0625** into C2 PROB to represent the corresponding probabilities

To obtain a random sample of 320 peas using the theoretical probabilities postulated by Mendel:

- Return to the Session window
- Choose **C**alc ▶ **R**andom Data ▶ **D**iscrete...
- Type **320** in the Generate rows of data text box and press [Tab]
- Type **SAMPLE** in the Store in column(s) text box and press [Tab]
- Select C1 TYPE for the Values in text box
- Select C2 PROB for the Probabilities in text box

The completed Discrete Distribution dialog box should look like Figure 5-7.

FIGURE 5-7

The completed Discrete Distribution dialog box from the Random Data submenu

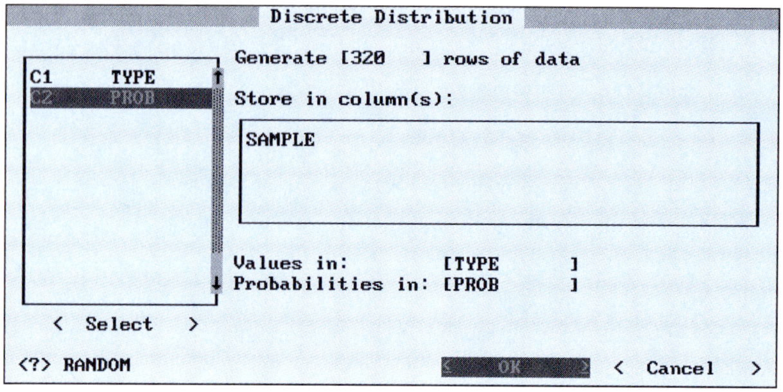

- Press [↵]
- Go to the Data worksheet

C3 SAMPLE now contains 320 entries consisting of the numbers 1, 2, 3, and 4. You can consider these 320 values the phenotypes from an experiment in which you planted 320 randomly selected peas. To count the number of 1s, 2s, 3s, and 4s in your sample:

- Return to the Session window
- Choose **Stat** ▶ **Tables** ▶ **Tally...**
- Select C3 SAMPLE as the variable
- Press [Alt]-P for **P**ercents and press [↵]

The frequency distribution for your sample appears in the Session window (Figure 5-8). Since the samples are generated randomly, your COUNT and PERCENT values will be slightly different from those in Figure 5-8.

FIGURE 5-8

Frequency distribution of phenotypes in the sample

```
MTB > Tally 'SAMPLE';
SUBC>   Counts;
SUBC>   Percents.

 SAMPLE  COUNT  PERCENT
      1    196    61.25
      2     50    15.62
      3     45    14.06
      4     29     9.06
     N=    320
```

The percentage of each phenotype in this simulation experiment is quite close to the probabilities theorized by Mendel. The smooth-yellow peas (1s) are high (61.25% versus 56.25%), the smooth-green peas (2s) are under-represented (15.62% versus 18.75%), as are the wrinkled-yellow peas (3s) (14.06 versus 18.75%), and the observed percentage of wrinkled-green peas (4s) is higher than the theoretical value (9.06% versus 6.25%).

In a matter of minutes, you were able to generate data similar to that on which Mendel based his conclusions. You will return to this case study and a data set similar to this in Tutorial 10.

You will now move from genetics to physiology class.

- Choose **F**ile ▶ Restart **M**initab

Case Study: Heights

Dr. Wei is a professor in the physiology department of the medical school on campus. She comes to you hoping that you can help her with a lecture she is preparing for her physiology class. She would like to show that many physiological variables in nature are approximately normally distributed. For example, she knows that the actual heights of college-age women are very close to a normal distribution, with a mean of 64 inches and a standard deviation of 3.1 inches, and would like to illustrate this using the height data for the 60 women in her class.

Dr. Wei had her students fill out a questionnaire that included heights and a number of other physiological variables. It strikes you that the best way to show the normal distribution of physiological variables might be to compare the *self-reported* female heights to a known normal distribution.

Generating Random Data from a Continuous Distribution

You suggest that Dr. Wei could simulate a sample of heights from the college-age female population, using the values $\mu = 64$ and $\sigma = 3.1$. She agrees to try it. To generate a sample of 60 observations from a normal population with mean 64 and standard deviation 3.1:

- Choose **C**alc ▶ **R**andom Data ▶ **N**ormal...

- Type **60** in the Generate —— rows of data text box and press [Tab]
- Type **'RAN HGTS'** in the Store in column(s) text box and press [Tab]
- Type **64** in the Mean text box and press [Tab]
- Type **3.1** in the Standard deviation text box

The completed Normal Distribution dialog box should look like Figure 5-9.

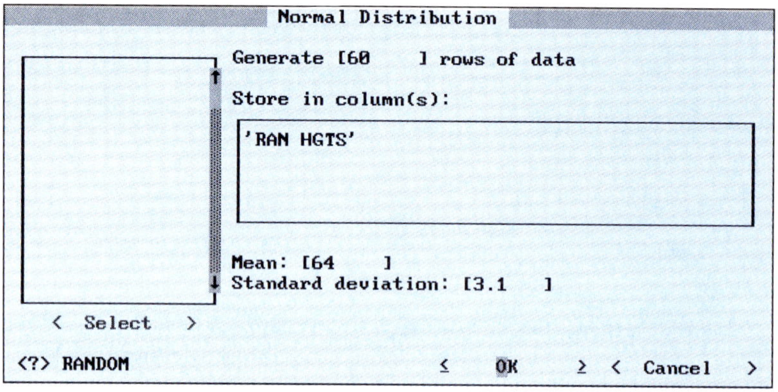

FIGURE 5-9

The completed Normal Distribution dialog box from the Random Data submenu

- Press [↵]
- Go to the Data worksheet

The worksheet contains 60 random values from a normal ($\mu = 64$ and $\sigma = 3.1$) distribution. You tell Dr. Wei to explain to her class that these data represent a random sample of the heights of 60 college-age women.

Note: Again, because randomly generated samples differ, your histograms may be slightly different.

Using this simulated sample, she can show the class how a sample from a normal distribution would appear in a graphical summary, and can compare this behavior to the class data she has collected. You first obtain a histogram of the randomly generated heights:

- Return to the Session window

- Choose **G**raph ▶ **H**istogram...
- Select C1 RAN HGTS
- Press [Alt]-O

The histogram appears in a graph screen (Figure 5-10).

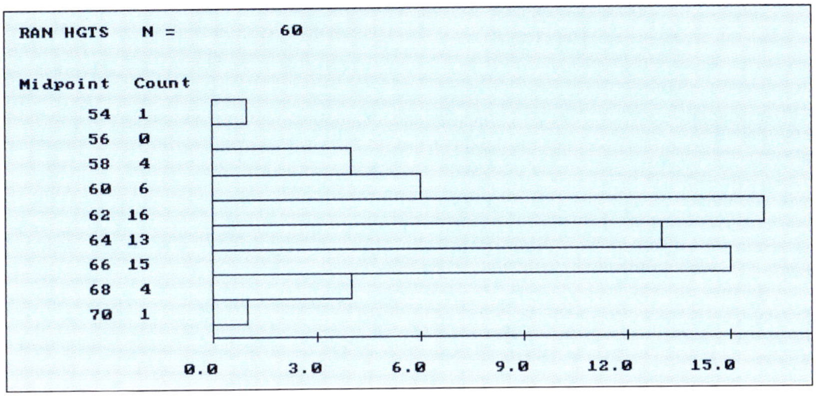

FIGURE 5-10
Histogram of random heights

The histogram does appear to be somewhat bell-shaped. This might be sufficient to convince her class, but there is another method of determining whether normality is a reasonable assumption.

- Press Q for Quit

Obtaining the Normal Probability Plot Using Normal Scores

A common graphical technique for checking whether a sample comes from a normal population is to obtain the normal probability plot (NPP). You can generate an NPP quite easily in Minitab using the Nscores and scatter plot commands.

- Choose **C**alc ▶ Functions and Statistics ▶ **F**unctions...
- Press [Tab]
- Select C1 RAN HGTS as the Input Column
- Type **NSCORES** in the Result in text box
- Press [Alt]-M to select Nor**m**al scores
- Press [↵]
- Go to the Data worksheet

MINITAB AT WORK

PUBLIC SAFETY: Six years after a rural university in Pennsylvania installed a nuclear reactor for educational purposes, concerned residents of the surrounding town claimed that the presence of the reactor was increasing infant mortality in the area. To support their contention, they presented the following data, which compared infant mortality in their town to that in another town similar in size and character.

A statistician examined the data to help determine whether the infant mortality rate over the nine-year period was unusually high. The statistician focused on several aspects of the claim; one was whether the town's 1968 rate of 10 infant deaths was unusually high, given a community where the average mortality rate was 6 deaths per year.

The statistician decided to see if randomly generated samples of similar data would contain any values as high as the 1968 value. He had Minitab randomly generate 100 Poisson distributions of nine-year spreads. He found that 58% of those randomly generated spreads contained one or more years with an infant mortality rate of at least 10. Since a majority of the spreads included a value as high as the 1968 rate, the statistician decided that the peak of 10 in 1968 was not uncommon in a situation with 6 deaths in an average year.

In the end no dangerous environmental effects were linked with the presence of the reactor and it was allowed to remain. The causes of infant mortality remain a vital concern, but it is important to recognize that peaks and valleys normally do occur in a nine-year period.

Minitab computes the normal scores and stores them in column C2 NSCORES.

- Return to the Session window

To obtain the NPP:

- Choose **G**raph ▶ Scatter **P**lot...
- Select C1 RAN HGTS for the Vertical axis
- Select C2 NSCORES for the Horizontal axis and press [Tab]
- Type . (period) for the Plotting symbol and press [↵]

The NPP appears on a separate graph screen (Figure 5-11).

FIGURE 5-11
Normal probability plot of randomly generated female heights

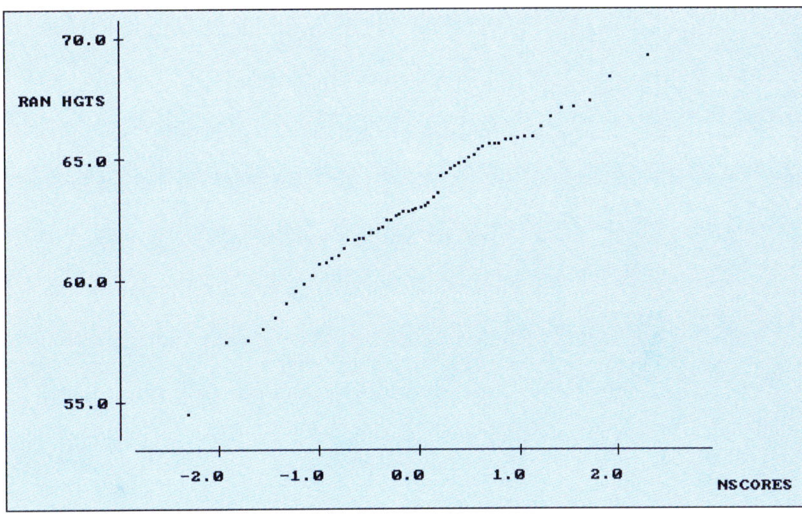

If the NPP is approximately a straight line, it is reasonable to conclude that the sample came from a population that is approximately normal. Since you generated the data from the normal distribution, a straight line fits very well, and the scatter plot will make a good illustration for Dr. Wei's lecture of how to show that a variable is approximately normally distributed. She can produce a similar NPP for the self-reported heights she collected from her class.

- Press Q for Quit

Dr. Wei has stored the female students' heights and an ID variable in the Minitab file HEIGHTS.MTW.

- Choose **F**ile ▶ Restart **M**initab

- Press [↵]
- Open HEIGHTS.MTW from the TUT5 directory

To produce the NPP you need to obtain the normal scores for the heights in C2 HEIGHTS and then obtain the scatter plot:

- Choose **C**alc ▶ **F**unctions and Statistics ▶ **F**unctions...
- Press [Tab]
- Select C2 HEIGHTS for the Input Column
- Type **NSCORES** in the Result in text box
- Press [Alt]-M for Nor**m**al
- Press [↵]

When Minitab has computed the normal scores:

- Choose **G**raph ▶ Scatter **P**lot...
- Select C2 HEIGHTS for the Vertical axis
- Select C3 NSCORES for the Horizontal axis and press [Tab]
- Type **.** (period) for the Plotting symbol and press [↵]

The NPP for the self-reported female heights appears in a graph screen (Figure 5-12).

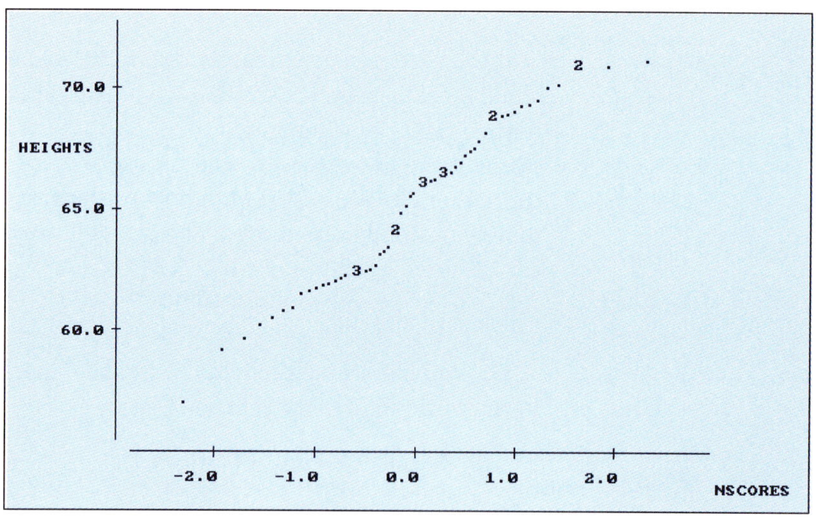

FIGURE 5-12
Normal probability plot of self-reported female heights for college-age women

While the plot may not be as straight as your simulation NPP, it is sufficiently close to a straight line. You report to Dr. Wei that, based on the NPP, self-reported heights of college-age women seem to be approximately normally distributed. She is pleased with the idea of comparing the simulation scatter plot to the actual scatter plot and plans to use both graphics for her lecture on the normal distribution of physiological variables.

- Press Q for Quit

Inverse Cumulative Functions for Continuous Distributions

Impressed with your work, Dr. Wei returns some time later to show you her follow-up work on self-reported heights. Using extensive information from her classes, she has found that self-reported heights of college-age women appear to be approximately normally distributed, with a mean of 64.25 and a standard deviation of 3.82.

Dr. Wei is planning another study that will investigate the relationship between bone structure and height. She plans to compare the bone structure distribution in four height groups. The height groups will be based on the quartiles of the self-reported height distribution. She asks you to find the quartiles.

To find the first quartile, Q_1 (the 25th percentile):

- Choose **Calc ▶ Probability Distributions ▶ Normal...**
- Press [Alt]-I for **I**nverse cumulative probability
- Press [Tab]
- Type **64.25** in the Mean text box and press [Tab]
- Type **3.82** in the Standard deviation text box
- Press [Alt]-N for Input co**n**stant and press [Tab]
- Type **.25** in the Input constant text box

The completed Normal Distribution dialog box should look like Figure 5-13.

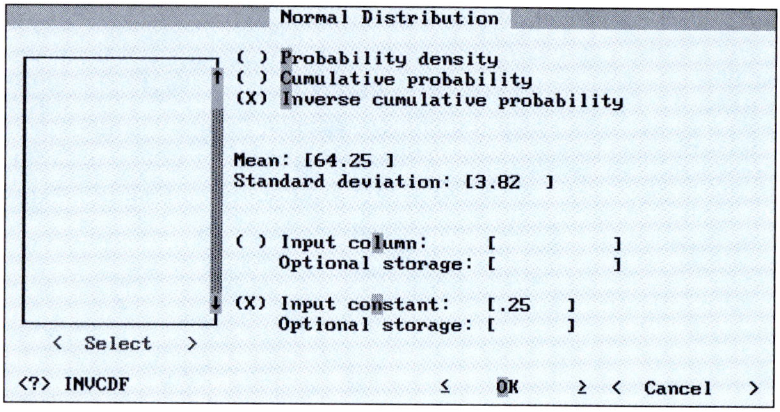

FIGURE 5-13
The completed Normal Distribution dialog box from the Probability Distributions submenu

- Press [↵]

The Session window displays the results, as shown in Figure 5-14.

FIGURE 5-14
The Session window, showing inverse cumulative values

```
MTB > InvCDF .25;
SUBC>   Normal 64.25 3.82.
    0.2500    61.6735
```

You conclude that 25% of the self-reported female heights are less than 61.67 inches. The first study group comprises women whose self-reported heights are less than 61.67 inches. The second group consists of women whose height range falls between 61.67 inches and the median of 64.25 inches.

To obtain the third quartile, Q_3 (75th percentile):

- Choose **E**dit ▶ Edit **L**ast Command Dialog...
- Press [Alt]-N for Input co**n**stant and press [Tab]
- Type **.75** in the Input constant text box and press [↵]

The third group consists of women with self-reported heights between 64.25 and 66.83 inches. The last group contains those women taller than 66.83 inches.

In the next tutorial you will learn another use of the inverse cumulative probability function.

Sampling from a Column

Dr. Wei is presenting a paper at a convention in Chicago and would like to have eight students in the class accompany her, four men and four women. To be fair she has asked you to use Minitab to select four female students at random from those whose heights are reported in C2 HEIGHTS. (She will select the male students in a similar manner.) Recall that Dr. Wei has included a student ID number in the Data worksheet (C1 ID).

To randomly select the four female students for the Chicago trip:

- Choose **C**alc ▶ **R**andom Data ▶ Sa**m**ple from Columns...
- Type 4 for Sample —— rows from column(s) and press [Tab]
- Select C1 ID and press [Tab]
- Type **CHICAGO** for Put samples in

The completed Sample From Columns dialog box should resemble Figure 5-15.

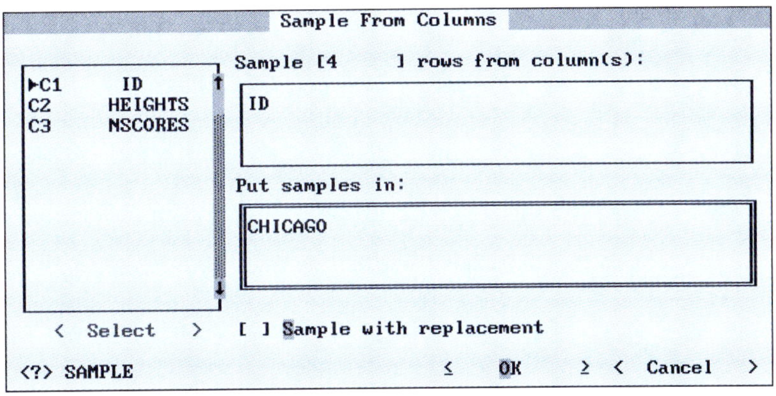

FIGURE 5-15
The completed Sample From Columns dialog box from the Random Data submenu

- Press [Alt]-O
- Go to the Data worksheet; if necessary, scroll to the top

The ID numbers of the four lucky students are displayed in C4 CHICAGO. Because the numbers are randomly selected, your selections will be different from those shown.

FIGURE 5-16

The Data worksheet, showing four randomly selected student IDs

→	ID C1	HEIGHTS C2	NSCORES C3	CHICAGO C4
1	441	65.0	-0.14548	861
2	805	71.3	2.31277	648
3	555	69.5	1.14165	712
4	390	62.8	-0.40450	918
5	49	67.1	0.44998	
6	820	62.1	-0.86503	
7	581	63.6	-0.27263	
8	298	63.4	-0.31594	
9	413	64.2	-0.20862	
10	648	61.7	-1.14165	
11	2	61.8	-1.06475	
12	639	61.0	-1.32015	
13	552	64.2	-0.20862	
14	968	66.2	0.06217	
15	483	70.2	1.32015	
16	597	62.5	-0.59290	
17	187	68.9	0.77735	
18	253	62.3	-0.74945	
19	155	66.9	0.40450	
20	577	66.7	0.35986	
21	114	66.6	0.27263	
22	961	68.0	0.64327	

To allow for the situation where you would want to sample with replacement (the same population member could be chosen more than one time), you could select the Sample with replacement option in the Sample From Columns dialog box.

Inform Dr. Wei that the following students were selected: 861, 648, 712, and 918 (of course, your numbers differ from these).

- Return to the Session window

In this tutorial you have worked with a few of the most commonly used distributions. In later tutorials you will see how other selections from the Probability Distributions commands can help solve statistical problems. In the next two tutorials you will see how to use Minitab to perform some parametric hypothesis tests.

If you plan to continue directly to the next tutorial:

- Choose **File** ▶ Restart **M**initab

If you want to take a longer break:

- Choose **File** ▶ **E**xit

Minitab Command Summary

The menus and commands introduced in or related to this tutorial are described in this section. You will find a complete explanation of all menus and commands in the Reference section of this manual.

Menu	Command	Function
Edit		
	Set Patterned Data	Generates sequences or repetitive patterns of numbers and stores the results in a column
Calc		
	Set Base	Allows the user to specify the "seed" number used to generate random data
	Random Data	Produces random samples from specified discrete and continuous distributions given below
	Sample From Columns	Takes random samples, with or without replacement, from a given column or columns
	Chisquare Normal F T Uniform Bernoulli Binomial Discrete Integer Poisson	Various continuous and discrete distributions from which random samples can be generated

Probability Distributions	Calculates probabilities, density function values, cumulative probabilities, and percentiles for the discrete and continuous random variables given below
Chisquare Normal F T Uniform Binomial Discrete Integer Poisson	Various continuous and discrete distributions on which probability distribution calculations are based

Review and Practice

Matching

Match the following terms to their definitions by placing the correct letter next to the term it explains.

____ Start at

____ Set Patterned Data

____ Cumulative probability

____ Random Data

____ Sample From Columns

____ Sample with replacement

____ Inverse cumulative probability

____ Normal score

a. Lets you enter sequences and/or repetitive patterns of data into the worksheet

b. Option on the Sample rows command that allows sampling with replacement from a row

c. Minitab option to obtain cumulative probabilities

d. Provides percentiles, quartiles, or deciles

e. Computes a normal score for use in normal probability plots

f. Beginning value for the Set Patterned Data command

Testing μ When σ Is Known

To perform a hypothesis test on the value of μ, the population mean, when the value of σ, the population standard deviation, is known, you will use the Z-test. As you can imagine, the population standard deviation is available only on rare occasions.

- Open CROWDS.MTW from the TUT6 directory

The worksheet contains female responses in C1, FEM RATE, and male responses in C2, MALERATE.

To see if for women there is significant evidence of a decrease in the mean from previous studies (15), set up the following hypotheses:

The null hypothesis, H_0: $\mu = 15$

The alternative hypothesis, H_1: $\mu < 15$, a decrease in crowdedness perception using white walls

Now perform the hypothesis test:

- Choose **S**tat ▶ **B**asic Statistics ▶ 1-Sample **Z**...
- Select C1 FEM RATE
- Press [Alt]-T for **T**est mean and press [Tab]
- Type **15** and press [Tab]
- Press [F4] to view the Alternative pop-up menu
- Press [↑] to choose the less than option and press [Tab]
- Type **3.5** in the Sigma text box

The completed 1-Sample Z dialog box should look like Figure 6-1.

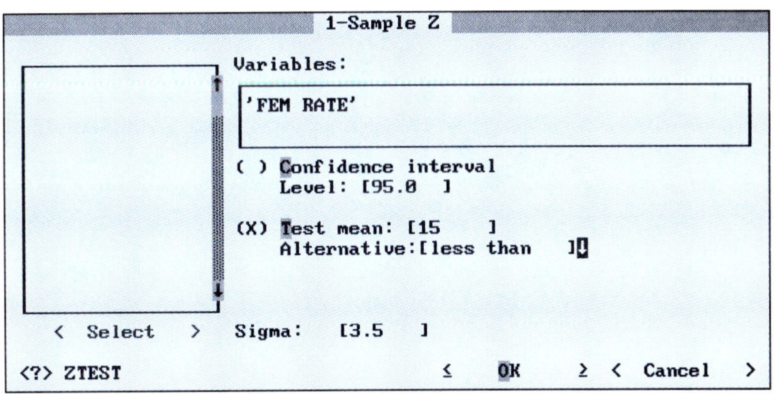

FIGURE 6-1
The completed 1-Sample Z dialog box from the Basic Statistics submenu from the Stat menu

- Press ↵

Now determine the critical z-value:

- Choose **C**alc ▶ **P**robability Distributions ▶ **N**ormal...
- Press Alt-I for **I**nverse cumulative probability
- Press Alt-N for Input co**n**stant and press Tab
- Type **0.05** in the Input constant text box and press ↵

The Session window (Figure 6-2) displays Minitab's commands and output corresponding to your menu choices.

FIGURE 6-2

Results of Z-test for female responses

Z-test output

```
MTB > ZTest 15 3.5 'FEM RATE';
SUBC>   Alternative -1.

TEST OF MU = 15.000 VS MU L.T. 15.000
THE ASSUMED SIGMA = 3.50

              N      MEAN    STDEV   SE MEAN         Z    P VALUE
FEM RATE     36    14.417    3.887     0.583     -1.00       0.16

MTB > InvCDF .05;
SUBC>   Normal 0.0 1.0.
    0.0500   -1.6449
```

Critical value

The subcommand Alternative –1 designates the left-tailed (less-than or lower-tailed) alternative hypothesis. Correspondingly, a right-tailed test would be designated +1 and a two-tailed test 0.

Assuming the null hypothesis is true, the sample mean of 14.417 has a z-score of –1.00. The critical z-value is –1.6449, so the test statistic of –1.00 does not fall in the rejection region. Fail to reject H_0. There is no significant evidence to conclude that the mean perceived crowdedness is less than 15 for women. On the basis of your data you cannot say that white walls had any effect on how crowded a group of women feel.

You can also decide to reject or fail to reject the null hypothesis using the p-value in the z-test output. When the p-value is less than your chosen level of significance, reject H_0. In this case the p-value of 0.16 is greater than 0.05, so your decision would be the same: fail to reject H_0 at the 0.05 level.

Now test the hypothesis that the mean response for men in a white room is less than 15:

- Choose **Stat** ▶ **Basic Statistics** ▶ 1-Sample **Z**...
- Select C2 MALERATE for the Variables text box
- Press [Alt]-T for **Test** mean and press [Tab]
- Type **15** and press [Tab]
- Press [↑] to select less than from the Alternative pop-up menu and press [Tab] (you don't have to press [F4] to see the menu unless you want to)
- Type **3.5** in the Sigma text box
- Press [↵]

The Session window should look like Figure 6-3.

FIGURE 6-3
Results of Z-test for male responses

```
MTB > ZTest 15 3.5 'MALERATE';
SUBC>   Alternative -1.

TEST OF MU = 15.000 VS MU L.T. 15.000
THE ASSUMED SIGMA = 3.50

              N      MEAN     STDEV   SE MEAN        Z    P VALUE
MALERATE     36    13.917     3.698     0.583    -1.86      0.032
```

For this test, the z-score is –1.86. Since the critical value at the 0.05 level of significance is –1.6449 (the same as that computed for the female test), the score of –1.86 falls in the critical region. So at the 0.05 level, reject H_0 and conclude that the mean male perception of crowdedness is less than 15. Men apparently feel less crowded in a white room than in a dark room.

Note that the p-value for this test is 0.032. Since this is less than 0.05, your decision would be to reject H_0 at the 0.05 level. However, if you were to perform the test at the .01 level, the decision would be to fail to reject H_0 since the p-value of 0.032 is greater than 0.01. Many statisticians feel that reporting test results in terms of the p-value avoids confusion since readers can use their own judgment as to whether the p-value is sufficiently small or not.

Computing a Confidence Interval for μ When σ Is Known

As part of your experimental psychology project, Dr. Ford would like you to estimate the mean perceived crowdedness for all adult men and women. Form a 90% confidence interval:

- Choose **Stat** ▶ **Basic Statistics** ▶ 1-Sample **Z**...
- Select C1 FEM RATE and C2 MALERATE and press [Tab]
- Type **90** in the Level text box and press [Tab]
- Type **3.5** in the Sigma text box

Note: Confidence levels can be entered in the Level text box as a whole number (90) or a decimal number (.90).

The completed 1-Sample Z dialog box should look like Figure 6-4.

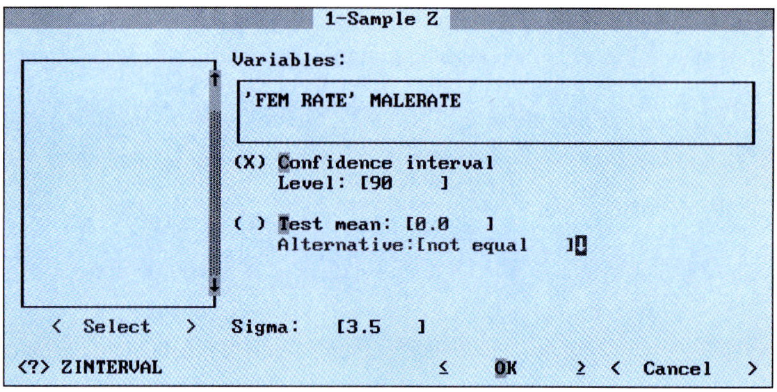

FIGURE 6-4
The completed 1-Sample Z dialog box from the Basic Statistics submenu

- Press [↵]

Figure 6-5 shows the results in the Session window.

FIGURE 6-5
The 90% confidence interval

```
MTB > ZInterval 90 3.5 'FEM RATE' 'MALERATE'.

THE ASSUMED SIGMA =3.50

              N      MEAN     STDEV  SE MEAN   90.0 PERCENT C.I.
FEM RATE     36    14.417     3.887    0.583  (  13.456,  15.377)
MALERATE     36    13.917     3.698    0.583  (  12.956,  14.877)
```

These results indicate that you can be 90% certain that:

- Women have a mean perception of crowdedness between 13.456 and 15.377.
- Men have a mean perception of crowdedness between 12.956 and 14.877.

Note that the confidence interval for women includes 15; however, the confidence level for men does not. This is consistent with the results of the hypothesis tests performed earlier.

- Choose **F**ile ▶ Restart **M**initab

Case Study: Revenues

As newly appointed district manager of Consolidated Stores, Inc., your task is to investigate revenues in various departments of the corporation in your district. Seven days out of the year have been randomly selected for each of the past four years, and daily revenues have been reported for the women's sportswear division. You have been told that mean revenues in the previous three years have been equal to $3500 a day and you would like to see if this amount has changed. You formulate your hypotheses:

$$H_0: \mu = 3500$$
$$H_1: \mu \neq 3500$$

Testing μ When σ Is Unknown

When checking records for past revenue figures in this particular department, you have found them to be nearly normally distributed (bell-shaped). You do not know the population standard deviation, so you cannot use a Z-test. The population is approximately normally distributed, so you can use a t-test.

- Open SALES.MTW in the TUT6 directory
- Choose **S**tat ▶ **B**asic Statistics ▶ **1**-Sample t...
- Select C1 1991

- Press [Alt]-T for **T**est mean and press [Tab]
- Type **3500** in the Test mean text box

Use the default alternative of not equal to perform a two-tailed test. The completed 1-Sample t dialog box should look like Figure 6-6.

FIGURE 6-6

The completed 1-Sample t dialog box from the Basic Statistics submenu

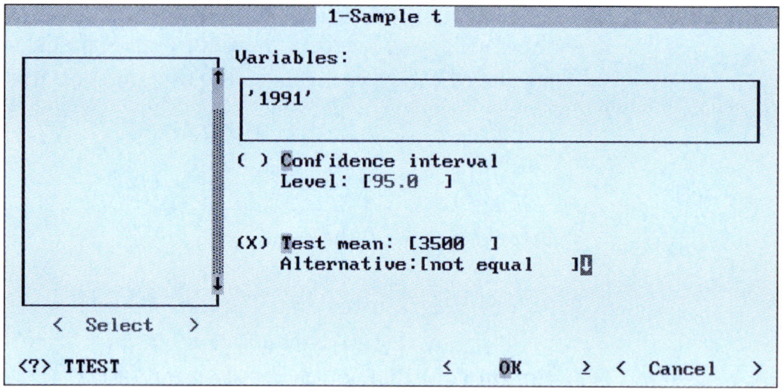

- Press [↵]

The Session window (Figure 6-7) appears.

FIGURE 6-7

Results of t-test

```
MTB > TTest 3500 '1991';
SUBC>   Alternative 0.

TEST OF MU = 3500.000 VS MU N.E. 3500.000

                N      MEAN     STDEV   SE MEAN        T    P VALUE
1991            7  2356.143  1347.778   509.412    -2.25      0.066
```

The sample mean sales of 2356 corresponds to the t value of –2.25. The corresponding p-value is 0.066. Since the p-value is greater than .05, fail to reject H_0 and conclude that there is no significant evidence of a change in revenues. The CEO will be pleased to hear that sales have not changed.

MINITAB AT WORK

RETAILING: Frozen foods are a common staple in many American households, especially frozen pizzas. Pizza producers must carefully monitor how bacteria respond to prolonged refrigeration temperatures. Microbiologists used Minitab to help determine how long pizza can be refrigerated without becoming a threat to public health.

In order to examine the effect of freezing on specific bacteria, researchers inoculated pizzas with measured amounts of *Escherichia coli* and other potential contaminants. They stored the pizzas at various temperatures, retrieving samples every other day for microbiological analysis. They counted colonies of bacteria at each testing and entered that data into Minitab. When they compared each day's count with the initial count, using a 1-sample t-test, they found that the *E. coli* colonies increased significantly (p-value < 0.05) between days 8 and 10.

This result suggests *E. coli* will grow when acceptable refrigeration temperatures are not maintained. Pizza producers could best safeguard public health by carefully monitoring bacteria levels before beginning the freezing process, while the vendors must ensure adequate refrigeration and carefully monitor shelf dates.

Computing a Confidence Interval for μ When σ Is Unknown

To compute a 95% confidence interval for the mean daily revenue in 1991:

- Choose **E**dit ▶ **E**dit **L**ast Command Dialog...
- Press [Alt]-C for **C**onfidence interval
- Press [↵]

The 95% confidence interval appears in the Session window, as shown in Figure 6-8.

FIGURE 6-8

The 95% confidence interval

```
MTB > TInterval 95.0 '1991'.

                N       MEAN     STDEV   SE MEAN    95.0 PERCENT C.I.
1991            7    2356.14   1347.78    509.41   ( 1109.31, 3602.98)
```

You can report, with 95% certainty, that the mean daily sales for 1991 is somewhere between $1,109 and $3,603.

- Choose **F**ile ▶ Restart **M**initab

Case Study: Election

You are working for Ann Gomez, one of two candidates running for the office of state senator. Gomez believes that she will win the election, which will take place in five days, because she thinks she has 51% voter support. She asks you to verify this. Earlier in the day, a random sample of 200 of the district's registered voters showed that 86 favor Ms. Gomez for senator (43% of the sample).

Ms. Gomez has asked that you test whether she has less than the needed 51% of the vote to win the election. She would also like you to estimate the percentage of support she can expect.

Testing and Obtaining a Confidence Interval for a Population Proportion

Use a 5% level of significance to determine if the data indicate that the true proportion of favorable voters is less than 51%. First formulate your hypotheses:

$$H_0: p = .51$$
$$H_1: p < .51$$

Minitab has no direct command for performing hypothesis tests on and obtaining a confidence interval for proportions. However, it can store a sequence of commands in a file called a *macro* that you can use to obtain both the test and the confidence interval. The commands necessary for performing this test are stored in PTEST.MTB on the backup Sample Files disk.

The test uses the normal approximation to the binomial and hence assumes np and n(1 – p) are both greater than 5. Since 200*0.51 = 102 > 5 and 200*(1 – 0.51) = 98 > 5, you proceed:

- Choose **File** ▶ Other **Files** ▶ **Execute** Macro...

The Execute Macro dialog box (Figure 6-9) appears.

FIGURE 6-9
The Execute Macro dialog box from the Other Files submenu

```
                 Execute Macro

Number of times to execute: [1      ]




<?> EXECUTE          <Select File>  <  Cancel    >
```

Accept the default value to execute the macro once.

- Press [↵]
- Select PTEST.MTB in the TUT6 directory

The Session window appears and you are asked to input values for p-naught (the hypothesized value of the population proportion), x (the observed number of successes), and n (the sample size).

Enter the values on one line at the DATA> prompt, separating the values by at least one space:

- Type **0.51 86 200** (put at least one space between each value)

The Session window should look like Figure 6-10.

FIGURE 6-10
The first DATA prompt for the PTEST.MTB macro

```
MTB > Execute 'A:\TUT6\PTEST.MTB' 1.

   At the "DATA>" prompt below, enter the following values:
   1.  p-naught, the hypothesized value of the population proportion;
   2.  x, the observed number of successes; and
   3   n, the sample size.

DATA> 0.51 86 200
```

- Press [↵]

Minitab then prompts you for the direction of your test (upper-tailed, two-tailed, or lower-tailed):

- Type **-1** to perform a lower-tailed test

The Session window should look like Figure 6-11.

FIGURE 6-11

The second DATA prompt for the PTEST.MTB macro

```
DATA> 0.51 86 200

Input:
    0.51     86.00    200.00


   At the "DATA>" prompt below, enter a
        1 to perform an upper-tailed test, or
        0 to perform a two-tailed test, or
       -1 to perform a lower-tailed test.

DATA> -1
```

- Press [↵]

After Minitab runs the test, the Session window should look like Figure 6-12.

FIGURE 6-12

PTEST.MTB results of the hypothesis test

```
DATA> -1

                    Ho: p = 0.5100  vs.  Ha: p   <   0.5100

                    z =-2.28525        p-value = 0.01115


   A confidence interval for the true population proportion will be
   produced below.  At the "DATA>" prompt below, enter the confidence
   level (95 for a 95% confidence interval) for the confidence interval.

DATA>
```

Minitab now prompts you for information on the confidence interval.

Before you continue, interpret the results of the hypothesis test. The null and alternative hypotheses are displayed, as is the z-statistic and the p-value. The Z-test statistic is –2.28525, with a p-value of 0.01115. Reject H_0. It appears that Ms. Gomez has less than 51% of the voters' support. You advise her of your results so she can plan accordingly.

To continue with the computations for obtaining the 95% confidence interval, at the DATA> prompt:

- Type **95** and press ↵

The Session window should resemble Figure 6-13.

FIGURE 6-13
Results of PTEST.MTB confidence interval computations

```
DATA> 95

CI Level
   95

    The 95% confidence interval is ( 0.3614  to  0.4986)
```

The lower confidence limit is .3614 and the upper confidence limit is .4986. You can be 95% certain that the proportion of voters who favor Ms. Gomez is between 36% and 50%.

These results indicate that Ms. Gomez does not have 51% voter support and is going to need to campaign hard in the next few days before the election if she expects to win.

In this tutorial you used Minitab to perform hypothesis tests and to form confidence intervals about the parameter of a single population. In the next tutorial you will learn to compare the difference between the parameters of two populations.

If you plan to continue directly to the next tutorial:

- Choose **F**ile ▶ Restart **M**initab

If you want to take a longer break:

- Choose **F**ile ▶ E**x**it

Minitab Command Summary

The menus and commands introduced in or related to this tutorial are described in this section. You will find a complete explanation of all menus and commands in the Reference section of this manual.

Menu	Command	Function
File		
	Other Files	
	Execute Macro	Executes a macro or a sequence of previously stored Minitab commands
Stat		
	Basic Statistics	
	1-Sample Z	Performs inferences (test and confidence intervals) on a population mean when σ is known
	1-Sample t	Performs inferences (test and confidence intervals) on a population mean when σ is unknown

Review and Practice

Matching

Match the following terms to their definitions by placing the correct letter next to the term it explains.

____ Confidence interval

____ 1-Sample t

____ PTEST.MTB

____ Alternative

____ sigma

____ Level

____ p-value

____ 1-Sample Z

____ Test mean

a. Provides a test of a population mean

b. The Minitab command used to perform 1-sample inference about a mean assuming σ is unknown

c. The name Minitab uses for the population standard deviation

d. Minitab's notation for the p-value used in testing hypotheses

e. Provides a confidence interval for a population mean

f. The Minitab command used to perform 1-sample inference about a mean assuming σ is known

g. The option on Minitab commands that allows you to change the confidence level of a confidence interval

h. Performs a test of population proportion and provide a confidence interval for the proportion

i. The Minitab subcommand that allows you to specify the direction of the alternative hypothesis

True/False

Mark the following statements T or F.

____ 1. Confidence levels can be entered as a percentage (99) or a decimal (.99) in Minitab.

____ 2. The population standard deviation must be known to perform a 1-sample test of a mean in Minitab.

____ 3. Confidence intervals and 1-sample tests are performed using the same Minitab command from the Stat menu.

____ 4. An upper-tailed test is the default alternative for a 1-sample test of a population mean.

____ 5. The confidence level for population confidence intervals can be set to any value you request.

____ 6. To perform the test of a proportion using the commands that Minitab has stored in a macro, you use the Other Files ▶ Execute Macro command from the File menu.

____ 7. An upper-tailed test is designated Alternative 0.

____ 8. Only a two-tailed test is performed using the PTEST macro.

____ 9. The default confidence level is 90% in Minitab's 1-sample confidence intervals.

____ 10. You will find most of Minitab's 1-sample inference commands under the File menu.

Practice Problems

1. National norms for weights and heights of first graders are 44.5 inches and 45.5 pounds. Use the WGTHGT.MTW data from the TUT6 directory to determine if this first grade class is "normal" with respect to weight and height. Refer to Tutorial 5, where you learned how to check for normality using normal probability plots.
2. Open PROF.MTW from the TUT6 directory.
   a. Obtain confidence intervals for the mean Course and Prof ratings at the university.
   b. Unstack the Course ratings into four columns using the year variable. Obtain confidence intervals for the mean course rating for each of the four years. What do you find?
   c. Code the professor ratings into a high/low group using 2 (AVERAGE) for the cut point. Use the Tally command to determine the number of profs in each group in your sample. Estimate, using 90% confidence, the percentage of professors at this university that the students consider average or above.
3. Using the HORSE.MTW data from the TUT6 directory, obtain a confidence interval for the mean number of species at the three locations perpendicular to the trail edge. What do you find?
4. Open PAY.MTW from the TUT6 directory. The industry average salary has been found to be approximately $35,000.00. Is this company's salary structure comparable to the industry?

TUTORIAL 7

Inference from Two Samples

In Tutorial 6 you performed hypothesis tests on the mean and the proportion of a single population. When examining male and female perceptions of crowdedness you may have wondered whether there was a *difference* between the means of these two distinct populations. Statisticians must often determine whether one group is inherently different from another because of some treatment or characteristic (in this case gender) or whether apparent differences should be attributed to sampling variation.

In this tutorial, you will investigate whether there is a difference in the crowdedness response between men and women, and then test whether gender or age makes a difference in mean diastolic blood pressure. Finally, you will perform a before-and-after test to ascertain whether aspirin has an effect on mean clotting times for adult males.

Objectives

In this tutorial you will learn to:

- test the difference between two population means when two independent samples are recorded in separate columns

- test the difference between two population means when two independent samples are stacked in a single column
- test the difference between two population means when two samples are paired (dependent samples)
- form a confidence interval for the difference between two population means when the sample is dependent

Testing the Difference Between Two Population Means Using Two Independent Samples in Separate Columns

Minitab offers several options for testing differences between two population means. Because the men and women were randomly and independently chosen for the crowdedness experiment, use the test for independent samples. Pose the hypotheses to test for a difference between mean male and female perceptions of crowdedness:

$$H_0: \mu_M = \mu_F$$
$$H_1: \mu_M \neq \mu_F$$

Now open the sample file and perform the t-test:

- Open CROWDST7.MTW from the TUT7 directory
- Choose **S**tat ▶ **B**asic Statistics ▶ **2**-Sample t...
- Press [Alt]-D for Samples in **d**ifferent columns and press [Tab]
- Select C1 FEM RATE for First and C2 MALERATE for Second

Since the samples are large, it is not necessary to assume equal variances, so leave the checkbox at the bottom empty. The completed 2-Sample t dialog box should look like Figure 7-1.

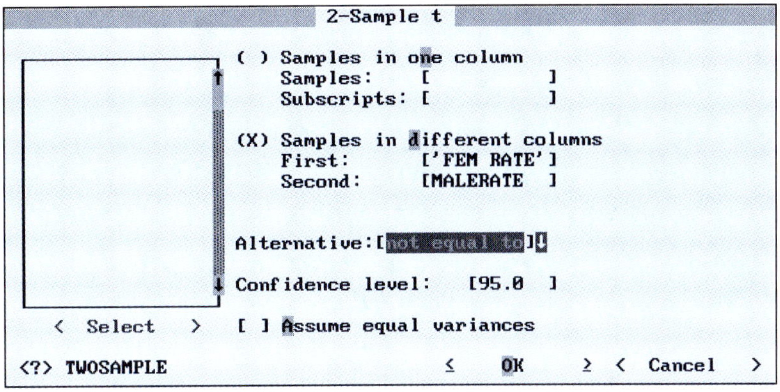

FIGURE 7-1

The completed 2-Sample t dialog box from the Basic Statistics submenu from the Stat menu

- Press [↵]

The results appear in the Session window (Figure 7-2).

FIGURE 7-2

Results of 2-Sample t test comparing mean female and male perceptions of crowdedness

```
MTB > TwoSample 95.0 'FEM RATE' 'MALERATE';
SUBC>   Alternative 0.

TWOSAMPLE T FOR FEM RATE VS MALERATE
            N      MEAN     STDEV   SE MEAN
FEM RATE   36     14.42      3.89      0.65
MALERATE   36     13.92      3.70      0.62

95 PCT CI FOR MU FEM RATE - MU MALERATE: (-1.28, 2.28)

TTEST MU FEM RATE = MU MALERATE (VS NE): T= 0.56  P=0.58  DF=  69
```

95 PCT CI

Minitab first presents summary information (sample size, mean, standard deviation, and standard error) for the women and men, and then displays the t-statistic (T=0.56), p-value (P=0.58), and degrees of freedom of the t-statistic (DF=69). Since the p-value of 0.58 exceeds the level of significance of 0.05, fail to reject the null hypothesis and conclude that there is no significant evidence of a difference between the mean perceptions of "crowdedness" for women and men. The differences in the sample means can be attributed to sampling variation.

Note that Minitab also provides a confidence interval for the difference in the means. The 95% confidence interval is (–1.28, 2.28).

- Choose File ▶ Restart Minitab

Case Study: Blood Pressure

As part of a study on the general health and fitness of college students, you want to test whether college men have a different diastolic blood pressure than college women.

You've collected data on age (C1 AGE), gender (C2 GENDER, recorded as 1=Female, 0=Male), height in centimeters (C3 HGT), diastolic and systolic blood pressure (C4 DBP, C5 SBP), smoking status (C6 SMOKER?, 1=yes, 0=no), and two variables that help determine fitness: the volume of air exhaled after one regular breath (C7 EX REG), and the volume of air exhaled after one deep breath (C8 EX MAX). (See the data set descriptions in Part III for a complete description of this data set.) The data have been stored in HEALTH.MTW.

Testing the Difference Between Two Population Means Using Two Independent Samples Stacked in a Single Column

- Open HEALTH.MTW from the TUT7 directory
- Go to the Data worksheet

First, formulate the pair of hypotheses:

$$H_0: \mu_M = \mu_F$$
$$H_1: \mu_M \neq \mu_F$$

In HEALTH.MTW male and female diastolic blood pressures are in one column (C4 DBP) with gender in another column (C2 GENDER). To perform the hypothesis test and obtain a 90% confidence interval for the difference in diastolic blood pressures of males and females:

- Return to the Session window
- Choose **S**tat ▶ **B**asic Statistics ▶ **2**-Sample t...

The two samples are in one column:

- Press [Tab]
- Select C4 DBP for the Samples text box
- Select C2 GENDER for the Subscripts text box and press [Tab] twice
- Type **90** for the Confidence level text box

Note: The Subscripts variable in a 2-Sample t test must be an integer and have two distinct values.

The completed 2-Sample t dialog box should look like Figure 7-3.

FIGURE 7-3
The completed 2-Sample t dialog box from the Basic Statistics submenu

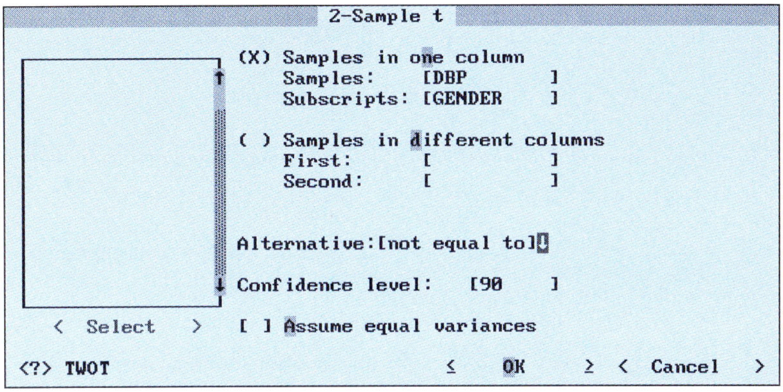

- Press [↵]

After Minitab performs the test, the Session window should look like Figure 7-4.

FIGURE 7-4
Results of t-test combining mean diastolic blood pressure by gender

```
MTB > TwoT 90 'DBP' 'GENDER';
SUBC>   Alternative 0.

TWOSAMPLE T FOR DBP
GENDER    N      MEAN     STDEV   SE MEAN
1        12      70.5      10.2       2.9
0         9     73.78      4.29       1.4

90 PCT CI FOR MU 1 - MU 0: (-9.0, 2.5)

TTEST MU 1 = MU 0 (VS NE): T= -1.00  P=0.33  DF=  15
```

90 PCT CI

The difference in sample means, 70.5 –73.78 = –3.28, corresponds to a t-value of –1.00 from a t-distribution with 15 degrees of freedom. The p-value for this test is 0.33, which is greater than 0.05. Therefore, fail to reject H_0 and conclude that there is no significant evidence of a difference between the mean diastolic blood pressures of college-age men and women. Note again that a confidence interval for the difference is also provided.

To pursue the investigation further, you ask: is age a factor in diastolic blood pressure? Do students under the age of 25 have lower diastolic blood pressure than their classmates who are over 25?

To assign identifying subscripts for the age variable:

- Choose **C**alc ► Code Data **V**alues...
- Select C1 AGE for Code data from columns and press [Tab]
- Type '**AGE CODE**' and press [Tab]
- Type **0:24**, press [Tab], type **1**, and press [Tab]
- Type **25:99**, press [Tab], and type **2**

The completed Code Data Values dialog box should look like Figure 7-5.

FIGURE 7-5

The completed Code Data Values dialog box from the Calc menu

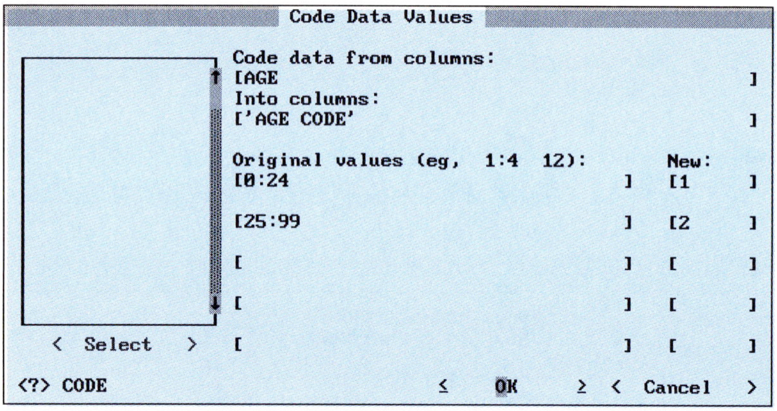

- Press [↵]

Next, formulate hypotheses to test whether younger students (AGE CODE 1 = ages 0–24) have lower blood pressure than older students (AGE CODE 2 = ages 25–99):

$$H_0: \mu_1 = \mu_2$$
$$H_1: \mu_1 < \mu_2$$

A check of the standard deviations of the two groups' diastolic blood pressures indicates that you can assume equal variances.

- Choose **S**tat ► **B**asic Statistics ► **2**-Sample t...
- Press [Tab]

- Select C4 DBP for Samples
- Select C9 AGE CODE for Subscripts and press [Tab]
- Press [↑] to choose the less than Alternative
- Press [Alt]-A for **A**ssume equal variances
- Press [↵]

The Session window should look like Figure 7-6.

FIGURE 7-6
Results of t-test comparing mean diastolic blood pressure by age

```
MTB > TwoT 95.0 'DBP' 'AGE CODE';
SUBC>   Alternative -1;
SUBC>   Pooled.

TWOSAMPLE T FOR DBP
AGE CODE    N      MEAN     STDEV   SE MEAN
1          13     70.77      7.33       2.0
2           8     73.75      9.71       3.4

95 PCT CI FOR MU 1 - MU 2: (-10.8, 4.8)

TTEST MU 1 = MU 2 (VS LT): T= -0.80  P=0.22  DF=  19

POOLED STDEV =        8.28
```

Since the p-value of 0.22 exceeds 0.05, fail to reject H_0 and conclude that there is no statistical evidence of a difference in the mean diastolic pressure of students under 25 and over 25 years old. Age does not appear to affect the diastolic blood pressure in younger age groups.

- Choose **F**ile ▶ Restart **M**initab

Testing the Difference Between Two Population Means Using Paired Samples

In the previous case studies in this tutorial, samples were drawn independently from each of two populations. Pairing subjects, like identical twins or before-and-after measurement of a subject, can eliminate the effect of extraneous variables. Such data are called *paired* or dependent data.

Case Study: Blood Clotting

In your experimental biology class, Professor Schwartz has asked you to investigate the theory that aspirin reduces a person's blood clotting ability. In this study, you first measured clotting times (the interval between the start of a prothrombin-thrombin reaction and the formation of the final clot) of twelve adult men before they took two aspirin tablets and then again three hours later.

- Open CLOTTING.MTW from the TUT7 directory

C1 BEFORE contains the clotting times (in seconds) before and C2 AFTER the clotting times after taking aspirin for each of the twelve men in the study. Assume that the difference between clotting time before and after taking aspirin follows a normal distribution. Compute the difference, D, between the clotting time before and after taking aspirin and place the result in C3:

- Choose **Calc** ▶ Functions and Statistics ▶ **General** Expressions...
- Type **'D=B-A'** in the New/modified variable text box and press [Tab] twice
- Type **C1-C2** in the Expression text box

The completed General Expressions dialog box should look like Figure 7-7.

FIGURE 7-7

The completed General Expressions dialog box from the Functions and Statistics submenu from the Calc menu

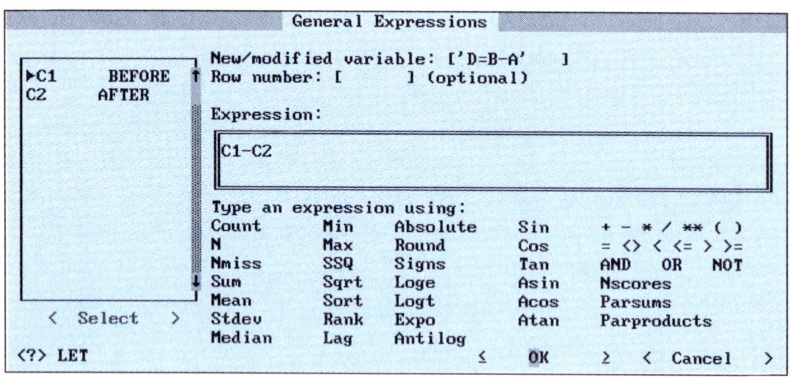

- Press [Alt]-O

MINITAB AT WORK

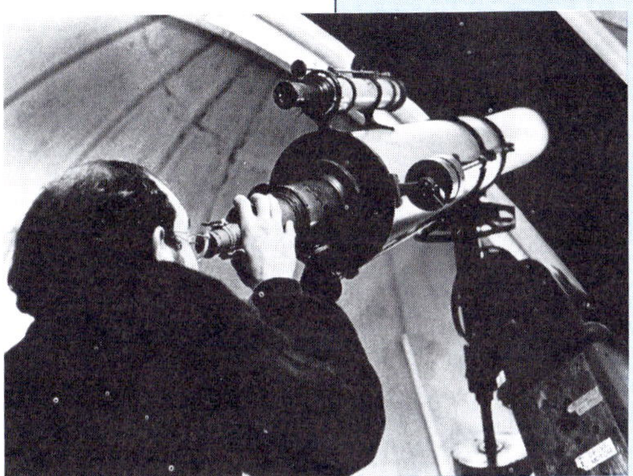

SCIENTIFIC RESEARCH: A supernova, the explosion of a star, is a rarely observed phenomenon, and researchers often study it by examining remnants it leaves behind. Astronomers have charted 29 supernova remnants (SNRs) in a nearby galaxy named the Large Magellanic Cloud. They predicted that SNRs produced by stars with relatively short lives would be close to areas of recent star formation, called H II regions. A physicist, a mathematician, and an undergraduate at a Colorado university teamed up to study the Large Magellanic Cloud supernovas by testing whether the remnants are indeed close to H II regions.

The team calculated the distance between each of the 29 known SNRs in the Large Magellanic Cloud and its nearest H II region and then found the mean distance. They used Minitab to simulate what the mean distance would have been had the SNRs been randomly distributed throughout the galaxy. A 2-sample t-test showed that the actual mean distance was significantly less than Minitab's randomly generated SNR locations had led them to expect.

They concluded that supernova remnants in the Large Magellanic Cloud are not randomly distributed; the SNRs cluster around areas of recent star formation and are likely to have resulted from the explosions of short-lived stars.

Minitab has stored each difference in C3. Next, form the hypotheses to test:

$$H_0: \mu_D = 0$$
$$H_1: \mu_D > 0$$

The hypothesis is upper-tailed, since the difference is the BEFORE time minus the AFTER time. If aspirin reduces the clotting time, the

AFTER time should be smaller, and the mean difference greater than zero.

To perform a paired t-test, use the 1-sample t-test used in Tutorial 6.

- Choose **S**tat ▶ **B**asic Statistics ▶ **1**-Sample t...
- Select C3 D=B-A
- Press [Alt]-T for **T**est mean

Because you are testing a mean difference of 0, accept the default.

- Press [Tab] twice and press [↓] to choose the greater than Alternative hypothesis

The completed 1-Sample t dialog box should look like Figure 7-8.

FIGURE 7-8

The completed 1-Sample t dialog box from the Basic Statistics submenu

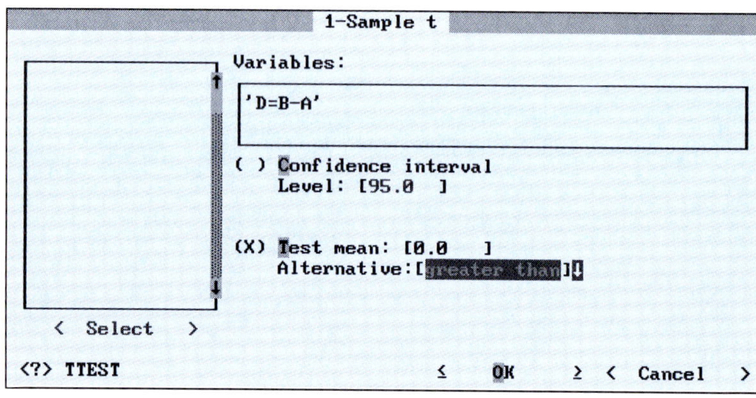

- Press [↵]

The results in the Session window should resemble Figure 7-9.

FIGURE 7-9

Results of t-test investigating the effect of aspirin on clotting time

```
MTB > Name c3 = 'D=B-A'
MTB > Let 'D=B-A' = C1-C2
MTB > TTest 0.0 'D=B-A';
SUBC>   Alternative 1.

TEST OF MU = 0.000 VS MU G.T. 0.000

                N      MEAN     STDEV   SE MEAN        T    P VALUE
D=B-A          12     0.108     0.507     0.146     0.74       0.24
```

The mean of the differences is 0.108 seconds, corresponding to a t-value of 0.74. Since the p-value for this test is 0.24 (greater than 0.10), fail to reject H_0 at the 10% level of significance. When you submit your study to Dr. Schwartz, you will report that this test does not provide significant evidence of any effect of aspirin on mean clotting time of males.

Calculating a Confidence Interval for the Difference Between Two Population Means Using Paired Samples

In order to obtain a 90% confidence interval, use the difference:

- Choose **E**dit ▶ Edit **L**ast Command Dialog...
- Press [Alt]-C and press [Tab]
- Type **90** in the Level text box

The completed 1-Sample t dialog box should resemble Figure 7-10.

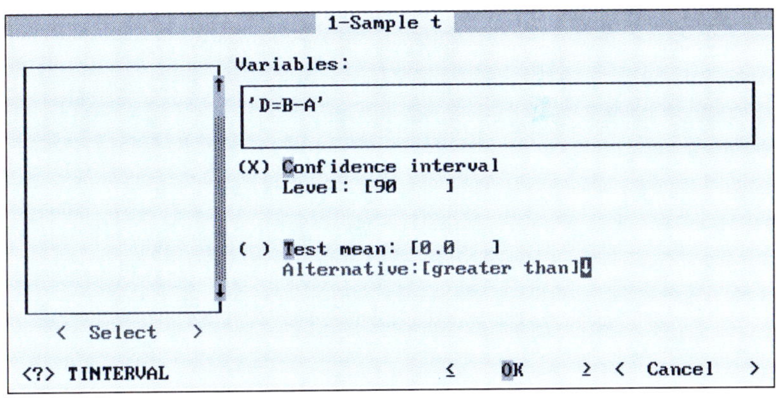

FIGURE 7-10
The completed 1-Sample t dialog box from the Basic Statistics submenu

- Press [↵]

The results in the Session window should resemble Figure 7-11.

```
MTB > TInterval 90 'D=B-A'.

                 N      MEAN     STDEV  SE MEAN    90.0 PERCENT C.I.
D=B-A           12     0.108     0.507    0.146  (  -0.155,    0.371)
```

FIGURE 7-11
Results of 90% confidence interval for difference in mean clotting time

The results indicate you can be 90% certain that, for men, the difference between mean clotting times before and after taking aspirin is between –0.155 and 0.371 seconds; the mean clotting time may be decreased by as much as 0.371 seconds, or it may be increased by as much as 0.155 seconds. Such a change in mean clotting time would not likely have much practical consequence. Your previous conclusion, that taking aspirin makes no difference in clotting time, is reinforced.

In this tutorial you focused on performing hypothesis tests on and computing confidence intervals for the difference between the means of two populations. Minitab can test independent samples, as in the case of the psychological crowdedness question and the blood pressure study, or it can test dependent samples, as in the case of the before-and-after aspirin test for blood clotting times. In the next tutorial you will learn how to compare the means of more than two populations.

If you plan to continue directly to the next tutorial:

- Choose **F**ile ▶ Restart **M**initab

If you want to take a longer break:

- Choose **F**ile ▶ E**x**it

Minitab Command Summary

The menus and commands introduced in or related to this tutorial are described in this section. You will find a complete explanation of all menus and commands in the Reference section of this manual.

Menu	Command	Function
Stat		
	Basic Statistics	
	1-Sample t	Performs inferences (tests and confidence intervals) on the differences between two population means using paired data
	2-Sample t	Performs inferences (tests and confidence intervals) on the differences between two population means using independent samples

Review and Practice

Matching

Match the following terms to their definitions by placing the correct letter next to the term it explains.

____ Level

____ Samples in one column

____ Assume equal variances

____ Samples in different columns

____ "not equal to" Alternative

____ Alternative 1

____ Basic Statistics

____ 2-Sample t

a. The default alternative hypothesis in Minitab commands

b. The Minitab option that lets you perform a 2-sample t-test assuming the variances of the populations are equal

c. Menu command on which all parametric two-sample commands are found

d. The Minitab command that performs inference on the difference between two population means using independent samples

e. Minitab subcommand that specifies an upper-tailed test be performed

f. Minitab option that specifies the degree of confidence for the interval estimate of the difference between two means

g. Minitab 2-sample test option that tests two population means using data in one column with a sample identifier in another column

h. Minitab 2-sample test option that tests two population means using sample data stored in two different columns

True/False

Mark the following statements T or F.

____ 1. Minitab can perform a 2-sample t-test if the data from the populations are stored in either one column or two.

____ 2. The Minitab menu command, Paired-T, is used to perform the paired t-test.

____ 3. The command 2-sample t is a Minitab menu command to perform a 2-sample t-test.

____ 4. Confidence intervals for the difference between two population means are included with the output of the test of the two population means.

____ 5. Minitab can perform independent, 2-sample t-tests assuming the population variances are equal or unequal.

____ 6. Only two-tailed 2-sample tests can be done in Minitab.

____ 7. The default confidence level for 2-sample confidence intervals is 95%.

____ 8. In a 2-sample test, a subscripts column is required when the two sample data are stored in a single column.

____ 9. If subscripts are used in the 2-sample t-test, then the subscript column must be numeric.

____ 10. Minitab automatically computes the differences for the paired t-test.

Practice Problems

1. Use the PROF.MTW data from the TUT7 directory to answer the questions below.

   a. Test whether first-year courses have a different mean rating than fourth-year courses. HINT: You will need to create a variable that is 1 for first-year courses, 2 for fourth-year courses, and missing for second- and third-year courses. Alternatively, you can unstack the course rating data into four columns as you did in a previous exercise and then use the appropriate columns.

   b. Repeat part a) using the Prof rating.

   c. Based on your results from a) and b), do students' opinions about their course instructors change over the course of their college careers?

2. Use the FISH.MTW data from the TUT7 directory to determine if the amount of time fish spend guarding and fanning their young is different for normal pH water and highly acidic water (pH = 5.5). Which is a more strenuous activity? What does it seem to say about the pH of water and fish activity?

3. Use the RIVERALL.MTW data set from the TUT7 directory and determine if the mean temperature of the river is different at site 2, directly upriver from the power plant, and site 3, directly downriver from the power plant's discharge from its cooling towers. You will need to create a new column that is 1 for site 2, 2 for site 3, and missing for all others. Use the Code Data Values command, recoding only the site 2 and 3 values. The other values will be coded as missing.

4. Use the SALES.MTW data set from the TUT7 directory to determine whether the sales for 1988–1991 are different. You want to compare each year's sales to every other year's sales. How many 2-sample tests will you need to do? Suppose you use an alpha of 5% for each test. What do you think is the probability of making a mistake in the total set of tests you just did? Equal to 5%? Much smaller than 5%? Much larger than 5%?

TUTORIAL 8

Comparing Population Means: Analysis of Variance

In Tutorial 7 you used Minitab to perform hypothesis tests comparing the means of two populations. Analysis of variance (ANOVA) is a statistical tool that lets you extend this capability and compare the means of several populations. In the first case study, as quality manager at an electronics company, you need to determine why your product's quality seems to vary depending on which of three shifts manufactured it. Since more than one factor often contributes to differences in measurements, later in the tutorial you will take the place of a data analyst trying to determine which combination of two factors, advertising medium (newspaper, radio, or television) and advertising agency (Ace or Best), will provide the greatest increase in sales per advertising dollar. In either situation, the ANOVA test requires three basic assumptions about the measurements in the study:

- The observations must be randomly selected
- The populations from which the observations are taken must all be normally distributed

- The variables in each group must come from populations with equal variances

Objectives

In this tutorial you will learn to:

- compare the means of several populations when all observations are in one column and all subscripts are in a second
- compare the means of several populations when the samples from each population are placed in different columns
- generate residual and fitted values
- perform a Tukey multiple comparison test to find which specific means are different from one another
- assess the effects of two factors on a response

Case Study: Electronics

You have just been promoted to quality manager at Flexible Circuits, Inc., a company specializing in the manufacture of parts for electronics components. Lately there have been complaints from the buyers about a lack of consistency in the diameters of the copper wire the company manufactures for stereo equipment. At the first stage of the plating process, the base wire is dipped in a copper micro-etch bath set at 95° F and left for 1 minute and 10 seconds. When removed from the bath, the plated wire is ready to be placed in the stereo.

The company has three separate shifts a day; you wonder if the variation in the diameters of the wires can be related to the shift during which they were made. Over the period of a week you randomly select several samples of wire from each of the three shifts, measure the diameters in microinches, and, in a Minitab worksheet, record the wire diameter in C1 DIAMETER and the shift during which it was made in C2 SHIFT. You save the worksheet in the file FLEXIBLE.MTW.

- Open FLEXIBLE.MTW from the TUT8 directory

Comparing the Means of Several Populations

When performing an ANOVA test, the relevant hypotheses for the copper wire experiment are:

H_0: The mean diameters of the copper wires from the three shifts are equal.

H_1: The mean diameters of the copper wires from the three shifts are not all equal.

To test the hypotheses using Minitab and the data you have collected:

- Choose **S**tat ► **A**NOVA ► **O**neway...
- Select C1 DIAMETER as the Response
- Select C2 SHIFT as the Factor

The completed Oneway Analysis of Variance dialog box from the Stat menu should resemble Figure 8-1.

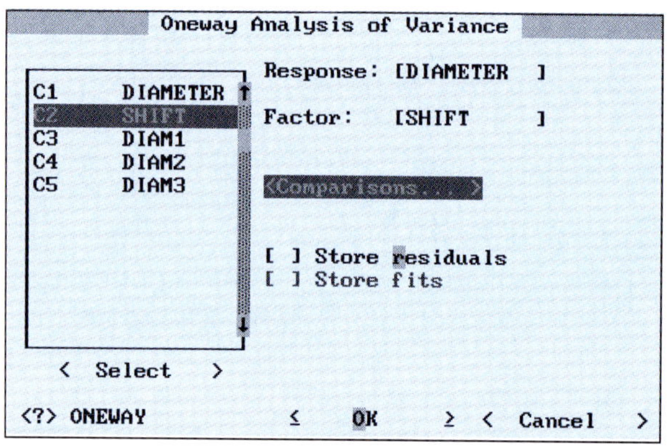

FIGURE 8-1
The completed Oneway Analysis of Variance dialog box from the Stat menu

- Press [Alt]-O

After the analysis is complete, the Session window should resemble Figure 8-2.

FIGURE 8-2

Results of oneway ANOVA of wire diameters

```
MTB > Oneway 'DIAMETER' 'SHIFT'.

ANALYSIS OF VARIANCE ON DIAMETER
SOURCE     DF        SS        MS         F        p
SHIFT       2     674.9     337.5      5.26    0.019
ERROR      15     962.7      64.2
TOTAL      17    1637.6
                                 INDIVIDUAL 95 PCT CI'S FOR MEAN
                                 BASED ON POOLED STDEV
LEVEL       N      MEAN     STDEV  --+---------+---------+---------+----
    1       9    70.333     9.760          (----*-----)
    2       6    65.000     5.060  (-------*------)
    3       3    83.333     6.028                 (---------*---------)
                                   --+---------+---------+---------+----
POOLED STDEV =    8.011                60        70        80        90
```

The Session window display includes four components:

- An ANOVA table including the F test result, 5.26, and corresponding p-value, 0.019. You would reject the null hypothesis at the 0.05 level (but fail to reject it at the 0.01 level).
- A descriptive summary of each shift (treatment) including the sample size, the sample mean, and the sample standard deviation.
- A diagram of the individual 95% confidence interval for each of the shifts (treatments), based on the pooled standard deviation. The * represents the sample mean and the ( ) the 95% confidence limits.
- The pooled standard deviation: in this case 8.011.

At this point in your analysis you have noticed some differences among the diameter means for the three shifts. The third shift appears to produce thicker wires than the first two shifts. You will follow up on this observation.

Fitted and Residual Values

Before you proceed, check to see whether the assumptions of the ANOVA are valid. If you select the Store residuals and Store fits checkboxes in the Oneway Analysis of Variance dialog box, Minitab stores the fitted values and the residual values in the next open columns. You can use the residuals and fitted values to determine whether the ANOVA assumptions are satisfied.

- Choose **Edit ▶ Edit Last Command Dialog...**
- Press [Alt]-R for Store **r**esiduals and [Alt]-F for Store **f**its
- Press [↵]

- Go to the Data worksheet

The Data worksheet displays columns containing the residuals and the fitted values. Compare the fitted values in C7 FITS1 to the sample means from Figure 8-2. Note that the fitted values (70.3333, 65.0000, and 83.3333) are the sample means of each shift. Minitab obtains the residuals, stored in C6 RESI1, by subtracting the corresponding fitted value (shift mean) from each wire diameter. You will use the residuals Minitab just computed to check the normality of the pooled samples.

- Return to the Session window

NScores and a Check for Normality

When performing an ANOVA test, you assume that all observations come from normally distributed populations. In order to determine if it is reasonable to assume the diameters of the wires are normally distributed, obtain the normal probability plot (NPP) (introduced in Tutorial 5) for the combined (pooled) samples.

First compute the normal score for each residual:

- Choose **Calc ▶ Functions and Statistics ▶ Functions...**
- Press Tab
- Select C6 RESI1 for Input column
- Type **NSCORES** in the Result in text box
- Press Alt-M for Normal scores

The completed Functions dialog box should resemble Figure 8-3.

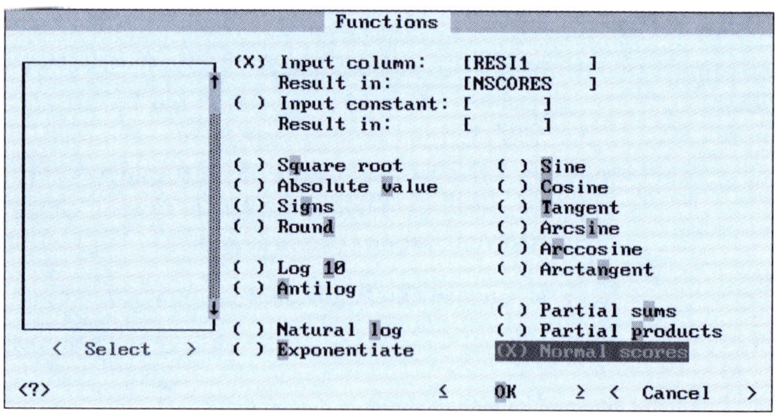

FIGURE 8-3

The completed Functions dialog box from the Functions and Statistics submenu

- Press [↵]

Minitab computes normal scores and stores them in C8 NSCORES.

Use a scatter plot to plot these normal scores against the residuals. If the plot is linear, then the normality assumption is reasonable.

- Choose **G**raph ▶ Scatter **P**lot...
- Select C8 NSCORES for the Vertical axis
- Select C6 RESI1 for the Horizontal axis and press [Tab]
- Type **.** (period) as the **P**lotting symbol
- Press [↵]

The scatter plot appears in its own graph screen (Figure 8-4).

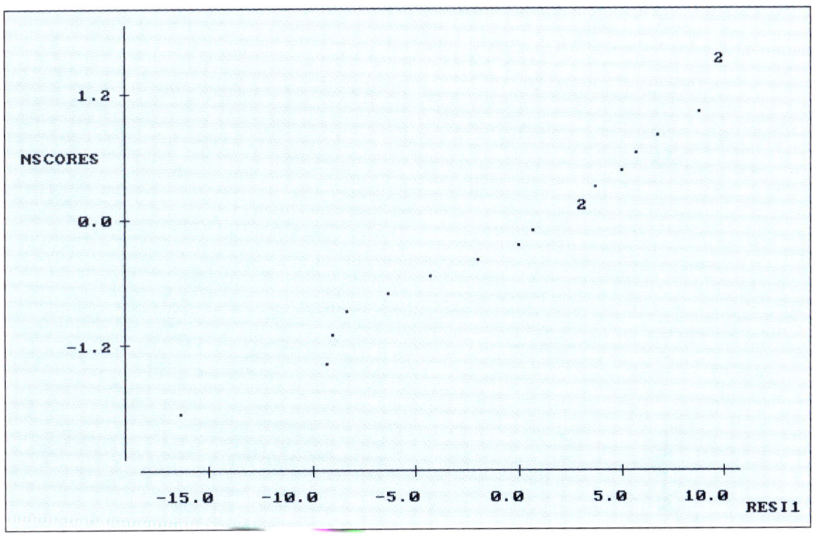

FIGURE 8-4
Scatter plot of normal scores versus residuals

Since the plot is approximately a straight line, you conclude that the assumption that the populations are approximately normally distributed is reasonable.

- Press Q for Quit

Checking for Constant Variance

To check for constant variance, use the graphical method of plotting the residuals versus the shift. (Alternatively, you could use the fitted values in place of the shift.) If the residuals have roughly the same range or vertical spread in each shift, then the constant or equal variance assumption would seem to be satisfied.

- Choose **E**dit ▶ Edit **L**ast Command Dialog...
- Select C6 RESI1 for the Vertical axis
- Select C2 SHIFT for the Horizontal axis
- Press [↵]

The resulting scatter plot appears in its own graph screen (Figure 8-5).

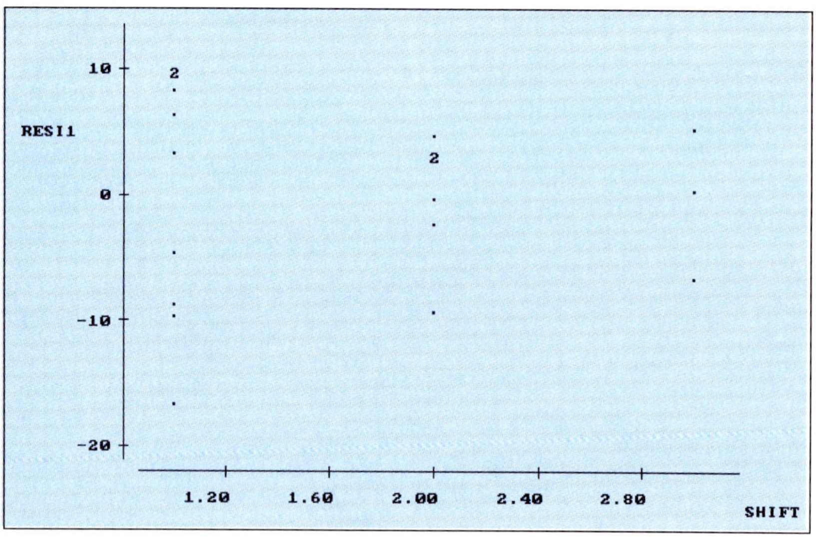

FIGURE 8-5
Scatter plot of residuals versus shift

The resulting residual plot indicates that the constant variance assumption does not appear to be violated. For the three shifts, the residuals have approximately the same range and hence the same variance.

- Press Q for Quit

Tukey Multiple Comparison Test

Recall that you rejected the null hypothesis of equality of means at the 0.05 level. You can use Minitab's multiple comparison capabilities to determine which means differ from one another. Minitab provides four different multiple comparison procedures: Tukey, Fisher, Dunnett, and Hsu. To illustrate, you will use the Tukey method. (Your professor can provide you with more information about the other procedures.)

For the Tukey multiple comparison test, you will form three null hypotheses:

$$H_0: \mu_1 = \mu_2$$
$$H_1: \mu_1 \neq \mu_2$$

$$H_0: \mu_1 = \mu_3$$
$$H_1: \mu_1 \neq \mu_3$$

$$H_0: \mu_2 = \mu_3$$
$$H_1: \mu_2 \neq \mu_3$$

The Tukey test forms confidence intervals for the differences between the means of shift 1 and shift 2, shift 1 and shift 3, and shift 2 and shift 3. To perform the Tukey multiple comparison:

- Choose **S**tat ▶ **A**NOVA ▶ **O**neway...
- Select C1 DIAMETER as the Response
- Select C2 SHIFT as the Factor
- Press [Alt]-C for **C**omparisons

In the Oneway Multiple Comparisons dialog box:

- Press the Space bar to select Tukey's
- Press [↵] twice

Note: The Tukey test may take a very long time when used on certain computers and for certain data sets.

Figure 8-6 shows the matrix of confidence intervals.

FIGURE 8-6
Results of Tukey multiple comparison

```
Tukey's pairwise comparisons

    Family error rate = 0.0500
Individual error rate = 0.0202

Critical value = 3.67

Intervals for (column level mean) - (row level mean)

                1          2

    2       -5.62
            16.29

    3      -26.86     -33.03
             0.86      -3.63
```

Reject the null hypothesis that the two means are equal whenever the confidence interval for the difference in the means does not contain 0.

A summary of the Tukey test follows:

Difference between	Confidence Interval 95% Family Confidence	Decision
Shift 1 and Shift 2	–5.62 to 16.29	Fail to reject $H_0{:}\mu_1=\mu_2$
Shift 1 and Shift 3	–26.86 to 0.86	Fail to reject $H_0{:}\mu_1=\mu_3$
Shift 2 and Shift 3	–33.03 to –3.63	Reject $H_0{:}\mu_2=\mu_3$

From the results of the Tukey test you determine that there is significant evidence of a difference between the mean diameters of the copper wire produced in shift 2 and shift 3. As quality manager you will investigate why.

Comparing the Means of Several Populations with Responses in Separate Columns

After some investigation, you determine that the temperature of the plating bath, which you have discovered varied quite a bit among shifts, might be a factor in causing the observed difference in wire diameter. So you have the temperature reset to 100° F and ensure it remains fixed for all three shifts.

Again you take random samples from each of the three shifts, but this time you put the data in three different columns (one for each shift): C3 DIAM1, C4 DIAM2, and C5 DIAM3. Repeat the ANOVA test to see if the diameter means for each shift are now the same. Use the Oneway (Unstacked) command that is appropriate when the sample data are stored in different columns.

- Choose Stat ► ANOVA ► Oneway (Unstacked)...
- Select C3 DIAM1, C4 DIAM2, and C5 DIAM3 as the Responses

The completed Oneway Analysis of Variance dialog box should look like Figure 8-7.

FIGURE 8-7

The completed Oneway Analysis of Variance dialog box from the Stat menu

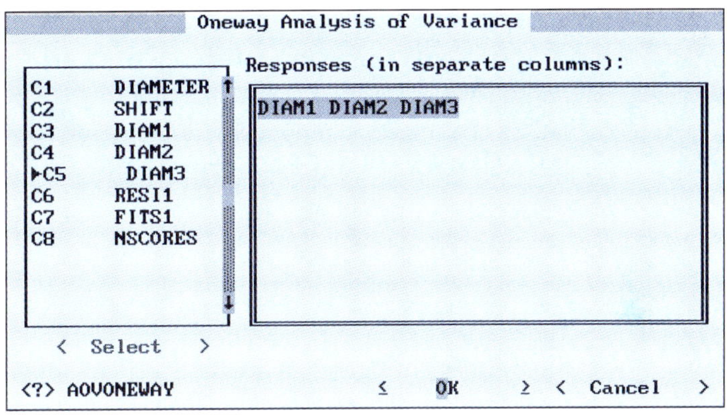

- Press [Alt]-O

The results, shown in Figure 8-8, appear in the Session window.

FIGURE 8-8

Results of oneway (unstacked) ANOVA of wire diameters

```
MTB > AOVOneway 'DIAM1' 'DIAM2' 'DIAM3'.

ANALYSIS OF VARIANCE
SOURCE     DF        SS        MS        F        p
FACTOR      2      18.4       9.2     0.14    0.870
ERROR      22    1443.0      65.6
TOTAL      24    1461.4
                                   INDIVIDUAL 95 PCT CI'S FOR MEAN
                                   BASED ON POOLED STDEV
 LEVEL      N      MEAN     STDEV  ----------+---------+---------+-----
DIAM1      12    68.750     9.372             (---------*--------)
DIAM2       7    69.714     6.651            (-----------*------------)
DIAM3       6    67.333     6.501    (-------------*------------)
                                   ----------+---------+---------+-----
POOLED STDEV =    8.099                     65.0      70.0      75.0
```

Minitab produces the same display for this test as it produced for the oneway test, in which all data were stacked in one column. This time the F-ratio is 0.14 with a p-value of 0.870; fail to reject the null hypothesis and conclude that there is now no significant evidence of difference among the wire diameters produced by the three shifts.

When the temperature of the plating bath was held constant at this value for all of the shifts, you found no difference in the mean wire diameter. You conclude that the differences in the diameters of the wires produced in different shifts might have been due to changes in the process temperature that occurred between shift 2 and shift 3. You make a note to tell production to monitor the process temperature and not let it vary.

You also recommend a follow-up study to determine the exact impact of temperature on the mean wire diameter. Perhaps the process can be optimized to produce wire diameters closer to specifications. You will return to this case study in Tutorial 12.

- Choose **F**ile ▶ Restart **M**initab

Assessing the Effects of Two Factors on a Response

You just analyzed the effect of a single factor with three levels (the three shifts during which a wire was manufactured). However, many responses are affected by more than one factor; statisticians must design experiments to take this into account.

Case Study: Marketing

The marketing department for Krunchy Cereal Company just hired you as data analyst. Krunchy has been working with two advertising agencies, Ace Ads and Best Ads. Each agency has been trying to increase sales by running promotions in three advertising media: newspaper, radio, and television. You begin your new job by determining which combination of ad agency and ad medium will produce the greatest increase in sales per advertising dollar.

For your experiment, you select twelve cities that are roughly the same size. You randomly assign two cities to receive an ad campaign prepared and transmitted by each of the six combinations of agency and medium. After one month, you compute the increase in sales per advertising dollar. To do this, you calculate the increase in sales over the same month last year and divide this by the amount of money spent on advertising. You record the results in a table (Figure 8-9):

FIGURE 8-9
Increase in sales per advertising dollar

	Ace Ad Agency (1)	**Best Ad Agency (2)**
Newspaper (1)	15.3	18.9
	12.7	22.4
Radio (2)	20.1	24.3
	17.4	28.8
Television (3)	12.7	12.5
	16.2	9.4

Krunchy uses Minitab for all its statistical research. Your co-worker, Manuel Gonzales, has entered the sales data in Figure 8-9 in a Minitab worksheet. The data are in column C1 SALESINC and the worksheet is saved in the file KRUNCHY.MTW so you can use an ANOVA test to see if agency and/or media affect sales increases.

- Open KRUNCHY.MTW from the TUT8 directory
- Go to the Data worksheet

Notice how Manuel has stored the data (Figure 8-10).

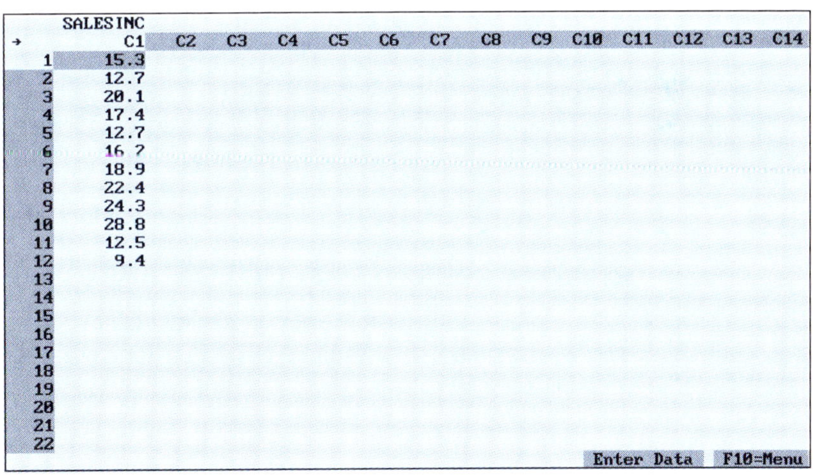

FIGURE 8-10
The KRUNCHY.MTW worksheet

The first six values in C1 SALESINC correspond to the Ace ad agency; the last six refer to Best. Likewise, the first two values and the seventh and eighth values correspond to the newspaper medium. The other values in C1 SALESINC correspond to the other advertising media.

To perform the two-factor ANOVA, you need to add two columns that identify, for each row of C1 SALESINC: 1) which medium was used and 2) which ad agency was used. These two columns correspond to the *factors.* You will use them to determine the effect of advertising medium and ad agency on sales increase.

Designate the three media of newspaper, radio, and television as 1, 2, and 3, respectively. In order to identify the media category for each row in C1, you could enter the numbers 1,1,2,2,3,3,1,1,2,2,3,3 (in that order) in column C2 of the worksheet. For small data sets like this one, this is the easiest method. Alternatively, you can use the Set Patterned Data command presented in Tutorial 5. For practice, use the latter method and enter this sequence of numbers:

- Return to the Session window
- Choose **E**dit ▶ **S**et Patterned Data...
- Type **MEDIUM** in the Put data into column text box and press [Tab] twice

Analyze the pattern of the data needed to enter (1,1,2,2,3,3,1,1,2,2,3,3). Notice that it is made up of the values 1, 2, and 3; these values start at 1, end at 3, and increment by 1. Each value is repeated two times and the whole list is repeated two times. To have Minitab enter this sequence:

- Type **1** in the Start at text box and press [Tab]
- Type **3** in the End at text box and press [Tab] twice
- Type **2** in the Repeat each value text box and press [Tab]
- Type **2** in the Repeat the whole list text box and press [↵]

Now store the values for the ad agency. Because there are two ad agencies, identify them as 1 for Ace and 2 for Best. The Ace values are the first six values in C1 SALESINC. The second six values are Best. Hence you need to enter the following pattern of numbers

(1,1,1,1,1,1,2,2,2,2,2,2) in C3 AGENCY. Use the Set Patterned Data command:

- Choose **E**dit ▶ Edit **L**ast Command Dialog...
- Type **AGENCY** in the Put data into column text box and press [Tab] three times

Analyze the pattern for the ad agency data. Notice that it is made up of the sequence 1,2; it starts at 1 and ends at 2, using an increment of 1. Each value is repeated six times and the whole list is repeated once.

- Type **2** in the End at text box and press [Tab] twice
- Type **6** in the Repeat each value text box and press [Tab]
- Type **1** in the Repeat the whole list text box and press [↵]
- Go to the Data worksheet

The Data worksheet should look like Figure 8-11.

FIGURE 8-11
The Data worksheet

→	SALESINC C1	MEDIUM C2	AGENCY C3	C4	C5	C6	C7	C8	C9	C10	C11	C12	C13
1	15.3	1	1										
2	12.7	1	1										
3	20.1	2	1										
4	17.4	2	1										
5	12.7	3	1										
6	16.2	3	1										
7	18.9	1	2										
8	22.4	1	2										
9	24.3	2	2										
10	28.8	2	2										
11	12.5	3	2										
12	9.4	3	2										
13													
14													
15													
16													
17													
18													
19													
20													
21													
22													

Enter Data F10=Menu

If columns two and three do not look exactly like those shown in Figure 8-11, erase them and start over. Try using the Set Patterned Data command again, or type in the values for C2 MEDIUM and C3 AGENCY.

CAUTION: It is very important that each of your columns have exactly the same number of entries. The ANOVA command you will use next requires that the response and factor columns contain identical numbers of rows. It is also critical that you have identified the correct factor levels for each data point. If you fail to do so, your analysis will be inaccurate.

You will test the following three sets of hypotheses:

H_0: There is no interaction between medium and agency used.
H_1: There is an interaction between medium and agency used.

H_0: There is no difference in the average increase in sales for different media.
H_1: There is a difference in the average increase in sales for different media.

H_0: There is no difference in the average increase in sales when using different ad agencies.
H_1: There is a difference in the average increase in sales when using different ad agencies.

Two Minitab commands will perform a multiway ANOVA: Twoway and Balanced ANOVA. Use the Twoway command when you have exactly two factors (as in the present example) and the Balanced ANOVA command when you have two or more factors.

Note: Both the Twoway and Balanced ANOVA commands require that all combinations of factor levels have an equal number of observations. That is, the data must be *balanced.*

In your example, each of the six media-agency combinations has two values, so the data are balanced. You will use the Balanced ANOVA command to investigate the effects of media and agency.

The Balanced ANOVA command accommodates many model types in which you can use crossed factors. (See your instructor for more information on the meaning and use of such factors.) In this case you will analyze only the medium factor, the agency factor, and the interaction between the two. Many texts designate this model as:

$$y_{ijk} = \mu + a_i + b_j + ab_{ij} + \epsilon_{k(ij)}.$$

Substituting the variable names for the factors ai and bj, the model is

$$y_{ijk} = \mu + \text{MEDIUM}_i + \text{AGENCY}_j + \text{MEDIUM*AGENCY}_{ij} + \epsilon_{k(ij)}.$$

Use Minitab to perform the analysis:

- Return to the Session window
- Choose **S**tat ▶ ANOVA ▶ **B**alanced ANOVA...
- Select C1 SALESINC as the Responses variable and press Tab
- Type **MEDIUM AGENCY MEDIUM*AGENCY** in the Model text box (do not forget the * between the second MEDIUM and AGENCY)

The completed Balanced Analysis of Variance dialog box should resemble Figure 8-12. Note the similarity between the model you enter in the Model text box and the second model described.

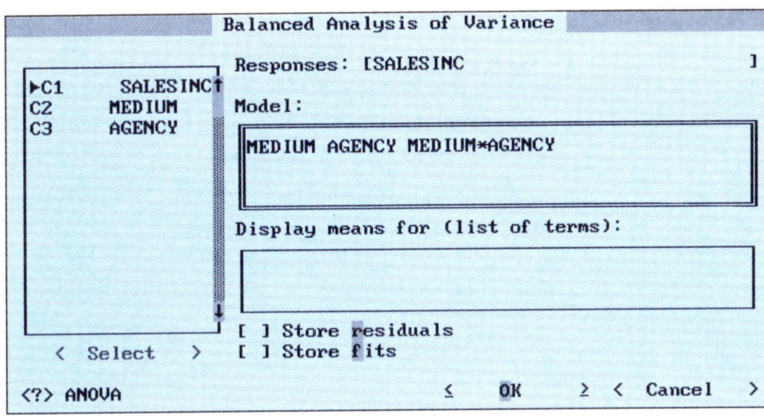

FIGURE 8-12
The completed Balanced Analysis of Variance dialog box from the Stat menu

- Press Alt-O

After Minitab completes the analysis, the Session window contains the results shown in Figure 8-13.

FIGURE 8-13

Results of sales ANOVA

```
MTB > ANOVA 'SALESINC' = MEDIUM AGENCY MEDIUM*AGENCY.

Factor      Type Levels Values
MEDIUM     fixed      3      1      2      3
AGENCY     fixed      2      1      2

Analysis of Variance for SALESINC

Source            DF         SS          MS       F      P
MEDIUM             2    198.332      99.166   17.39  0.003
AGENCY             1     39.967      39.967    7.01  0.038
MEDIUM*AGENCY      2     77.345      38.673    6.78  0.029
Error              6     34.205       5.701
Total             11    349.849
```

The first column in the upper table lists the factors; the second column identifies them as fixed. (The difference between fixed and random factors is an involved topic. See your instructor for more information.) The next column tells you that the Medium variable had three levels (corresponding to newspaper, radio, television) and the Agency variable had two (Ace and Best). The remaining columns simply list the values for each factor (1, 2, and 3 for Medium, and 1 and 2 for Agency). The lower table is the standard ANOVA table; it lists the sources of variation (medium, agency, interaction, and error), the F-ratios for each test, and the corresponding p-values.

The following table uses information from the ANOVA table to describe the results of the test.

Test	Effect	F-ratio	p-value	Decision
1.	MEDIUM*AGENCY	6.78	0.029	Reject H_0; conclude there is significant interaction between medium and agency
2.	MEDIUM	17.39	0.003	Reject H_0; conclude different media affect increase in sales differently
3.	AGENCY	7.01	0.038	Reject H_0; conclude different agencies affect increase in sales differently

(The order of Minitab's display is slightly different.)

The results indicate a significant interaction between medium and agency (p-value = 0.029). You conclude that the ad agency's effect is not constant for the three media: the two agencies produce different sales increases, depending upon the medium used.

If the interaction were not significant, you would then test the last two sets of hypotheses. However, if the interaction is significant, you need to interpret the results of tests 2 and 3 with care. Your instructor can provide you with more details.

Now that you have concluded that the combined choice of agency and medium does affect sales increases, you decide to include the mean sales increase per advertising dollar for each of the three media, each of the two agencies, and each of the six combinations in the study as part of a report you are preparing. To obtain these means:

- Choose **E**dit ▶ Edit **L**ast Command Dialog...
- Press Tab twice
- Type **MEDIUM AGENCY MEDIUM*AGENCY** in the Display means for text box

The completed Balanced Analysis of Variance dialog box should look like Figure 8-14.

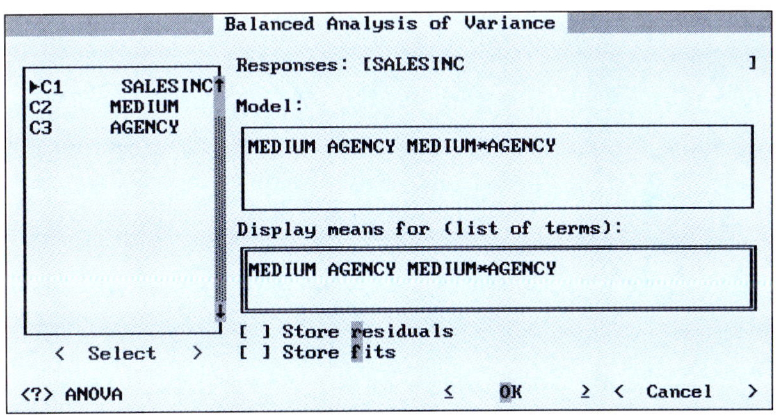

FIGURE 8-14
The completed Balanced Analysis of Variance dialog box

- Press Alt-O

The results appear in Figure 8-15.

FIGURE 8-15

Average sales increases for the different media, agencies, and combinations of media and agencies

```
 MEANS

MEDIUM   N  SALESINC
     1   4    17.325
     2   4    22.650
     3   4    12.700

AGENCY   N  SALESINC
     1   6    15.733
     2   6    19.383

MEDIUM AGENCY   N  SALESINC
     1      1   2    14.000
     1      2   2    20.650
     2      1   2    18.750
     2      2   2    26.550
     3      1   2    14.450
     3      2   2    10.950
```

Advertising medium 2 (radio) had the highest sales increase per advertising dollar (22.650); Best Ads (2) had a higher increase than did Ace. Check the combination (2,2) to see that the highest increase occurred when Best Ad Agency used radio for its advertisements. The poorest results occurred when Best Ad Agency (2) used television (3). Possibly they spent too much money for air time, making their strategy too expensive. When you present your report, you will recommend using more radio advertisements designed by Best Ad Agency. If Krunchy insists on television ads, recommend that they use Ace Ads for this medium.

You can see that using Minitab's analysis of variance capability gives you real assistance in making decisions in any discipline. As quality manager for Flexible Circuits, Inc., you used an ANOVA test to affirm the second and third shifts produced different products; changing the process eliminated this difference. As a data analyst at the Krunchy Cereal Company you performed ANOVA tests on two factors to determine where advertising money could be spent most effectively. In both capacities, you used Minitab to provide the company with invaluable help.

If you plan to continue directly to the next tutorial:

- Choose **F**ile ▶ Restart **M**initab

If you want to take a longer break:

- Choose **F**ile ▶ E**x**it

Minitab Command Summary

The menus and commands introduced in or related to this tutorial are described in this section. You will find a complete explanation of all menus and commands in the Reference section of this manual.

Menu	Command	Function
Stat		
	ANOVA	
	Oneway	Performs a oneway analysis of variance when the response is stored in one column and the sample indicator or subscript is stored in another column
	Oneway (Unstacked)	Performs a oneway analysis of variance when the response is stored in separate columns
	Twoway	Performs a twoway analysis of variance when the response is stored in one column and the two factor level indicators or subscripts are stored in two other columns; the data must be balanced
	Balanced ANOVA	Performs a multiway analysis of variance when the response is stored in one column and the factor level indicators or subscripts are stored in other columns; the data must be balanced

Review and Practice

Matching

Match the following terms to their definitions by placing the correct letter next to the term it explains.

___ model

___ Store fits

___ Response variable

___ Store residuals

___ balanced

___ Comparisons

___ factor

___ *

a. Performs multiple comparisons of the means in a oneway ANOVA using the Oneway command

b. Specifies that residuals should be stored in the next open column

c. Specifies that fitted values should be stored in the next open column

d. Denotes interaction between effects

e. Denotes that there are equal numbers of observations for each factor combination

f. Denotes the relationship between the response variable and the factors

g. In ANOVA, denotes the variable or variables that affect a continuous variable

h. In ANOVA, denotes the continuous variable whose mean is affected by the factors

True/False

Mark the following statements T or F.

___ 1. Minitab's Twoway command allows for unbalanced data, whereas the Balanced ANOVA command must have balanced data.

___ 2. Residuals and fitted values can be stored using any of the ANOVA commands.

___ 3. Multiple comparisons can be performed only in the "stacked" Oneway command.

___ 4. For the Oneway command, the "fits" can be saved without saving the "residuals."

____ 5. The user specifies the columns to store the residuals and/or fitted values in ANOVA commands.

____ 6. Multiway ANOVA can be performed using the Balanced ANOVA command.

____ 7. 95% confidence intervals for each population mean are part of the default output for the ANOVA command.

____ 8. More than one Response variable can be used in the Balanced ANOVA command.

____ 9. Only two multiple comparison procedures are available in the Oneway command.

____ 10. The NSCORES function is useful in determining if the populations are normally distributed.

Practice Problems

1. Using the PASTA.MTW data from the TUT8 directory, determine if the cost and calories per servings are different for different quality ratings. Since some of the ratings occur only once or twice, you will need to combine some of the ratings. What would be one logical way of doing this?

2. Use the TECHN.MTW data set from the TUT8 directory to determine if the average salary is different within different departments at Technitron.

3. Use the PROF.MTW data from the TUT8 directory to determine if students' ratings of courses and professors are different for the different levels of courses: 100 level courses, 200 level courses, and so forth.

4. Use the SALES.MTW data set from the TUT8 directory to determine if the sales are different for different years. What would you report to your manager based on these results?

TUTORIAL 9

Examining Linear Relationships Between Variables: Regression

In this tutorial, you return to the role of the managerial consultant hired to analyze the salary structure of Technitron, Inc. Your preliminary report, which contained pictorial displays of the salaries in the sales department, was well received; Technitron has asked that you now analyze the relationship between salary and the other variables for the entire company. You will begin with a simple linear regression problem: relating salary to one other variable, years at the company. Later in the tutorial you will use Minitab to do a multiple regression analysis on Technitron's salary structure; this is a much more complex problem because it relates salary to several independent variables. Finally, you will use stepwise regression to select the variables that best predict salary.

Objectives

In this tutorial you will learn to:

- use simple linear regression to describe a linear relationship between two variables

- perform multiple regression analysis to investigate the form of the linear relationship between one variable and several other variables
- use stepwise regression to explore the relative importance of predictor variables

Finding a Straight Line Fit to Data: Simple Linear Regression

To the original salary data on the sales department at Technitron from Tutorial 1, you have added information on employees in the purchasing, advertising, and engineering departments. These new data are saved in the file TECHN.MTW on your backup Sample Files disk. There is information on 46 employees and the following variables are stored in the file: C1 SALARY, C2 YRS EM (years at Technitron), C3 PRIOR YR (prior years of experience), C4 EDUC (number of years of education), C5 ID (company identification number), C6 GENDER (coded 0=male, 1=female), C7 DEPT (coded 1=sales, 2=purchasing, 3=advertising, and 4=engineering), and C8 SUPER (number of employees supervised).

You will begin your investigation by analyzing the relationship between salaries at Technitron and the length of time an employee has been at the company. Verify that the relationship between these variables is linear.

- Open TECHN.MTW from the TUT9 directory
- Choose **G**raph ▶ Scatter **P**lot...
- Select C1 SALARY for the Vertical axis
- Select C2 YRS EM for the Horizontal axis
- Press [↵]

The scatter plot should resemble Figure 9-1.

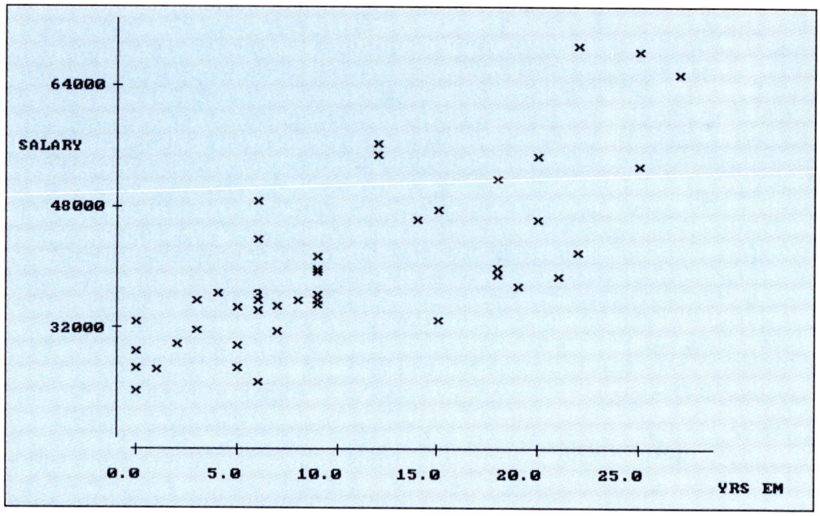

FIGURE 9-1
Scatter plot of salary versus years employed

The plot suggests a positive linear trend. Measure the strength of the linear relationship by computing the correlation coefficient:

- Press Q for Quit
- Choose **S**tat ▶ **B**asic Statistics ▶ **C**orrelation...
- Select C1 SALARY and C2 YRS EM as the Variables
- Press Alt-O

The Session window reports a correlation coefficient of 0.765. Since this value is somewhat close to 1, it seems there is a linear relationship between salary and years employed at Technitron. You are now ready to obtain the linear equation that relates salary to years employed:

- Choose **S**tat ▶ **R**egression ▶ **R**egression...
- Select C1 SALARY as the Response
- Select C2 YRS EM for the Predictors text box

The completed Regression dialog box should look like Figure 9-2.

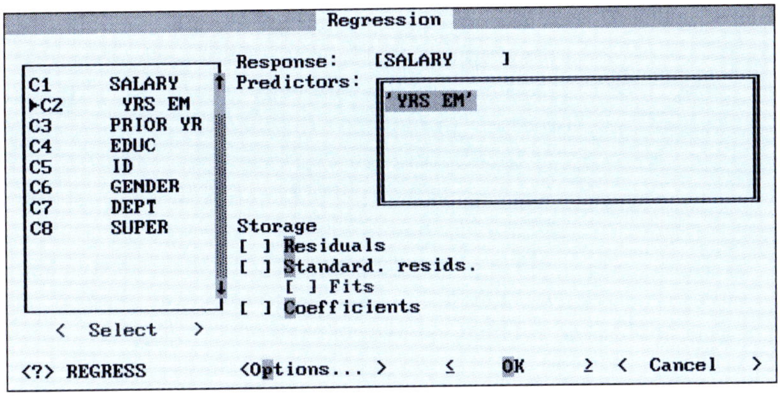

FIGURE 9-2
The completed Regression dialog box from the Stat menu

- Press [Alt]-O

When the analysis is complete, the Session window display should resemble Figure 9-3.

FIGURE 9-3
Results of salary regression analysis

Regression equation

```
The regression equation is
SALARY = 28394 + 1107 YRS EM

Predictor       Coef      Stdev    t-ratio       p
Constant       28394       1794      15.83   0.000
YRS EM        1107.2      140.4       7.88   0.000

s = 7162        R-sq = 58.5%      R-sq(adj) = 57.6%

Analysis of Variance

SOURCE        DF          SS          MS        F        p
Regression     1  3187557888  3187557888    62.15    0.000
Error         44  2256693504    51288488
Total         45  5444251648

Unusual Observations
Obs.   YRS EM    SALARY      Fit  Stdev.Fit  Residual   St.Resid
 15      12.0     56326    41681       1082     14645      2.07R
 40      22.0     69246    52753       1950     16493      2.39R

R denotes an obs. with a large st. resid.
```

Predictor table — ANOVA table — Unusual observations table

- Scroll to the top of the screen if necessary

The first line of the regression analysis reports the estimated regression equation:

SALARY = 28394 + 1107 YRS EM

Using this equation, you would predict a starting salary of \$28,394 for an individual who is new to Technitron (YRS EM = 0). The formula adds \$1107 (slope) for each year of employment at Technitron. Therefore, an employee with five years of experience has a predicted salary of \$33,930.

The predictor table contains the estimate for each of the regression coefficients and their standard deviations, as well as the t-statistics and p-values for testing the hypothesis that the coefficient is zero (the variable has no significant effect on the response variable).

The p-value of 0.000 for YRS EM in the predictor table indicates that there is a significant evidence of a non-zero slope.

The rest of the display contains information that will help you assess the usefulness of the model, as described in the following paragraphs.

The next line includes s, the estimated standard deviation around the regression line; R-sq, the coefficient of determination; and R-sq(adj), the R^2 value adjusted for degrees of freedom. The R^2 value indicates that 58.5% of the salary variation can be explained by the linear relationship to the number of years employed at the company. The higher the R^2 value, the better the data fit the regression equation.

Minitab computes an F-ratio to test the hypothesis that all of the predictor coefficients are zero and prints the result in an ANOVA table. In this model, the F-value of 62.15 corresponds to a p-value of 0.000, so there is statistically significant evidence that the predictor variable YRS EM has an effect on the response variable, SALARY. This indicates that the YRS EM coefficient is not zero.

In the unusual observations table, Minitab produces a list of outliers or influence points that have a standardized residual of more than 2 or less than –2 or an X value that is substantially different from the other X values in the data. For example, the employees in row 15 (12 years employed and a salary of 56326) and row 40 (22 years employed and a salary of 69246) are reported as unusual observations. You will look into these outliers and report possible causes.

Minitab can also compute (and store for later use) the *fitted values* and *residuals* for each observation. The fitted values and residuals can then be used to check assumptions, predict salaries, and investigate possible salary inequities.

To compute the fitted and residual values and save them in the worksheet:

- Choose **E**dit ▶ Edit **L**ast Command Dialog...

The Regression dialog box reappears.

- Press [Alt]-R, [Alt]-S, and [Alt]-F to select the **R**esiduals, **S**tandard. resids., and **F**its checkboxes
- Press [↵]
- Go to the Data screen
- If necessary, scroll right so that columns C9, C10, and C11 are visible

Minitab computes the residuals, standardized residuals, and fitted values for each observation in the data set (Figure 9-4; only the top portion of the worksheet is presented). In addition, Minitab automatically places the data in columns and names the columns.

FIGURE 9-4

The Data worksheet showing standardized residuals, fits, and residuals

SRES1	FITS1	RESI1
C9	C10	C11
-1.33399	48324.1	-9339.1
-1.71313	45002.4	-12082.4
-0.62215	33930.3	-4382.3
-1.45786	35037.5	-10288.5
-1.57655	52753.0	-10864.0
-0.02680	31715.8	-187.8
-1.85685	51645.7	-12854.7
-1.21358	48324.1	-8496.1
0.08522	28394.2	590.8
0.63287	28394.2	4387.8
1.22379	35037.5	8636.5
0.53526	31715.8	3751.2
-0.10486	30608.6	-732.6
-0.27230	38359.1	-1928.1
2.06870	41680.8	14645.2
0.21730	35037.5	1533.5
-0.40830	38359.1	-2891.1
-0.26195	28394.2	-1816.2
0.35923	45002.4	2533.6
-0.68368	28394.2	-4740.2
-1.70302	49431.3	-11883.3
0.53433	32823.0	3755.0

The new columns contain the following information:

Column No. and Name	Function
C9 SRES1	Converts each residual to a standard score. Unusual observations are determined by extreme standard scores—often those beyond two standard deviations from zero.
C10 FITS1	Lists each employee's salary as predicted by the regression equation. Compare the result on the third line with your earlier result.
C11 RESI1	Records the difference between each employee's actual salary and predicted (fitted) salary.

To graph the fitted values of the regression equation:

- Return to the Session window
- Choose **G**raph ▶ Scatter **P**lot...
- Select C10 FITS1 for the Vertical axis
- Select C2 YRS EM for the Horizontal axis
- Press [↵]

The graph of the fitted regression line appears (Figure 9-5).

FIGURE 9-5
Scatter plot of fitted values versus years employed

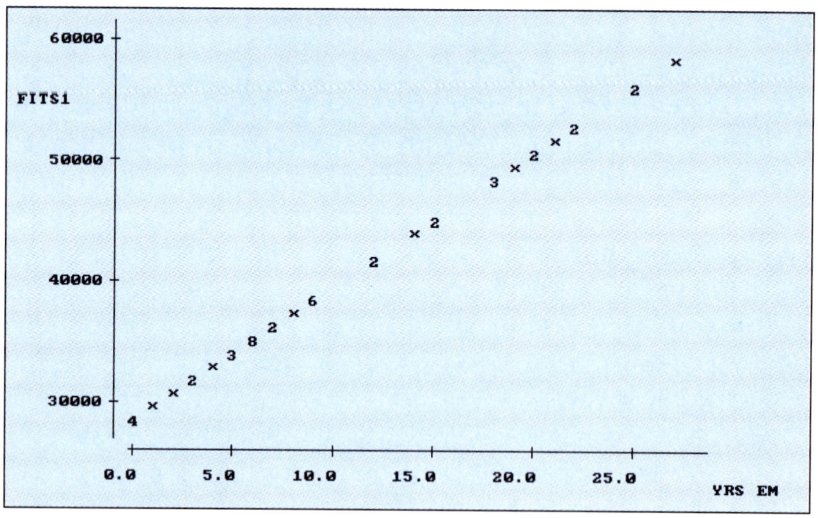

To see how well the line fits the data, construct a multiple scatter plot that displays both the actual values and the fitted values:

- Press Q for Quit
- Choose **G**raph ▶ **M**ultiple Scatter Plot...

For the plot of the fitted points on the regression line:

- Select C10 FITS1 for the first Vertical axis
- Select C2 YRS EM for the first Horizontal axis

For the plot of the data points:

- Select C1 SALARY for the second Vertical axis
- Select C2 YRS EM for the second Horizontal axis

To have Minitab draw a line through the estimated regression equation points:

- Press [Alt]-L for **L**ines
- Select C10 FITS1 for the Y column
- Select C2 YRS EM for the X column
- Press [↵] twice

The multiple scatter plot appears (Figure 9-6).

FIGURE 9-6
Multiple scatter plot of actual values (B) and fitted values (A)

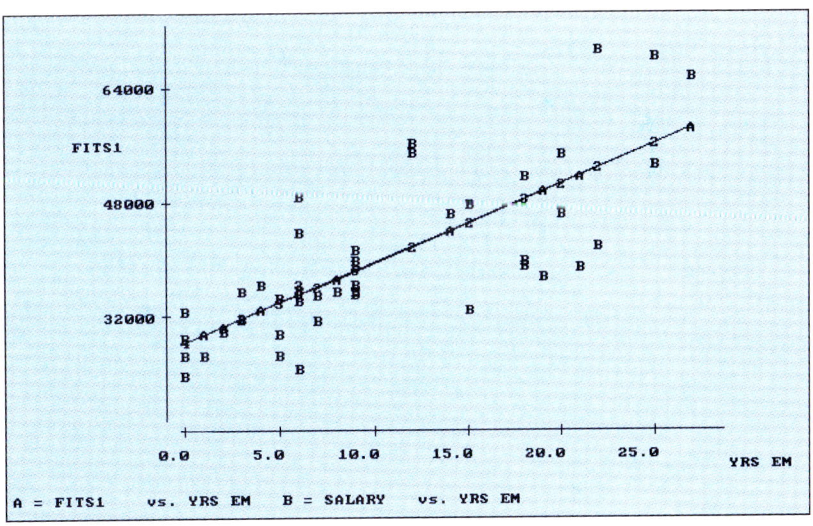

Minitab constructs a line through the fitted values (points designated by A). Data points are represented by B. You conclude that there is quite a bit of variation around the regression line. Salary at Technitron is not based solely on time with the company; there are other factors involved. You will try to further explain salary using additional predictor variables.

- Press Q for Quit

Polynomial Regression Models

You have just examined the simplest case, where salary is expressed as a linear function of years employed. Perhaps this relationship can be better described by a curve. Use the General Expressions command to create a second-order variable, $(\text{YRS EM})^2$. With this new variable, you can form a quadratic (polynomial) equation for SALARY.

- Choose **C**alc ▸ **F**unctions and Statistics ▸ **G**eneral Expressions...
- Type **'YRS**2'** in the New/modified variable text box and press [Tab] twice
- Type **C2**2** in the Expression text box and press [Alt]-O
- Go to the Data worksheet and scroll right to view C12

Minitab has recorded a new variable, the square of each term in C2, in C12 YRS**2.

- Return to the Session window

  Now try a regression model for salary using C2 and C12:

- Choose **S**tat ▸ **R**egression ▸ **R**egression...
- Select C1 SALARY as the Response
- Select C2 YRS EM and C12 YRS**2 as the Predictors
- Press [Alt]-O

Figure 9-7 displays the results of the polynomial regression.

FIGURE 9-7
Results of polynomial regression

```
MTB > Name c12 = 'YRS**2'
MTB > Let 'YRS**2' = C2**2
MTB > Regress 'SALARY' 2 'YRS EM' 'YRS**2'.

The regression equation is
SALARY = 29323 + 863 YRS EM + 9.7 YRS**2

Predictor        Coef        Stdev     t-ratio        p
Constant        29323         2640       11.11    0.000
YRS EM          863.3        523.9        1.65    0.107
YRS**2           9.74        20.14        0.48    0.631

s = 7225        R-sq = 58.8%       R-sq(adj) = 56.9%

Analysis of Variance

SOURCE        DF          SS          MS          F        p
Regression     2  3199762944  1599881472      30.65    0.000
Error         43  2244488448    52197404
Total         45  5444251648

SOURCE        DF      SEQ SS
YRS EM         1  3187557888
YRS**2         1    12205007

Unusual Observations
Obs.  YRS EM    SALARY       Fit Stdev.Fit  Residual   St.Resid
 15     12.0     56326     41086      1644     15240      2.17R
 40     22.0     69246     53031      2050     16215      2.34R
 41     27.0     65487     59734      3956      5753      0.95 X

R denotes an obs. with a large st. resid.
X denotes an obs. whose X value gives it large influence.
```

- Scroll up to see the second-order equation

$$\text{SALARY} = 29323 + 863 \text{ YRS EM} + 9.7 \text{ YRS**2}$$

Using this model, an employee with five years of experience would have a predicted (fitted) salary = $29323 + 863(5) + 9.7(5^2) = 33{,}880.5$.

The predictor table reports that the YRS EM coefficient has a p-value of 0.107; it is not significant in this model. The quadratic term, YRS**2, has a p-value of 0.631; it is also not significant.

The polynomial regression explains 58.8% of the variation—not much better than the simple linear regression model used earlier.

The ANOVA table reports an F-ratio of 30.65. The corresponding p-value of 0.000 indicates that at least one of the coefficients in the model is not zero. The results indicate that SALARY depends on YRS EM or the quadratic term YRS**2.

Minitab can include not only higher powers of a variable but other functions as well. In certain cases, it is common to use the logarithm of a variable; if a term is cyclic in nature, it is sometimes advisable to include the cosine of that variable. Minitab allows you to form a new column and use the regression command with these variables.

Multiple Linear Regression

Your intuition tells you that salary is probably determined by many factors other than years employed. To investigate, you will model salary as a function of years employed, prior years of experience, years of education, and number of employees supervised. To fit a multiple regression model:

- Choose **S**tat ▶ **R**egression ▶ **R**egression...
- Select C1 SALARY as the Response
- Select C2 YRS EM, C3 PRIOR YR, C4 EDUC, and C8 SUPER as the Predictors
- Press Alt-O
- Scroll up the Session window to see the results (Figure 9-8)

FIGURE 9-8
Results of multiple linear regression

```
MTB > Regress 'SALARY' 4 'YRS EM' 'PRIOR YR' 'EDUC' 'SUPER'.

The regression equation is
SALARY = 24496 + 655 YRS EM - 161 PRIOR YR + 1636 EDUC + 179 SUPER

Predictor        Coef       Stdev     t-ratio        p
Constant        24496        2049       11.95    0.000
YRS EM          655.3       139.6        4.69    0.000
PRIOR YR       -161.1       231.5       -0.70    0.490
EDUC           1636.4       406.1        4.03    0.000
SUPER          178.80       97.59        1.83    0.074

s = 5643          R-sq = 76.0%       R-sq(adj) = 73.7%

Analysis of Variance

SOURCE         DF           SS           MS          F        p
Regression      4   4138631168   1034657792      32.49    0.000
Error          41   1305620224     31844396
Total          45   5444251648

SOURCE         DF       SEQ SS
YRS EM          1   3187557888
PRIOR YR        1       160191
EDUC            1    844012864
SUPER           1    106900216

Unusual Observations
Obs.   YRS EM     SALARY         Fit Stdev.Fit  Residual    St.Resid
  1      18.0      38985       50785      1745    -11800      -2.20R
  2      15.0      32920       49285      1700    -16365      -3.04R
 40      22.0      69246       62839      3535      6407       1.46 X
 41      27.0      65487       69693      3779     -4206      -1.00 X
 42       6.0      48695       45610      4249      3085       0.83 X

R denotes an obs. with a large st. resid.
X denotes an obs. whose X value gives it large influence.
```

The contents of the display are explained in the following paragraphs. The multiple regression equation is:

SALARY = 24496 + 655 YRS EM –
161 PRIOR YR + 1636 EDUC + 179 SUPER

Minitab also displays the t-ratio for each of the coefficients and the corresponding p-values. The predictor table indicates that there is significant evidence that the coefficients for years employed and education are different from zero, but there is not significant evidence that the coefficients for prior years and number of employees supervised—given that the other variables are in the model—are different from zero.

This model explains 76.0% of the variation in salary at Technitron. The addition of other variables has substantially improved your model over the linear and quadratic (polynomial) models considered earlier.

The ANOVA table (which tests the hypothesis that all predictor coefficients are zero) reports a p-value of 0.000; you can conclude that at least one of the coefficients is different from zero.

The content and interpretation of the SEQ SS table following the ANOVA table is rather involved. See your instructor for details.

Minitab has noted several unusual observations in the data set. There are two outliers (observations in rows 1 and 2) and three influence points (in rows 40, 41, and 42). You would investigate these values further before making your final report.

To determine the effect of qualitative data, such as gender, on salary and include it as a predictor, the variable must first be "dummied up." A *dummy variable* is one that takes on two values—typically 0 and 1. Recall that C6 GENDER is already coded in this form (0=male and 1=female). To include C6 GENDER in the regression equation:

- Choose **S**tat ▶ **R**egression ▶ **R**egression...
- Select C1 SALARY as the Response variable
- Select C2 YRS EM, C3 PRIOR YR, C4 EDUC, C6 GENDER, and C8 SUPER as the Predictors
- Press [Alt]-O

The Session window reports the results of the multiple regression:

$$\text{SALARY} = 25801 + 638 \text{ YRS EM} - 209 \text{ PRIOR YR} + 1605 \text{ EDUC} - 1627 \text{ GENDER} + 183 \text{ SUPER}$$

When GENDER=0 for male employees, $(-1627)(0) = 0$ is added to the equation when computing salaries of male employees. For female employees GENDER=1, so $(-1627)(1) = -1627$ is added to female salaries. Using this equation, a woman with the same years employed, same prior years of experience, same education, and supervising the same number of employees earns, on the average, $1627 less than a man with the same qualifications. Is this a case for sex discrimination? The p-value for the coefficient of gender, 0.359, indicates that there is not significant evidence that the coefficient is different from zero, so you cannot infer any sex discrimination from the results.

The R^2 value of 76.5% indicates this model fits the data reasonably well. However, there are several insignificant variables. You might simplify your model without decreasing its predictive ability by omitting these insignificant variables.

Stepwise Multiple Regression

Whenever you have a large list of potential independent variables, it is difficult to decide which to include. In the last section you saw that the coefficient for the prior years of experience did not have a significant value in that model, so perhaps it should be left out of the model. The stepwise regression procedure yields a model that contains only those terms with significant F-values at specified levels. To determine which variables are significant predictors of salary at Technitron, you will perform a stepwise regression using SALARY as the response variable and the variables C2 YRS EM, C3 PRIOR YR, C4 EDUC, C6 GENDER, and C8 SUPER as potential predictors.

By specifying different subcommands, you can have Minitab select variables in three different ways:

Stepwise selection At each step Minitab calculates an F-statistic for each predictor in the equation. If the F-value associated with any predictor is less than the specified value of FREMOVE (default=4), Minitab removes that variable with the smallest F value from the model. Minitab then calculates a new regression equation, prints the result and proceeds to the next step. At the next step, Minitab tries to add a variable by calculating an F-statistic for each predictor not in the equation. It then includes the variable with the largest F, provided its F-statistic exceeds a specified value (default=4). If no predictor can be added or deleted, the stepwise procedure stops.

Forward selection Minitab adds predictor variables one at a time. None are removed. To do a forward selection, set F to remove at 0. (Since F-statistics are the t-values squared, they can never be less than 0.)

Backward elimination Minitab begins with an equation that contains all predictors. It then removes predictors as in the stepwise procedure; none are allowed to re-enter the equation. To do backward elimina-

MINITAB AT WORK

ECOLOGY: Ecologists who study the reproductive success of fish that tend their young on river and lake bottoms need efficient ways to count the young that each adult produces. An ecologist in Ontario, Canada, developed just such a technique for one species of fish, the rock bass. He used Minitab to investigate the accuracy of his procedure.

The ecologist used an ordinary plastic kitchen meat baster to suction the newly hatched rock bass young from their nests. The male parent guarded the empty nest while the ecologist placed the young in a pan on the river bank, photographed each brood several times, and then quickly returned it to the parent who resumed caring for its brood with no apparent behavioral changes. The technique resulted in no detectable harm to either parent or progeny.

Back in the lab the ecologist gridded each photograph, counted the number of young in each grid square, and from those numbers determined a total count. He suspected that his counting method became less accurate the more young there were in a brood, so differences in the counts of various photographs for the same brood should have increased with increasing brood size.

To test this prediction, the ecologist used Minitab's regression capabilities to produce an equation relating the average count of young from photographs of the same brood to the variability of those counts: $\ln(\text{variance} + 1) = 0.092 + 0.129(\text{mean count})$. This outcome convinced the ecologist that his initial suspicions were true: with more young, his counts did tend to vary more from photo to photo. By calculating the confidence limits about the regression line, the ecologist could test his subsequent use of the technique. For any new nest, if the count variance for a particular mean fell outside the regression confidence limits, the ecologist would quickly know to check for possible counting errors.

tion, set F to enter at 10000 (a value virtually impossible to attain) and list all predictors on the Enter subcommand.

Stepwise Selection

To do a general stepwise regression:

- Choose **Stat ▶ Regression ▶ Stepwise...**
- Select C1 SALARY as the Response
- Select C2 YRS EM, C3 PRIOR YR, C4 EDUC, C6 GENDER, and C8 SUPER as Predictors
- Press Alt-O

The Session window displays the results of the stepwise regression (Figure 9-9).

FIGURE 9-9
Results of stepwise regression

```
MTB > Stepwise 'SALARY' 'YRS EM' 'PRIOR YR' 'EDUC' 'GENDER'  'SUPER';
SUBC>   FEnter 4.0;
SUBC>   FRemove 4.0.

 STEPWISE REGRESSION OF  SALARY  ON  5 PREDICTORS, WITH N =   46

    STEP         1        2
CONSTANT     24582    23177

EDUC          3010     1916
T-RATIO       8.19     5.05

YRS EM                  672
T-RATIO                4.75

S             7002     5738
R-SQ         60.37    73.99
 MORE? (YES, NO, SUBCOMMAND, OR HELP)
SUBC>
```

The display in the Session window contains the following information. (For each step, you read down the column to obtain information about the variable entered or removed, as well as summary information about the regression model.)

Step 1: Minitab entered the EDUC variable because it had the highest F-ratio of all variables not in the regression equation. The one-variable equation is SALARY = 24582 + 3010 EDUC. The T-ratio of 8.19 provides a test of the hypothesis that coefficient of EDUC = 0. The estimated standard deviation around the regression line is 7002. This model explains 60.37% of the variation in salary.

Step 2: Of the remaining variables, Minitab determines that YRS EM produced the largest F-ratio that is greater than 4; it adds (or enters) that variable to the equation to produce an estimated regression model of SALARY = 23177 + 1916 EDUC + 672 YRS EM. The T-ratios are 5.05 and 4.75, respectively. This model explains 73.99% of the variation in salary.

Because no other variables meet the criteria that allow them to be added or removed, Minitab stops and asks you if you want to perform another step.

- Type **YES** at the SUBC> prompt and press [↵]

Minitab reports that no variables have been entered or removed. The default stepwise process has ended. None of the remaining variables can be entered into the regression equation and none of the variables in the regression equation can be removed.

Normally, you would type NO to end the stepwise command, but this time you explore another issue.

In the real world, there may be certain variables that you must include in the equation. For example, at Technitron, the number of employees supervised is an indication of the level of responsibility held by each employee; management has deemed this an important variable. To force it into your equation:

- Type **ENTER 'SUPER'.** (be sure to include the period at the end) and press [↵]

Step 3: Minitab adds SUPER to the model with EDUC and YRS EM. Note that the T-ratio for SUPER is 1.74. This model accounts for 75.73% of the variation in salary.

Step 4: Minitab determines that SUPER is not significant and removes it from the regression equation, returning you to the regression equation of Step 2.

Using the ENTER or REMOVE subcommands, you can add or remove variables and readily determine their impact on the model.

You have finished using the stepwise command. Because you will not enter any other variables into the model:

- Type **NO** and press [↵]

Forward Selection

To use the forward selection stepwise regression procedure:

- Choose **E**dit ▶ Edit **L**ast Command Dialog...
- Press [Alt]-P for O**p**tions

The Stepwise Options subdialog box (Figure 9-10) appears.

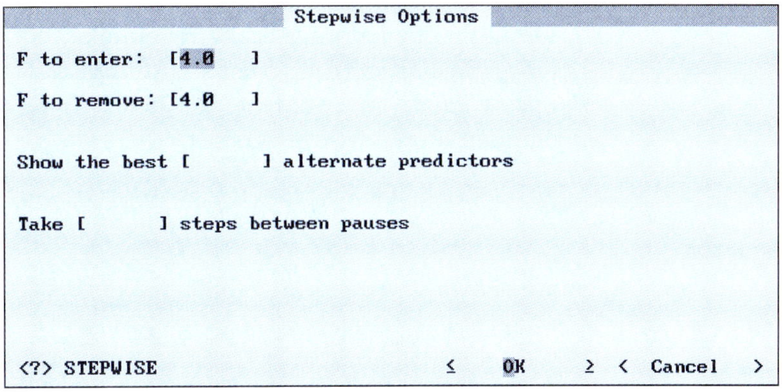

FIGURE 9-10

The Stepwise Options subdialog box

Recall (from the introduction to forward selection earlier in this section) that you set the F to remove value (FREMOVE) to zero in order to perform a forward selection stepwise regression.

- Press [Tab] and type **0** in the F to remove text box
- Press [↵] twice

The forward selection results are displayed in Figure 9-11.

FIGURE 9-11

Results of forward selection stepwise regression

```
MTB > Stepwise 'SALARY' 'YRS EM' 'PRIOR YR' 'EDUC' 'GENDER'  'SUPER';
SUBC>   FEnter 4.0;
SUBC>   FRemove 0.

 STEPWISE REGRESSION OF  SALARY  ON  5 PREDICTORS, WITH N =   46

    STEP         1         2
CONSTANT     24582     23177

EDUC          3010      1916
T-RATIO       8.19      5.05

YRS EM                   672
T-RATIO                 4.75

S             7002      5738
R-SQ         60.37     73.99
 MORE? (YES, NO, SUBCOMMAND, OR HELP)
SUBC>
```

The results are identical to the first two steps of the general stepwise method used earlier (Figure 9-9). Your conclusions would remain the same. To end the forward selection procedure without entering any other variables:

- Type **NO** and press [↵]

Backward Elimination

Recall that to perform a backward elimination, you use the stepwise procedure but set the F to enter criteria very large. That way a variable, once deleted, can never enter the model. To perform the backward elimination stepwise regression:

- Choose **S**tat ▶ **R**egression ▶ **S**tepwise...
- Select C1 SALARY as the Response
- Select C2 YRS EM, C3 PRIOR YR, C4 EDUC, C6 GENDER, and C8 SUPER as Predictors and press [Tab]
- Select C2 YRS EM, C3 PRIOR YR, C4 EDUC, C6 GENDER, and C8 SUPER for the Enter text box
- Press [Alt]-P to open the Stepwise Options dialog box
- Type **10000** in the F to enter text box and press [↵] twice

The backward elimination stepwise regression begins with all the predictors in the equation and ends when no variable in the model has an F-statistic less than 4. The four steps (Figure 9-12) are shown in the Session window.

FIGURE 9-12
Results of backward elimination stepwise regression

```
MTB > Stepwise 'SALARY' 'YRS EM' 'PRIOR YR' 'EDUC' 'GENDER'  'SUPER';
SUBC>   Enter 'YRS EM' 'PRIOR YR' 'EDUC' 'GENDER'  'SUPER';
SUBC>   FEnter 10000;
SUBC>   FRemove 4.0.

 STEPWISE REGRESSION OF  SALARY  ON  5 PREDICTORS, WITH N =   46

    STEP         1        2        3        4
CONSTANT     25801    24655    23783    23177

YRS EM         638      646      659      672
T-RATIO       4.53     4.60     4.75     4.75

PRIOR YR      -209
T-RATIO      -0.88

EDUC          1605     1615     1639     1916
T-RATIO       3.93     3.97     4.06     5.05

GENDER       -1627    -1295
T-RATIO      -0.93    -0.76

SUPER          183      165      165
T-RATIO       1.87     1.73     1.74

S             5653     5637     5608     5738
R-SQ         76.52    76.07    75.73    73.99
 MORE? (YES, NO, SUBCOMMAND, OR HELP)
SUBC>
```

Step 1: All variables are included.

Step 2: PRIOR YR is eliminated and the others remain.

Step 3: GENDER is eliminated.

Step 4: SUPER is eliminated.

The backward elimination process is complete. The only variables left have F-statistics that are greater than 4. Backward elimination results in the same two variables (YRS EM and EDUC) in the salary equation. To end the Stepwise command:

- Type **NO** and press [↵]

All three stepwise procedures identified the same variables as important: YRS EM and EDUC. (Frequently the three procedures will yield different regression equations.) You decide to include the variable SUPER even though it was not selected as significant. Therefore, to model salaries at Technitron, you will use years employed, education, and number of people supervised.

You have completed your regression analysis on the salaries at Technitron and are ready to submit your recommendations. Stepwise analysis helped you determine the best variables to use as predictors. You will recommend the model that uses prior years at Technitron, years of education after high school, and number of employees supervised to determine the salary structure. You will review the salaries of those individuals whose standardized residuals fall below –2 to determine why their salaries are far from the estimated average salary of such employees. Your results will be valuable to management when determining raises next year.

If you plan to continue directly to the next tutorial:

- Choose **F**ile ▶ Restart **M**initab

If you want to take a longer break:

- Choose **F**ile ▶ E**x**it

Minitab Command Summary

The menus and commands introduced in or related to this tutorial are described in this section. You will find a complete explanation of all menus and commands in the Reference section of this manual.

Menu	Command	Function
Stat		
	Fit Intercept	Allows the intercept to be included or excluded in a regression model; allows one to perform regression through the origin
	Regression	
	Regression	Performs simple linear or multiple regression
	Stepwise	Performs stepwise regression, using backward elimination, forward selection, or both

Minitab Session Command

BRIEF K	Controls the amount of output from the Regression and ARIMA commands displayed in the Session window, with K=1 producing the least output and K=3 (4 for ARIMA) the most; must be issued as a command in the Session window

Review and Practice

Matching

Match the following terms to their definitions by placing the correct letter next to the term it explains.

____ SRES

____ FITS

____ F to remove

____ Remove

____ Enter

____ F to enter

____ predictors

____ BRIEF

a. Sets the F-ratio for removal criteria of independent variables in a stepwise procedure

b. Sets the F-ratio for inclusion criteria of independent variables in a stepwise procedure

c. Name given to the column of standardized residuals

d. Name given to the column of fitted or predicted values

e. Controls the amount of output produced by the Regression command

f. Minitab's name for the independent variables

g. Adds one or more variables from the regression model in the Stepwise command

h. Deletes one or more variables from the regression model in the Stepwise command

True/False

Mark the following statements T or F.

____ 1. The Regression command is used to perform simple linear regression, quadratic regression, and multiple regression.

____ 2. The fitted values alone can be saved in the worksheet.

____ 3. Minitab can perform linear and nonlinear regression.

____ 4. The Correlation command outputs both the sample correlation and the p-value for testing that the correlation is zero.

____ 5. To end the Stepwise command you type END at the subcommand prompt.

____ 6. Outlier observations are automatically displayed in the regression output.

____ 7. The Stepwise command can perform a forward selection by setting the FREMOVE value to a large value.

____ 8. Fitted values can be saved to the worksheet only if the residual values are saved.

____ 9. Even if the residual and fitted values are not saved, Minitab displays these values for unusual observations.

____ 10. Minitab denotes the standard deviation of the regression line as s.

Practice Problems

1. The amount of output that is displayed in the Session window from the Regression command is determined by the current value of the BRIEF variable. To request different amounts of output from the Regression command, issue the command BRIEF K in the Session window, where K is 1, 2, or 3. The default value is 2, so what you see in Figure 9-8, for example, is the default amount of output. The higher the value of K specified, the greater the amount of output. To explore the BRIEF command, review the section on the polynomial regression. Use the three different levels of BRIEF to compare and contrast the amount and kind of output produced by each level of BRIEF. The BRIEF command also works with the ARIMA command that you will see in Tutorial 13.

2. In Tutorial 1 you worked with the snowfall data for a small town in the upper Midwest. The data are actually arranged in chronological order starting with the total snowfall for 1977. Residents have claimed that the snow totals seem to be less than they once were. Use the data to determine whether there is any statistical evidence that the amount of snow has been decreasing over the years. The data have been saved in the file SNOWFALL.MTW in the TUT9 directory. Use the Set Patterned Data command to enter the year data in another column and perform a regression analysis of the data.

3. One of the larger components of a movie's cost is the cost of advertising. Below are the costs in millions of dollars for ten movies randomly selected from each of the past twelve years, starting with 1979.

   4 2 11 12 26 74 141 184 278 446 447 504

   You are curious whether there appears to be a trend in movie advertising expenses. Determine whether any relation exists between year and movie advertising expenses. HINT: A plot, in this case, is very revealing! How might you make your plot more linear?

4. Use the COMPUTER.MTW data set from the TUT9 directory to determine which of the variables in the data set affect the price of a computer. Note that many of the variables are not numeric; you will need to "dummy them up" (provide numeric equivalents).

TUTORIAL 10

Analyzing Categorical Data

Most of data you worked with in previous tutorials were numeric. Now you will see how to use Minitab to make statistical decisions about categorical data. First you will perform a goodness-of-fit test for a genetics experiment. Then you will test for independence of variables as an engineer and as a managerial consultant. In all three cases you will use the chi-square distribution.

Objectives

In this tutorial you will learn to:

- compare an observed distribution to a hypothesized distribution
- test the relationship between two categorical variables using a contingency table in the worksheet
- test the relationship between two categorical variables, having Minitab construct the contingency table using data in the worksheet

Comparing an Observed Distribution to a Hypothesized Distribution

In Tutorial 6 you learned how to test data from binomial experiments (having two categorical outcomes for each trial, such as winning or losing an election). You will now look at multinomial experiments that have more than two categorical outcomes for each trial. Recall that in genetics class you analyzed Mendel's experiment with garden peas in which he hypothesized that the four phenotypes—(1) smooth-yellow, (2) smooth-green, (3) wrinkled-yellow, and (4) wrinkled-green—would be produced in a 9:3:3:1 ratio. In genetics lab, Dr. Michaels has asked you to grow garden peas in carbon-dioxide–deficient soil and determine whether this changes the phenotype ratio. You will use a chi-square goodness-of-fit test with:

> H_0: There is no change in distribution. The peas planted in carbon-dioxide–deficient soil reproduce in a 9:3:3:1 phenotype ratio.
> H_1: The distribution changes.

- Open GENETICS.MTW from the TUT10 directory

The first two columns of this worksheet display the four numeric values of the phenotypes (C1 TYPE) and the corresponding Mendelian probabilities (C2 PROB). C3 PHENO lists the phenotypes from your random sample of 200 peas grown in carbon-dioxide–deficient soil. Minitab does not have a single command to perform the chi-square goodness-of-fit test, but in earlier tutorials you have seen the commands necessary to perform the test.

You will use Minitab to perform the chi-square goodness-of-fit calculations, using the formula:

$$\chi^2 = \sum \frac{(\text{Obs} - \text{Exp})^2}{\text{Exp}}$$

where Obs and Exp are the observed and expected number of peas with a given phenotype. You then will calculate the p-value by comparing the observed chi-square results to a chi-square distribution with $4 - 1 = 3$ degrees of freedom.

For your sample data, use the Tally command to compute the observed values for each of the four categories:

- Choose **Stat ▶ Tables ▶ Tally...**
- Select C3 PHENO for the Variables text box

- Press [Alt]-O

The Session window displays the counts (Figure 10-1).

FIGURE 10-1
Tally of phenotype distribution

```
MTB > Tally 'PHENO';
SUBC>   Counts.

   PHENO  COUNT
       1     94
       2     50
       3     44
       4     12
      N=    200
```

Store these observed values in C4:

- Go to the Data screen
- Assign the name OBSERVED to column C4
- Type **94, 50, 44,** and **12** in the first four rows of C4 (be sure to press [↵] after typing the last number)
- Return to the Session window

Since you assume H_0 is true, obtain the expected number for each phenotype by multiplying its probability (stored in C2 PROB) by the sample size, 200. To have Minitab compute the expected frequencies:

- Choose **C**alc ▶ **F**unctions and Statistics ▶ **G**eneral Expressions...
- Type **EXPECTED** in the New/modified variable text box and press [Tab] twice
- Type **'PROB'*200** in the Expression text box and press [Alt]-O
- Go to the Data screen

C5 EXPECTED now contains the expected numbers: 112.5, 37.5, 37.5, and 12.5.

- Return to the Session window

To compute the chi-square statistic, first compute the $(\text{Obs} - \text{Exp})^2/\text{Exp}$ value for each phenotype:

- Choose **E**dit ▶ Edit **L**ast Command Dialog...

- Type **CHISQR** in the New/modified variable text box and press [Tab] twice
- Type **(C4-C5)**2/C5** in the Expression text box and press [Alt]-O
- Go to the Data worksheet

The Data worksheet should resemble Figure 10-2.

FIGURE 10-2

The Data worksheet with chi-square values

OBSERVED	EXPECTED	CHISQR
C4	C5	C6
94	112.5	3.04222
50	37.5	4.16667
44	37.5	1.12667
12	12.5	0.02000

To obtain the chi-square statistic, sum the individual chi-square values in C6 CHISQR and store that sum in constant location K1 for later use (refer to Tutorial 2, Column Summaries, if you want to review constants):

- Return to the Session window
- Choose **Calc** ▶ **Functions and Statistics** ▶ **Column Statistics...**
- Press [Tab]
- Select C6 CHISQR as the Input variable
- Press [Alt]-R for Store **r**esult in and press [Tab]
- Type **K1**
- Press [↵]

The chi-square statistic is 8.3556, the sum of C6 CHISQR (Figure 10-3).

FIGURE 10-3

The Session window with the chi-square statistic

```
MTB > Name c5 = 'EXPECTED'
MTB > Let 'EXPECTED' = 'PROB'*200
MTB > Name c6 = 'CHISQR'
MTB > Let 'CHISQR' = (C4-C5)**2/C5
MTB > Sum 'CHISQR' K1.
   SUM     =      8.3556
MTB >
```

To determine whether there is significant evidence that the relative frequencies differ from the hypothesized ratio of 9:3:3:1, compute the p-value of the observed statistic:

- Choose **C**alc ▶ Probability **D**istributions ▶ **C**hisquare...
- Press [Alt]-C for **C**umulative probability and press [Tab]
- Type **3** in the Degrees of freedom text box
- Press [Alt]-N for Input co**n**stant and press [Tab]
- Type **K1** and press [Tab]
- Type **K2** in the Optional storage text box and press [↵]

The cumulative probability function computes the probability of a value being less than or equal to the input value. To compute the p-value:

- Type **LET K3=1-K2** after the Minitab prompt (MTB >) in the Session window and press [↵]
- Type **PRINT K3** and press [↵]

The bottom of the Session window should resemble Figure 10-4.

FIGURE 10-4
The Session window with p-value of 0.0392075

```
MTB > CDF K1 K2;
SUBC>   Chisquare 3.
MTB > LET K3=1-K2
MTB > PRINT K3
K3       0.0392075
MTB >
```

Since the p-value of the chi-square statistic is 0.0392075, reject the null hypothesis at the 0.05 level and conclude that the distribution has changed. In your lab report, note that growing garden peas in carbon-dioxide–deficient soil changes the phenotype distribution from the Mendelian ratio of 9:3:3:1.

- Choose **F**ile ▶ Restart **M**initab

Case Study: Transistors

You are now working in the engineering department of Flexible Circuits, Inc., where you design parts for electronic equipment. There have been some problems with a particular transistor and the vice president wants you to locate the source of the difficulty. You suspect that the quality of the transistor might depend on the day of the week it was produced, so you select a random sample of 510 transistors from stock and classify each (using its lot number) by the day it was produced. You ask a team to rate each transistor for quality. They report the number of transistors in each rating for each day. The data have been stored in the file TRANS.MTW.

Testing the Relationship Between Two Categorical Variables in a Contingency Table

- Open TRANS.MTW from the TUT10 directory
- Go to the Data worksheet

The Data worksheet displays the contingency table. The first column lists the quality ratings for the parts. The next five columns list the number of transistors that received ratings in each category by day of the week. (The fair and poor categories have been combined to ensure that there are not too many cells with small frequencies.)

- Return to the Session window

To test for the independence of variables, first formulate the hypotheses:

H_0: Product quality and day of manufacture are independent.
H_1: Product quality and day of manufacture are dependent.

To run the test:

- Choose **Stat** ▶ **Tables** ▶ Chisquare **Test**...
- Select C2 MON, C3 TUE, C4 WED, C5 THU, and C6 FRI

The completed Chisquare Test dialog box should resemble Figure 10-5.

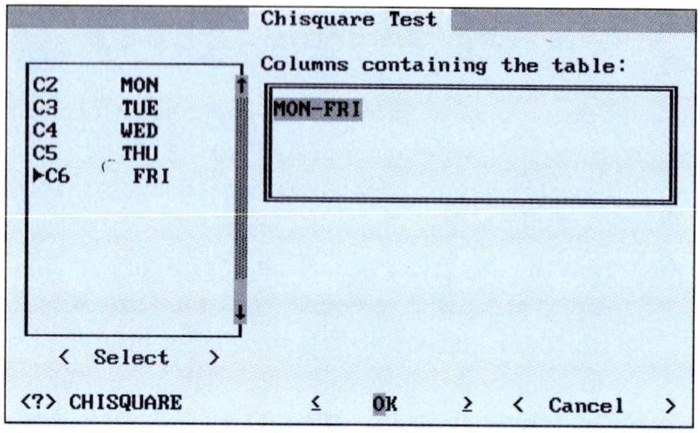

FIGURE 10-5

The completed Chisquare Test dialog box from the Tables submenu

- Press [Alt]-O

The results of the chi-square test appear in the Session window (Figure 10-6).

FIGURE 10-6

The Session window with the chi-square test results

```
MTB > ChiSquare 'MON'-'FRI'.

Expected counts are printed below observed counts

          MON      TUE      WED      THU      FRI    Total
   1       44       74       79       72       31      300
        47.65    69.41    77.06    68.24    37.65

   2       25       19       27       21       12      104
        16.52    24.06    26.71    23.65    13.05

   3       12       25       25       23       21      106
        16.84    24.53    27.23    24.11    13.30

Total      81      118      131      116       64      510

ChiSq =  0.279 +  0.303 +  0.049 +  0.208 +  1.174 +
         4.356 +  1.065 +  0.003 +  0.298 +  0.085 +
         1.389 +  0.009 +  0.182 +  0.051 +  4.455 = 13.906
df = 8
```

Minitab prints the expected counts below the observed counts for each cell. It then lists the individual chi-square values from each cell and sums them to obtain the chi-square statistic, 13.906. From this, you can see which cells contribute the most to the chi-square total. Note that on Friday, more FAIRPOOR transistors than expected are produced; on Monday more GOOD transistors are produced (1=EXCELLENT; 2=GOOD; 3=FAIRPOOR). The degrees of freedom of the chi-square statistic (df = 8) is given last.

To determine the p-value for this test:

- Choose **Calc** ▶ **Probability Distributions** ▶ **Chisquare...**
- Press [Alt]-C for **C**umulative probability and press [Tab]
- Type **8** in the Degrees of freedom text box
- Press [Alt]-N for Input co**n**stant and press [Tab]
- Type **13.906** in the Input constant text box and press [Tab]
- Type **K1** and press [↵]

After the MTB > prompt in the Session window:

- Type **LET K2=1-K1** and press [↵]
- Type **PRINT K2** and press [↵]

Minitab prints a value of 0.0841846, K2, the p-value, so fail to reject H_0. Inform the vice president that transistor quality and the day of manufacture are independent. However, because the results are significant at the 0.10 level and because of the large number of defective transistors produced on Friday, you will pursue the question further. You recommend that more data be collected and the process be observed in greater detail.

- Choose **F**ile ▶ Restart **M**initab

Testing the Relationship Between Two Categorical Variables Using Raw Data

It is not necessary to place the data in a contingency table to perform a chi-square test of independence. You can tell Minitab where the raw data are stored; the program will count the observed frequencies and compile the contingency table for you. Return to the case study in which you acted as a managerial consultant at Technitron.

- Open TECH.MTW from the TUT10 directory

If your data are not numeric, you would need to convert them to numeric values using the Convert command. Refer to Tutorial 4, Converting Alpha Data to Numeric, for more information. Recall, however, from Tutorial 9 that the department data have already been coded for you so that 1=sales, 2=purchasing, 3=advertising, and 4=engineering.

To continue your study of salaries at Technitron, you would like to ascertain whether there is a relationship between salary and the department in which an individual works. First, set up the two hypotheses:

H_0: Salary levels and department are independent.
H_1: Salary levels and department are not independent.

Collapse the salary data into a small number of categories by using the Code Data Values command.

CAUTION: When you use the Chisquare command from the previous section, Minitab warns you if you have too many cell counts below 5. However, the Tables command you will use next does not issue this warning; keep this in mind when defining your categories.

- Choose **C**alc ▶ Code Data **V**alues...
- Select C1 SALARY for the Code data from columns text box and press [Tab]
- Type **SALCODE** for the Into columns text box and press [Tab]
- Type **23000:34999** for the first Original values text box, press [Tab], type **1**, and press [Tab]
- Type **35000:44999**, press [Tab], type **2**, and press [Tab]
- Type **45000:99999**, press [Tab], type **3**, and press [↵]

Now have Minitab create the contingency table from the data in C7 DEPT and C9 SALCODE:

- Choose **S**tat ▶ **T**ables ▶ **C**ross Tabulation...
- Select C7 DEPT and C9 SALCODE for the Classification variables
- Press [Alt]-A for Chisquare **a**nalysis

The completed Cross Tabulation dialog box should look like Figure 10-7.

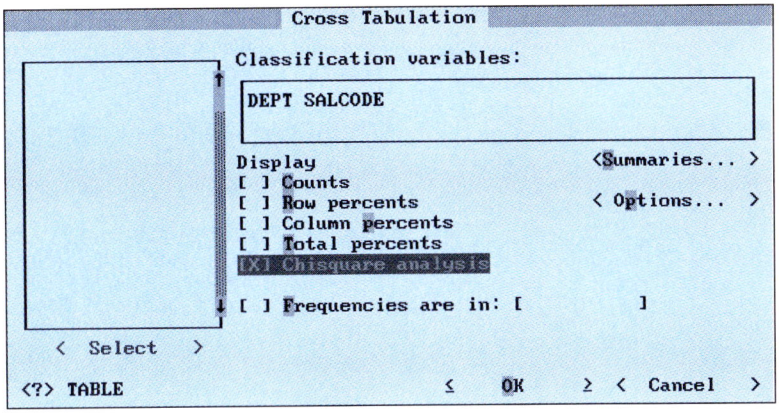

FIGURE 10-7

The completed Cross Tabulation dialog box from the Tables submenu

- Press [↵]

The contingency table and the results of the chi-square test are displayed in the Session window (Figure 10-8).

FIGURE 10-8

The Session window, showing contingency table and results of the chi-square test

```
MTB > Table 'DEPT' 'SALCODE';
SUBC>   ChiSquare.


 ROWS: DEPT      COLUMNS: SALCODE

              1        2        3       ALL

  1           6        4        0        10
  2           2        5        1         8
  3           2        2        3         7
  4           6        7        8        21
 ALL         16       18       12        46

CHI-SQUARE =      8.947    WITH D.F. =     6

  CELL CONTENTS --
                 COUNT
```

Minitab displays the four departments (1–4) in the first column. The next three columns contain the counts of the coded salary ranges. Each cell contains a count. The chi-square statistic (8.947) and the degrees of freedom for this table (6) are displayed last, with a note that the contents of each cell represent a count.

MINITAB AT WORK

EDUCATION: Medical education experts overseeing the training of young physicians are concerned that doctors do not write prescriptions accurately enough. The Department of Medical Education at a Pittsburgh research hospital decided to test this concern by conducting a study of prescriptions written by residents studying to become doctors.

They collected copies of prescriptions written by residents over a four-month period and then recorded and categorized error types, hoping to be able to find patterns that could be corrected. Error categories included omissions, ambiguities, and mistakes. (Contrary to popular belief, unreadable handwriting is rarely a problem, though the use of Latin terms, abbreviations, and unfamiliar drug names makes it seem so to patients.)

The educators used Minitab's chi-square test to determine error rates for each category. When they studied Minitab's displays, they found that most errors occurred when residents did not provide enough information to the pharmacist.

Experience seemed to be a good teacher, though; third-year residents made half as many errors as first-year residents. Studies of this kind use Minitab to show medical educators how to teach residents to be better communicators—and, at the same time, better doctors.

Compute the p-value to determine whether the chi-square statistic of 8.947 (with 6 degrees of freedom) is significant:

- Choose **C**alc ► **P**robability Distributions ► **C**hisquare...
- Press [Alt]-C for **C**umulative probability and press [Tab]
- Type **6** in the Degrees of freedom text box
- Press [Alt]-N for Input co**n**stant and press [Tab]

- Type **8.947** in the Input constant text box and press [Tab]
- Type **K1** in the Optional storage text box and press [↵]
- In the Session window, type **LET K2=1-K1** after the MTB > prompt and press [↵]
- Type **PRINT K2** and press [↵]

The Session window (Figure 10-9) shows that the p-value represented by K2 for this test is 0.176403.

FIGURE 10-9

The p-value for the chi-square statistic

```
MTB > CDF 8.947 K1;
SUBC>   Chisquare 6.
MTB > LET K2=1-K1
MTB > PRINT K2
K2        0.176403
```

On the basis of the p-value, you fail to reject H_0. Your data indicate that salary level and department are not significantly related. You see approximately the same distribution of salary ranges in each of the departments.

You would like more detail on the salary distribution. In particular, you would like the percentage of employees in each salary category. The Tables command offers subcommand options that display more information:

- Choose **S**tat ▶ **T**ables ▶ **C**ross Tabulation...
- Select C7 DEPT and C9 SALCODE for the Classification variables
- Press [Alt]-C for **C**ounts, and then press [↓] and the Space bar to select the Row percents, Column percents, and Total percents checkboxes
- Press [↵]

Each cell (shown in Figure 10-10) now contains the row percent, the column percent, and the total percent as well as the count, as described by Minitab at the bottom of the output.

FIGURE 10-10

The Session window, with percentages of employees in each salary category

```
MTB > Table 'DEPT' 'SALCODE';
SUBC>   Counts;
SUBC>   RowPercents;
SUBC>   ColPercents;
SUBC>   TotPercents.

 ROWS: DEPT      COLUMNS: SALCODE

              1         2         3       ALL

  1           6         4         0        10
          60.00     40.00        --    100.00
          37.50     22.22        --     21.74
          13.04      8.70        --     21.74

  2           2         5         1         8
          25.00     62.50     12.50    100.00
          12.50     27.78      8.33     17.39
           4.35     10.87      2.17     17.39

  3           2         2         3         7
          28.57     28.57     42.86    100.00
          12.50     11.11     25.00     15.22
           4.35      4.35      6.52     15.22

  4           6         7         8        21
          28.57     33.33     38.10    100.00
          37.50     38.89     66.67     45.65
          13.04     15.22     17.39     45.65

 ALL         16        18        12        46
          34.78     39.13     26.09    100.00
         100.00    100.00    100.00    100.00
          34.78     39.13     26.09    100.00

  CELL CONTENTS --
                    COUNT
                    % OF ROW
                    % OF COL
                    % OF TBL
```

Engineering employees earning between 23000 and 34999

Look at the cell describing employees in the engineering department (C7 DEPT=4) who earn between $23000 and $34999 (C9 SALCODE=1). There are six individuals in this category, representing 28.57% of the engineering department, and 37.50% of all employees whose salaries fall in this lowest salary category. The individuals in this cell represent 13.04% of the company's employees.

Note that the chi-square test is an option for the Cross Tabulation command. Typically, however, you would request the summary information and the test on the same command.

The Cross Tabulation command can handle more than two columns of categorical variables. If you specify more than two classification variables, Minitab forms the table from the first two columns and then performs a separate chi-square test of independence for each combination of values in the remaining columns.

In this tutorial you saw how to use the chi-square statistic to perform goodness-of-fit tests and tests for independence of variables on categorical data. In the next tutorial you will learn how to use Minitab to perform nonparametric analyses—analyses in which you make fewer assumptions about the distribution of the data.

If you plan to continue directly to the next tutorial:

- Choose **File** ▶ Restart **Minitab**

If you want to take a longer break:

- Choose **File** ▶ **Exit**

Minitab Command Summary

The menus and commands introduced in or related to this tutorial are described in this section. You will find a complete explanation of all menus and commands in the Reference section of this manual.

Menu	Command	Function
Stat		
	Tables	
	Cross Tabulation	Performs a contingency table analysis using numeric raw data, from which Minitab computes the contingency table
	Tally	Tabulates numeric raw data into counts
	Chisquare Test	Minitab command to perform a contingency table analysis using a table in the worksheet

Review and Practice

Matching

Match the following terms to their definitions by placing the correct letter next to the term it explains.

____ DF

____ Rowpercents

____ observed frequency

____ Chisquare

____ K

____ Colpercents

____ contingency table

a. A table of observed counts of a sample classified with respect to two or more criteria

b. The number of sample items with a given characteristic

c. Minitab subcommand to the Tables command to provide row percentage summaries

d. Minitab subcommand to the Tables command to provide column percentage summaries

e. Minitab subcommand to the Tables command that will generate the chi-square test of independence

f. Minitab notation for the degrees of freedom of a chi-square statistic

g. Minitab notation for a stored constant

True/False

Mark the following statements T or F.

____ 1. Chi-square goodness-of-fit tests are done in Minitab using the FIT command.

____ 2. When computing p-values for the chi-square test, intermediate results must always be stored as constants.

____ 3. If more than two columns are specified on the Cross Tabulation command, one chi-square analysis is performed for the complete table.

____ 4. Row, column, and total percents are options on both the Cross Tabulation and Tally commands.

____ 5. Alpha data columns can be used in the Cross Tabulation command, but not the Tally command.

____ 6. In the Tally command both the cell chi-square value and its standardized value can be obtained by selecting the appropriate checkboxes.

____ 7. The chi-square's p-value is provided when a chi-square test of independence is performed in both the Cross Tabulation and Tally outputs.

____ 8. The Sum function is the default function for the Column Statistics command.

____ 9. In addition to the chi-square statistic, the contribution of each cell is also printed in the Chisquare Test command.

____ 10. Marginal totals are automatically given in the Cross Tabulation command.

Practice Problems

1. Many states have lotto games. In a certain state, you pay $1 and choose six numbers between 1 and 47. If your numbers match those selected, you win. Each Friday the state publishes a summary of how many times each number has been drawn in all of the drawings. If the drawings are random, you would expect to see each number the same number of times.

   The file LOTTO.MTW from the TUT10 directory contains state lotto information. Rows 1 through 47 contain the frequency with which that number has been drawn over the past three years of a particular state's bi-weekly lotto drawing. Determine if there is any indication that the drawings are not being done randomly.

2. Use the PROF.MTW data from the TUT10 directory to determine whether the level of the class and the instructor's rating are independent. You need to code the instructor's rating variable, using the following intervals: 1:1.99, 2:2.49, 2.50:2.99, 3:3.49, and 3.50:4.00.

3. Use the RADON.MTW data set from the TUT10 directory to determine if radon levels depend on the age, amount of insulation, and proximity to a sump pump. Code the radon values as follows: 0:4.99, 5:7.50, 7.51:9.99, 10:14.99, 15:50. Note that you will need to recode some of your variables after observing your output.

TUTORIAL 11

Analyzing Data with Nonparametric Methods

Until now, the techniques you have used to make inferences about parameters have required random samples and approximately normally distributed populations. In this tutorial you will learn how to check data for randomness and how to analyze data from populations that are not necessarily normally distributed. Techniques that require less stringent assumptions about the nature of the population probability distribution are called *nonparametric* statistical methods.

Objectives

In this tutorial you will learn to:

- check a sampling process for randomness
- compare the median of a sample to a constant
- compare the medians of two populations
- compare the centers of more than two populations

Checking a Sampling Process for Randomness with the Runs Test

To use the tests shown in previous tutorials, you had to assume that the data were randomly selected. The *runs test* is a procedure that can test for randomness.

In Tutorial 7 you were introduced to the blood-clotting data; you investigated whether aspirin affects a person's blood-clotting time. The data were stored in the order in which the subjects were selected for the study. In retrospect, you wonder whether the subjects in your sample were selected randomly. You will check to determine if the observed pattern of BEFORE times can be considered random.

- Open CLTNGT11.MTW from the TUT11 directory
- Go to the Data screen to look at the data

Recall that C1 and C2 contain the number of seconds it took for blood to clot before and after taking aspirin. The twelve clotting times before aspirin (in seconds) are: 11.3, 11.0, 11.0, 11.5, 11.8, 11.3, 12.5, 13.0, 13.0, 12.0, 12.0, and 12.3. You are suspicious because the first six values are smaller than the average of the twelve observations (11.89) and the last six are larger. The selection process does not appear to be random. To determine whether you have statistical evidence of non-randomness, perform the runs test.

A run is a series of consecutive observations that fall above a specified constant (the default is the sample mean) or consecutive observations that fall on or below the specified constant. You will use Minitab to determine whether your data have too few or too many runs.

First set up the hypotheses:

H_0: The sampling process is random.
H_1: The sampling process is not random.

Use Minitab to test the null hypothesis.

- Return to the Session window
- Choose **S**tat ▶ **N**onparametrics ▶ **R**uns Test...
- Select C1 BEFORE for the Variables text box

The completed Runs Test dialog box should look like Figure 11-1.

FIGURE 11-1

The completed Runs Test dialog box from the Nonparametrics submenu

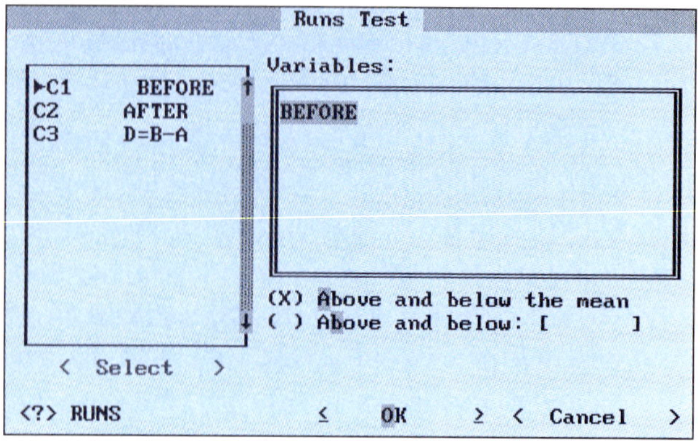

- Press Alt-O

The Session window (Figure 11-2) contains the results.

FIGURE 11-2

The Session window, showing the results of the runs test

```
MTB > Runs 'BEFORE'.

   BEFORE

   K =      11.8917

   THE OBSERVED NO. OF RUNS =    2
   THE EXPECTED NO. OF RUNS =    7.0000
    6 OBSERVATIONS ABOVE K     6 BELOW
 * N SMALL--FOLLOWING APPROX. MAY BE INVALID
             THE TEST IS SIGNIFICANT AT  0.0025
```

The constant Minitab used was the sample mean, K = 11.8917; there were two observed runs. You can verify this from the raw data. When there are too many or too few runs, the sample is in non-random order.

Minitab calculates that the expected number of runs, assuming a random sample, is 7; it displays the number of observations above and below the constant. The p-value for this test is 0.0025, so reject H_0 at the 0.05 level. Minitab warns you that, because the sample size is small, you should consider your results as approximate. Nonetheless, the p-value is sufficiently small to convince you that the subjects for your study may not have been randomly selected. Your results in Tutorial 7 should be viewed with caution.

- Choose **F**ile ▶ Restart **M**initab

Testing the Population Median

In Tutorial 6 you used a t-test and constructed a confidence interval to make inferences about the value of a population mean under the assumption that the populations were nearly normal. Minitab offers two nonparametric techniques (the Sign and Wilcoxon tests) that test the central tendency of a population that is not necessarily normal.

To illustrate one of these nonparametric tests, you will use the yearly sales data in SALES.MTW.

- Open SALES.MTW from the TUT11 directory
- Go to the Data screen

Because management was concerned that sales had fallen off from previous levels of approximately 4000 per day, test whether the 1991 median daily sales is less than 4000. First, form the hypotheses:

$$H_0\text{: Median} = 4000.$$
$$H_1\text{: Median} < 4000.$$

The Data screen shows that six of the seven data values in 1991 were below and one was above the null hypothesis median. Is this significant evidence? Perform the Wilcoxon test:

- Return to the Session window
- Choose **S**tat ▶ **N**onparametrics ▶ 1-Sample **W**ilcoxon...
- Select C1 1991 for the Variables text box
- Press [Alt]-T for **T**est median and press [Tab]
- Type **4000** in the Test median text box and press [Tab]
- Press [↑] to choose the less than option from the Alternative pop-up menu

The completed 1-Sample Wilcoxon dialog box should look like Figure 11-3.

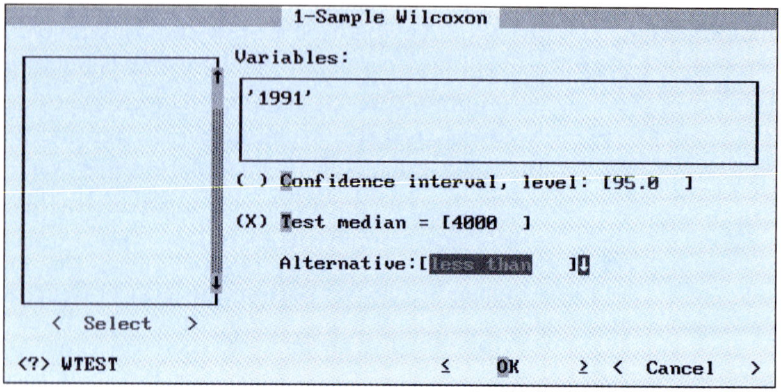

FIGURE 11-3
The completed 1-Sample Wilcoxon dialog box from the Nonparametrics submenu

- Press [↵]

The results of the test appear in the Session window (Figure 11-4).

FIGURE 11-4
The Session window, showing results of the Wilcoxon test

```
MTB > WTest 4000 '1991';
SUBC>   Alternative -1.

TEST OF MEDIAN = 4000 VERSUS MEDIAN L.T. 4000

                 N FOR   WILCOXON              ESTIMATED
             N    TEST  STATISTIC   P-VALUE       MEDIAN
1991         7       7        1.0     0.017         2112
```

The p-value for this test is 0.017. The estimated median of 2112 suggests that 1991 sales have indeed fallen from previous levels. Note that the median of the seven observations is 2080; 2112 is the median of the Walsh averages (pairwise averages of all pairs of data points).

Some statisticians maintain that if parametric and nonparametric procedures yield the same results, then the assumptions underlying the parametric procedures are reasonable. This provides a quick method for "checking" the validity of assumptions in parametric analyses.

Minitab can form a confidence interval for the median, just as it did for the mean.

- Choose **E**dit ▶ Edit **L**ast Command Dialog...
- Press [Alt]-C for **C**onfidence interval
- Press [↵]

Minitab displays the 94.8% confidence interval for the median (1198, 3877), as shown in Figure 11-5.

FIGURE 11-5
The nonparametric confidence interval

```
MTB > WInterval 95.0 '1991'.

                  ESTIMATED    ACHIEVED
              N      MEDIAN  CONFIDENCE  CONFIDENCE INTERVAL
1991          7        2112        94.8  (     1198,     3877)
```

In many nonparametric procedures, the degree of confidence generated will not be exactly what you requested; here Minitab achieved a 94.8% level confidence interval. It would appear that median daily sales have fallen from at least $123 to as much as $2802 below the previous year's sales of $4000. Is it time to start looking for a new job?

- Choose **File ▶ Restart Minitab**

Comparing the Medians of Two Populations

In Tutorial 7 you learned to perform t-tests for the equality of two population means, assuming normality. The Mann-Whitney (Wilcoxon) procedure is a nonparametric counterpart of the 2-sample t-test. It uses a 2-sample rank test to compare two population medians; it can compute the corresponding point and confidence interval estimates of the difference between these medians.

Case Study: Banking

In your finance course, you are researching banking industry profits for 1991. You want to determine if there has been a change from 1990. The file BANKING.MTW contains data from FDIC research on first-quarter bank profits (in billions of dollars) for 1991 and 1990. Ten states' (not necessarily the same ten states) first-quarter profits were selected each year.

- Open BANKING.MTW from the TUT11 directory
- Go to the Data screen

MINITAB AT WORK

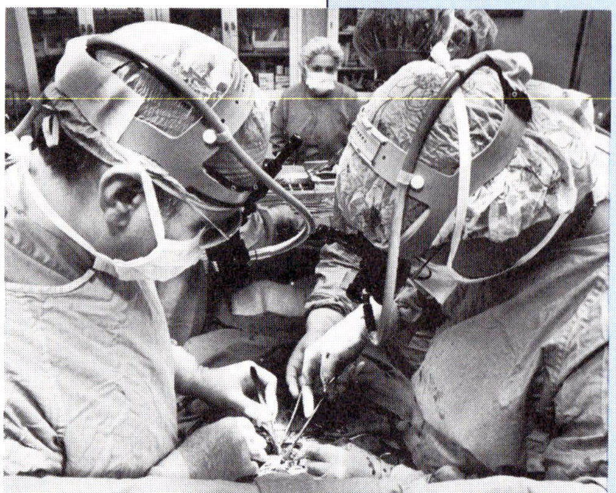

MEDICAL DIAGNOSTICS: Although most of us associate heart failure with older people, it can affect children and infants when the main artery of the heart, the aorta, becomes obstructed and blood cannot flow freely. Doctors treat these blockages by inserting small balloons into the constricted aorta and inflating them to clear the obstruction.

A pediatrician at a midwestern university hospital used the balloon treatment on 30 children, ages 14 days to 13 years, who had obstructed aortas. He monitored their recovery carefully to see what factors would predict whether the operation was a success. One factor the pediatrician used was the measurement of aorta diameter at five points. In a normal aortic valve, the diameters at all five locations would be the same, and the variance in diameter measurements would be zero.

The pediatrician used Minitab's Mann-Whitney test to compare diameter variances of two groups of patients: those who eventually required a second balloon treatment and those who did not. The results indicated that the children who would completely recover showed a greater decline in diameter variance than those who would require more surgery. This result gave the pediatrician another diagnostic tool to predict whether more treatment would be needed at a later date for a particular patient. Being able to predict patients' future needs enables doctors to better treat them in the present.

Because the population (the 50 states) does not have an infinite (or even reasonably large) number of values, you decide that it is probably not normal. You will use the Mann-Whitney nonparametric procedure.

Formulate the hypotheses:

H_0: The median bank profits for 1991 and 1990 are equal.
H_1: The median profits for 1991 are less than the median profits for 1990 for these states.

To perform the test:

- Return to the Session window
- Choose **S**tat ▶ **N**onparametrics ▶ **M**ann-Whitney...
- Select C1 1991 for the First Sample
- Select C2 1990 for the Second Sample and press [Tab]
- Press [↑] to choose the less than option from the Alternative pop-up menu (the median of the first sample C1 1991 is less than the median of the second sample C2 1990)

The completed Mann-Whitney dialog box should look like Figure 11-6.

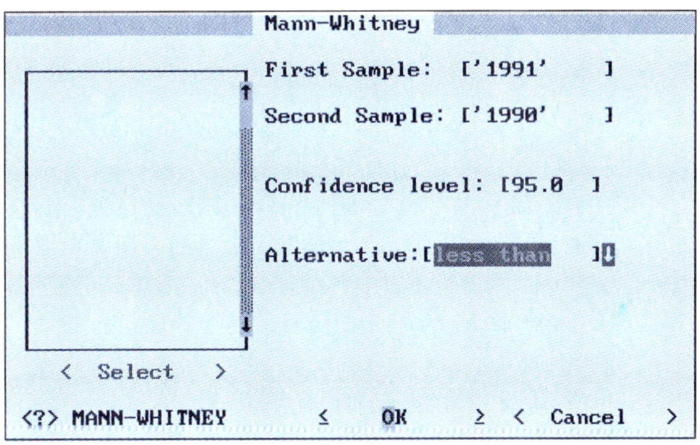

FIGURE 11-6
The completed Mann-Whitney dialog box from the Nonparametrics submenu

- Press [↵]

The results of the test appear in the Session window (Figure 11-7).

FIGURE 11-7
Results of the Mann-Whitney test

```
MTB > Mann-Whitney 95.0 '1991' '1990';
SUBC>   Alternative -1.

Mann-Whitney Confidence Interval and Test

1991        N =  10      Median =        309.5
1990        N =  10      Median =        343.0
Point estimate for ETA1-ETA2 is         -24.0
95.5 pct c.i. for ETA1-ETA2 is (-184.1,109.8)
W = 99.0
Test of ETA1 = ETA2  vs.  ETA1 l.t. ETA2 is significant at 0.3388
The test is significant at 0.3387 (adjusted for ties)

Cannot reject at alpha = 0.05
```

Minitab first lists medians for each of the years and then gives the point estimate for the difference (ETA1 – ETA2 = –24.0 billion!). The 95.5% confidence interval for the difference in population medians is from –184.1 to 109.8. Minitab reports the test statistic of 99.0 and a p-value of 0.3388, so you cannot reject H_0 at the 0.05 level. Conclude that there has been no change in median profit from the first quarter of 1990 to that of 1991. Relieved, you decide to leave the money you earned last summer in your local branch of the Fly-By-Night International Bank.

- Choose **F**ile ▶ Restart **M**initab

Comparing the Centers of K Populations

In Tutorial 8, you used analysis of variance to compare the means of more than two populations. To perform ANOVA, you had to assume parametric normality for each population. The Kruskal-Wallis H-test is a nonparametric counterpart of ANOVA. It is a generalization of the Mann-Whitney (Wilcoxon) test.

You will run a Kruskal-Wallis test on the data in FLEXIBLE.MTW to test whether there is a difference among the diameters of the wires manufactured in the three production shifts.

- Open FLXBLT11.MTW from the TUT11 directory
- Go to the Data screen

When you analyzed this data using ANOVA in Tutorial 8, you found that there is significant evidence (p = 0.019) that the three shifts produced different mean diameters of copper wire. You will re-analyze this data using the nonparametric analysis of variance procedure; if you obtain similar results, you can be more confident that your assumptions for the parametric procedure were correct.

To use the Kruskal-Wallis procedure, the samples must be random and independent, with five or more measurements from each. You must list the data in one column (called the Response) and the subscripts in a second column (called the Factor). The data in C1 do not satisfy the conditions of the test, since there are only three measures from shift 3. Accordingly, Minitab warns you that one of your samples is small, so you should consider your results approximate.

To perform the Kruskal-Wallis test:

- Return to the Session window
- Choose **S**tat ▶ **N**onparametrics ▶ **K**ruskal-Wallis...
- Select C1 DIAMETER as the Response
- Select C2 SHIFT as the Factor

The completed Kruskal-Wallis dialog box should look like Figure 11-8.

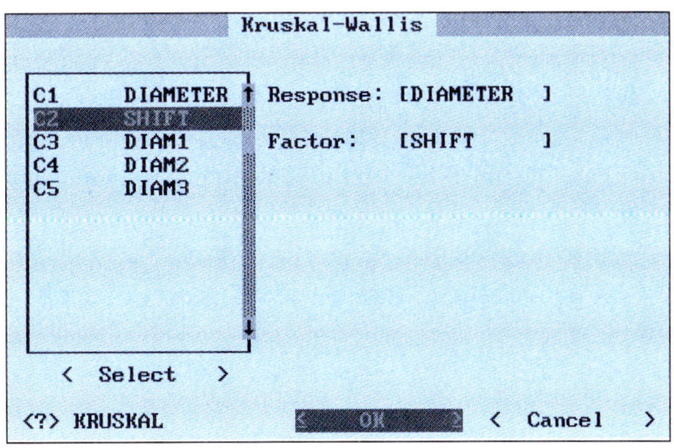

FIGURE 11-8
The completed Kruskal-Wallis dialog box from the Nonparametrics submenu

- Press [↵]

The Session window shows the results of the test (Figure 11-9).

FIGURE 11-9
Results of the Kruskal-Wallis test

```
MTB > Kruskal-Wallis 'DIAMETER' 'SHIFT'.

LEVEL     NOBS    MEDIAN  AVE. RANK   Z VALUE
    1        9     74.00        9.3     -0.18
    2        6     66.50        6.7     -1.59
    3        3     84.00       15.8      2.25
OVERALL     18                  9.5

H = 5.93  d.f. = 2  p = 0.052
H = 5.95  d.f. = 2  p = 0.052 (adj. for ties)

* NOTE  * One or more small samples
```

Minitab first reports summary statistics for each shift. The median diameter is highest for shift 3 (84.00 microinches) and smallest for shift 2 (66.50). The Kruskal-Wallis H value is 5.93, with a p-value of 0.052. (The Kruskal-Wallis H value, adjusted for ties in the sample, and the corresponding p-value are also given.) You conclude that there is significant evidence that the median diameter of copper wires is different for the three shifts. You might suggest that management implement a quality-control program.

This p-value is similar to the result you obtained earlier using parametric ANOVA techniques; you can infer that your previous assumptions were not seriously violated.

In this tutorial you learned to use nonparametric procedures that correspond to parametric procedures seen in Tutorials 6, 7, and 8. Nonparametric techniques test hypotheses on the median of a single population or compare medians of more than one population; they are useful when the underlying assumption of normality is not justified. Using ranked and sorted data, pairwise averages, differences, slopes, and other Minitab commands, you can perform many other nonparametric inference procedures, such as the Spearman's rank correlation.

In the next tutorial you will see how Minitab can be used in a quality control setting to monitor the output of a production process. You will also see the runs test applied to data collected over time.

If you plan to continue directly to the next tutorial:

- Choose **F**ile ► Restart **M**initab

If you want to take a longer break:

- Choose **File ▶ Exit**

Minitab Command Summary

The menus and commands introduced in or related to this tutorial are described in this section. You will find a complete explanation of all menus and commands in the Reference section of this manual.

Menu	Command	Function
Stat		
	Nonparametrics	
	1-Sample Sign	Performs a nonparametric one-sample Sign inference (test or confidence interval) on a median
	1-Sample Wilcoxon	Performs a nonparametric Wilcoxon one-sample inference (test or confidence interval) on a median
	Mann-Whitney	Performs a two-sample nonparametric inference (test or confidence interval) on two medians
	Kruskal-Wallis	Minitab command to perform a nonparametric comparison of more than two medians
	Runs Test	Performs a test to evaluate random order of data
	Pairwise Averages	Computes Walsh averages; computes the average of each pair of data points in a column, including each value with itself
	Pairwise Differences	Computes the difference between all possible pairs of data values in two columns
	Pairwise Slopes	Computes the slopes using each pair of data values in two columns

Review and Practice

Matching

Match the following terms to their definitions by placing the correct letter next to the term it explains.

____ H

____ ETA1–ETA2

____ nonparametric

____ K

____ estimated median

____ run

____ Factor

____ Response

a. A series of Minitab statistical techniques that do not assume the population(s) possess any particular distributional form

b. Minitab notation for the difference between two population medians

c. A sequence of observations all sharing a similar characteristic

d. Minitab notation for the column in which the data are stored for the Kruskal-Wallis command

e. Minitab notation for the test statistic from the Kruskal-Wallis test

f. Minitab notation for the constant that is used in the runs test to identify a run

g. Minitab name for the median estimated using the median value of all pairwise averages of data values

h. Minitab dialog box notation for the subscript column used in the Kruskal-Wallis command

True/False

Mark the following statements T or F.

____ 1. The Runs Test command requires numeric data since a run is determined by comparing a data value to a number.

____ 2. Confidence intervals corresponding to exact levels of confidence can always be obtained using Minitab nonparametric commands.

____ 3. Only two-tailed tests can be performed using Minitab nonparametric tests.

____ 4. The Runs Test command allows you to input any number to define runs.

____ 5. Confidence intervals are part of the default output of the Wilcoxon command.

____ 6. The Kruskal-Wallis command requires that the data be in one column and a subscript identifier in another column.

____ 7. The default null hypothesis value for the median in the Wilcoxon command is zero.

____ 8. The sample median is the default value used to identify runs in the Runs Test command.

____ 9. The Mann-Whitney command assumes that the two samples of data are stored in different columns.

____ 10. The desired confidence level can be specified as any value in the Wilcoxon command.

Practice Problems

1. Open SNOWFALL.MTW from the TUT11 directory. Perform a runs test on the snowfall data. Recall that the data were presented in chronological order. Based on your results, can the residents claim that it has been snowing less in recent years?

2. Open the GRADES.MTW data from the TUT11 directory. Use nonparametric tests to answer the following:

   a. Is the median score different from 75% on the three exams?

   b. Did the class perform the same on exams 2 and 3?

   c. Determine whether the class's median score was different on the three exams. (Hint: You will need to stack the exam data in one column *and* save the subscripts in another.)

3. In Tutorial 1 you studied the TV viewing times of ten married couples. Open TVVIEW.MTW from the TUT11 directory.

   a. Compare the median TV viewing times of husbands and wives.

b. Use the difference in TV viewing times to determine if the median difference is non-zero.

c. What can you conclude about the TV viewing habits of husbands and wives?

4. The file VPVH.MTW from the TUT11 directory contains data about the TV viewing habits of various age/gender groups for various kinds of entertainment. Refer to the data set descriptions in Part III for details on this data set. Compare the median viewers per viewing households for the four groups for each of the program types. Summarize your findings.

TUTORIAL 12

Statistical Process Control

There is natural variability in any set of measurements. Statistical process control (SPC) is used in industry to monitor a process and to achieve a high level of quality by meeting certain specifications. In this tutorial, you return to the role of quality manager at Flexible Circuits, Inc.; you will to learn how to construct and interpret various types of SPC graphs in Minitab.

Objectives

In this tutorial you will learn to:

- construct an $\overline{X}$ chart to monitor the mean of a process
- construct a range chart to monitor variability in a process
- construct an individuals chart to monitor individual observations from a process
- construct a proportion chart that will monitor the proportion of defective wires produced

Recall from Tutorial 8 that Flexible Circuits, Inc. designs and manufactures parts for electronics equipment. Your company's engineers have specified that the copper-plated wires be 70 ± 3 microinches in diameter to fit into the electronic equipment for which they are manufactured. Recently, however, many of the wires, which are copper-plated in a microetch process, have been out of specification. You will use SPC in an attempt to investigate this problem.

First you will determine whether the process is "in control"—that is, whether the mean and variability of the process are stable and any variation in the process is due to random causes. Suspecting a problem, you have sampled five consecutive wires (subgroups of size 5) each hour for 21 consecutive hours, measured their diameters in microinches, and placed the results in C1 DIAMETER of FLEX2.MTW.

- Open FLEX2.MTW from the TUT12 directory

Constructing an Xbar Chart

To determine whether the mean of the copper-plating microetching process is "in control," you will produce an $\overline{X}$ chart to look at the 21 sample means:

- Choose **Stat ▸ SPC Charts ▸ Xbar...**
- Select C1 DIAMETER for the Variables text box and press [Tab] twice
- Type **5** in the Subgroup size text box

Minitab can perform eight different tests to determine if there are any extreme observations, any unusual sequences, or runs in the data. To have Minitab perform these eight Tests For Special Causes:

- Press [Alt]-G for All eight

The completed Xbar Chart dialog box should resemble Figure 12-1.

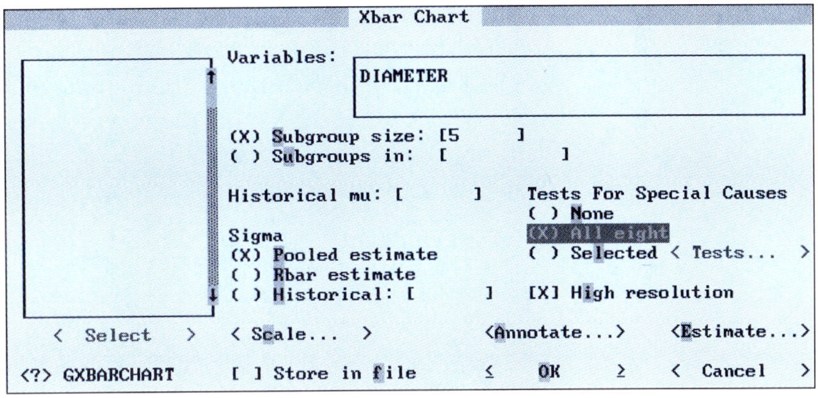

FIGURE 12-1
The completed Xbar Chart dialog box from the SPC Charts submenu

- Press ↵

Minitab computes the 21 sample means (using subgroups of size 5) and plots them on the $\overline{X}$ chart that appears in a graph screen (Figure 12-2).

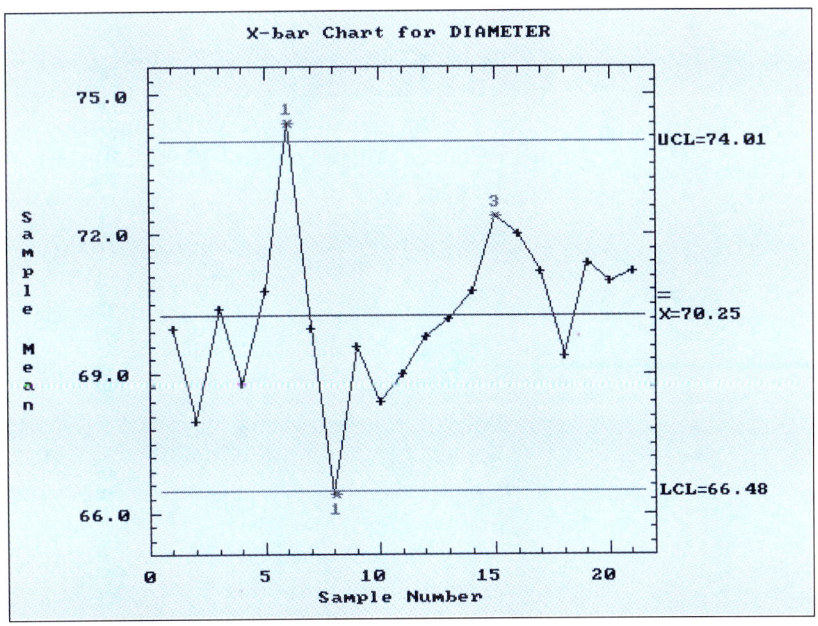

FIGURE 12-2
X-bar chart for DIAMETER

Minitab marks the center line at 70.25. It also places the upper-control-limit (UCL) line at 74.01 and a lower-control-limit (LCL) line at 66.48. Each of these limits is three standard deviations from the mean. The $\overline{X}$ chart shows that the process is out of control, because there are two points that have failed Test 1 and one that has failed Test 3. To view the details of these results:

- Press Q for Quit

The Session window should look like Figure 12-3.

FIGURE 12-3

The Session window, showing results of test failures

```
MTB > GXbarChart 'DIAMETER' 5;
SUBC>   Test 1:8.
Test results for chart of DIAMETER

TEST 1. One point beyond zone A.
Test Failed at points: 6 8

TEST 3. Six points in a row all increasing or all decreasing.
Test Failed at points: 15
```

Minitab reports that Test 1 failed at points 6 and 8; these sample averages fell beyond the control limits. Test 3 failed at point 15, where Minitab found an unusual run of six points in a row where values were all increasing. Unusual runs might indicate that the process is drifting away from the target value of 70 microinches. To take a second look at the $\overline{X}$ chart:

- Choose **E**dit ▶ Edit **L**ast Command Dialog...
- Press Alt-O

The copper-plating process appears to vary widely. The $\overline{X}$ chart shows that the sixth sample average was more than three standard deviations *above* the overall average of 70.25. Two samples later, it was three standard deviations *below* this average. You suspect that one of the foremen may have observed the large average at hour 6 and adjusted the process downward—but perhaps too far down.

The six increasing values Minitab noted in the Session window appear immediately after this low point. Perhaps the same person noted the extremely small diameters and adjusted the process upward. However, this time it appears that the change was less extreme. In any case, there may be some external source of variation in the plating process.

- Press Q for Quit

Constructing a Range Chart

The variability of any process should also be investigated because process variability determines the control limits for the process mean. To determine if the variability of the process is stable and random, you will investigate the spread in your samples. You have the option of using the sample range (R) or sample standard deviation (S) in Minitab (R charts and S charts, respectively). For small samples such as this, the R chart is appropriate.

To obtain the chart for your data:

- Choose **Stat** ▶ SP**C** Charts ▶ **R**...
- Select C1 DIAMETER for the Variables text box and press Tab twice
- Type **5** in the Subgroup size text box

The completed R Chart dialog box should resemble Figure 12-4.

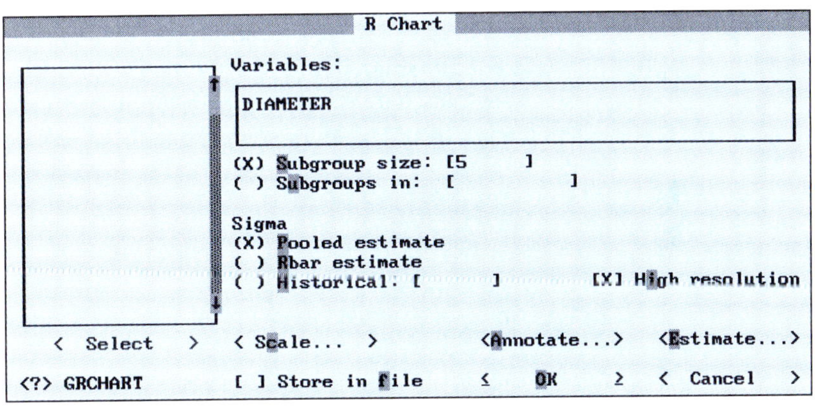

FIGURE 12-4
The completed R Chart dialog box from the SPC Charts submenu

- Press ↵

Minitab computes the range of each of the 21 groups of five samples, then plots them on the chart (Figure 12-5).

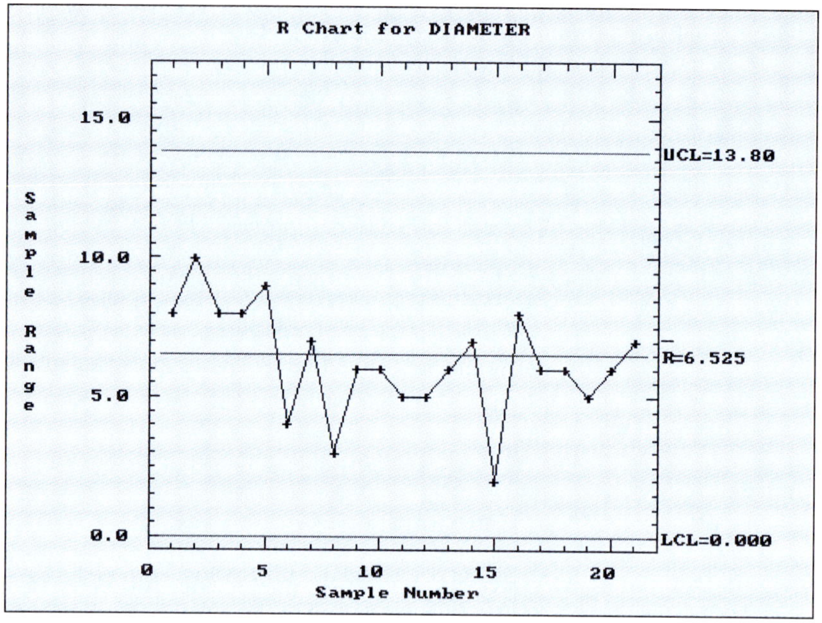

FIGURE 12-5
The R chart for DIAMETER

Minitab draws the center line at 6.525 (the average of the sample ranges); it draws the lower and upper control limits at 0.000 and 13.80, respectively. The R chart indicates that process variability is not out of control. The observed variation in the range of the wire diameters appears to be random.

You conclude that the copper-plating process is prone to large changes in the mean or center, but that it does produce consistent thicknesses. You recommend that management meet with the process personnel to determine the source of the variability seen in the $\overline{X}$ chart. Perhaps together they can identify the cause and avoid the problem in the future.

- Press Q for Quit

Constructing an Individuals Chart

Your initial analysis of the copper-plating process has piqued your interest. Perhaps you can isolate why the mean wire thickness process went out of control. In addition, the production engineer would like to know what fraction of the production is within the specification limits of 70 ± 3 microinches. To investigate this, you will analyze each wire individually using an individuals chart. Specify the control limits (70 + 3 = 73 and 70 − 3 = 67), the center line (historical mu = 70) and the process variability $\sigma = 1$. (Note that for individual values the control limits are determined by center line $\pm 3 * \sigma$. Since $3 * \sigma = 3$, $\sigma = 1$.)

To obtain the individuals chart:

- Choose **Stat** ▶ SPC Charts ▶ **I**ndividuals...
- Select C1 DIAMETER for the Variables text box and press Tab
- Type **70** in the Historical mu text box
- Press Alt-H for **H**istorical under Sigma and press Tab
- Type **1** in the Historical text box

The completed Individuals Chart dialog box should resemble Figure 12-6.

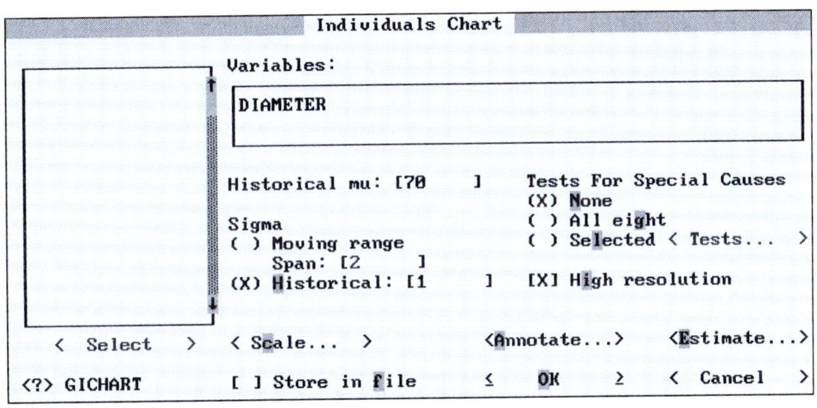

FIGURE 12-6
The completed Individuals Chart dialog box from the SPC Charts submenu

- Press ↵

The I (individuals) chart appears in its own graph screen (Figure 12-7).

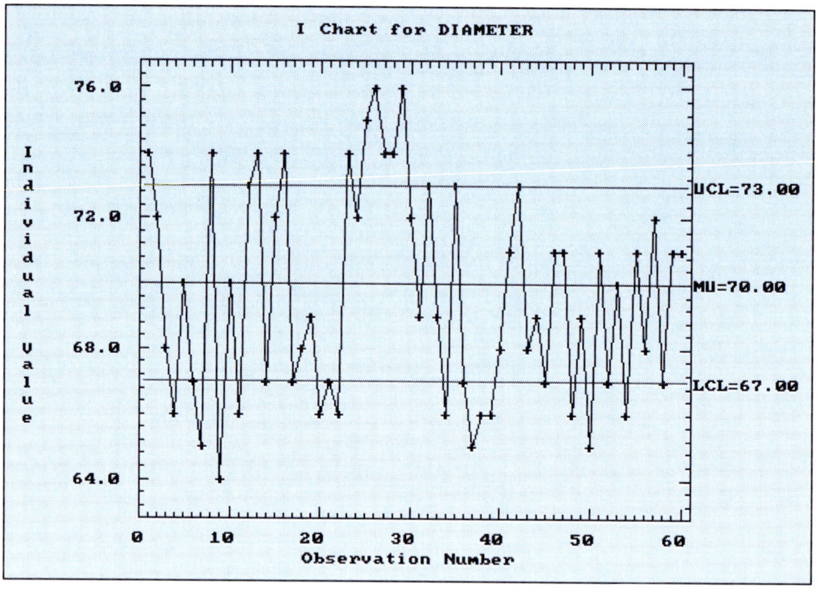

FIGURE 12-7
The I chart for DIAMETER, showing the first 60 observations

Notice that only the first 60 observations are included in this individuals chart. In a data set this large, not all observations appear at the same time; the remaining 45 appear on a second chart, which you will examine next.

Recall that the data in C1 DIAMETER represent consecutive hours of the day, with five consecutive observations per hour. Hence, observations 1 to 40 were produced during the first shift, 41 to 80 during the second shift, and 81 to 105 during the third shift. Analysis of the graph is revealing. There would appear to be quite a problem on the first shift. Ten of the forty wires (25%) are too thick and ten are too narrow; 50% are not usable in the electronic equipment. The production engineer has a major problem to address.

To investigate the second shift, look at both this chart and the next (Figure 12-8):

- Press N for Next

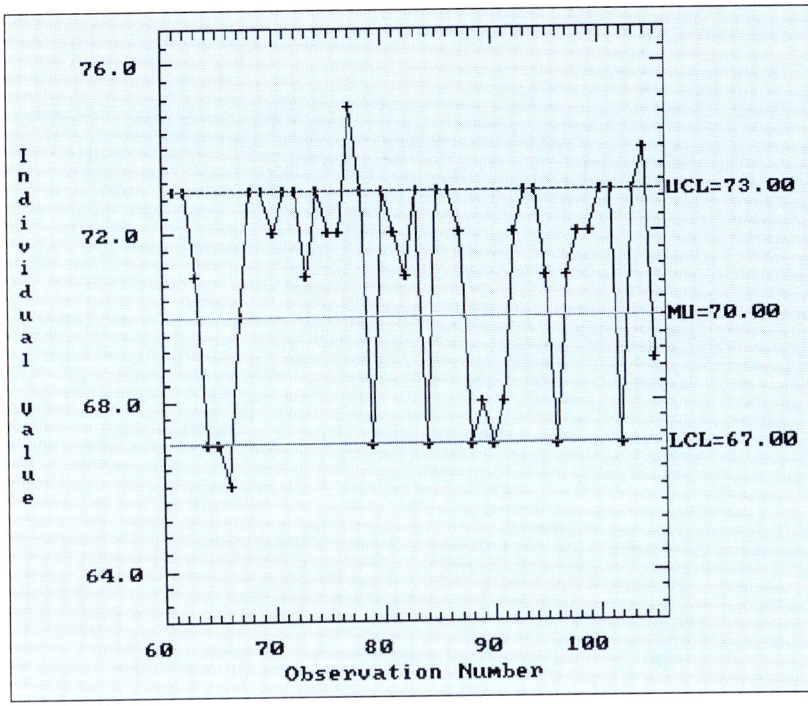

FIGURE 12-8
The I chart for DIAMETER, showing the remaining 45 observations

Quality is somewhat better on the second shift (observations 41 to 80). Only 5/40, or 12.5%, defective wires were produced on the second shift. This is still unacceptable, however.

For the third shift (observations 81 to 105), only one defect out of 25 (just 4%!) was found in the sample. You should investigate the third shift to discover what they are doing right.

You also note that near the end of each of the first two shifts the wire thicknesses tended to increase. You didn't see this pattern for the third shift, but you only monitored the first five hours of that shift. Perhaps after running an entire shift, the machinery overheats and deposits too much copper on the wires? To pursue the matter further, you will review your results with production personnel to pinpoint the cause for this increase. You might also design an experiment to evaluate potential causes for this increase in wire thickness.

- Press Q for Quit

Constructing a Moving Range Chart

Several days after meeting with plant personnel to address the results of your initial analysis, you resample the data and systematically select one wire every twelve minutes from each shift during one day's production (for a total of 40 observations per shift). You store the data in C2 SHIFT 1, C3 SHIFT 2, and C4 SHIFT 3.

In your first investigation you selected five consecutive wires. Now you have selected only one wire; with only one unit in your sample you cannot estimate process variability using only one sample. Instead, you use the moving range—the range of two or more consecutive observations—to investigate the variability of the process during the third shift:

- Choose **S**tat ▶ SP**C** Charts ▶ **M**oving Range...
- Select C4 SHIFT 3 for the Variables text box

The completed Moving Range Chart dialog box should resemble Figure 12-9.

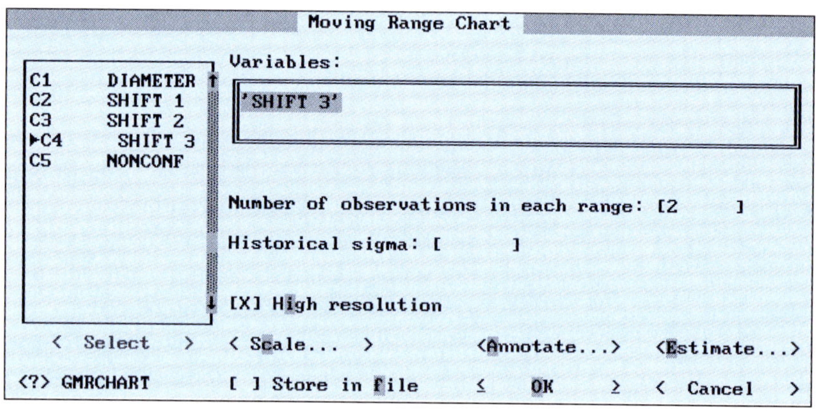

FIGURE 12-9
The completed Moving Range Chart dialog box from the SPC Charts submenu

- Press Alt-O

The moving range chart appears in a separate graph screen (Figure 12-10).

FIGURE 12-10

The moving range chart for SHIFT 3

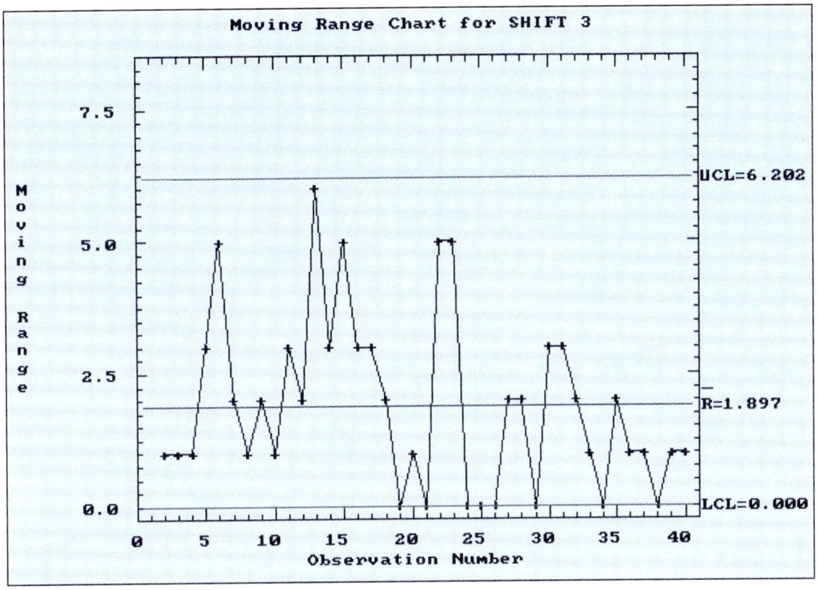

Process variability is in control, at least for the third shift. None of the moving ranges of size two exceed the control limits. You conclude that the variability in wire diameters observed in your sample can be attributed to random or natural variation alone.

To pursue the matter further, you would need to investigate process variability during the other two shifts, as well as their process mean, by using moving averages. You will perform these additional analyses in the practice problems at the end of this tutorial.

- Press Q for Quit

Constructing a Proportion Chart

Several weeks after instituting new production procedures for the copper-plating process, the production engineer asks you to formally investigate product quality by studying the proportion of defective wires. You both hope the new procedure has reduced the proportion of defective wires to about 2%.

To help you in your investigation, you randomly sample 200 wires per day for a whole month. You enter the results (the number of wires from the daily sample that do not meet the specifications—i.e., the nonconforming wires) in C5 NONCONF. In SPC jargon, this is known as *attribute data* since each wire is classified as defective or not defective. Contrast this type of data to that seen earlier—the measured diameter of the wire—which is called *variables data.*

To analyze attribute data, use P (proportion) charts:

- Choose **Stat** ► SPC Charts ► **P...**
- Select C5 NONCONF for the Variables text box and press [Tab] twice
- Type **200** for the Subgroup size text box and press [Tab]
- Type **0.02** in the Historical p text box (this is the production engineer's goal)

The completed P Chart dialog box should resemble Figure 12-11.

FIGURE 12-11

The completed P Chart dialog box from the SPC Charts submenu

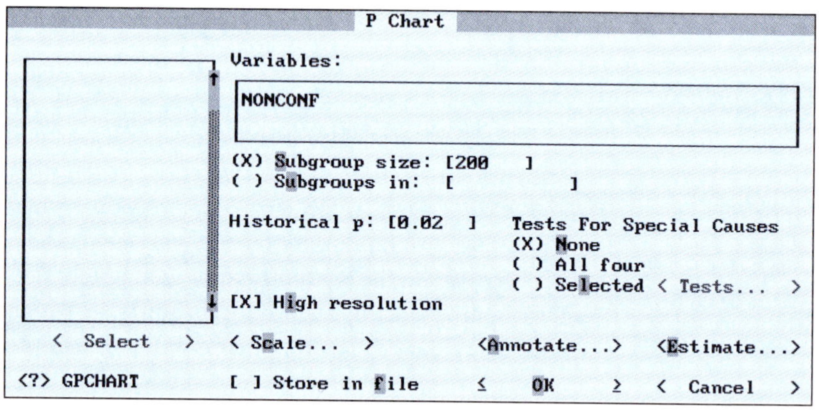

- Press [↵]

The P chart appears in its own graph screen (Figure 12-12).

FIGURE 12-12
The P chart for NONCONF

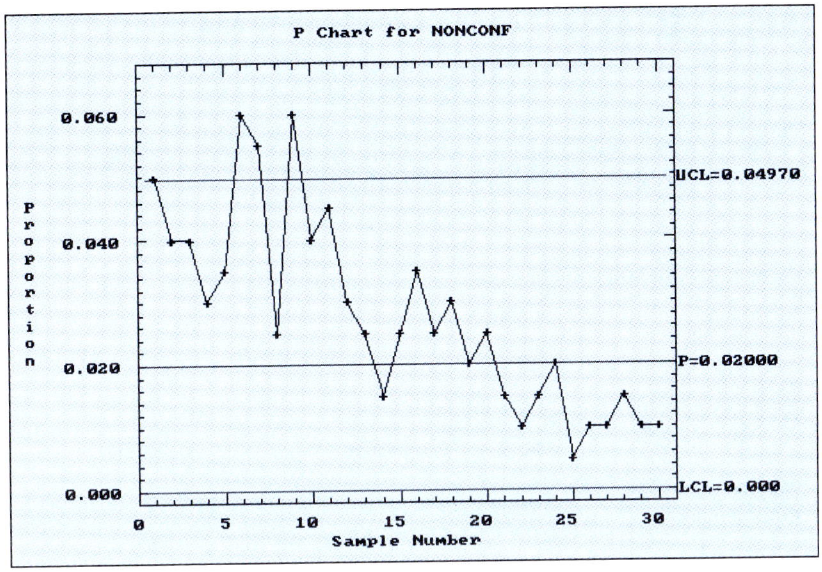

In the first third of the month there were four samples above the upper control limit. From there on, the proportion of defective wires steadily declined and appeared to level off at around 1.5%. You reason that the plating process personnel simply needed some time to adjust to the new procedures. Once they adjusted, the product quality improved substantially; now the process is operating in an acceptable manner. To ensure continued stability, you recommend that SPC charts be used routinely to monitor the process on an ongoing basis. If the process goes "out of control," the problem can be addressed quickly.

- Press Q for Quit

You have seen only a small part of Minitab's SPC capabilities. Minitab can also chart standard deviations, moving averages, numbers of defects (instead of the proportion of defective wires), and numbers of defects per unit—all methods that are used routinely in the monitoring and analysis of a process.

In the next tutorial you will learn how to use Minitab to analyze and forecast trends in time series data.

If you plan to continue directly to the next tutorial:

- Choose **File** ▶ **Restart Minitab**

If you want to take a longer break:

- Choose **File** ▶ **Exit**

Minitab Command Summary

The menus and commands introduced in or related to this tutorial are described in this section. You will find a complete explanation of all menus and commands in the Reference section of this manual.

Menu	Command	Function
Stat		
	SPC Charts	
	Xbar	Constructs an $\overline{X}$ chart for variables data stored in a column
	R	Constructs a range chart using the variables data in a column
	S	Constructs a standard deviation chart using the variables data in a column
	Individuals	Constructs an individuals chart using the variables data in a column
	Moving Range	Constructs a moving range chart
	EWMA	Constructs an exponentially weighted moving average chart
	Moving Average	Constructs a moving average chart
	P	Constructs a proportions defective chart using attribute data stored in a column
	NP	Constructs a number defective chart using attribute data stored in a column
	C	Constructs a number of defects per unit using attribute data stored in a column for constant sample size

U	Constructs a number of defects per unit using attribute data stored in a column for varying sample sizes

Review and Practice

Matching

Match the following terms to their definitions by placing the correct letter next to the term it explains.

____ Number of observations in each range

____ Individuals

____ Sigma historical

____ Historical mu

____ Subgroup size

____ Tests For Special Causes

a. Fixes the center line at a specified value in an $\overline{X}$ chart

b. Fixes the variability value in a SPC chart at a specified value

c. Requests all or a selected subset of tests that check for nonrandom occurrences be performed on SPC data

d. Allows the user to specify the size of the samples in SPC charts

e. Determines the number of consecutive observations used in computing a moving range

f. Refers to variables data consisting of samples of size one

True/False

Mark the following statements T or F.

____ 1. The control limits and center line can be directly specified in Minitab's SPC commands.

____ 2. SPC charts can either be high-resolution or character-based displays.

____ 3. Minitab can fit up to 120 points on a single SPC chart.

____ 4. There are nine special-cause tests that can be performed in the Xbar command.

____ 5. There are four Tests For Special Causes in the P chart command.

____ 6. Multiple columns can be specified in the Xbar Chart command.

____ 7. The default number of values used in computing the moving range is 2.

____ 8. Details of the special-cause tests are included in the graph screen along with the chart.

____ 9. The Subgroup Size subcommand is required in all of Minitab's SPC commands.

____ 10. Special-cause tests can be requested in the Moving Range command.

Practice Problems

1. Use the data in FLEX2.MTW from the TUT12 directory to complete the SPC analysis of the data from shifts 1 through 3. Specifically:

   a. Investigate the variability in the copper-plating process on shifts 2 and 3. You have already found that process variability is in control during shift 3. Can the same be said of shifts 1 and 2?

   b. Investigate the process mean by obtaining the moving average of the data from shifts 1, 2, and 3. Use a moving average of size three. Is the process mean in control for all three shifts?

2. In the illustration of proportion charts (P charts) given in this tutorial, you used the production engineer's goal of 2% defective to determine the center line and control limits. Redo the analysis letting Minitab use the sample proportion to compute the center line and control limits. Can you explain why your results differ?

TUTORIAL 13

Time Series Analysis

In Tutorial 9 you used regression analysis first to determine a suitable model and then to predict a response variable from one or more predictor variables. When data are obtained from observations over equally spaced intervals of time, Minitab can help you determine an appropriate model that describes the observed time series and then use that model to predict or forecast future values of the series.

Objectives

In this tutorial you will learn to:

- construct a time series plot
- use the autocorrelation and partial autocorrelation plots to identify a model
- transform a time series
- use Box-Jenkins autoregressive integrated moving average (ARIMA) techniques to model and forecast a time series

Case Study: Environment

During the summer of 1988, one of the hottest on record in the Midwest, a graduate student in environmental science studied the impact of an electric generating plant along a river for the state Environmental Protection Agency. The EPA worried that the plant's use of river water for cooling was raising the temperature of the water and endangering the aquatic habitants that lived there. They established a site directly downstream from the cooling discharge outlets of the plant, where they measured the water temperature hourly for 95 consecutive hours. You are now working for the EPA on this project and will use time series methods to analyze the problem.

You will perform the time series analysis in four phases:

Phase I: Investigate the autocorrelation and partial autocorrelation structure of the time series to determine an appropriate model.

Phase II: Transform the data (if necessary) using lags and differences to obtain a stationary time series.

Phase III: Fit an adequate ARIMA Box-Jenkins model.

Phase IV: Apply the model to forecast future values.

- Open RIVER3.MTW from the TUT13 directory
- Go to the Data worksheet to look at the data

C1 HOUR lists the time of day (in military format) for each measurement; C2 TEMP gives the temperature measurement in °C. The other columns in RIVER3.MTW contain other measurements, which will be used in the practice problems at the end of this tutorial. (See the data set description for this file in Part III for more details on these measurements.)

Plotting a Time Series

To begin your study, construct a time series plot to get a picture of the temperature data over the time period:

- Return to the Session window

- Choose **Stat** ▶ Time **S**eries ▶ **T**ime Series Plot...
- Select C2 TEMP for the Series text box
- Press Alt-P for **P**eriod and press Tab
- Type **24**

The completed Time Series Plot dialog box should look like Figure 13-1.

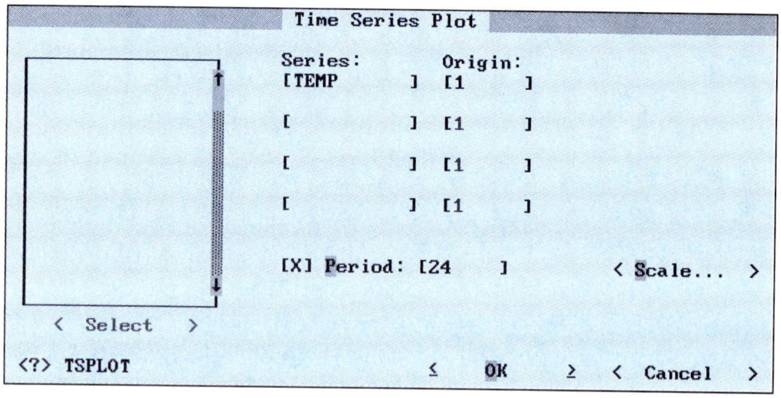

FIGURE 13-1

The completed Time Series Plot dialog box from the Time Series submenu

- Press ↵

The time series plot appears in the Session window (Figure 13-2). Your screen will show this plot in two consecutive screens; scroll or page up to see the second screen.

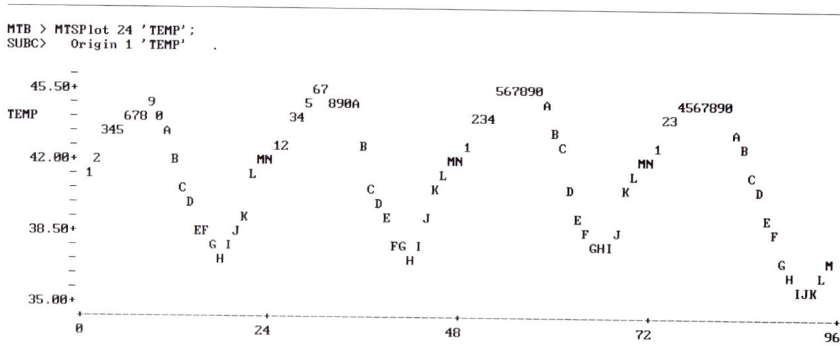

FIGURE 13-2

The Session window, showing the time series plot of temperature

- Scroll up the Session window to see the beginning of the plot

Minitab plots temperature on the vertical axis and the hour on the horizontal axis. It assigns a symbol (a digit or a letter of the alphabet) to each hour of the day and uses these symbols as the plot character for that hour. Minitab begins with the digits 1 (for 1400 = 2 P.M.), 2 (1500 = 3 P.M.), and 3 (1600 = 4 P.M.). Since the period you specified in the plot (24 hours) is more than 9, Minitab uses 0 for 2200 = 10 P.M., then A for 2300 = 11 P.M., B for 2400 = 12 P.M., and so on up to N for 1300 = 1 P.M. After N, the series starts again with 1, 2, 3, and so on. Although this time series has a period of 24, you can plot a time series with any period up to 36 units (since Minitab can use 10 digits and 26 letters).

The plot indicates a cyclical pattern beginning with temperatures at 3 P.M. (marked by the digit 2) around 42 degrees, then rising for the next four hours, then falling until they reach a low of about 37 degrees at 7 A.M. (represented by the letter H). The cycle of rising and falling temperatures repeats through the next 24-hour period but with some variation. The peaks and valleys occur roughly 24 hours apart; this suggests that your ARIMA model might include a periodic component. (In time series terminology, this is commonly referred to as a seasonal component, even though the cycle might be over hours or days.) Your ARIMA model could include a 24-hour seasonal component.

Checking the Autocorrelation and Partial Autocorrelation Plots

For time series data, autocorrelation and partial autocorrelation measure the degree of relationship between observations K time periods (or lags) apart. The autocorrelation and partial autocorrelation plots provide valuable information to help you identify an appropriate ARIMA model:

- Choose **Stat** ▶ **Time Series** ▶ **Autocorrelation...**
- Select C2 TEMP for the Series text box
- Press [Alt]-N for **Number of lags** and press [Tab]
- Type **24**

The completed Autocorrelation Function dialog box should look like Figure 13-3.

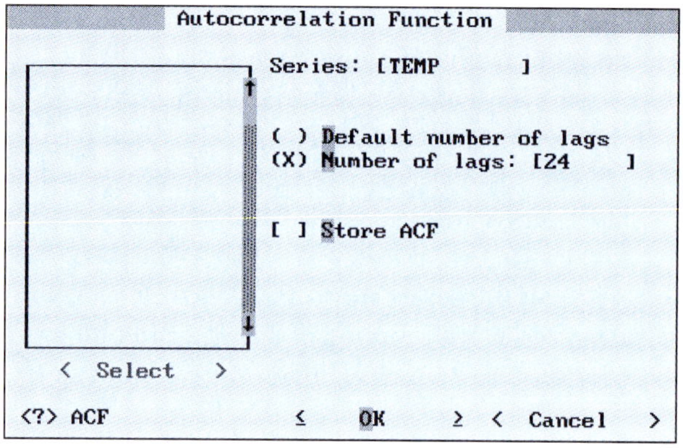

FIGURE 13-3
The completed Autocorrelation Function dialog box from the Time Series submenu

- Press ↵

The autocorrelation plot shown in Figure 13-4 appears in the Session window.

FIGURE 13-4
The complete autocorrelation plot in the Session window

Autocorrelation

Lags

```
MTB > ACF 24 'TEMP'.

ACF of TEMP

          -1.0 -0.8 -0.6 -0.4 -0.2  0.0  0.2  0.4  0.6  0.8  1.0
            +----+----+----+----+----+----+----+----+----+----+
  1   0.949                          XXXXXXXXXXXXXXXXXXXXXXXXX
  2   0.836                          XXXXXXXXXXXXXXXXXXXXXX
  3   0.675                          XXXXXXXXXXXXXXXXXX
  4   0.477                          XXXXXXXXXXXXX
  5   0.261                          XXXXXXXX
  6   0.039                          XX
  7  -0.172                      XXXXX
  8  -0.355                 XXXXXXXXXX
  9  -0.504             XXXXXXXXXXXXXX
 10  -0.611           XXXXXXXXXXXXXXXX
 11  -0.673         XXXXXXXXXXXXXXXXXX
 12  -0.696         XXXXXXXXXXXXXXXXXX
 13  -0.679         XXXXXXXXXXXXXXXXXX
 14  -0.623          XXXXXXXXXXXXXXXXX
 15  -0.532             XXXXXXXXXXXXXX
 16  -0.409                XXXXXXXXXXX
 17  -0.263                   XXXXXXXX
 18  -0.097                        XXX
 19   0.076                          XXX
 20   0.243                          XXXXXXX
 21   0.394                          XXXXXXXXXXX
 22   0.524                          XXXXXXXXXXXXXX
 23   0.617                          XXXXXXXXXXXXXXXX
 24   0.662                          XXXXXXXXXXXXXXXXXX
```

- Scroll up the Session window as necessary to view the plot

The autocorrelation plot resembles a sine pattern. This suggests that temperatures close in time are strongly and positively correlated while temperatures about 12 hours apart are strongly and negatively correlated. (The large positive autocorrelation at lag 24 is indicative of the seasonal component of 24 hours.) The pattern in the autocorrelation plot suggests that your ARIMA model may have an autoregressive (AR) component. The two large, positive autocorrelations at lags 1 and 2 call for an AR component of degree 2.

Now obtain a plot of the partial autocorrelation function to provide further information about an appropriate ARIMA model:

- Choose Stat ▶ Time Series ▶ Partial Autocorrelation...
- Select C2 TEMP for the Series text box
- Press [Alt]-**N** for **N**umber of lags and press [Tab]
- Type **24**

The completed Partial Autocorrelation Function dialog box should look like Figure 13-5.

FIGURE 13-5
The complete Partial Autocorrelation Function dialog box from the Time Series submenu

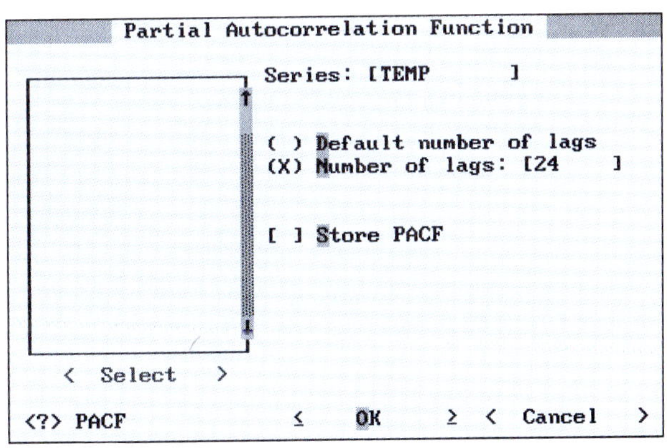

- Press [↵]

The partial autocorrelation plot appears (Figure 13-6) in the Session window.

FIGURE 13-6
The partial autocorrelation plot in the Session window

```
MTB > PACF 24 'TEMP'.

PACF of TEMP

                 -1.0 -0.8 -0.6 -0.4 -0.2  0.0  0.2  0.4  0.6  0.8  1.0
                    +----+----+----+----+----+----+----+----+----+----+
  1   0.949                                  XXXXXXXXXXXXXXXXXXXXXXXXX
  2  -0.660                 XXXXXXXXXXXXXXXXXX
  3  -0.287                           XXXXXXXX
  4  -0.234                            XXXXXXX
  5  -0.086                                XXX
  6  -0.164                              XXXXX
  7  -0.011                                  X
  8   0.025                                  XX
  9  -0.079                                XXX
 10  -0.031                                 XX
 11  -0.079                                XXX
 12  -0.140                              XXXXX
 13  -0.072                                XXX
 14   0.036                                  XX
 15   0.041                                  XX
 16   0.098                                  XXX
 17   0.074                                  XXX
 18   0.160                                  XXXXX
 19   0.007                                  X
 20  -0.017                                  X
 21   0.020                                  X
 22   0.139                                  XXXX
 23  -0.095                                XXX
 24  -0.128                               XXXX
```

- Scroll up the Session window to see the beginning of the plot

The plot has two large partial autocorrelations (spikes) at lags 1 and 2; it also suggests an AR component of degree 2. Later in this tutorial you will fit an ARIMA model based on your findings thus far.

Transforming a Time Series

Luckily, your river data are fairly well-behaved, as evidenced by your time series plot (Figure 13-2). If you were to draw a horizontal line at the mean of the series, you would see that the data oscillate with the same cyclical pattern. A time series like this, whose mean and variance do not change with time, is called *stationary.*

A time series that appears to wander and does not systematically fluctuate around a single value is called *nonstationary.* By lagging and differencing a nonstationary time series, you can make it stationary. Just to get some practice using these commands, you will obtain lags and differences for the river data, even though the river data appear to be stationary already.

Think of lagging as time shifting: it shifts each element in a time series plot to a later point so that it lags behind by the number of time units you specify. When you lag a column in Minitab and store the lagged data, the new column is identical to the former one, except that the entries have been shifted down or lagged by a specified number of rows. The empty rows at the beginning of the resulting column contain * to indicate missing values.

- Choose **Stat** ▶ Time **S**eries ▶ **L**ag...
- Select C2 TEMP for the Series text box
- Type **LAGS** for the Put lags in text box

The completed Lag dialog box should look like Figure 13-7.

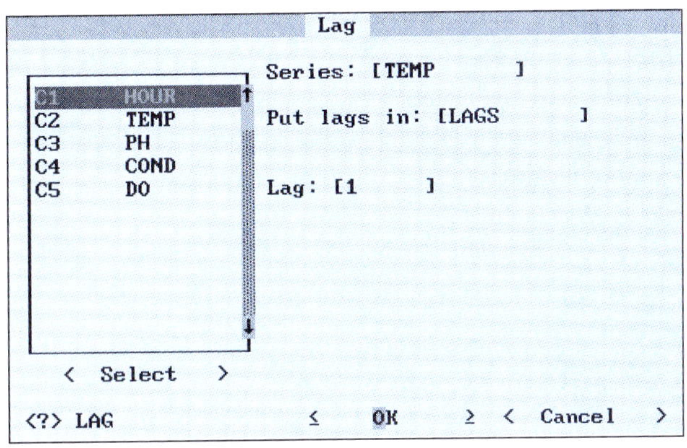

FIGURE 13-7
The completed Lag dialog box from the Time Series submenu

- Press ↵
- Go to the Data screen

Compare the temperature data in C2 with the data in column C6 LAGS (Figure 13-8). Note that a value in C6 LAGS is one row lower than the corresponding value in C2 TEMP. The first entry in C6 LAGS is missing.

FIGURE 13-8

Lagged temperature data in C6

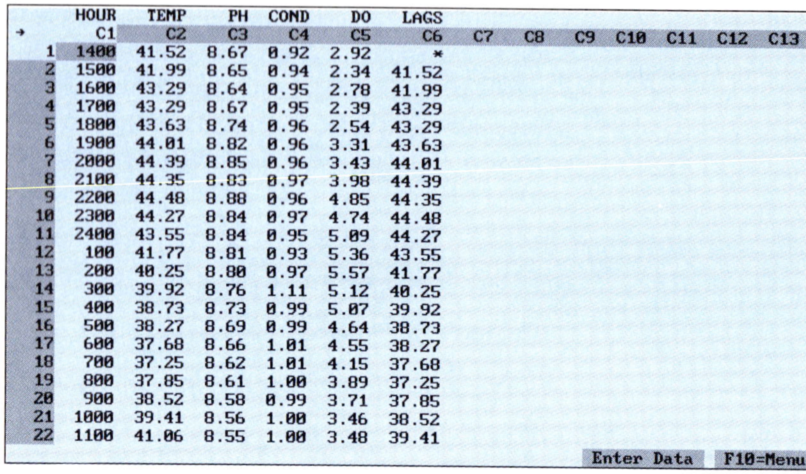

	HOUR C1	TEMP C2	PH C3	COND C4	DO C5	LAGS C6	C7	C8	C9	C10	C11	C12	C13
1	1400	41.52	8.67	0.92	2.92	*							
2	1500	41.99	8.65	0.94	2.34	41.52							
3	1600	43.29	8.64	0.95	2.78	41.99							
4	1700	43.29	8.67	0.95	2.39	43.29							
5	1800	43.63	8.74	0.96	2.54	43.29							
6	1900	44.01	8.82	0.96	3.31	43.63							
7	2000	44.39	8.85	0.96	3.43	44.01							
8	2100	44.35	8.83	0.97	3.98	44.39							
9	2200	44.48	8.88	0.96	4.85	44.35							
10	2300	44.27	8.84	0.97	4.74	44.48							
11	2400	43.55	8.84	0.95	5.09	44.27							
12	100	41.77	8.81	0.93	5.36	43.55							
13	200	40.25	8.80	0.97	5.57	41.77							
14	300	39.92	8.76	1.11	5.12	40.25							
15	400	38.73	8.73	0.99	5.07	39.92							
16	500	38.27	8.69	0.99	4.64	38.73							
17	600	37.68	8.66	1.01	4.55	38.27							
18	700	37.25	8.62	1.01	4.15	37.68							
19	800	37.85	8.61	1.00	3.89	37.25							
20	900	38.52	8.58	0.99	3.71	37.85							
21	1000	39.41	8.56	1.00	3.46	38.52							
22	1100	41.06	8.55	1.00	3.48	39.41							

Enter Data F10=Menu

The Differences command computes differences of observations that are a specified lag apart. If you specify a lag of one, Minitab computes differences between adjacent values in the time series and stores them in a column. To apply the Differences command to the temperature data and use the default of lag 1:

- Return to the Session window
- Choose **Stat** ▶ Time **S**eries ▶ **D**ifferences...
- Select C2 TEMP for the Series text box
- Type **DIFF** in the Put differences in text box

The completed Differences dialog box should look like Figure 13-9.

FIGURE 13-9

The completed Differences dialog box from the Time Series submenu

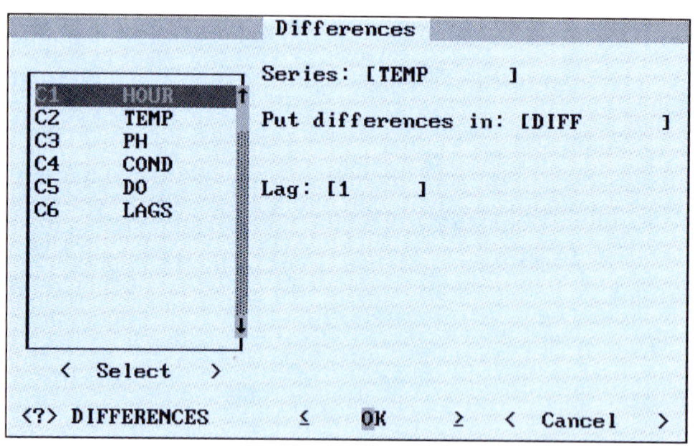

- Press [↵]
- Go to the Data worksheet

The differences of lag 1 of the temperature data appear in column C7 DIFF (Figure 13-10).

FIGURE 13-10
The Data worksheet, showing LAGS and DIFF columns

LAGS C6	DIFF C7
*	*
41.52	0.47000
41.99	1.30000
43.29	0.00000
43.29	0.34000
43.63	0.38000
44.01	0.38000
44.39	-0.04000
44.35	0.13000
44.48	-0.21000
44.27	-0.72000
43.55	-1.78000
41.77	-1.52000
40.25	-0.33000
39.92	-1.19000
38.73	-0.46000
38.27	-0.59000
37.68	-0.43000
37.25	0.60000
37.85	0.67000
38.52	0.89000
39.41	1.65000

C7 DIFF contains the differences between adjacent values in the time series for C2 TEMP. Equivalently, C7 DIFF is the difference between columns C2 TEMP and C6 LAGS.

- Return to the Session window

Recall that the shape of your time series plot indicates whether the time series is stationary or nonstationary. Consider taking differences when the time series plot indicates a nonstationary time series. You can then use the resulting differenced data as your time series, plotting the differenced time series and determining if it is stationary.

Box-Jenkins (ARIMA) Analysis of a Time Series

Your study of the autocorrelation and partial autocorrelation plots suggested that you should consider an ARIMA model with an AR component of degree 2, called AR 2, and 24-hour seasonal AR component of degree 1, called SAR 1. Hoping to keep the model as simple as possible, you first try a model with AR 2.

MINITAB AT WORK

STOCK MARKET: Stock market analysts must be able to accurately model and predict prices to make wise decisions about futures trade contracts. A mathematician in South Carolina used Minitab's ARIMA capability to model the Chicago Board of Trade's wheat contract.

The mathematician assumed that the current wheat contract price is a function of previous price trends; it is this statistical dependence that time series analysis studies. He used 1,054 previous wheat contract prices over a period of four years and entered that data into Minitab. Testing several different configurations led him to a successful model that used an autoregressive component of 1, a differencing component of 1, and a moving average of 2.

Once Minitab helps identify a statistically correct model, a stock market or commodities analyst can use Minitab's forecasting capability to predict future wheat contract prices and maybe even catch a short-term profit.

You will use the ARIMA command to estimate the parameters for this model and investigate its fit.

- Choose **S**tat ▶ Time **S**eries ▶ A**R**IMA...
- Select C2 TEMP for the Series text box
- Type **2** for the Autoregressive component

Note: The two columns next to Autoregressive, Differencing, and Moving average correspond to the nonseasonal and seasonal components of the ARIMA model, respectively. You can have Minitab difference the time series directly in the ARIMA model by specifying a Differencing value.

The completed ARIMA dialog box should resemble Figure 13-11.

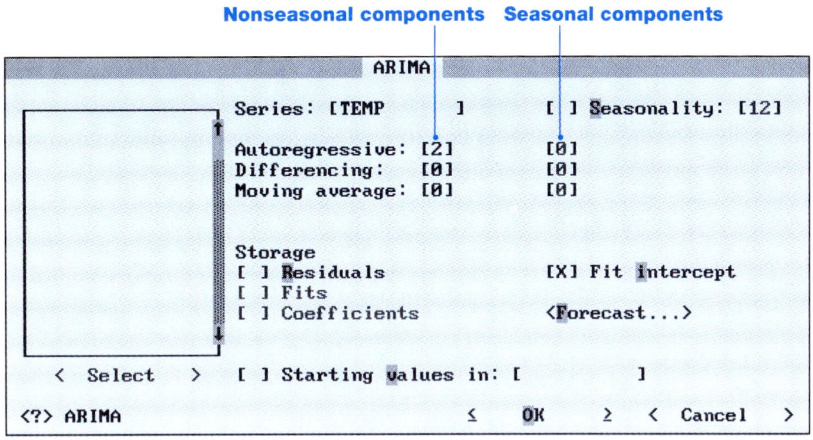

FIGURE 13-11
The completed ARIMA dialog box from the Time Series submenu

- Press [↵]

Note: Estimating the parameters in an ARIMA model is an iterative process. Be patient; in some cases it takes Minitab quite a while to perform all of the calculations. Using simple models helps.

- Scroll up the Session window to view the results of the ARIMA analysis (Figure 13-12)

FIGURE 13-12
Iteration estimates from the ARIMA analysis

```
MTB > ARIMA 2 0 0 'TEMP';
SUBC>   Constant.

Estimates at each iteration
Iteration        SSE      Parameters
    0        556.993    0.100     0.100    33.408
    1        460.739    0.250     0.020    30.500
    2        376.654    0.400    -0.064    27.719
    3        301.680    0.550    -0.147    24.946
    4        235.665    0.700    -0.231    22.175
    5        178.590    0.850    -0.315    19.407
    6        130.437    1.000    -0.399    16.642
    7         91.060    1.150    -0.482    13.864
    8         60.775    1.300    -0.566    11.108
    9         39.313    1.450    -0.650     8.349
   10         26.743    1.600    -0.734     5.609
   11         22.933    1.733    -0.810     3.203
   12         22.919    1.742    -0.815     3.069
   13         22.919    1.742    -0.816     3.060
Relative change in each estimate less than  0.0010
```

Minitab provides a history of this iterative process, giving the sum of squared errors (SSE) and the parameter estimates for each iteration. In Figure 13-12 the parameter estimates correspond to the two AR 2 components and the constant parameters, respectively. If the estimates do not converge after 25 iterations, Minitab will stop the process.

Next comes a detailed display of the final parameter estimates, as shown in Figure 13-13.

FIGURE 13-13

Final parameter estimates from the ARIMA analysis

```
Final Estimates of Parameters
Type         Estimate      St. Dev.   t-ratio
AR    1        1.7421        0.0629     27.70
AR    2       -0.8156        0.0639    -12.76
Constant      3.05974       0.05129     59.66
Mean          41.6198        0.6977

No. of obs.:   95
Residuals:     SS =  22.8843   (backforecasts excluded)
               MS =   0.2487   DF = 92

Modified Box-Pierce chisquare statistic
Lag                    12              24              36              48
Chisquare    25.2(DF=10)     48.7(DF=22)     58.4(DF=34)     76.7(DF=46)
```

The first autoregressive coefficient (AR 1) is estimated to be 1.7421, with a standard deviation of 0.0629 and a t-ratio of 27.70. The second autoregressive coefficient (AR 2) is estimated to be –0.8156 with a standard deviation of 0.0639 and a t-ratio of –12.76. The constant term is estimated as 3.05974.

You conclude that both the AR 1 and AR 2 parameters are significantly different from 0 since the t-ratios are so large. You would compute the estimated temperature at time T as follows:

TEMP at time T = 3.05974 + 1.7421 * TEMP (at time T-1) –
0.8156 * TEMP (at time T-2)

The last part of the display shown in Figure 13-13 (the modified Box-Pierce chi-square statistic) measures how well the model fits the data.

For the following hypotheses, chi-square statistics are computed at lags of 12, 24, 36, and 48:

H_0: The specified ARIMA model fits the data.
H_1: The specified ARIMA model does not fit the data.

To check the significance of the value for the lag of 12:

- Choose **C**alc ▶ **P**robability Distributions ▶ **C**hisquare...
- Press [Alt]-C for **C**umulative probability and press [Tab]
- Type **10** in the Degrees of freedom text box
- Press [Alt]-N for Input co**n**stant and press [Tab]
- Type **25.2** and press [Tab]
- Type **K1** in the Optional storage text box and press [↵]

After the MTB > prompt in the Session window:

- Type **LET K2=1-K1** and press [↵]
- Type **PRINT K2** and press [↵]

The p-value for the test is K2 0.00497365, so the chi-square statistic is significant. If you check the p-values for the other chi-square statistics, you will find them also to be small. So your specified ARIMA model does not fit the data. If you are primarily interested in forecasting future values of the series, check the forecasts. It may be that your model will be adequate for your purposes, even though the model does not "fit" by this test.

Forecasting Using ARIMA

Once you have decided upon a model, the final step is to forecast future values. To predict temperatures for the next 48 hours and store the forecasts and prediction limits:

- Choose **S**tat ▶ Time **S**eries ▶ **A**RIMA...
- Select C2 TEMP for the Series text box
- Type **2** for the Autoregressive component
- Press [Alt]-F for **F**orecast

In the ARIMA - Forecasts subdialog box:

- Type **48** in the Leads text box and press [Tab] twice
- Type **FORECAST** in the Forecasts text box and press [Tab]
- Type **LOWER** in the Lower limits text box and press [Tab]

- Type **UPPER** in the Upper limits text box

The completed ARIMA - Forecasts subdialog box should resemble Figure 13-14.

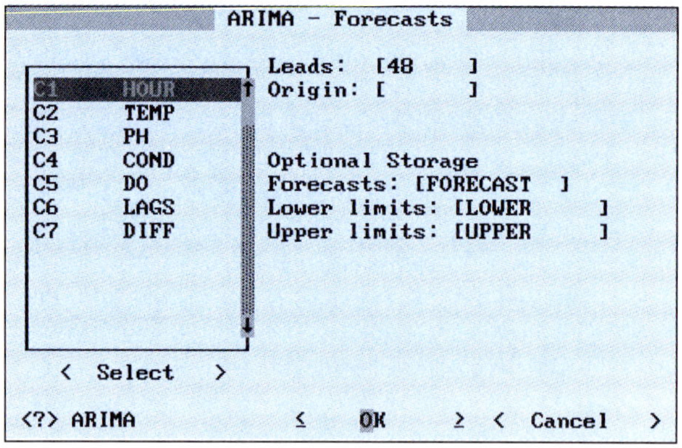

FIGURE 13-14
The completed ARIMA - Forecasts subdialog box

- Press [↵] twice

Forecasts with 95% confidence limits are displayed in the Session window (Figure 13-15).

Note: Minitab estimates the parameters again, so it may take quite a while before the forecasts are displayed.

Your forecasts display the same pattern as your data. They peak around period 104, corresponding to 9 P.M. (the same time you saw peaks in your data). The valleys occur around 9 A.M. Surprisingly, your forecast intervals are fairly narrow; you would have thought otherwise, on the basis of the Box-Pierce tests. The first forecasts are roughly ± 1.0 degrees and later become ± 6.0 degrees. As you recall from your statistics course, forecast intervals increase as you forecast further into the future. If the weather pattern remains constant, you would expect the river temperature to be close to the forecast values.

Although Minitab found your ARIMA (2,0,0) (0,0,0) (0) model to fit poorly, the forecasts generated by the model are useful. You might consider other models. For example, an ARIMA (2,0,0) (1,1,0) (24) or ARIMA (2,1,0) (1,0,0) (24) model both fit very well. You might try these models and compare forecasts from these models with those in Figure 13-15.

FIGURE 13-15
Forecasts using ARIMA

Forecasts from period 95

Period	Forecast	95 Percent Limits Lower	95 Percent Limits Upper	Actual
96	38.2048	37.2271	39.1825	
97	39.1938	37.2298	41.1577	
98	40.1787	37.2521	43.1053	
99	41.0879	37.3090	44.8668	
100	41.8685	37.3945	46.3426	
101	42.4869	37.4912	47.4826	
102	42.9275	37.5760	48.2790	
103	43.1907	37.6249	48.7565	
104	43.2898	37.6164	48.9632	
105	43.2479	37.5352	48.9606	
106	43.0940	37.3751	48.8130	
107	42.8602	37.1407	48.5797	
108	42.5782	36.8477	48.3088	
109	42.2778	36.5204	48.0353	
110	41.9845	36.1873	47.7817	
111	41.7184	35.8758	47.5610	
112	41.4942	35.6080	47.3803	
113	41.3205	35.3985	47.2426	
114	41.2009	35.2532	47.1486	
115	41.1341	35.1708	47.0974	
116	41.1154	35.1446	47.0861	
117	41.1371	35.1639	47.1104	
118	41.1904	35.2169	47.1639	
119	41.2654	35.2917	47.2390	
120	41.3526	35.3777	47.3276	
121	41.4434	35.4658	47.4210	
122	41.5304	35.5491	47.5117	
123	41.6079	35.6226	47.5933	
124	41.6720	35.6829	47.6611	
125	41.7205	35.7283	47.7126	
126	41.7526	35.7584	47.7468	
127	41.7690	35.7736	47.7644	
128	41.7714	35.7755	47.7674	
129	41.7622	35.7661	47.7584	
130	41.7443	35.7482	47.7404	
131	41.7205	35.7243	47.7166	
132	41.6937	35.6974	47.6900	
133	41.6664	35.6698	47.6630	
134	41.6407	35.6438	47.6376	
135	41.6182	35.6209	47.6155	
136	41.6000	35.6024	47.5976	
137	41.5866	35.5887	47.5844	
138	41.5781	35.5800	47.5761	
139	41.5742	35.5761	47.5723	
140	41.5744	35.5763	47.5726	
141	41.5779	35.5798	47.5761	
142	41.5839	35.5857	47.5820	
143	41.5913	35.5932	47.5895	

In this tutorial you have seen how to analyze a time series with Box-Jenkins ARIMA techniques. Autocorrelation and partial autocorrelation plots, together with lagging and differencing transformations, guided the model-identification stage. The interactive nature of Minitab makes it possible to try as many preliminary models as your patience allows before you settle on a final model and begin to make forecasts. The techniques you have used in this tutorial represent a very powerful and flexible tool that can fit virtually any forecasting model.

In the final tutorial, you will see the macro capability of Minitab. This macro function allows you to store and execute a repetitive sequence of commands, creating new Minitab commands to perform special statistical analyses.

If you plan to continue directly to the next tutorial:

- Choose **F**ile ▶ Restart **M**initab

If you want to take a longer break:

- Choose **F**ile ▶ E**x**it

Minitab Command Summary

The menus and commands introduced in or related to this tutorial are described in this section. You will find a complete explanation of all menus and commands in the Reference section of this manual.

Menu	Command	Function
Stat		
	Time Series	
	Differences	Computes and saves the differences of a time series
	Lag	Forms the lag of a time series
	Time Series Plot	Plots a times series
	Autocorrelation	Plots the autocorrelations of a time series
	Partial Autocorrelation	Plots the partial autocorrelations of a time series

Cross Correlation	Computes the cross correlation between two time series
ARIMA	Fits a specified autoregressive integrated moving average model to time series data stored in a column and can provide forecasts

Review and Practice

Matching

Match the following terms to their definitions by placing the correct letter next to the term it explains.

____ Fit intercept

____ Fits

____ Time Series Plot

____ Lag

____ Number of lags

____ Forecast

____ Differences

a. Specifies the number of autocorrelations and partial autocorrelations to compute and display in the autocorrelation and partial autocorrelation plots

b. Computes and saves the time series forecasts in the next available column

c. Shifts a specified column of data down a specified number of rows and saves the results in a column

d. Computes and stores the difference between observations in a given column a specified number of rows apart

e. Command found on both the Stat ▶ Time Series submenu and Graph menus that displays the plot of a time series

f. Saves the fitted time series values in the next available column

g. Requests that an intercept term be included in the model

True/False

Mark the following statements T or F.

____ 1. When you use the Differences command, storing the differences in a column is optional.

____ 2. Forecasts of future events are always performed when you use the ARIMA command.

____ 3. The default period for time series plots is 12.

____ 4. Before you have Minitab compute differences, you must issue the Lag command.

____ 5. P-values, determining the significance of the ARIMA model's fit, are part of the ARIMA output.

____ 6. In the ARIMA command, you can request interval forecasts of any specified confidence level.

____ 7. You can save any combination of fitted, residual, and coefficient estimates using the ARIMA command.

____ 8. Autocorrelation and partial autocorrelation plots always output a test of significance.

____ 9. P-values for the t-ratio tests of the ARIMA parameters are not given in the ARIMA output, but you can compute them using the Probability Distributions command.

____ 10. When forecasting using ARIMA, you can save any combination of the forecasts, upper limits, or lower limits.

Practice Problems

1. Open the RIVER3.MTW data set from the TUT13 directory. Three other river characteristics were measured in addition to the river's temperature: the pH, conductivity, and dissolved oxygen content. The pH (PH) measures the acidity/alkalinity of the water. Conductivity (COND) is a measure of electrical resistance of the water and the dissolved oxygen (DO) measures the amount of oxygen in the water.

   Perform a time series analysis of these other characteristics. Your analysis should mirror that of the tutorial. That is, for each characteristic, you should plot the series, obtain the autocorrelation and partial autocorrelation plots, and finally fit and forecast an appropriate ARIMA model.

2. In the river study, several sites along the river were monitored. Site 2 was directly upriver from the plant's intake pipes. Redo the analysis of this tutorial using the site 2 data. The data for site 2 are in the file RIVER2.MTW in the TUT13 directory.

TUTORIAL 14

Macros

In addition to using Minitab's menu commands, you can also write and use your own stored sets of commands, called macros. In this tutorial you will see how to write macros that perform repetitive analyses. You can also use macros to perform statistical analyses that do not exist as commands in Minitab's menus. This macro feature of Minitab essentially gives you the power to "program" in Minitab.

Objectives

In this tutorial you will learn to:

- create a macro in Minitab by cutting and pasting commands within the Session window
- execute a macro more than once
- create a macro using a word processor
- make macros more flexible

Menu Commands and the Minitab Command Language

A macro is a series of Minitab commands stored in a file. Minitab macro files must be in ASCII format. When you store a macro, Minitab automatically saves the file in the ASCII format and adds the extension .MTB to the file name.

To practice writing a macro, you will investigate statistical confidence intervals. (Recall that the level of confidence (say 90%) of a confidence interval is the percentage of *all* such confidence intervals that trap the population mean.) You will "simulate" what would happen if you were to repeat the experiment an infinite number of times.

In this tutorial you will first generate random samples of data from a normal population with mean = 10 and $\sigma = 4$ and store these samples in columns. You will then obtain confidence intervals for the mean and finally determine how many of them actually include the population mean (10).

In earlier tutorials you issued Minitab commands primarily through menu choices. With few exceptions, you can also issue these commands by typing them in the Session window. To use Minitab's macro feature to its fullest, you must "know" the commands and subcommands by name. If you read the commands Minitab prints in the Session window as it executes your choices, you can become familiar with Minitab's command language.

Note: To find the Session command equivalent for any menu command, you can also consult Appendix A, Session Command/Menu Command Cross Reference or Chapter 2, Session Window Menu Reference, in the Reference Section.

As you generate the simulation data consisting of 30 observations stored in each of 25 columns, watch the commands that appear in the Session window.

- Choose **C**alc ▶ **R**andom Data ▶ **N**ormal...
- Type **30** in the Generate rows of data text box and press [Tab]
- Type **C1-C25** in the Store in column(s) text box and press [Tab]
- Type **10** in the Mean text box and press [Tab]
- Type **4** in the Standard deviation text box and press [↵]

Two lines appear in the Session window, as shown in Figure 14-1.

FIGURE 14-1
The Session window, showing the Random command

```
MTB > Random 30 C1-C25;
SUBC>   Normal 10 4.
```

The Minitab command to generate random data is called Random. The "30" after Random in the Session window corresponds to the number of rows of random values for each sample generated. The "C1–C25" tells Minitab to store the results in columns 1 through 25 inclusive. The semicolon at the end of the line indicates that a subcommand follows.

The subcommand "Normal 10 4" tells Minitab what distribution to sample from, in this case a normal distribution with mean = 10 and $\sigma = 4$. The period at the end of the subcommand indicates that no other subcommands follow.

Now compute the 25 90% confidence intervals for the population mean using the 25 samples stored in columns C1–C25 because you know the population standard deviation is 4. Use the 1-Sample Z command:

- Choose **S**tat ▶ **B**asic Statistics ▶ 1-Sample **Z**...
- Type **C1-C25** in the Variables text box and press [Tab] twice
- Type **90** in the Level text box and press [Tab]
- Type **4** in the Sigma text box and press [↵]

The Session window displays 25 confidence intervals for each mean.

- Press [PgUp] to see the beginning of the Session window

First look at the commands Minitab used (Figure 14-2). The command used to obtain confidence intervals for a population mean when the population standard deviation is known is ZInterval. The desired degree of confidence (90) comes next, then the population sigma (4), and finally the columns containing the data (C1–C25).

Now look at the 25 90% confidence intervals.

FIGURE 14-2

The 90% confidence intervals

```
MTB > Random 30 C1-C25;
SUBC>   Normal 10 4.
MTB > ZInterval 90 4 C1-C25.

THE ASSUMED SIGMA =4.00

              N      MEAN     STDEV   SE MEAN    90.0 PERCENT C.I.
C1           30     9.218     3.632     0.730  (   8.016,  10.421)
C2           30    10.392     3.546     0.730  (   9.189,  11.595)
C3           30     9.462     4.473     0.730  (   8.260,  10.665)
C4           30    11.182     4.359     0.730  (   9.979,  12.384)
C5           30     8.878     4.097     0.730  (   7.676,  10.081)
C6           30     8.487     3.837     0.730  (   7.284,   9.689)
C7           30    10.888     4.425     0.730  (   9.685,  12.091)
C8           30     9.471     5.447     0.730  (   8.269,  10.674)
C9           30     9.086     3.995     0.730  (   7.884,  10.289)
C10          30    10.195     4.248     0.730  (   8.992,  11.398)
C11          30    10.399     3.815     0.730  (   9.196,  11.601)
C12          30    10.130     3.700     0.730  (   8.927,  11.332)
C13          30    10.146     4.652     0.730  (   8.944,  11.349)
C14          30    10.778     3.539     0.730  (   9.576,  11.981)
C15          30    10.254     3.865     0.730  (   9.051,  11.456)
C16          30    11.812     3.870     0.730  (  10.609,  13.014)
C17          30    12.233     2.970     0.730  (  11.031,  13.436)
C18          30     9.792     4.168     0.730  (   8.589,  10.995)
C19          30    10.708     3.985     0.730  (   9.506,  11.911)
C20          30    10.021     3.913     0.730  (   8.818,  11.223)
C21          30    10.759     4.056     0.730  (   9.557,  11.962)
C22          30    10.915     4.486     0.730  (   9.713,  12.118)
C23          30    10.260     4.005     0.730  (   9.058,  11.463)
C24          30    10.179     4.239     0.730  (   8.976,  11.381)
C25          30    10.193     4.556     0.730  (   8.991,  11.396)
```

- Press Ctrl-End to see the bottom of the list

Your results will differ from Figure 14-2 since your random samples are different. Of the 25 90% confidence intervals generated for this tutorial, three (C6, C16, and C17) do not contain the population mean, 10. Although your results will be different, you would expect that approximately 10% of your confidence intervals would not contain the mean.

Take this idea one step further; generate 100 samples and see how many confidence intervals fail to trap the mean. You could simply repeat the preceding steps three more times, but it is simpler to store these commands in a macro and then execute the macro.

To store commands in a macro:

- Choose **F**ile ▶ Other **F**iles ▶ Start Storing **M**acro...
- Press Tab, open the TUT14 directory to store your macro, and press Shift-Tab

- Type **CONFINTS** in the File name text box
- Press [↵]

The Session window shows the corresponding Minitab command (Store) followed by the drive, directory, and filename 'A:\TUT14\CONFINTS'. Note that the prompt in the Session window has changed from MTB > to STOR>, indicating that Minitab is storing commands for a macro. When Minitab is in this mode, it does not execute any commands issued, but simply stores them.

At this point you have several options. You could type the macro commands in the Session window. This requires that you have a very good knowledge of the command language. Also, when typing commands into a macro, you need to be very careful. If you make a typing mistake and happen to notice it before you press [↵], you can go back and fix it. But once you've pressed [↵] you cannot make any changes to that line.

Your second alternative is to use the menus and let Minitab translate the menu command into its own language equivalent and store it in the macro. A word of caution here also. Some commands might not work because Minitab will not execute a command that uses columns that do not yet have data.

The third and easiest alternative is to copy and paste the commands you just used. This method has the advantage of letting you try the commands in a given sequence beforehand, verifying that the macro performs as intended. Also, since you are copying and pasting commands that have worked correctly, there will be no typos.

To copy and paste previously executed commands, first move to the beginning of the Session window:

- Press [Ctrl]-[Home]

The commands you need are all there, and you can copy them using the Edit menu's cut and paste capabilities.

- Use [↓] to move the cursor to the beginning of the line that contains the Random command
- Press and hold [Shift] as you use [↓] to scroll through the line containing the ZInterval command (the first three command lines should be highlighted)

- Release [Shift]

Your screen should look like Figure 14-3.

FIGURE 14-3
Highlighted commands in the Session window

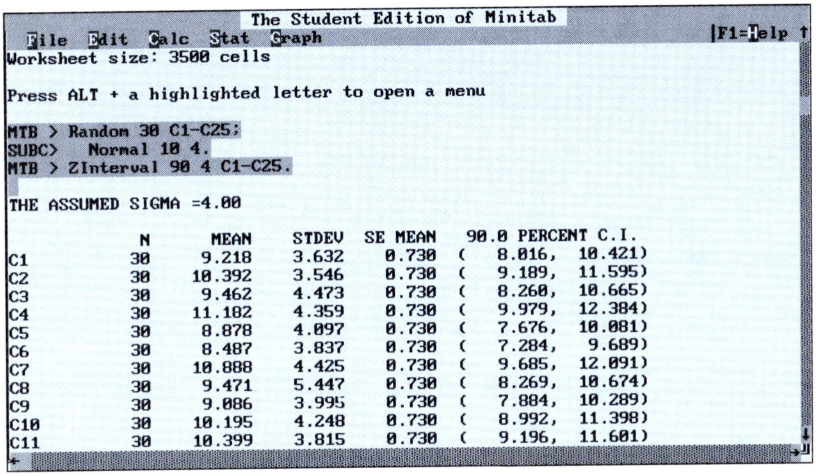
```
                     The Student Edition of Minitab
 File  Edit  Calc  Stat  Graph                                   |F1=Help
Worksheet size: 3500 cells

Press ALT + a highlighted letter to open a menu

MTB > Random 30 C1-C25;
SUBC>   Normal 10 4.
MTB > ZInterval 90 4 C1-C25.

THE ASSUMED SIGMA =4.00

             N      MEAN     STDEV   SE MEAN    90.0 PERCENT C.I.
C1          30     9.218     3.632     0.730  (   8.016,   10.421)
C2          30    10.392     3.546     0.730  (   9.189,   11.595)
C3          30     9.462     4.473     0.730  (   8.260,   10.665)
C4          30    11.182     4.359     0.730  (   9.979,   12.384)
C5          30     8.878     4.097     0.730  (   7.676,   10.081)
C6          30     8.487     3.837     0.730  (   7.284,    9.689)
C7          30    10.888     4.425     0.730  (   9.685,   12.091)
C8          30     9.471     5.447     0.730  (   8.269,   10.674)
C9          30     9.086     3.995     0.730  (   7.884,   10.289)
C10         30    10.195     4.248     0.730  (   8.992,   11.398)
C11         30    10.399     3.815     0.730  (   9.196,   11.601)
```

- Choose **E**dit ▶ **C**opy Commands Only

You are now ready to insert or paste the commands after the STOR> prompt:

- Choose **E**dit ▶ **P**aste

Minitab automatically types the commands after the STOR> prompt. They are not actually stored until you press [↵]. This gives you the opportunity to edit them if you want.

Note: Before you store the commands, check to make sure that Minitab copied all three highlighted lines. If you did not place the cursor at the *beginning* of the line containing the Random command, that line was not copied.

To store the commands:

- Press [↵]

Minitab places each command line on a separate STOR> line. To end the macro:

- Choose **F**ile ▶ Other **F**iles ▶ Stop Storing **M**acro...

Your screen should look like Figure 14-4. Notice that the Minitab Command Language equivalent of the Stop Storing Macro menu command is End.

FIGURE 14-4

The completed macro, shown in the Session window

```
STOR> Random 30 C1-C25;
STOR>   Normal 10 4.
STOR> ZInterval 90 4 C1-C25.
STOR>
STOR> End.
```

You are now ready to run, or execute, the macro. In Tutorial 6 you saw how to execute the PTEST macro that was stored on the Sample Files disk. To execute the macro you just created:

- Choose **F**ile ▶ Other **F**iles ▶ **E**xecute Macro...
- Press [↵] to execute the macro once
- Select CONFINTS.MTB from the TUT14 directory
- Press [↵]

Watch the Session window as Minitab executes the macro; all commands and results are displayed. The macro stops when Minitab encounters the last command of the macro, "End."

If you inspect the 25 confidence intervals shown in Figure 14-5, note that this time only one does not include 10 (C25). Remember that your output differs from this.

FIGURE 14-5
Additional confidence intervals

THE ASSUMED SIGMA =4.00

	N	MEAN	STDEV	SE MEAN	90.0 PERCENT C.I.
C1	30	9.262	4.264	0.730	(8.059, 10.464)
C2	30	10.193	3.581	0.730	(8.990, 11.395)
C3	30	10.276	4.153	0.730	(9.074, 11.479)
C4	30	10.086	3.357	0.730	(8.884, 11.289)
C5	30	9.417	4.109	0.730	(8.215, 10.620)
C6	30	9.342	3.906	0.730	(8.139, 10.544)
C7	30	9.212	3.960	0.730	(8.009, 10.415)
C8	30	9.931	3.512	0.730	(8.728, 11.133)
C9	30	8.868	4.247	0.730	(7.665, 10.071)
C10	30	10.147	4.481	0.730	(8.944, 11.350)
C11	30	10.030	4.394	0.730	(8.827, 11.232)
C12	30	9.664	4.012	0.730	(8.461, 10.866)
C13	30	10.958	3.293	0.730	(9.755, 12.160)
C14	30	10.438	3.878	0.730	(9.235, 11.640)
C15	30	10.862	4.815	0.730	(9.659, 12.064)
C16	30	10.114	3.682	0.730	(8.911, 11.317)
C17	30	10.243	4.457	0.730	(9.041, 11.446)
C18	30	9.069	3.728	0.730	(7.866, 10.271)
C19	30	10.005	3.552	0.730	(8.803, 11.208)
C20	30	9.316	3.947	0.730	(8.113, 10.518)
C21	30	9.643	3.993	0.730	(8.440, 10.846)
C22	30	10.570	4.241	0.730	(9.368, 11.773)
C23	30	11.167	3.476	0.730	(9.965, 12.370)
C24	30	9.269	3.890	0.730	(8.066, 10.471)
C25	30	8.348	3.897	0.730	(7.146, 9.551)

So far, 4 confidence intervals out of the 50 generated for this tutorial have not contained the mean. In the next section you will generate 50 more confidence intervals and see how many out of your 100 do not contain 10 (you would expect 10). Ninety percent of confidence intervals with a confidence level of 90% should include the true population mean.

Executing a Macro Several Times

To obtain 50 more confidence intervals, you can have Minitab execute the macro twice more. Macros can be executed as many times as you want.

- Choose **File** ▶ Other **Files** ▶ Execute Macro...
- Type **2** in the Number of times to execute text box and press ↵
- Select CONFINTS.MTB in the TUT14 directory

Note: To run or execute a macro from the Session window, you would use the format: EXECUTE, the macro's filename (in single quotes), and the number of times you want the macro to be executed.

It takes Minitab a while to complete these computations. The 50 additional confidence intervals generated for this tutorial are shown in Figure 14-6.

FIGURE 14-6

Additional 50 confidence intervals

```
             N      MEAN     STDEV   SE MEAN      90.0 PERCENT C.I.
C1          30    10.045     3.909     0.730   (   8.843,   11.248)
C2          30     9.125     3.603     0.730   (   7.922,   10.327)
C3          30     8.986     3.995     0.730   (   7.784,   10.189)
C4          30     9.929     4.076     0.730   (   8.727,   11.132)
C5          30     9.197     3.782     0.730   (   7.994,   10.399)
C6          30     8.848     3.576     0.730   (   7.645,   10.050)
C7          30    10.894     3.827     0.730   (   9.692,   12.097)
C8          30     8.626     3.227     0.730   (   7.423,    9.829)
C9          30     9.244     3.401     0.730   (   8.041,   10.446)
C10         30     9.875     4.460     0.730   (   8.672,   11.078)
C11         30    11.443     3.750     0.730   (  10.240,   12.645)
C12         30    11.358     3.493     0.730   (  10.155,   12.561)
C13         30     9.422     3.385     0.730   (   8.219,   10.624)
C14         30    11.250     3.993     0.730   (  10.048,   12.453)
C15         30     9.463     4.396     0.730   (   8.261,   10.666)
C16         30    11.439     4.158     0.730   (  10.237,   12.642)
C17         30    11.499     3.580     0.730   (  10.297,   12.702)
C18         30    10.093     3.989     0.730   (   8.891,   11.296)
C19         30     9.513     3.366     0.730   (   8.311,   10.716)
C20         30    10.137     4.810     0.730   (   8.934,   11.339)
C21         30    10.412     4.752     0.730   (   9.209,   11.614)
C22         30     9.333     3.935     0.730   (   8.131,   10.536)
C23         30     9.714     4.177     0.730   (   8.512,   10.917)
C24         30     9.924     4.175     0.730   (   8.721,   11.126)
C25         30     9.988     3.246     0.730   (   8.785,   11.191)

MTB >
MTB > End.
MTB > Random 30 C1-C25;
SUBC>   Normal 10 4.
MTB > ZInterval 90 4 C1-C25.

THE ASSUMED SIGMA =4.00

             N      MEAN     STDEV   SE MEAN      90.0 PERCENT C.I.
C1          30     9.980     3.604     0.730   (   8.777,   11.183)
C2          30    10.070     3.269     0.730   (   8.867,   11.272)
C3          30    11.185     4.241     0.730   (   9.982,   12.388)
C4          30    10.474     3.372     0.730   (   9.271,   11.676)
C5          30     9.063     5.419     0.730   (   7.861,   10.266)
C6          30     9.459     3.973     0.730   (   8.256,   10.662)
C7          30     9.315     4.568     0.730   (   8.112,   10.517)
C8          30    11.397     3.080     0.730   (  10.195,   12.600)
C9          30    10.101     3.844     0.730   (   8.898,   11.304)
C10         30     9.745     3.704     0.730   (   8.542,   10.947)
C11         30     9.184     4.191     0.730   (   7.981,   10.387)
C12         30    10.600     4.952     0.730   (   9.397,   11.802)
```

C13	30	10.735	3.137	0.730	(9.533, 11.938)
C14	30	10.341	4.229	0.730	(9.138, 11.543)
C15	30	10.874	3.841	0.730	(9.671, 12.076)
C16	30	10.197	3.378	0.730	(8.995, 11.400)
C17	30	9.540	4.427	0.730	(8.337, 10.742)
C18	30	10.299	3.467	0.730	(9.097, 11.502)
C19	30	10.282	3.906	0.730	(9.080, 11.485)
C20	30	9.230	4.196	0.730	(8.028, 10.433)
C21	30	11.055	3.746	0.730	(9.853, 12.258)
C22	30	9.186	3.279	0.730	(7.983, 10.388)
C23	30	9.454	3.203	0.730	(8.251, 10.656)
C24	30	10.821	3.338	0.730	(9.618, 12.023)
C25	30	11.482	3.166	0.730	(10.280, 12.685)

Of the 50 additional confidence intervals, eight do not contain the mean (C8, C11, C12, C14, C16, and C17 in the first set of 25 confidence intervals and C8 and C25 in the second set).

Now consider the results of the 100 confidence intervals shown in this book. Twelve did not contain 10. Your results, if taken in conjunction with the results presented here, represent 200 samples. Of this total, you should observe approximately 20 confidence intervals that do not contain the mean.

To get an accurate picture, many statisticians believe simulations should include more than 1,000 replications; some even advocate 10,000. If you were to continue generating confidence intervals, you would see that the percentage of CI's that include the mean would approach 90%. Using macros and Minitab's capability of generating random data from almost any distribution, you can perform simulations that investigate many other statistical properties.

In the next section, you will see another major use of macros—to create a set of commands to perform an analysis or special function that does not exist in Minitab.

Creating a Macro Using a Word Processor

In this section you will create a macro that will perform a chi-square goodness-of-fit (GOF) test for a set of data. You will use the genetics data from Tutorial 10 to verify your macro.

A macro can be just a set of commands copied from the Session window, or it can be generalized and annotated. Macros of the second kind may become quite long, so it is easiest to write them in a word processor or text editor. You could write them in Minitab, but you would have no opportunity to go back and edit the command entries. So for this section you need access to a text editor or word processor that can handle ASCII text. Minitab macros must be saved in text (ASCII) format.

- Choose **File** ▶ **Exit**
- Press [↵] to exit without saving the worksheet
- Open your word processing program

Now recall the commands you will need in your macro. In the genetics example in Tutorial 10, there were four phenotype categories, stored in C1 TYPE. You had stored the hypothesized probabilities corresponding to the phenotypes in C2 PROB. The observed phenotypes (from your experiment in which you grew 200 peas in carbon-dioxide–deficient soil) were stored in C3 PHENO; the observed frequency of each phenotype category was stored in C4 OBSERVED. A copy of this data set with this information is on your Sample Files disk in the TUT14 directory. You will open it later when you restart Minitab.

When you performed the chi-square GOF test in Tutorial 10, you used the Minitab menus to perform four tasks:

- You computed the expected frequency of each phenotype by multiplying each expected probability in C2 by 200 (the total number of peas sampled); you stored those frequencies in C5.
- You then computed the chi-square values for each phenotype ((C4-C5)**2/C5) and stored them in C6.
- You computed the chi-square GOF statistic by summing C6.
- You computed the p-value using the Probability Distributions command and the General Expressions (LET) command.

The Minitab commands to perform these four tasks are:

- LET C5 = C2*200
- LET C6 = (C4-C5)**2/C5
- LET K1 = SUM(C6)
- CDF K1 K2;
CHISQUARE 3.
LET K3 = 1-K2
PRINT K1 K3

You could verify these commands by repeating the steps from Tutorial 10 and looking at the commands that appears in the Session window.

To create your macro, use your word processor to create a file named GOF.MTB and type these commands into the file:

- Type **LET C5 = C2*200** and press ↵
- Type **LET C6 = (C4-C5)**2/C5** and press ↵
- Type **LET K1 = SUM(C6)** and press ↵
- Type **CDF K1 K2;** (do not forget the ;) and press ↵
- Type **CHISQUARE 3.** (do not forget the .) and press ↵
- Type **LET K3 = 1-K2** and press ↵
- Type **PRINT K1 K3** and press ↵

The text should look like Figure 14-7, which shows the GOF macro in a popular word processor.

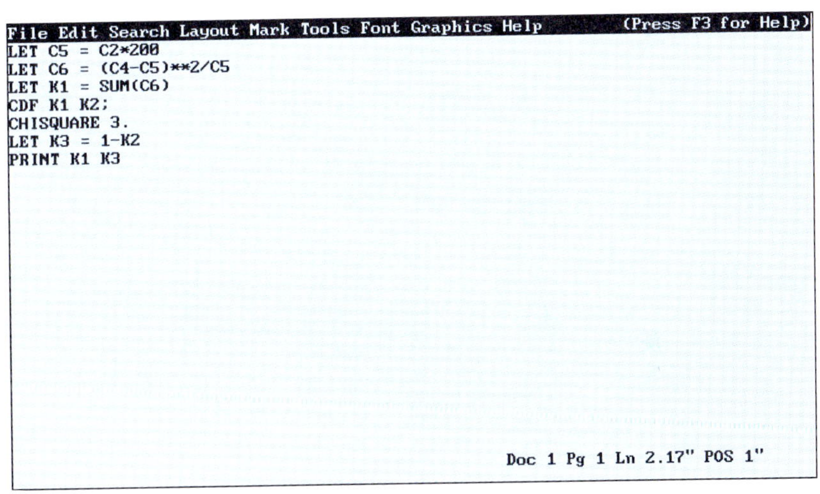

FIGURE 14-7
The GOF macro in a word processing file

After you finish typing these commands, go back and verify that each line is correct. You are now ready to save the macro in a file:

- Save the document as a text (ASCII) file named GOF.MTB in the TUT14 directory of the Sample Files disk

Note: When you create a macro in a word processor, you don't need to save it with the .MTB file extension, but you must save the file in text or ASCII format. If you fail to do so, Minitab will be unable to read it.

When you have saved the file in the TUT14 directory, you are ready to execute it from Minitab. To do that:

- Exit your word processor
- Start Minitab
- Open GENEST14.MTW from the TUT14 directory
- Go to the Data worksheet

Verify that the data described earlier are stored in the columns indicated and then execute the macro you just created:

- Return to the Session window
- Choose **F**ile ▶ Other **F**iles ▶ **E**xecute Macro...
- Press [↵] to execute the macro once
- Select GOF.MTB from the TUT14 directory
- Press [↵]

The Session window shows the macro commands and results (Figure 14-8).

FIGURE 14-8
GOF.MTB results from the Session window

```
MTB > Execute 'A:\TUT1 \GOF.MTB' 1.
MTB > LET C5 = C2*200
MTB > LET C6 = (C4-C5)**2/C5
MTB > LET K1 = SUM(C6)
MTB > CDF K1 K2;
SUBC> CHISQUARE 3.
MTB > LET K3 = 1-K2
MTB > PRINT K1 K3
K1       8.35556
K3       0.0392075
```

Minitab executes each command you typed in your macro. At the end of the commands, Minitab reports the chi-square statistic and the p-value, K1 8.35556 and K3 0.0392075, respectively. Compare the results in Figure 14-8 to those in Tutorial 10.

Your results should be the same. If they are not, go back to your word processor and reenter the commands, typing very carefully and verifying each line. When you are sure of your typing, continue by saving the file as you did previously. Run the new macro and verify that it is working properly before continuing to the next section.

You now have a GOF test macro: it is essentially a new Minitab command. When you need to perform a chi-square GOF test, you can use this macro. However, in its present form the macro will work only with certain data sets. In the next section you will modify this macro and make it more flexible.

Generalizing a Macro

The GOF.MTB macro from the previous section will perform a chi-square GOF test on a data set, but only if the expected probabilities and observed frequencies are stored in columns C2 and C4, respectively. The macro also assumes that there are exactly four categories (since a chi-square with 3 degrees of freedom was used to compute the p-value) and that the sample size is 200. You will generalize the macro so that it will automatically determine the appropriate sample size and the appropriate number of categories; you will also annotate it for future reference.

The macro still requires the user to enter the hypothesized probabilities in C2 and observed frequencies in C4.

You need to make the changes to the macro in your word processor. To do that:

- Choose **File** ▶ **Exit** and press [↵]
- Start your word processor and open GOF.MTB

Now make the three changes. You can have Minitab determine the sample size by summing the observed frequencies in C4. So replace the 200 in the first line of your macro with SUM(C4):

- Delete 200 in the first line of the macro
- Type **SUM(C4)** in its place

Next, you need to determine the degrees of freedom of the chi-square statistic. The degrees of freedom is the number of categories minus one. Since the p-value computations depend on this value, you need to have the value computed and stored before the CDF command is executed in the macro.

- Insert a blank line before the CDF command

Now write instructions to have Minitab count the number of rows in C4 (you could also use C2) using the Count command; use Let to have Minitab store this value in a constant location (K4) and subtract one to yield the degrees of freedom. (This can all be done in a single command.)

- Type **LET K4 = COUNT(C4)-1** on the blank line

Have Minitab use this value when computing the p-value. To do that:

- Delete the 3 in the CHISQUARE line (be careful not to delete the period at the end of the line)
- Type **K4** in its place

Finally, you would like to add some annotation to the macro so that you know its restrictions and exactly what the macro expects to find in various columns. To add annotation to a macro use the NOTE command (or a #). Minitab ignores any information following NOTE or #.

The macro expects that the hypothesized probabilities are stored in column C2 and that the observed counts are in C4. You should note all of this at the beginning of your macro, so:

- Make room at the top of your macro for notes

You are now ready to add notes that will inform the user that:

- This is a chi-square goodness-of-fit test
- The hypothesized probabilities must be stored in C2
- The observed frequencies must be stored in C4

To add these notes at the beginning of the macro:

- Type **NOTE CHISQUARE GOODNESS-OF-FIT PROCEDURE** and press [↵]
- Type **NOTE HYPOTHESIZED PROBABILITIES MUST BE IN C2** and press [↵]
- Type **NOTE OBSERVED FREQUENCIES MUST BE IN C4**

You also decide to label the macro output so that K1 and K3 are identified as the chi-square GOF test statistic and the p-value, respectively.

- Insert a blank line after the line of the macro that reads LET K3 = 1-K2
- Type **NOTE K1 IS THE STATISTIC AND K3 IS THE P-VALUE**

You are ready to save the file. Before you do, verify that the macro resembles the one in Figure 14-9.

FIGURE 14-9
The generalized GOF.MTB macro in a word processing file

```
File Edit Search Layout Mark Tools Font Graphics Help          (Press F3 for Help)
NOTE CHISQUARE GOODNESS-OF-FIT PROCEDURE
NOTE HYPOTHESIZED PROBABILITIES MUST BE IN C2
NOTE OBSERVED FREQUENCIES MUST BE IN C4
LET C5 = C2*SUM(C4)
LET C6 = (C4-C5)**2/C5
LET K1 = SUM(C6)
LET K4 = COUNT(C4)-1
CDF K1 K2;
CHISQUARE K4.
LET K3 = 1-K2
NOTE K1 IS THE STATISTIC AND K3 IS THE P-VALUE
PRINT K1 K3

C:\MINITAB\TUTDATA\GOF.MTB                          Doc 1 Pg 1 Ln 3" POS 1"
```

After you have verified that your macro is identical to that in Figure 14-9:

- Save the macro as a text (ASCII) file (still named GOF.MTB) in the TUT14 directory
- Exit from your word processor
- Start Minitab
- Open GENEST14.MTW from the TUT14 directory

You are now ready to run the generalized macro:

- Choose **File** ▶ Other **Files** ▶ **Execute** Macro...
- Press [↵] to execute the macro once
- Select GOF.MTB from the TUT14 directory

Minitab displays the Session window as the macro is executing. When it finishes (assuming your changes are correct), your screen should look like Figure 14-10.

FIGURE 14-10
The Session window, showing results of the GOF.MTB macro

```
MTB > Execute 'A:\TUT14\GOF.MTB' 1.
MTB > NOTE CHISQUARE GOODNESS-OF-FIT PROCEDURE
MTB > NOTE HYPOTHESIZED PROBABILITIES MUST BE IN C2
MTB > NOTE OBSERVED FREQUENCIES MUST BE IN C4
MTB > LET C5 = C2*SUM(C4)
MTB > LET C6 = (C4-C5)**2/C5
MTB > LET K1 = SUM(C6)
MTB > LET K4 = COUNT(C4)-1
MTB > CDF K1 K2;
SUBC> CHISQUARE K4.
MTB > LET K3 = 1-K2
MTB > NOTE K1 IS THE STATISTIC AND K3 IS THE P-VALUE
MTB > PRINT K1 K3
K1      8.35556
K3      0.0392075
```

First check to verify that the test statistic and p-value are identical to those you produced earlier. Always check your macro using results that you have previously verified. You know that the statistic should be 8.35556 and the p-value 0.0392075; if your macro yields different results, you know there is an error that you need to correct.

The Session window displays the notes that you added; whenever you return to this macro in the future you will know what it does and what needs to be stored in the worksheet before it is executed.

Notes can also help you identify output; for example, in GOF.MTB the values of K1 and K3 are identified as the test statistic and p-value, respectively. Notes serve two purposes: to describe output and to describe the macro.

In the future, when you need to perform a GOF test, you can simply execute the macro GOF.MTB.

Other Enhancements to Macros

In this section you will see some other macro functions that you can use by examining the PTEST.MTB macro from Tutorial 6. This macro, written by Minitab programmers, has quite a few tricks and techniques that make macros very general. You will execute it and then follow along to note the function of the macro steps.

- Choose **F**ile ► Restart **M**initab

Figure 14-11 shows the entire PTEST.MTB macro. You could also view this file in your word processor.

FIGURE 14-11

Complete listing of the PTEST.MTB macro

PTEST.MTB

Nonechoed #'s

```
noecho                      #macro commands will not be printed to the screen
#
#  Binomial parameter:a confidence interval and hypothesis test.
#
#  Written:  9/5/91  Cathy Akritas  Minitab Inc.
#
#
#  USER INPUT:
#   k90 = p-naught, the hypothesized value of the population proportion
#   k89 = p-hat, the observed value of p, the sample proportion
#   k88 = n, the size of the sample that p-hat is based on
#   k81 = indicator used to specify the type of hypothesis test, 1 = upper-
#         tailed test, 2 = a lower-tailed test, and 3 = two-tailed test.
#   c90 = confidence level of the confidence interval for p
#
#  SCRATCH:
#   k82 = Normal cdf at absolute value of Z.
#   k83 = Absolute value of Z.
#   k84 = 2-tailed p-value.
#   k85 = Upper-tail p-value.
#   k86 = Lower-tail p-value.
#   k87 = Z.
#   c93 = For printing, "<", "not =", or ">".
#  c100 = p-naught, for printing purposes
#   c97 = value of the test statistic, z
#   c96 = contains the p-value for the specified hypothesis test
#   c89 = lower endpoint of the confidence interval
#   c87 = upper endpoint of the confidence interval
#
```

Echoed notes

```
note
note     At the "DATA>" prompt below, enter the following values:
note     1.  p-naught, the hypothesized value of the population proportion;
note     2.  x, the observed number of successes; and
note     3   n, the sample size.
note
```

SET command

```
set 'terminal'  c100;       #accepts input from user, p-naught, p-hat, and n
nobs = 3.                   #Minitab expects 3 pieces of information
name c100 'Input:'          #name the input data column
print c100                  #show the user the input values
copy c100 k90 k89 k88       #copy input data into constants, used in calculations
let k89 = k89 / k88
note
```

Direction of test

```
note     At the "DATA>" prompt below, enter a
note          1 to perform an upper-tailed test, or
note          0 to perform a two-tailed test, or
note         -1 to perform a lower-tailed test.
note
set 'terminal' c100;        #accepts input from the user
nobs = 1.                   #waiting for 1 piece of information
let k81 = c100(1) + 2       #k81 = type of hypothesis test to be performed

# The z-test statistic = (phat - pnaught)/sqrt(phat(1-phat)/n)

let k87 = (k89 - k90) / sqrt (k89*(1-k89)/k88)
```

p-values computed

```
# Calculate p-value from z for all 3 alternatives

cdf k87 k86                 # cdf(z) = p-value for the lower-tailed test
let k85 = 1- k86            #(1-cdf(z)) = p-value for upper-tailed test
let k83 = absolute(k87)     #k83 = absolute value of z,
cdf k83 k82                 #2*(1-cdf(absolute(z)) = p-value for two-tailed test
let k84 = 2*(1-k82)
```

```
erase c100 c97 c96        #empty out future storage columns
copy k90 c100             #copy p-naught into c100, use later in output
copy k87 c97              #copy z into c97, use later in reporting reults
copy k86 k84 k85 c96      #copy the p-values into c96
set c93;                  #c93 used in reporting the type of test selected
format (a6).
  <
not =
  >
end
```

Output of appropriate p-value

```
copy  c93 c96 c93 c96;  #copy the p-value column and the type of test column,
use k81.                #but only use row that corresponds to specified test
print c100 c93 c100 c97 c96; #print the results
format ('                 Ho: p = ',f6.4,'  vs.  Ha: p ',a6,f6.4,//,&
'                       z =',f8.5,'       p-value =', f8.5).
note
note    A confidence interval for the true population proportion will be
note    produced below.  At the "DATA>" prompt below, enter the confidence
note    level (95 for a 95% confidence interval) for the confidence interval.
note
```

Input of confidence level

```
set 'terminal' c90;       #c90 = confidence level, specified by the user
nobs = 1.                 #waiting for one piece of information
name c90 'CI Level'
print c90                 #show the user the confidence level
# k90 is used in finding the critical value, Z(alpha/2) used in the confidence
let k90 =  (c90(1)/100) + (1-c90(1)/100)/2
invcdf k90 k91          #k91 = critical value used in confidence interval
let c89 = k89 - k91*sqrt(k89*(1-k89)/k88) #c89 is the lower endpoint
let c87 = k89 + k91*sqrt(k89*(1-k89)/k88) #c87 is the upper endpoint
```

Formatted output of confidence interval

```
print c90 c89 c87;        #report the results
format ('   The ',i2,'% confidence interval is (', f7.4,'  to  ',f6.4,')').

erase k81-k90 c90 c93 c100
echo                      #restore the screen echo feature
```

Quickly browse through the PTEST.MTB macro. The programmer who created this macro annotated it extensively. Almost every line uses either NOTE or #. This makes it easy for you to follow the details of the macro and make any necessary changes.

Now, execute the PTEST.MTB macro:

- Choose **File** ▶ Other Files ▶ **Execute Macro...**
- Press [↵] to execute the macro once
- Select PTEST.MTB from the TUT14 directory

The Session window appears (Figure 14-12). At this point the macro is waiting for you to enter the test null value of p and the sample results. Before you enter these values, notice the commands that Minitab has executed from the macro.

FIGURE 14-12

The first prompt of PTEST.MTB macro in the Session window

```
MTB > Execute 'A:\TUT14\PTEST.MTB' 1.

  At the "DATA>" prompt below, enter the following values:
  1.  p-naught, the hypothesized value of the population proportion;
  2.  x, the observed number of successes; and
  3   n, the sample size.

DATA>
```

In Figure 14-11, the first command in the PTEST.MTB macro is NOECHO. In Figure 14-12, notice that Minitab has not "echoed" the commands executed in the macro. (Remember that when you executed your GOF.MTB macro, Minitab repeated every command of the macro in the Session window.) The NOECHO command is useful if you do not want the Session window "cluttered up" with commands. The NOECHO command also suppresses the display of the MTB > prompt in the Session window.

The NOECHO command is usually the first command in the macro. To turn the echo function back on, the ECHO command should be the last command in the macro before END, as shown in Figure 14-11.

Next, notice the difference between comments that use NOTE and #. When the NOECHO command is used, Minitab echoes NOTE lines in the Session window, but not # lines. None of the USER INPUT lines were echoed in the Session window because they are preceded by a #. However, every line that begins with NOTE is echoed. By using NOTE and # selectively, you can tailor your output as you need.

The programmer tells you, up front, what constants are used and what they relate to. For example, the hypothesized value of p will be stored in K90, the sample size in K88, and so on. By storing results and values in constant locations near K100 and column values around C100, you are less likely to write over information in your worksheet. This is a wise practice.

The PTEST.MTB macro is *interactive,* meaning that the program stops and asks you for a response. You, the user, supply it with information, namely, p-naught, x, and n, the sample size. At the moment, PTEST.MTB is stopped at the SET 'TERMINAL' C100 command and is waiting for you to type the three requested values, which will be stored in C100.

To make a macro interactive, the programmer used the SET command to store the values the user inputs from the terminal (i.e., the keyboard) in column C100. The NOBS 3 subcommand tells Minitab to accept only three values from the keyboard. If too many or too few values are entered, Minitab informs you.

Enter the sample information to continue the macro:

- Type **0.51 86 200** and press ↵

After recording the values you entered (Figure 14-13), Minitab asks for the direction of your test and waits for you to respond.

FIGURE 14-13

The results of the PTEST.MTB macro in the Session window

```
DATA> 0.51 86 200

Input:
    0.51     86.00    200.00


   At the "DATA>" prompt below, enter a
        1 to perform an upper-tailed test, or
        0 to perform a two-tailed test, or
       -1 to perform a lower-tailed test.

DATA>
```

Respond to perform a lower-tailed test:

- Type **-1** and press ↵

If you continue to follow the macro commands, you will note that it computes p-values in much the same way as you did when you created the GOF.MTB macro. For example, the default CDF command is used, corresponding to a standard normal distribution. The macro then computes all three p-values, corresponding to upper-tailed, lower-tailed, and two-tailed tests.

Using an innovative technique, the macro outputs the appropriate p-value for the alternative you specify. Notice the USE subcommand, which allows you to select the appropriate alternative hypothesis and p-value by specifying the appropriate row of columns.

Finally, enter the desired level of confidence for the confidence interval for p:

- Type **95** and press ↵

Continue reading down the macro and note the use of the FORMAT subcommand when printing results. The result is the informative output seen in the Session window (Figure 14-14).

FIGURE 14-14
Output from the PTEST.MTB macro

```
DATA> -1

                    Ho: p = 0.5100  vs.  Ha: p   <   0.5100

                    z =-2.28525      p-value = 0.01115

  A confidence interval for the true population proportion will be
  produced below.  At the "DATA>" prompt below, enter the confidence
  level (95 for a 95% confidence interval) for the confidence interval.

DATA> 95

CI Level
  95

   The 95% confidence interval is ( 0.3614  to  0.4986)
```

The FORMAT subcommand uses Fortran notation. You can also include words as part of the output to make the results more coherent. (For more information about Fortran notation, see the Reference section in Part IV of this book.)

Although it is not covered here, you might want to take some additional time and work your way through this macro command by command to see exactly where the programmer stored the various quantities. Because the programmer documented every step, it can be instructive to work your way through.

Given Minitab's many functions, it is easy to build your own set of unique programs. The only limits are your imagination. If you are interested in learning more about macros, ask your instructor for more information. If you want to pursue it yourself, refer to the discussion of macros in the Reference section (Part IV of this book).

Congratulations! You have seen what Minitab is capable of doing—but this is only the beginning. If you use Minitab in your school or on the job, you will continue to find new and interesting features that show just how powerful a program it is.

Minitab Command Summary

The menus and commands introduced in or related to this tutorial are described in this section. You will find a complete explanation of all menus and commands in the Reference section of this manual.

Menu	Command	Function
File		
	Other Files	
	Start Recording History	Stores executed commands in a file, which can then be edited in a word processor and used as a macro
	Stop Recording History	Stops entering commands into the file
	Start Storing Macro	Stores commands in a file, called a macro, that can be executed any number of times
	Stop Storing Macro	Stops entering commands into the macro file
	Execute Macro	Executes the commands in a macro file a user-specified number of times

Review and Practice

Matching

Match the following terms to their definitions by placing the correct letter next to the term it explains.

____ 'TERMINAL'

____ NOBS

____ END

____ ASCII

a. Minitab notation for the keyboard, when user enters information a macro is executing

b. Stops entering commands in a macro

c. Stores commands in a macro file

____ STOR>

____ NOTE

____ #

____ STORE

d. Similar to the NOTE command

e. Minitab prompt when a macro is being created in Minitab

f. Determines the number of values to be typed

g. Allows the user to document a macro by including comments in the macro that annotate the function of the macro; can also be used in the Minitab Session window

h. Acronym that means the same thing as a text-formatted file

True/False

Mark the following statements T or F.

____ 1. Minitab macros created in a word processor must be saved in ASCII or text format.

____ 2. Minitab adds the .MTB extension to macros created using the Store command.

____ 3. Minitab can execute a macro created in a word processor if the macro filename has an .MTB extension.

____ 4. Macros can be executed at most three times.

____ 5. Once a command is entered in a macro in Minitab, the command cannot be changed using Minitab.

____ 6. The STOR> prompt in the Session window indicates that Minitab is waiting for a command to store in a macro.

____ 7. The Stop Storing Macro menu command is equivalent to the END command in the Session window.

____ 8. Files referred to in Minitab commands are enclosed in single quotes.

___ 9. When storing commands in a Minitab macro, the commands are simultaneously executed in the Session window.

___ 10. Files created with a word processor are automatically in ASCII or text format.

Practice Problems

1. Using a word processor, change the sample size in each column of the CONFINTS macro from 30 to 5 and save the macro as CONFINTS5.MTB. Execute the macro four times. How has the smaller sample size affected your results? How many of the confidence intervals do not contain the mean? Should the smaller sample size affect this? What can you say about the sizes (i.e., lengths) of your confidence intervals? Would you expect this to happen?

2. Create a new macro that performs the same computations as CONFINTS but uses the t distribution (i.e., assume you do not know sigma).

3. Many states have daily "numbers" games or lotteries. Most have 3-number games and some also have 4-number games. You bet on a certain number; if that number is chosen, you win.

   In some states the 3-digit number is selected as follows (the 4-digit number is similar): there are three bins labeled 1, 2, and 3. In each bin are ten identical ping pong balls, each labeled with a digit from 0 to 9. One ball is selected randomly from each bin and the resulting 3-digit number is the winning number.

   After monitoring the outcomes for about a month and a half (after 40 numbers have been drawn), you decide to check if the numbers are being chosen randomly. One way to check would be to determine if the digits 0 to 9 are uniformly distributed. Use the information below and the GOF macro to determine if the digits are uniformly distributed.

Digit:	0	1	2	3	4	5	6	7	8	9
Freq:	9	11	11	9	11	24	6	13	17	9

4. Create a macro that is similar to the CONFINTS.MTB macro, but will generate data from a chi-square distribution with 8 degrees of freedom. The variance of a chi-square (8df) is 2*8=16, so sigma is 4. Generate 100 95% confidence intervals using normal theory results (use ZInterval) and decide whether it is wise to use normal theory results (based on samples of n=30) when the population is clearly not normal.

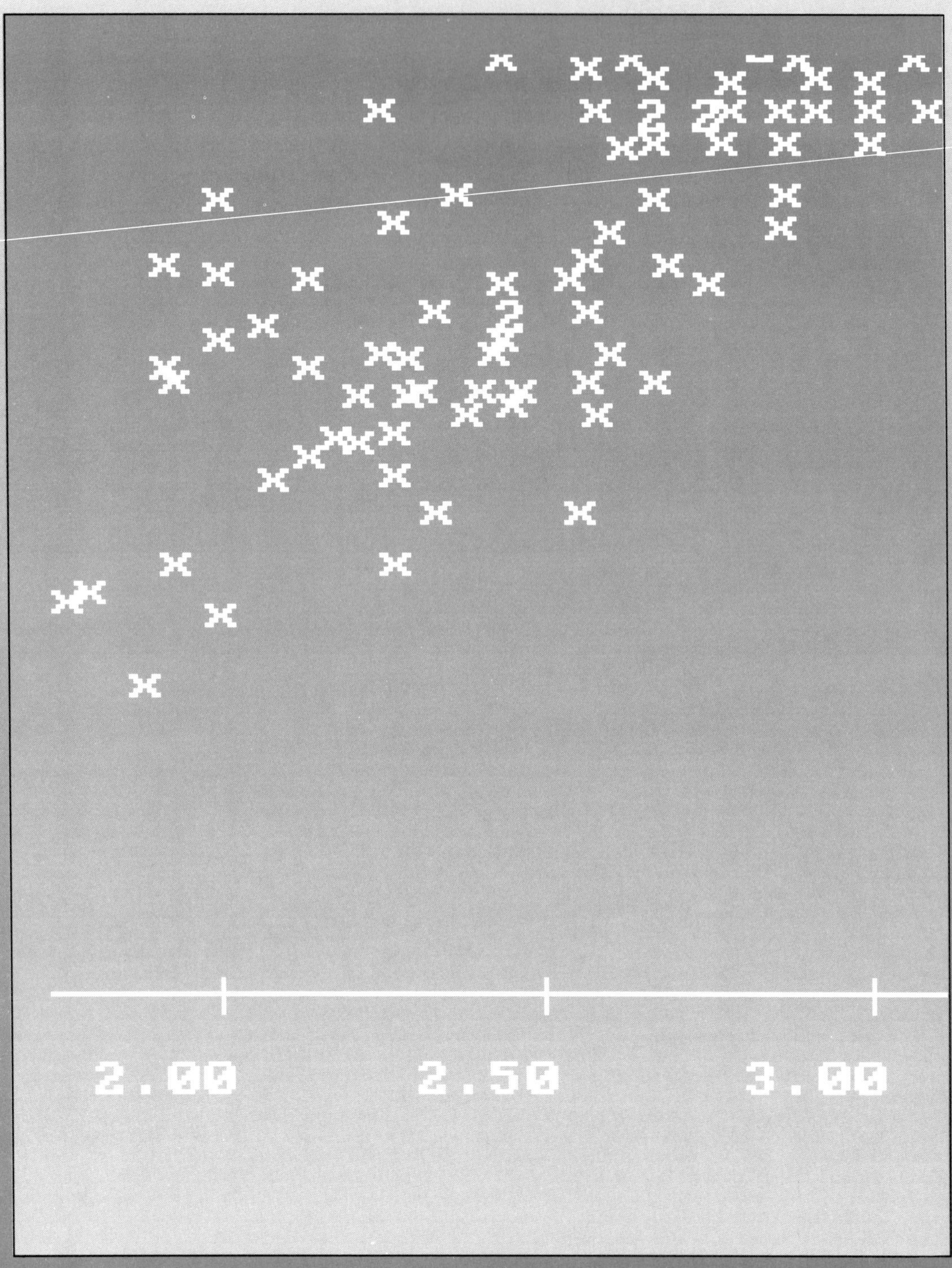
2.00
2.50
3.00

PART III

Exploring Data

This section contains descriptions of all the data sets used in *The Student Edition of Minitab*, as well as for extra, larger data sets that students can explore on their own once they have completed the tutorials.

All descriptions include:

- a discussion of the source of the data and its contents;
- a listing of each variable name, its column number, a count of non-missing values, and description.

The section is divided into three parts:

1. Exploring Data: Other Data Sets
These data sets are not used in the tutorials or exercises, and present opportunities for students to analyze data using the statistical techniques presented in the tutorials.

2. Exploring Data: Larger Data Sets
These large data sets are not used in the tutorials or exercises. Their descriptions include suggestions for analysis, as well as larger questions about relationships among variables that students can answer using their own knowledge of Minitab gained in the tutorials.

3. Data Sets Used in Tutorials and Exercises
This section contains descriptions of all data sets used in the tutorials and exercises. Each one is cross referenced to the tutorial(s) in which it is used, either in the tutorial itself, or the exercises. When they are finished with the tutorials, students can explore these data sets further, using whatever Minitab techniques they choose.

Exploring Data: Other Data Sets

ACCOUNTS.MTW

As branch manager of Fly-By-Night International Bank's largest branch, you want to see your customers served quickly, especially when they are opening a new account. You would like it to take no more than six minutes to fill out and process all of the paper work to open any kind of new account.

Your assistant manager measures the time (in minutes) it takes to process five randomly selected "new account" customers each day for 40 consecutive days.

Column	Name	Count	Description
C1	CUST 1	40	Time for the first randomly selected customer on a given day to be processed
C2	CUST 2	40	Time for the second randomly selected customer on a given day to be processed
C3	CUST 3	40	Time for the third randomly selected customer on a given day to be processed
C4	CUST 4	40	Time for the fourth randomly selected customer on a given day to be processed
C5	CUST 5	40	Time for the fifth randomly selected customer on a given day to be processed

FOOTBALL.MTW

The data below come from a newspaper article listing the salaries of all players on a professional football team prior to the start of the 1991 season.

Column	Name	Count	Description
C1-A	POSITION	50	The position of the player
C2	EXPERNCE	50	The years experience of the player
C3	1990 SAL	47	The 1990 salary of the player
C4	1991 SAL	39	The 1991 salary of the player
C5	1992 SAL	19	The 1992 salary of the player
C6	BONUS	17	The signing bonus the player received

GOLF.MTW

A college student, who is also an avid golfer, kept track of his golf scores in the fall of 1991. Based on playing nine holes he recorded his score, how many greens he hit in regulation, and how many pars or better he made for the nine holes.

Column	Name	Count	Description
C1	SCORE	22	The score for nine holes of golf
C2	REGLTN	22	The number of greens made in the regulation number of strokes
C3	PARS	22	The number of pars or better (i.e., pars, birdies, eagles, etc.) made in the nine holes

HWASTE.MTW

New and abandoned hazardous waste sites are being discovered across the U.S. For each region of the country the number of hazardous waste sites found in each state in the region was determined.

Column	Name	Count	Description
C1	NORTHWST	7	The number of hazardous waste sites found in each state in the northwestern part of the U.S.
C2	SOUTHWST	6	The number of hazardous waste sites found in each state in the southwestern part of the U.S.
C3	MIDWEST	7	The number of hazardous waste sites found in each state in the midwestern part of the U.S.
C4	SOUTHCEN	7	The number of hazardous waste sites found in each state in the south central part of the U.S.
C5	SOUTHEAS	12	The number of hazardous waste sites found in each state in the southeastern part of the U.S.
C6	NORTHEAS	9	The number of hazardous waste sites found in each state in the northeastern part of the U.S.

NIELSEN.MTW

Each year the Nielsen company does an extensive survey of TV viewing habits of the US population. Many of the surveys are done by age and gender groups because sponsors are very interested in what age and gender person watches specific programs. (For example, see the VPVH.MTW data set.)

This data set concerns the trends of TV stations and TV sets in the U.S. over the years. It also contains information about weekly TV viewing habits.

Column	Name	Count	Description
C1	YEAR	25	Year
C2	TV STNS	17	The number of TV stations both VHF and UHF
C3	NUM TVS	17	The number of households in the U.S. with TVs in 1,000
C4	CABLE	14	The number of cable stations operating
C5	SUBSCBRS	16	The number of cable subscribers in 1,000
C6	TIME	20	The average number of hours of viewing per TV household per week

PAPER.MTW

A large metropolitan newspaper buys its newsprint from a supplier in the northwest. A quality engineer inspects each roll of paper that is used by the newspaper. The engineer is especially concerned about small holes in the paper, since if there is a hole, the print is lost and this makes it difficult, if not impossible, to read an article or ad.

Each roll is sampled six times. The sampling involves taking 1.5- by 2-foot sections of the paper (this corresponds roughly to the final dimension of a page of the newspaper) and counting the number of holes (or flaws) larger than 1 millimeter in diameter found in the section.

Column	Name	Count	Description
C1	SAMPLE 1	35	The number of holes per 1.5 × 2 foot section of newspaper in the first sample
C2	SAMPLE 2	35	The number of holes per 1.5 × 2 foot section of newspaper in the second sample
C3	SAMPLE 3	35	The number of holes per 1.5 × 2 foot section of newspaper in the third sample
C4	SAMPLE 4	35	The number of holes per 1.5 × 2 foot section of newspaper in the fourth sample
C5	SAMPLE 5	35	The number of holes per 1.5 × 2 foot section of newspaper in the fifth sample
C6	SAMPLE 6	35	The number of holes per 1.5 × 2 foot section of newspaper in the sixth sample

REPORTS.MTW

Many universities around the country are part of a small town or city. In many cases the student population dwarfs the town or city's full-time resident population. This file contains data on the total number of police reports for each month over the past six and a half years. A police report was defined as any arrest or any formal statement taken by the police department. Hence the reports cover the spectrum of charges and complaints; these include noise violations, burglary, and assaults.

Column	Name	Count	Description
C1	YEAR	80	Year
C2	MONTH	80	Month
C3	TOTAL	80	The total number of police reports for the month

SALAMDER.MTW

Fourteen salamanders were housed in individual cages. During the period of study, the salamanders were exposed to normal conditions, and each cage was monitored separately. The activity level in each cage was measured hourly over the course of six days, for a total of 144 hourly assessments. These results were subsequently used to compare other experimental conditions (not included in this data set).

Column	Name	Count	Description
C1	ACTIVITY	144	The daily activity level for 14 salamanders

STEALS.MTW

Early in the 1991 major league baseball season, Rickey Henderson of the Oakland Athletics baseball team became the stolen base leader, passing Lou Brock. Newspapers reported the number of bases Mr. Henderson stole for each day of the week. This information is saved in this file.

Column	Name	Count	Description
C1-A	DAY	7	The day of the week
C2	BASES	7	The total number of bases that Mr. Henderson stole on the given day of the week

TBILLS.MTW

This file contains information on the bid and asking price and yield of treasury bills for 34 selected days in 1991.

Column	Name	Count	Description
C1	BID	34	The price bid for a treasury bill on a selected day

C2	ASK	34	The asking price for a treasury bill on a selected day
C3	CHANGE	29	The change in the price
C4	YIELD	34	The yield of the bill on the selected day

USDEMOG.MTW

Census values for the U.S. are given. The estimated population of the U.S. as well as population density of the U.S. are provided.

Column	Name	Count	Description
C1	YEAR	35	Year
C2	US POPLN	21	Population of the U.S. in millions
C3	POP DENS	21	Population density of the U.S. in people per square mile

Exploring Data: Larger Data Sets

LAKES.MTW

An extensive study was done to determine if characteristics of lakes in Wisconsin had changed over the last 60 years. Historical data were obtained on 149 lakes between 1925 and 1931. Similar data were obtained on these same lakes between 1979 and 1983.

Information collected included physical characteristics of the lake such as maximum depth and surface area, as well as the kind of lake it was. Other variables included the total area of the lake's watershed and the percentage of the lake that was bog. The amount of development was also included and is represented by the number of permanent dwellings that are within 100 meters of the shore.

In addition, several water quality variables were measured. These included the pH, alkalinity, conductivity, and calcium. Since measurement techniques had changed from 1925 to 1979, measurements were adjusted to be comparable. The data given represent the adjusted values.

Column	Name	Count	Description
C1	LAKE ID	149	An identification number given to each lake
C2	TYPE	149	The type of lake (1=seepage; 2=drained; 3=drainage; 4=spring)
C3	DEPTH	149	Maximum lake depth in meters
C4	AREA	149	Lake surface area in hectares
C5	WS AREA	149	Watershed area in hectares
C6	% BOG	148	Percentage of lake that is bog
C7	DW HIST	148	Number of lakeshore dwellings, circa 1930
C8	DW CURNT	149	Number of lakeshore dwellings, circa 1980
C9	PH HIST	149	Historical pH reading
C10	PH CURNT	149	Current pH reading
C11	COND HST	149	Historical conductivity reading
C12	COND CUR	149	Current conductivity reading
C13	ALK HIST	149	Historical alkalinity reading
C14	ALK CURN	149	Current alkalinity reading
C15	CA HIST	116	Historical calcium reading
C16	CA CURNT	149	Current calcium reading

Suggestions for Analysis

1. Summarize each of the variables in the data set.
2. Plot each of the current lake variables versus the historical variables. If the slope between the historical and current measurements differs from 1, then one of the measurements is biased relative to the other measurement. Do any of the relationships suggest a bias?
3. Compare the current and historical measurements to determine if there has been any change in the lake characteristics.

4. Create a new variable that records the maximum of the number of dwellings in 1930 and the number of dwellings in 1980 for each lake. Define undeveloped lakes as those with no permanent dwellings. Define low developed lakes as those with 1 to 20 dwellings per lake, moderately developed lakes as those with 21 to 43 dwellings per lake, and highly developed lakes as those with 44 or more dwellings. Determine if the lake characteristics have changed over time for these different groups of lakes.

5. Larger lakes can certainly support a larger number of dwellings. Create a new variable that is the ratio of the number of dwellings per hectare of lake area. Form four equal-size groups using this variable and determine if the lake characteristics have changed over time for these different groups of lakes.

6. You can also do both questions 4 and 5 using the information for the historical or current time periods alone. Do your answers change if you restrict your attention to one time period alone?

LANGUAGE.MTW

One way of measuring people's attitudes toward others is to ask them to evaluate speakers of other languages. However, if the speakers they rate are different, one does not know whether to attribute variability in ratings to the speaker or to the language. In a technique called the matched guise technique, pioneered by Wallace Lambert at McGill University, subjects are asked to listen to a number of language segments and rate certain qualities of the speaker, such as friendliness, honesty, and trustworthiness. However, three of the segments they hear are actually the same speaker, using different language "guises." Differences in ratings of that speaker, then, can be attributed to attitudes toward those languages and those who speak them.

In the data set LANGUAGE.MTW, students at an American high school were asked to rate five language segments for various qualities, on a 1 to 5 bipolar rating scale. (The qualities were determined in a prior survey that asked students which qualities they considered most important for friendship.) The language segments were:

Segment A: the language of a recently arrived immigrant group

Segment C: English

Segment E: French

Segments B and D were "distractor" languages, and are not included in this data set. Students filled out questionnaires with background information on their experience with other languages, length of time they lived in the area, and gender.

The immigrant language used was the language of a rather large, recently arrived immigrant population. This study attempted to determine if high school age students held significantly negative attitudes toward speakers of the immigrants' language. It was predicted that they would have positive attitudes toward English and French.

For all questions that were answered on a 1–5 bipolar rating scale, 1 was the most negative (inconsiderate, unfriendly, etc.), and 5 was the most positive (considerate, friendly, etc.).

Column	Name	Count	Description
C1	IMM CONS	59	Immigrant language: Is the person considerate? (1=inconsiderate, 2=somewhat inconsiderate, 3=neutral, 4=somewhat considerate, 5=considerate)
C2	IMM FRND	59	Immigrant language: Is the person friendly?
C3	IMM TRST	59	Immigrant language: Is the person trustworthy?
C4	IMM HON	59	Immigrant language: Is the person honest?
C5	IMM HLP	57	Immigrant language: Is the person helpful?
C6	IMM UND	58	Immigrant language: Is the person understanding?
C7	IMM RESP	59	Immigrant language: Is the person responsible?
C8	IMM ?	59	Can you identify this language? (0=no, 1=yes)
C9	ENG CONS	59	English language: Is the person considerate?

C10	ENG FRND	59	English language: Is the person friendly?
C11	ENG TRST	59	English language: Is the person trustworthy?
C12	ENG HON	59	English language: Is the person honest?
C13	ENG HLP	59	English language: Is the person helpful?
C14	ENG UND	58	English language: Is the person understanding?
C15	ENG RESP	59	English language: Is the person responsible?
C16	ENG ?	59	Can you identify this language? (0=no, 1=yes)
C17	FRN CONS	58	French language: Is the person considerate?
C18	FRN FRND	58	French language: Is the person friendly?
C19	FRN TRST	58	French language: Is the person trustworthy?
C20	FRN HON	58	French language: Is the person honest?
C21	FRN HLP	58	French language: Is the person helpful?
C22	FRN UND	57	French language: Is the person understanding?
C23	FRN RESP	58	French language: Is the person responsible?
C24	FRN ?	59	Can you identify this language? (0=no, 1=yes)
C25	ENGLISH?	59	Is English your native language? (1=yes, 2=no)
C26	STATE?	59	Have you lived in this state all your life? (0=no, 1=yes)

C27	LANGTIME	45	For how many years have you studied a language at school? (0=none, 1=0–1 years, 2=1–2 years, 3=2+ years)
C28	2ND LANG	45	How, if at all, are you exposed to a language other than English in your home? (0=not exposed at all, 1=speak one, 2=hear one but do not understand, 3=hear one and do understand)
C29	TIME 2 L	37	How long have you been exposed to a language other than English in your home? (0=0 years, 1=1–7 years, 2=8–15 years)
C30	GENDER	42	The sex of the student (0=female, 1=male)

Suggestions for Analysis

1. Obtain boxplots for each of the three languages for each of the seven qualities that were rated.
2. Obtain descriptive statistics for each of the qualities for each of the languages.

Each of the following can be asked of each rating quality separately or of the average rating, averaged across all seven qualities.

1. Compare the ratings of the three languages.
2. Compare the ratings of the three languages between those students whose native language is and is not English.
3. Compare the ratings of the three languages between those students who have lived and not lived in the state their entire life.
4. Compare the ratings of the three languages among students who have studied a foreign language in high school for different numbers of years.
5. How do the ratings of the three languages change if the student is exposed to another language at home?

6. How do the ratings of the three languages change depending upon the length of time the student has been exposed to another language at home?

7. Compare the ratings of the three languages between male and female students.

S&P500.MTW

A professor in a business school at a southern university monitored the stock market over several years. In this data set are 500 consecutive daily high, low, and closing values for the Standard and Poor's 500 Cash (Spot) Index.

Column	Name	Count	Description
C1	HIGH	500	The high value of Standard and Poor's 500 Cash (Spot) Index on a given day
C2	LOW	500	The low value of Standard and Poor's 500 Cash (Spot) Index on a given day
C3	CLOSE	500	The closing value of Standard and Poor's 500 Cash (Spot) Index on a given day

Suggestions for Analysis

1. Since the data are daily data, obtain a time series plot of each of the variables.

2. Take first differences of the closing price data and obtain the time series plot of these data.

3. Obtain the autocorrelation and partial autocorrelation plots of the closing data and the differenced closing data.

4. Perform an ARIMA analysis of the closing price data.

5. Perform similar analyses of the high and low price data for each day.

6. Obtain the range (i.e., the high minus the low price) for each day. Summarize these ranges. Does a time series plot of the ranges suggest that time series analysis could be used to analyze these ranges?

SALARY.MTW

A small private college does a yearly study of its faculty's salaries. Information on gender, department, years at the school, beginning salary, current salary, and an "experience" variable are recorded. The experience variable is a summary of many other variables that are all combined to come up with an "experience" score. The higher the score the more experience the person had when they first started. The faculty member's current rank is also measured.

Column	Name	Count	Description
C1	ID	171	The college's identification number for the faculty
C2-A	GENDER	171	The gender of the faculty member coded F and M
C3	GENDER N	171	The gender of the faculty member coded 0=F and 1=M
C4	START YR	171	The starting year of the faculty member
C5	DEPTCODE	171	The department of the faculty member coded as a number
C6	BEGIN $	171	The starting salary of the faculty member
C7	1991 $	171	The current salary (1991) of the faculty member
C8	EXPERNC	171	The "experience variable" value when the person started at the college
C9	RANKCODE	171	The current rank of the faculty member where 1=instructor, 2=assistant professor, 3=associate professor, and 4=professor

Suggestions for Analysis

1. Obtain summary statistics for the percentage of females/males, starting year, percentages in each department, ranks, and percentage of males and females in each department and each rank.
2. Obtain summary information about the average salary at the college, separately for each gender, each department, each rank, and each gender by department and rank.
3. Obtain summary information about the average salary increase (in dollars) separately for each gender, each department, each rank, and each gender by department and rank.
4. Obtain summary information about the average salary increase (as a percentage) separately for each gender, each department, each rank, and each gender by department and rank.
5. What has been the average yearly salary increase for the college?
6. Compare the salaries of females and males at the college.
7. Are the salaries different for the different departments?
8. What effect do department and gender have on salary?
9. Compare the effect of current rank on the salary structure.
10. Are current rank and gender related?
11. Are department and gender related?
12. Which variable has the greatest effect on current salary?

WHEAT.MTW

A professor in a business school at a southern university studied wheat futures. This data set contains the daily high, low, and closing values for wheat futures for 500 consecutive days, representing approximately 1½ year's data. In addition, the number of wheat future contracts traded on the day is recorded.

Column	Name	Count	Description
C1	HIGH	500	The high value of wheat futures traded on that day

C2	LOW	500	The low value of wheat futures traded on that day
C3	CLOSE	500	The closing value of wheat futures traded on that day
C4	VOLUME	500	The total number of contracts traded on that day

Suggestions for Analysis

1. Because the data are daily data, obtain a time series plot of each of the variables.
2. Take first differences of the closing price data and obtain the time series plot of these data.
3. Obtain the autocorrelation and partial autocorrelation plots of the closing data and the differenced closing data.
4. Perform an ARIMA analysis of the closing price data.
5. Perform similar analyses of the high and low price data for each day.
6. Obtain the range (i.e., the high minus the low price) for each day of trading. Summarize these ranges. Does the time series plot suggest that time series analysis could be used to analyze these ranges?

Data Sets Used in Tutorials and Exercises

BANKING.MTW

Banking profits for the first quarter of the year were obtained for all banks in a state in the years 1991 and 1990. Ten states were chosen randomly each year and the profits were obtained from FDIC records.

The total first-quarter profits for each of the 10 states are stored in separate columns, each year's data in one column.

Column	Name	Count	Description
C1	1991	10	First-quarter 1991 banking profits in billions for all banks in 10 randomly selected states

C2	1990	10	First-quarter 1990 banking profits in billions for all banks in 10 randomly selected states

Used in: Tutorial 11, Analyzing Data with Nonparametric Methods

CLOTTING.MTW

Aspirin is routinely prescribed by doctors to heart attack patients to prevent the formation of obstructions in the arteries due to blood clots. A study was done to investigate whether the formation of blood clots is affected by aspirin. Twelve adult men were used in the study. The time for these twelve men's blood to clot was measured by the time from the start of a prothrombin-thrombin reaction to the formation of the final clot. The clotting time was measured before the men took two aspirin and then three hours after taking the aspirin.

Column	Name	Count	Description
C1	BEFORE	12	The time for a clot to form, before taking aspirin
C2	AFTER	12	The time for a clot to form, after taking aspirin

Used in: Tutorial 7, Inference from Two Samples
Tutorial 11, Analyzing Data with Nonparametric Methods

COMPUTER.MTW

A student was interested in purchasing a computer. After saving up some money from various summer jobs, the student began to research prices and equipment. The student decided to purchase a high-performance computer, so that it would be usable throughout her college years and well beyond. The college recommends that students purchase DOS personal computers, so her efforts were directed at investigating these kinds of machines. To research the cost, she bought several personal computer magazines, and recorded the prices and features of various computers advertised. This data set contains the result of the student's efforts.

Column	Name	Count	Description
C1	CPU	35	The type of CPU used in the computer
C2	SPEED	35	The speed of the CPU
C3	HD	35	The size of the hard disk drive in megabytes
C4	FLOPPY	35	The number of floppy drives included
C5	MEMORY	35	The RAM size in megabytes
C6-A	MONITOR	35	Color or monochrome display
C7-A	MOUSE	35	Is a mouse included?
C8-A	SOFTWARE	35	Is software included?
C9	PRICE	35	The cost of the system in $

Used in: Tutorial 1, Working with Data (exercises)
Tutorial 2, Summarizing, Transforming, and Manipulating Data (exercises)
Tutorial 9, Examining Linear Relationships Between Variables: Regression (exercises)

CROWDS.MTW

In a study of perceived crowdedness and the color of the walls of a room, an experimental psychology professor selected 36 unacquainted female and 36 unacquainted male subjects. The female subjects were all brought into a room in which the walls had been painted a dark green. At the end of one hour each subject was asked to rate how crowded the subject felt on a scale of 1 to 30, with 30 being the most crowded. The experiment was repeated with the male subjects.

The perceived crowdedness of each female subject is recorded in column C1 and the male values are recorded in column C2.

Column	Name	Count	Description
C1	FEM RATE	36	The perceived crowdedness of females in the study

C2	MALERATE	36	The perceived crowdedness of males in the study

Used in: Tutorial 6, Inference from One Sample
Tutorial 7, Inference from Two Samples

FISH.MTW

Scientists are concerned with the effects of acid rain on aquatic life. Studies have shown that at very low pH levels (around pH 3, which is very acidic), many fish die. In the environment, however, the decrease in pH from naturally occurring levels (of around 7) is rather gradual and rarely are very low pH values seen. Values in the range of 6.5 to 5.5 are quite common. Scientists are interested in the effects of this lowered pH on fish, particularly in how the lowered pH adversely changes the parental behavior in fish. Fish offspring that are not cared for adequately have a lower survival rate.

In one study, a certain species of fish was investigated and several parental behaviors observed. Guarding is an important activity because it ensures that the fish eggs and young are safe from predators. Fanning the eggs is also important since it keeps oxygenated water circulating over the eggs and hence increases the chances of survival of the eggs. Pairs of fish were exposed to water of varying pH levels and the percentage of time each fish spent guarding and fanning their young was recorded. The values given are the averages of approximately 10 fish.

Column	Name	Count	Description
C1	pH	80	The level of pH the fish were exposed to: 7.0, 6.5, 6.0, and 5.5
C2	DAY	80	The day of the study, 1 to 10 days
C3-A	GENDER	80	The gender of the fish, M or F
C4	GUARDING	80	The average time spent guarding the young
C5	FANNING	80	The average time spent fanning the young

Used in: Tutorial 3, Graphical Methods for Describing Data (exercises)
Tutorial 7, Inference from Two Samples (exercises)

FLEXIBLE.MTW

Flexible Circuits, Inc. is a company specializing in the manufacture of parts used in various electronic components. Their products include copper wires used in stereo equipment. These copper wires are subjected to a plating process in which they are dipped in a micro-etch bath, set at 95 degrees F, for 1 minute and 10 seconds. The diameters of the wires must meet certain specifications if they are to be acceptable to the purchaser.

A study was done to investigate the apparent lack of consistency of the wire diameters from shift to shift. Two studies were done. In the first study, the temperature of the bath was set at 95 degrees F and wires were randomly selected from each shift's production: nine wires from the first shift, six wires from the second, and three from the third shift. The wire diameter is stored in column C1 DIAMETER and the shift that it came from in column C2 SHIFT.

In the second study, the temperature of the bath was set to 100 degrees F. Twenty-five samples were taken: twelve from shift 1, seven from shift 2, and six from shift 3. These data are stored in columns C3 DIAM1, C4 DIAM2, and C5 DIAM3, respectively.

Column	Name	Count	Description
C1	DIAMETER	18	The diameter in microinches of wires used in stereo equipment
C2	SHIFT	18	The shift during which the wire was produced
C3	DIAM1	12	Wire diameters in microinches taken from shift 1
C4	DIAM2	7	Wire diameters in microinches taken from shift 2
C5	DIAM3	6	Wire diameters in microinches taken from shift 3

Used in: Tutorial 8, Comparing Population Means: Analysis of Variance
Tutorial 11, Analyzing Data with Nonparametric Methods

FLEX2.MTW

In another study of the diameters of the copper-plated wires manufactured by the Flexible Circuits, Inc., the stability of the production process was investigated. The company's engineers have specified that the wires have diameters of 70 microinches plus or minus 3 microinches. Five wires were randomly selected each hour for 21 consecutive hours.

Several weeks later, after instituting new guidelines for the production process, wire diameters were selected systematically every 12 minutes during each of the three shift's production on a given day. These data are stored in columns C2 SHIFT 1, C3 SHIFT 2, and C4 SHIFT 3, respectively.

As a final study of the wire production process, the plant engineer wanted to determine what fraction of the wires produced were defective, that is, did not meet the specifications that had been set forth by the engineering staff. Two hundred wires were randomly selected each day for an entire month and the number of nonconforming or defective wires out of 200 is stored in C5 NONCONF.

Column	Name	Count	Description
C1	DIAMETER	105	Wire diameters, sampled 5 per hour for 21 hours
C2	SHIFT 1	40	Wire diameter, systematically selected every 12 minutes from shift 1
C3	SHIFT 2	40	Wire diameter, systematically selected every 12 minutes from shift 2
C4	SHIFT 3	40	Wire diameter, systematically selected every 12 minutes from shift 3
C5	NONCONF	30	The number of defective (nonconforming) wires out of 200 wires selected randomly each day for a month

Used in: Tutorial 12, Statistical Process Control

GENETICS.MTW

This is the result of a study to determine whether carbon-dioxide–deficient soil changes the distribution of phenotypes of peas. Two hundred randomly chosen peas were grown in carbon-dioxide–deficient soil and the phenotype of each of these peas was determined.

Column	Name	Count	Description
C1	TYPE	4	Phenotype of pea: 1=smooth-yellow, 2=smooth-green, 3=wrinkled-yellow, 4=wrinkled-green
C2	PROB	4	Mendelian probabilities of each phenotype
C3	PHENO	200	Phenotype code for each of 200 randomly chosen peas grown in carbon-dioxide–deficient soil

Used in: Tutorial 10, Analyzing Categorical Data
Tutorial 14, Macros

GRADES.MTW

This data set is the grade summary for a social studies class in a secondary school. Three tests scores have been recorded for the 24 students in the class.

Column	Name	Count	Description
C1-A	LAST NAM	24	The last name of the student
C2-A	FIRST	24	The first name of the student
C3	TEST1	24	The score (out of 100) on the first test
C4	TEST2	24	The score (out of 100) on the second test
C5	TEST3	24	The score (out of 100) on the third test

Used in: Tutorial 1, Working with Data
Tutorial 2, Summarizing, Transforming, and Manipulating Data
Tutorial 3, Graphical Methods for Describing Data (exercises)
Tutorial 11, Analyzing Data with Nonparametric Methods (exercises)

HEALTH.MTW

As part of a study investigating the general health of college students, information was collected from 21 randomly chosen college students.

Column	Name	Count	Description
C1	AGE	21	The age of the student in years
C2	GENDER	21	The gender of the student: coded as 0=male, 1=female
C3	HGT	21	The height of the student in centimeters
C4	DBP	21	The diastolic blood pressure of the student
C5	SBP	21	The systolic blood pressure of the student
C6	SMOKER?	21	The smoking status of the student: coded as 0=no and 1=yes
C7	EX REG	21	The volume of air exhaled after a regular breath
C8	EX MAX	21	The volume of air exhaled after one deep breath

Used in: Tutorial 7, Inference from Two Samples

HEIGHTS.MTW

A professor in the Physiology department of a medical school collected data on the self-reported heights of 60 females in an introductory physiology class. Students were asked to provide their height (in inches) the first day of class.

Column	Name	Count	Description
C1	ID	60	The student's ID #
C2	HEIGHTS	60	The self reported heights (in inches) of 60 college females

Used in: Tutorial 5, Distributions and Random Data

HORSE.MTW

Officials at a western national park were concerned about the following issue. Horses are rented by concessions outside the park for use in riding trails in the park. Park officials are concerned that plant seeds eaten by the horses while grazing in pastures outside the park will pass through the horses and be deposited along the trails in the park. These seeds could then spread to displace the park's natural fauna.

A graduate student in botany investigated this problem by studying several pedestrian/equestrian trails in the park to determine whether the diversity of plant species was affected by the presence of horses on the trail. (Her study included much more data than are presented in this data set.)

The student selected six trails from the park, two low-usage trials, two moderate-usage trails, and two high-usage trails. The amount of usage corresponded to the amount of time the trail was used by horses. The low-usage trails were actually "none," in that horses were not permitted on these trails.

At systematic distances from the beginning of each trail, the student determined the number of species present along the trail. She determined the number of species present at three spots at each site along the trail: 1) within a 1/2-square-meter area directly adjacent to the trail, 2) 1 meter from the edge of the trail and adjacent to her first area, and 3) 5 meters from the edge of the trail in the interior. The three locations are named EDGE1, EDGE2, and INTERIOR.

Column	Name	Count	Description
C1	TRAIL	289	Trail number 1–6; 1 and 2 are low usage, 3 and 4 moderate, and 5 and 6 high usage

C2	DISTNCE	289	Distance of site from the beginning of the trail in meters
C3	EDGE1	289	Number of species adjacent to trail
C4	EDGE2	289	Number of species 1 meter off of the trail
C5	INTERIOR	289	Number of species 5 meters off of the trail

Used in: Tutorial 4, Numerical Methods for Describing Data (exercises)
Tutorial 6, Inference from One Sample (exercises)

KRUNCHY.MTW

The marketing department of Krunchy Cereal Company did a study to determine which of two advertising companies (Ace or Best) to use to advertise their product lines. Each of the two companies uses three different advertising media in their ad campaigns: newspaper, radio, and TV. On a trial basis both companies and all three ad campaign types were used in a preliminary study. Twelve comparable cities were randomly selected and two cities were used for each company and media type combination. The sales increase per advertising dollar was computed after each ad campaign.

Column	Name	Count	Description
C1	SALESINC	12	Sales increase per advertising dollar for a city
C2	MEDIUM	12	The medium used in the advertising campaign coded as 1=newspaper, 2=radio, 3=TV
C3	AGENCY	12	The ad agency used in the campaign coded as 1=Ace and 2=Best

Used in: Tutorial 3, Graphical Methods for Describing Data (exercises)
Tutorial 8, Comparing Population Means: Analysis of Variance

LOTTO.MTW

A state lotto randomly selects 6 numbers from the numbers 1 through 47. There are two drawings per week. To check whether the drawings are done in a random fashion, a student monitored the game for several years and based on information provided by the local newspaper determined the number of times each of the numbers 1 through 47 had been drawn over the course of the past three years. Hence there were a total of 156 drawings.

Column	Name	Count	Description
C1	OBSERVED	47	The observed number of times each number has been drawn

Used in: Tutorial 10, Analyzing Categorical Data (exercises)

PASTA.MTW

The nutritionist at a local hospital investigated the different pasta brands that were available from the hospital's food supplier. Each brand that was available from the supplier was rated by several members of the hospital's nutrition department. The average rating for each brand of pasta was recorded as well as the cost and calories per 10-oz. serving of the pasta.

Column	Name	Count	Description
C1-A	RATING	15	The rating of a particular brand of pasta
C2	CENT/SER	15	The cost (in cents) per 10-oz. serving of the pasta
C3	CAL/SER	15	The calories per 10-oz. serving of the pasta

Used in: Tutorial 1, Working with Data (created by student)
Tutorial 4, Numerical Methods for Describing Data
Tutorial 8, Comparing Population Means: Analysis of Variance (exercises)

PAY.MTW

This data set contains the salary information of the 11 salaried employees in the sales department of the Technitron company. This data set is part of the larger data set described later, TECHN.MTW, which contains the salary information of all salaried employees in four departments at Technitron.

Column	Name	Count	Description
C1	SALARY	11	The salary of an employee in the sales department
C2	YRS EM	11	The number of years employed at Technitron
C3	PRIOR YR	10	The number of prior years' experience
C4	EDUC	10	Years of education after high school
C5	(age variable deleted in tutorials)		
C6	ID	11	The company identification number for the employee
C7-A	GENDER	11	The gender of the employee
C8	GENDER N	11	The coded gender of the employee where 0=female and 1=male

Used in: Tutorial 1, Working with Data
Tutorial 3, Graphical Methods for Describing Data
Tutorial 6, Inference from One Sample (exercises)

PROF.MTW

Student governments at many universities perform annual surveys of courses, commonly referred to as "Course/Prof" surveys. The purpose of these surveys is to provide some information for students when selecting courses and instructors.

The data set provided is one such survey taken at a university. Only a fraction of all classes were actually surveyed and this data includes a sample of those. This data set contains the results of 146 surveys from a variety of disciplines, and the results from 4 of the 11 statements the students were asked to respond to. These are:

1. The course stimulated your interest in this area of study.
2. The instructor presented course material in an effective manner.
3. Overall, I would rate this course as:
4. Overall, I would rate this instructor as:

The possible responses were:

For questions 1 and 2:

0=strongly disagree, 1=disagree, 0=neutral, 3=agree, 4=strongly agree

For questions 3 and 4:

0=poor, 1=below average, 0=average, 3=above average, 4=excellent

The survey was administered to 15 members of the class. Some surveys were not returned and some classes had fewer than 15 students so the sample size is occasionally less than 15.

The data set contains the course number (with an explanation of the prefixes below), the average response to questions 1 through 4, the number of questionnaires returned, and the class size.

The departmental prefixes are:

ACC = Accounting
AER = Aeronautics
ARC = Architecture
ART = Art
ATH = Anthropology
CHM = Chemistry
COM = Communication
DSC = Decision Sciences
ECO = Economics
EDL = Educational Leadership
EDP = Educational Psychology
EDT = Teacher Education
EGR = Manufacturing Engineering
ENG = English
FIN = Finance
FRE = French
FST = Film Studies

GEO = Geology
GER = German
HST = History
ITS = International Studies
JPN = Japanese
LAT = Latin Language and Literature
MBI = Microbiology
MGT = Management
MKT = Marketing
MTH = Mathematics
MUS = Music
PHL = Philosophy
PHS = Physical Education, Health, and Sports Studies
PHY = Physics
POL = Political Science
PPS = Paper Science and Engineering
PSY = Psychology
RUS = Russian
SAN = Systems Analysis
SOC = Sociology
SPN = Spanish
STA = Statistics
WMS = Women's Studies
ZOO = Zoology

Column	Name	Count	Description
C1-A	DEPT	146	Department of the course; see prefix list above
C2	NUMBER	146	Course number, 100=first year, 200=sophomore, 300=junior, 400=senior
C3	INTEREST	146	Interest in class statement
C4	MANNER	146	Manner of presentation statement

C5	COURSE	146	Course rating statement
C6	INSTRUCR	146	Instructor rating statement
C7	RESPONDS	146	Number of questionnaires returned
C8	SIZE	130	Number of students in class
C9	YEAR	146	The level or year of the class

Used in: Tutorial 4, Numerical Methods for Describing Data
Tutorial 6, Inference from One Sample (exercises)
Tutorial 7, Inference from Two Samples (exercises)
Tutorial 8, Comparing Population Means: Analysis of Variance (exercises)
Tutorial 10, Analyzing Categorical Data (exercises)

RADON.MTW

A television station in southwestern Ohio did a survey to determine the radon levels in homes in its viewing area. Questionnaires and radon detection kits were sent to all viewers who requested one. Below is part of the resulting data. Only certain questions from the full questionnaire are included.

Column	Name	Count	Description
C1	RADON	513	The radon measurement in pico curies
C2	AGE	483	The age of the house in years
C3	DAYS	478	The number of days the kit was exposed
C4	INSULATE	535	The amount of insulation in the house: 0=poor, 1=average, 2=excellent
C5	SUMP?	526	Was the sample taken near a sump pump? 0=yes, 1=no

Used in: Tutorial 2, Summarizing, Transforming, and Manipulating Data (exercises)
Tutorial 10, Analyzing Categorical Data (exercises)

RIVER1.MTW
RIVER2.MTW
RIVER3.MTW
RIVER4.MTW
RIVER5.MTW
RIVERALL.MTW

During the summer of 1988, one of the hottest on record in the midwest, a graduate student in Environmental Science did a study for a state Environmental Protection Agency. She studied the impact of an electric generating plant along a river by observing several water characteristics at five sites along the river. Site #1 was approximately 4 miles upriver from the electrical plant, about 6 miles down river from a moderately large midwestern city, and directly down river from a large suburb of this city. Site #2 was directly up river from the cooling inlets of the plant. Site #3 was directly down river from the cooling discharge outlets of the plant. Site #4 was approximately ¾ of a mile down river from site #3, and site #5 was approximately 6 miles down river from site #3.

The EPA was most concerned with the plant's use of river water for cooling. They were concerned that the plant was raising the temperature of the water and hence endangering the aquatic species that lived in the river.

The student anchored data sounds (canisters that float in the river) at five sites and took hourly measurements of the temperature, pH, conductivity, and dissolved oxygen content. They are battery-operated and self-contained. She left them there for five consecutive days.

The data sets RIVER1.MTW through RIVER5.MTW contain the recordings for a separate site and hence do not include columns C6 SITE and C7 HOUR1 described below. RIVERALL.MTW contains the recordings from all five sites and includes all of the columns described below.

Column	Name	Count	Description
C1	HOUR	*	The hour of the measurement in military time
C2	TEMP	*	The temperature in degrees C of the river at the given hour

C3	PH	*	The pH of the river at the given hour
C4	COND	*	The conductivity in electrical potential of the river at the given hour
C5	DO	*	The dissolved oxygen content of the river at the given hour
C6	SITE	*	The site number
C7	HOUR1	*	The hour recorded as a number from 1 through 100

* The counts for the different data sets are: RIVER1.MTW = 95; RIVER2.MTW = 95; RIVER3.MTW = 95, RIVER4.MTW = 96, RIVER5.MTW = 97; RIVERALL.MTW = 478.

Used in: Tutorial 7, Inference from Two Samples (RIVERALL.MTW) (exercises)
Tutorial 13, Time Series Analysis (RIVER2.MTW and RIVER3.MTW)

SALES.MTW

Consolidated Stores Inc. investigated the revenues from the women's sportswear division over the years 1988 through 1991. Seven days were randomly selected each year and the total revenue from this division was recorded.

Column	**Name**	**Count**	**Description**
C1	1991	7	The daily revenues of the women's sportswear division for 7 randomly selected days in 1991
C2	1990	7	The daily revenues of the women's sportswear division for 7 randomly selected days in 1990
C3	1989	7	The daily revenues of the women's sportswear division for 7 randomly selected days in 1989

C4	1988	7	The daily revenues of the women's sportswear division for 7 randomly selected days in 1988

Used in: Tutorial 4, Numerical Methods for Describing Data (exercises)
Tutorial 6, Inference from One Sample
Tutorial 7, Inference from Two Samples (exercises)
Tutorial 8, Comparing Population Means: Analysis of Variance (exercises)
Tutorial 11, Analyzing Data with Nonparametric Methods

SNOWFALL.MTW

Using data collected at the weather station outside of a small midwest town, a college student recorded the yearly snowfall for the town for the past 15 years, back to 1976.

Column	Name	Count	Description
C1	SNOWFALL	15	The snowfall in inches for the past 15 winters for a small midwest town
C2	RAIN	15	The equivalent rainfall in inches

Used in: Tutorial 2, Summarizing, Transforming, and Manipulating Data (exercises)
Tutorial 9, Examining Linear Relationships Between Variables: Regression (exercises)
Tutorial 11, Analyzing Data with Nonparametric Methods (exercises)

TECHN.MTW

This data set contains the salary information of all salaried employees in four departments at the Technitron company. The data set PAY.MTW is a subset of this larger data set.

Column	Name	Count	Description
C1	SALARY	46	The salary of an employee

C2	YRS EM	46	The number of years employed at Technitron
C3	PRIOR YR	46	The number of prior years' experience
C4	EDUC	46	Years of education after high school
C5	ID	46	The company identification number for the employee
C6	GENDER	46	The coded gender of the employee where 0=female and 1=male
C7	DEPT	46	The department of the employee coded as 1=sales, 2=purchasing, 3=advertising, and 4=engineering
C8	SUPER	46	The number of employees supervised by this employee

Used in: Tutorial 8, Comparing Population Means: Analysis of Variance (exercises)
Tutorial 9, Examining Linear Relationships Between Variables: Regression
Tutorial 10, Analyzing Categorical Data

TRANS.MTW

As part of a study investigating the quality of transistors produced at Flexible Circuits, Inc., 510 transistors were sampled from stock and were classified with respect to the day of the week the transistor was manufactured and the quality of the transistor. The data are stored in a contingency table format.

Column	Name	Count	Description
C1-A	(no name)	3	A description of the quality of the transistors
C2	MON	3	The number of transistors manufactured on Monday, classified by the quality of the transistor
C3	TUE	3	The number of transistors manufactured on Tuesday, classified by the quality of the transistor

C4	WED	3	The number of transistors manufactured on Wednesday, classified by the quality of the transistor
C5	THU	3	The number of transistors manufactured on Thursday, classified by the quality of the transistor
C6	FRI	3	The number of transistors manufactured on Friday, classified by the quality of the transistor

Used in: Tutorial 10, Analyzing Categorical Data

TVVIEW.MTW

Ten married couples were randomly selected and the husband and wife were asked the average amount of time (in hours) each spent watching TV per week.

Column	Name	Count	Description
C1	HUSBAND	10	The average number of hours spent watching TV per week by the husband
C2	WIFE	10	The average number of hours spent watching TV per week by the wife
C3	TOTAL	10	The total average number of hours spent watching TV per week by the husband and wife
C4	DIFF	10	The difference between the average number of hours spent watching TV per week by the husband and wife

Used in: Tutorial 2, Summarizing, Transforming, and Manipulating Data (exercises)
Tutorial 4, Numerical Methods for Describing Data (exercises)
Tutorial 11, Analyzing Data with Nonparametric Methods (exercises)

VPVH.MTW

Each year the Nielsen company does an extensive survey of TV viewing habits of the U.S. population. Many of the surveys are done by age and gender groups because sponsors are very interested in what age and gender person watches specific programs.

This data set contains the VPVH's estimates for several different categories of television programming. The VPVH estimate is the estimated number of viewers per 1000 viewing households tuned to a station or program. This data set includes the ten VPVH estimates for each of four commonly surveyed gender/age groups (Men age 18–34, Women age 18–34, Men age 55+, and Women 55+) for the following kinds of programs: Network Movies, Situation Comedy, and Sports. For the Sports program, only data for the two male age groups were given.

Column	Name	Count	Description
C1	MOVIES	40	The VPVH data for top ten network movies
C2	COMEDY	40	The VPVH data for top ten situation comedies
C3	SPORTS	40	The VPVH data for the top ten sporting events
C4-A	GROUP	40	The gender/age group
C5	GROUP N	40	The gender/age group coded numerically

Used in: Tutorial 11, Analyzing Data with Nonparametric Methods (exercises)

WGTHGT.MTW

A young college graduate in his first teaching assignment in a local school district decided to introduce his first grade classes to statistics. As a class exercise, he brought in a scale and a tape measure and recorded the heights (in inches) and weights (in pounds) of all 73 students in his two homeroom classes.

Column	Name	Count	Description
C1	WEIGHT	73	Weight in pounds of first grader
C2	HEIGHT	73	Height in inches of first grader

Used in: Tutorial 6, Inference from One Sample (exercises)

```
-0.4 -0.2  0.0  0.2  0.4  0.6  0.8
--+----+----+----+----+----+----+-
            XXXXXXXXXXXXXXXXXXXXXX
            XXXXXXXXXXXXXXXXXXXXXX
            XXXXXXXXXXXXXXXXXX
            XXXXXXXXXXXXX
            XXXXXXXX
            XX
        XXXXX
   XXXXXXXXXX
XXXXXXXXXXXXX
XXXXXXXXXXXXX
XXXXXXXXXXXXX
XXXXXXXXXXXXX
XXXXXXXXXXXXX
XXXXXXXXXXXXX
XXXXXXXXXXXXX
  XXXXXXXXXXX
     XXXXXXXX
          XXX
            XXX
            XXXXXXX
            XXXXXXXXXXX
            XXXXXXXXXXXXXX
            XXXXXXXXXXXXXXXX
```

PART IV

Reference

CHAPTER 1

Special Topics

This chapter describes selected Minitab topics that either do not correspond to specific menu commands or are described indirectly or in a variety of places in the tutorials. The topics are:

- Working with Menus, Dialog Boxes, and the Keyboard
- Alpha Data
- File Types
- Importing and Exporting Data

Working with Menus, Dialog Boxes, and the Keyboard

Working with Menus

The menu bar at the top of the Session window contains Minitab's main menus: File, Edit, Calc, Stat, and Graph. You can issue nearly all of Minitab's commands through these menus. An ellipsis (...) following a command indicates that a dialog box appears when you choose the command; you use the dialog box to communicate with Minitab. The >> symbol to the right of a command indicates that a submenu containing additional commands opens when you choose that command, as shown here.

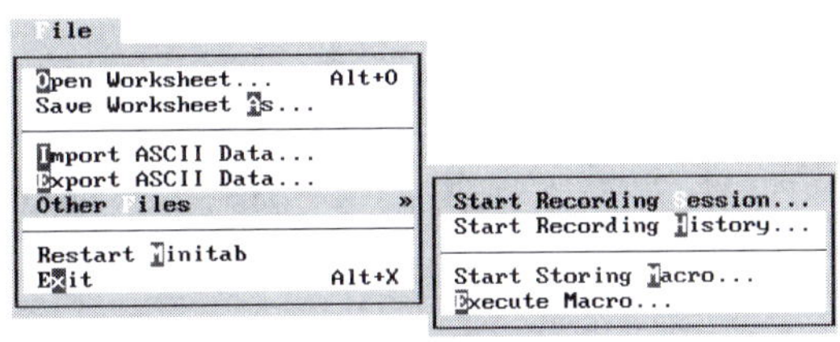

A few menu commands have keyboard shortcuts; when these are available, they are displayed on the menu to the right of the command name (for example, Alt + O is the shortcut for the Open Worksheet... command on the File menu). You can use the keyboard shortcuts to issue commands without opening the menus.

If a menu command is dimmed, the item is currently unavailable. Sometimes whole menus are dimmed, indicating that all the commands in the menu are unavailable.

Opening a Menu

To open a Minitab menu:

- Move to the menu bar by pressing [F10]
- Use the arrow keys to move to the menu name
- Press [↵] to open the menu

To open a menu in one step, press and hold [Alt] as you press the highlighted letter for that menu name.

Choosing a Command/Opening a Submenu

To choose menu commands, you:

- Use the arrow keys to highlight the command or submenu name
- Press [↵]

As a shortcut, while the menu is open, simply press the highlighted letter in the command or submenu name.

Closing a Menu

To close a menu without choosing a command:

- Press [Esc]

Mouse Techniques

Minitab supports but does not require the use of a mouse. Since Minitab uses only the left mouse button, all references to the mouse button mean the left button. Minitab uses four basic mouse operations:

Pointing

- Move the mouse so that the cursor is on an item

Clicking

- Point to an item
- Without moving the mouse, press and release the mouse button

Double-clicking

- Point to an item
- Without moving the mouse, press and release the mouse button twice in rapid succession

Dragging

- Press and hold down the mouse button
- Move the mouse so that the mouse pointer is in another location
- Release the mouse button

Using the Mouse on Menus

- To open a menu, click the menu name
- To choose a command from an open menu, click the command name
- To close a menu or submenu without making a choice, move the mouse pointer off the menu and click

The Data Screen Menu

To open the Data screen menu, press [F10] or click the "F10=Menu" box at the bottom of the screen. Choose commands from this menu as you would from the menus in the Session window.

About the Alt *Key Shortcuts*

You may not be able to use Alt in combination with a letter as a shortcut if other software uses the same key combination as Minitab. However, Minitab never *requires* the use of Alt; there is always an alternative way to perform the same action.

Working with Dialog Boxes

Most menu commands display a dialog box for choosing variables and options. Many dialog boxes also have subdialog boxes that contain less frequently used options. The following three examples introduce you to the use of dialog boxes in Minitab.

Example 1: The Normal Distribution Dialog Box

The notation, "Choose Calc ▶ Random Data ▶ Normal..." means that you should choose the Normal command from the Random Data submenu in the Calc menu. The Normal command opens the Normal Distribution dialog box.

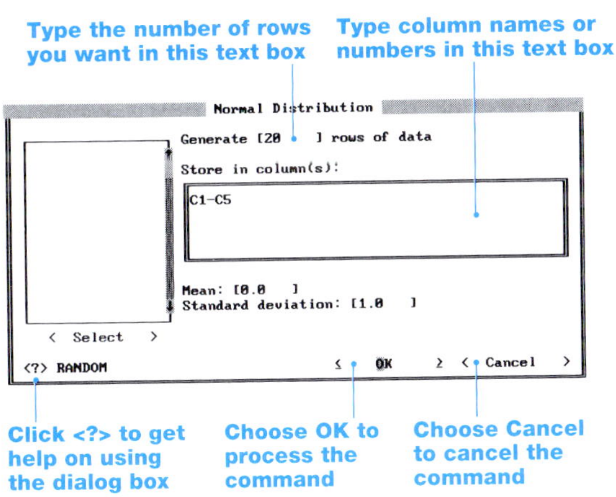

To indicate the amount of data you want Minitab to generate:

- Type the number of rows of data you want in the first text box
- Move the text cursor, indicated by the blinking underscore, to the second text box by pressing Tab

To tell Minitab where to store the random data:

- Type column names or numbers in the second text box; separate them with blanks, not commas

If you type a name that has not already been assigned to a column, Minitab automatically chooses an unused column and assigns it the name.

The text boxes labeled Mean and Standard deviation contain default values. If you want some other value:

- Move to the appropriate box by pressing Tab or, if you are using a mouse, clicking the border of the box

This highlights the current text. Any characters you type will automatically replace the highlighted text.

To get help:

- Press F1 or click the <?> button

To cancel the dialog box without issuing any commands:

- Press Esc or click Cancel

To begin processing the command:

- Press Alt-O (this means you should press and hold Alt and then press O; make sure to use the letter O, not the digit zero) or click OK

Example 2: The Regression Dialog Box

- Choose Stat ▶ Regression ▶ Regression...

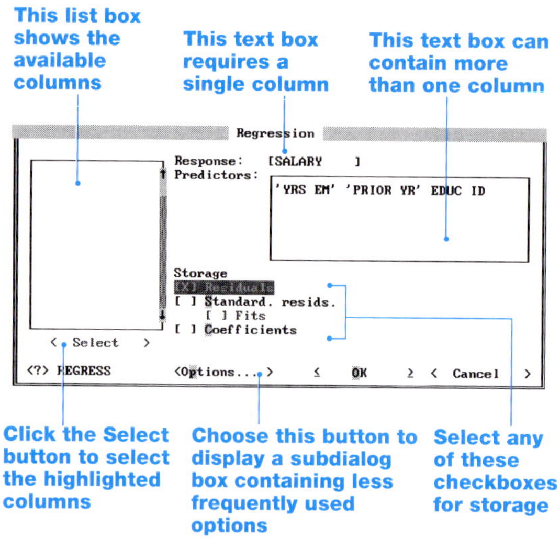

Specify the column C1 as the response variable:

- Make sure the cursor is in the text box labeled Response; use [Tab] if it is not
- Press [F2] to activate the list box and highlight the first column there
- Press [F2] again to place that column in the text box with the cursor

> **Mouse Users:**
>
> - Make sure the cursor is in the text box labeled Response; if it is not, click the Response text box with the mouse
> - Click C1 in the list box to highlight it
> - Click Select
>
> (You may also double-click C1 to place it in the active text box.)

To specify columns C2 through C5 as the predictors:

- Make sure the cursor is in the text box labeled Predictors
- Press [F2] to move to the list box
- Move the triangular pointer to C2 by pressing [↓]
- Press the Space bar to highlight C2
- Repeat this process to highlight C3, C4, and C5, then press [F2] again

> **Mouse Users:**
>
> - Click C2, C3, C4, and C5 to highlight them
> - Click Select
>
> (You may also double-click each column you want to select.)

As you place columns in the active text box, the text cursor remains in the text box, allowing you to add more columns. Note that Minitab abbreviates a set of consecutive columns with a dash. If you prefer, you can type column names or numbers (for example, C1) in the text boxes, separating them with blanks.

To store any of the items listed under Storage:

- Use [Tab] to move to the Residuals checkbox
- Press the Space bar to *toggle* its setting (that is, check it or remove the check)

> **Mouse Users:**
>
> - You can also click any checkbox to toggle its setting

Since the checkboxes for storage are logically related, they are grouped in a *field* that you navigate using the arrow keys rather than [Tab].

For each checkbox you select, Minitab automatically chooses an unused column or stored constant. If the storage is in a column, Minitab assigns it an appropriate name.

To display a subdialog box containing less frequently used options:

- Tab to the Options button and press the Space bar, or click the Options button

This opens the Options subdialog box. After making your choices:

- Choose OK to return to the main dialog box
- If you decide that you don't want to change anything in the subdialog box, choose Cancel

Whenever the label of a command ends with an ellipsis (...), choosing the command displays a subdialog box. Since you can always cancel the subdialog box, there is no danger in exploring these options.

Example 3: The 1-Sample t Dialog Box

- Choose Stat ▶ Basic Statistics ▶ 1-Sample t...

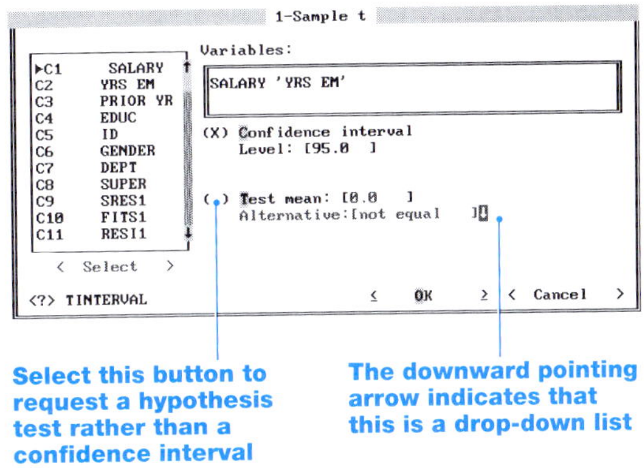

Specify the variable or variables to analyze by typing column names or numbers in the first text box or by selecting them from the list box.

To select the hypothesis test (the Test mean button) rather than the confidence interval:

- Press [Tab] to move to the Confidence interval option button
- Press [↓] to select the Test mean option (the hypothesis test)

> **Mouse Users:**
>
> - Click the Test mean option

To choose an alternative hypothesis:

- Press [Tab] twice to move to the Alternative drop-down list
- Press [F4] to open the list
- Use the arrow keys to move the cursor to your choice
- Press [F4] to accept your choice and close the list

Mouse Users:

- Click the arrow to the right of the Alternative line
- Click your choice

Moving Around a Dialog Box

You can move from place to place by pressing [Tab] to go forward or [Shift]-[Tab] to go backward. You move from one option button to another or among a set of related checkboxes by pressing [↑] and [↓].

Text Boxes: When typing, you should separate columns and constants with blanks, not commas.

To edit text in a text box, you can move the cursor around within the text box, switch between Insert and Overstrike modes, and delete blocks of text.

To move the cursor around in the text box:

- Use the arrow keys, [Home], [End], [PgUp], and [PgDn]

Mouse Users:

- Click anywhere in the text box

When you move into a text box, you are in Insert mode. You can switch between Insert and Overstrike modes by pressing [Ins]. In Overstrike mode, the cursor is a blinking underscore. In Insert mode, it is a blinking block.

To delete a block of text:

- First highlight the block by holding [Shift] down while you use the arrow keys, [Home], [End], [PgUp], and [PgDn]
- Delete the highlighted block by pressing [Del] or the backspace key, or by typing any character

Mouse Users:

- Point to the beginning of the text you want to highlight
- Press and hold the mouse button down and drag to the end
- Release the mouse button
- Delete the highlighted block by pressing [Del] or the backspace key, or by typing any character.

To remove the highlighting:

- Press any directional key or click anywhere in the box

When you move into a text box by pressing [Tab] or [Shift]-[Tab] or by clicking on its border, Minitab highlights its previous contents. To replace the contents, simply start typing. To edit the contents, press any directional key or check anywhere in the box, then make any desired changes.

Option Buttons: Use option buttons to select among exclusive options. A set of option buttons is always grouped into a field. Moving to a different button in the set selects the new button (although you can change the selection as often as you want until you're ready to select OK).

- Use the arrow keys to move from one option button to another in the same set
- As a shortcut, move directly to the button and select it by pressing [Alt] in combination with the highlighted letter in its label

> **Mouse Users:**
>
> - Point to any portion of the button or its label and click

Checkboxes:

- Move to the checkbox by pressing [Tab] or [Shift]-[Tab]
- Press the Space bar to toggle the checkbox
- As a shortcut, press [Alt] in combination with the highlighted letter in its label to move directly to the checkbox and toggle it

> **Mouse Users:**
>
> - Point to any portion of the checkbox or its label and click

Command Buttons: You choose a command button (OK, Cancel, and so forth) when you're ready to perform an action.

- Move to the button by pressing [Tab] or [Shift]-[Tab]
- Press the Space bar to choose the button
- If a letter in the label of a command button is highlighted, you can press [Alt] in combination with the highlighted letter to move directly to the button and choose it

> **Mouse Users:**
>
> - Click the button

The [↵] Key: Pressing [↵] in dialog boxes performs different actions, depending on the situation. When the cursor is in a multi-line text box, pressing [↵] moves the cursor to the next line in the text box. Otherwise, pressing [↵] is equivalent to choosing the OK command button or other highlighted command buttons enclosed by < >.

Drop-down Lists: Use a drop-down list to select among exclusive options.

- Press [F4] to open a drop-down list
- Move the cursor to your choice using the arrow keys
- Press [F4] to accept the choice
- You can also move through the choices using the arrow keys, without opening the list

> **Mouse Users:**
>
> - Click the downward pointing arrow at the right of the Alternative line to open the drop-down list
> - Click your choice

Selecting Columns from a List Box: It is often more convenient to select columns from the list box than to type the column names or numbers. To do this:

- Place the text cursor in the desired text box
- Press [F2] to move to the list box

- Highlight the column(s) you want
- Press F2 again to select them

When the text box can contain just a single column, use the arrow keys to highlight the column you want (you won't need to press the Space bar). When the text box can contain more than one column, use the arrow keys to move the triangular pointer to each column you want, then press the Space bar to highlight it. If you make a mistake, press the Space bar again to remove the highlight.

Mouse Users:

- Highlight the column or columns you want
- Click the Select button

When the text box can contain just a single column, click the column you want to highlight it. Double-clicking a column also selects it. When the text box can contain more than one column, click each column you want to highlight (click again to remove a highlight), then click select. Double-clicking a column highlights that column and selects all highlighted columns.

Abbreviating a Range

You can abbreviate a range of columns or stored constants using a dash. For example, C3-C7 is short for C3, C4, C5, C6, and C7. If C3 and C7 are named 'First' and 'Last', respectively, you can type this as First-Last, First-C7, or C3-Last.

Column Names in Text Boxes

A name consists of 1 to 8 characters, with no leading or trailing spaces, and no single quotation marks (') or octothorpes (#). Also, a name cannot consist of a single *. You cannot use special characters (such as Alt or Ctrl) in names. Names are not case-sensitive.

With certain exceptions, you can type names starting with a letter and consisting only of letters and digits without quotation marks. The exceptions are any names that might be mistaken for column numbers or stored constant numbers; for example, C2 or K3. In particular, if a name consists of the letter C or K followed by one or more digits, it must be enclosed in single quotation marks. In any case, such names are best avoided because of the confusion they are likely to produce.

Any other name must be enclosed in single quotation marks. A name starting with anything other than a letter, or containing any character other than a letter or a digit, must be enclosed in single quotation marks.

Incidentally, all but a handful of Minitab's session commands require all names to be enclosed in single quotation marks.

Missing Value Code

Minitab's missing value code * can be typed in text boxes without being enclosed in quotation marks.

Choosing OK

When you select or click OK, Minitab executes the commands you have entered into the dialog boxes. All menu commands have counterparts, called session commands, in Minitab's own language. When you select commands, Minitab displays the session commands in the Session window after the MTB > prompt. Minitab executes the commands just as if you had typed them at the MTB > prompt.

A command may display its results in the Session window or in a separate graph screen. Some commands do not display any results, but their effect on the worksheet is reflected in the Data screen.

When you use the Edit ▶ Copy Columns... command you can use or omit rows equal to a specified numeric value or range but you cannot use or omit rows equal to a specified alpha value.

When you use the Calc ▶ Unstack... command to unstack columns using subscripts, the subscripts must be numeric, not alpha.

Alpha Data

Minitab handles two types of data: numeric data (numbers) and alpha data (other characters). Most of your work will be done with numbers and most Minitab commands handle only numbers. In Minitab, alpha data are used primarily as labels.

Each alpha item (one row of a column) may be up to 80 characters. You may use any characters (letters, numbers, punctuation symbols, blanks). Any single column cannot contain both alpha and numeric data: any numbers that appear in an alpha column are treated as alpha characters and cannot be used for computations.

You can use alpha data with the following commands:

File ▶	Open Worksheet...	RETRIEVE
	Save Worksheet...	SAVE
	Import ASCII Data...	READ, SET, INSERT
	Export ASCII Data...	WRITE
Edit ▶	Display Data...	PRINT
	Set Patterned Data...	SET
Calc ▶	Sort...	SORT
	Delete Rows...	DELETE
	Erase Variables...	ERASE
	Copy Columns...	COPY
	Stack...	STACK
	Unstack...	UNSTACK
	Convert...	CONVERT
	Concatenate...	CONCATENATE

File Types

In Minitab, you will use three different types of files: files that contain data, files that contain Minitab commands, and files that contain Minitab output. This section describes how you can use these files. See the next section, Importing and Exporting Data, for additional information.

Filenames

You can enter the filename of your choice when you are saving a file. Filenames may include any characters except for leading blanks and the symbols # and '. Filenames in Minitab have an extension—a three-letter ending that tells you what kind of file it is.

When used in a session command, enclose filenames in single quotation marks or apostrophes. For example:

MTB > SAVE 'SCHOOLS'

creates the file SCHOOLS.MTW.

File Types

You may use seven different types of files, as summarized in the table at the end of this section. The first three store data, the next two store Minitab output, and the last two store session commands. Each is associated with one or more Minitab commands, and each has a specific default file extension.

Files That Store Data

Saved Worksheet: A saved worksheet (default extension .MTW) contains all the information in the current worksheet, including columns, column names, constants, and Data screen settings. Use saved worksheets when you are using Minitab on only one type of computer. Saved worksheets are a very efficient way to store data and are very fast to retrieve. You cannot edit or print saved worksheets outside of Minitab, nor can you import them into other applications. Use the portable format or data file format, described next, for this purpose.

Portable Worksheet: Except for Data screen settings, portable worksheets (extension .MTP) contain the same information as a saved worksheet. Use portable worksheets to transfer your worksheet data from Minitab on one type of computer to Minitab on another type of computer: for example, from Minitab on a mainframe to Minitab on a PC. Portable worksheets are not as fast to retrieve as saved worksheets.

Data File: Data files (extension .DAT) contain columns of data in a text (ASCII) file; they do not include stored constants. Data files do not include column names. Use data files to transfer worksheet data between Minitab and other applications like a spreadsheet or a data base.

Files That Store Minitab Output

Outfile: An outfile (.LIS) stores a record of your Minitab session (all commands and output except for high-resolution graphs) in a text (ASCII) file. Use outfiles to keep a permanent record of your session and to produce reports. You can print an outfile or edit it with any text editor or word processor.

Graphics File: A graphics file stores a high-resolution graph in a device-dependent format. Use graphics files to store your graphs and charts to print or to include in a report. There are two types of graphics files: printer graphics files (.PRI file extension), and plotter graphics files (.PLT file extension).

Files That Store Minitab Commands

Macro File: A macro file (.MTB) is a text (ASCII) file of session commands that you can execute in a batch. Use macro files to automate Minitab procedures you perform often or to extend Minitab's functionality. You can create a macro file using Minitab or (if you want to edit the file) any word processor or text editor.

STARTUP.MTB: STARTUP.MTB is a special macro file that, if it exists, automatically executes when you start a new Minitab session. It is a handy tool for users who want to avoid entering the same commands every time they start Minitab.

Journal File: A journal file (.MTJ) is a text (ASCII) file that records the session commands you execute during your Minitab session. Since a journal file is a text file, you can print it or edit it with other software. You can also execute a journal file as a macro file.

File Types Used By Minitab

File Type	Created By	Used By	File Extension
Saved Worksheet (machine-specific)	File ▶ Save Worksheet As (SAVE)	File ▶ Open Worksheet (RETRIEVE)	.MTW
Portable Worksheet (text file)	Same as above, with "Portable" option selected (SAVE; PORTABLE)	Same as above, with "Portable" option selected (RETRIEVE; PORTABLE)	.MTP
Data File (text file)	File ▶ Export ASCII Data (WRITE); other software	File ▶ Import ASCII Data (READ, SET, INSERT); other software	.DAT
Outfile (text file)	File ▶ Other Files ▶ Start Recording Session (OUTFILE)	A word processor or editor	.LIS
Graphics File (device-specific file)	"Store in file" option selected in dialog box (GOPTIONS; PRINTER) (GOPTIONS; PLOTTER)	Other software	.PRI .PLT
Macro (text file)	File ▶ Other Files ▶ Start Storing Macro (STORE); word processor	File ▶ Other Files ▶ Execute Macro (EXECUTE)	.MTB
Journal (text file)	File ▶ Other Files ▶ Start Recording History (JOURNAL)	File ▶ Other Files ▶ Execute Macro (EXECUTE); word processor	.MTJ

Importing and Exporting Data

Overview of Lotus 1-2-3/Symphony Interface

You can use the Lotus 1-2-3/Symphony Interface to transfer data between the Minitab worksheet and a Lotus spreadsheet file generated by the following Lotus products (referred to as "Lotus" in this chapter):

Lotus 1-2-3, version 2.x or 3.x	(.WK1 file extension)
Lotus 1-2-3, version 1a	(.WKS file extension)
Lotus 1-2-3, version 1	(.WKS file extension)
Symphony, version 2.x	(.WR1 file extension)
Symphony, version 1.1 or 1.2	(.WR1 file extension)
Symphony, version 1.0	(.WRK file extension)

After you have entered data using either Minitab or Lotus, you can use features of both programs to analyze and plot data.

Setting Up Your Computer to Use the Lotus Interface

If you are transferring a worksheet between Minitab and Lotus 1-2-3, Version 2.x, you can skip this setup section because the default option for worksheet transfer is Lotus 1-2-3, Version 2.x. However, if you want to transfer a worksheet to any other Lotus product, you must first use MSETUP to select the desired Lotus product. You can run MSETUP from the DOS prompt before you start Minitab or you can type the SYSTEM command at the MTB > prompt to exit from Minitab to DOS and then run MSETUP. Use the step-by-step procedure below to select a Lotus 1-2-3/Symphony option.

How to Select the Lotus 1-2-3/Symphony Interface

Whether you are at the MTB > prompt or at the DOS prompt, the procedure to activate MSETUP begins with the same step.

- If you are at the MTB > prompt, exit from Minitab to DOS by typing:

  SYSTEM

- Make the directory that contains the Minitab program files the default directory (if it is not already). For example, if the directory is named MINITAB and it is a sub-directory of the root directory, type:

  CD \MINITAB

- To start MSETUP, at the DOS prompt, type:

  MSETUP

- From the MSETUP main menu, select Set Lotus 1-2-3/Symphony Interface Default
- From the Lotus 1-2-3/Symphony Interface menu, select the Lotus or Symphony option that you want to activate (be sure to press [↵], not [Esc], to select the option)
- Use [Esc] to return to the DOS prompt

If you started at the MTB > prompt in the first step, return to the MTB > prompt by typing:

EXIT

Numerical Precision

Minitab stores numbers in single precision, which provides accuracy to six significant digits. Lotus spreadsheets are stored in double precision, which provides accuracy beyond six digits. You'll notice differences between Minitab and Lotus in the storage of numbers with more than six digits.

How to Save and Retrieve Lotus Files

The instructions in this section explain how to save and retrieve Lotus files using the File menu commands Save Worksheet... and Open Worksheet....

To save a Lotus file:

- Choose File ▶ Save Worksheet...
- Select the Lotus 1-2-3 worksheet checkbox from the Save As dialog box

To open Lotus files:

- Choose File ▶ Open Worksheet...
- Select the Lotus 1-2-3 worksheet checkbox from the Open dialog box

The following instructions describe how to save and retrieve Lotus files using the session commands.

Saving Minitab to Lotus

To save a Minitab worksheet as a Lotus spreadsheet file that Lotus can retrieve, use the Minitab SAVE command with the subcommand LOTUS. Minitab adds a filename extension based on the Lotus product selected in MSETUP. For example, enter:

```
MTB > SAVE 'OUTFILE';
SUBC>    LOTUS.
```

Retrieving Lotus into Minitab

To retrieve a saved Lotus spreadsheet file into a Minitab worksheet, use the Minitab RETRIEVE command with the subcommand LOTUS. Minitab adds a filename extension based on the Lotus product you selected in MSETUP. For example, enter:

```
MTB > RETRIEVE 'INFILE';
SUBC>    LOTUS.
```

Lotus to Minitab Conversion

You can use two different approaches to convert a Lotus spreadsheet file to a Minitab worksheet. The first or default approach converts the entire Lotus spreadsheet file to a Minitab worksheet, maintaining Lotus's row/column orientation; it also imposes a number of restrictions on what can be converted. The second approach uses Lotus named ranges to specify Minitab column contents; it is by far the more flexible of the two methods.

Default Conversion

The default conversion uses the following rules to make the transfer from Lotus to Minitab:

- A Minitab column is created for every Lotus column that contains an entry.
- The Lotus row/column orientation is maintained.
- Only numeric data are converted. Alpha data, @ERR, and @NA entries are converted to the missing value symbol, *.
- Minitab columns are named with the corresponding Lotus column name, like A, B, and so on.

Example of Default Conversion: The following spreadsheet was saved by Lotus 1-2-3, Version 2.0, as EXAMPLE1.WK1 without named ranges.

	A	B	C	D	E	F	G
1	Column1	Column2	1	Column5	Column6	Comp9	Col-error
2	1	0.2	NA	this	11	1.1	12
3	11	-0.02	56	is	junk	2.2	ERR
4	111	-0.002	0.12	a	22	3.3	25
5	1111	-0.0002	NA	column	junk	4.4	ERR
6	11111	-0.00002	1.12	with	33	5.5	38
7	111111	-0.00000	-0.45	a		6.6	6
8	-111111	0.000002	34.44	lot	44	7.7	51
9	-11111	0.00002	11.11	of		8.8	8
10	-1111	0.0002	-55.57	text	55	9.9	64
11	-111	0.002	NA			-8.9	-9
12	-11	0.02	NA		66	-7.8	58
13	-1	0.2	NA			-6.7	-7
14					77	-5.6	71
15					NA	-4.5	ERR
16					88	-3.4	84
17					NA	-2.3	ERR
18					99	-1.2	97
19					NA	-0.1	ERR

Minitab supplies the filename extension .WK1 to this spreadsheet file: EXAMPLE1.WK1. The following Minitab command retrieves this file:

```
MTB > RETRIEVE 'EXAMPLE1';
SUBC>     LOTUS.
```

The default conversion of the EXAMPLE1 spreadsheet file produced the following Minitab worksheet:

MTB > INFO

COLUMN	NAME	COUNT	MISSING
C1	A	13	1
C2	B	13	1
C3	C	13	5
C4	D	10	10
C5	E	19	10
C6	F	19	1
C7	G	19	6

CONSTANTS USED: NONE

MTB > PRINT C1-C7

	A	B	C	D	E	F	G
1	*	*	1.00	*	*	*	*
2	1	-0.200000	*	*	11	1.1	12
3	11	-0.020000	56.00	*	*	2.2	*
4	111	-0.002000	0.12	*	22	3.3	25
5	1111	-0.000200	*	*	*	4.4	*
6	11111	-0.000020	1.12	*	33	5.5	38
7	111111	-0.000002	-0.45	*	*	6.6	6
8	-111111	0.000002	34.44	*	44	7.7	51
9	-11111	0.000020	11.11	*	*	8.8	8
10	-1111	0.000200	-55.57	*	55	9.9	64
11	-111	0.002000	*		*	-8.9	-9
12	-11	0.020000	*		66	-7.8	58
13	-1	0.200000	*		*	-6.7	-7
14					77	-5.6	71
15					*	-4.5	*
16					88	-3.4	84
17					*	-2.3	*
18					99	-1.2	97
19					*	-0.1	*

Named Ranges

Using Lotus named ranges, you can convert either the entire spreadsheet or a specified subset of the spreadsheet to specific Minitab columns or constants. Refer to Lotus documentation for a full description of the /RN command and named ranges. Minitab uses the following rules in converting named ranges:

- Only named ranges that conform to the following naming conventions will be converted:

COLxx	Numeric data, xx = a Minitab column number from 1 to 100.
ACOLxx	Alpha data, xx = a Minitab column number from 1 to 100.
KONxx	Constants, xx = a Minitab constant number from 1 to 100.

- If the first cell in a numeric column (COLxx) is alpha, Minitab uses the cell as the Minitab column name. If the first cell in an alpha column (ACOLxx) starts with an &, Minitab uses the cell as the Minitab column name.
- @NA and @ERR entries, numeric values in alpha columns, alpha values in numeric columns, and null cells in numeric columns are converted to missing. Null cells in alpha columns are converted to blanks.

Example of Named Ranges Conversion

The following spreadsheet was saved by Lotus 1-2-3, Version 2.0, as EXAMPLE2.WK1 with the following named ranges:

KON2	A3
KON3	A4
KON4	A5
KON5	A6
KON6	A7
COL2	B2..B12
COL4	C2..C11
COL7	D2..D15
COL8	E2..E15
ACOL10	F2..F14

	A	B	C	D	E	F
1	KONstant	Col2	Col4	Col7	Col8	Acol10
2		integers	large	twoplace	missings	&alphacol
3	1	6	123456	14	NA	abcde
4	0.000001	4	234567	79	NA	fghi
5	123456	9	345678	88	NA	jkl
6	-123.123	-5	-456789	44	NA	mn
7	NA	-4	-567890	18	NA	o
8		3	678901	53	NA	pq
9		-7	789012	23	NA	rst
10		1	8901234	73	NA	uvwx
11		-3	1111111	56	NA	1.1
12		4		42	NA	asdfs
13				40	NA	asdfa
14				27	NA	asd
15				61	NA	

Minitab supplied the filename extension .WK1 to the spreadsheet file: EXAMPLE2.WK1. The following command retrieved the file:

```
MTB > RETRIEVE 'EXAMPLE2';
SUBC>   LOTUS.
```

The named range conversion of the EXAMPLE2 spreadsheet file produced the following Minitab worksheet:

```
MTB > INFO

  COLUMN      NAME        COUNT    MISSING
  C2          integers       10
  C4          large           9
  C7          twoplace       13
  C8          missings       13         13
A C10         alphacol       12

CONSTANTS USED: K2   K3   K4   K5   K6

MTB > PRINT K2 K3 K4 K5 K6
K2     1.00000
K3     0.000001000
K4     123456
K5     -123.123
K6     *

MTB > PRINT C2 C4 C7 C8 C10

ROW   integers      large   twoplace   missings   alphacol
  1          6     123456         14          *   abcde
  2          4     234567         79          *   fghi
  3          9     345678         88          *   jkl
  4         -5    -456789         44          *   mn
  5         -4    -567890         18          *   o
  6          3     678901         53          *   pq
  7         -7     789012         23          *   rst
  8          1    8901234         73          *   uvwx
  9         -3    1111111         56          *   1.1
 10          4                    42          *   asdfs
 11                               40          *   asdfa
 12                               27          *   asd
 13                               61          *
```

Minitab to Lotus Conversion

Minitab creates a Lotus spreadsheet file when you save your Minitab worksheet with the SAVE command and LOTUS subcommand. The resulting spreadsheet contains Minitab columns and constants enclosed in named ranges. The name of each named range appears in the first row of the spreadsheet above the range it defines. Minitab converts alpha data to text and missing data to @NA. Minitab column names appear as the first cell in the Lotus named range.

Example of Minitab to Lotus Conversion

The following Minitab worksheet will be saved as a Lotus spreadsheet:

```
MTB > INFO

   COLUMN     NAME       COUNT    MISSING
   C1                       10
A  C2         alphacol      10
   C5         twelve        12          1

CONSTANTS USED: K2   K75

MTB > PRINT K2 K75
K2       100.100
K75      200.200
MTB > PRINT C1 C2 C5

ROW          C1    alphacol    twelve
  1     0.81493    abc              1
  2     1.22108    defg             2
  3     0.41226    hijkl            3
  4     0.09872                     4
  5    -0.09351                     5
  6     0.50996    mnop             6
  7     0.36813    qrs              *
  8    -0.04499    2.5              8
  9    -0.43454    more             9
 10     0.42606    text            10
 11                                11
 12                                12
```

Minitab adds the filename extension .WK1 to the Minitab worksheet and saves it as the Lotus 1-2-3, Version 2.0, spreadsheet file EXAMPLE3.WK1, using the following command:

MTB > SAVE 'EXAMPLE3';
SUBC> LOTUS.

After entering Lotus 1-2-3 and retrieving EXAMPLE3, you will see the following spreadsheet:

	A	B	C	D	E
1	KONstant		Col1	Acol2	Col5
2				&alphacol	twelve
3	100.0999		0.814930	abc	1
4	200.1999		1.221084	defg	2
5			0.412259	hijkl	3
6			0.098722		4
7			-0.09351		5
8			0.509961	mnop	6
9			0.368134	qrs	NA
10			-0.04498	2.5	8
11			-0.43454	more	9
12			0.426064	text	10
13					11
14					12

The EXAMPLE3 spreadsheet automatically contains the following named ranges:

COL1	C3..C12
ACOL2	D2..D12
COL5	E2..E14
KON2	A3
KON75	A4

The named ranges generated when converting from Minitab to Lotus can perform a named range conversion in the opposite direction (that is, from Lotus to Minitab).

Note: Most Lotus worksheet operations, such as column delete and move, do not update named ranges. Before converting back to Minitab, be sure to update any named ranges that have been relocated or increased in size.

CHAPTER 2

Session Window Menu Reference

Using the Session Window

Most menus you will use in Minitab are available only from the Session window. (Chapter 3 of the Reference section contains information on using the Data screen menu.) The Session window displays the results of commands that produce numerical summaries, character-style graphs, and statistical analyses. In addition, you can type Session commands and data directly into the Session window after the MTB > prompt.

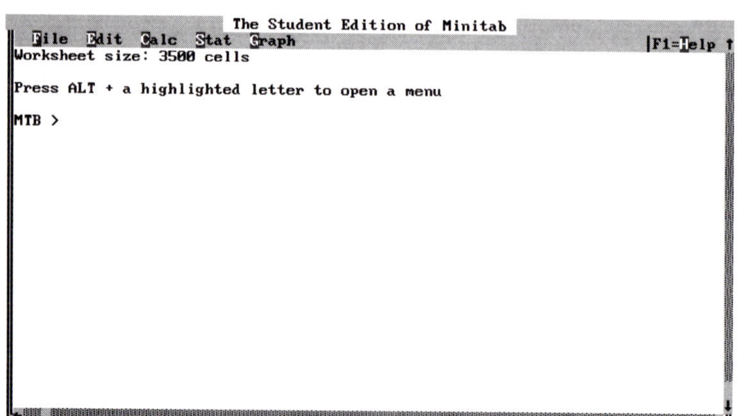

Scrolling Around the Session Window

The Session window automatically scrolls to keep the most recent line of output visible. To interrupt this automatic scrolling, press the Pause key. To resume, press [↵].

You can scroll up and down or from side to side to view the contents of the Session window. [PgUp] or [PgDn] scrolls up or down one page. [Ctrl]-[Home] or [Ctrl]-[End] scrolls to the top or bottom. [Ctrl]-[PgUp] or [Ctrl]-[PgDn] scrolls left or right one page.

Mouse Users:

Click the vertical scroll bar above or below the scroll box to scroll up or down one page. Click the horizontal scroll bar to the left or right of the scroll box to scroll left or right one page. Click a scroll arrow to scroll one line or character at a time. Point at a scroll arrow, press and hold down the mouse button to scroll continuously; release the mouse button to stop scrolling.

Saving the Contents of the Session Window

There is a limit to the amount of text the Session window can contain. When the Session window reaches the limit of text it can contain, it discards the first half of the contents without warning. By default, the Session window can hold 8192 characters. If you have extra conventional memory available, you can increase the limit using a command line option at the DOS prompt. For example, the command:

MINITAB -S 16384

would allow the Session window to store twice as much information. The number you enter in the MINITAB -S command must be between 2000 and 64000. If you want to save your entire session, use File ▶ Other Files ▶ Start Recording Session at the start of the Minitab session to save the contents of the Session window to a file.

Using Cut, Copy, and Paste

Sometimes it is convenient to edit a copy of a previously executed session command and re-enter it. (The previous command could be one that you typed or one generated from a menu.) You can highlight any block of text in the Session window, copy it, and paste it at the current input prompt, using the Edit menu's cut, copy, and paste commands. To do this, you highlight text by using the directional arrow keys to place the cursor at the beginning of the text to be copied, then press and hold [Shift] as you move the arrow keys to highlight the text you want. You can then Cut or Copy the highlighted text and Paste it at the MTB > prompt. Minitab does not read the pasted text until you press [↵], so you have a chance to edit it first. Tutorial 14 describes how to copy and paste Session window text.

Mouse Users:

You can also use the mouse to highlight text by moving the cursor before the text, pressing and holding the mouse button, then dragging until the text is highlighted.

Note: When you copy commands from the Session window, you must highlight the entire MTB > prompt or else Minitab will not read the first line.

Stored Constants

You can use up to 100 stored constants, each of which can contain a single number. Minitab automatically assigns certain values to the last three stored constants; that is, the missing value code * is K98, e (2.718...) is K99, and π (3.141...) is K100. If necessary, you can assign other values to these constants.

Basic Syntax Rules for Session Commands

If you use the Session window to issue commands, use the syntax conventions given after the dialog box commands for each individual menu item. See Chapter 4 of the Reference section, Minitab Command Language, for more information.

1. You need only type the first four letters of a command or subcommand.
2. Do not use the symbols & . + ; - : # or [Tab] as extra text; these symbols have specific meanings. Type comments, including any symbols you want, after the comment symbol #, which may be used at the beginning of any line.
3. Abbreviate a list of consecutive columns or stored constants with a dash (-). PRINT K2-K4 means PRINT K2 K3 K4.
4. Start each command or subcommand on a new line.
5. Continue a command, subcommand, or row of data onto the next line with a continuation symbol, & or ++.
6. You can type in lowercase or uppercase letters, or combination of the two.
7. Many commands have subcommands that provide Minitab with more information. To use a subcommand, end the command line with a semicolon (;). Then type your subcommands, each on a new line, ending each line with a (;). When you are finished, type the last subcommand and end with a period (.).
8. To interrupt macros, displays of data, and printing, you can type [Ctrl]-[Break].

Additional information on session command syntax appears on the Help menu under the heading Session Commands.

Session Window Menu Reference

This Menu Reference provides you with a complete index to all commands available in Session window menus, organized by menu and cross referenced to the tutorials that introduce them.

Each menu on the main Session window menu bar lists a number of commands. An arrow (>>) to the right of a command indicates that a submenu appears when you select that item. Ellipses (...) after a command indicate that, when you choose that command, a dialog box appears. You can execute from the keyboard any menu command that is accompanied by the [Alt], [Ctrl], or [Shift] keys and a keyboard character. (Keyboard shortcuts appear in this chapter, to the right of the commands they represent.)

If a menu command is dimmed, the item is currently unavailable. Sometimes whole menus are dimmed, indicating that all the commands in the menu are unavailable.

Each entry in this section includes a description of the command and all related dialog box selections. The equivalent session command syntax is also provided, with subcommands indented. When the session command syntax specifies a C, the argument must be a column. An E indicates that you may use a column, stored constant, or number as an argument. K refers to a constant. Brackets [ ] enclose optional arguments. Boldface type indicates elements you must include. Italicized or non-bolded text is informational. The following example illustrates these conventions:

PCHART *number of nonconformities are in*
C...C, *sample size* = **E**
P = **K**
SUBGROUP *size is* **K**
TEST K...K

See Chapter 4, Minitab Command Language, for information on using session command syntax.

Most command descriptions conclude with an example that illustrates using both the menu commands and session commands. Most of the examples use data sets from *The Student Edition of Minitab* Sample Files disk. In some cases, the data sets in the examples use columns added in the tutorials.

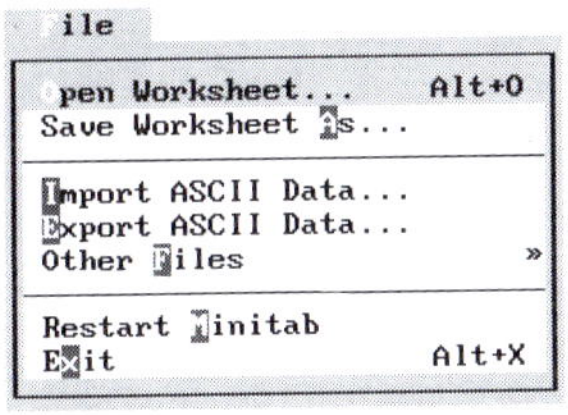

The File Menu

The **F**ile menu contains all the commands necessary to create, maintain, and use Minitab files. File menu options also allow you to access non-Minitab files.

Open Worksheet... Alt-O

The **O**pen Worksheet... command retrieves a previously saved Minitab worksheet. The data in the new worksheet replaces the current worksheet.

All output from previous worksheet computations remain in the Session window until you end the Minitab session (or until you reach the storage capacity of the window). If you want to clear the Session window, choose **F**ile ▶ Restart **M**initab before opening a worksheet.

The Open Dialog Box

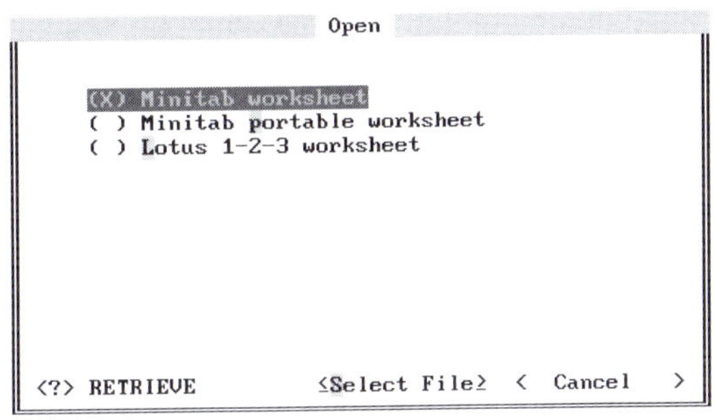

Options in the Open Dialog Box

Select one of the three options by placing an X in front of the option you want to use.

Minitab worksheet: This option retrieves a previously saved Minitab worksheet that can contain columns, column names, and stored constants. It also retrieves any Data screen settings saved with the worksheet.

Minitab **p**ortable worksheet: This subcommand retrieves a saved worksheet created by Minitab on a different computer system and saved using the Portable subcommand. This allows Minitab worksheets to be transferred between computer systems (say from an IBM PC to a VAX). This retrieval takes longer than that of a regular saved Minitab worksheet; you should use this subcommand only when transferring worksheets between dissimilar computers.

Lotus 1-2-3 worksheet: This option retrieves a spreadsheet in Lotus 1-2-3 format or a Symphony spreadsheet file. Minitab automatically looks for the appropriate file extension. Many applications, including Excel, Quattro, and Lotus 1-2-3 Release 3, can save data in a Minitab-supported Lotus format. This subcommand enables you to import data from several different applications. See the section on Importing and Exporting Data in Chapter 1, Special Topics, for more information.

Select File: This button opens the Open File dialog box that you use to specify which worksheet you want to open.

The Open File Dialog Box

Menu commands that read or write files display this dialog box. It contains a list box that allows you to browse through your directories and disk drives to find the file you want.

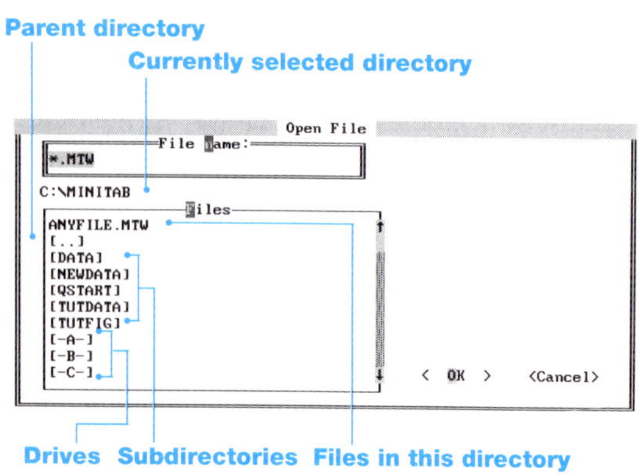

Options in the Open File Dialog Box

File name: If you want to type the name of the worksheet you want to open, do so here. Be sure to include the drive and directory if they are different from the one currently selected (shown in the line between the two boxes). Initially, the File name text box contains a highlighted default (called a *mask*) that can be used to determine which file names are displayed in the Files list box. The wildcard characters * and ? perform the same functions in the Minitab mask as they do in the DOS command DIR. For example, type ***.*** to have all files in the selected directory listed. Type **P*.MTW** to see all files beginning with P and having the extension .MTW. After you change the mask and press [↵], Minitab updates the list in the Files text box.

Currently selected directory: Between the File name text box and the Files text box is a line of text that indicates the current drive and directory (and subdirectories). This line always displays the drive and directory that are currently selected.

Files: The Files list box displays a list of files and subdirectories in the current directory (shown on the line between the two list boxes) as well as all the drives on your computer. The box lists files in the current directory first, and then the parent directory (the directory above the current one, designated by [..]). Next the box lists the subdirectories within the current directory. Subdirectories are enclosed in brackets: for example, [DATA]. Drives are also indicated by brackets, as in [-A-].

Session Command Syntax for Open Worksheet...

RETRIEVE *the worksheet saved in*
  ['**FILENAME**']
 PORTABLE
 LOTUS

See also Tutorial 1.

Save Worksheet As...

The Save Worksheet As... command copies the current worksheet, including the columns, data, column names, constants, and Data screen settings, into a saved file.

The Save As Dialog Box

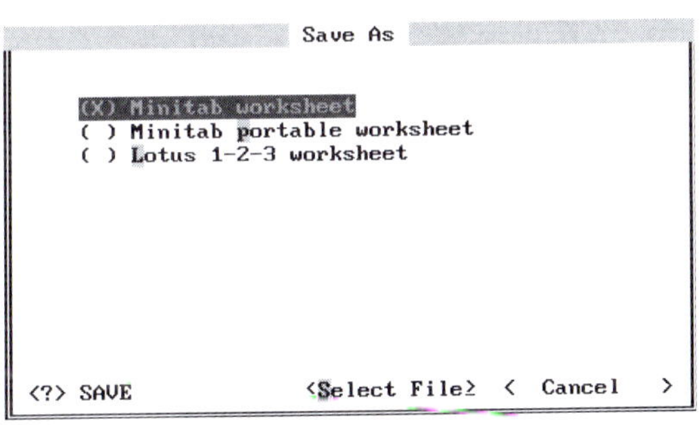

Options in the Save As Dialog Box

Minitab worksheet: This option saves the worksheet as a Minitab worksheet with the extension .MTW; the worksheet can contain columns, column names, and stored constants. This option also saves any Data screen settings.

Minitab portable worksheet: This subcommand saves the Minitab worksheet in a portable format that can be retrieved on another computer system. This allows Minitab worksheets to be transferred between computer systems (say from an IBM PC to a VAX). Saving worksheets in a portable format takes longer than saving them as regular Minitab worksheets; use this option only when transferring worksheets from Minitab on one type of computer to Minitab on another type of computer (e.g., IBM to a mainframe).

Lotus 1-2-3 worksheet: This option saves the Minitab worksheet as a file that can be retrieved by Lotus 1-2-3 and automatically gives the worksheet the appropriate file extension. This subcommand enables you to export data to several different applications. See the section on Importing and Exporting Data in Chapter 1, Special Topics, for more information.

Select File: This button opens the dialog box that you use to specify the worksheet name and the storage location you want. See File ▶ Open Worksheet... for information on the Select File dialog box.

Session Command Syntax for Save Worksheet As...

SAVE *the worksheet in* ['**FILENAME**']
 PORTABLE
 LOTUS

Import ASCII Data...

The Import ASCII Data... command enters text or ASCII data, one row at a time, into one or more worksheet columns. Text or data may be imported either from the keyboard or from a data file. If the Replace existing data option in the ASCII Data dialog box is selected, any existing values in the columns are erased. You can also insert data before existing data, after existing data, or between consecutive rows. Each row of data must start on a new line and contain one value per column. At least one space or comma should separate the numbers as delimiters unless they have been formatted differently (see the description of the Import ASCII Data - Format subdialog box). The missing value code (*) and data in exponential (scientific) notation, such as 1.23E-2, are valid entries. Minitab ignores letters or words on the data line unless you use the Import ASCII Data - Format subdialog box. You may enter up to 80 characters into an alpha column using the READ, SET, and INSERT commands.

The Import ASCII Data Dialog Box

Options in the Import ASCII Data Dialog Box

Put data in column(s): You must tell Minitab where to put the imported data.

Replace existing data, if any: This option is selected by default. Unless you select one of the following three options, Minitab replaces existing data in the specified columns with the imported data.

Insert before existing data: Select this option to have Minitab insert the imported data before existing data.

Insert between rows — and —: Minitab inserts the imported data between the two rows you specify, moving the existing data down.

Insert after existing data: Minitab inserts the imported data after the worksheet's existing data.

Read from keyboard instead of file: Instead of entering data from a file, you can type it in the Session window. When you select this option, Minitab displays a DATA> prompt, after which you can enter the first row of the data. When you press [↵], a new DATA> prompt appears; use it to enter the second row, and so on. When you are finished entering your data, type **END** on a line by itself.

The Import ASCII Data - Format Subdialog Box

The Format subcommand is similar to a Fortran format statement. It specifies where and how the data appear on the data line. The allowable format statements are:

Statement	Explanation
Fw	F format—for numeric data
Fw.d	F format—for numeric data with decimal places specified
Gw	G format—for numeric data
Gw.d	G format—for numeric data with significant digits specified
Ew	E format—exponential format for numbers
Ew.d	E format—with significant digits specified
'string'	Quoted string
Aw	A format—for alphanumeric data

X	X format—skip a space
Tn	T format—move to position n
n	Repeat factor
(	Open parenthesis
)	Close parenthesis
,	Comma—used to separate format items
/	Slash—go to a new output line

Options in the Import ASCII Data - Format Subdialog Box

Read only the first — rows: Minitab imports only the (specified) first portion of the file.

Blank delimited (numeric data only): By default, Minitab accepts data separated by at least one space or comma.

Formatted: To import data using a format with or without delimiters, enter a Fortran format statement using the Fortran commands previously described.

Session Command Syntax for Import ASCII Data...

READ *the data* [*in* **'FILENAME'**] *into* **C...C**
    FORMAT (Fortran format statement)
    NOBS = **K**

SET *the data* [*in* **'FILENAME'**] *into column* **C**
    FORMAT (Fortran format statement)
    NOBS = **K**

INSERT *the data* [*in* **'FILENAME'**] [*between* **K K**] *into* **C...C**
    FORMAT (Fortran format statement)
    NOBS = **K**

Type **END** when you are finished, unless you are using the NOBS subcommand to indicate how many rows will be entered.

Example: Using Import ASCII Data...

The following dialog boxes and equivalent Session window commands illustrate how to import the grades data from the ASCII file GRADES.DAT in Tutorial 1.

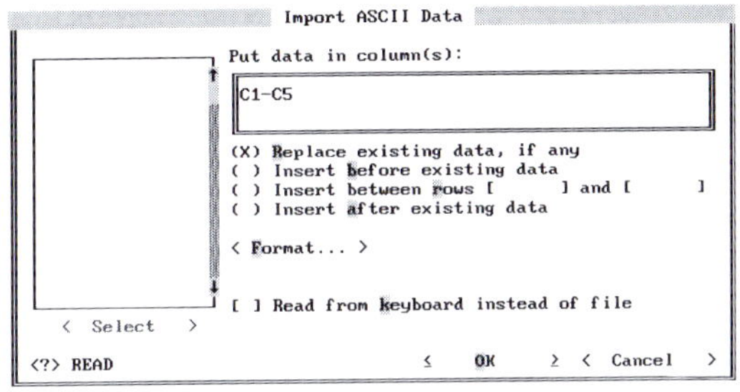

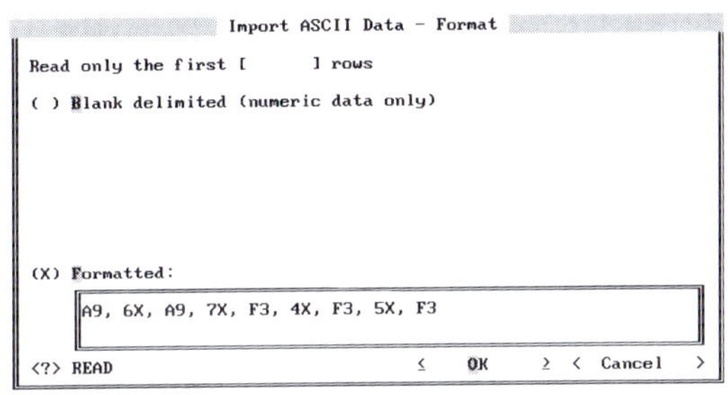

After executing these commands, Minitab produces a dialog box that you use to select GRADES.DAT:

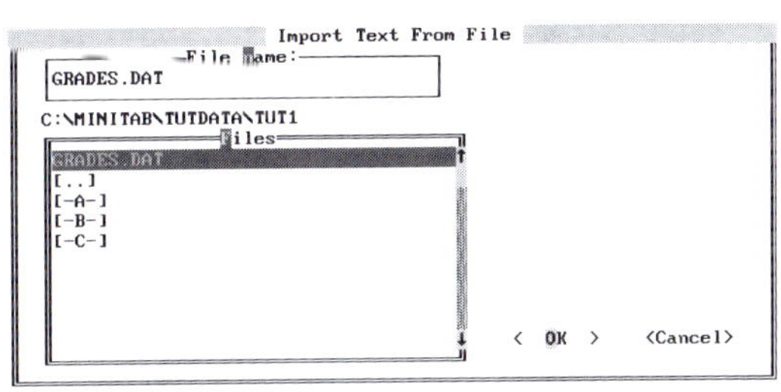

When you press [↵], Minitab imports the ASCII file into a worksheet.

```
MTB > Read 'C:\MINITAB\TUTDATA\TUT1\GRADES.DAT' C1-C5;
SUBC>   Format (A9, 6X, A9, 7X, F3, 4X, F3, 5X, F3).
```

The imported data can be seen in the Data worksheet.

→	C1	C2	C3	C4	C5
1	ADAMS	JAMES	72	93	93
2	BENSON	MELISSA	99	86	83
3	BROWN	LAMAR	59	59	90
4	DOUGHERTY	MEGAN	79	69	60
5	DOUGLAS	JASON	48	77	25
6	GIGLIOTTI	ANDREW	78	94	50
7	GOLDBERG	JONATHAN	98	98	94
8	GREEN	JENNIFER	92	91	99
9	KENNEDY	KEVIN	71	78	62
10	LEE	SANG	64	68	97
11	MCCLURE	MARK	49	79	43
12	MESSINA	STEVEN	94	93	95
13	NORMAN	BARBARA	99	95	84
14	NOWICKI	AMY	91	81	79
15	PATEL	HIMA	90	100	62
16	PIERSON	RICHARD	100	77	100
17	ROJAS	LUIS	73	79	83
18	RYAN	MATT	77	79	85
19	SCHMIDT	NANCY	83	79	52
20	SCOTT	MICHAEL	81	75	100
21	SHEPPARD	KATHLEEN	94	97	100
22	SMITH	HOLLY	82	51	25

See also Tutorial 1.

Export ASCII Data...

The Export ASCII Data... command exports data in text or ASCII format to a file. The exported file can be edited, printed, or used in packages other than Minitab. Only column data (no stored constants) are written to the specified file. Minitab adds the default file extension .DAT to your filename.

The Export ASCII Data Dialog Box

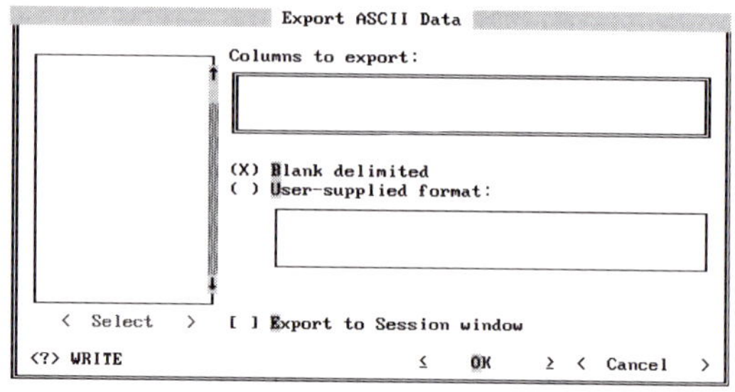

Options in the Export ASCII Data Dialog Box

Columns to export: You must specify the columns to be written out. When exporting columns of unequal length, Minitab adds missing value symbols (*) to the shorter numeric column(s).

Blank delimited: By default, Minitab uses blanks to separate columns. If data from all columns do not fit one line, Minitab uses the continuation symbol (&) at the end of the line and continues the data on the next line.

User-supplied format: To export data in Fortran format with or without delimiters, enter a Fortran format statement. Fortran conventions are listed in the format subdialog box in the File ► Import ASCII Data... section.

Export to Session window: Minitab displays the data in the Session window.

Session Command Syntax for Export ASCII Data...

WRITE [*to* **'FILENAME'**] *the data in columns*
C...C
FORMAT (Fortran format statement)

PRINT E...E
FORMAT (Fortran format statement)

Files created with WRITE may be imported into Minitab using the READ, SET, or INSERT commands.

Other Files

Choosing Other **F**iles opens a submenu that allows you to record the output and/or commands you issue in a given session, or to create and execute macros.

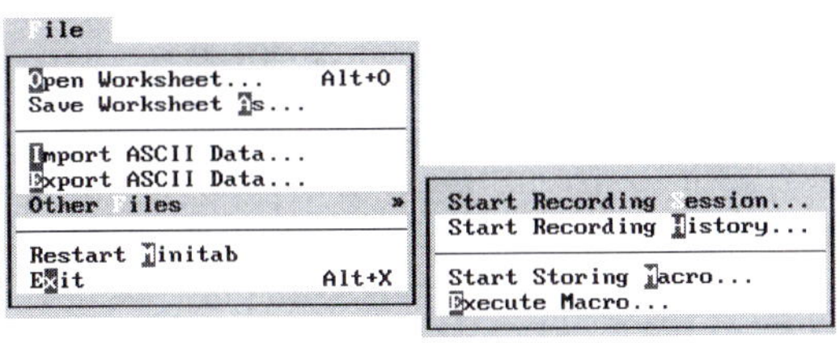

Start Recording Session...

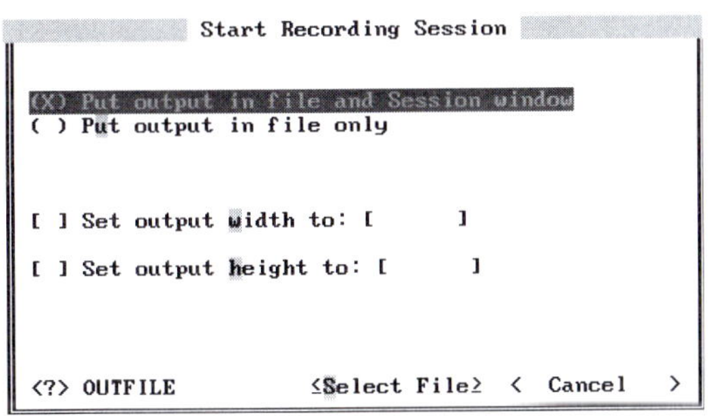

The Start Recording Session... command stores the Minitab output in a file. Minitab saves all the commands and output produced after the Start Recording Session... command is issued in the specified file until you end the session or choose Stop Recording Session.... (When you start recording the session, the Start Recording Session... command automatically changes to Stop Recording Session....) After you exit from Minitab, you can view and edit the new file with any word processing program; you can also print the file.

High-resolution graphics cannot be stored in an outfile. To save a graph as a separate file, use the Store in file option that appears under the high-resolution option in various graph dialog boxes.

Options in the Start Recording Session Dialog Box

Put output in file and Session window: By default, Minitab displays the session commands and output in the Session window and also writes them to a file.

P**u**t output in file only: Minitab directs commands and output to a file, but not to the Session window.

Set output **w**idth to: The default width is 79 characters, corresponding to the width of most screens. To change the line width, enter any number from 30 to 132. Some commands cannot produce output narrower than 70 spaces.

Set output **h**eight to: You can change the number of lines per page of your output. Minitab tries not to split a logical block of output across page breaks, so some pages may be less than the height you specify.

Select File: See the File ▶ Open Worksheet... command for information on the Select File dialog box. Minitab adds the default extension .LIS to the filename. If you do not want an extension, end the name with a period. If you use the same filename with this command later, Minitab will ask if you want to add to the existing file. If you answer yes, Minitab adds the new output to the end of the original file. If you answer no, you must enter another filename.

Session Command Syntax for Start Recording Session...

OUTFILE ['**FILENAME**']
  OW *output width is* **K** *spaces*
  OH *output height is* **K** *lines*
  NOTERMINAL *sends output only to the outfile*
NOOUTFILE *ends the recording session*

See also Tutorial 2.

Start Recording History...

The Start Recording **H**istory... command lets you record commands, but no output, in a standard ASCII file that can be printed and edited by any word processor. Minitab adds the extension .MTJ to the filename. When you have finished recording the commands you want to save, choose Stop Recording History.... (When you start recording, the Start Recording History... command automatically changes to Stop Recording History....) See the File ▶ Open Worksheet... command for information on the files dialog box that resembles the Record History in File dialog box.

Session Command Syntax for Start Recording History...

JOURNAL ['**FILENAME**']
NOJOURNAL

Start Storing Macro...

Minitab's macro feature is very useful. You can store commands that you use frequently so that you need not retype them each time. For example, you can use a macro to loop through columns or rows of a worksheet, repeating the same analysis on each column or row. Macros also give you the opportunity to use Minitab as a programming language to perform operations not provided in the menus. Your macros can inform users and even interact with them.

The Start Storing **M**acro... command operates in the same way as Start Recording History... except that the commands that you enter at the STOR> prompt aren't executed until the macro is executed. Start Recording History... keeps track of each command as it is executed. When you have finished recording the commands you want to save, choose Stop Storing Macro.... (When you start recording commands, the Start Storing Macro... command automatically changes to Stop Storing Macro.)

See the Open File dialog box described under the File ▶ Open Worksheet... command for information on the Store Macro In File dialog box. Minitab automatically adds the extension .MTB and stores the macro as a standard ASCII file; you can use a word processing program to edit or print it.

For more information, see Chapter 5, Macros, at the end of this Reference section.

Session Command Syntax for Start Recording Macro...

STORE [*in* '**FILENAME**'] *the following Minitab commands*
END *of stored commands*
NOECHO *the commands that follow*
ECHO *the commands that follow*
YESNO K
NOTE [any text]
\#   [any text]

The NOTE and # commands also work in a non-macro mode as independent commands. NOTE is similar to beginning a line with the symbol #. However, NOTE cannot be used among data lines for READ, SET, and INSERT, while # can.

See also Tutorial 14.

Execute Macro...

The Execute Macro... command executes any macro you have stored (see Start Storing Macro...). Macros may be nested; you can write one macro that executes another. You can nest a maximum of five macros.

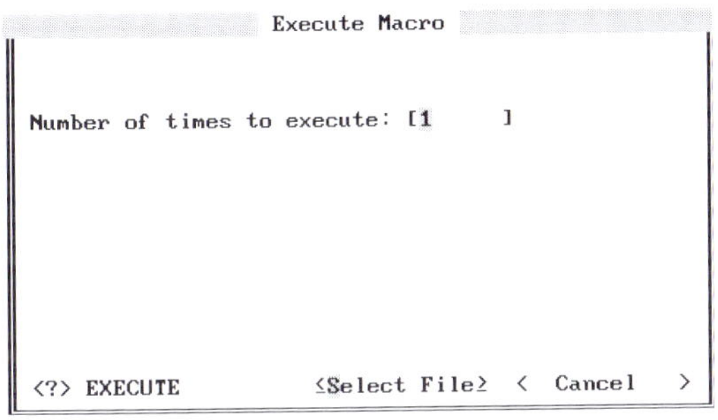

Options in the Execute Macro Dialog Box

Number of times to execute: By default, Minitab executes a macro only once. The opportunity to execute a macro several times is useful for simulations.

Select File: The subdialog box that appears is similar to the Open File dialog box described under the File ▶ Open Worksheet... command. In this case, you select the macro you want to execute rather than the worksheet you want to open.

Session Command Syntax for Execute Macro...

EXECUTE *the commands* [*stored in* **'FILENAME'**] [**K** *times*]

See also Tutorial 14.

Restart Minitab

The Restart Minitab command starts Minitab over, just as if you had quit and then started again from the DOS prompt. However, it is faster because you don't actually exit from the program. It is a convenient way to clear the Session window, erase all data from the Data worksheet, and reset all parameters and commands to their defaults. If any changes have been made, Minitab asks if you want to save the worksheet. You also have the opportunity of saving the current worksheet in a Portable or Lotus format. See the File ▶ Save Worksheet As... command for more information.

Session Command Syntax for Restart Minitab

RESTART

See also Tutorial 1.

Exit

Alt-X

Choose Exit to exit from Minitab; if there is a worksheet open, you have the opportunity to save it as a Minitab worksheet or in a Portable or Lotus format. See the File ▶ Save Worksheet As... command for more information.

Session Command Syntax for Exit

STOP

See also Tutorial 1.

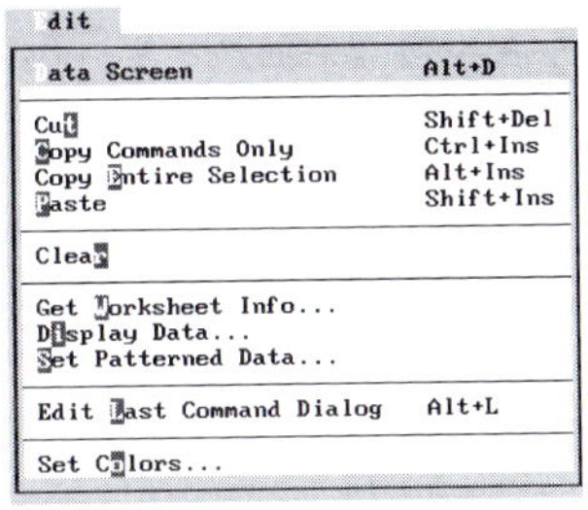

The Edit Menu

The **E**dit menu provides the commands needed to work with data and commands in the Session window. You can cut, copy, paste, and clear items in the Session window, display worksheet information and the data in the current worksheet, generate patterned data, return to previous commands, and save color preferences for the Minitab display.

Data Screen Alt-D

Choosing the **D**ata Screen command displays Minitab's Data screen rather than the Session window. Pressing Alt-M returns you to the Session window.

Cut Shift-Del

The Cu**t** command removes highlighted text that follows a pending command entered after the MTB > prompt (that is, a command that you have not yet executed by pressing ↵). Minitab stores the text to the clipboard, a temporary storage location. You can paste the section at the active MTB > prompt using the Edit ▶ Paste command. Minitab does not read the pasted commands until you press ↵; you can edit them before that time. This procedure is useful when you are typing a very long command. If you cut another section, it replaces the current contents of the clipboard.

You must highlight the entire MTB > prompt to ensure that the first line is included in the copied text. See the section Using Cut, Copy, and Paste earlier in this chapter for more information.

Copy Commands Only Ctrl-Ins

The **C**opy Commands Only command copies only the commands from a highlighted Session window selection and stores them until you choose Edit ▶ Paste. Minitab reads the commands when you press ↵. You must highlight the entire MTB > prompt to ensure including the first line in the copied text. See the section Using Cut, Copy, and Paste earlier in this chapter for more information.

Copy Entire Selection Alt-Ins

The Copy Entire Selection command works the same way as Copy Commands Only except that it includes the output as well as the commands.

Paste Shift-Ins

The Paste command inserts the contents of the clipboard after the active MTB > prompt. You can edit the pasted text before executing it. Press ↵ to have Minitab execute what you have pasted.

Clear

The Clear command removes highlighted text. It is similar to the Cut command.

Get Worksheet Info...

The Get Worksheet Info... command displays (in the Session window) information on nonempty columns and constants in the current worksheet.

The Get Worksheet Info Dialog Box

Options in the Get Worksheet Info Dialog Box

Include all columns and constants: The Session window displays a list of all columns, column names, number of rows, number of missing values, and stored constants.

Include only: Minitab displays information only on the columns you select.

Session Command Syntax for Get Worksheet Info...

INFORMATION [*on* **C...C**]

Example: Using Get Worksheet Info...

The Get Worksheet Info dialog box and the equivalent Session window commands that follow illustrate how Minitab displays information on the PROF.MTW data set from Tutorial 4.

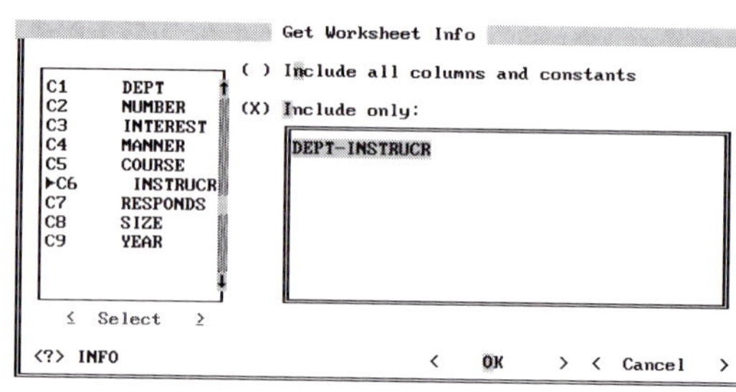


```
MTB > Info 'DEPT'-'INSTRUCR'.
```

These commands produce the following display of information in the Session window:

```
    COLUMN     NAME       COUNT
A   C1         DEPT         146
    C2         NUMBER       146
    C3         INTEREST     146
    C4         MANNER       146
    C5         COURSE       146
    C6         INSTRUCR     146
```

Display Data...

The Display Data... command lists the data in the current worksheet in the Session window.

The Display Data Dialog Box

Options in the Display Data Dialog Box

Columns and constants to display: You can list any combination of columns or constants in any order. If you list only one column, Minitab prints it across the Session window; if you list multiple columns, they appear vertically. Minitab chooses the number of decimal digits for displayed value.

Session Command Syntax for Display Data...

PRINT *the data in* **E...E**

  FORMAT (format statement)

If you want to format the data display in the Session window, use the PRINT command with the FORMAT subcommand and a Fortran format statement as specified in the section on the File ▶ Import ASCII Data - Format subdialog box.

Example: Using Display Data...

The following dialog box and equivalent Session window commands illustrate how to display some of the PROF.MTW data set from Tutorial 4 in the Session window.

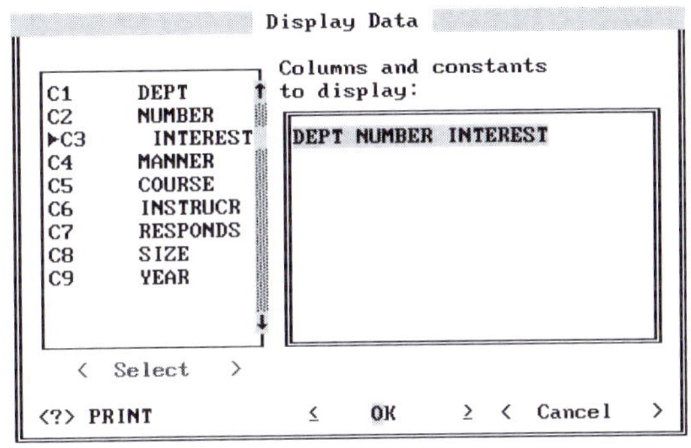


```
MTB > Print 'DEPT' 'NUMBER' 'INTEREST'.
```

These commands produce the following display in the Session window (only the first portion is visible in the illustration):

```
ROW   DEPT  NUMBER  INTEREST

  1   ACC     221     2.07
  2   ACC     221     2.40
  3   ACC     321     2.64
  4   ACC     344     3.42
  5   AER     101     3.25
  6   ARC     426     3.29
  7   ART     111     2.47
  8   ART     111     3.00
  9   ART     211     3.17
 10   ART     485     3.60
 11   ATH     155     2.50
 12   ATH     212     2.92
 13   CHM     111     1.44
 14   CHM     141     2.17
 15   CHM     142     1.38
 16   COM     193     3.71
```

See also Tutorial 2.

Set Patterned Data...

The Set Patterned Data... command enters repetitive data into a column.

The Set Patterned Data Dialog Box

Options in the Set Patterned Data Dialog Box

Put data into column: Name or indicate the storage location.

Patterned sequence: By default, Minitab creates a sequence of repetitive data according to your specifications. It can start and end with either a number or a stored constant.

Start at: Type the first number or constant.

End at: Type the last number or constant.

Increment: Type the increment you want to use.

Arbitrary list of constants: Use this command when the numbers aren't sequential.

Repeat each value: Indicate the number of times you want each value repeated.

Repeat the whole list: Indicate the number of times you want the entire list repeated.

Session Command Syntax for Set Patterned Data...

SET *data* [*from* **'FILENAME'**] *into* **C**
END *indicates you are finished*

The patterned sequence of numbers is a list of numbers that uses parentheses ( ), colons :, and slashes / to indicate the pattern as in 2(30:40/5)3. The 30:40/5 in the parentheses produces a list of values from 30 to 40 using an increment of 5. Each value is repeated 3 times and the entire list is repeated twice. The values in the parentheses can also be a list of values, separated by spaces.

Example: Using Set Patterned Data...

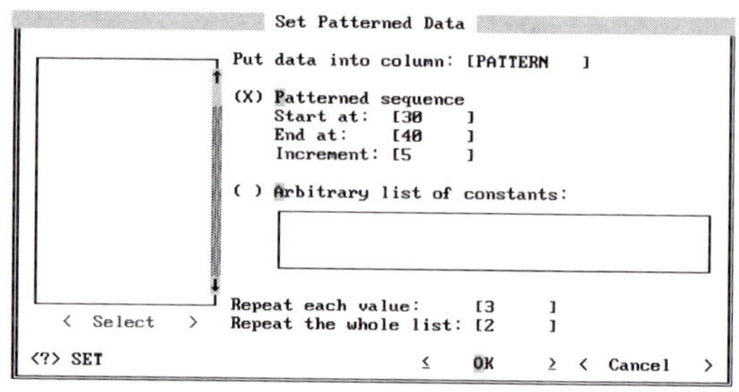


```
MTB > Name c1 = 'PATTERN'
MTB > Set 'PATTERN'
DATA>   2( 30 : 40 / 5 )3
DATA>   End.
```

These commands produce the following data, which are displayed in the Data worksheet:

→	PATTERN C1
1	30
2	30
3	30
4	35
5	35
6	35
7	40
8	40
9	40
10	30
11	30
12	30
13	35
14	35
15	35
16	40
17	40
18	40

See also Tutorial 5.

Edit Last Command Dialog [Alt]-L

The Edit Last Command Dialog command displays the last dialog box you used to generate a session command. If you plan to rerun a procedure with only minor changes, this command can save time and effort.

See also Tutorial 1.

Set Colors...

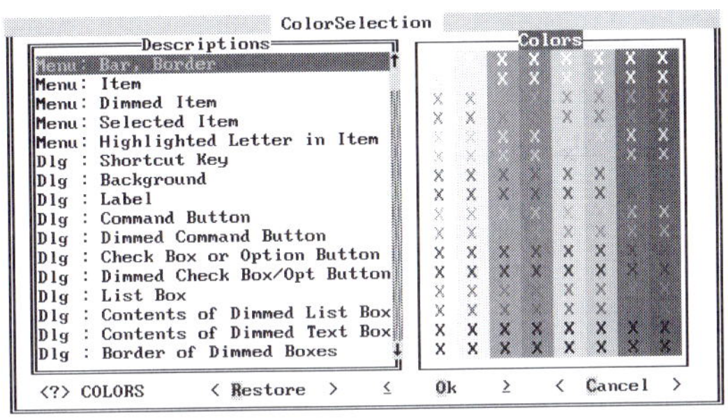

The Set Colors... command sets the colors of various screen elements. In the Color Selections dialog box, scroll through the Descriptions window to highlight the item you want to change. Position the cursor (using the directional arrow keys or the mouse) over the color combination of foreground and background color you want. Choose OK to accept the color changes you have made, Cancel to discard them, or Restore to restore the default colors.

When you select OK and change the colors, Minitab saves the new color settings in a file named MINITAB.INI in your current directory. The next time you start Minitab from that directory, Minitab reads this file and sets screen colors accordingly.

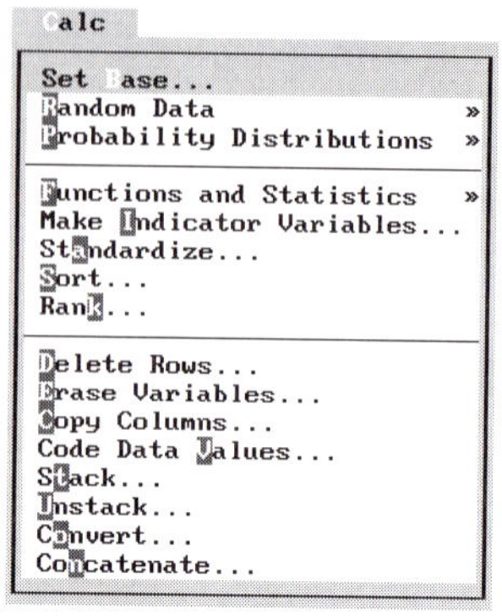

The Calc Menu

The Calc menu contains three groups of commands: distributions and random data, mathematical transformations, and worksheet operations.

Set Base...

The Set **B**ase... command fixes a starting point for Minitab's random number generator. Minitab has a long string of "random" numbers available. If it always started at the beginning of the list, you would always get the same data. To avoid this, most computers use the time of day (in seconds or fractions of a second) to choose a "random" starting point in the string.

Minitab normally chooses its own random starting point for this process so that you don't see the same random data each session. When you need to generate the same random data, use the Set Base... option to tell the random number generator where to begin.

The Set Base Dialog Box

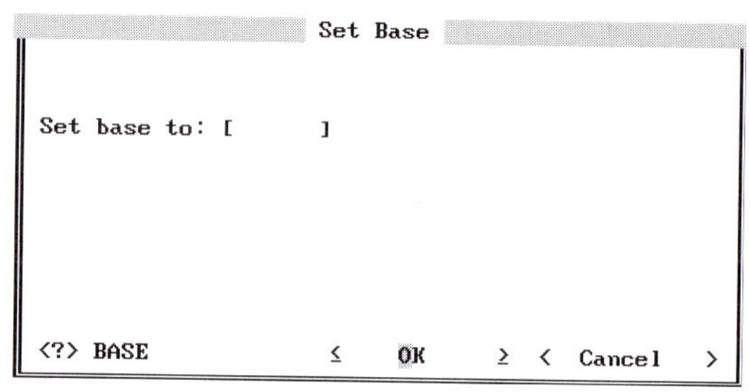

Options in the Set Base Dialog Box

Set base to: Type a single integer to begin the random number sequence.

Session Command Syntax for Set Base...

BASE K

Random Data

Choosing **R**andom Data displays a submenu that contains commands for generating a random sample of numbers. The sample may be obtained from one of the given distributions listed. Alternatively, a random sample can be obtained from any existing column in the worksheet.

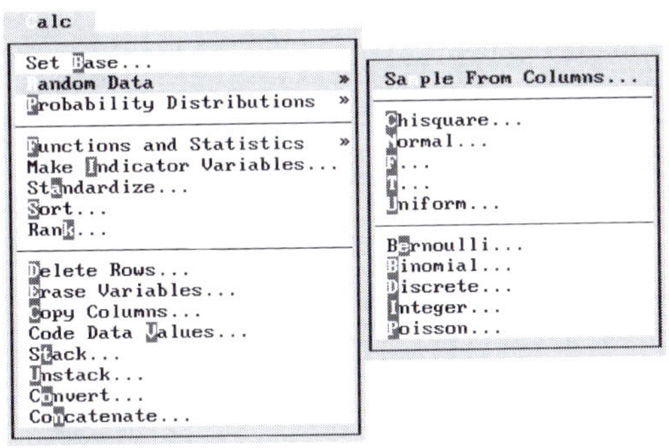

Sample From Columns...

Using the Sa**m**ple From Columns... command, you can randomly sample rows from one or more columns. If you sample from several columns at once, they must all have the same length; Minitab selects the same rows from each. When sampling without replacement, the number of rows to be sampled must be no more than the number of rows in the sampled columns.

Options in the Sample From Columns Dialog Box

Sample — rows from column(s): Enter the number of rows you want Minitab to sample.

Put samples in: Name or designate the column(s) where the sampled values are to be stored.

Sample with replacement: By default, Minitab samples without replacement, so the same row cannot be selected more than once. Select this checkbox to sample with replacement.

Session Command Syntax for Sample From Columns

SAMPLE K *rows from* **C...C** *put in* **C...C**
REPLACE

Example: Using Sample From Columns...

The following dialog box and equivalent Session window commands illustrate how to sample four student ID numbers, stored in C1 ID, from the self-reported heights data set, HEIGHTS.MTW, from Tutorial 5:

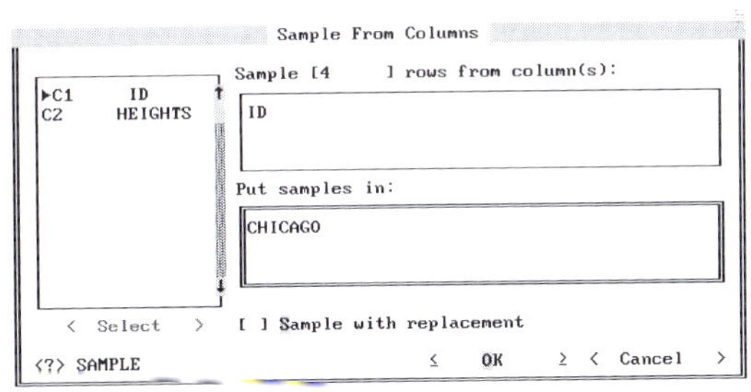


```
MTB > Name c3 = 'CHICAGO'
MTB > Sample 4 'ID' 'CHICAGO'.
```

Minitab randomly selects four ID numbers and stores them in C3 'CHICAGO', as seen in the Data screen:

→	ID C1	HEIGHTS C2	CHICAGO C3
1	441	65.0	820
2	805	71.3	670
3	555	69.5	552
4	390	62.8	679
5	49	67.1	
6	820	62.1	
7	581	63.6	
8	298	63.4	
9	413	64.2	
10	648	61.7	
11	2	61.8	
12	639	61.0	
13	552	64.2	
14	968	66.2	
15	483	70.2	
16	597	62.5	
17	187	68.9	
18	253	62.3	
19	155	66.9	
20	577	66.7	
21	114	66.6	
22	961	68.0	

Options on the Random Data Submenu

Distributions available on the Random Data submenu are: Chisquare, Normal, F, T, Uniform, Bernouilli, Binomial, Discrete, Integer, and Poisson.

All dialog boxes on the Random Data submenu function the same way. The Chisquare Distribution dialog box illustrates the main elements.

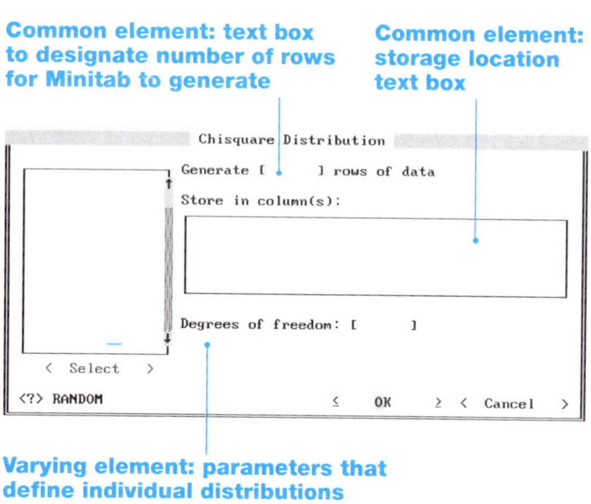

Common Elements

All the Random Data dialog boxes have two common elements:

Generate — rows of data: Indicate here the number of rows of random data you would like Minitab to generate.

Store in column(s): Designate the columns into which Minitab should put the data it generates.

Varying Elements

Each of the Random Data dialog boxes contains parameters that define individual distributions. For example, the Chisquare distribution is defined by Degrees of freedom. Other options are listed below.

Defining Parameters for the Random Data Dialog Boxes

Distributions depend on parameters—numbers or values that determine a particular distribution. For example, the normal distribution is defined by two parameters—the mean and the standard deviation. The following paragraphs describe the parameters used by each type of distribution.

Chisquare and T distributions: Defined by values for Degrees of freedom.

Normal distribution: Defined by a Mean and Standard deviation.

F distribution: Defined by values for Numerator and Denominator degrees of freedom.

Uniform distribution: Defined by values for Lower endpoint and Upper endpoint.

Binomial distribution: Defined by values for Number of trials and Probability of success.

Discrete distribution: Defined by Values in and Probabilities in.

Integer distribution: Defined by Minimum value and Maximum value.

Poisson distribution: Defined by the Mean value.

Session Command Syntax for Random Data Distributions

RANDOM K *observations into column* **C...C**
  BERNOULLI p = **K**
  BINOMIAL n = **K**, p = **K**
  CHISQUARE *degrees of freedom* = **K**
  DISCRETE *values in* **C** *probabilities in* **C**
  F *df numerator* = **K** *df denominator* = **K**
  INTEGER *discrete uniform distribution on* **K** *to* **K**
  NORMAL [*mean* = **K** [*standard deviation* = **K**]]
  POISSON *mean* = **K**
  T *degrees of freedom* = **K**
  UNIFORM *continuous distribution* [*on* **K** *to* **K**]

Example: Using Random Data

The following dialog box and equivalent Session window commands illustrate how to generate a sample of ten observations (for example, female heights in inches) from a normal population with mean 64 and standard deviation 3.1.

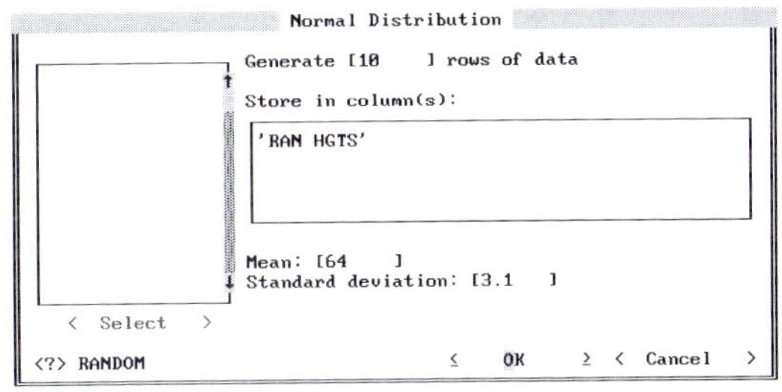


```
MTB > Name c1 = 'RAN HGTS'
MTB > Random 10 'RAN HGTS';
SUBC>   Normal 64 3.1.
```

These commands produce a new column in the Data worksheet (RAN HGTS), containing 10 rows of randomly generated data, distributed normally.

→	RAN HGTS C1
1	68.2105
2	62.7713
3	61.9228
4	66.7603
5	64.0310
6	66.4253
7	64.2524
8	61.6878
9	67.2406
10	66.1496

See also Tutorial 5.

Probability Distributions

When you choose Probability Distributions, a submenu containing the following distributions is displayed: Chisquare, Normal, F, T, Uniform, Binomial, Discrete, Integer, and Poisson.

Options on the Probability Distributions Submenu

The Probability Distributions submenu contains commands for continuous and discrete distributions. You can calculate probabilities, probability densities, cumulative probabilities, and inverse cumulative probabilities directly from the dialog box for each individual distribution.

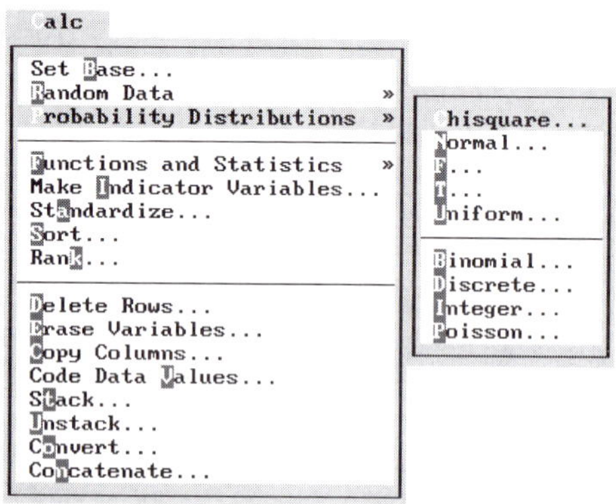

All dialog boxes on the Probability Distributions submenu function the same way. The first one on the submenu, Chisquare..., illustrates the main components.

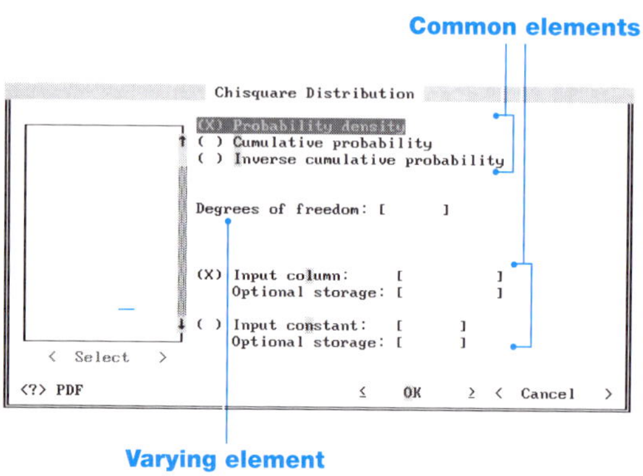

Probability Distributions Dialog Boxes

Each of the Probability Distributions dialog boxes contains parameters that define individual distributions. For example, the Chisquare Distribution is defined by Degrees of freedom. Other options are listed below.

Probability (or Probability density): For discrete distributions (Binomial, Discrete, Integer, and Poisson), the Probability option appears and Minitab calculates the probability of the values indicated in the Input column text box. If you omit this argument, Minitab produces a full table of probabilities for the discrete distribution chosen. For continuous distributions (Chisquare, Normal, F, T, and Uniform), the Probability density option appears and Minitab calculates the continuous probability density function, the height of the curve, for each number specified.

Cumulative probability: This command computes cumulative probabilities for the given values from a specified distribution. The cumulative distribution function for a random variable gives the probability that its value is less than or equal to x, computing the probability for a constant or for each number in a column.

Inverse cumulative probability: This command computes the inverse of the cumulative distribution function, giving the value associated with a given cumulative probability. It is convenient to use this command to look up critical values for T, F, and other distributions rather than searching through tables. For the continuous distributions (Chisquare, Normal, F, T, and Uniform), the Inverse cumulative probability exists for all probabilities between 0 and 1. Whether or not it exists for all probabilities depends on the distribution. For the discrete distributions (Binomial, Discrete, Integer, and Poisson), there may be no value that corresponds exactly to a given probability, in which case the two closest values are given.

Input column or constant: Indicate the column or constant you want to evaluate.

Optional storage: Indicate the location where you want to store the calculated values.

Defining Parameters for the Probability Distributions Dialog Boxes

Distributions depend on parameters—numbers or values that determine a particular distribution. For example, the normal distribution is defined by two parameters—the mean and the standard deviation. The following paragraphs describe the parameters used by each type of distribution.

Chisquare and **T** distributions: Defined by values for Degrees of freedom.

Normal distribution: Defined by a Mean and Standard deviation.

F distribution: Defined by values for Numerator and Denominator degrees of freedom.

Uniform distribution: Defined by values for Lower endpoint and Upper endpoint.

Binomial distribution: Defined by values for Number of trials and Probability of success.

Discrete distribution: Defined by Values in and Probabilities in.

Integer distribution: Defined by Minimum value and Maximum value.

Poisson distribution: Defined by the Mean value.

Session Command Syntax for Probability Distributions

PDF *for values in* **E** [*put into* **E**]
CDF *for values in* **E** [*put into* **E**]
INVCDF *for values in* **E** [*put into* **E**]

The session commands PDF, CDF, and INVCDF are equivalent to the Probability or Probability density command, the Cumulative probability command, and the Inverse cumulative probability command, respectively. Use the following subcommands for these three commands:

BINOMIAL *n* = **K** *p* = **K**
CHISQUARE *degrees of freedom* = **K**
DISCRETE *values in* **C** *probabilities in* **C**
F *df numerator* = **K** *df denominator* = **K**
INTEGER *discrete uniform distribution on* **K** *to* **K**
NORMAL [*mean* = **K** [*standard deviation* = **K**]]
POISSON *mean* = **K**
T *degrees of freedom* = **K**
UNIFORM *continuous distribution* [*on* **K** *to* **K**]

Example: Using Probability Distributions

The following Normal Distribution dialog box and equivalent Session window commands show how to calculate and store the cumulative probabilities associated with self-reported female height data stored in C2 of HEIGHTS.MTW from Tutorial 5.

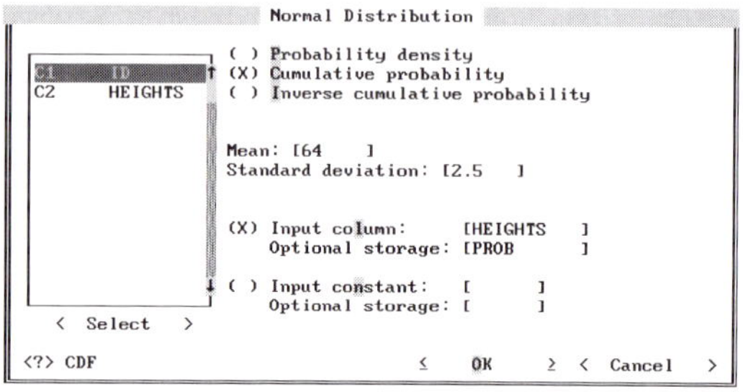


```
MTB > Name c3 = 'PROB'
MTB > CDF 'HEIGHTS' 'PROB';
SUBC>   Normal 64 2.5.
```

The cumulative probability associated with each self-reported height value appears in the Data worksheet; the first portion of the probability data is shown in the following figure:

	ID	HEIGHTS	PROB
→	C1	C2	C3
1	441	65.0	0.655422
2	805	71.3	0.998250
3	555	69.5	0.986097
4	390	62.8	0.315614
5	49	67.1	0.892512
6	820	62.1	0.223627
7	581	63.6	0.436440
8	298	63.4	0.405165
9	413	64.2	0.531881
10	648	61.7	0.178786
11	2	61.8	0.189430
12	639	61.0	0.115070
13	552	64.2	0.531881
14	968	66.2	0.810570
15	483	70.2	0.993431
16	597	62.5	0.274253
17	187	68.9	0.975002
18	253	62.3	0.248252
19	155	66.9	0.876976
20	577	66.7	0.859929
21	114	66.6	0.850830
22	961	68.0	0.945201

See also Tutorial 5.

Functions and Statistics

The **F**unctions and Statistics submenu gives you access to arithmetic and mathematical transformations on columns, rows, stored constants, and numbers. The commands are grouped under the following headings: General Expressions... (does arithmetic using algebraic expressions), Functions... (transforms columns of data by using functions), Column Statistics... (calculates statistics on individual variables in your data set), and Row Statistics... (calculates statistics on individual cases).

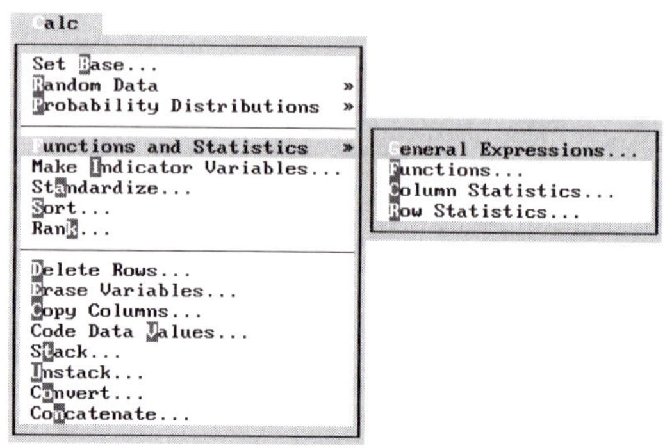

The General Expressions Dialog Box

The **G**eneral Expressions... command allows you to assign new values to one element in a column, to a constant, or to an entire column.

Options in the General Expressions Dialog Box

New/modified variable: Name the variable or designate the column you want to create or modify.

Row number: Designate an individual row number if you want to modify one element in a column.

Expression: Type the mathematical operation you want Minitab to perform in this text box. The usual ordering of arithmetic operations holds:

1. Expressions within () are evaluated first.
2. ** is performed first, then * and /, then finally + and -.
3. Operations of "equal order" are performed from left to right.

No extra text is allowed (except after #). Parentheses may be nested up to nine deep. The total length of the expression, including continuation lines, may not exceed 78 characters.

1. Arithmetic Operations:

+	addition
–	subtraction
*	multiplication
/	division
**	exponentiation

2. Comparisons:

=	or EQ (equal to)
~=	or NE (not equal to)
<	or LT (less than)
>	or GT (greater than)
<=	or LE (less than or equal to)
>=	or GE (greater than or equal to)

3. Logical Operators:

&	or AND (and)
~	or NOT (not)
|	or OR (or)

With comparisons and logical operators, the result is set to 1 if the expression is true and 0 if it is false. With logical operators involving numbers, 0 represents false and all nonzero numbers are treated as true. For example, 1&5 evaluates to 1 (for true) and 0&5 evaluates to 0 (for false).

You may use the missing data code with comparisons = and ~=. For example, the expression C1 ~= '*' puts a 1 in all rows where C1 has a nonmissing value, and a 0 where it has a missing value.

Include parentheses around the argument of the function—that is, SQRT (C1), not SQRT C1. The argument may be a variable, stored constant, or number. The values used in the function are the values of the argument.

4. Functions that operate on column values or on a single value:

SQRT	Calculates square roots. Applied to negative numbers, the result is * (missing value).
ABSOLUTE	Calculates absolute values.
ROUND	Rounds numbers to the nearest integer. Numbers halfway between two integers are rounded up in magnitude.
SIGNS	Converts negative numbers, zero, and positive numbers to −1, 0 and +1, respectively, printing a summary table. You may optionally store the new values in a column.
LOGE	Calculates logarithms to the base e (natural logarithms). LOGE of 0 or a negative number results in * (missing value).
LOGT	Calculates logarithms to the base 10. LOGT of 0 or a negative number results in * (missing value).
EXPO	Calculates the power of e to the argument value.
ANTILOG	Calculates the power of 10 to the argument value.

SIN	Calculates the trigonometric function sine, requiring the argument in radians.
COS	Calculates the trigonometric function cosine, requiring the argument in radians.
TAN	Calculates the trigonometric function tangent, requiring the argument in radians.
ASIN	Calculates the inverse sine, giving results in radians.
ACOS	Calculates the inverse cosine, giving results in radians.
ATAN	Calculates the inverse tangent, giving results in radians.
NSCORES	Computes normal scores for use in probability plots.
PARSUMS	Calculates partial sums. The sum of the first *i* rows of the input column is put in the ith row of the storage column.
PARPRODUCTS	Calculates partial products. The product of the first *i* rows of the input column is put into the ith row of the storage column.

5. Functions that operate on columns only:

COUNT	Gives the total number of values, including missing values.
N	Number of values in the arguments.
NMISS	Number of missing values in the arguments.
SUM	Sums the values of the arguments.
MEAN	Gives the mean of a column.
STDEV	Computes the sample standard deviation of a column.
MEDIAN	Calculates the median of a column.
MIN	Gives the minimum value in a column.
MAX	Gives the maximum value in a column.
SSQ	Calculates the uncorrected sum of squares of the column.
SORT	Sorts one or more columns.
RANK	Computes ranks of the values in a column.
LAG	Lags data.

Many of these functions can be issued as direct commands from the Calc ► Functions and Statistics ► Functions... or Column Statistics... dialog boxes. See those sections for further explanation.

Session Command Syntax for General Expressions...

LET E = *expression*

You can use the following arithmetic operations as functions within a LET command using the conventions described in the previous section or as independent commands with the following forms:

ADD E *to* **E**...*to* **E** *put into* **E**
SUBTRACT E *from* **E** *put into* **E**
MULTIPLY E *by* **E**...*by* **E** *put into* **E**
DIVIDE E *by* **E** *put into* **E**
RAISE E *to the power of* **E** *put into* **E**

With the LET command, use arithmetic symbols (+, –, *, /, **) to represent the five previous operators.

ABSOLUTE *value of* **E** *put into* **E**
SIGNS *of* **E** *put into* **E**
SQRT *of* **E** *put into* **E**
ROUND E *to integer put into* **E**
LOGE (natural logarithms) *of* **E** *put into* **E**
LOGTEN (logarithms—base 10) *of* **E** *put into* **E**
EXPONENTIATE (e to the power) *of* **E** *put into* **E**
ANTILOG (10 to the power) *of* **E** *put into* **E**
NSCORE (normal scores) *of* **C** *put into* **C**
SIN *of* **E** *put into* **E**
COS *of* **E** *put into* **E**
TAN *of* **E** *put into* **E**
ASIN (arcsin) *of* **E** *put into* **E**
ACOS (arccosine) *of* **E** *put into* **E**
ATAN (arctangent) *of* **E** *put into* **E**
PARSUMS (partial sums) *of* **C** *put into* **C**
PARPRODUCTS (partial products) *of* **C** *put into* **C**

You can also use the following functions within a LET command: COUNT, N, NMISS, SUM, MEAN, STDEV, MEDIAN, MIN, MAX, SSQ, SORT, RANK, LAG.

The Session window expression syntax is generally the same as that described in the Expression text box selection. See the sections on Column Statistics... and Row Statistics... later in this chapter for the syntax of those specific commands.

Example: Using General Expressions...

The following example shows how to compute individual chi-square values for the observed and expected values for growing peas in carbon-dioxide–deficient soil. The data set GENETICS.MTW in Tutorial 10 contains the phenotypes. The observed values for each type, 94, 50, 44, and 12, are stored in C4, while the expected values, 112.5, 37.5, 37.5, and 12.5, are stored in C5.

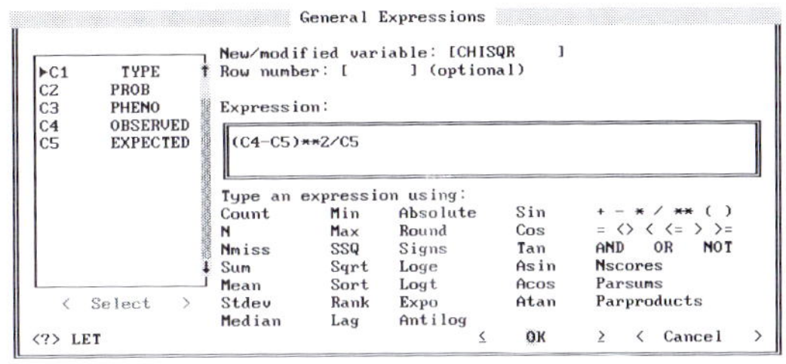


```
MTB > Name c6 = 'CHISQR'
MTB > Let 'CHISQR' = (C4-C5)**2/C5
```

These commands produce the following chi-square values in C6 CHISQR:

	TYPE	PROB	PHENO	OBSERVED	EXPECTED	CHISQR
↓	C1	C2	C3	C4	C5	C6
1	1	0.5625	2	94	112.5	3.04222
2	2	0.1875	3	50	37.5	4.16667
3	3	0.1875	1	44	37.5	1.12667
4	4	0.0625	1	12	12.5	0.02000

See also Tutorial 1.

The Functions Dialog Box

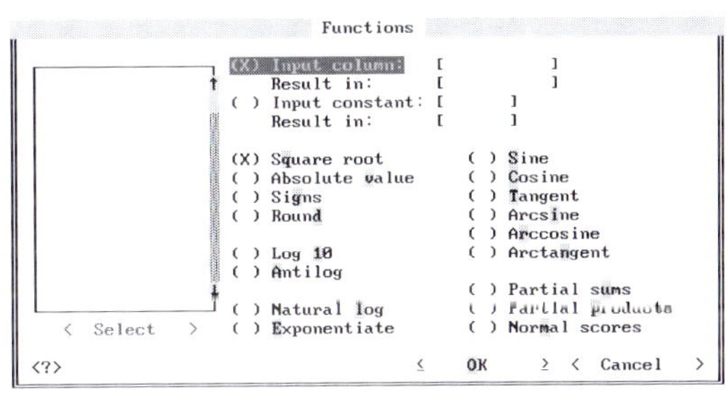

The Functions... command includes a useful subset of the commands available on the Functions and Statistics submenu. It can perform various functions on a column or constant, displaying the results and optionally storing them in a column or constant.

Options in the Functions Dialog Box

Input column: Indicate the argument here.

Result in: Indicate the name or column where you want the result to be stored.

Square root, Absolute value, etc.: Select the function you want to use.

See the General Expressions... section of the Calc ▶ Functions and Statistics submenu for an explanation of each function and the equivalent Session window syntax.

See also Tutorial 5.

The Column Statistics Dialog Box

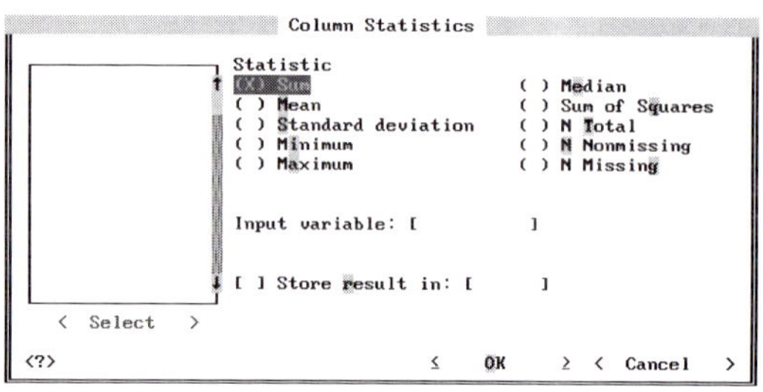

The Column Statistics... command calculates various statistics on the variable you indicate, displaying the results and optionally storing them in a constant.

Options in the Column Statistics Dialog Box

Statistic: See the Calc ▶ Functions and Statistics ▶ General Expressions... section for an explanation of the individual statistics you can choose.

Input variable: Indicate the variable in this text box.

Store result in: Indicate the constant storage location.

Session Command Syntax for Column Statistics...

COUNT *the number of values in* **C** [*put into* **K**]
N *count the non-missing values in* **C** [*put into* **K**]
NMISS *count the missing values in* **C** [*put into* **K**]
SUM *the values in* **C** [*put into* **K**]
MEAN *of the values in* **C** [*put into* **K**]
STDEV *standard deviation of* **C** [*put into* **K**]
MEDIAN *of the values in* **C** [*put into* **K**]
MINIMUM *of the values in* **C** [*put into* **K**]
MAXIMUM *of the values in* **C** [*put into* **K**]
SSQ (uncorrected) *sum of squares of* **C** [*put into* **E**]

See also Tutorial 2.

The Row Statistics Dialog Box

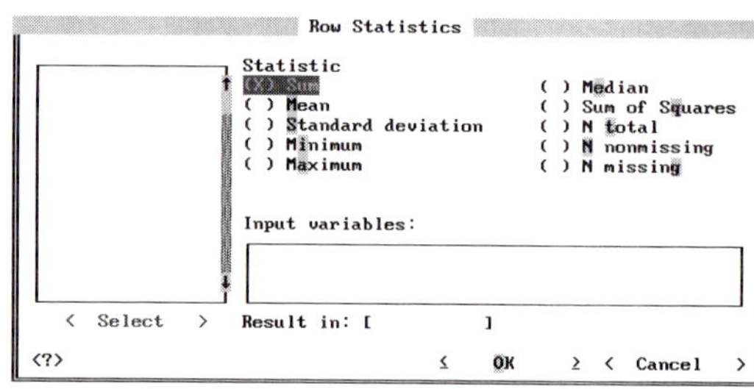

The row functions compute one number for each row in a set of columns. You can use them only as standalone commands, and the answers are always stored in the corresponding rows of the new variable.

Options in the Row Statistics Dialog Box

Statistic: See the Calc ▶ Functions and Statistics ▶ General Expressions... section for an explanation of the individual statistics you can choose.

Input variables: Indicate the column(s) or constants you want to use in this text box.

Result in: Name or indicate a column as the storage location.

Session Command Syntax for Row Statistics...

RCOUNT *total number of values in row of* **E...E** *put in* **C**
RN *number of non-missing values in row of* **E...E** *put in* **C**
RNMISS *number of missing values per row of* **E...E** *put in* **C**
RSUM *sum of all values on row* of **E...E** *put in* **C**
RMEAN *average of all values on row of* **E...E** *put in* **C**
RSTDEV *stand. dev. of all values on row of* **E...E** *put in* **C**
RMEDIAN *median value in row of* **E...E** *put in* **C**
RMINIMUM *smallest number in row of* **E...E** *put in* **C**
RMAXIMUM *largest number in row of* **E...E** *put in* **C**
RSSQ *sum of the squared values in row of* **E...E** *put in* **C**

See also Tutorial 2.

Make Indicator Variables...

The Make Indicator Variables... command creates indicator (dummy) variables that you can use in regression analysis. The variables are formed from a subscript column containing consecutive integers; the subscript column must contain integers from –10000 to +10000 or missing values. You can create up to 100 indicator variables.

If there are K distinct possible levels, then you must give K storage columns. The first storage column will contain 1 in every row that has the smallest number in the levels column, and a 0 in all other rows. The second storage column will contain a 1 in every row that has the second smallest level number, a 0 in all other rows, and so on. For example, if the range of the data in the levels column is between 2 and 6, you need five storage columns—regardless of whether the levels column contains all values between 2 and 6.

The Make Indicator Variables Dialog Box

Options in the Make Indicator Variables Dialog Box

Indicator variables for: Designate the column you want to create an indicator variable for.

Put in: Indicate the names or columns where the results should be stored.

Session Command Syntax for Make Indicator Variables...

INDICATOR *variables for values in* **C** *put into* **C...C**

Example: Using Make Indicator Variables...

The following dialog box and equivalent Session window commands show how to create indicator variables for the department variable,

C7 DEPT, at Technitron, Inc. from the TECHN.MTW data set from Tutorial 9. You can then use the indicator variables in a regression analysis to determine the effect of department on salary.

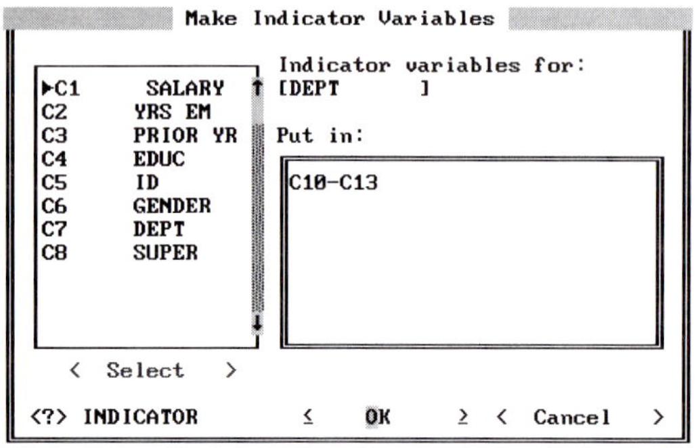


```
MTB > Indicator 'DEPT' C10-C13.
```

These commands produce four new columns that indicate whether a given employee is from a given department. Only the first portion is shown in the following illustration.

DEPT C7	SUPER C8	C9	C10	C11	C12	C13	C14
1	5		1	0	0	0	
1	4		1	0	0	0	
1	0		1	0	0	0	
1	1		1	0	0	0	
1	7		1	0	0	0	
1	6		1	0	0	0	
1	9		1	0	0	0	
1	5		1	0	0	0	
1	4		1	0	0	0	
1	0		1	0	0	0	
2	2		0	1	0	0	
2	3		0	1	0	0	
2	5		0	1	0	0	
2	2		0	1	0	0	
2	6		0	1	0	0	
2	2		0	1	0	0	
2	5		0	1	0	0	
2	2		0	1	0	0	
3	4		0	0	1	0	
3	2		0	0	1	0	
3	6		0	0	1	0	
3	8		0	0	1	0	

Enter Data F10=Menu

Standardize...

The Standardize... command allows you to center and scale columns of data.

The Standardize Dialog Box

Options in the Standardize Dialog Box

Input column(s): Indicate the variable(s) you want to standardize.

Put results in: Name or indicate the column(s) where the results will be stored.

Subtract mean and divide by SD: Transforms the column by subtracting its mean and dividing the result by the standard deviation.

Subtract mean: Transforms the column by subtracting its mean.

Divide by SD: Transforms the column by dividing by its standard deviation.

Subtract — and divide by —: Transforms the column by subtracting a specified value and dividing by a specified value.

Make range from — to —: Transforms the column by doing a linear transformation within the range you specify.

Session Command Syntax for Standardize...

CENTER C...C *put into* **C...C**
  LOCATION [*subtracting* **K...K**]
  SCALE [*dividing by* **K...K**]
  MINMAX [*min* = **K** *max* = **K**]

Example: Using Standardize...

The following example standardizes test grades in the GRADEST2.MTW data set from Tutorial 2.

```
                              Standardize
 ▶C3     TEST1   ↑ Input column(s):
  C4     TEST2     ┌──────────────────────────────────┐
  C5     TEST3     │TEST1-TEST3                        │
                   └──────────────────────────────────┘
                   Put results in:
                   ┌──────────────────────────────────┐
                   │STD1 STD2 STD3                     │
                   └──────────────────────────────────┘
                   (X) Subtract mean and divide by SD
                   ( ) Subtract mean
                 ↓ ( ) Divide by SD
                   ( ) Subtract [0.0     ] and divide by [1.0     ]
   <  Select  >    ( ) Make range from [-1.0   ] to [1.0    ]

 <?> CENTER                        <  OK    >  <  Cancel  >
```

```
MTB > Name c6 = 'STD1' c7 = 'STD2' c8 = 'STD3'
MTB > Center 'TEST1'-'TEST3' 'STD1' 'STD2' 'STD3'.
```

These commands produce the following display (only the first portion is shown):

	LAST NAM C1	FIRST C2	TEST1 C3	TEST2 C4	TEST3 C5	STD1 C6	STD2 C7	STD3 C8	C9	C10
1	ADAMS,	JAMES	72	93	93	-0.51215	0.88157	0.76592		
2	BENSON,	MELISSA	99	86	83	1.21635	0.35451	0.35376		
3	BROWN,	LAMAR	59	59	90	-1.34439	-1.67844	0.64227		
4	DOUGHERTY,	MEGAN	79	69	60	-0.06402	-0.92550	-0.59419		
5	DOUGLAS,	JASON	48	77	25	-2.04859	-0.32314	-2.03672		
6	GIGLIOTTI,	ANDREW	78	94	50	-0.12804	0.95687	-1.00634		
7	GOLDBERG,	JONATHAN	98	98	94	1.15233	1.25805	0.80713		
8	GREEN,	JENNIFER	92	91	99	0.76822	0.73098	1.01321		
9	KENNEDY,	KEVIN	71	78	62	-0.57617	-0.24784	-0.51176		
10	LEE,	SANG	64	68	97	-1.02429	-1.00079	0.93078		
11	MCCLURE,	MARK	49	79	43	-1.98457	-0.17255	-1.29484		
12	MESSINA,	STEVEN	94	93	95	0.89626	0.88157	0.84835		
13	NORMAN,	BARBARA	99	95	84	1.21635	1.03216	0.39498		
14	NOWICKI,	AMY	91	81	79	0.70420	-0.02196	0.18890		
15	PATEL,	HIMA	90	100	62	0.64018	1.40864	-0.51176		
16	PIERSON,	RICHARD	100	77	100	1.28037	-0.32314	1.05442		
17	ROJAS,	LUIS	73	79	83	-0.44813	-0.17255	0.35376		
18	RYAN,	MATT	77	79	85	-0.19206	-0.17255	0.43619		
19	SCHMIDT,	NANCY	83	79	52	0.19206	-0.17255	-0.92391		
20	SCOTT,	MICHAEL	81	75	100	0.06402	-0.47373	1.05442		
21	SHEPPARD,	KATHLEEN	94	97	100	0.89626	1.18275	1.05442		
22	SMITH,	HOLLY	82	51	25	0.12804	-2.28080	-2.03672		

Enter Data F10=Menu

See also Tutorial 2.

Sort...

The Sort... command sorts data (alpha or numeric) in order by rows, according to the values in the column(s) you indicate, and then stores the rearranged data. By default, Minitab sorts the first column, carrying along additional columns that you specify. When two or more values are equal for all sorting variables, Minitab maintains the original order of the column.

When sorting alpha data, Minitab converts the "words" into uppercase and alphabetizes them. If two words are the same when converted to uppercase, then SORT compares the original upper- and lowercase values. The first letter that differs in case determines the order. Lowercase is sorted before uppercase. If the "words" contain special symbols (such as ? or %), then SORT uses the ASCII collating sequence to determine their order. If two words are exactly the same, SORT leaves them in the original order. Missing values in numeric columns (*'s) are sorted last. Missing values in alpha columns are blanks and are sorted first.

The Sort Dialog Box

Options in the Sort Dialog Box

Sort column(s): Indicate the column(s) you want to sort.

Put into: Name or indicate the columns where the results should be stored. You can select the same columns you want to sort; Minitab replaces the unsorted data with the sorted.

Sort by column: You can select up to four columns by which to sort. To sort by more than four columns, use the session command SORT with the BY subcommand.

Descending: The default sort order is ascending; select descending to change the order.

Session Command Syntax for Sort...

SORT *data in* **C** [*carry along corresponding rows of* **C...C**], *put into* **C** [*corresponding rows into* **C...C**]
  BY C...C
  DESCENDING C...C

Example: Using Sort...

The following dialog box and equivalent Session window commands illustrate how to sort students by their test grades, from best score to worst score, using the GRADEST2.MTW data set from Tutorial 2.

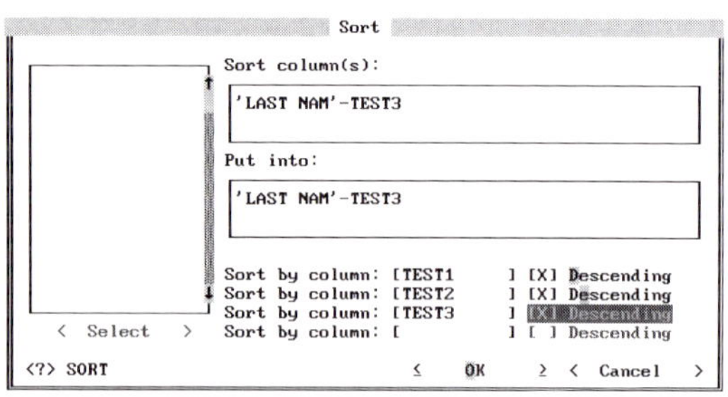


```
MTB > Sort 'LAST NAM'-'TEST3' 'LAST NAM'-'TEST3';
SUBC>   By 'TEST1' 'TEST2' 'TEST3';
SUBC>   Descending 'TEST1' 'TEST2' 'TEST3'.
```

These commands re-order the rows in the Data worksheet, using the first test as the first ordering criterion and test two and three as the second and third criteria:

→	LAST NAM C1	FIRST C2	TEST1 C3	TEST2 C4	TEST3 C5
1	PIERSON,	RICHARD	100	77	100
2	NORMAN,	BARBARA	99	95	84
3	BENSON,	MELISSA	99	86	83
4	GOLDBERG,	JONATHAN	98	98	94
5	SHEPPARD,	KATHLEEN	94	97	100
6	MESSINA,	STEVEN	94	93	95
7	GREEN,	JENNIFER	92	91	99
8	NOWICKI,	AMY	91	81	79
9	PATEL,	HIMA	90	100	62
10	WATSON,	KEISHA	88	93	41
11	SCHMIDT,	NANCY	83	79	52
12	SMITH,	HOLLY	82	51	25
13	SCOTT,	MICHAEL	81	75	100
14	DOUGHERTY,	MEGAN	79	69	60
15	GIGLIOTTI,	ANDREW	78	94	50
16	RYAN,	MATT	77	79	85
17	ROJAS,	LUIS	73	79	83
18	ADAMS,	JAMES	72	93	93
19	KENNEDY,	KEVIN	71	78	62
20	LEE,	SANG	64	68	97
21	THOMPSON,	SUSAN	59	60	84
22	BROWN,	LAMAR	59	59	90

See also Tutorial 2.

Rank...

The Rank... command assigns rank scores to values in a column; 1 to the smallest value in the column, 2 to the next smallest value, and so on. When Minitab encounters a tie, it assigns the average of the ranks.

The Rank Dialog Box

Options in the Rank Dialog Box

Rank data in: Indicate the column you want to rank.

Put ranks in: Name or indicate the location where the results will be stored.

Session Command Syntax for Rank...

RANK *the data in* **C** *put ranks in* **C**

Example: Using Rank...

The following dialog box and equivalent Session window commands illustrate how to obtain the ranks of students based on their first test scores. The data are stored in C3 of GRADEST2.MTW from Tutorial 2.

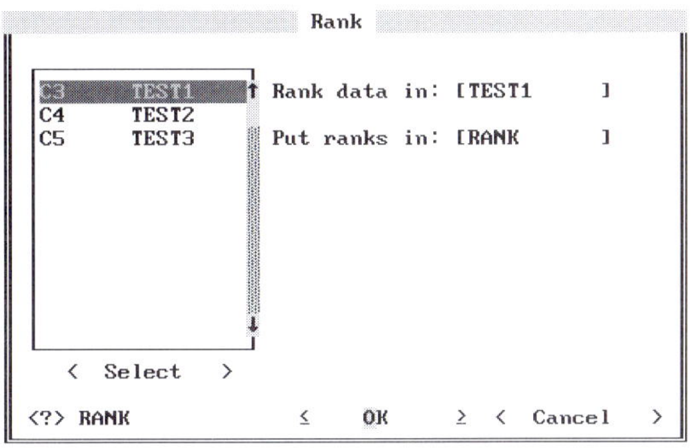


```
MTB > Name c6 = 'RANK'
MTB > Rank 'TEST1' 'RANK'.
```

These commands produce a column that gives the rank of each student in the class based on their score on the first test. The first portion of the data appears in the following illustration:

	LAST NAM	FIRST	TEST1	TEST2	TEST3	RANK
→	C1	C2	C3	C4	C5	C6
1	PIERSON,	RICHARD	100	77	100	24.0
2	NORMAN,	BARBARA	99	95	84	22.5
3	BENSON,	MELISSA	99	86	83	22.5
4	GOLDBERG,	JONATHAN	98	98	94	21.0
5	SHEPPARD,	KATHLEEN	94	97	100	19.5
6	MESSINA,	STEVEN	94	93	95	19.5
7	GREEN,	JENNIFER	92	91	99	18.0
8	NOWICKI,	AMY	91	81	79	17.0
9	PATEL,	HIMA	90	100	62	16.0
10	WATSON,	KEISHA	88	93	41	15.0
11	SCHMIDT,	NANCY	83	79	52	14.0
12	SMITH,	HOLLY	82	51	25	13.0
13	SCOTT,	MICHAEL	81	75	100	12.0
14	DOUGHERTY,	MEGAN	79	69	60	11.0
15	GIGLIOTTI,	ANDREW	78	94	50	10.0
16	RYAN,	MATT	77	79	85	9.0
17	ROJAS,	LUIS	73	79	83	8.0
18	ADAMS,	JAMES	72	93	93	7.0
19	KENNEDY,	KEVIN	71	78	62	6.0
20	LEE,	SANG	64	68	97	5.0
21	THOMPSON,	SUSAN	59	60	84	3.5
22	BROWN,	LAMAR	59	59	90	3.5

See also Tutorial 2.

Delete Rows...

The **D**elete Rows... command deletes selected rows from columns in the worksheet and adjusts the remaining rows to fill in the gaps.

The Delete Rows Dialog Box

Options in the Delete Rows Dialog Box

Delete rows: Type the row numbers you want to delete, using a colon (:) to indicate an inclusive range.

From columns: Enter the desired columns.

Session Command Syntax for Delete Rows...

DELETE *rows* **K...K** *in columns* **C...C**

Example: Using Delete Rows...

Say you have a data set that looks like this:

↓	C1	C2	C3	C4	C5
1	1	6	11	16	21
2	2	7	12	17	22
3	3	8	13	18	23
4	4	9	14	19	24
5	5	10	15	20	25
6					

Use the following dialog box and equivalent Session window commands to delete rows 3 and 4:

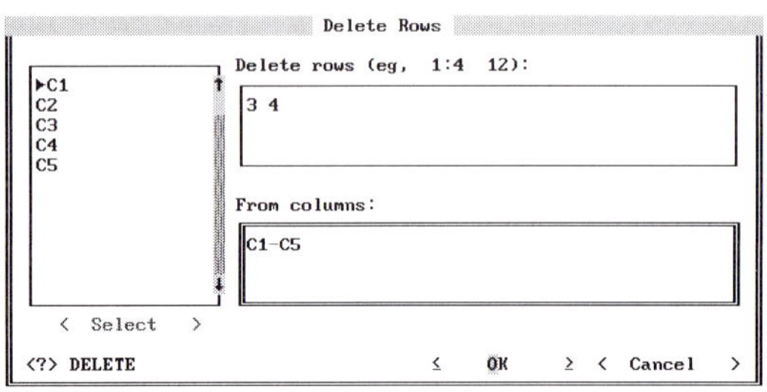


```
MTB > Delete 3 4 C1-C5
```

These commands delete the third and fourth row and move all others up two rows so that the Data worksheet now contains only the following rows:

↓	C1	C2	C3	C4	C5
1	1	6	11	16	21
2	2	7	12	17	22
3	5	10	15	20	25
4					
5					
6					

See also Tutorial 1.

Erase Variables...

The **E**rase Variables... command removes any combination of columns and constants from the current worksheet but has no effect on saved worksheet files. You can use this command to erase data you no longer need. Corresponding column names are also erased.

The Erase Variables Dialog Box

Options in the Erase Variables Dialog Box

Columns and constants to erase: Indicate here what Minitab should erase.

Session Command Syntax for Erase Variables...

ERASE E...E

Example: Using Erase Variables...

Say you have a data set with the following columns:

↓	C1	C2	C3	C4	C5
1	1	6	11	16	21
2	2	7	12	17	22
3	5	10	15	20	25

Use the following dialog box and equivalent Session window commands to erase C2 and C3.

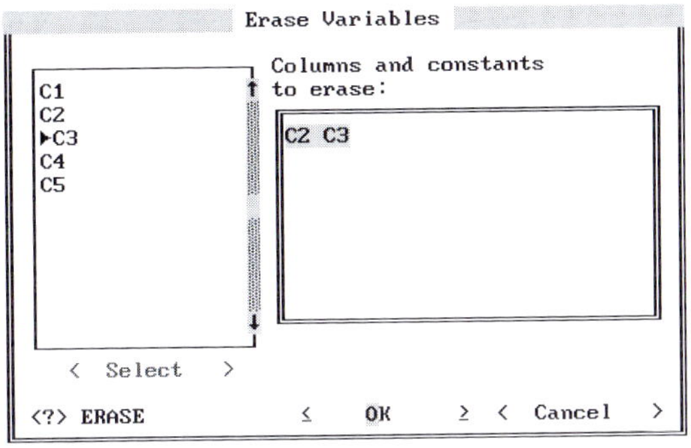

MTB > Erase C2 C3.

Columns C2 and C3 now are both blank. Note that, unlike Delete Rows, remaining columns are not moved together. Erased columns remain in the Data worksheet, but they are now empty and unnamed.

↓	C1	C2	C3	C4	C5
1	1			16	21
2	2			17	22
3	5			20	25

See also Tutorial 1.

Copy Columns...

The **C**opy Columns... command copies data to and from columns and constants, including all rows or a specified subset.

The Copy Columns Dialog Box

Options in the Copy Columns Dialog Box

Copy from column(s): Specify the column(s) you want to copy.

To columns: Name or indicate the location where the copies will be stored.

The Copy - Use Rows Subdialog Box

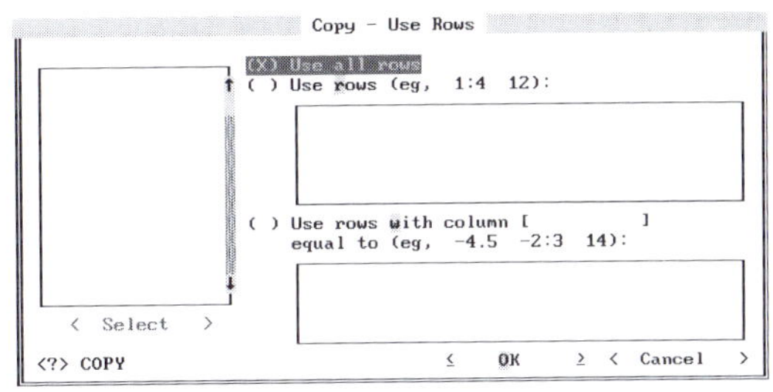

The Copy - Use Rows subdialog box lets you make a subset of your data by copying only select rows.

Use **a**ll rows: By default, Minitab copies all rows of the column you select to copy.

Use **r**ows: Minitab copies only the individual row numbers you specify. Use a colon (:) to indicate an inclusive range.

Use rows **w**ith column — equal to: Minitab copies rows with specified values in a designated column which need not be one of the columns that is copied. Use a colon (:) to indicate an inclusive range.

The Copy - Omit Rows Subdialog Box

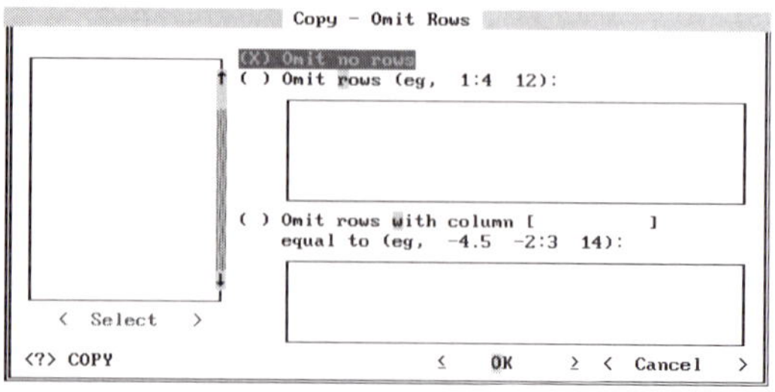

Use the Copy - Omit Rows subdialog box to omit certain rows from the columns you select to copy.

Omit **n**o rows: By default, Minitab does not omit any rows of the column you are copying.

Omit **r**ows: Minitab omits only the rows you specify. Use a colon (:) to indicate an inclusive range.

Omit rows **w**ith column — equal to: Minitab omits rows with specified values in a designated column, which need not be one of the columns that is copied.

Session Command Syntax for Copy Columns...

COPY *from* **C...C** *into* **C...C**
  USE *rows* **K...K**
  USE *rows where* **C** = **K...K**
  OMIT *rows* **K...K**
  OMIT *rows where* **C** = **K...K**

The command can also take the form:

COPY *from constants* **K...K** *into* **K...K**
COPY *from* **C** *into constants* **K...K**
COPY *from constants* **K...K** *into* **C**

Example: Using Copy Columns...

For the following data set, assume you want to copy C2 into C4:

↓	C1	C2	C3
1	1	6	11
2	2	7	12
3	3	8	13
4	4	9	14
5	5	10	15
6			

The following dialog box and equivalent Session window commands copy C2 into C4.

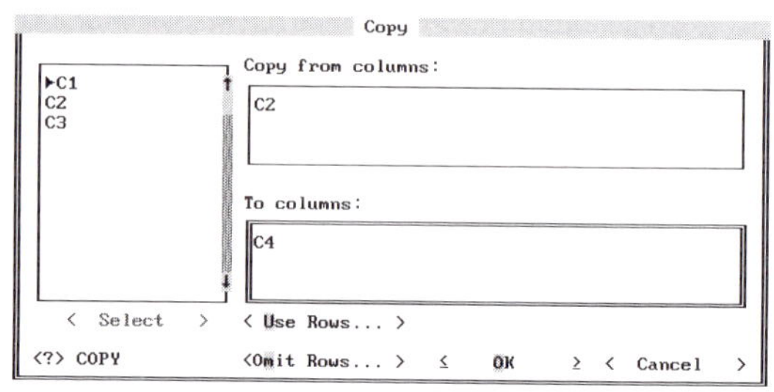


```
MTB > Copy C2 C4.
```

These commands produce a new column, C4, containing the same values as C2:

↓	C1	C2	C3	C4
1	1	6	11	6
2	2	7	12	7
3	3	8	13	8
4	4	9	14	9
5	5	10	15	10
6				

See also Tutorial 1.

Code Data Values...

The Code Data Values... command recodes one or more columns. It searches the specified columns for a value or set of values and replaces them with a new value. You can recode only numeric columns.

The Code Data Values Dialog Box

Options in the Code Data Values Dialog Box

Code data from columns: Indicate the column(s) you want to code.

Into columns: Name or indicate the location where Minitab should store the coded values.

Original values: Use a colon (:) to indicate a range of values.

New: Type the number you want to represent the range of original values.

Session Command Syntax for Code Data Values...

CODE (K...K) *to* K...(K...K) *to* K *for data in* C...C *put into* C...C

Example: Using Code Data Values...

The following dialog box and equivalent Session window commands code each student's test average (stored in C9 AVERAGE) to a number that represents his or her final grade, using the GRADEST2.MTW data set from Tutorial 2. Any score in the range 90–100 is coded as a 4 (or an A); any score from 80–89 is coded as a 3 (or a B), and so on.

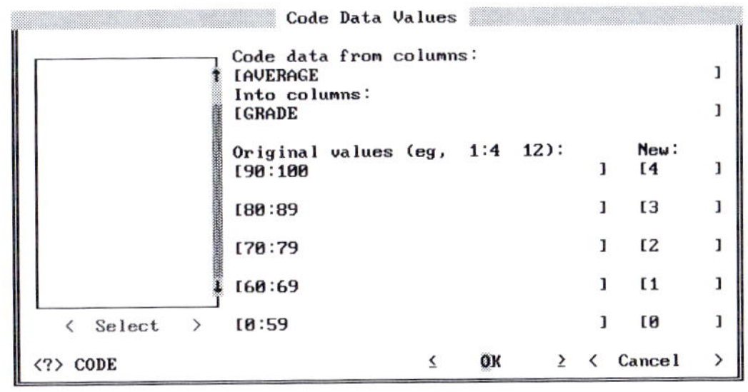


```
MTB > Name c10 = 'GRADE'
MTB > Code (90:100) 4 (80:89) 3 (70:79) 2 (60:69) 1 (0:59) 0 'AVERAGE'
CONT>     'GRADE'
```

These commands produce a new column, GRADE, that shows each student's numeric grade. Use the Convert... command (described later in this section) to translate the numerical grade into an alphabetic grade.

	FIRST	TEST1	TEST2	TEST3	AVERG	RMEAN	RMEDIAN	AVERAGE	GRADE	
→	C2	C3	C4	C5	C6	C7	C8	C9	C10	C11
1	KATHLEEN	94	97	100	97.0000	97.0000	97	97	4	
2	JONATHAN	98	98	94	96.6667	96.6667	98	97	4	
3	JENNIFER	92	91	99	94.0000	94.0000	92	94	4	
4	STEVEN	94	93	95	94.0000	94.0000	94	94	4	
5	BARBARA	99	95	84	92.6667	92.6667	95	93	4	
6	RICHARD	100	77	100	92.3333	92.3333	100	92	4	
7	MELISSA	99	86	83	89.3333	89.3333	86	89	3	
8	JAMES	72	93	93	86.0000	86.0000	93	86	3	
9	MICHAEL	81	75	100	85.3333	85.3333	81	85	3	
10	HIMA	90	100	62	84.0000	84.0000	90	84	3	
11	AMY	91	81	79	83.6667	83.6667	81	84	3	
12	MATT	77	79	85	80.3333	80.3333	79	80	3	
13	LUIS	73	79	83	78.3333	78.3333	79	78	2	
14	SANG	64	68	97	76.3333	76.3333	68	76	2	
15	ANDREW	78	94	50	74.0000	74.0000	78	74	2	
16	KEISHA	88	93	41	74.0000	74.0000	88	74	2	
17	NANCY	83	79	52	71.3333	71.3333	79	71	2	
18	KEVIN	71	78	62	70.3333	70.3333	71	70	2	
19	LAMAR	59	59	90	69.3333	69.3333	59	69	1	
20	MEGAN	79	69	60	69.3333	69.3333	69	69	1	
21	SUSAN	59	60	84	67.6667	67.6667	60	68	1	
22	MARK	49	79	43	57.0000	57.0000	49	57	0	

Enter Data F10=Menu

See also Tutorial 2.

Stack...

The Stack... command stacks blocks of columns and/or constants on top of each other, storing the result in new columns. Minitab always places the first block on top of the second block, and so on. Columns within each block must be of the same length.

The Stack Dialog Box

Options in the Stack Dialog Box

Stack the following blocks: Indicate the columns or blocks of columns you want to stack.

And put in: Name or indicate the storage location.

Put subscripts in: You can create a column of subscripts that identify the column where the values in the stacked column originated. Minitab gives the rows from the first block of values the subscript 1, the rows from the second block the subscript 2, and so on.

Session Command Syntax for Stack...

STACK (E...E) *on top of* (E...E) *put in* (C...C)
  SUBSCRIPTS *put into* C

Example: Using Stack...

The following dialog box and equivalent Session window commands illustrate how to stack the three test scores stored in C3–C5 into one column, using the GRADEST2.MTW data set from Tutorial 2.

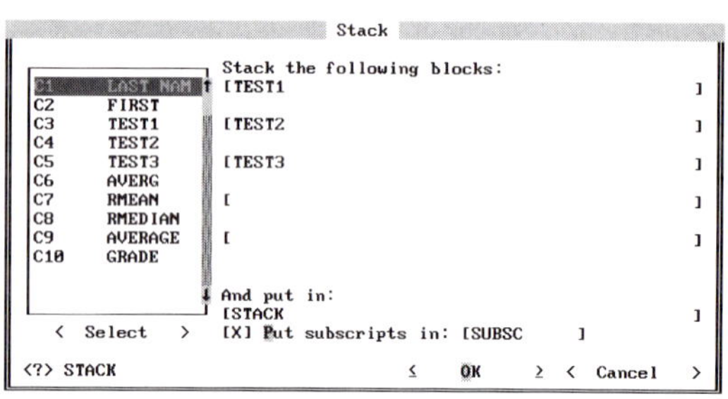


```
MTB > Name c11 = 'STACK' c12 = 'SUBSC'
MTB > Stack ('TEST1') ('TEST2') ('TEST3') ('STACK');
SUBC>   Subscripts 'SUBSC'.
```

These commands produce the following column of stacked data (only the first portion of output is shown):

	TEST2	TEST3	AVERG	RMEAN	RMEDIAN	AVERAGE	GRADE	STACK	SUBSC		
→	C4	C5	C6	C7	C8	C9	C10	C11	C12	C13	C14
1	97	100	97.0000	97.0000	97	97	4	94	1		
2	98	94	96.6667	96.6667	98	97	4	98	1		
3	91	99	94.0000	94.0000	92	94	4	92	1		
4	93	95	94.0000	94.0000	94	94	4	94	1		
5	95	84	92.6667	92.6667	95	93	4	99	1		
6	77	100	92.3333	92.3333	100	92	4	100	1		
7	86	83	89.3333	89.3333	86	89	3	99	1		
8	93	93	86.0000	86.0000	93	86	3	72	1		
9	75	100	85.3333	85.3333	81	85	3	81	1		
10	100	62	84.0000	84.0000	90	84	3	90	1		
11	81	79	83.6667	83.6667	81	84	3	91	1		
12	79	85	80.3333	80.3333	79	80	3	77	1		
13	79	83	78.3333	78.3333	79	78	2	73	1		
14	68	97	76.3333	76.3333	68	76	2	64	1		
15	94	50	74.0000	74.0000	78	74	2	78	1		
16	93	41	74.0000	74.0000	88	74	2	88	1		
17	79	52	71.3333	71.3333	79	71	2	83	1		
18	78	62	70.3333	70.3333	71	70	2	71	1		
19	59	90	69.3333	69.3333	59	69	1	59	1		
20	69	60	69.3333	69.3333	69	69	1	79	1		
21	60	84	67.6667	67.6667	60	68	1	59	1		
22	79	43	57.0000	57.0000	49	57	0	49	1		

Enter Data F10=Menu

See also Tutorial 2.

Unstack...

The Unstack... command separates one block of values into several shorter blocks of columns or constants according to subscript values in a column you specify. Minitab stores rows from the block with the smallest subscript in the first block, rows with the next smallest subscript in the second block, and so on. If you do not use a subscript, Minitab assumes that each row from the first column should be put in a separate block.

The Unstack Dialog Box

Options in the Unstack Dialog Box

Unstack: Indicate the column(s) you want Minitab to unstack.

Using subscripts in: The subscripts must be integers from −10000 to +10000 or missing values (*). They need not be in order or consecutive.

Into blocks: Name or indicate the storage locations.

Session Command Syntax for Unstack...

UNSTACK (C...C) *into* **(E...E)** ... **(E...E)**
  SUBSCRIPTS *are in* **C**

Example: Using Unstack...

The following dialog box and equivalent Session window commands illustrate how to unstack all test scores into three columns (TEST1, TEST2, and TEST3), using the GRADEST2.MTW data set from Tutorial 2.

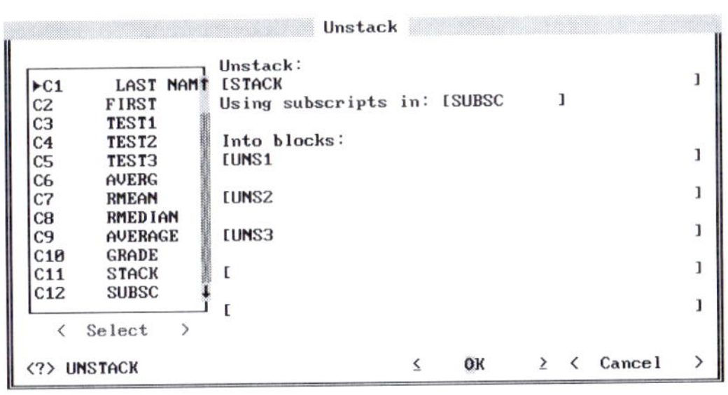


```
MTB > Name c13 = 'UNS1' c14 = 'UNS2' c15 = 'UNS3'
MTB > Unstack ('STACK') ('UNS1') ('UNS2') ('UNS3');
SUBC>   Subscripts 'SUBSC'.
```

These commands produce the following columns in the Data worksheet:

	AVERG	RMEAN	RMEDIAN	AVERAGE	GRADE	STACK	SUBSC	UNS1	UNS2	UNS3	
→	C6	C7	C8	C9	C10	C11	C12	C13	C14	C15	C16
1	97.0000	97.0000	97	97	4	94	1	94	97	100	
2	96.6667	96.6667	98	97	4	98	1	98	98	94	
3	94.0000	94.0000	92	94	4	92	1	92	91	99	
4	94.0000	94.0000	94	94	4	94	1	94	93	95	
5	92.6667	92.6667	95	93	4	99	1	99	95	84	
6	92.3333	92.3333	100	92	4	100	1	100	77	100	
7	89.3333	89.3333	86	89	3	99	1	99	86	83	
8	86.0000	86.0000	93	86	3	72	1	72	93	93	
9	85.3333	85.3333	81	85	3	81	1	81	75	100	
10	84.0000	84.0000	90	84	3	90	1	90	100	62	
11	83.6667	83.6667	81	84	3	91	1	91	81	79	
12	80.3333	80.3333	79	80	3	77	1	77	79	85	
13	78.3333	78.3333	79	78	2	73	1	73	79	83	
14	76.3333	76.3333	68	76	2	64	1	64	68	97	
15	74.0000	74.0000	78	74	2	78	1	78	94	50	
16	74.0000	74.0000	88	74	2	88	1	88	93	41	
17	71.3333	71.3333	79	71	2	83	1	83	79	52	
18	70.3333	70.3333	71	70	2	71	1	71	78	62	
19	69.3333	69.3333	59	69	1	59	1	59	59	90	
20	69.3333	69.3333	69	69	1	79	1	79	69	60	
21	67.6667	67.6667	60	68	1	59	1	59	60	84	
22	57.0000	57.0000	49	57	0	49	1	49	79	43	

Enter Data F10=Menu

See also Tutorial 2.

Convert...

The Convert... command converts numeric data to alpha data and vice versa using codes you specify. You need two worksheet columns to serve as a conversion table: one listing alpha expressions and one listing the corresponding numbers.

The Convert Dialog Box

Options in the Convert Dialog Box

Original data: Indicate the column that contains the data you want to convert.

Converted data: Name or indicate the storage location for the converted data.

Conversion Table, Original: Indicate the column that contains the first part of the conversion table (that is, the values you want to convert).

Conversion Table, Converted: Indicate the column that contains the second part of the conversion table (that is, the codes you will use to represent the original data).

Session Command Syntax for Convert...

CONVERT *using conversion table in* **C C**
convert **C** *to* **C**

Example: Using Convert...

The following dialog box and equivalent Session window commands illustrate how to convert alpha pasta ratings stored in C1 RATING to numeric data, using the PASTAT4.MTW data set from Tutorial 4. First, set up the conversion table in columns C4 and C5 in the Data worksheet:

→	RATING C1	CENT/SER C2	CAL/SER C3	CONVA C4	CONVN C5	C6	C7	C8	C9	C10	C11
1	VERY GOOD	44	335	EXCELLENT	1						
2	FAIR	22	350	VERY GOOD	2						
3	VERY GOOD	16	350	GOOD	3						
4	GOOD	16	355	FAIR	4						
5	GOOD	18	375	POOR	5						
6	FAIR	22	390								
7	EXCELLENT	16	340								
8	POOR	80	445								
9	GOOD	25	380								
10	VERY GOOD	20	365								
11	GOOD	23	405								
12	GOOD	13	335								
13	VERY GOOD	27	355								
14	GOOD	47	480								
15	GOOD	23	350								
16											
17											
18											
19											
20											
21											
22											

Enter Data F10=Menu

Then fill in the dialog box as shown:

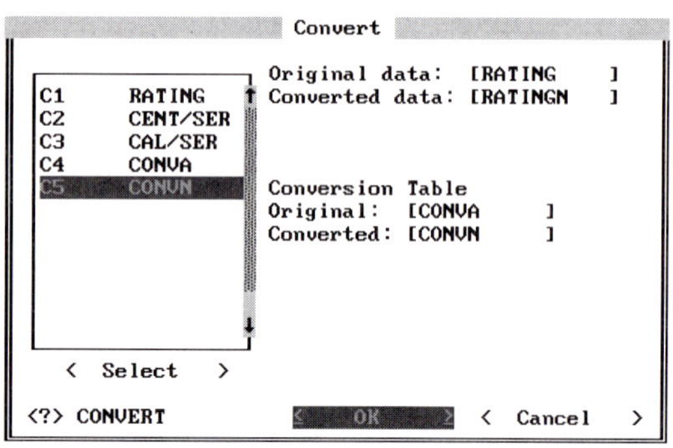


```
MTB > Name c6 = 'RATINGN'
MTB > Convert 'CONVA' 'CONVN' 'RATING' 'RATINGN'.
```

These commands produce a new column, RATINGN, shown in the Data worksheet:

→	RATING C1	CENT/SER C2	CAL/SER C3	CONVA C4	CONVN C5	RATINGN C6	C7	C8	C9	C10
1	VERY GOOD	44	335	EXCELLENT	1	2				
2	FAIR	22	350	VERY GOOD	2	4				
3	VERY GOOD	16	350	GOOD	3	2				
4	GOOD	16	355	FAIR	4	3				
5	GOOD	18	375	POOR	5	3				
6	FAIR	22	390			4				
7	EXCELLENT	16	340			1				
8	POOR	80	445			5				
9	GOOD	25	380			3				
10	VERY GOOD	20	365			2				
11	GOOD	23	405			3				
12	GOOD	13	335			3				
13	VERY GOOD	27	355			2				
14	GOOD	47	480			3				
15	GOOD	23	350			3				
16										
17										
18										
19										
20										
21										
22										

Enter Data F10=Menu

See also Tutorial 4.

Concatenate...

The Concatenate... command combines two or more alpha columns side by side and stores them in one new column. The old columns must contain alpha data (strings of letters or other symbols); the new column will also be an alpha column, up to 80 characters wide.

The Concatenate Dialog Box

Options in the Concatenate Dialog Box

Concatenate alpha columns: List the columns in the order you want them to appear in the new column.

Put result in: Name or indicate the storage location for the new variable.

Session Command Syntax for Concatenate...

CONCATENATE C...C *put into* C

Example: Using Concatenate...

The following dialog box and equivalent Session window commands combine the first and last names of the students, stored in C1 and C2, into a single column, using the GRADEST2.MTW data set from Tutorial 2.

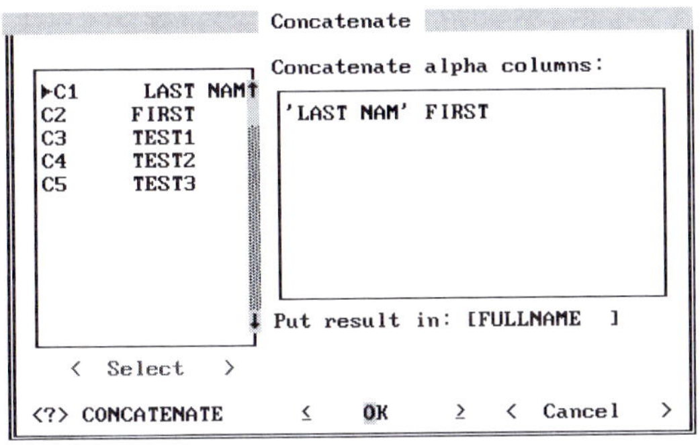


```
MTB > Name c6 = 'FULLNAME'
MTB > Concatenate 'LAST NAM' 'FIRST' 'FULLNAME'.
```

These commands produce a column containing the full name of each student; the column may be seen in the Data worksheet.

	LAST NAM	FIRST	TEST1	TEST2	TEST3	FULLNAME			
→	C1	C2	C3	C4	C5	C6	C7	C8	C9
1	ADAMS,	JAMES	72	93	93	ADAMS, JAMES			
2	BENSON,	MELISSA	99	86	83	BENSON, MELISSA			
3	BROWN,	LAMAR	59	59	90	BROWN, LAMAR			
4	DOUGHERTY,	MEGAN	79	69	60	DOUGHERTY, MEGAN			
5	DOUGLAS,	JASON	48	77	25	DOUGLAS, JASON			
6	GIGLIOTTI,	ANDREW	78	94	50	GIGLIOTTI, ANDREW			
7	GOLDBERG,	JONATHAN	98	98	94	GOLDBERG, JONATHAN			
8	GREEN,	JENNIFER	92	91	99	GREEN, JENNIFER			
9	KENNEDY,	KEVIN	71	78	62	KENNEDY, KEVIN			
10	LEE,	SANG	64	68	97	LEE, SANG			
11	MCCLURE,	MARK	49	79	43	MCCLURE, MARK			
12	MESSINA,	STEVEN	94	93	95	MESSINA, STEVEN			
13	NORMAN,	BARBARA	99	95	84	NORMAN, BARBARA			
14	NOWICKI,	AMY	91	81	79	NOWICKI, AMY			
15	PATEL,	HIMA	90	100	62	PATEL, HIMA			
16	PIERSON,	RICHARD	100	77	100	PIERSON, RICHARD			
17	ROJAS,	LUIS	73	79	83	ROJAS, LUIS			
18	RYAN,	MATT	77	79	85	RYAN, MATT			
19	SCHMIDT,	NANCY	83	79	52	SCHMIDT, NANCY			
20	SCOTT,	MICHAEL	81	75	100	SCOTT, MICHAEL			
21	SHEPPARD,	KATHLEEN	94	97	100	SHEPPARD, KATHLEEN			
22	SMITH,	HOLLY	82	51	25	SMITH, HOLLY			

Enter Data F10=Menu

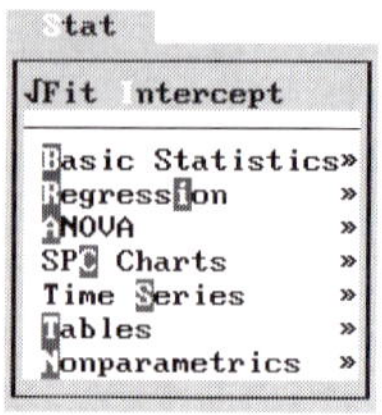

The Stat Menu

The **S**tat menu contains the commands needed to perform a variety of statistical analyses: basic statistics, regression, analysis of variance, statistical process control, time series, contingency table analysis, and nonparametric statistics.

Fit Intercept

The Fit **I**ntercept command fits regression equations with or without a constant or intercept term. By default, there is a checkmark to the left of this command, indicating that Minitab will fit a constant term (the y-intercept of the regression line) to all regression and time series models. Choosing this command removes the checkmark, causing Minitab to omit the constant term from subsequent regression and time series models until you replace the checkmark or end the session. When you omit the constant term, Minitab excludes the R^2 value from the Session window display.

Session Command Syntax for Fit Intercept

NOCONSTANT *omits y-intercept*
CONSTANT *fits y-intercept*

Basic Statistics

The **B**asic Statistics command calculates basic statistics, including descriptive statistics, z- and t-tests, correlation, and covariance, for the variable(s) you specify.

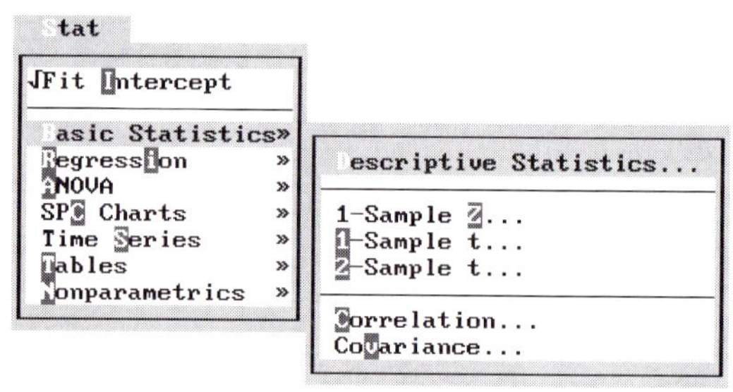

Descriptive Statistics Dialog Box

The **D**escriptive Statistics... command calculates the following summary statistics for one or more columns and displays them in the Session window. If you want to calculate these statistics individually and store them as constants, you can do so using Calc ▶ Functions and Statistics ▶ Column Statistics... (except for Q1 and Q3).

N	number of nonmissing observations
N*	number of missing observations (if there are none, Minitab does not include this column)
MEAN	average value
MEDIAN	middle value
TRMEAN	a 5% trimmed mean; Minitab removes the smallest 5% and largest 5% and computes the mean of the remaining values
STDEV	standard deviation
SEMEAN	standard error of the mean
MIN	smallest number
MAX	largest number
Q1	first quartile (25th percentile)
Q3	third quartile (75th percentile)

Options in the Descriptive Statistics Dialog Box

Variables: Indicate the variable(s) you want described.

By variable: Minitab displays descriptive statistics separately for each value of the variable you select here. The By variable must contain integers from –9999 to +9999 or missing values (*).

Session Command Syntax for Descriptive Statistics...

DESCRIBE *the data in* **C...C**
BY C

Example: Using Descriptive Statistics...

Use the following dialog box and equivalent Session window commands to calculate descriptive statistics for the variable C3 INTEREST (how much interest students express for their classes) by their year in college, stored in C9 YEAR, using the PROF.MTW data set from Tutorial 8.

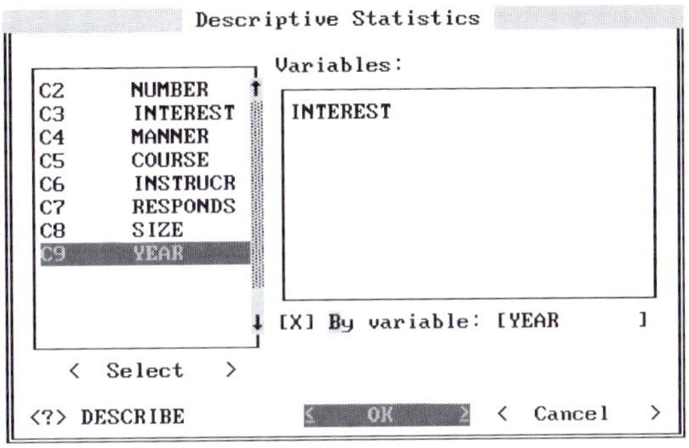


```
MTB > Describe 'INTEREST';
SUBC>   By 'YEAR'.
```

These commands produce the following display in the Session window:

```
           YEAR      N     MEAN   MEDIAN   TRMEAN    STDEV   SEMEAN
INTEREST      1     46   2.4937   2.5000   2.4964   0.6046   0.0891
              2     45   2.6818   2.7300   2.6751   0.6174   0.0920
              3     34    2.636    2.615    2.638    0.602    0.103
              4     21    2.786    3.000    2.834    0.685    0.149

           YEAR    MIN      MAX       Q1       Q3
INTEREST      1 1.1000   3.7100   2.1600   2.8725
              2 1.4600   4.0000   2.0700   3.0950
              3  1.560    3.930    2.287    3.145
              4  1.000    3.670    2.295    3.290
```

See also Tutorial 4.

The 1-Sample Z Dialog Box

The 1-Sample **Z**... command performs a one-sample z-test or calculates a confidence interval for the mean—assuming that the standard deviation (sigma) is known—on one or more columns of data.

Options in the 1-Sample Z Dialog Box

Variables: Indicate the column(s) you want Minitab to use.

Confidence interval: Minitab calculates a separate one-sample confidence interval for the mean of one or more variables with standard deviation σ known.

Level: Indicate the level of confidence desired; the default is 95%. If you specify a fraction, Minitab automatically multiplies it by 100 (that is, .80 becomes 80%).

Test mean: Minitab performs a separate one-sample test with standard deviation σ known for each variable. By default Minitab does a test with the null hypothesis value = 0; however, you can specify any test value.

Alternative: You can specify less than (lower-tailed), the default not equal (two-tailed), or greater than (upper-tailed) for the kind of test you want (one-sided or two-sided).

Sigma: Enter the value for sigma here.

Session Command Syntax for 1-Sample Z...

ZTEST [*of* μ = **K**] *assumed* σ = **K** *on* **C...C**
  ALTERNATIVE = **K** (Specify K as –1 (lower-tailed), 0 (two-tailed), or +1 (upper-tailed).)
ZINTERVAL [**K**% *confidence*] *assumed* σ = **K**
  for data in **C...C**

Example: Using 1-Sample Z...

The following dialog box and equivalent Session window commands test whether female subjects perceive a room with white walls as less crowded than a room with dark green walls, using C1 FEM RATE of the CROWDS.MTW data set from Tutorial 6.

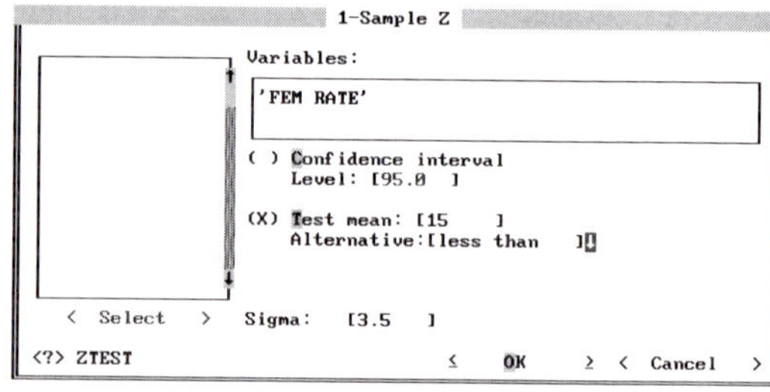


```
MTB > ZTest 15 3.5 'FEM RATE';
SUBC>   Alternative -1.
```

These commands produce the following display in the Session window:

```
TEST OF MU = 15.000 VS MU L.T. 15.000
THE ASSUMED SIGMA = 3.50

             N      MEAN     STDEV   SE MEAN         Z    P VALUE
FEM RATE    36    14.417     3.887     0.583     -1.00       0.16
```

See also Tutorial 6.

The 1-Sample t Dialog Box

The 1-Sample t command performs a t-test or t-confidence interval for the mean of each column listed.

Options in the 1-Sample t Dialog Box

Variables: Indicate the variable(s) you want Minitab to test.

Confidence interval: Minitab calculates a separate one-sample t-confidence interval for the mean of one or more variables (assumed to be normal) without knowing their standard deviations σ. The procedure uses values from the student's t-distribution.

Level: Indicate the level of confidence desired; the default is 95%. If you specify a fraction, Minitab automatically multiplies it by 100 (that is, .80 becomes 80%).

Test mean: Minitab performs a separate one-sample t-test of the mean for each variable where the standard deviation is not known. By default, Minitab does a test with the null hypothesis value = 0; however, you can specify any test mean value.

Alternative: You can specify less than (lower-tailed), the default not equal (two-tailed), or greater than (upper-tailed) for the kind of test you want (one-sided or two-sided).

Session Command Syntax for 1-Sample t...

TTEST [μ = **K**] *on* **C...C**
  ALTERNATIVE = **K** (Specify K as –1 (lower-tailed), 0 (two-tailed), or +1 (upper-tailed).)
TINTERVAL [K% *confidence*] *for data in* **C...C**

Example: Using 1-Sample t...

The following dialog box and equivalent Session window commands investigate whether 1991 sales revenues, stored in C1 1991, which have equalled $3500 a day, have changed, using the SALES.MTW data from Tutorial 6.

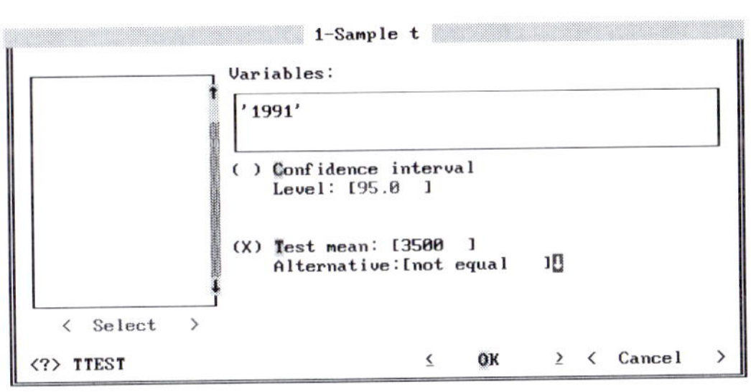


```
MTB > TTest 3500 '1991';
SUBC>   Alternative 0.
```

These commands produce the following display in the Session window:

```
TEST OF MU = 3500.000 VS MU N.E. 3500.000

              N      MEAN     STDEV   SE MEAN         T    P VALUE
1991          7  2356.143  1347.778   509.412     -2.25      0.066
```

See also Tutorial 6.

The 2-Sample t Dialog Box

The 2-Sample t... command performs a two (independent) sample t-test and generates a confidence interval.

Options in the 2-Sample t Dialog Box

Samples in one column: By default, Minitab assumes the samples are in the same column, differentiated by subscript values in a second column. (This is the TWOT session command.)

Samples: Indicate the sample location.

Subscripts: Indicate the subscript location. The subscript tells Minitab to which of the two populations each value belongs. Subscripts may be any integers from –9999 to +9999 or the missing value symbol (*). The subscript column must contain two different integers.

Samples in different columns: Choose this alternative if the samples you will compare are in two separate columns. (This is the TWOSAMPLE session command.)

First: Indicate the location of the first sample.

Second: Indicate the location of the second sample.

Alternative: You can specify less than (lower-tailed), not equal to (two-tailed), or greater than (upper-tailed) for the kind of test you want (one-sided or two-sided).

Confidence level: Indicate the level of confidence desired; the default is 95%. If you specify a fraction, Minitab automatically multiplies it by 100 (that is, .80 becomes 80%).

Assume equal variances: By default, Minitab does not assume that the populations have equal variances.

Session Command Syntax for 2-Sample t...

TWOSAMPLE [**K**% *confidence*] *for data in* **C** *and* **C**

ALTERNATIVE = **K** (Specify K as –1 (lower-tailed), 0 (two-tailed), or +1 (upper-tailed).)

POOLED

TWOT [**K**% *confidence*] *for data in* **C**, *subscripts in* **C**

ALTERNATIVE = **K** (Specify K as –1 (lower-tailed), 0 (two-tailed), or +1 (upper-tailed).)

POOLED

Example: Using 2-Sample t...

The following dialog box and equivalent Session window commands test whether there is a difference between male (C2 MALERATE) and female (C1 FEM RATE) mean perceptions of crowdedness in a small room with green walls, using the CROWDST7.MTW data set from Tutorial 7.

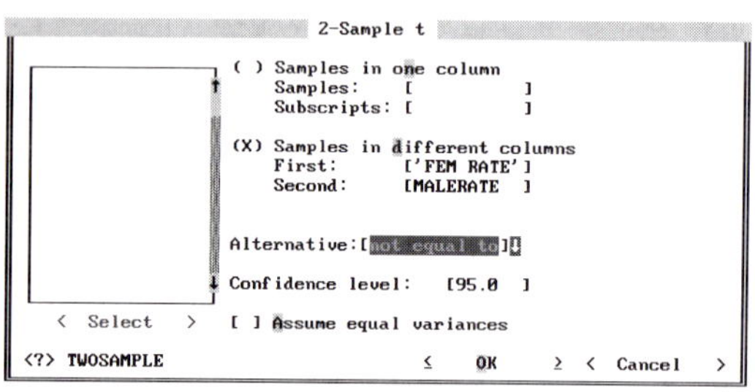


```
MTB > TwoSample 95.0 'FEM RATE' 'MALERATE';
SUBC>   Alternative 0.
```

These commands produce the following display in the Session window:

```
TWOSAMPLE T FOR FEM RATE VS MALERATE
            N      MEAN     STDEV   SE MEAN
FEM RATE   36     14.42      3.89      0.65
MALERATE   36     13.92      3.70      0.62

95 PCT CI FOR MU FEM RATE - MU MALERATE: (-1.28, 2.28)

TTEST MU FEM RATE = MU MALERATE (VS NE): T= 0.56  P=0.58  DF=  69
```

See also Tutorial 7.

The Correlation Dialog Box

The Correlation... command calculates the correlation between each pair of variables you list. Minitab does not use the pairs of column values where one or both values are missing (called "pairwise deletion").

You can calculate Spearman's rho (rank correlation) between pairs of nonmissing data by ranking both columns (use Calc ▶ Rank...) and correlating the ranks (delete rows that contain missing data first).

Options in the Correlation Dialog Box

Variables: If you list two columns, Minitab calculates the (Pearson product moment) correlation coefficient for the pair. If you list more than two columns, Minitab calculates the correlation for every possible pair, printing the lower triangle of the correlation matrix.

Session Command Syntax for Correlation...

CORRELATION *the data in* **C...C**

Example: Using Correlation...

The following dialog box and equivalent Session window commands determine the correlation to provide numerical information about the direction and the strength of the linear relationship between cents per serving (C2 CENT/SER),calories per serving (C3 CAL/SER), and taste rating (C7 RATING N) using the PASTAT4.MTW data set from Tutorial 4.

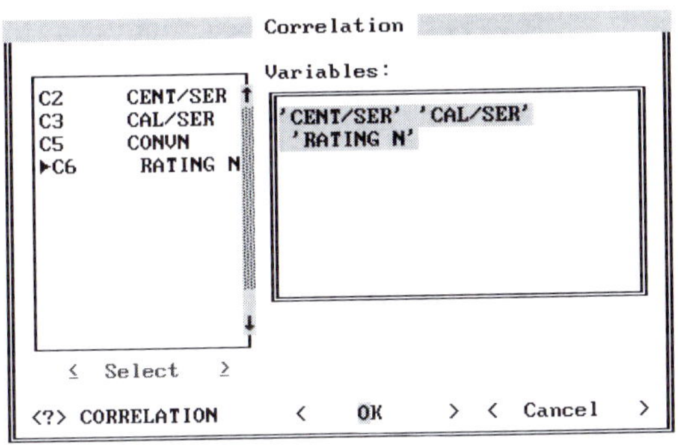


```
MTB > Correlation 'CENT/SER' 'CAL/SER'  'RATING N'.
```

These commands produce the following display in the Session window:

```
          CENT/SER  CAL/SER
CAL/SER   0.655
RATING N  0.495     0.508
```

See also Tutorial 4.

The Covariance Dialog Box

The Covariance... command calculates and displays the covariance between each pair of variables you select in a Session window matrix. If some data are missing, Minitab calculates the covariance between each pair of columns using all rows that have values in both columns.

Options in the Covariance Dialog Box

Variables: Indicate the desired variables here.

Session Command Syntax for Covariance...

COVARIANCE *for* C...C

Example: Using Covariance...

The following dialog box and equivalent Session window commands find the covariance between cents per serving (C2 CENT/SER) and calories per serving (C3 CAL/SER), using the PASTAT4.MTW data set from Tutorial 4.

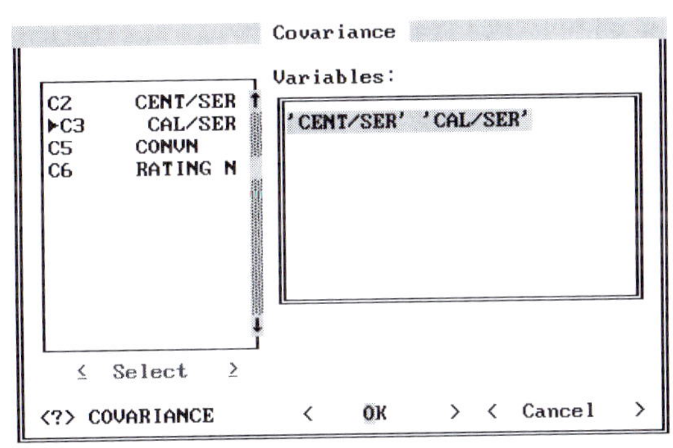


```
MTB > Covariance 'CENT/SER' 'CAL/SER'.
```

These commands produce the following display in the Session window. Note that Minitab computes the covariance of each indicated variable with itself; this is just the variance of the variable.

```
          CENT/SER   CAL/SER
CENT/SER   304.981
CAL/SER    476.214  1732.857
```

See also Tutorial 4.

Regression

The **R**egression command gives you two options: Regression... to fit a linear (simple, polynomial, and multiple) regression model to the data you specify, and Stepwise... to do stepwise regression, forward selection, and backward elimination.

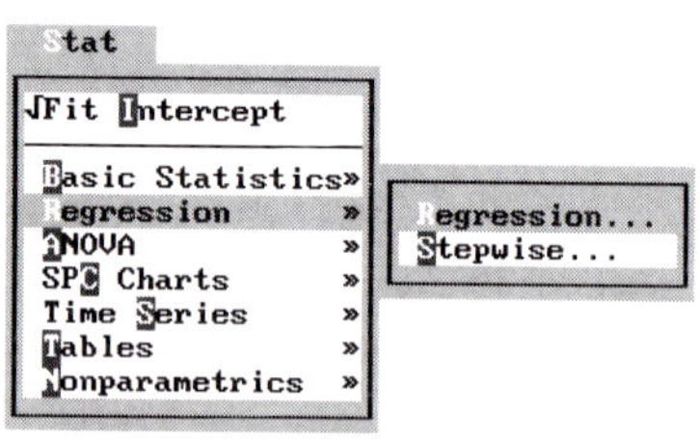

The Regression Dialog Box

The **R**egression... command fits a linear equation to your data by the least-squares method.

Options in the Regression Dialog Box

Response: Indicate the dependent or y variable you want to regress. Minitab does not use observations that contain missing values, either in the dependent or one or more of the independent variables (see Minitab Help in the Regression dialog box for exceptions).

Predictors: List the predictor variables you want to include in your model.

Storage: Minitab can store additional regression information, depending on which storage checkboxes you select. Minitab automatically names these columns.

Residuals: Minitab stores the residuals (the difference between observed and fitted values) in the next available column.

Standard. resids.: Minitab stores the standardized residuals in the next available column.

Fits: Minitab stores the fitted values in the next available column.

Coefficients: Minitab stores the coefficients of the regression model equation in the next available column.

The Regression Options Subdialog Box

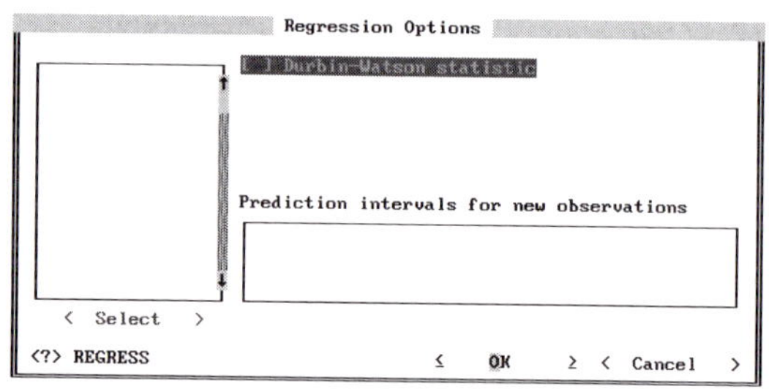

Durbin-Watson statistic: Minitab performs the Durbin-Watson test of autocorrelation in the data, using only nonmissing observations.

Prediction intervals for new observations: Minitab computes fitted values based on the regression equation, along with their 95% confidence intervals and 95% prediction intervals for predictor values specified here. Specify one column or constant for each predictor. If you specify an unusual case, Minitab prints an X at the end of the output line, and indicates extreme cases with XX.

Session Command Syntax for Regression...

REGRESS *y in* **C** *on* **K**, *predictors in* **C...C**
  [*standardized residuals in* **C** [*fitted values in* **C**]]
  NOCONSTANT
  COEFFICIENTS *put into* **C**
  PREDICT *for* **E...E**
  RESIDUALS *put into* **C**
  DW (*Durbin-Watson statistic*)
BRIEF *output code* **K**

The NOCONSTANT subcommand fits the regression equation without the y-intercept term.

The BRIEF command controls the amount of output for subsequent REGRESS commands and is not available as a menu command. K is an integer from 0 to 3. The larger the value of K, the more output. BRIEF 2 is the default (that is, what you get if no BRIEF command is specified). The levels of output are as follows:

- K = 0 Minitab prints nothing, but stores all requested output.
- K = 1 Minitab prints the regression equation, table of coefficients, s, R^2, adj. R^2, and the usual analysis of variance table (SS Regression, SSE, and SS Total).
- K = 2 In addition to the BRIEF 1 output, Minitab prints the sequential analysis of variance table (provided there are two or more predictors), and the "unusual observations" table.
- K = 3 In addition to the output from BRIEF 1 and 2, Minitab prints the full table of fits and residuals.

Example: Using Regression...

The following dialog box and equivalent Session window commands produce a regression model for C1 SALARY using years employed (C2), prior years of experience at Technitron (C3), and years of education (C4) as predictor variables. The data are stored in TECHN.MTW from Tutorial 9.

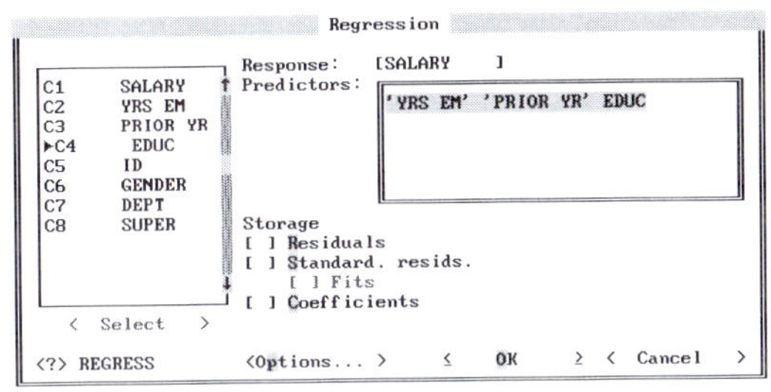


```
MTB > Regress 'SALARY' 3 'YRS EM' 'PRIOR YR' 'EDUC'.
```

These commands produce the following Session window display (only the first portion is shown):

```
The regression equation is
SALARY = 23480 + 671 YRS EM - 74 PRIOR YR + 1926 EDUC

Predictor        Coef       Stdev    t-ratio        p
Constant        23480        2028      11.58    0.000
YRS EM          671.3       143.2       4.69    0.000
PRIOR YR        -73.8       232.8      -0.32    0.753
EDUC           1925.9       384.4       5.01    0.000

s = 5799         R-sq = 74.1%      R-sq(adj) = 72.2%

Analysis of Variance
```

See also Tutorial 9.

The Stepwise Regression Dialog Box

The Stepwise... command performs a stepwise regression to find the subset of independent variables that best predict the dependent variables.

You can vary the basic procedure to allow for forward selection or backward elimination. The method alternates between stages of adding and removing variables until no more predictors can enter or leave the model. After each screenful of output, Minitab asks, MORE? You can answer YES to continue or NO to quit. You may also alter the model from the Session window using the subcommands listed in the Session Command Syntax section.

1. Default Procedure: In step one, Minitab calculates an F-statistic for each predictor already in the model. If that value is less than the value specified in the F to remove text box (of the Stepwise Options subdialog box) for any predictor, Minitab removes the predictor with the lowest F-statistic and prints output from the resulting model. In step two, Minitab calculates an F-statistic for each predictor not in the current model. If any value is greater than the value specified in the F to enter text box (of the Stepwise Options subdialog box) for any predictor, Minitab enters the predictor with the highest F-statistic and prints the output from the resulting model.
2. Forward Selection: This method adds predictors to the model as in the default procedure, but never removes any. Set the F to remove text box value to 0.
3. Backward Elimination: This method begins with a model containing all possible predictors and removes them one at a time without ever reentering any. Set the F to enter text box value to 10000 (a value virtually impossible to obtain) and list all predictors in the Enter text box.

Options in the Stepwise Regression Dialog Box

Response: Indicate the dependent or y variable you want to regress. Minitab does not use observations that contain missing values, either in the dependent or one or more of the independent variables (see Minitab Help from the dialog box for exceptions).

Predictors: List the predictor variables you want to include in your model.

Enter: List the variables you want Minitab to start with in the initial stepwise model. If their F-statistic falls below the value in the F to remove text box (in the Stepwise Options subdialog box), Minitab will remove them.

Force: Variables listed here are never removed from the regression model. You can change their status at the MORE? prompt using the Session window REMOVE or ENTER subcommands.

Options in the Stepwise Options Subdialog Box

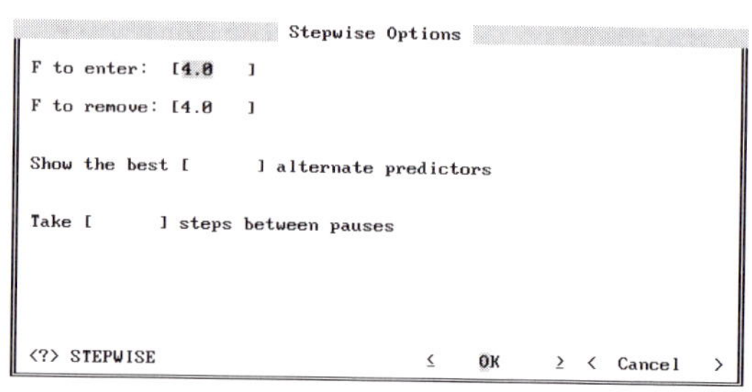

F to enter: You can change the minimum F-value required to enter a predictor variable into a model from the default value of 4. This value must be greater than or equal to the F to remove value. Any variable not yet in the model is entered if its F value is the largest and exceeds this value.

F to remove: You can set this F-value to remove a predictor variable from the model. The default value is 4. If any default predictors in the model have F statistics that are below this value, Minitab removes that variable with the smallest F from the equation.

Show the best — alternate predictors: For each step in which Minitab adds a variable to the model, it prints the next K best alternatives in terms of the F-value, along with their t-statistics. Each t-value shown is obtained by replacing the variable actually chosen by the alternative variable. The default value of K is 0.

Take — steps between pauses: You can set the number of steps of output printed; K can be any number from 1 up to the maximum allowed by the width of your screen (or by the OW—Output Width—command). Use smaller values when you want to intervene in the variable selection procedure more often.

Session Command Syntax for Stepwise...

STEPWISE *regression of y in* **C** *on the predictors* **C...C**
  FENTER = K
  FREMOVE = K
  FORCE C...C
  ENTER C...C
  REMOVE C...C
  BEST K *alternative predictors*
  STEPS = K
NOCONSTANT

The REMOVE subcommand (available only through the Session window) lets you indicate variables to be removed from the current model. Any of them may reenter the model at the next step if its F-value exceeds FENTER. Models are fit with a constant term (y-intercept) unless the NOCONSTANT subcommand is used or the NOCONSTANT command was issued previously.

Example: Using Stepwise...

The following dialog box and equivalent Session window commands illustrate how to use Stepwise... to fit a model that predicts salary at Technitron, Inc., starting with the number of people an employee supervises. The data are stored in TECHN.MTW from Tutorial 9.

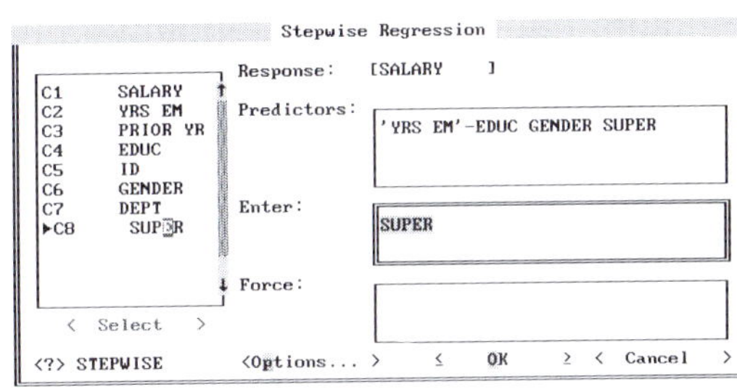


```
MTB > Stepwise 'SALARY' 'YRS EM'-'EDUC' 'GENDER' 'SUPER';
SUBC>   Enter 'SUPER';
SUBC>   FEnter 4.0;
SUBC>   FRemove 4.0.
```

These commands produce the following display in the Session window:

```
STEPWISE REGRESSION OF  SALARY  ON  5 PREDICTORS, WITH N =   46

   STEP         1        2        3        4
CONSTANT    36616    28189    23783    23177

SUPER         564      317      165
T-RATIO      4.88     3.12     1.74

YRS EM                 960      659      672
T-RATIO               7.82     4.75     4.75

EDUC                           1639     1916
T-RATIO                        4.86     5.85

S            9475     6542     5688     5738
R-SQ        27.45    66.28    75.73    73.99
 MORE? (YES, NO, SUBCOMMAND, OR HELP)
SUBC> N
```

See also Tutorial 9.

ANOVA

The **ANOVA** menu contains commands for analysis of variance. You have the options of a oneway ANOVA, with the response in one column and subscripts in another, or with each sample in a separate column, and of a twoway ANOVA or an ANOVA for balanced models.

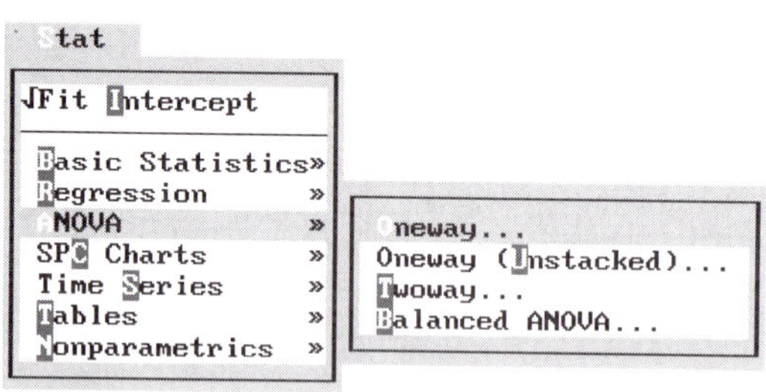

Oneway Analysis of Variance Dialog Box

The **Oneway...** command computes a one-way analysis of variance on data in a single column with subscripts in a second column.

Options in the Oneway Analysis of Variance Dialog Box

Response: Indicate the column containing the variable you want to analyze.

Factor: This column contains the codes identifying the factor level or group number; subscripts may be any integers from –10000 to +10000 or missing values (*). They need not be consecutive. The Edit ▶ Set Patterned Data... command is useful for entering subscripts.

Store residuals: Minitab stores residuals in the next available column.

Store fits: Minitab stores the fitted values (the group mean) in the next available column.

The Oneway Multiple Comparisons Subdialog Box

Minitab can perform multiple comparisons using four different methods that provide confidence intervals for the differences between means.

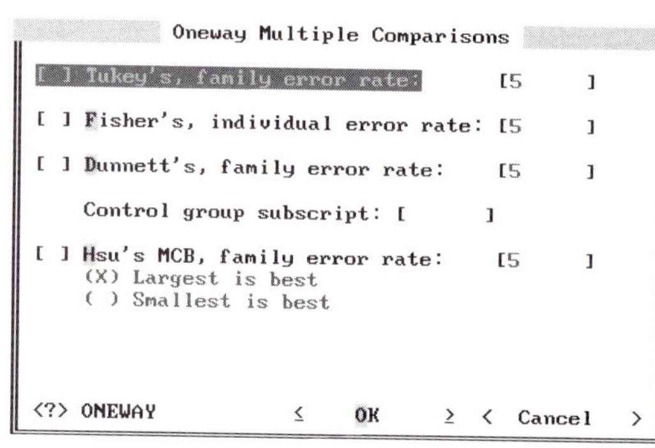

Tukey's, family error rate: The Tukey comparison provides confidence intervals for all pairwise differences between level means using Tukey's method. The default error rate is 5%.

Fisher's, individual error rate: The Fisher comparison provides confidence intervals for all pairwise differences between level means using Fisher's LSD procedure. The default error rate is 5%.

Dunnett's, family error rate: The Dunnett comparison provides a two-sided confidence interval for the difference between each treatment mean and a control mean. The default error rate is 5%.

Control group subscript: When using Dunnett's procedure, specify the control group factor level value here.

Hsu's MCB, family error rate: The Hsu MCB comparison provides a confidence interval for the difference between each level mean and the best of the other level means (you have two choices). The default error rate is 5%.

Largest is best: By default, Minitab uses the largest mean.

Smallest is best: You can have Minitab consider the smallest mean as the best mean.

Session Command Syntax for Oneway...

ONEWAY *on the data in* **C**, *subscripts in* **C**
  [*residuals in* **C** [*fitted values in* **C**]]
 TUKEY [*family error rate* **K**]
 FISHER [*individual error rate* **K**]
 DUNNETT [*family error rate K*] *control level is* **K**
 MCB [*family error rate* **K**] *best is* **K**

Example: Using Oneway...

The following dialog box and equivalent Session window commands illustrate using an analysis of variance to test whether a lack of consistency in the diameters of the copper wire manufactured for stereo equipment can be traced to shifts, using the FLEXIBLE.MTW data set from Tutorial 8. For this ANOVA, the diameter values are stored in C1, while the shifts in which they were produced are stored in C2.

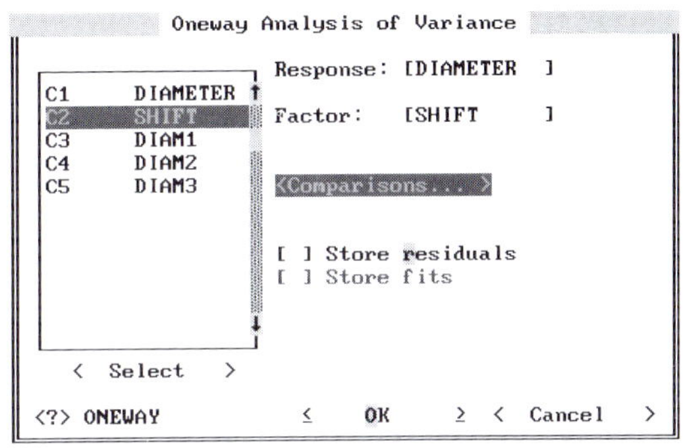


```
MTB > Oneway 'DIAMETER' 'SHIFT'.
```

These commands produce the following display in the Session window:

```
ANALYSIS OF VARIANCE ON DIAMETER
SOURCE     DF        SS        MS        F        p
SHIFT       2     674.9     337.5     5.26    0.019
ERROR      15     962.7      64.2
TOTAL      17    1637.6
                                  INDIVIDUAL 95 PCT CI'S FOR MEAN
                                  BASED ON POOLED STDEV
 LEVEL      N      MEAN     STDEV  --+---------+---------+---------+----
     1      9    70.333     9.760        (----*-----)
     2      6    65.000     5.060  (------*------)
     3      3    83.333     6.028              (----------*----------)
                                   --+---------+---------+---------+----
POOLED STDEV =    8.011             60        70        80        90
```

See also Tutorial 8.

The Oneway Analysis of Variance (Unstacked) Dialog Box

The Oneway (Unstacked)... command computes a one-way analysis of variance between two or more columns.

Options in the Oneway Analysis of Variance Dialog Box

Responses (in separate columns): List the response variables. Minitab does not require that each column have the same number of observations.

Session Command Syntax for Oneway (Unstacked)...

AOVONEWAY *on the data in* **C...C**

Example: Using Oneway (Unstacked)...

As in the previous example, the following dialog box and equivalent Session window commands illustrate using an analysis of variance to test whether a lack of consistency in the diameters of the copper wire manufactured for stereo equipment can be traced to shifts. The diameter values for each shift are stored in three columns: C3, C4, and C5. The data are in FLEXIBLE.MTW from Tutorial 8.

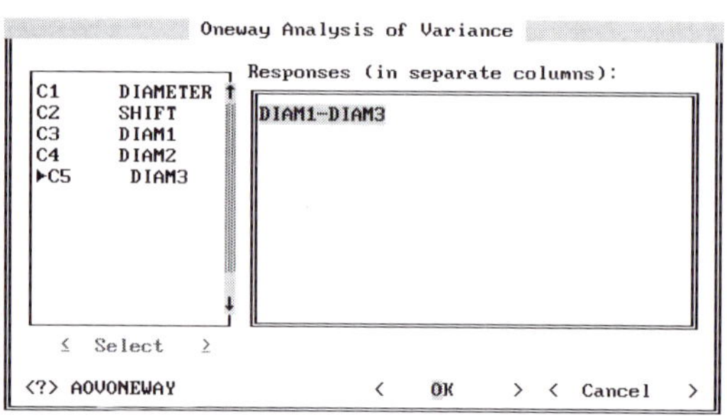


```
MTB > AOVOneway 'DIAM1'-'DIAM3'.
```

These commands produce the following display in the Session window:

```
ANALYSIS OF VARIANCE
SOURCE     DF        SS        MS        F        p
FACTOR      2      18.4       9.2     0.14    0.870
ERROR      22    1443.0      65.6
TOTAL      24    1461.4
                                 INDIVIDUAL 95 PCT CI'S FOR MEAN
                                 BASED ON POOLED STDEV
 LEVEL      N      MEAN     STDEV  ---------+---------+---------+------
DIAM1      12    68.750     9.372         (--------*--------)
DIAM2       7    69.714     6.651        (----------*-----------)
DIAM3       6    67.333     6.501  (------------*-----------)
                                   ---------+---------+---------+------
POOLED STDEV =    8.099                  65.0      70.0      75.0
```

See also Tutorial 8.

The Twoway Analysis of Variance Dialog Box

The Twoway... command performs a two-way analysis of variance for balanced data. In a two-way analysis of variance, data are classified by two sets of factors representing treatments or blocks, each having two or more levels. The number of levels in the first factor times the number of levels in the second factor equals the number of cells, which represents the number of different factor-level combinations. Each of these cells must contain an equal number of observations (that is, the data must be balanced).

Options in the Twoway Analysis of Variance Dialog Box

Response: Indicate the response variable containing the sample data.

Row factor: Indicate the first factor. This column may contain any integers between –10000 and +10000 or missing values (*). They need not be consecutive.

Column factor: Indicate the second factor. This column must contain integers between –10000 and +10000 or missing values (*). They need not be consecutive.

Display means: Minitab calculates marginal means and 95% confidence intervals for each level of either or both factor columns using the Student's t-distribution, MS ERROR degrees of freedom, and a pooled standard deviation equal to $\sqrt{\text{MS ERROR}}$.

Store residuals: Minitab stores the residuals in the next available column.

Store fits: Minitab stores the fitted value for each group if you do not use the additive subcommand.

Fit additive model: Minitab fits a model without an interaction term.

Session Command Syntax for Twoway...

TWOWAY *for the data in* **C**, *subscripts in* **C** *and* **C** [*store residual values in* **C** [*fits in* **C**]]
  ADDITIVE *model*
  MEANS *for the subscripts in* **C** [**C**]

Example: Using Twoway...

The following dialog box and equivalent Session window commands compute a two-way analysis of variance between advertising medium (newspaper, radio, and television) and agency (Ace Ads and Best Ads) to determine whether there is a significant effect of these two factors on the average increase in the sales of Krunchy Cereal, using the KRUNCHY.MTW data set from Tutorial 8.

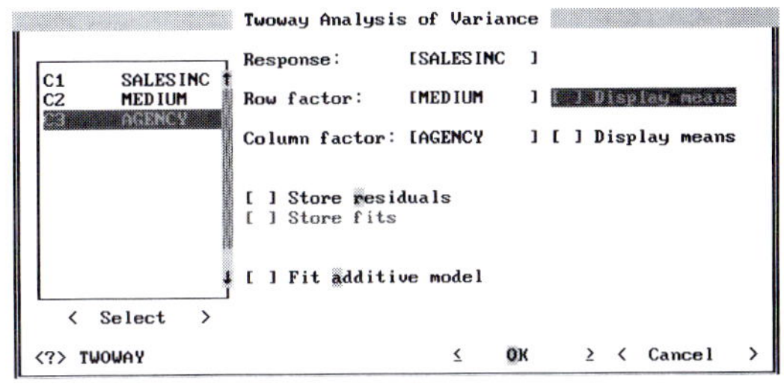


```
MTB > Twoway 'SALESINC' 'MEDIUM' 'AGENCY'.
```

These commands produce the following display in the Session window:

```
ANALYSIS OF VARIANCE  SALESINC

SOURCE         DF        SS        MS
MEDIUM          2    198.33     99.17
AGENCY          1     39.97     39.97
INTERACTION     2     77.35     38.67
ERROR           6     34.21      5.70
TOTAL          11    349.85
```

See also Tutorial 8.

The Balanced Analysis of Variance Dialog Box

The Balanced ANOVA... command does analysis of variance for multi-way balanced designs (all cells must have the same number of observations), and one-way analysis of variance for unbalanced designs.

Options in the Balanced Analysis of Variance Dialog Box

Responses: List the responses here.

Model: This command uses a simplified version of a model as it appears in many textbooks. Use an * between factors to include an interaction term. You may omit the quotes around variable names in this text box. You can abbreviate a model using a | or ! to indicate crossed factors and a – to remove terms. Models with many terms can take a long time to compute. The following two examples will get you started. See Minitab Help or your instructor to learn more.

1. Two factors crossed: Y = A B A*B (this model was used in the previous Twoway example)
2. Three factors crossed: Y = A B C A*B A*C B*C A*B*C

Display means for (list of terms): Minitab displays a table of means corresponding to each term. Specify the list of terms, both main effects and interactions, as you did for the Model text box. For example, the list of terms A, B, D, A*B*D displays four tables: one table for each main effect and one for the three-way interaction.

Store residuals: Minitab stores the residuals in the next available columns, using one column for each response.

Store fits: Minitab stores one fitted value for each observation in the data set in the next available columns, using one column for each response.

Session Command Syntax for Balanced ANOVA...

ANOVA *model*
  FITS C...C
  RESIDUALS C...C
  MEANS *term list*

Example: Using Balanced ANOVA...

The following dialog box and equivalent Session window commands compute a balanced analysis of variance between advertising medium (newspaper, radio, and television) and agency (Ace Ads and Best Ads) to determine whether there is a significant effect of these two factors on the average increase in the sale of Krunchy Cereal. The data are stored in KRUNCHY.MTW from Tutorial 8.

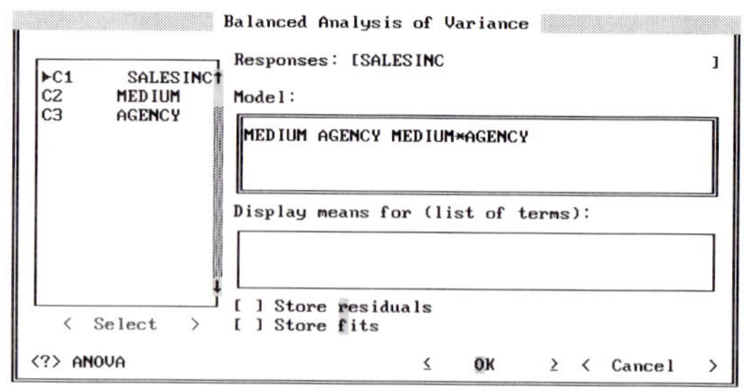


```
MTB > ANOVA 'SALESINC' = MEDIUM AGENCY MEDIUM*AGENCY.
```

These commands produce the following display in the Session window:

```
Factor      Type  Levels Values
MEDIUM     fixed       3      1      2      3
AGENCY     fixed       2      1      2

Analysis of Variance for SALESINC

Source            DF         SS         MS        F       P
MEDIUM             2    198.332     99.166    17.39   0.003
AGENCY             1     39.967     39.967     7.01   0.038
MEDIUM*AGENCY      2     77.345     38.673     6.78   0.029
Error              6     34.205      5.701
Total             11    349.849
```

See also Tutorial 8.

SPC Charts

Minitab can produce eleven different kinds of statistical process control (SPC) charts. These charts, used to study the variation in a process, display two basic types of data, variables and attributes. The first seven charts (Xbar, R, S, Individuals, Moving Range, EWMA, and Moving Average) display variables data—for example, measurements of thickness, pressure, or temperature. The last four charts (P, NP, C, and U) display attributes data—counts, usually of the number of defects or nonconformities in a sample.

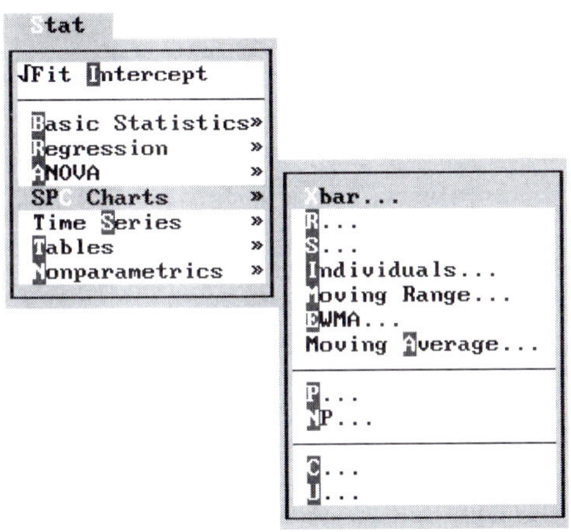

In all charts, the data consist of samples taken, usually over time. A summary statistic (like a sample mean or sample proportion) is calculated and plotted against the sample number. This plot is the control chart. Minitab draws three lines on the chart:

1. The center line, an estimate of the average value of the summary statistic.
2. An upper control limit (UCL), drawn at 3σ limits (standard deviations) above the center line.
3. A lower control limit (LCL), drawn at 3σ limits (standard deviations) below the center line.

If the process is "in control," or stable, it is very unlikely that a point (a value of the summary statistic) will fall outside the control limits. Any point that does so should be investigated.

Minitab omits missing observations (*) from the calculations.

The Xbar Chart Dialog Box

The **X**bar... command displays a separate chart of sample means for each variable.

Options in the Xbar Chart Dialog Box

Variables: Enter the variable(s) you are investigating.

Subgroup size: If you choose a constant subgroup size of, say, 5, then Minitab takes the first five rows as the first sample, the second five rows as the second sample, and so on, plotting the mean of each subgroup.

Subgroups in: If you choose a column with subscript values, Minitab forms a new subgroup every time the value in that column changes and plots each subgroup's mean. If the subgroups are not equal, the control limits will not be straight lines but will vary with the subgroup size. If the subgroup sizes do not vary much, you may want to force the control limits into straight lines by specifying a fixed subgroup size. Use the Subgroup Size subcommand in the Xbar - Estimation of Mu and Sigma subdialog box so you do not affect the data being plotted.

Historical mu: Minitab uses as the center line either a mean you specify here or a mean estimated from the data.

Sigma: Minitab computes the upper and lower control limits using either a pooled estimate, an Rbar estimate, or a standard deviation that you specify.

Pooled estimate: By default, Minitab uses the pooled standard deviation to estimate σ.

Rbar estimate: Minitab estimates σ by using a function of the sample ranges.

Historical: You can specify the standard deviation.

High resolution: Minitab's default setting produces a high-resolution chart that appears on a separate graphic screen. You can select this checkbox to turn off the default (remove the X); the chart then appears in the Session window in a character-based format.

Store in file: You can store the high-resolution chart in a file; Minitab gives the file the .PRI extension that indicates a printer file. It can take several minutes to store a high-resolution plot in a file, depending on your computer. The Store Graph in File dialog box resembles the File ▶ Open Worksheet dialog box. Refer to that command for more information.

Tests For Special Causes: Minitab can perform eight tests for special causes to detect specific patterns in the data plotted on the chart that calls for further investigation. Subgroup sizes must be equal. When a point fails a test, Minitab marks it with the test number on the plot and displays the test description in the Session window.

None: Minitab omits the tests for special causes.

All eight: Minitab performs all eight tests; see Minitab Help for a description.

Selected: You can specify which of the eight tests Minitab should perform. When you select this option, the Tests... button is activated.

Highlight this button and press [↵] to display the Xbar - Tests subdialog box.

Xbar - Tests Subdialog Box

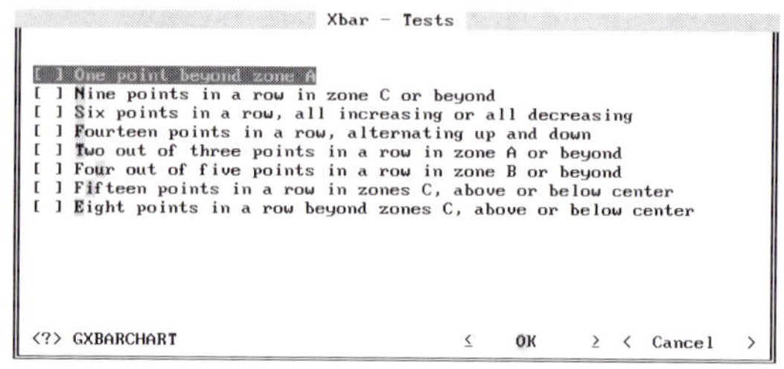

Choose which tests you want Minitab to perform from the list in the subdialog box. You may select as many tests as you want by checking the selection box.

The Xbar - Scale Subdialog Box

Use the Scale... command to control the range of your plot's Vertical and Horizontal axes. Minitab displays only the points between the minimum and maximum positions.

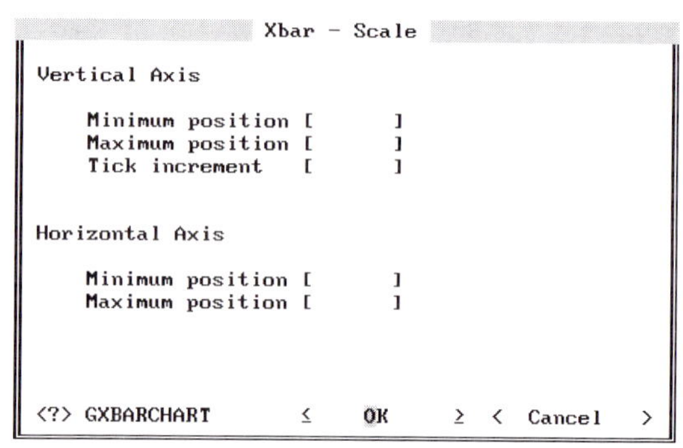

Minimum position: Set the minimum position here.

Maximum position: Set the maximum position here.

Tick increment: You can specify the increment that marks the distance between tick marks (+) on the axes.

The Xbar - Annotate Chart Subdialog Box

Use the **A**nnotate... command to supply labels for your plots.

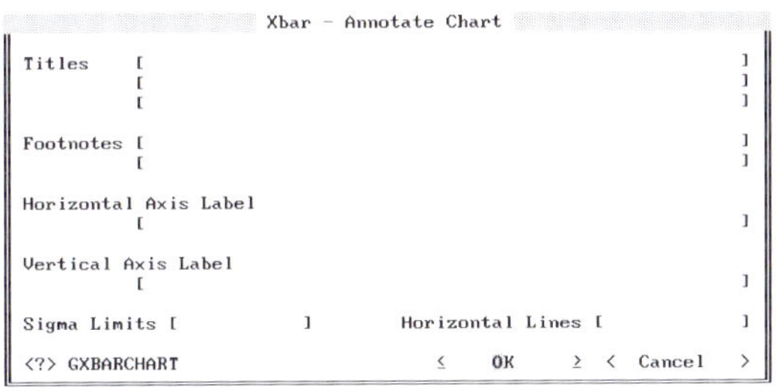

Titles: You can include three lines of text at the top of the graph.

Footnotes: You can have two lines of text at the bottom of the graph, below the horizontal axis label.

Horizontal Axis Label: Minitab automatically labels the horizontal axis with the column name, but you can replace that label with one of your own.

Vertical Axis Label: Minitab automatically labels the vertical axis with the column name, but you can replace that label with one of your own.

Sigma Limits: You can define what multiples of σ Minitab uses to compute the upper and lower control limits. The default is 3.

Horizontal Lines: You can add horizontal reference lines to a chart; if you do so, Minitab will not display the lower and upper control limits unless you change the default σ limits.

The Xbar - Estimation of Mu and Sigma Subdialog Box

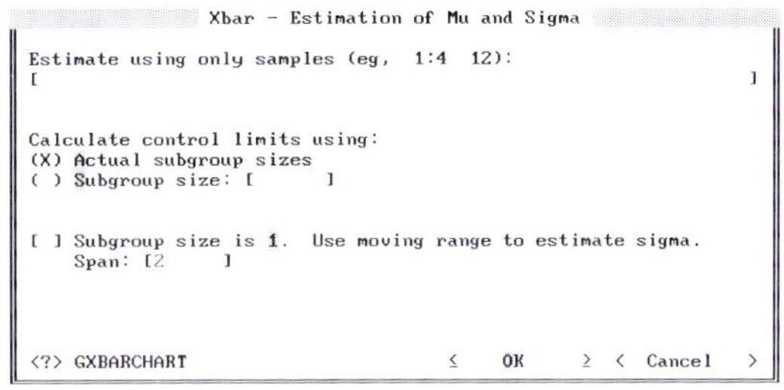

Estimate using only samples: By default, Minitab estimates the parameters for establishing the control limits using all samples, but you can use only specified subgroups of the data by listing individual sample numbers or a range of samples. Note that this refers to entire samples, not individual observations. If you want to omit one observation from a sample, change that value to * (the missing value code).

Calculate control limits using: You have two options for computing the control limits: actual subgroup size or specified subgroup size.

Actual subgroup sizes: This is the default setting; Minitab uses the subgroup sizes as given in the parent dialog box.

Subgroup size: If the sample sizes are unequal, set the sample size here to force straight control limits.

Subgroup size is **1**: Minitab estimates process variation using the sample standard deviations of each subgroup. If the subgroup size is 1, you cannot calculate sample standard deviations. Estimate the process variation using moving ranges instead. This allows you to specify the number of observations to calculate the moving range. The default is 2.

Session Command Syntax for Xbar...

Character-based

XBARCHART *for* **C...C**, *subgroups are in* **E**
  MU = **K**
  SIGMA = **K**
  RBAR
  SUBGROUP *size is* **K**
  RSPAN = **K**
  TEST K...K

High-resolution

GXBARCHART *for* **C...C**, *subgroups are in* **E**
  MU = **K**
  SIGMA = **K**
  RBAR
  SUBGROUP *size is* **K**
  RSPAN = **K**
  TEST K...K

Minitab uses the following subcommands in all control charts:

  SLIMITS *are* **K...K**
  HLINES *at* **E...E**
  ESTIMATE *using just samples* **K...K**

  XSTART *at* **K** [*end at* **K**]
  YSTART at K [*end at* **K**]
  YINC = **K**

  XLABEL '*text*'
  YLABEL '*text*'
  TITLE '*text*'
  FOOTNOTE '*text*'

  FILE ['**FILENAME**']

Example: Using Xbar...

The following dialog box and equivalent Session window commands produce an Xbar chart for a sampling of 5 wire diameters every hour for 21 hours (stored in C1 DIAMETER) to see if the process producing the wires is in control, using the FLEX2.MTW data set from Tutorial 12.

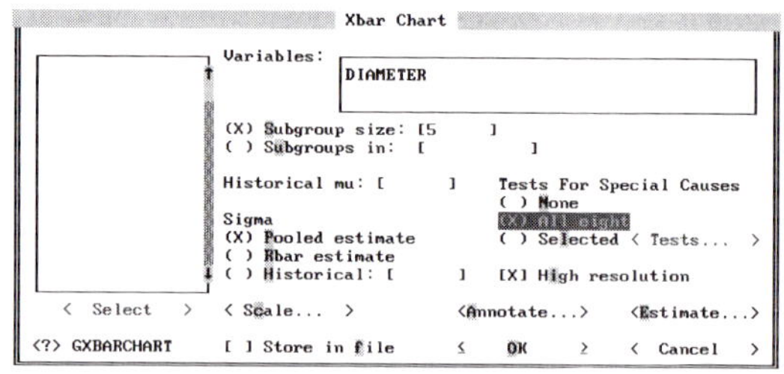


```
MTB > GXbarChart 'DIAMETER' 5;
SUBC>   Test 1:8.
```

These commands produce the following chart in a separate graph screen:

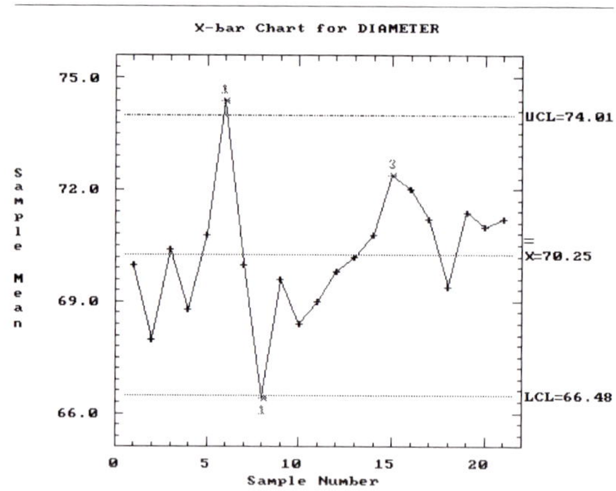

See also Tutorial 12.

The R Chart Dialog Box

The **R**... command displays a chart of sample ranges. See Stat ▶ SPC Charts ▶ Xbar... for an example of statistical process control charts.

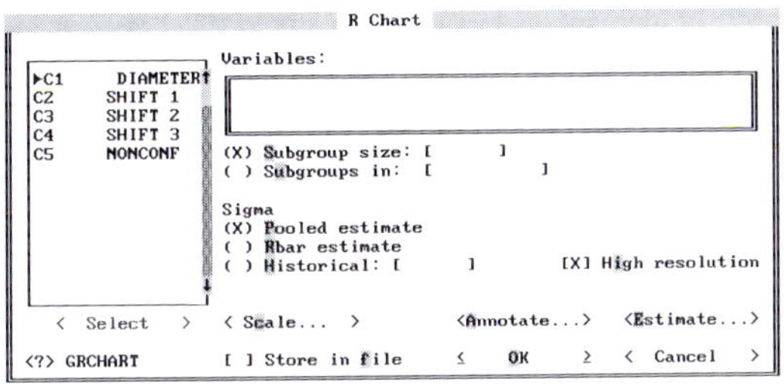

Options in the R Chart Dialog Box

Variables: Enter the variable(s) you are investigating.

Subgroup size: If you choose a constant subgroup size of, say, 5, then Minitab takes the first 5 rows as the first sample, the second 5 rows as the second sample, and so on, plotting the range of each subgroup.

Subgroups in: If the subgroup sizes are not constant, you need to specify a subscript column. If you choose a column with subscript values, Minitab forms a new subgroup every time the value in that column changes and plots each subgroup's range. If the subgroups are not equal, the control limits will not be straight lines but will vary with the subgroup size. If the subgroup sizes do not vary much, you may want to force the control limits to be straight lines by specifying a fixed subgroup size using the Subgroup size subcommand in the R Chart - Estimation of Sigma subdialog box.

Sigma: To compute the upper and lower control limits, Minitab uses either a pooled estimate, an Rbar estimate, or a historical standard deviation that you specify.

Pooled estimate: By default, Minitab uses the pooled standard deviation to estimate σ.

Rbar estimate: Minitab estimates σ by using a function of the sample ranges.

Historical: You can specify the population or historical standard deviation; Minitab uses this value to determine the center line, as well as the lower and upper control limits.

High resolution: Minitab's default setting produces a high-resolution chart that appears in a separate graphic screen. You can select this checkbox to turn off the default; the chart then appears in the Session window in a character-based format.

Store in file: You can store the high-resolution chart in a file; Minitab gives the file the .PRI extension that indicates a printer file. It can take several minutes to store a high-resolution plot in a file, depending on your computer. The Store Graph in File dialog box resembles the File ▶ Open Worksheet dialog box. Refer to that command for more information.

Scale... and Annotate...: See Stat ▶ SPC Charts ▶ Xbar... for information on these commands.

The R Chart - Estimation of Sigma Subdialog Box

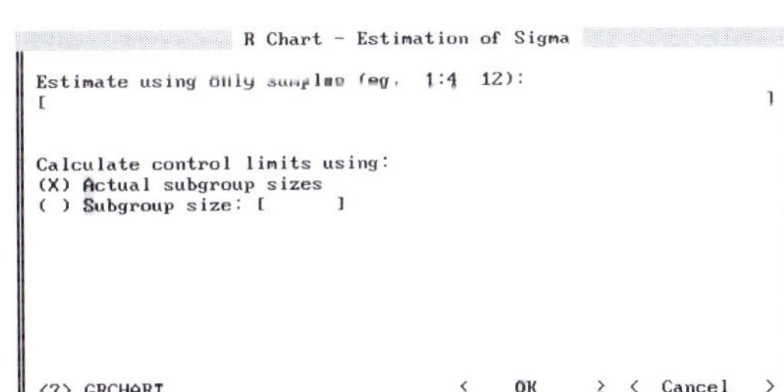

Estimate using only samples: By default, Minitab estimates the parameters using all samples, but you can use only specified subgroups of the data by listing individual sample numbers or a range of samples. Note that this refers to entire samples, not individual observations. If you want to omit one observation from a sample, change that value to * (the missing value code).

Calculate control limits using: You have two options for computing the control limits: actual subgroup size or specified subgroup size.

Actual subgroup sizes: This is the default setting; Minitab uses the subgroup sizes as given in the parent dialog box.

Subgroup size: If the sample sizes are unequal, set the sample size here to force straight control limits. This command will not affect the data plotted.

Session Command Syntax for R...

Character-based

RCHART *for* **C...C**, *subgroups are in* **E**
  SIGMA = **K**
  RBAR
  SUBGROUP *size is* **K**

High-resolution

GRCHART *for* **C...C**, *subgroups are in* **E**
  SIGMA = **K**
  RBAR
  SUBGROUP *size is* **K**

All statistical process control charts also use the list of subcommands shown in the Stat ▶ SPC Charts ▶ Xbar... Session Command Syntax section.

See also Tutorial 12.

The S Chart Dialog Box

The **S**... command displays a chart of sample standard deviations.

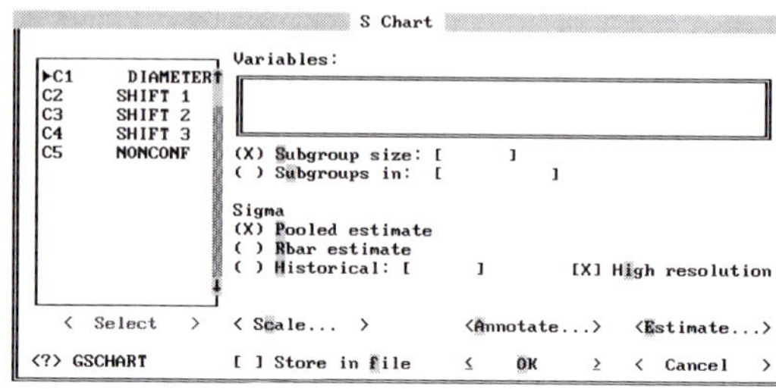

Options in the S Chart Dialog Box

Variables: Enter the variable(s) you are investigating.

Subgroup size: If you choose a constant subgroup size of, say, 5, then Minitab takes the first 5 rows as the first sample, the second 5 rows as the second sample, and so on, plotting the standard deviations of each subgroup.

Subgroups in: If the subgroup sizes are not constant, you need to specify a subscript column. If you choose a column with subscript values, Minitab forms a new subgroup every time the value in that column changes and plots each subgroup's mean. If the subgroups are not equal, the control limits will not be straight lines but will vary with the subgroup size. If the subgroup sizes do not vary much, you may want to force the control limits to be straight lines by specifying a fixed subgroup size (using the Subgroup size subcommand in the S Chart - Estimation of Sigma dialog box).

Sigma: To compute the upper and lower control limits, Minitab uses either a pooled estimate, an Rbar estimate, or a historical standard deviation that you specify.

Pooled estimate: By default, Minitab uses the pooled standard deviation to estimate σ.

Rbar estimate: Minitab estimates σ by using a function of the sample ranges.

Historical: You can specify the population or historical standard deviation; Minitab uses this value to determine the center line, as well as the lower and upper control limits.

Hi**g**h resolution: Minitab's default setting produces a high-resolution chart that appears on a separate graphic screen. You can select this checkbox to turn off the default; the chart then appears in the Session window in a character-based format.

Store in **f**ile: You can store the high-resolution chart in a file; Minitab gives the file the .PRI extension that indicates a printer file. It can take several minutes to store a high-resolution plot in a file, depending on your computer. The Store Graph in File dialog box resembles the File ► Open Worksheet dialog box. Refer to that command for more information.

S**c**ale... and **A**nnotate...: See Stat ► SPC Charts ► Xbar... for information on these commands.

The S Chart - Estimation of Sigma Subdialog Box

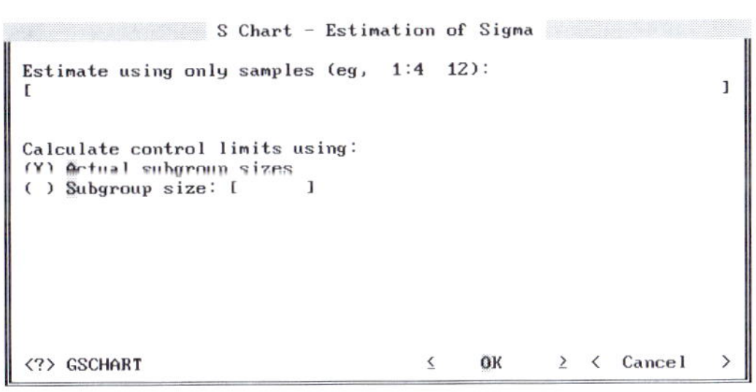

Estimate using only samples: By default, Minitab estimates the parameters using all samples, but you can use only specified subgroups of the data by listing individual sample numbers or a range of samples. Note that this refers to entire samples, not individual observations. If you want to omit one observation from a sample, change that value to * (the missing value code).

Calculate control limits using: You have two options for computing the control limits: actual subgroup size or specified subgroup size.

Actual subgroup sizes: This is the default setting; Minitab uses the subgroup sizes as given in the parent dialog box.

Subgroup size: If the sample sizes are unequal, set the sample size here to force straight control limits. This command will not affect the data plotted.

Session Command Syntax for S...

Character-based

SCHART *for* **C...C**, *subgroups are in* **E**
  SIGMA = **K**
  RBAR
  SUBGROUP *size is* **K**

High-resolution

GSCHART *for* **C...C**, *subgroups are in* **E**
  SIGMA = **K**
  RBAR
  SUBGROUP *size is* **K**

All statistical process control charts also use the list of subcommands shown in the Stat ► SPC Charts ► Xbar... Session Command Syntax section.

The Individuals Dialog Box

The **I**ndividuals... command displays a chart of individual observations. Each sample contains just one observation. See Stat ▶ SPC Charts ▶ Xbar... for an example of statistical process control charts.

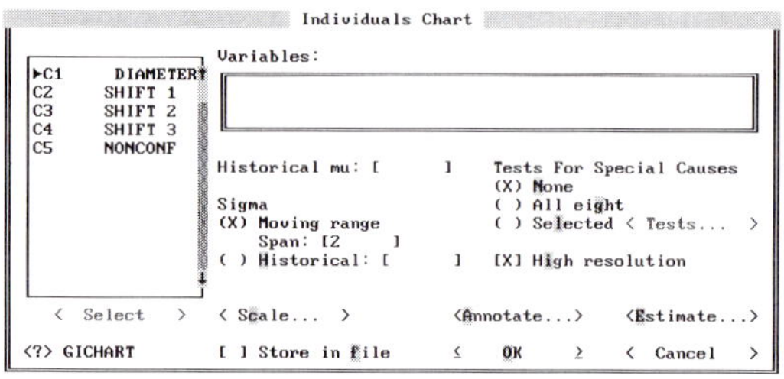

Options in the Individuals Chart Dialog Box

Variables: Enter the variable(s) you are investigating.

Historical mu: By default, Minitab uses, as the center line, the mean estimated from all the data. If you want to use a particular or historical value, enter it here.

Sigma: To compute the upper and lower control limits, Minitab uses either a moving range or a historical standard deviation that you specify.

Moving range: In an individuals chart, Minitab estimates the parameter σ from moving ranges. It cannot be estimated from the sample standard deviations, since there is just one observation per sample.

Span: The moving range span specifies the number of consecutive values to use to compute the moving range; the default is 2.

Historical: You can specify the population or historical value of the standard deviation.

H**i**gh resolution: Minitab's default setting produces a high-resolution chart that appears in a separate graphic screen. You can select this checkbox to turn off the default; the chart then appears in the Session window in a character-based format.

Store in **f**ile: You can store the high-resolution chart in a file; Minitab gives the file the .PRI extension that indicates a printer file. It can take several minutes to store a high-resolution plot in a file, depending on your computer. The Store Graph in File dialog box resembles the File ▶ Open Worksheet dialog box. Refer to that command for more information.

Tests For Special Causes: Minitab performs eight tests for special causes to detect specific patterns in the data plotted on the chart that calls for further investigation. When a point fails a test, Minitab marks it with the test number on the plot.

None: Minitab omits the tests for special causes.

All ei**g**ht: Minitab performs all eight tests; see Minitab Help for a description.

Selected Tests: You can specify which of the eight tests Minitab should perform.

S**c**ale... and **A**nnotate...: See Stat ▶ SPC Charts ▶ Xbar... for information on these commands.

The Estimate Subdialog Box

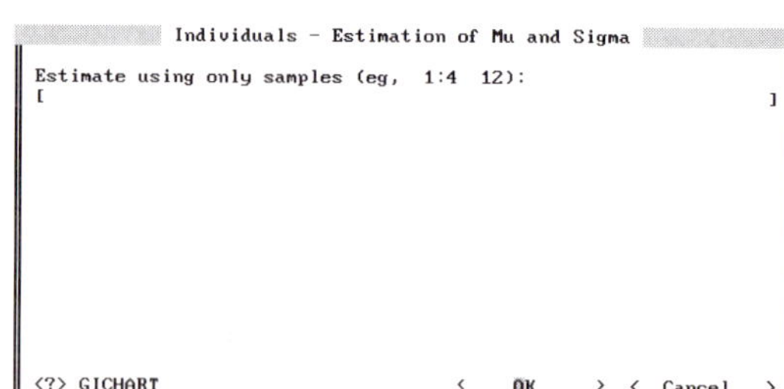

Estimate using only samples: By default, Minitab estimates the parameters using all samples, but you can use only specified subgroups of the data by listing individual sample numbers or a range of samples. Note that this refers to entire samples, not individual observations.

Session Command Syntax for Individuals...

Character-based

ICHART *for* **C...C**
MU = K
SIGMA = K
RSPAN = K
TEST K...K

High-resolution

GICHART *for* **C...C**
MU = K
SIGMA = K
RSPAN = K
TEST K...K

All statistical process control charts also use the list of subcommands shown in the Stat ▶ SPC Charts ▶ Xbar... Session Command Syntax section.

See also Tutorial 12.

The Moving Range Chart Dialog Box

The Moving Range... command displays a separate moving range chart for each variable you indicate. Each sample consists of a single observation. Minitab forms moving ranges from the observations and plots them on the chart. If an observation is missing, Minitab sets all moving ranges that use that observation to missing and a gap appears in the center line and control limits. See Stat ▶ SPC Charts ▶ Xbar... for an example of statistical process control charts.

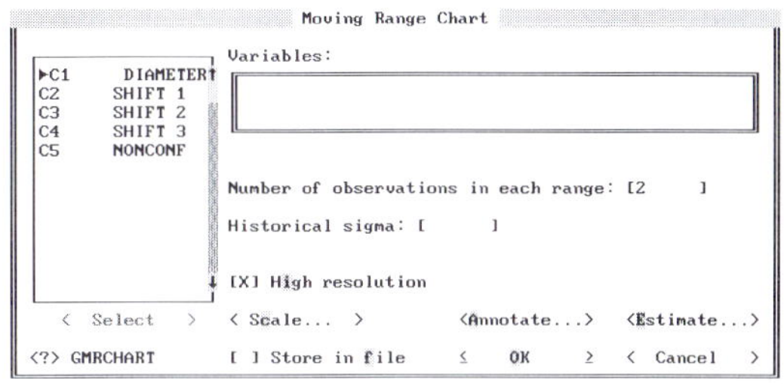

Options in the Moving Range Chart Dialog Box

Variables: Indicate the variable(s) you want to investigate.

Number of observations in each range: Specify the number of consecutive observations to use in computing the moving range.

Historical sigma: If you specify σ, Minitab uses this value to determine the center line and upper and lower control limits. The default is 2.

High resolution: Minitab's default setting produces a high-resolution chart that appears in a separate graphic screen. You can select this checkbox to turn off the default; the chart then appears in the Session window in a character-based format.

Store in file: You can store the high-resolution chart in a file; Minitab gives the file the .PRI extension that indicates a printer file. It can take several minutes to store a high-resolution plot in a file, depending on your computer. The Store Graph in File dialog box resembles the File ▶ Open Worksheet... dialog box. Refer to that command for more information.

Scale... and Annotate...: See Stat ▶ SPC Charts ▶ Xbar... for information on these commands.

The Moving Range Chart - Estimation of Sigma Subdialog Box

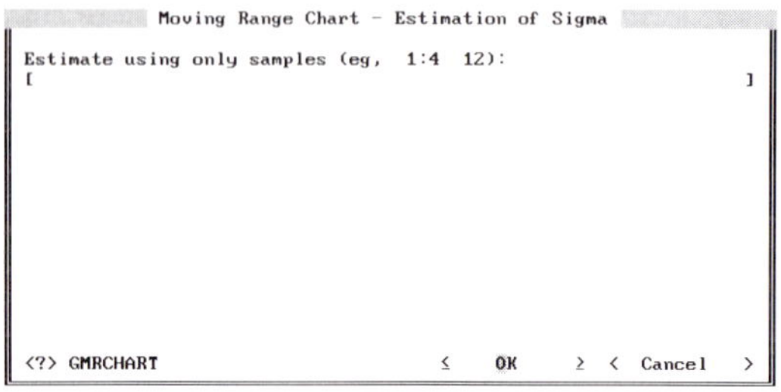

Estimate using only samples: By default, Minitab estimates the parameters using all samples, but you can use only specified subgroups of the data by listing individual sample numbers or a range of samples. Note that this refers to entire samples, not individual observations.

Session Command Syntax for Moving Range...

Character-based

MRCHART *for* **C...C**
  SIGMA = **K**
  RSPAN = **K**

High-resolution

GMRCHART *for* **C...C**
  SIGMA = **K**
  RSPAN = **K**

All statistical process control charts also use the list of subcommands shown in the Stat ▶ SPC Charts ▶ Xbar... Session Command Syntax section.

See also Tutorial 12.

The EWMA Chart Dialog Box

The EWMA... command displays a separate chart of exponentially weighted moving averages for each variable you list. This chart is also called a geometrically weighted moving average chart. See Stat ▶ SPC Charts ▶ Xbar... for an example of statistical process control charts.

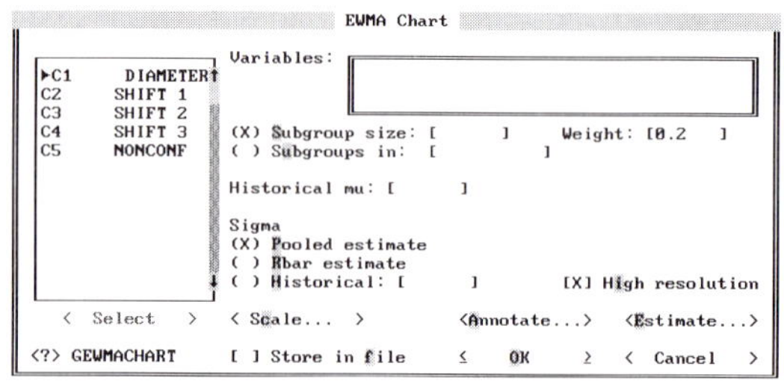

Options in the EWMA Chart Dialog Box

Variables: Enter the variable(s) you are investigating.

Subgroup size: If you choose a constant subgroup size of, say, 5, then Minitab takes the first 5 rows as the first sample, the second 5 rows as the second sample, and so on, plotting the mean of each subgroup. Means are calculated and then exponentially weighted.

Subgroups in: Specify subscript columns if the subgroup sizes are not constant. If you choose a column with subscript values, Minitab forms a new subgroup every time the value in that column changes and plots each subgroup's mean. If the subgroups are not equal, the control limits will not be straight lines but will vary with the subgroup size. If the subgroup sizes do not vary much, you may want to force the control limits to be straight lines by specifying a fixed subgroup size (using the Subgroup size subcommand in the EWMA - Estimation of Mu and Sigma subdialog box).

Weight: Specify the weight used in the exponentially weighted moving average between 0 and 1. The default is 0.2.

Historical mu: By default the control chart center line is estimated from the data. To use a specific center line, specify the value here.

Sigma: To compute the upper and lower control limits, Minitab uses either a pooled estimate, an Rbar estimate, or a historical standard deviation that you specify.

Pooled estimate: By default, Minitab uses the pooled standard deviation to estimate σ.

Rbar estimate: Minitab estimates σ by using a function of the sample ranges.

Historical: You can specify the standard deviation and Minitab uses this value to determine the center line, as well as the lower and upper control limits.

High resolution: Minitab's default setting produces a high-resolution chart that appears on a separate graphic screen. You can select this checkbox to turn off the default; the chart then appears in the Session window in a character-based format.

Store in file: You can store the high-resolution chart in a file; Minitab gives the file the .PRI extension that indicates a printer file. It can take several minutes to store a high-resolution plot in a file, depending on your computer. The Store Graph in File dialog box resembles the File ► Open Worksheet dialog box. Refer to that command for more information.

Scale... and Annotate...: See Stat ► SPC Charts ► Xbar... for information on these commands.

The EWMA - Estimation of Mu and Sigma Subdialog Box

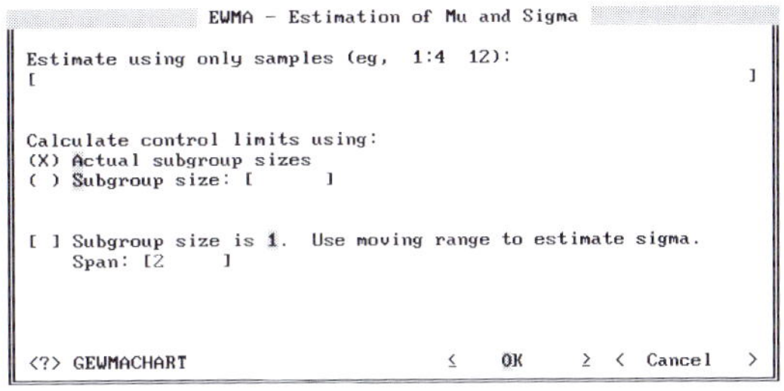

Estimate using only samples: By default, Minitab estimates the parameters using all samples, but you can use only specified subgroups of the data by listing individual sample numbers or a range of samples. Note that this refers to entire samples, not individual observations. If you want to omit one observation from a sample, change that value to * (the missing value code).

Calculate control limits using: You have two options for computing the control limits: actual subgroup size or specified subgroup size.

Actual subgroup sizes: This is the default setting; Minitab uses the subgroup sizes as given in the parent dialog box.

Subgroup size: If the sample sizes are unequal, set the sample size here to force straight control limits.

Subgroup size is 1: If the subgroup size is 1 and you want to specify the number of observations used in calculating the moving range, supply the desired span.

Span: Minitab estimates the span using the sample standard deviations of each subgroup. If the subgroup size is 1, you cannot calculate sample standard deviations. Estimate using moving ranges instead. This allows you to specify the number of observations to calculate the moving range. The default is 2.

Session Command Syntax for EWMA...

Character-based

EWMACHART *for* **C...C**, *subgroups are in* **E**
  MU = **K**
  SIGMA = **K**
  RBAR
  SUBGROUP *size is* **K**
  WEIGHT = **K**
  RSPAN = **K**

High-resolution

GEWMACHART *for* **C...C**, *subgroups are in* **E**
  MU = **K**
  SIGMA = **K**
  RBAR
  SUBGROUP *size is* **K**
  WEIGHT = **K**
  RSPAN = **K**

All statistical process control charts also use the list of subcommands shown in the Stat ▶ SPC Charts ▶ Xbar... Session Command Syntax section.

The Moving Average Chart Dialog Box

The Moving Average... command displays a separate chart of moving averages for each variable. See Stat ▶ SPC Charts ▶ Xbar... for an example of statistical process control charts.

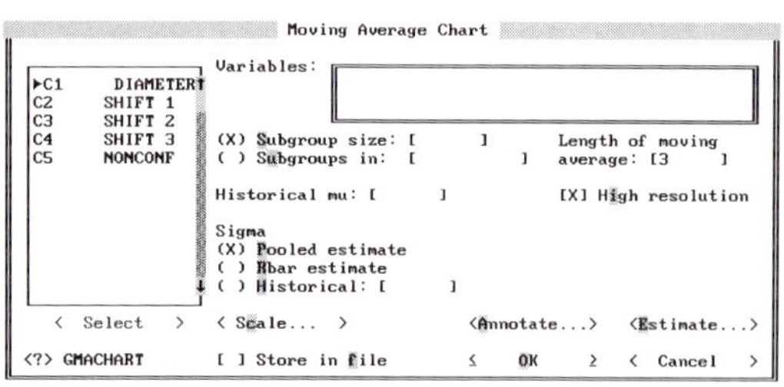

Options in the Moving Average Chart Dialog Box

Variables: Enter the variable(s) you are investigating.

Subgroup size: If you choose a constant subgroup size of, say, 5, then Minitab takes the first 5 rows as the first sample, the second 5 rows as the second sample, and so on. Moving averages are formed from these means.

Subgroups in: Use a subscript column if the subgroup sizes are different. If you choose a column with subscript values, Minitab forms a new subgroup every time the value in that column changes and plots each subgroup's mean. If the subgroups are not equal, the control limits will not be straight lines but will vary with the subgroup size. If the subgroup sizes do not vary much, you may want to force the control limits to be straight lines by specifying a fixed subgroup size (using the Subgroup size subcommand).

Length of moving average: Specify the number of consecutive sample means to be used in computing a moving average. Minitab first forms sample averages, using the subgroup size you specify. Then, to compute the moving average, Minitab averages a consecutive number of these sample averages. For example, the following table contains eight sample means and uses a span of three.

sample	1	2	3	4	5	6	7	8
sample mean	14.00	9.00	7.00	9.00	13.00	4.00	9.00	11.00
moving average	14.00	11.50	10.00	8.33	9.67	8.67	8.67	8.00

The moving average for sample 1 is just the first mean, 14. For sample 2 it is the average of the first two means, (14 + 9) / 2 = 11.5. These two are special because we do not have three means to average yet. Because of this, the upper and lower control limits will be farther out than for the rest of the samples. The rest follow the general pattern. The moving average for sample 3 is the average of the first three means, that is (14 + 9 + 7) / 3 = 10. For the fourth sample it is the average of the next three means, that is (9 + 7 + 9) / 3 = 8.33. In general, the moving average for sample i is the average of the means for samples *i* - 2, *i* - 1, and *i*. Minitab plots the moving averages on the chart.

Historical mu: By default, the center line is the average of all subgroup sample averages. To set the center line at a certain value, enter that value here.

Sigma: To compute the upper and lower control limits, Minitab uses either a pooled estimate, an Rbar estimate, or a historical standard deviation that you specify.

Pooled estimate: By default, Minitab uses the pooled standard deviation to estimate σ.

Rbar estimate: Minitab estimates σ by using a function of the sample ranges.

Historical: You can specify the standard deviation and Minitab will use this value to determine the lower and upper control limits.

High resolution: Minitab's default setting produces a high-resolution chart that appears on a separate graphic screen. You can select this checkbox to turn off the default; the chart then appears in the Session window in a character-based format.

Store in file: You can store the high-resolution chart in a file; Minitab gives the file the .PRI extension that indicates a printer file. It can take several minutes to store a high-resolution plot in a file, depending on your computer. The Store Graph in File dialog box resembles the File ▶ Open Worksheet dialog box. Refer to that command for more information.

Scale... and Annotate...: See Stat ▶ SPC Charts ▶ Xbar... for information on these commands.

The Moving Average - Estimation of Mu and Sigma Subdialog Box

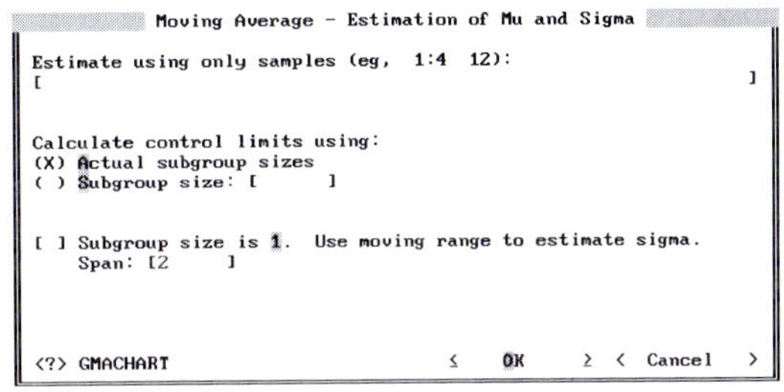

Estimate using only samples: By default, Minitab estimates the parameters using all samples, but you can use only specified subgroups of the data by listing individual sample numbers or a range of samples. Note that this refers to entire samples, not individual observations. If you want to omit one observation from a sample, change that value to * (the missing value code).

Calculate control limits using: You have two options for computing the control limits—actual subgroup size or specified subgroup size.

Actual subgroup sizes: This is the default setting; Minitab uses the subgroup sizes as given in the parent dialog box.

Subgroup size: If the sample sizes are unequal, set the sample size here to force straight control limits.

Subgroup size is 1: If the subgroup size is 1 and you want to specify the number of observations used in calculating the moving range, supply the desired span.

Span: Minitab estimates the process variation using the sample standard deviations of each subgroup. If the subgroup size is 1, you cannot calculate sample standard deviations. Estimate the process variation using moving ranges instead. This allows you to specify the number of observations to calculate the moving range. The default is 2.

Session Command Syntax for Moving Average Chart...

Character-based

MACHART *for* **C...C**, *subgroups are in* **E**
  MU = **K**
  SIGMA = **K**
  RBAR
  SUBGROUP *size is* **K**
  SPAN = **K**
  RSPAN = **K**

High-resolution

GMACHART *for* **C...C**, *subgroups are in* **E**
  MU = **K**
  SIGMA = **K**
  RBAR
  SUBGROUP *size is* **K**
  SPAN = **K**
  RSPAN = **K**

All statistical process control charts also use the list of subcommands shown in the Stat ▶ SPC Charts ▶ Xbar... Session Command Syntax section.

The P Chart Dialog Box

The **P**... command displays a separate chart (proportion of nonconformities) for each variable you list. See Stat ▶ SPC Charts ▶ Xbar... for an example of statistical process control charts.

Options in the P Chart Dialog Box

Variables: Enter the variable(s) you want to investigate. Each row corresponds to one sample that is assumed to have come from a binomial distribution with parameters n and p. The column(s) contain the number of nonconforming items in the sample. Minitab plots the proportion of nonconforming items corresponding to each sample.

Subgroup size: If the subgroup size (n) is the same for all samples, specify the value here.

Subgroups in: Enter the column with different sample sizes here.

Historical p: You can specify the parameter, p, of the binomial distribution. Minitab uses this value for the center line and in calculating the upper and lower control limits.

High resolution: Minitab's default setting produces a high-resolution chart that appears in a separate graphic screen. You can select this checkbox to turn off the default; the chart then appears in the Session window in a character-based format.

Store in file: You can store the high-resolution chart in a file; Minitab gives the file the .PRI extension that indicates a printer file. It can take several minutes to store a high-resolution plot in a file, depending on your computer. The Store Graph in File dialog box resembles the File ▶ Open Worksheet dialog box. Refer to that command for more information.

Tests For Special Causes: Minitab can perform four tests for special causes to detect specific patterns in the data plotted on the chart that call for further investigation. Subgroup sizes must be equal. When a point fails a test, Minitab marks it with the test number on the plot. An explanation of the test can be found in the Session window output.

None: Minitab omits the tests for special causes.

All four: Minitab performs all four tests; see Minitab Help for a description. See also the discussion of the Xbar Chart dialog box for more details.

Selected Tests: You can specify which of the four tests Minitab should perform from the P-Tests subdialog box.

Scale... and **A**nnotate...: See Stat ▶ SPC Charts ▶ Xbar... for information on these commands.

The P Chart - Estimation of Mu and Sigma Subdialog Box

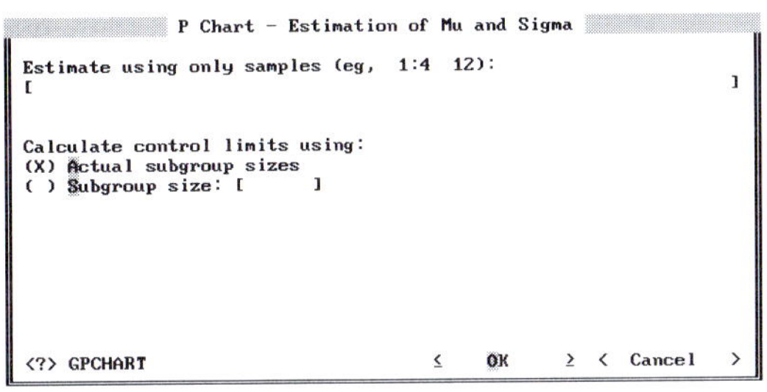

Estimate using only samples: By default, Minitab estimates the parameters using all samples, but you can use only specified subgroups of the data by listing individual sample numbers or a range of samples.

Calculate control limits using: You have two options for computing the control limits: actual subgroup size or specified subgroup size.

Actual subgroup sizes: This is the default setting; Minitab uses the subgroup sizes as given in the parent dialog box.

Subgroup size: If the sample sizes are unequal, set the sample size here to force straight control limits. This command will not affect the data plotted.

Session Command Syntax for P...

Character-based

PCHART *number of nonconformities are in*
    C...C, *sample size* = **E**
  P = **K**
  SUBGROUP *size is* **K**
  TEST K...K

High-resolution

GPCHART *number of nonconformities are in*
    C...C, *sample size* = **E**
  P = **K**
  SUBGROUP *size is* **K**
  TEST K...K

All statistical process control charts also use the list of subcommands shown in the Stat ▶ SPC Charts ▶ Xbar... Session Command Syntax section.

Example: Using P...

The following dialog box and equivalent Session window commands produce a P chart for a data set that contains the number of defective plastic soda bottle containers (C1) for a sample size of either 2000 or 3000 (C2). The data set is shown in the following display:

↓	C1	C2
1	51	3000
2	35	3000
3	21	3000
4	32	2000
5	48	2000
6	19	2000
7	12	2000
8	31	3000
9	18	3000
10	35	3000
11	33	3000
12	41	3000
13	45	3000

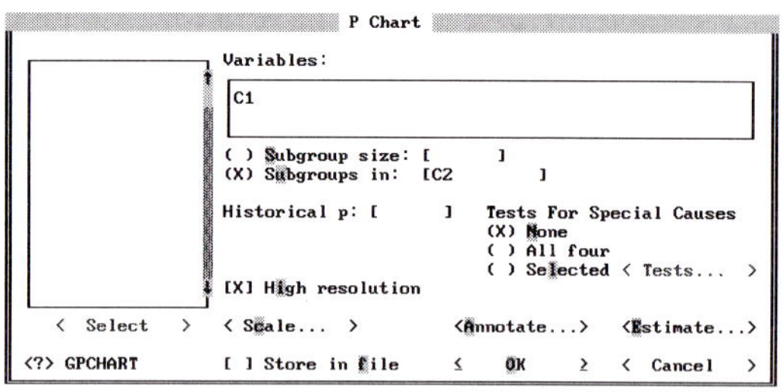


```
MTB > GPChart C1 C2.
```

These commands produce the following chart in a separate graph screen:

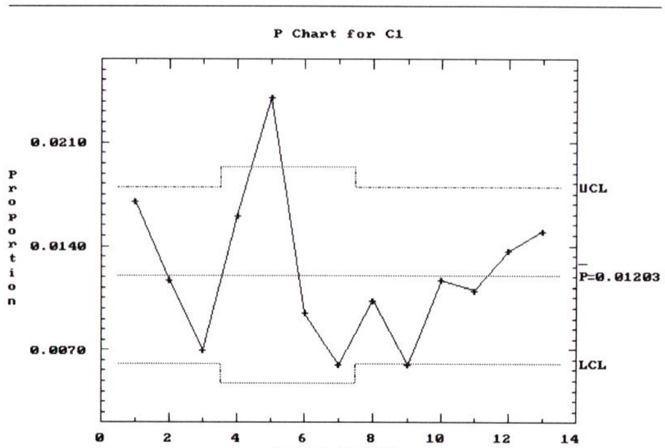

See also Tutorial 12.

The NP Dialog Box

The NP... command displays a separate number of nonconformities chart for each variable and plots the number of nonconformities. See Stat ► SPC Charts ► Xbar... for an example of statistical process control charts. The session command is NPCHART and GNPCHART; refer to the P... command for more details. The dialog box and Session window subcommands and command formats are identical for P... and NP....

The C Dialog Box

The C... command displays a separate chart for Poisson counts for each variable you list. See Stat ► SPC Charts ► Xbar... for an example of statistical process control charts.

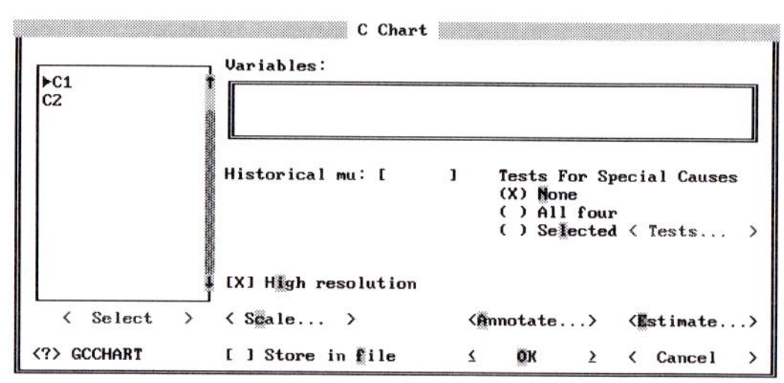

Options in the C Chart Dialog Box

Variables: Indicate the variable(s) you want to investigate. Each row corresponds to one sample. The sample is assumed to have come from a Poisson distribution with mean μ. The variable(s) contain the number of nonconformities in the sample (that is, the value of the Poisson variable). Minitab plots the number of nonconformities corresponding to each sample on the chart.

Historical mu: You can specify the mean of the Poisson distribution. Minitab uses this value to compute the center line, as well as the upper and lower control limits.

High resolution: Minitab's default setting produces a high-resolution chart that appears in a separate graphic screen. You can select this checkbox to turn off the default; the chart then appears in the Session window in a character-based format.

Store in file: You can store the high-resolution chart in a file; Minitab gives the file the .PRI extension that indicates a printer file. It can take several minutes to store a high-resolution plot in a file, depending on your computer. The Store Graph in File dialog box resembles the File ▶ Open Worksheet dialog box. Refer to that command for more information.

Tests For Special Causes: Minitab can perform four tests for special causes to detect specific patterns in the data plotted on the chart that calls for further investigation. Subgroup sizes must be equal. When a point fails a test, Minitab marks it with the test number on the plot.

None: Minitab omits the tests for special causes.

All four: Minitab performs all four tests; see Minitab Help for a description.

Selected Tests: You can specify which of the four tests Minitab should perform from the C - Tests subdialog box.

Scale... and Annotate...: See Stat ▶ SPC Charts ▶ Xbar... for information on these commands.

The C Chart - Estimation of Mu and Sigma Subdialog Box

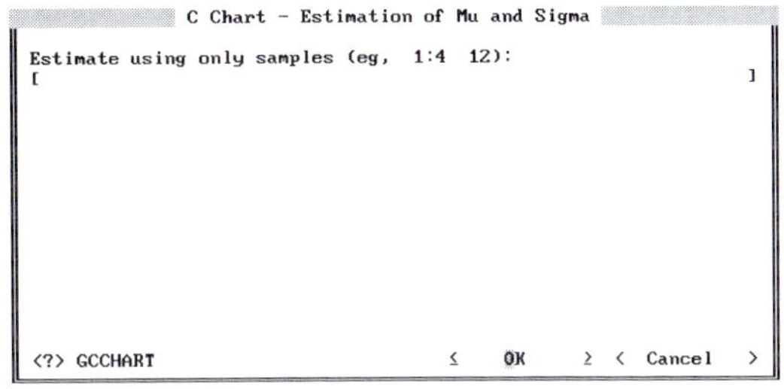

Estimate using only samples: By default, Minitab estimates the parameter using all samples. Alternatively, you can use a subset of the data by listing individual sample (or row) numbers or a range of samples.

Session Command Syntax for C...

Character-based

CCHART *number of nonconformities are in*
C...C
MU = K
TEST K...K

High-resolution

GCCHART *number of nonconformities are in*
C...C
MU = K
TEST K...K

All statistical process control charts also use the list of subcommands shown in the Stat ▶ SPC Charts ▶ Xbar... Session Command Syntax section.

The U Chart Dialog Box

The U... command displays a separate chart for Poisson counts per unit for each variable. See Stat ▶ SPC Charts ▶ Xbar... for an example of statistical process control charts.

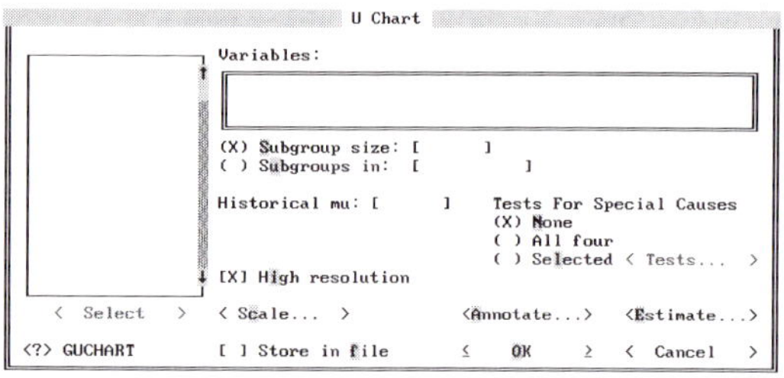

Options in the U Chart Dialog Box

Variables: Enter the variable(s) you are investigating. Each row corresponds to one sample that is assumed to have come from a Poisson distribution with mean μ. The variable(s) contain the number of nonconforming items in the sample. Minitab plots the average number of nonconformities per unit on the chart. If the sample sizes are not equal, the Poisson mean is different for each sample.

Subgroup size: You can specify the size of the sample, the parameter n, through a fixed subgroup size.

Subgroups in: Enter the column with different sample sizes here.

Historical mu: You can specify the mean of the Poisson distribution. Minitab uses this value to compute the center line, as well as upper and lower control limits.

High resolution: Minitab's default setting produces a high-resolution chart that appears in a separate graphic screen. You can select this checkbox to turn off the default; the chart then appears in the Session window in a character-based format.

Store in file: You can store the high-resolution chart in a file; Minitab gives the file the .PRI extension that indicates a printer file. It can take several minutes to store a high-resolution plot in a file, depending on your computer. The Store Graph in File dialog box resembles the File ▶ Open Worksheet dialog box. Refer to that command for more information.

Tests For Special Causes: Minitab can perform four tests for special causes to detect specific patterns in the data plotted on the chart that calls for further investigation. Subgroup sizes must be equal. When a point fails a test, Minitab marks it with the test number on the plot.

None: Minitab omits the tests for special causes.

All four: Minitab performs all four tests; see Minitab Help for a description.

Selected Tests: You can specify which of the four tests Minitab should perform from the U - Tests subdialog box.

Scale... and Annotate...: See Stat ▶ SPC Charts ▶ Xbar... for information on these commands.

The U Chart - Estimation of Mu and Sigma Subdialog Box

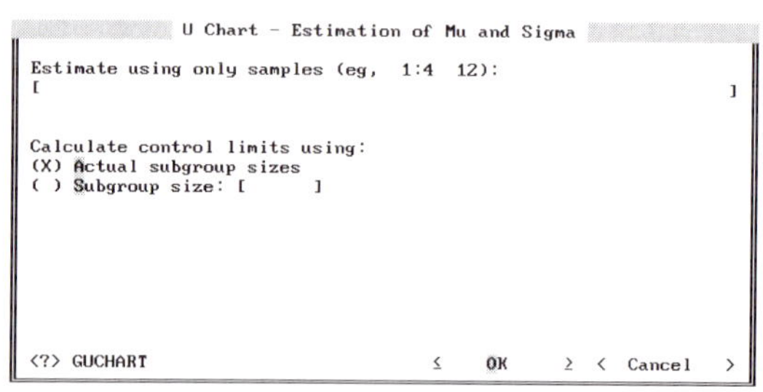

Estimate using only samples: By default, Minitab estimates the parameters using all samples, but you can use only specified subgroups of the data by listing individual sample numbers or a range of samples.

Calculate control limits using: You have two options for computing the control limits: actual subgroup size or specified subgroup size.

Actual subgroup sizes: This is the default setting; Minitab uses the subgroup sizes as given in the parent dialog box.

Subgroup size: If the sample sizes are unequal, set the sample size here to force straight control limits. This command will not affect the data plotted.

Session Command Syntax for U...

Character-based

UCHART *number of nonconformities are in*
C...C, *sample size* = **E**
MU = **K**
SUBGROUP *size is* **K**
TEST K...K

High-resolution

GUCHART *number of nonconformities are in*
C...C, *sample size* = **E**
MU = **K**
SUBGROUP *size is* **K**
TEST K...K

All statistical process control charts also use the list of subcommands shown in the Stat ► SPC Charts ► Xbar... Session Command Syntax section.

Time Series

The Time Series menu contains a list of commands that you can use to investigate the behavior of data collected over time. You can use Minitab to lag, difference, and plot a series, determine an appropriate model that describes the observed time series, and then use the model to predict or forecast future values of the series.

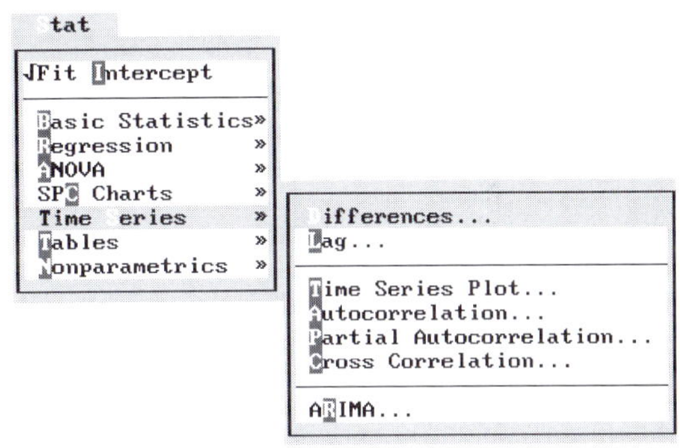

The Differences Dialog Box

The Differences... command computes differences between the elements of a column.

Options in the Differences Dialog Box

Series: Indicate the variable for which you want to compute differences.

Put differences in: Name or indicate the column to store the differences.

Lag: Minitab subtracts from each row the element K rows above, and stores the differences in a new column. The first K rows of the new column will contain asterisks. The default lag is 1.

Session Command Syntax for Differences...

DIFFERENCES [*with lag* **K**] *for data in* **C** *put into* **C**

Example: Using Differences...

The following dialog box and equivalent Session window commands compute differences of lag 2 for C1, which contains the numbers 1, 3, 8, 12, and 7.

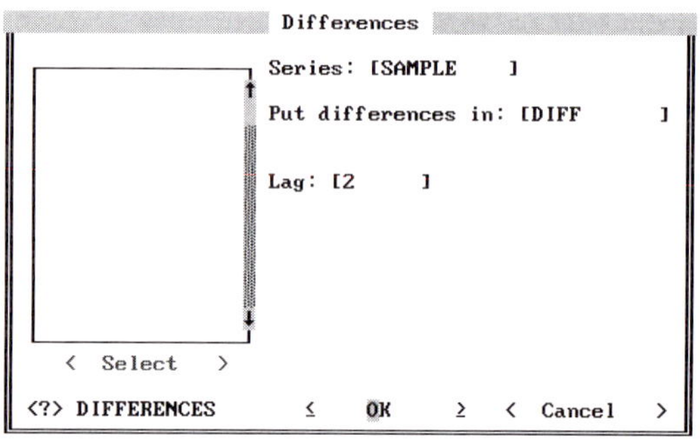


```
MTB > Name c2 = 'DIFF'
MTB > Differences 2 'SAMPLE' 'DIFF'.
```

These commands produce a new column, C2 DIFF, shown in the Data worksheet. Since the lag is 2, *'s are put in the first two rows of C2. Row 3 of C2 contains 7 (8–1), row 4 contains 9 (12–3), and row 5 contains –1 (7–8).

↓	C1 SAMPLE	C2 DIFF
1	1	*
2	3	*
3	8	7
4	12	9
5	7	-1
6		

See also Tutorial 13.

The Lag Dialog Box

The **Lag...** command moves numbers in a column down a specified number of rows.

Options in the Lag Dialog Box

Series: Indicate the variable you want to lag.

Put lags in: Name or indicate the storage column.

Lag: Minitab moves the row elements of a column down K rows, with 1 as the default, storing the result in a new column of the same length. There will be K missing value symbols (*) at the top of the output column. The output column has the same number of rows as the input column, so the last K values from the input column are not lagged.

Session Command Syntax for Lag...

LAG [*of length* **K**] *data in* **C** *put into* **C**

Example: Using Lag...

The following dialog box and equivalent Session window commands compute the lags of the following observations in C1 SAMPLE: 5, 3, 18, 7, 10, and 2, using a lag of 3 and stores the results in the next available column, naming the column LAGS.

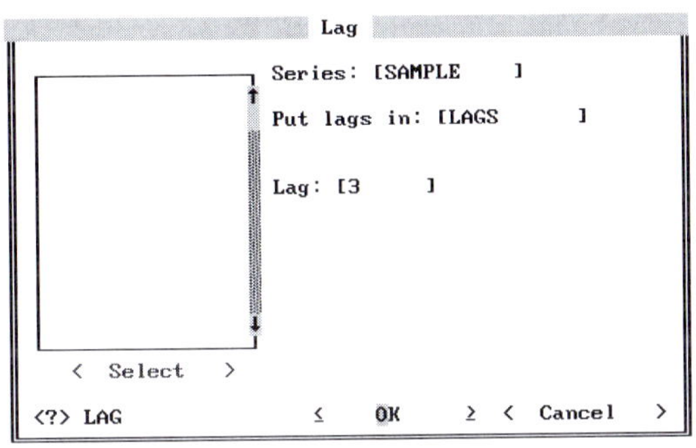


```
MTB > Name c2 = 'LAGS'
MTB > Lag 3 'SAMPLE' 'LAGS'.
```

These commands produce a new column, C2 LAGS, that contains the lagged values, shown in the Data worksheet.

↓	SAMPLE C1	LAGS C2
1	5	*
2	3	*
3	18	*
4	7	5
5	10	3
6	2	18

See also Tutorial 13.

The Time Series Plot Dialog Box

This command is covered in detail under Graph ▶ Time Series Plot... later in this chapter.

See also Tutorial 13.

The Autocorrelation Function Dialog Box

The **A**utocorrelation... command displays the plot of the autocorrelations for a time series.

Options in the Autocorrelation Function Dialog Box

Series: Indicate the variable you want to investigate.

Default number of lags: If you don't specify K, Minitab sets K = $\sqrt{n} + 10$, where n is the number of observations in the series. Minitab computes the autocorrelation of the time series for time lags varying from 1 to K.

Number of lags: Specify the number of lags.

Store ACF: Store the autocorrelation values in a new column if you want; Minitab chooses the next available column if you enter a name that does not correspond to an existing one.

Session Command Syntax for Autocorrelation...

ACF [*up to* **K** *lags*] *for data in* **C** [*put into* **C**]

Example: Using Autocorrelation...

The following dialog box and equivalent Session window commands compute the autocorrelations for observations of river temperatures (stored in C2 TEMP) taken upstream from a power plant over a period of time with a 24-hour lag, using the RIVER2.MTW data set from Tutorial 13.

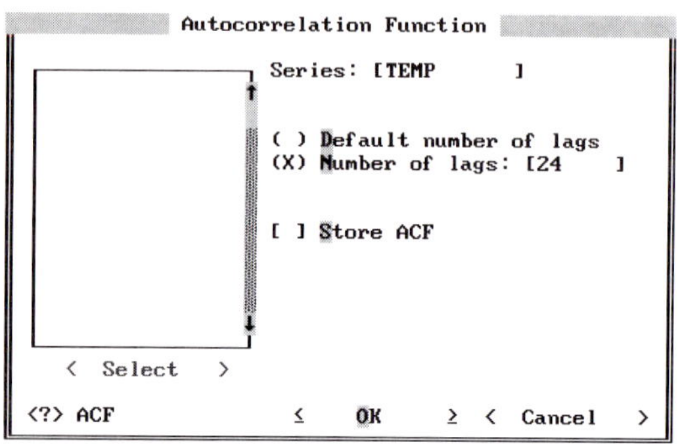


```
MTB > ACF 24 'TEMP'.
```

These commands produce the following autocorrelation plot in the Session window (only the first 20 rows are shown in this figure):

```
            -1.0 -0.8 -0.6 -0.4 -0.2  0.0  0.2  0.4  0.6  0.8  1.0
              +----+----+----+----+----+----+----+----+----+----+
  1   0.843                              XXXXXXXXXXXXXXXXXXXXXX
  2   0.703                              XXXXXXXXXXXXXXXXXXX
  3   0.550                              XXXXXXXXXXXXXXX
  4   0.380                              XXXXXXXXXX
  5   0.231                              XXXXXXX
  6   0.079                              XXX
  7  -0.067                            XXX
  8  -0.187                       XXXXXX
  9  -0.265                     XXXXXXXX
 10  -0.352                   XXXXXXXXXX
 11  -0.379                   XXXXXXXXXX
 12  -0.380                   XXXXXXXXXX
 13  -0.361                   XXXXXXXXXX
 14  -0.292                     XXXXXXXX
 15  -0.212                       XXXXXX
 16  -0.126                         XXXX
 17  -0.013                            X
 18   0.056                            XX
 19   0.112                            XXXX
 20   0.205                            XXXXXX
```

See also Tutorial 13.

The Partial Autocorrelation Function Dialog Box

The Partial Autocorrelation... command displays a plot of the partial autocorrelations for a time series.

Options in the Partial Autocorrelation Function Dialog Box

Series: Indicate the variable you want to investigate.

Default number of lags: If you don't specify K, Minitab sets $K = \sqrt{n} + 10$, where n is the number of observations in the series. Minitab computes the partial autocorrelation of the time series for time lags varying from 1 to K.

Number of lags: Specify the number of lags.

Store PACF: Store the PACF (partial autocorrelation function) values in a new column if you want; Minitab chooses the next available column, if you enter a name that does not correspond to an existing column.

Session Command Syntax for Partial Autocorrelation...

PACF [*up to* **K** *lags*] *for data in* **C** [*put into* **C**]

Example: Using Partial Autocorrelation...

The following dialog box and equivalent Session window commands compute the partial autocorrelations for observations of river temperatures (stored in C2 TEMP) taken upstream from a power plant over a period of time with a 24-hour lag, using the RIVER2.MTW data set from Tutorial 13.

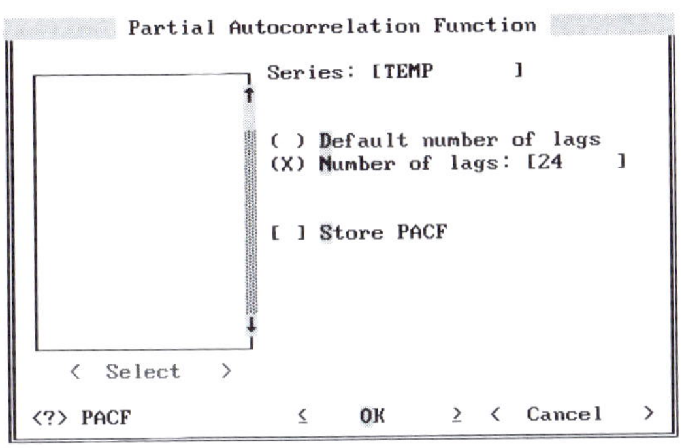


```
MTB > PACF 24 'TEMP'.
```

These commands produce the following display in the Session window (only the first 20 rows are shown in the figure):

```
           -1.0 -0.8 -0.6 -0.4 -0.2  0.0  0.2  0.4  0.6  0.8  1.0
             +----+----+----+----+----+----+----+----+----+----+
 1   0.843                            XXXXXXXXXXXXXXXXXXXXXX
 2  -0.023                           XX
 3  -0.128                         XXXX
 4  -0.161                        XXXXX
 5  -0.052                           XX
 6  -0.123                         XXXX
 7  -0.118                         XXXX
 8  -0.068                          XXX
 9   0.018                            X
10  -0.157                        XXXXX
11   0.049                            XX
12   0.004                            X
13  -0.009                            X
14   0.079                            XXX
15   0.042                            XX
16   0.010                            X
17   0.102                            XXXX
18  -0.102                         XXXX
19  -0.009                            X
20   0.166                            XXXXX
```

See also Tutorial 13.

The Cross Correlation Function Dialog Box

The **C**ross Correlation... command displays a plot of the the cross correlations between two time series.

Options in the Cross Correlation Function Dialog Box

First series: Indicate the first time series.

Second series: Indicate the second time series.

Default number of lags: If you don't specify K, Minitab sets K = $\sqrt{n}$ + 10, where n is the number of observations in the series. Minitab computes and graphs the cross correlations between two time series for time lags varying from –K to K.

Number of lags: You can specify the number of lags.

Session Command Syntax for Cross Correlation...

CCF [*up to* **K** *lags*] *between data in* **C** *and* **C**

Example: Using Cross Correlation...

The following dialog box and equivalent Session window commands cross correlate river temperatures (stored in C2 TEMP) taken hourly upstream from a power plant with the pH value of the water (stored in C3 PH), using the RIVER2.MTW data set from Tutorial 13.

```
                Cross Correlation Function
 ┌──────────────┐ First series:  [TEMP       ]
 │              ↑
 │              │ Second series: [PH         ]
 │              │
 │              │ ( ) Default number of lags
 │              │ (X) Number of lags: [24     ]
 │              │
 │              ↓
 └──────────────┘
    < Select >

 <?> CCF               <  OK  >  < Cancel >
```

```
MTB > CCF 24 'TEMP' 'PH'.
```

These commands produce the following display in the Session window (only a portion of the output is displayed):

```
          -1.0 -0.8 -0.6 -0.4 -0.2  0.0  0.2  0.4  0.6  0.8  1.0
            +----+----+----+----+----+----+----+----+----+----+
-24   0.381                          XXXXXXXXXXX
-23   0.331                          XXXXXXXXX
-22   0.231                          XXXXXXX
-21   0.093                          XXX
-20  -0.053                         XX
-19  -0.201                     XXXXXX
-18  -0.303                  XXXXXXXXX
-17  -0.392                XXXXXXXXXXX
-16  -0.489              XXXXXXXXXXXXX
-15  -0.555            XXXXXXXXXXXXXXX
-14  -0.590           XXXXXXXXXXXXXXXX
-13  -0.585           XXXXXXXXXXXXXXXX
-12  -0.539             XXXXXXXXXXXXXX
-11  -0.473              XXXXXXXXXXXXX
-10  -0.377                 XXXXXXXXXX
 -9  -0.229                    XXXXXXX
 -8  -0.076                        XXX
 -7   0.071                          XXX
 -6   0.242                          XXXXXXX
 -5   0.374                          XXXXXXXXXX
```

The ARIMA Dialog Box

The ARIMA... (autoregressive integrated moving average) command fits seasonal or nonseasonal models to a time series and lets you predict future values.

Options in the ARIMA Dialog Box

Series: Indicate the time series data you want to fit.

Seasonality: You can define the number of units in a complete cycle; the default is 12. The seasonal model uses three parameters designated P, D, and Q.

Autoregressive: Give the order of the autoregressive (AR) component (p). Specify the order of the seasonal component (P) in the second text box.

Differencing: Give the number of differences (d) used to discount trends over time. There must be at least three data points left after differencing. Specify the number of differences for the seasonal component (D) in the second text box.

Moving average: Give the order of the moving average (MA) component (q). Specify the order of the seasonal component (Q) in the second text box.

There are a number of specifications you must observe:

1. At least one of the p/P or q/Q parameters must be non-zero, and none may exceed five.

2. The maximum number of parameters to be estimated is ten.

3. There must be at least three data points left after differencing. That is, S*D + d + 2 must be less than the number of points, where S is the length of a season.

4. The maximum "back order" for the model is 100. In practice, this condition is always satisfied if S*D + d + p + P + q + Q is at most 100.
5. The ARIMA model normally includes a constant term only if there is no differencing (that is, d = D = 0).
6. Missing observations are only allowed at the beginning or the end of a series, not in the middle.
7. The seasonal component of this model is multiplicative, and thus is appropriate when the amount of cyclical variation is proportional to the mean.

Storage: You can store the following values in the worksheet for further analysis:

Residuals: Minitab stores residuals in the next available column.

Fits: Minitab stores fits in the next available column.

Coefficients: Minitab stores estimated coefficients in the next available column.

Fit intercept: By default, Minitab includes a constant term in the ARIMA model.

Starting values in: You can specify the initial parameter values, entering them in the order that the parameters appear on the output: p (AR values), P (seasonal AR values), q (MA values), Q (seasonal MA values), and then (optionally) the constant. The default starting value for all coefficients is 0.1.

The ARIMA - Forecasts Subdialog Box

The Forecasts... command requests Minitab to predict future values for the time series. Results may be stored in the worksheet for future use.

Leads: Specify the number of forecasts you want Minitab to generate.

Origin: The default origin is the end of the series (that is, the forecasts are for the future). You can specify a different origin if you want.

Forecasts: Name a location and Minitab stores forecasted values; store the forecasts if you want to plot them.

Lower limits: Name a location and Minitab stores the lower confidence limits for the forecasts.

Upper limits: Name a location and Minitab stores the upper confidence limits for the forecasts.

Session Command Syntax for ARIMA...

ARIMA *p* = **K** *d* = **K** *q* = **K** [*P* = **K** *D* = **K** *Q* = **K**
 S = **K**] *for data in* **C** [*put residuals into* **C**
 [*predicted values into* **C** [*coefficients into*
 C]]]
 CONSTANT
 NOCONSTANT
 STARTING *values in* **C**
 FORECAST [*Origin* = **K**] *up to* **K** *leads* [*store*
 forecasts in **C** [*confidence limits in* **C C**]]
BRIEF *output code* **K**

BRIEF controls the amount of output produced by the ARIMA command; it is not available as a menu command. K is an integer from 0 to 4. BRIEF 2 is the default output. The levels of output are as follows:

K = 0 Minitab prints nothing but stores all requested output.

K = 1 Minitab prints the table of final estimates, differencing information, residual sum of squares, and number of observations.

K = 2 In addition, Minitab prints the table of estimates at each iteration. If back forecasts are not dying out rapidly, Minitab also prints them.

K = 3 In addition, Minitab prints the correlation matrix of the estimated parameters.

K = 4 Minitab prints the back forecasts regardless of status.

Example: Using ARIMA...

The following dialog boxes and equivalent Session window commands fit an ARIMA model for observations of river temperatures (stored in C2 TEMP) taken upstream from a power plant over a period of time, and predict temperatures for the next six hours, storing the forecasts and prediction limits. The data are stored in RIVER2.MTW from Tutorial 13.

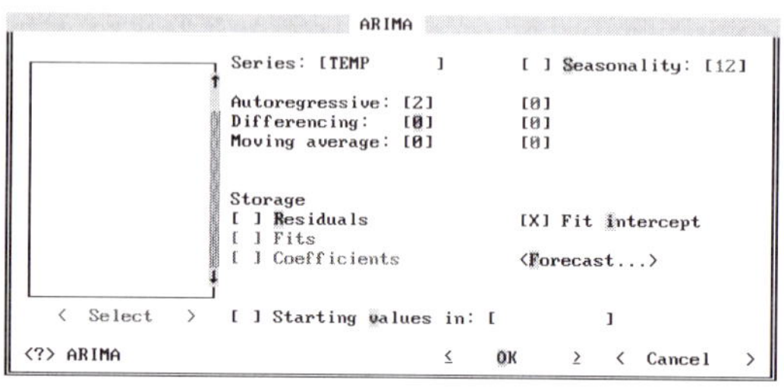

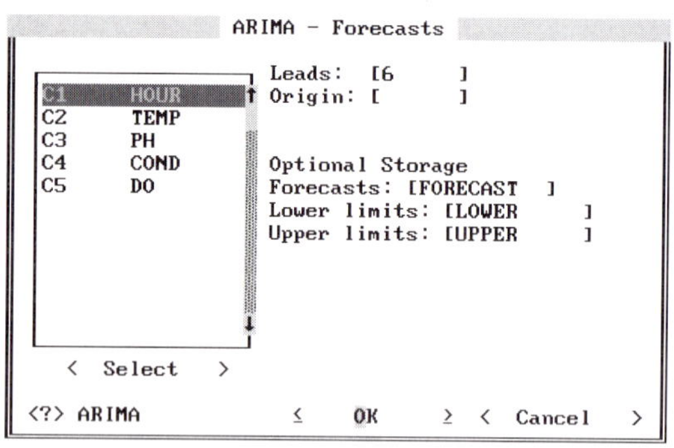


```
MTB > Name c6 = 'FORECAST' c7 = 'LOWER' c8 = 'UPPER'
MTB > ARIMA 2 0 0 'TEMP';
SUBC>   Constant;
SUBC>   Forecast 6 'FORECAST' 'LOWER' 'UPPER'.
```

These commands produce the following display in the Session window (only a portion of the output is shown):

```
Constant     4.07464       0.07452      54.68
Mean        31.5973        0.5779

No. of obs.:  95
Residuals:    SS =  47.1021  (backforecasts excluded)
              MS =   0.5120  DF = 92

Modified Box-Pierce chisquare statistic
Lag                 12              24              36              48
Chisquare     10.7(DF=10)     33.3(DF=22)     58.3(DF=34)     78.9(DF=46)

Forecasts from period 95
                                  95 Percent Limits
Period       Forecast          Lower          Upper          Actual
  96          30.0795         28.6768        31.4822
  97          30.2829         28.3901        32.1757
  98          30.4595         28.2691        32.6499
  99          30.6124         28.2231        33.0017
 100          30.7448         28.2167        33.2728
 101          30.8593         28.2321        33.4865
```

See also Tutorial 13.

Tables

The Tables menu lists the commands Minitab provides to analyze categorical data.

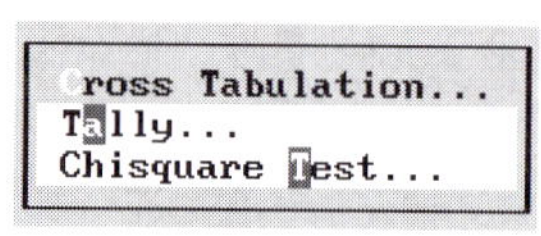

The Cross Tabulation Dialog Box

The Cross Tabulation... command produces one-way or multi-way contingency tables and tables of statistics for associated variables. With the Cross Tabulation... menu commands, you can only obtain summary statistics (MEANS, MEDIANS, etc.) for the same set of associated variables; for summary statistics of a specific column, use the Session window TABLE command and specify the desired column(s) in the subcommand.

Options in the Cross Tabulation Dialog Box

Classification variables: The values in the first column that you list determine the row headings of the table, and the values in the second column determine the column headings. Minitab produces a separate table for every possible combination of values from the remaining columns. All columns used must contain integers between –10000 and +10000 or the missing value symbol (*). The maximum number of classification variables is 10.

Display: You can request that Minitab display certain summary values in each cell of the contingency table.

Counts: Minitab prints the total number of values (missing and nonmissing) for each cell and for the margins.

Row percents: Minitab displays the percentage each cell represents of the total observations in the row.

Column percents: Minitab displays the percentage each cell represents of the total observations in the column.

Total percents: Minitab displays the percentage each cell represents of all the observations in the table.

Chisquare analysis: Minitab prints the chi-square statistic, used to test the independence of the row and column variables in a two-way table, together with its associated degrees of freedom. By default, Minitab prints the observed count for each cell. If you want more information, you must execute this command in the Session window. The following data are printed in each cell, depending on the value of the Chisquare subcommand output code K (its default is 1):

K = 1 Observed count for each cell.
K = 2 Observed and expected counts for each cell.
K = 3 Observed counts, expected counts, and the standardized residuals for each cell, which Minitab computes as (observed count – expected count) divided by the square root of the expected count.

Frequencies are in: The Cross Tabulation... command normally assumes that each row in the first column you list refers to one case. Sometimes you may find it necessary to combine the raw-data values into partial or full-frequency counts. Check this box to tell Minitab where to find the frequencies (or weights) for each row.

The Cross Tabulation Summaries Subdialog Box

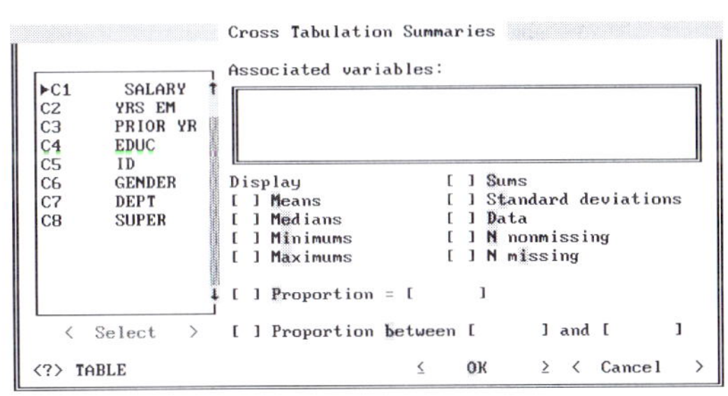

The Cross Tabulation Summaries... command can also be used to obtain summary statistics on a continuous variable for each cell. For example, it can obtain cell means and standard deviations in ANOVA settings.

Associated variables: Specify the continuous variable(s) to be summarized.

Display: Minitab displays any combination of the following column summaries that you check: Means, Medians, Minimums, Maximums, Sums, Standard deviations, Data, N nonmissing, or N missing.

Proportion =: Minitab prints the proportion of observations with a specified value for each cell and for the margins. There should not be any missing value symbols (*) in columns listed with this subcommand.

Proportion between — and —: Minitab prints the proportion of observations for a range of values for each cell and for the margins. There should not be any missing value symbols (*) in columns listed with this subcommand.

The Cross Tabulation Options Subdialog Box

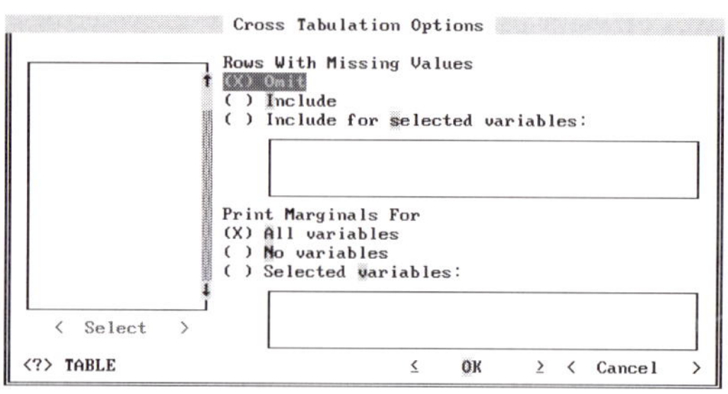

Rows With Missing Values: Minitab adds a row or column labeled MISSING to the display. This row or column contains counts of the missing observations in each cell for any variables that have missing values.

Omit: By default, Minitab omits this option.

Include: If you can select this option, Minitab includes missing value summaries for all variables.

Include for selected variables: Select this option to have Minitab include missing value summaries for the indicator variable(s).

Print Marginals For: Minitab displays the row and column marginal statistics for the designated classification variables.

All variables: By default, Minitab displays marginal statistics for all classification variables.

No variables: You can instruct Minitab not to display the statistics for any classification variables.

Selected variables: You can select the classification variables for which Minitab will display marginal statistics.

Session Command Syntax for Cross Tabulation...

TABLE *the classification variables in* **C...C**
MEANS *for* **C...C**
MEDIANS *for* **C...C**
SUMS *for* **C...C**
MINIMUMS *for* **C...C**
MAXIMUMS *for* **C...C**
STDEV *for* **C...C**
STATS *for* **C...C**
DATA *for* **C...C**
N *for* **C...C**
NMISS *for* **C...C**
PROPORTION *of cases* = **K** [*through* **K**] *in* **C...C**
COUNTS
ROWPERCENTS
COLPERCENTS
TOTPERCENTS
CHISQUARE *analysis* [*output code* = **K**]
MISSING *level for the classification variable* **C...C**
NOALL *in margins*
ALL *for the classification variables* **C...C**
FREQUENCIES *are in* **C**

Example: Using Cross Tabulation...

The following dialog box and equivalent Session window commands produce a contingency table for the coded salary value (C9 SALCODE) and the department (C7 DEPT) in which an employee works at Technitron Co., using the TECH.MTW data set that you modified in Tutorial 10.

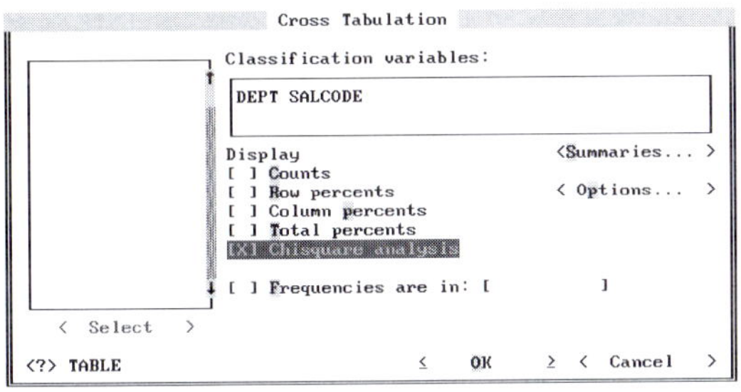


```
MTB > Table 'DEPT' 'SALCODE';
SUBC>   ChiSquare.
```

These commands produce the following contingency table and chi-square test in the Session window:

```
 ROWS: DEPT      COLUMNS: SALCODE

             1         2         3       ALL

  1          6         4         0        10
  2          2         5         1         8
  3          2         2         3         7
  4          6         7         8        21
 ALL        16        18        12        46

CHI-SQUARE =     8.947    WITH D.F. =     6

  CELL CONTENTS --
                    COUNT
```

See also Tutorial 10.

The Tally Dialog Box

The Tally... command tallies information for each variable you list.

Options in the Tally Dialog Box

Variables: Indicate which variables you want Minitab to tally. They must represent classification variables (such as gender, group number, or year) and contain only integers between –9999 and +9999 or missing value symbols (*).

Display: Minitab can display summary values for each distinct value in the column.

Counts: Minitab displays the number of times each distinct value occurs in the columns listed. This is the default.

Percents: Minitab displays the relative frequency of each nonmissing value in the columns listed.

Cumulative counts: Minitab displays cumulative counts of the nonmissing values in each column listed.

Cumulative percents: Minitab displays cumulative relative frequencies of the nonmissing values in each column listed.

Session Command Syntax for Tally...

TALLY *the data in* C...C
  COUNTS
  PERCENTS
  CUMCOUNTS *cumulative counts*
  CUMPERCENTS *cumulative percentages*
  ALL *four statistics above*

Example: Using Tally...

The following dialog box and equivalent Session window commands tally the number of peas (stored in C3 PHENO) occurring in each of the four phenotypes predicted by Mendel. These peas, however, were grown in carbon-dioxide–deficient soil. The data are stored in GENETICS.MTW from Tutorial 10.

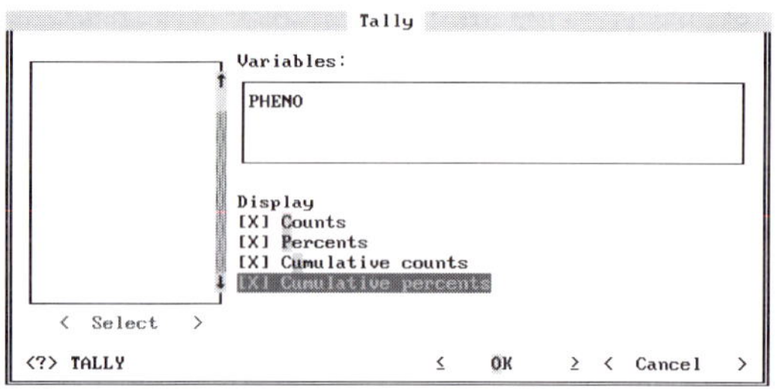


```
MTB > Tally 'PHENO';
SUBC>   Counts;
SUBC>   Percents;
SUBC>   CumCounts;
SUBC>   CumPercents.
```

These commands produce the following tally table in the Session window:

PHENO	COUNT	PERCENT	CUMCNT	CUMPCT
1	94	47.00	94	47.00
2	50	25.00	144	72.00
3	44	22.00	188	94.00
4	12	6.00	200	100.00
N=	200			

See also Tutorials 4 and 10.

The Chisquare Test Dialog Box

The Chisquare Test... command does a chi-square test of association for the table of counts given in the columns you indicate.

Minitab prints a table of observed values and expected values, the total chi-square statistic as the sum of its components from each cell of the table, and the number of degrees of freedom. Minitab also lists the number of cells with small expected frequencies (less than five), if any.

Options in the Chisquare Test Dialog Box

Columns containing the table: You may specify up to seven columns; they must contain integer values.

Session Command Syntax for Chisquare Test...

CHISQUARE *analysis of the table in* **C...C**

Example: Using Chisquare Test...

The following dialog box and equivalent Session window commands perform a chi-square test on data containing tallied ratings of transistor quality, stored in C2 MON–C6 FRI, using the TRANS.MTW data set from Tutorial 10.

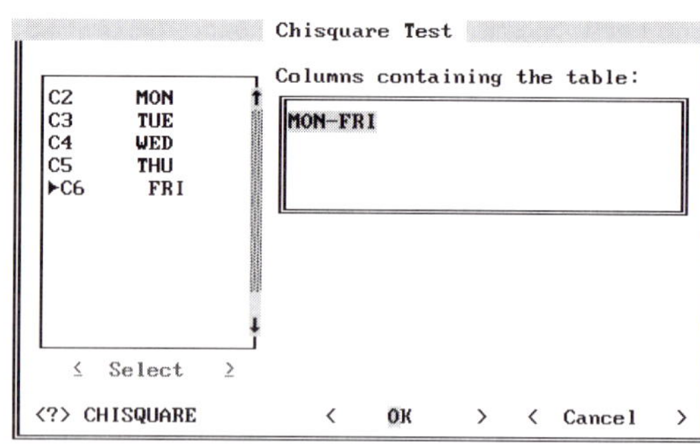


```
MTB > ChiSquare 'MON'-'FRI'.
```

These commands produce the following display in the Session window:

```
Expected counts are printed below observed counts

          MON      TUE      WED      THU      FRI    Total
  1        44       74       79       72       31      300
        47.65    69.41    77.06    68.24    37.65

  2        25       19       27       21       12      104
        16.52    24.06    26.71    23.65    13.05

  3        12       25       25       23       21      106
        16.84    24.53    27.23    24.11    13.30

Total      81      118      131      116       64      510

ChiSq =  0.279 +  0.303 +  0.049 +  0.208 +  1.174 +
         4.356 +  1.065 +  0.003 +  0.298 +  0.085 +
         1.389 +  0.009 +  0.182 +  0.051 +  4.455 = 13.906
df = 8
```

See also Tutorial 10.

Nonparametrics

The **N**onparametrics menu allows you to analyze data from populations that are not necessarily normally distributed.

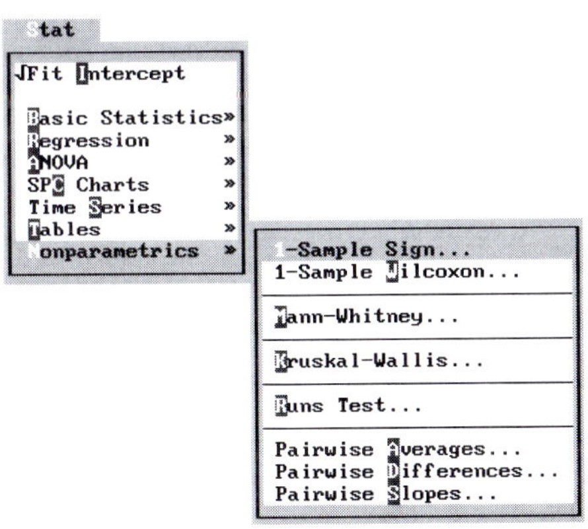

The 1-Sample Sign Dialog Box

The **1**-Sample Sign... command computes a nonparametric sign test for the median for one or more columns or a sign confidence interval for the median.

Options in the 1-Sample Sign Dialog Box

Variables: Indicate the variable(s) you want Minitab to use.

Confidence interval, level: Minitab calculates three confidence intervals for the median for each column listed: one with confidence just above K, one with confidence just below K, and a middle interval which approximates K using nonlinear interpolation. By default, K = 95%.

Test median =: Minitab performs a sign-test, using the null value you specify.

Alternative: Use this pop-up menu to indicate whether you want Minitab to compute a less than (lower-tailed), not equal to (two-tailed), or greater than (upper-tailed) test (one-sided or two-sided). A two-tailed test is the default.

Session Command Syntax for 1-Sample Sign...

STEST [*median* = **K**] *on data in* **C...C**
  ALTERNATIVE = **K** (Specify K as –1 (lower-tailed), 0 (two-tailed), or +1 (upper-tailed).)
SINTERVAL [*confidence* = **K**] *on data in* **C...C**

When you use the ALTERNATIVE subcommand, indicate the lower-tailed test by –1 and the upper-tailed test by +1.

Example: Using 1-Sample Sign...

The following dialog box and equivalent Session window commands obtain a confidence interval for the median TV viewing time of husbands (stored in C1 HUSBAND), using the TVVIEW.MTW data set from Tutorial 11.

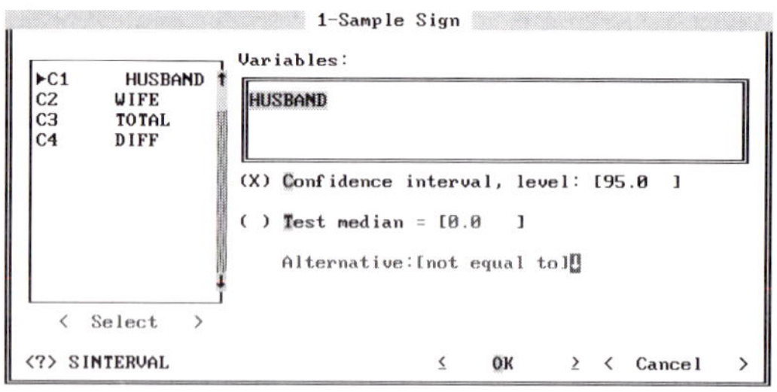


```
MTB > SInterval 95.0 'HUSBAND'.
```

These commands produce the following display in the Session window:

```
SIGN CONFIDENCE INTERVAL FOR MEDIAN

                              ACHIEVED
             N    MEDIAN    CONFIDENCE     CONFIDENCE INTERVAL    POSITION
HUSBAND     10     32.00      0.8906       (   27.00,    38.00)          3
                              0.9500       (   24.95,    39.71)        NLI
                              0.9785       (   21.00,    43.00)          2
```

The 1-Sample Wilcoxon Dialog Box

The 1-Sample **W**ilcoxon... command performs either a one-sample Wilcoxon test of the median or a Wilcoxon confidence interval for the median. This command is the nonparametric equivalent to the 1-Sample t... command.

Options in the 1-Sample Wilcoxon Dialog Box

Variables: Indicate the variable(s) you want to use. Minitab assumes that each column of data is a random sample from a continuous, symmetric population.

Confidence interval, level: By default, Minitab calculates an approximate 95% confidence interval; you can specify another level of confidence.

Test median: Minitab performs a one- or two-sided test, using an hypothesized median value of zero or one that you specify.

Alternative: Use this pop-up menu to indicate whether you want Minitab to compute a less than (lower-tailed), not equal to (two-tailed), or greater than (upper-tailed) test (one-sided or two-sided).

Session Command Syntax for 1-Sample Wilcoxon...

WTEST [*of median* **K**] *on the data in* **C...C**
  ALTERNATIVE = **K** (Specify K as –1 (lower-tailed), 0 (two-tailed), or +1 (upper-tailed).)
WINTERVAL [**K**% *confidence*] *for data in* **C...C**

Example: Using 1-Sample Wilcoxon...

The following dialog box and equivalent Session window commands test whether median daily sales in 1991 (stored in C1 1991) have fallen from their previous levels of $4,000 per day, using the SALES.MTW data set from Tutorial 11.

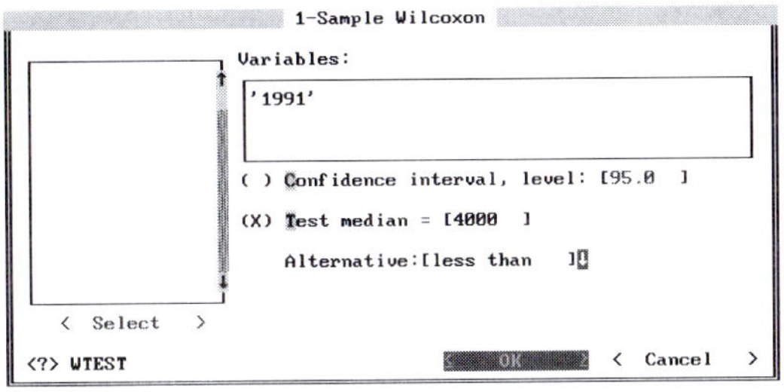


```
MTB > WTest 4000 '1991';
SUBC>   Alternative -1.
```

These commands produce the following display in the Session window:

```
TEST OF MEDIAN = 4000 VERSUS MEDIAN L.T. 4000

                 N FOR   WILCOXON             ESTIMATED
            N    TEST   STATISTIC   P-VALUE      MEDIAN
1991        7       7         1.0     0.017        2112
```

See also Tutorial 11.

The Mann-Whitney Dialog Box

The Mann-Whitney... command performs a two-sample rank test for the difference between two population medians, and calculates corresponding point and confidence interval estimates. It is sometimes called the two-sample Wilcoxon rank sum test.

Options in the Mann-Whitney Dialog Box

First Sample: Indicate the first variable.

Second Sample: Indicate the second variable.

Confidence level: Minitab uses a 95% confidence interval level by default. The attained level of confidence will be as close as possible to the requested level.

Alternative: Use this pop-up menu to indicate whether you want Minitab to compute a less than (lower-tailed), not equal to (two-tailed), or greater than (upper-tailed) test (one-sided or two-sided).

Session Command Syntax for Mann-Whitney...

MANN-WHITNEY [*alternative* **K**] [**K**% *confidence*] *for the data in* **C** *and* **C**
  ALTERNATIVE = **K** (Specify K as –1 (lower-tailed), 0 (two-tailed), or +1 (upper-tailed).)

Example: Using Mann-Whitney...

The following dialog box and equivalent Session window commands test whether banking industry profits for 1991 (stored in C1 1991) have changed from 1990 (stored in C2 1990), using the BANKING.MTW data set from Tutorial 11.

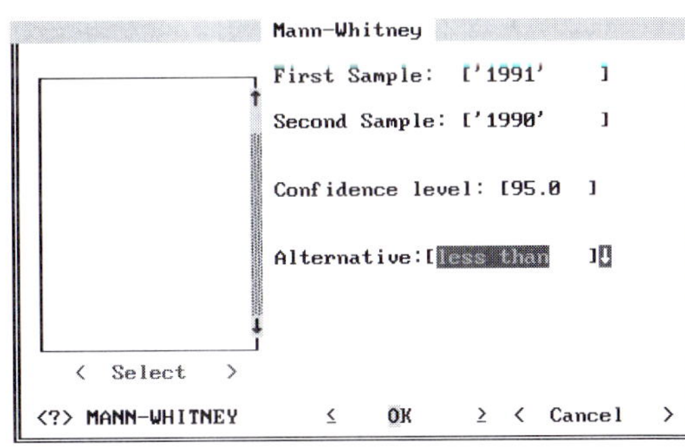


```
MTB > Mann-Whitney 95.0 '1991' '1990';
SUBC>   Alternative -1.
```

These commands produce the following display in the Session window:

```
Mann-Whitney Confidence Interval and Test

1991        N =  10      Median =        309.5
1990        N =  10      Median =        343.0
Point estimate for ETA1-ETA2 is          -24.0
95.5 pct c.i. for ETA1-ETA2 is (-184.1,109.8)
W = 99.0
Test of ETA1 = ETA2  vs.  ETA1 l.t. ETA2 is significant at 0.3388
The test is significant at 0.3387 (adjusted for ties)

Cannot reject at alpha = 0.05
```

See also Tutorial 11.

The Kruskal-Wallis Dialog Box

The **Kruskal-Wallis...** command is a nonparametric test for differences among several population medians. It extends the Mann-Whitney test to any number of groups, and represents a nonparametric alternative to the one-way analysis of variance.

Options in the Kruskal-Wallis Dialog Box

Response: This column contains data from all the samples.

Factor: This column identifies the group (an integer from –10,000 to +10,000) of the data in the Response column.

Session Command Syntax for Kruskal-Wallis...

KRUSKAL-WALLIS *test for data in* **C** *groups in* **C**

Example: Using Kruskal-Wallis...

The following dialog box and equivalent Session window commands test whether there is a difference among the diameters of the wires (stored in C1 DIAMETER) produced in three different production shifts (stored in C2 SHIFT), using the FLXBLT11.MTW data set from Tutorial 11.

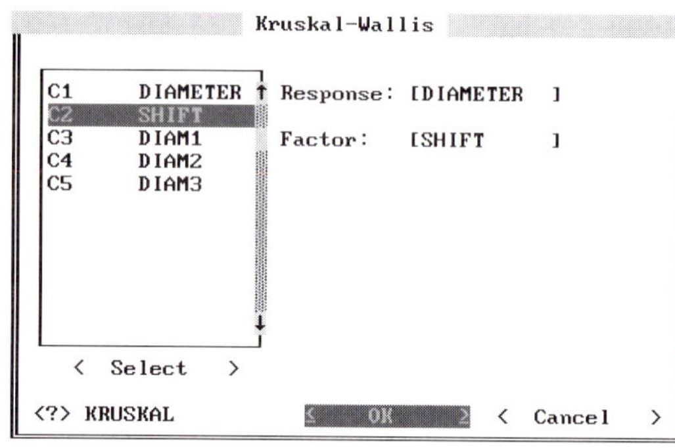


```
MTB > Kruskal-Wallis 'DIAMETER' 'SHIFT'.
```

These commands produce the following display in the Session window:

```
LEVEL      NOBS     MEDIAN  AVE. RANK   Z VALUE
    1         9      74.00        9.3     -0.18
    2         6      66.50        6.7     -1.59
    3         3      84.00       15.8      2.25
OVERALL      18                   9.5

H = 5.93  d.f. = 2  p = 0.052
H = 5.95  d.f. = 2  p = 0.052 (adj. for ties)

* NOTE  * One or more small samples
```

See also Tutorial 11.

The Runs Test Dialog Box

The **R**uns Test... command performs a two-sided runs test to determine if the selection process is random. A run is a series of one or more observations in a row that are greater than a given number, or one or more observations in a row that are less than or equal to that number.

Options in the Runs Test Dialog Box

Variables: Indicate the variable(s) you want to test.

Above and below the mean: By default, Minitab uses the mean to determine the number of runs.

Ab**o**ve and below: Specify the value that Minitab should use to determine runs.

Session Command Syntax for Runs Test...

RUNS *test [above and below* **K**] *for data in* **C...C**

Example: Using Runs Test...

The following dialog box and equivalent Session window commands will determine whether blood clotting data were collected in random order, using C1 BEFORE from the Tutorial 11 CLTNGT11.MTW data set.

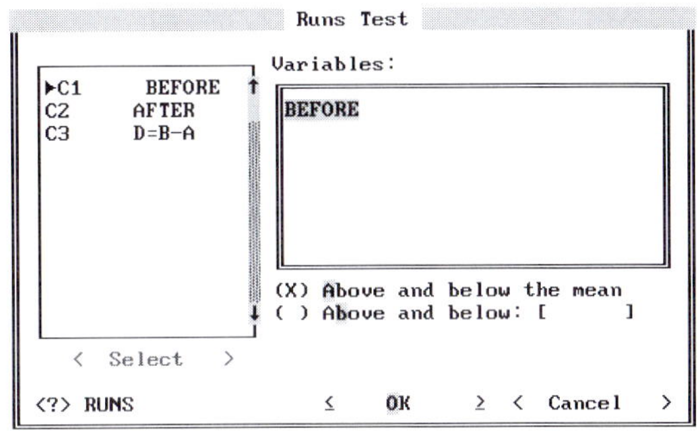


```
MTB > Runs 'BEFORE'.
```

These commands produce the following display in the Session window:

```
 BEFORE

 K =     11.8917

 THE OBSERVED NO. OF RUNS =    2
 THE EXPECTED NO. OF RUNS =    7.0000
  6 OBSERVATIONS ABOVE K     6 BELOW
* N SMALL--FOLLOWING APPROX. MAY BE INVALID
            THE TEST IS SIGNIFICANT AT  0.0025
```

See also Tutorial 11.

The Pairwise Averages Dialog Box

The Pairwise **A**verages... command calculates the averages of all pairs of values in a column, including the average of each value with itself. For n data values, Minitab stores n (n + 1) / 2 pairwise (or Walsh) averages.

Options in the Pairwise Averages Dialog Box

Averages for: Indicate the column for which you want to obtain averages.

Put in: Name or indicate the storage location.

Put indices in: Name two locations and Minitab also stores the indices i and j for each average $(x_i + x_j) / 2$.

Session Command Syntax for Pairwise Averages...

WALSH *averages for* **C** *put into* **C** [*put indices into* **C** *and* **C**]

Example: Using Pairwise Averages...

The following dialog box and equivalent Session window commands obtain Walsh averages for C1, which contains the values 1, 2, and 3.

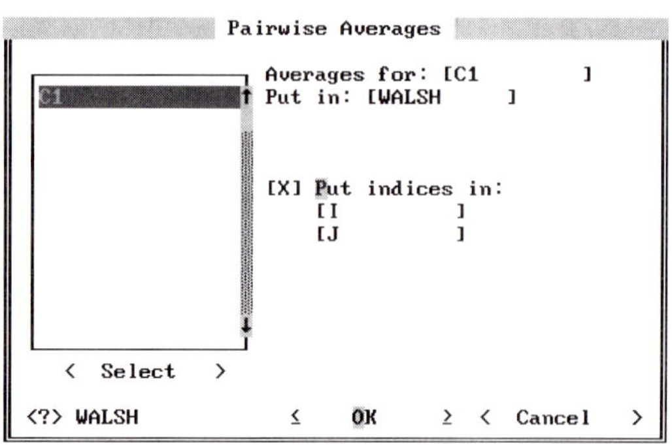


```
MTB > Name c2 = 'WALSH' c3 = 'I' c4 = 'J'
MTB > Walsh C1 'WALSH' 'I' 'J'.
```

These commands produce the following columns in the Data worksheet:

		WALSH	I	J
→	C1	C2	C3	C4
1	1	1.0	1	1
2	2	1.5	1	2
3	3	2.0	2	2
4		2.0	1	3
5		2.5	2	3
6		3.0	3	3

The Pairwise Differences Dialog Box

The Pairwise Differences... command computes all possible differences between pairs of elements from two columns. It uses the form $x_i - y_j$ where x_i is a value from the first column and y_j is a value from the second.

Options in the Pairwise Differences Dialog Box

First variable: Indicate the first variable.

Second variable: Indicate the second variable.

Put differences in: Name or indicate the storage location.

Put indices in: If you name or indicate two more locations, Minitab stores the row numbers i and j used for each difference.

Session Command Syntax for Pairwise Differences...

WDIFF *for* **C** *and* **C** *put into* **C** [*put indices in* **C** *and* **C**]

Example: Using Pairwise Differences...

The following dialog box and equivalent Session window commands obtain pairwise differences for C1 (which contains the values 1, 2, and 3) and C2 (which contains the values 10, 12, and 13).

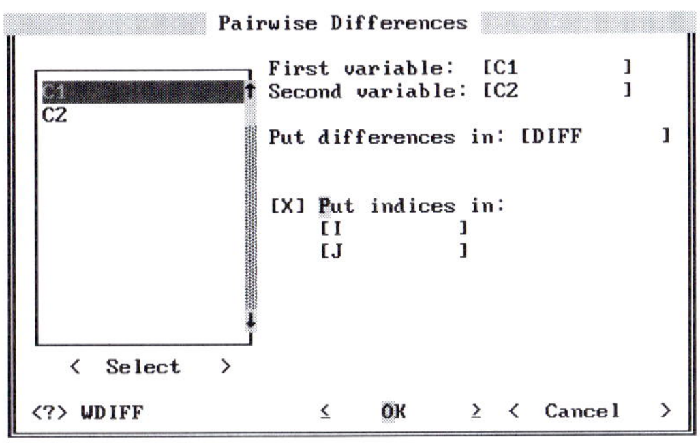


```
MTB > Name c3 = 'DIFF' c4 = 'I' c5 = 'J'
MTB > WDifferences C1 C2 'DIFF' 'I' 'J'.
```

These commands produce the following columns in the Data worksheet:

↓	C1	C2	DIFF C3	I C4	J C5
1	1	10	-9	1	1
2	2	12	-11	1	2
3	3	13	-12	1	3
4			-8	2	1
5			-10	2	2
6			-11	2	3
7			-7	3	1
8			-9	3	2
9			-10	3	3

The Pairwise Slopes Dialog Box

The Pairwise Slopes... command computes slopes for all pairs of rows from two columns of equal length. There pairwise slopes can be used to find robust estimates of the slope of a line through the data from two columns. There will be n(n – 1) / 2 slopes. If any observations are missing or the slope is undefined, the slope is computed as missing.

Options in the Pairwise Slopes Dialog Box

Y column: Specify the y-variable.

X column: Specify the x-variable.

Put slopes in: Name or indicate the storage location.

Put indices in: If you name or indicate two more locations, Minitab stores the row indices i and j for each slope computed.

Session Command Syntax for Pairwise Slopes...

WSLOPE *y in* **C** *x in* **C** *put slopes in* **C** [*put indices in* **C C**]

Example: Using Pairwise Slopes...

The following dialog box and equivalent Session window commands obtain pairwise slopes for C1 (which contains values 3, 5, 2, and 6) and C2 (which contains values 1.1, 2.0, 1.1, and 3.0), using C2 as the y-variable and C1 as the x-variable.

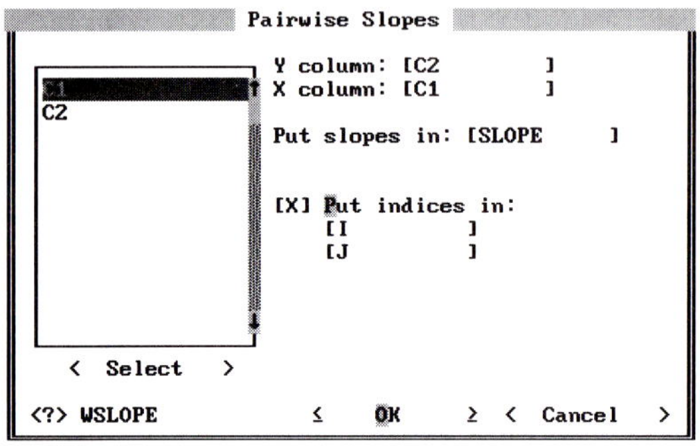


```
MTB > Name c3 = 'SLOPE' c4 = 'I' c5 = 'J'
MTB > WSlopes C2 C1 'SLOPE' 'I' 'J'.
```

These commands produce the following columns in the Data worksheet:

			SLOPE	I	J
↓	C1	C2	C3	C4	C5
1	3	1.1	0.45000	2	1
2	5	2.0	0.00000	3	1
3	2	1.1	0.30000	3	2
4	6	3.0	0.63333	4	1
5			1.00000	4	2
6			0.47500	4	3

```
Graph
Set Options...
Histogram...
Boxplot...
Dotplot...
Stem-and-Leaf...
Scatter Plot...
Multiple Scatter Plot...
Time Series Plot...
Pseudo 3-D Plot...
```

The Graph Menu

The **G**raph menu offers five different command groups: options, displays of single columns, displays of multiple columns, time series displays, and a pseudo three-dimensional plot. Some of the Graph commands include subcommands that allow you to customize the appearance of your plot with colors, lines, notes, labels, and size.

Set Options...

The Set **O**ptions... command allows you to specify the height and width of all subsequent graphs. This command controls the height of the following plots: time series plot, scatter plot, multiple scatter plot, pseudo 3-D plot, and all the statistical process control charts. It controls the width of the following plots: dotplot, boxplot, scatter plot, multiple scatter plot, and pseudo 3-D plot. You must use the Session window command OW (output width) to control the width of time series plots and all the statistical process control charts.

The Set Options Dialog Box

```
                     Set Options
High Resolution Graphs

    (X) No change to hard-copy device
    ( ) Hard-copy device is a printer
    ( ) Hard-copy device is a plotter

    Height: [        ] (Default = 3.3 inches)
    Width:  [        ] (Default = 5.7 inches)

Character Graphs

    Height: [        ] (Default = 17 lines)
    Width:  [        ] (Default = 57 characters)

<?>                  ≤   OK   ≥  <  Cancel  >
```

Options in the Set Options Dialog Box

There are two groups of settings, for high-resolution graphs and character-based graphs. You should set the device for high-resolution graphs if you want to print or plot the graph from the graph screen using the Print option.

Height: You can specify heights from 5 to 400 lines; the default is 17 lines. For high-resolution graphs, the default is 3.3″.

Width: You can specify widths from 10 to 150 spaces; the default is 57 characters. For high-resolution graphs, the default is 5.7″.

Note: Scales tend to be better if you use odd numbers.

Session Command Syntax for Set Options...

HEIGHT *of all plots that follow is* **K** *lines*
WIDTH *of all plots that follow is* **K** *spaces*

Histogram...

Histograms give an overview of the distribution of data in a single column. Minitab divides the data into intervals and displays the count of observations in each interval both numerically and graphically. Character-based histograms use a horizontal line of *'s to represent data points. If there are more than 50 observations in an interval, Minitab indicates how many observations each * represents. Observations falling on an interval boundary are put in the interval that has the larger midpoint. Minitab can display up to 100 levels in a single histogram. Minitab uses bars instead of * lines for high-resolution graphs, and the data may be divided into a maximum of 18 classes.

The Histogram Dialog Box

Options in the Histogram Dialog Box

Variables: Indicate the variable(s) you want to display as histograms in this text box.

By variable: Minitab produces a separate histogram for each value of the By variable, which must contain integers from –9999 to +9999 or missing data (*). There may be up to 20 distinct groups.

Same scale for all variables: Select this checkbox to force Minitab to draw all displays on axes with the same scale (based on the extremes of all the data).

First midpoint and Last midpoint: You can specify the midpoint for the first and last plotting intervals. Any observations beyond these intervals are omitted from the display.

Interval width: You can specify the distance between midpoints or, equivalently, the width of each bar of the histogram.

High resolution: Minitab's default setting produces a high-resolution histogram that appears on a separate graphic screen. You can select this checkbox to turn off the default; the histogram then appears in the Session window in a character-based format.

Store in file: You can store the high-resolution graph in a file; Minitab gives the file the .PRI extension that indicates a printer file. It can take several minutes to store a high-resolution plot in a file, depending on your computer. The Store Graph in File dialog box resembles the File ▶ Open Worksheet dialog box. Refer to that command for more information.

Session Command Syntax for Histogram...

Character-based

HISTOGRAM *of the data in* **C...C**
  INCREMENT = **K**
  START *at* **K** [*end at* **K**]
  BY C
  SAME *scales for all columns*

High-resolution

GHISTOGRAM *of the data in* **C...C**
  INCREMENT = **K**
  START *at* **K** [*end at* **K**]
  BY C
  SAME *scales for all columns*

  FILE ['FILENAME']

Example: Using Histograms...

The following dialog box and equivalent Session window commands show a histogram of salary data (stored in C1 SALARY) at Techni-tron Co., divided into intervals of 4000, using the PAYT3.MTW data set from Tutorial 3.

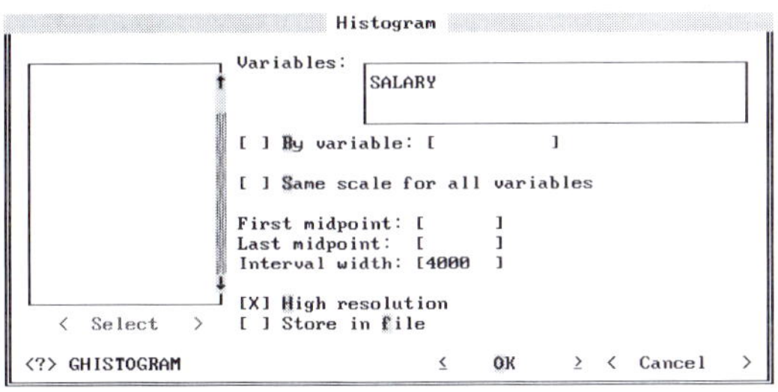


```
MTB > GHistogram 'SALARY';
SUBC>   Increment 4000.
```

These commands produce the following histogram:

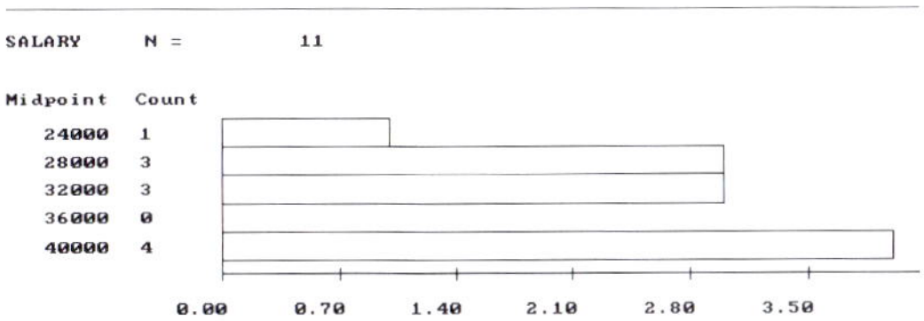

See also Tutorial 3.

Boxplot...

Boxplots give an overview of the values in a single column and allow you to identify extreme values. The **B**oxplot... command can also depict a confidence interval for the population median. The boxplot display consists of a rectangular box, representing roughly the middle 50% of the data, and lines (or "whiskers") extending to either side, indicating the extent of the data. Minitab marks the median value with a tick mark + inside the box. Approximate first and third quartiles are represented by the left and right sides of the box. Minitab considers any value lying between one and one-half and three times the box width beyond the box ends as possible *outliers* and marks them with an *. Any more remote value is considered an extreme outlier and is plotted with a 0.

The Boxplot Dialog Box

Options in the Boxplot Dialog Box

Variable: Indicate the variable you want displayed as a boxplot for this text box.

By variable: You can produce separate boxplots for each distinct value of the By variable. This allows you to compare several groups of data. Levels of the By variable must be integers between –10000 and +10000 or missing values (*). They need not be consecutive. Up to 100 distinct levels are allowed.

Use levels: Use this option with By variable when you want to rearrange or omit the displays for some subgroups. One boxplot is drawn for each of the By variable subscript values (levels) listed, in the order you indicate.

Notch, confidence level: Minitab includes parentheses (notches) that indicate the limits of confidence interval for the population median, calculated using the same interval computed by the SINTERVAL command. Minitab's default confidence level is 90%. Minitab uses a priority system to determine what symbols to display in the boxplot. If the median falls on the same space as a notch (CI parenthesis), the notch is not displayed. Similarly, if the median and a box edge fall on the same space, the box edge is not displayed.

Axis: You can customize the boxplot display by choosing Minimum position or Maximum position to specify the first and optionally the last tick mark + on the horizontal axis.

Tick increment: You can specify the distance between the tick marks.

High resolution: Minitab's default setting produces a high-resolution boxplot that appears in a separate graphic screen. You can select this checkbox to turn off the default; the boxplot then appears in the Session window in a character-based format.

Store in file: You can store the high-resolution chart in a file; Minitab gives the file the .PRI extension that indicates a printer file. It can take several minutes to store a high-resolution plot in a file, depending on your computer. The Store Graph in File dialog box resembles the File ▶ Open Worksheet dialog box. Refer to that command for more information.

Condensed display: Minitab displays each boxplot with only one line instead of three. Normally it uses three lines.

You can specify the boxplot width using the Graph ▶ Set Options... command.

Session Command Syntax for Boxplot...

Character-based

BOXPLOT *for data in* **C**
  START *at* **K** [*end at* **K**]
  INCREMENT = **K**
  NOTCH [**K**% *confidence*] *sign confidence interval*
  BY C
  LEVELS K...K [*for* **C**]
  LINES = **K**

High-resolution

GBOXPLOT *for data in* **C**
  START *at* **K** [*end at* **K**]
  INCREMENT = **K**
  NOTCH [**K**% *confidence*] *sign confidence interval*
  BY C
  LEVELS K...K [*for* **C**]
  LINES = **K**
  FILE ['**FILENAME**']

Example: Using Boxplots...

The following example shows the dialog box and equivalent Session window commands used to create a boxplot of salary data (stored in C1 SALARY) by gender (stored in C8 GENDER N) at Technitron Co., using the PAYT3.MTW data set from Tutorial 3:

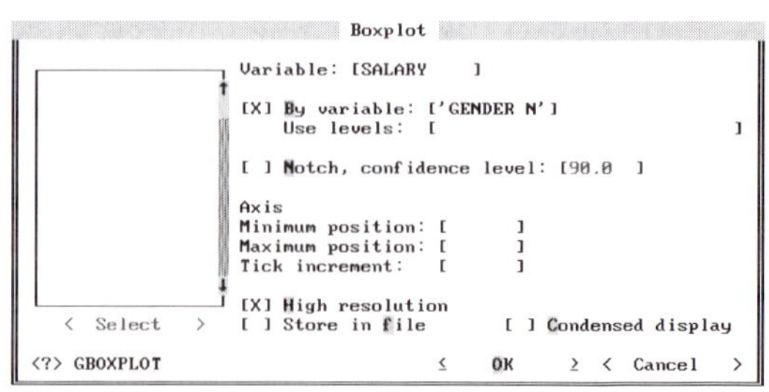

```
MTB > GBoxPlot 'SALARY';
SUBC>   By 'GENDER N'.
```

These commands produce the following box-plot:

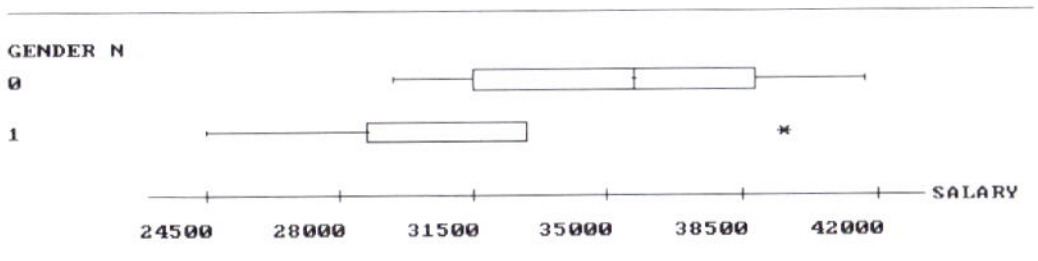

See also Tutorial 3.

Dotplot

A dotplot is a horizontal histogram showing distributional characteristics of a single variable. The **D**otplot... command plots data as dots (one dot represents one observation) above a horizontal axis that covers the entire range of observations. Only character-based dotplots are available.

The Dotplot Dialog Box

Options in the Dotplot Dialog Box

Variables: Indicate the variable(s) for which you want dotplots.

By variable: You can produce a separate dotplot for each value in the By variable, which may contain integers between –10000 and +10000 or the missing value symbol (*).

Same scale for all variables: This option forces Minitab to use the same scale in drawing the dotplots for all columns listed (based on the extremes of the data).

First midpoint and Last midpoint: You can specify the first and last plotting position of the data.

Tick increment: This subcommand controls the distance between tick marks ┼ on the horizontal axis.

You can specify dotplot width using the Graph ► Set Options... command.

Session Command Syntax for Dotplot...

DOTPLOT *of the data in* **C...C**
  INCREMENT = **K**
  START *at* **K** [*end at* **K**]
  BY C
  SAME *scales for all columns*

Example: Using Dotplot...

The following dialog box and equivalent Session window commands produce a dotplot of salary (stored in C1 SALARY) at Technitron Co., with a tick increment of 5000, beginning with 20,000, using the PAYT3.MTW data set from Tutorial 3:

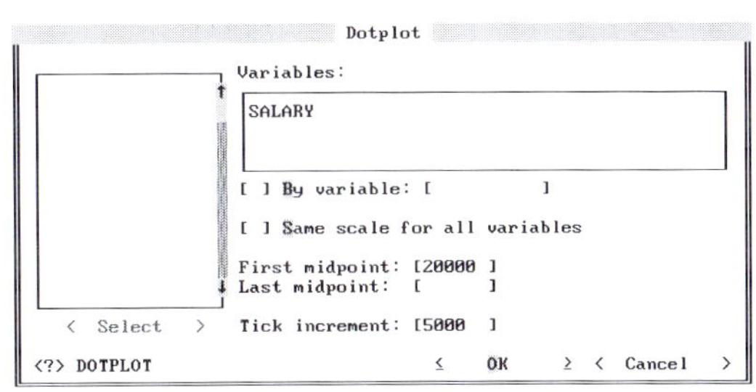

```
MTB > DotPlot 'SALARY';
SUBC>   Start 20000;
SUBC>   Increment 5000.
```

These commands produce the following display:

```
            .            :.   .  :            :  .   .
     +---------+---------+---------+---------+-----SALARY
   20000     25000     30000     35000     40000
```

See also Tutorial 3.

Stem-and-Leaf...

Stem-and-leaf plots are histograms with digits from the actual data values. The display has three columns. The column on the left is a cumulative count of values from the top of the figure down and from the bottom of the figure up to the middle. The number in parentheses is the count of values in the row containing the median. Parentheses around the median row are omitted if the median falls between two lines of the display.

Each number in the second column is called a *stem,* while the numbers to its right are the *leaves,* each of which is a single digit to place after the stem digits, representing one data value. The leaf unit tells you where to put the decimal place in each number.

The Stem-and-Leaf Dialog Box

Options in the Stem-and-Leaf Dialog Box

Variables: Indicate the variable(s) you would like to display.

By variable: This option produces stem-and-leaf displays for the subsets defined by distinct values in the By variable, which must contain integers from –10000 to +10000 or missing values (*). This option cannot be used with the Trim outliers option.

Trim outliers: You can trim all outliers (see the section describing Boxplot... for an explanation of outliers) and shows them on special lines labeled LO and HI. This option cannot be used with By variable.

Increment: You can control vertical scaling by setting the increment between display lines (the difference between the smallest possible values on adjacent lines).

Session Command Syntax for Stem-and-Leaf...

STEM-AND-LEAF *of the data in* **C...C**
  TRIM *outliers*
  INCREMENT = **K**
  BY C

Example: Using Stem-and-Leaf...

The following dialog box and equivalent Session window commands show how to produce a stem-and-leaf display of salary data (stored in C1 SALARY) at Technitron Co., using the PAYT3.MTW data set from Tutorial 3.

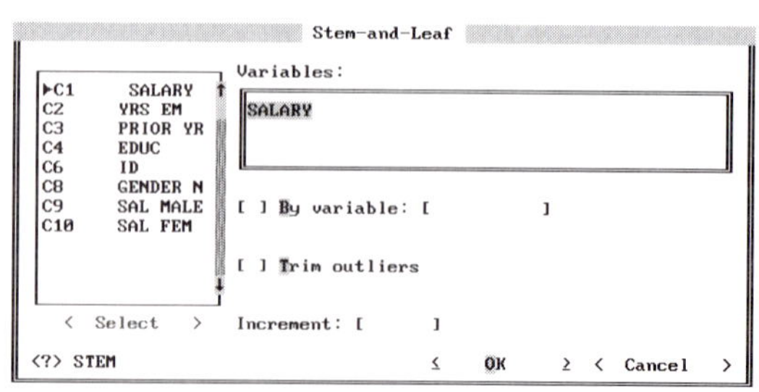

```
MTB > Stem-and-Leaf 'SALARY'.
```

These commands produce the following display:

```
Stem-and-leaf of SALARY    N  = 11
Leaf Unit = 1000

   1    2 4
   1    2
   4    2 889
   5    3 1
  (2)   3 22
   4    3
   4    3
   4    3 889
   1    4 1
```

See also Tutorial 3.

Scatter Plot...

Scatter plots show the relationship between two variables by plotting one column against another. You can have Minitab incorporate a third variable in the plot by "tagging" plotted points using a Tag variable. You can also use other subdialog boxes that allow you to label the scatter plot. Minitab plots individual points with an * or x (or whatever plotting symbol you choose; the example in this section uses a $). When two or more points coincide, Minitab prints a count instead. If more than nine points fall on the same spot, the symbol + is printed.

The Scatter Plot Dialog Box

Options in the Scatter Plot Dialog Box

Vertical axis and Horizontal axis: Indicate the variables you want to plot against each other in these text boxes.

Plotting symbol: You can define the plotting symbol with any single keyboard number, letter, or symbol. By default, Minitab plots points with an x (for high-resolution plots) or * (for character-based plots).

Use tags in: Indicate the tag variable you want to use. Minitab marks each data point with a letter coded to its tag variable value, using the following codes:

Tag variable value:											
...	−2	−1	0	1	2	3	...	26	27	28	...
Plot character:											
...	X	Y	Z	A	B	C	...	Z	A	B	...

High resolution: Minitab's default setting produces a high-resolution scatter plot that appears in a separate graphic screen. You can select this checkbox to turn off the default; the scatter plot then appears in the Session window in a character-based format.

Store in file: You can store the high-resolution chart in a file; Minitab gives the file the .PRI extension that indicates a printer file. It can take several minutes to store a high-resolution plot in a file, depending on your computer. The Store Graph in File dialog box resembles the File ► Open Worksheet dialog box. Refer to that command for more information.

Symbol colors in: You can use this option (when producing a high-resolution scatter plot) to plot subgroups of points with different colors, specified through integer numbers in a column, that must be the same length as the columns being plotted. The colors associated with different integers are:

0 white
1 black
2 red
3 green
4 blue
5 cyan (light blue)
6 magenta
7 yellow

Colors can be used to emphasize group membership. If you had coded C1 'GENDER' with 3 = male and 4 = female, you could select C1 for the Symbol colors in text box, and in the plot Minitab would color all data points representing males green (3) and all data points representing females blue (4).

The Lines Subdialog Box

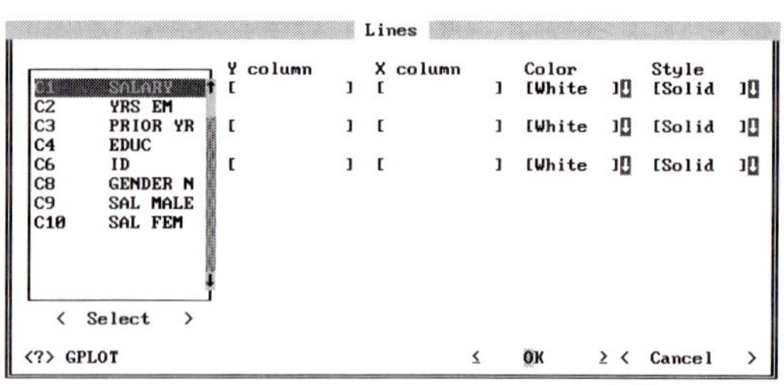

Use the **L**ines... command to connect data points defined in two columns.

Y column and X column: Specify the Y and X columns(s). Minitab connects the points in the order you give them; there cannot be any missing values (*).

Color: You can select the color for each line if your hardware supports colors.

Style: You can select a line style; the pop-up menu shows the available styles.

The Annotate Scatter Plot Subdialog Box

Use the **A**nnotate... command to give your plots labels.

Titles: You can include three lines of text at the top of the graph.

Footnotes: You can have two lines of text at the bottom of the graph, below the horizontal axis label.

Horizontal Axis Label: Minitab automatically labels the horizontal axis with the column name, but you can replace that label with one of your own.

Vertical Axis Label: Minitab automatically labels the vertical axis with the column name, but you can replace that label with one of your own.

The Plot Scale Subdialog Box

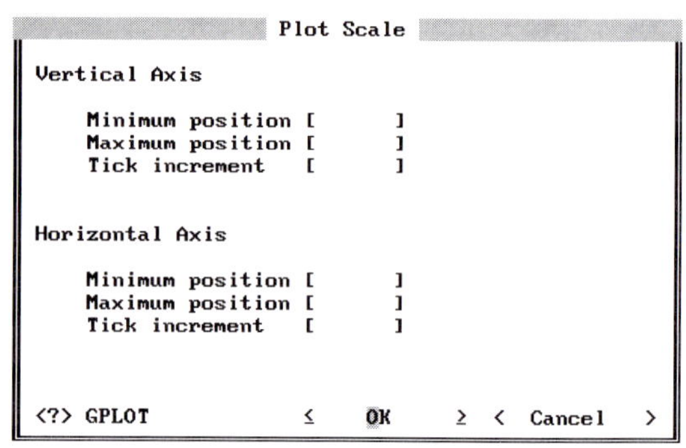

Use the Plot Scale... command to control the range of your plot's vertical and horizontal axes.

Minimum position: Use to set the minimum position.

Maximum position: Use to set the maximum position.

Tick increment: You can specify the increment that marks the distance between tick marks ⸸ on both axes.

You can specify scatter plot height and width using the Graph ▶ Set Options command.

Session Command Syntax for Scatter Plot...

Character-based

PLOT C *vs.* **C**
  LPLOT C *vs.* **C** *using letters as coded in* **C**
  YSTART *from* **K** [*to* K]
  YINCREMENT = **K**
  XSTART *from* **K** [*to* **K**]
  XINCREMENT = **K**

  TITLE '*Name*'
  FOOTNOTE '*Name*'
  XLABEL '*Name*'
  YLABEL '*Name*'

High-resolution

GPLOT C *vs.* **C**
  GLPLOT C *vs.* **C** *tagged by* **C**
  YSTART *from* **K** [*to* **K**]
  YINCREMENT = **K**
  XSTART *from* **K** [*to* **K**]
  XINCREMENT = **K**

  LINES [*style* = **K** [*color* = **K**]] *connecting pairs in* **C C**
  SYMBOL '*symbol*' (*only works with GPLOT*)
  COLOR = **C**

  TITLE '*Name*'
  FOOTNOTE '*Name*'
  XLABEL '*Name*'
  YLABEL '*Name*'

  FILE ['**FILENAME**']

Example: Using Scatter Plot...

The following example shows a scatter plot of salary data (C1 SALARY) by number of years employed at Technitron Co. (C2 YRS EM), using the Annotate... command. In the Session window commands, the last four subcommands are from the Annotate Scatter Plot subdialog box. The data set is PAYT3.MTW from Tutorial 3.

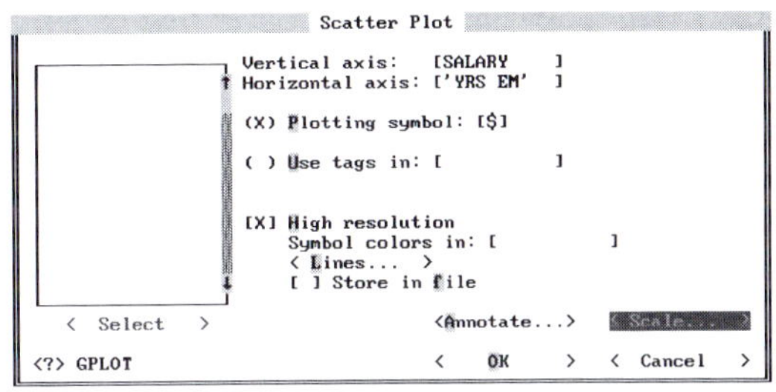

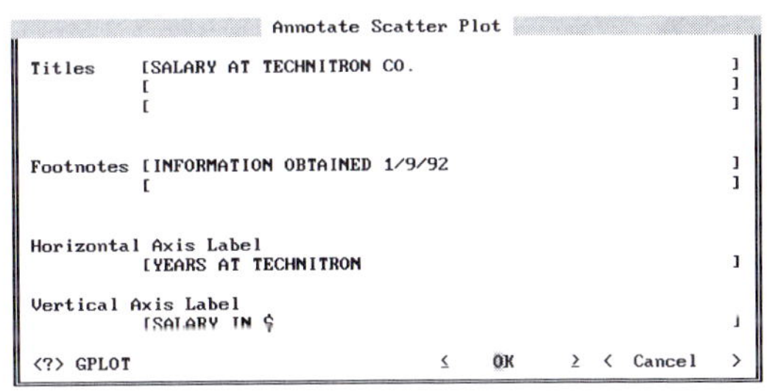


```
MTB > GPlot 'SALARY' 'YRS EM';
SUBC>   Symbol '$';
SUBC>   Title 'SALARY AT TECHNITRON CO.';
SUBC>   Footnote 'INFORMATION OBTAINED 1/9/92';
SUBC>   XLabel 'YEARS AT TECHNITRON';
SUBC>   YLabel 'SALARY IN $'.
```

These commands produce the following scatter plot:

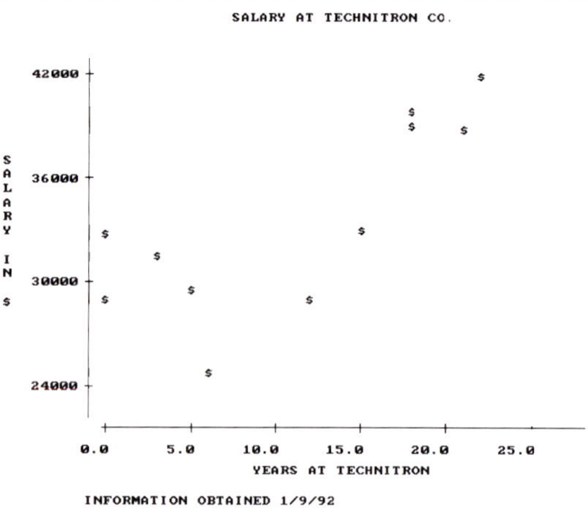

See also Tutorial 3.

Multiple Scatter Plot...

The **M**ultiple Scatter Plot... command displays several scatter plots on a single set of axes. Minitab plots the first pair of columns with the symbol A, the second with B, and so on. Up to four pairs of columns for the vertical and horizontal axes may be plotted. If more than four pairs of columns need to be plotted, use the Session window command. If several points fall on the same spot, a count is given. If the count is over 9, a + is used.

The Multiple Scatter Plot Dialog Box

Options in the Multiple Scatter Plot Dialog Box

Vertical axis and Horizontal axis: Indicate the variables that you want to plot against each other.

High resolution: Minitab's default setting produces a high-resolution multiple scatter plot that appears in a separate graphics screen. You can select this checkbox to turn off the default; the multiple scatter plot then appears in the Session window in a character-based format.

Store in **f**ile: You can store the high-resolution chart in a file; Minitab gives the file the .PRI extension that indicates a printer file. It can take several minutes to store a high-resolution plot in a file, depending on your computer. The Store Graph in File dialog box resembles the File ▶ Open Worksheet dialog box. Refer to that command for more information.

Symbol colors in, **L**ines..., **A**nnotate..., Scale...: See the section called Options in the Scatter Plot Dialog Box for information on these options.

You can specify multiple scatter plot height and width using the Graph ▶ Set Options command.

Session Command Syntax for Multiple Scatter Plot...

Character-based

MPLOT C *vs.* **C ..., C** *vs.* **C**
  YSTART *from* **K** [*to* **K**]
  YINCREMENT *1* = **K**
  XSTART *from* **K** [*to* **K**]
  XINCREMENT = **K**

  TITLE '*Name*'
  FOOTNOTE '*Name*'
  XLABEL '*Name*'
  YLABEL '*Name*'

High-resolution

GMPLOT C *vs.* **C...C** *vs.* **C**
  YSTART *from* **K** [*to* **K**]
  YINCREMENT = **K**
  XSTART *from* **K** [*to* **K**]
  XINCREMENT = **K**

  LINES [*style* = **K** [*color* = **K**]] *connecting pairs in* **C C**
  COLOR = **C**

  TITLE '*Name*'
  FOOTNOTE '*Name*'
  XLABEL '*Name*'
  YLABEL '*Name*'

  FILE ['**FILENAME**']

Example: Using Multiple Scatter Plot...

The following dialog box and Session window commands generate a multiple scatter plot that shows how salaries at Technitron Co. (C1 SALARY) relate to several different variables (C2 YRS EM, C3 PRIOR YR, and C4 EDUC), using the PAYT3.MTW data set from Tutorial 3:

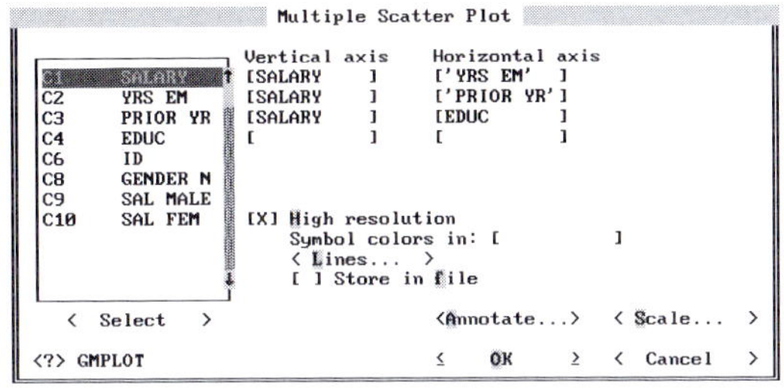


```
MTB > GMPlot 'SALARY' 'YRS EM' 'SALARY' 'PRIOR YR' 'SALARY' 'EDUC'.
```

These commands produce the following display:

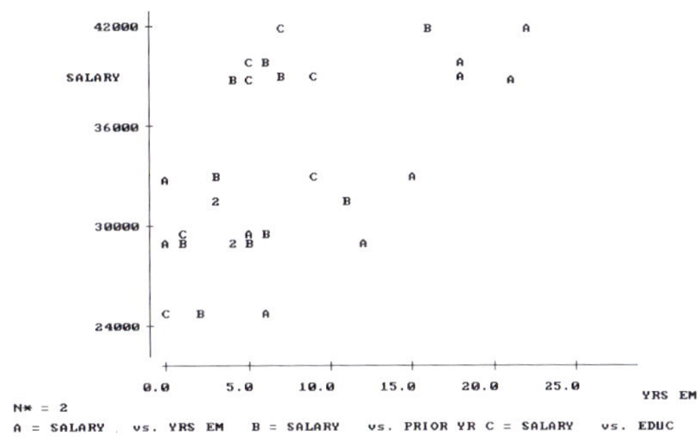

See also Tutorial 3.

Time Series Plot...

You can produce a time series plot with one or more series plotted on the vertical axis versus the integers 1, 2, 3, ... on the horizontal axis. Often the data are a series of observations made at equally spaced intervals of time, such as monthly sales figures or yearly growth increments.

The Time Series Plot Dialog Box

Options in the Time Series Plot Dialog Box

Series: Specify the column (vertical axis) you want to plot against time (horizontal axis). If you specify more than one time series, they are plotted on the same graph. In this case, Minitab uses special plot symbols and explains them at the bottom of the graph.

Origin: You can specify the scale of numbers to use when labeling the horizontal axis. The first point will be plotted directly above the number you specify.

Period: Minitab uses periodic numbers as plotting symbols. If you specify a period length of 5, each group of five observations is be plotted with the numbers 1, 2, 3, 4, 5. For a period length of greater than 9, data are plotted with a 0 for 10, A for 11,...Z for 36. The period sets the distance between tick marks. It may be any positive integer up to 36; the default is 10.

The Plot Scale Subdialog Box

```
                     Plot Scale
Vertical Axis

    Minimum position [        ]
    Maximum position [        ]
    Tick increment   [        ]


Time Axis

    First time [        ]
    Last time  [        ]



<?> TSPLOT          < OK >  < Cancel >
```

Use the Scale... command to control the range of your plot's vertical and time axes.

Vertical Axis: You can control the range and scale of the vertical axis.

Minimum position and Maximum position: Indicate the desired range of the vertical axis in these text boxes.

Tick increment: You can specify the tick increment that marks the distance between tick marks on the vertical axis.

Time Axis: Indicate the desired time range in these text boxes.

First time and Last time: You can control the subset of the time series that will be plotted. If you set the First time at 15, then the first point plotted is the 15th observation. The First time and Last time specified interact with the Origin for the time series. With Origin set to 1921, First time set to 1930, and Last time set to 1950, just those observations from 1930 to 1950 are plotted.

You can specify the height of your time series plot using the Graph ► Set Options... command. You can specify width only through the Session window, using the command OW (output width).

Session Command Syntax for Time Series Plot...

To plot a single time series:

TSPLOT [*with period* **K**] *time series data in* **C**
  INCREMENT = **K**
  START *at* **K** [*end at* **K**]
  ORIGIN = **K**
  TSTART *at* **K** [*end at* **K**]

To plot multiple time series on the same graph:

MTSPLOT [*with period* **K**] *time series data in* **C...C**
  INCREMENT = **K**
  START *at* **K** [*end at* **K**]
  ORIGIN = **K**
  TSTART *at* **K** [*end at* **K**]

Example: Using Time Series Plot...

The following dialog box and equivalent Session window commands will produce a time series plot that shows river temperatures (stored in C2 TEMP) taken upstream from a power plant over a period of time, using the RIVER2.MTW data set from Tutorial 13:

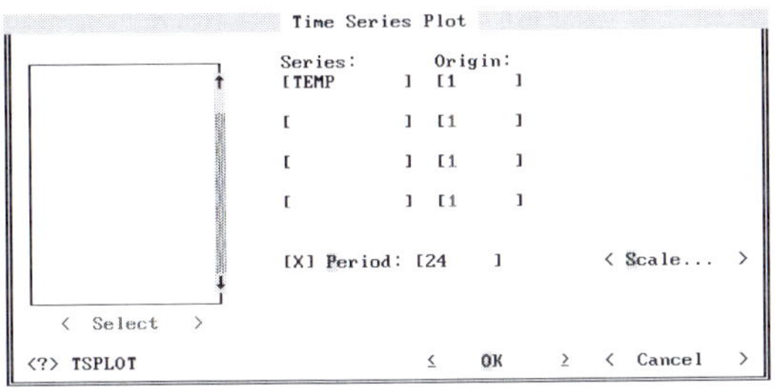


```
MTB > MTSPlot 24 'TEMP';
SUBC>    Origin 1 'TEMP'    .
```

These commands produce the following display (the first portion is shown):

```
            -
            -
   35.00+
            -
 TEMP       -
            -                                     0A
            -                                   89   BC
   32.50+            9                      4  7       D
            -      567  0A                23 5           E
            -                                6            F
            -  234    8    B DE                            GHIJ   N
            -                C  FGH                              KLM
   30.00+ 1                       IJK    1
            -                        LMN
            -
            -
            -
            +-------------------------+-------------------------+
            0                        24                        48
```

See also Tutorial 13.

Pseudo 3-D Plot...

The Pseudo 3-D Plot... command produces a pseudo three-dimensional plot of three different variables. Minitab represents the first column on the y-axis of the plot and the second column on the x-axis of the plot. The z column is represented with a set of special plotting symbols. The plotting symbol used for z is "0" if z is more than one standard deviation below its mean, "." if z is within one standard deviation below the mean, "/" if z is within one standard deviation above the mean, or "X" if z is more than one standard deviation above the mean. If several points fall on the same spot, Minitab prints a count instead.

The Pseudo 3-D Plot Dialog Box

Options in the Pseudo 3-D Plot Dialog Box

Third axis: The z-variable.
Vertical axis: The y-variable.
Horizontal axis: The x-variable.

High resolution: Minitab's default setting produces a high-resolution pseudo 3-D plot that appears in a separate graphics screen. You can select this checkbox to turn off the default; the plot then appears in the Session window in a character-based format.

Store in file: You can store the high-resolution chart in a file; Minitab gives the file the .PRI extension that indicates a printer file. It can take several minutes to store a high-resolution plot in a file, depending on your computer. The Store Graph in File dialog box resembles the File ▶ Open Worksheet dialog box. Refer to that command for more information.

Symbol colors in, Lines..., Annotate..., Scale...: See the section called Options in the Scatter Plot Dialog Box for information on these commands.

You can specify 3-D plot height and width using the Graph ► Set Options command.

Session Command Syntax for Pseudo 3-D Plot...

Character-based

TPLOT *y in* **C** *vs. x in* **C** *vs. z in* **C**
  YSTART *from* **K** [**to K**]
  YINCREMENT = **K**
  XSTART *from* **K** [*to* **K**]
  XINCREMENT = **K**

  TITLE '*Name*'
  FOOTNOTE '*Name*'
  XLABEL '*Name*'
  YLABEL '*Name*'

High-resolution

GTPLOT *y in* **C** *vs. x in* **C** *vs. z in* **C**
  YSTART *from* **K** [*to* **K**]
  YINCREMENT = **K**
  XSTART *from* **K** [*to* **K**]
  XINCREMENT = **K**

  LINES [*style* = **K** [*color* = **K**]] *connecting pairs in* **C C**
  COLOR = **C**

  TITLE '*Name*'
  FOOTNOTE '*Name*'
  XLABEL '*Name*'
  YLABEL '*Name*'

  FILE ['**FILENAME**']

Example: Using Pseudo 3-D Plot...

The following dialog box and Session window commands produce a pseudo three-dimensional plot on a data set created with the Set Patterned Data... and General Expressions... commands:

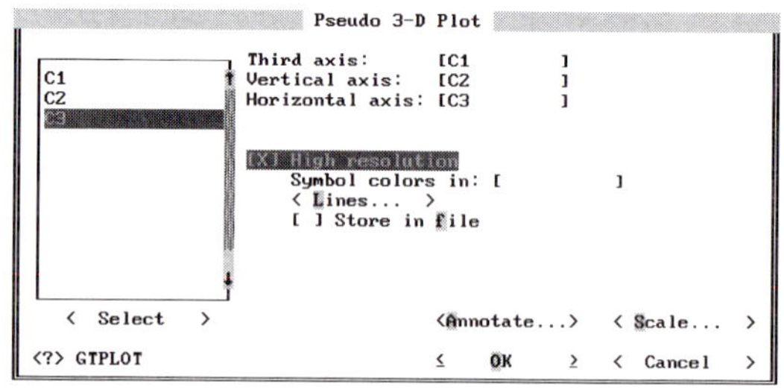


```
MTB > Set C1
DATA> 1( 0 : 1 / 0.1 )10
DATA> End.
MTB > Set C2
DATA> 10( 0 : 1 / 0.1 )1
DATA> End.
MTB > Let C3 = SIN (C1**2 + C2**2)
MTB > GTPlot C2 C3 C1.
```

These commands produce the following display:

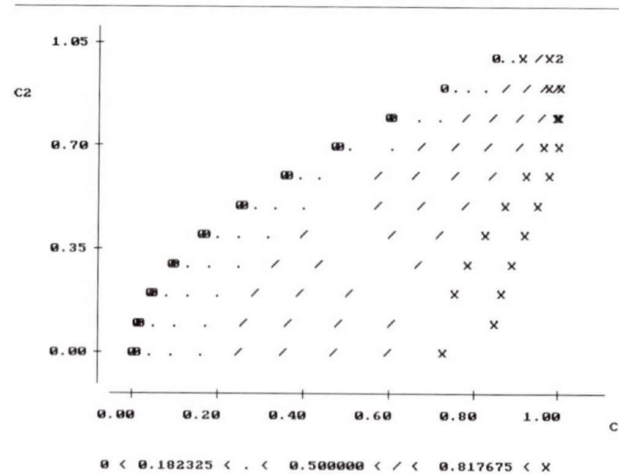

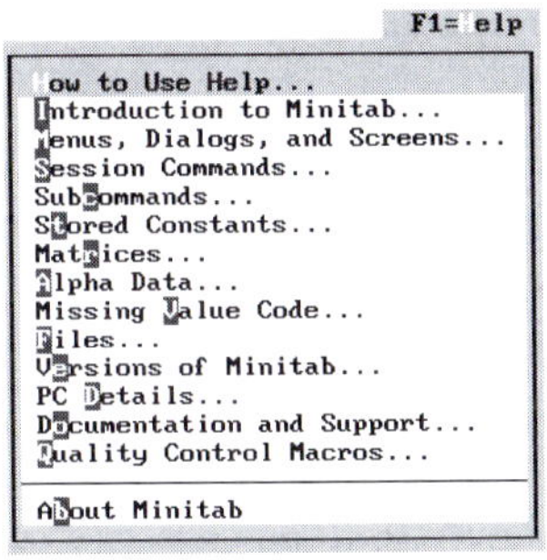

The Help Menu

The Session window **H**elp menu lists a number of different topics that you can select to display on-screen information. You can get help for specific commands by selecting the <?> in individual dialog boxes, or by typing **HELP** after the MTB > prompt in the Session window. Type **HELP OVERVIEW** to list overview topics in the Session window, and type **HELP COMMANDS** to list command topics in the Session window. To get help on an individual command, type, for example, **HELP REGRESS**. Typing **HELP REGRESS DW** explains the DW subcommand of REGRESS. To learn about getting help in the Data worksheet, see the Help Menu section in Chapter 3 of this Reference section.

How to Use Help...

How to Use Help... explains the three ways to reach Minitab's Help function, as well as how to print any Help selection. It also explains conventions used in the Help display.

Introduction to Minitab...

Introduction to Minitab... explains Minitab's structure and the extent of its storage and display capabilities.

Menus, Dialogs, and Screens...

Menus, Dialogs, and Screens... provides a thorough summary of the basic key or mouse functions that operate and navigate Minitab's menus, dialog boxes, and screens, and explains the various parts of each. It also provides a discussion of mistakes, files, drives, and directories.

Session Commands...

Session Commands... shows you how to issue commands by typing them in the Session window after the MTB > prompt, bypassing the dialog boxes. It explains the conventions and rules you must follow to type the commands so Minitab can read them.

Subcommands...

Subcommands... concludes the Session Commands... option by explaining how to issue subcommands through the Session window.

Stored Constants...

Stored Constants... explains how to store and use constants in Minitab.

Matrices...

Matrices... are not included in *The Student Edition of Minitab.*

Alpha Data...

Alpha Data... explains how to use alpha data in the Data screen, listing Session window commands that handle alpha data as well as notes on alpha data conventions.

Missing Value Code...

Missing Value Code... explains how to indicate missing values in data sets, and describes how Minitab handles them.

Files...

Files... lists and explains Minitab's seven file types: outfile (.LIS), saved worksheet (.MTW), portable worksheet (.MTP), data file (.DAT), macro file (.MTB), journal file (.MTJ), and graphics file (.PRI).

Versions of Minitab...

Versions of Minitab... discusses Minitab's availability on different computer systems.

PC Details...

PC Details... documents sizes and defaults of Minitab's components. It also includes hints on using Minitab with DOS (giving the formal DOS syntax for running Minitab), interrupting macros, and selecting colors.

About Minitab

About Minitab displays Minitab's opening screen.

CHAPTER 3

Data Editor Menu Reference

Using the Data Editor

Minitab provides many different ways to enter and edit data. If you want to enter data from the keyboard, edit individual values, or view your data, you should work in the Data screen and use the features described in this chapter. If you want to enter patterned data (for example, the integers between 1 and 100), choose Edit ▶ Set Patterned Data... from the Session window menu to save time. If you want to edit and manipulate larger blocks of data, or if you want to erase columns, use the commands in the Calc menu, also available from the Session window.

The Data Screen

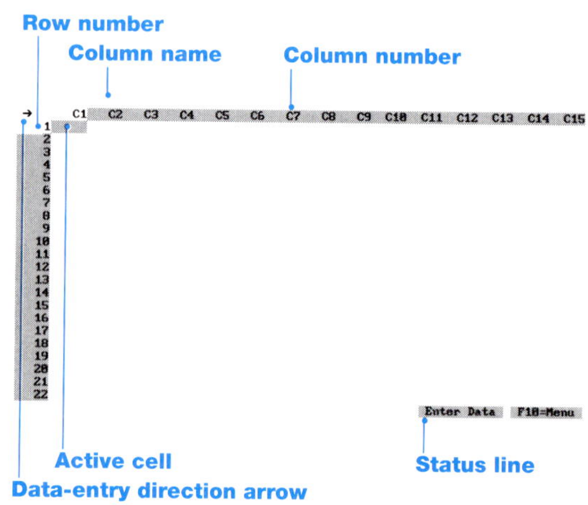

Each column contains data for one variable, and each row contains one set of observations. You can use up to 100 columns and as many rows as your worksheet size will allow. When you start Minitab, the Session window displays the worksheet size, the maximum number of cells that can be occupied. The largest possible worksheet is 3,500 cells. If you have less than 475,000 bytes available when you start Minitab, your worksheet size is reduced. See Appendix B, Additional Installation and System Notes, for more information.

By default, columns are four characters wide, the data-entry directional arrow points right, and the display mode is uncompressed (that is, Minitab does not hide empty, unnamed columns from display). You can override those defaults any time while you are in the Data screen. When you open a saved worksheet, Minitab automatically retrieves the Data screen settings that were in effect when you saved that worksheet.

The highlighted cell is the current active cell. To enter a new value into the active cell, type the value. It overrides the previous contents of the cell.

When you are editing a cell (using the Edit within a Cell command from the Data screen menu), the status line in the lower right corner of the screen changes from Enter Data to Edit Cell. A box appears indicating that you are in the Insert mode; you can toggle between Insert and Overwrite modes by pressing [Ins] or by using the mouse to click the box. In the Insert mode, what you type is added to the text already in the cell; in the Overwrite mode, what you type replaces the text in the cell.

The directional keys behave differently when editing a cell than when entering data. When editing a cell, the arrow, [Home], and [End] keys move the cursor within the cell. When entering data, those keys move the active cell in the worksheet.

If you have made changes to a cell and have not yet pressed [↵] or moved the active cell, you can restore the previous value by pressing [Esc]. You can erase columns from the Session window (see Calc ▶ Erase Variables...) but not from the Data screen. See the Quick Reference Card for a full documentation of keyboard or mouse operations used in the Data worksheet.

Data Editor Quick Reference

The Basics

To enter the Data screen: From the Session window menu, choose Edit ▶ Data Screen, or press [Alt]-D

To open the Data screen menu: Press [F10], or click F10=Menu in the bottom right corner of the screen

To close the Data screen menu: Press [Esc], or click outside the menu

To get help in the Data screen: Choose Menu ▶ Help, or press [F1]

To switch to the Session window: Choose Menu ▶ Go to Minitab Session, or press [Alt]-M

Editing the Data Worksheet

To enter a new value into the active cell: Type the value (it overwrites the previous contents of the cell)

To edit the active cell: Choose Menu ▶ Edit within a Cell, or press [F2], or click the active cell

To switch between Insert and Overwrite modes while editing the active cell: Press [Ins], or click Insert/Overwrite on the status line

To delete the active cell and move all cells in the column up: Choose Menu ▶ Delete Cell, or press [F8]

To delete the active row and move all cells in all columns up: Choose Menu ▶ Delete Row, or Press [Shift]-[F8]

To insert one cell above the active cell: Choose Menu ▶ Insert Cell, or press [F7]

To insert one row above the active cell: Choose Menu ▶ Insert Row, or press [Shift]-[F7]

To restore the previous value of the current cell: Press [Esc]

To name a column: Move to the name row (the top row of the column, above the column number) and enter the column name, or choose Menu ▶ Name Columns, or press [Alt]-N

To delete a column name: Move the active cell to the column name, then press [F8]

Changing the Display of Columns

To specify the format of a column (width, decimal digits, etc.): Choose Menu ▶ Format Columns, or press [F9]

To set compressed mode on or off (hide or display empty, unnamed columns): Choose Menu ▶ Compress, or press [F4]

Moving the Active Cell Around the Data Screen

To move the active cell...

to the beginning of the current worksheet: Press [Ctrl]-[Home]

to the end of the current worksheet (the last row in the last column): Press [Ctrl]-[End]

one screen to the right or left: While holding down [Ctrl], press an arrow key

one screen up or down: Press [PgUp] or [PgDn]

to a specific row and/or column: Choose Menu ▶ Go to Cell..., or press [F5]

to the beginning of the next row or column, depending on the data-entry direction arrow ([→] or [↓], respectively): Choose Menu ▶ Go to Next Row/Column, or press [F6]

to the beginning of the current row or column, depending on the data-entry direction arrow: Press [Home]

to the end of the current row or column, depending on the data-entry direction arrow ([→] or [↓], respectively): Press [End]

one cell to the right or down, depending on the data-entry direction arrow ([←] or [↓], respectively): Press [↵]

To change the direction of the data-entry direction arrow: Choose Menu ▶ Change Entry Direction, or press [F3], or click the data-entry direction arrow

Note: If the Data Editor operations don't seem to be working, it may be because you have a pending data cell. Move the active cell by pressing [↵] or an arrow key, or press [Esc] to remove the pending status.

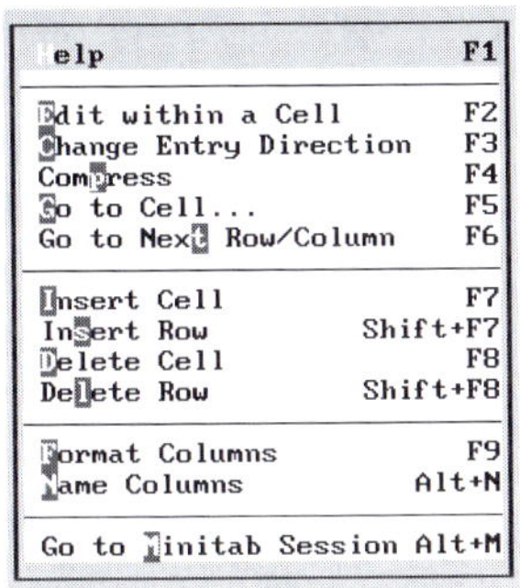

The Data Screen Menu Reference

The Data screen menu lists the commands you need to navigate and edit the Data worksheet. Each command is accompanied by a keyboard equivalent or key combination that you can use to bypass the menu. The Data screen menu is accessible only when the Data screen is active.

Help [F1]

The **H**elp command opens the Help menu. See the section called Data Screen Help Menu, later in this chapter, for information on how to get help.

Edit within a Cell [F2]

The **E**dit within a Cell command lets you change characters within a cell, using the backspace key or [→] or [←] and [Del].

Change Entry Direction [F3]

The **C**hange Entry Direction command changes the direction of the data-entry direction arrow. Depending on the direction of this arrow, pressing [↵] will either move you down one row [↓] or across one column [→].

Compress [F4]

The Com**p**ress command hides empty, unnamed columns from the Data worksheet display. Choose this command again to change the display to its original, uncompressed format.

Go to Cell... [F5]

The **G**o to Cell... command is used to move the active cell to a specified column and row. The column and row numbers must be entered in the Go To a Cell dialog box.

The Go To a Cell Dialog Box

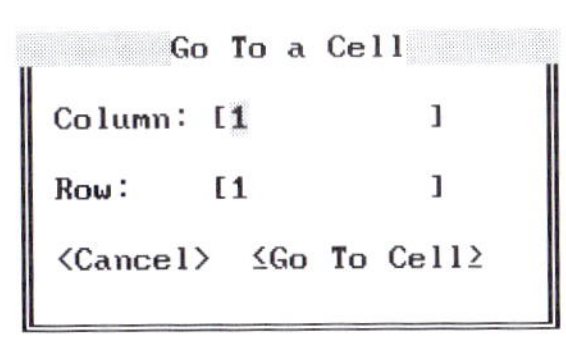

Options in the Go To a Cell Dialog Box

Column: Specify the column number that contains the cell you want to reach.

Row: Specify the row number that contains the cell you want to reach.

Go to Next Row/Column — F6

The Go to Next Row/Column command moves the active cell to the beginning of the next row or column, depending on the direction of the data-entry arrow (→ or ↓, respectively).

Insert Cell — F7

The Insert Cell command inserts one cell above the active cell and moves the remaining cells in the column down.

Insert Row — Shift-F7

The Insert Row command inserts one row above the active row and moves the rest down.

Delete Cell — F8

The Delete Cell command deletes the active cell and moves the remaining cells up.

Delete Row — Shift-F8

The Delete Row command deletes the active row and moves the rest up. To delete a block of rows, go to the Session window and choose Calc ▶ Delete Rows.... Using that command, you can specify the range of rows; Minitab deletes the entire range in one step.

Format Columns — F9

The Format Columns command specifies how a column of data is displayed on the screen. For example, it changes the width of the column or the number of decimal digits displayed. Formatting a column does not actually change the values in a column; it just changes how those values are displayed.

As data are entered in a column, initially the column's format width and number of decimals displayed is determined automatically by Minitab, to best accommodate the data in the column. Initially, all columns have a width of four characters; this is the minimum column width Minitab displays.

When you choose Format Columns, two rows labeled FMT (for format) and A/F (for Automatic/Fixed) appear at the bottom of the screen.

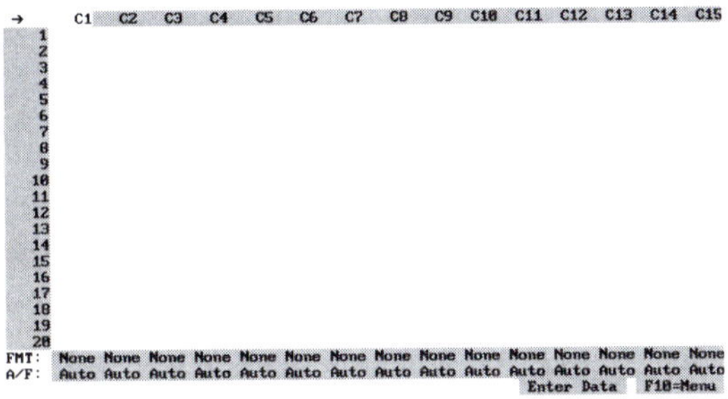

To format a column, use the arrow keys or the mouse to highlight the FMT row of the column you want to change. Type in the format and press [↵]. The corresponding A/F row will change to Fix, if the column was previously in Auto format mode. For example, typing the format F7.2, for a numeric column, changes the column width to seven characters and displays two decimal places. Alpha column width can be increased or decreased using the Aw format, where w is a number indicating the desired width of the column.

To return a column to the automatic format mode, type A in the A/F row of the column and press [↵]; to make the format fixed, type F and press [↵].

Press [Esc] to exit from the Format Columns command.

Name Columns [Alt]-N

The **N**ame Columns command moves the active cell to the top row (above the column numbers) so you can enter column names.

Go to Minitab Session [Alt]-M

The Go to **M**initab Session command makes the Session window the active screen.

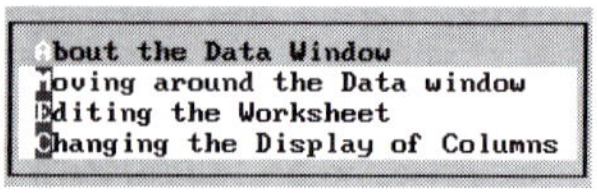

The Data Screen Help Menu

The Data Screen Help menu lists four selections that you can choose to learn more about using the Data worksheet.

About the Data Window

The **A**bout the Data Window option explains the setup of the Data screen and summarizes the menu commands available for working with data in a spreadsheet environment.

Moving around the Data window

The **M**oving around the Data window option lists the keyboard and mouse functions that you can use to navigate the Data worksheet most efficiently.

Editing the Worksheet

The **E**diting the Worksheet option explains the keyboard methods used to edit an existing worksheet.

Changing the Display of Columns

The **C**hanging the Display of Columns selection explains how to format columns or to use the Data worksheet's compressed mode.

CHAPTER 4

Minitab Command Language

Session Commands

When you execute a command by choosing it from a menu, Minitab displays the corresponding session command in the Session window. You can also execute a command by typing or pasting it into the Session window directly.

Session commands start with a command word like READ, ERASE, REGRESS, or PLOT. You usually follow this word with a list of *arguments* that could be columns, constants, numbers, filenames, or text strings. A few commands like LET and ANOVA allow fairly complicated expressions, but most use just a simple list of arguments. Each command must start on a new line and can be typed in upper- or lowercase letters.

Subcommands

Many commands have subcommands that provide additional information. To use a subcommand, put a semicolon at the end of the main command line. This tells Minitab that subcommands will follow. Then type the subcommands. Start each on a new line, ending each line with a semicolon. When you are done, end the last subcommand with a period. Here is a simple example:

```
TABLE C1 C2;
MEANS C10;
MEDIANS C10;
COUNTS.
```

If you forget to end the last subcommand with a period and use another semicolon, simply type a period, all by itself, on the next subcommand line. If you want to cancel the whole command, type **ABORT** as the next subcommand. Typing ABORT is the same as selecting Cancel in the dialog boxes.

Syntax Rules for Session Commands

- You need type only the first four letters of a command or a subcommand.
- You may include extra text with any commands except LET and ANOVA. However, never use the symbols & . + ; - : # as extra text.
- Type comments, including any symbols you want, after the comment symbol #. You may use # on any command line, subcommand line, data line, and as the first symbol on a line.
- Abbreviate a list of consecutive columns, stored constants, or matrices with a dash. For example, READ C2-C5 is the same as READ C2 C3 C4 C5, and PRINT K5-K2 is the same as PRINT K5 K4 K3 K2.
- Start each command and subcommand on a new line.
- Continue a command, subcommand, or row of data onto the next line with the continuation symbols & or ++.

The session commands below are all equivalent. In this example, columns C1 through C4 are named 'A', 'B', 'C', and 'D'.

```
HISTOGRAM C1 C2 'C' 'D'
HISTOGRAM C1 - C4
HISTOGRAM of the data for males in 'A' &
   -'B' and females in 'C'-'D'
HISTOGRAM C1 - C4    # data from June &
   24, 1987
HIST C1 - C4
HISTOGRAM C1 C2 & C3 C4
hist c1-c4
```

Using Symbols

*, Missing Values

Minitab uses an * in numeric columns and a blank in alpha columns to represent missing values in a column.

Most commands exclude from analysis all cases with a missing value in any input variable. For example, scatter plots exclude points where both x, y coordinates are not present; Minitab displays the number of excluded points. Regression commands use only those cases that have the dependent and all the independent variables present.

When an arithmetic command operates on a missing value, Minitab sets the result equal to *. For example, if you add columns C1 and C2, Minitab stores the sum in C3 as shown below:

```
C1    C2    C3
 5     7    12
 2  +  *  =  *
 4     6    10
```

You can use * just as you would use a number in many commands. For example, when you copy columns you can use or omit rows equal to *. The time series commands LAG and DIFFERENCE produce output columns with *'s at the top.

To code numbers to the missing value symbol *, choose Code Data Values... from the Calc menu, using * for the New value. Alternatively, you can use the session command CODE. When you use * in a session command, however, you must enclose it in single quotation marks. For example:

```
CODE (2:4) '*' C1 C3
```

#, Comment Symbol

Minitab ignores everything you type between a # symbol and the end of a line. You can use the symbol to include comments on command lines, subcommand lines, data lines, or on lines by themselves.

Session Command Syntax

[any text]

&, Continuation Symbol

You can type an & at the end of any line to indicate that the command, subcommand, or data row continues on to the next line. Minitab returns with a CONT> prompt.

Session Commands Not Available Through the Menus

The following Session commands are not available through the menus:

ADD	NOTE	BATCH
SUBTRACT	OW	NOECHO
MULTIPLY	IW	ECHO
DIVIDE	BRIEF	YESNO
RAISE	TSHARE	GOPTIONS

The functionality of the commands ADD, SUBTRACT, MULTIPLY, DIVIDE, and RAISE is available through the Functions and Statistics submenu of the Calc menu. The rest of the commands are useful primarily for writing macros. The CK capability (i.e., looping) cannot be used with menu commands. Use Minitab Help for more information on these commands; type **HELP** and then the name of any of these commands after the MTB > prompt in the Session window. Chapter 5, Macros, also explains the CK feature.

Certain limitations apply to the menu command equivalents of some session commands:

CDF	CDF with no argument for discrete distributions is not available.
CENTER	Only 0 or 1 values are allowed for LOCATION and SCALE.
CODE	Only five sets of old/new values are allowed.
COPY	Copying from or to constants is not allowed.
INVCDF	INVCDF with no argument for discrete distributions is not available.
LET	A subscript of a column on the left side cannot be an expression; it can only be a positive integer constant (stored or stated).
LPLOT	Only six LINE subcommands are allowed.
MPLOT	Only four (y, x) pairs are allowed. Only six LINE subcommands are allowed.
MTSPLOT	Only four series are allowed.
NAME	Not directly available. Columns can be named in a dialog box when they are created and on the Data worksheet.
PDF	PDF with no argument for discrete distributions is not available.
PLOT	Only six LINE subcommands are allowed.
PRINT	FORMAT subcommand not available.

REGRESS	Only one PREDICT subcommand is allowed. The NOCONSTANT and TOLERANCE subcommands are not available.
Rowwise statistics	(RCOUNT, RN, RNMISS, RSUM, RMEAN, RSTDEV, RMEDIAN, RMINIMUM, RMAXIMUM, RSSQ) Empty columns are not allowed.
SET	FORMAT and NOBS subcommands not available, the form of the data is restricted, and data cannot be read from a file.
SORT	Only four BY variables are allowed.
SPC charts	The HLINES subcommand can only be specified using constants, not columns.
STACK	Only five blocks are allowed.
STEPWISE	No dialog box is provided for the interactive part of STEPWISE.
TABLE	The same set of auxiliary variables must be used for all of the summary statistics (MEANS, MEDIANS, etc.). No control over the level of output from the CHISQUARE subcommand is available; the default level is used.
UNSTACK	Only five blocks are allowed.

CHAPTER 5

Macros

A *macro* is a set of commands stored in a file. You can execute a macro through the File menu by choosing Other Files and then Execute Macro... or through the Session window by typing:

EXECUTE '*filename*' [**K** *times*]

The optional argument K can be any integer; by default, Minitab executes macros once. The default file extension for macros is .MTB.

Macros allow you to:

- Store commands that you will use repeatedly, so you do not have to retype them each time.
- Repeat a block of commands many times. This is useful for simulations.
- Loop through columns of the worksheet, doing the same analysis on each block of columns.
- Loop through rows of the worksheet, doing the same analysis on each block of rows.
- Use Minitab as a programming language to perform operations not provided as standalone commands. You can even write an interactive macro that pauses during execution, prompts the user for information, and then continues with execution.

To interrupt the execution of a macro, press Ctrl-Break. Minitab executes the command in progress before it stops the macro.

A Simple Example

Each month, a laboratory sends you data on three chemical measurements: YIELD, CHEM1, and CHEM2. You always do the same analysis: descriptive statistics, plots of YIELD versus the two other measures, a regression, and a residual plot. Suppose you use a text editor or word processor to create the following file called ANALYSIS.MTB:

```
NAME C1 = 'YIELD' C2 = 'CHEM1' C3 =
   'CHEM2'
DESCRIBE C1-C3
PLOT C1 C2
PLOT C1 C3
REGRESS C1 2 C2 C3 C10 C11
NAME C10 = 'RESIDS' C11 = 'FITS'
PLOT C10 C11
```

Suppose you put the data for January in the file JAN.DAT, with the yield data in C1, the chemical 1 data in C2, and the chemical 2 data in C3. You could enter your data by choosing Import ASCII Data from the File menu and selecting the file JAN.DAT. Then you could do your analysis by executing the ANALYSIS macro through the Execute Macro dialog box. You can repeat this analysis each month.

How to Create Macros

There are three ways to create macros:

- With a text editor, as you just did. If you use a text editor, store the file in a standard (usually ASCII) format. If you create a macro with a word processor, save the file as text only.
- With the command JOURNAL (File ▶ Other Files ▶ Start Recording History...). This command stores a copy of all commands used in a Minitab session in a file with the extension .MTJ. When you execute this file, you must provide the .MTJ extension.
- With the command STORE (File ▶ Other Files ▶ Start Storing Macro...). It allows you to create a macro during your Minitab session.

Looping Through Commands

Suppose you want to train your eye to judge normal probability plots. You decide to generate 20 plots for data from a normal distribution. First store the following commands in a file called NPLOT.MTB:

```
RAND 50 C1
NSCORES C1 C2
NAME C1 = 'DATA' C2 = 'NSCORES'
PLOT C1 C2
```

To execute this file 20 times and get 20 different normal probability plots, either use the Execute Macro dialog box or type:

```
EXECUTE 'NPLOT' 20
```

You can also loop through rows of data. Suppose you have a full year of the laboratory data from the first example, one month stacked on top of another, in a file called LAB.DAT. There are now four variables, C1 YIELD, C2 CHEM1, C3 CHEM2, and C4 MONTH. To do the same analysis as before, separately for each month (in C4), store the following commands in the file YEAR.MTB:

```
NAME C11 = 'YIELD' C12 = 'CHEM1' C13&
   = 'CHEM2' C20 = 'RESIDS' C21 = 'FITS'
COPY C1-C3 C11-C13;
   USE C4 = K1
PRINT K1
DESCRIBE C11-C13
PLOT C11 C12
PLOT C11 C13
REGRESS C11 2 C12 C13 C20 C21
PLOT C20 C21
LET K1 = K1 + 1
```

Then, to analyze the file LAB.DAT, type:

LET K1 = 1
READ 'LAB' C1-C4
EXECUTE 'YEAR' 12

Looping Through Columns

A special feature, sometimes called the CK capability, allows you to loop through columns of the worksheet. Suppose you have a file, MYDATA.DAT, containing 21 variables, and you want to plot the last variable versus each of the first 20 variables in 20 separate plots. First store the following commands in a file called PLOTS.MTB:

PLOT C21 CK1
LET K1 = K1 + 1

Then type:

READ 'MYDATA' C1-C21
LET K1 = 1
EXECUTE 'PLOTS' 20

The first time through the loop, K1 = 1. This value is substituted for the K1 in the PLOT command, giving PLOT C21 C1. The next time through the loop, K1 = 2, giving PLOT C21 C2, and so on.

The next example shows how to accumulate column statistics in one column. Suppose you have data in C1 through C30 and you want to compute the mean of each column and store those means in C40. Store the following commands in the file MEAN.MTB:

LET C40(K1) = MEAN(CK1)
LET K1 = K1 + 1

Then type:

LET K1 = 1
EXECUTE 'MEAN' 30

The first time through the loop, K1 = 1, so row 1 of C40 will equal the mean of C1. The next time through the loop, K1 = 2, so row 2 of C40 will equal the mean of C2, and so on.

Conditional Execution and Nesting Macros

If the argument K on EXECUTE is zero or negative, then the macro is not executed. This feature allows you to do conditional execution. As an example, modify the macro MEAN so that it accumulates means for just those columns that have more than 9 observations. You will need two files. MEAN10.MTB contains:

```
LET K3 = (COUNT(CK1) > 9)
EXECUTE 'OVER9' K3
LET K1 = K1 + 1
```

and OVER9.MTB contains:

```
LET C40(K2) = MEAN(CK1)
LET K2 = K2 + 1
```

To use this macro, type:

LET K1 = 1
LET K2 = 1
EXECUTE 'MEAN10' 30

First notice that you have nested two macros, that is, MEAN10 calls (or executes) OVER9. Nesting helps you write fairly sophisticated macros. You can nest macros up to five deep on most computers.

To see how this macro works, consider a worksheet with three columns. Suppose C2 has 23 observations, C2 has 7, and C3 has 35. When you first execute MEAN10, K1 = K2 = 1. Then K3 = 1 since COUNT (C1) > 9. Since K3 = 1, OVER9 is executed once, MEAN (C1) is stored in C40 (1), and K2 = 2. For the second time through the loop, K2 = 2 and K1 = 2. This time K3 = 0 since COUNT (C2) < 9, and OVER9 is not executed. For the third time through the loop, K1 = 3 and K2 = 2. Then K3 = 1 since COUNT (C3) > 9, OVER9 is executed, and MEAN (C3) is stored in C40 (2).

Interactive Macros

It is possible to write a Minitab macro that will execute, pause for user input, and then continue executing. You can do this with the special filename TERMINAL with the READ, SET, and INSERT commands.

Suppose you have two macros. The first, PLANTS.MTB, is the same as before. The second, TOMATO.MTB, contains:

```
NOECHO
NOTE How many tomato plants do you
NOTE have this month?
SET 'TERMINAL' C50;
  NOBS = 1.
COPY C50 K50
EXEC 'PLANTS'
ECHO
```

When you type EXECUTE 'TOMATO', Minitab prints the note "How many tomato plants do you have this month?" The terminal then waits for you to respond. You type a number and press [↵]. The subcommand NOBS = 1 tells SET to expect just one number. This means the user of the macro does not have to type the word END to signal the end of typing data to SET. The macro TOMATO then executes with the correct number of plants.

Using YESNO

The YESNO command:

```
YESNO K
```

also takes input from the terminal. It prompts the user for a decision to execute or skip a block of commands. YESNO reads a YES or NO response from the terminal and changes the value of its argument, K, accordingly. YESNO sets K = 1 when the user responds YES and K = 0 when the user responds NO. YESNO takes only one argument and it must be a stored constant. Any response beginning with an upper- or lowercase Y is interpreted as a YES; any beginning with an upper- or lowercase N as a NO. All other responses are invalid; the user receives the message "Please answer Yes or No" and is given another opportunity. If Minitab does not obtain a valid response after five tries, it assumes a NO answer.

YESNO does not issue a prompt; it only reads a response. When you write a macro, you must use the NOTE command to prompt the user.

Using NOECHO and ECHO

The command NOECHO suppresses the printing of the Minitab prompt and commands, and ECHO turns it back on. Normally NOECHO is the first command in a command file and ECHO is the last. If the NOECHO command is used, then only output and the comments on NOTE commands are printed. Minitab does not print any commands or comments beginning with the # symbol.

APPENDIX A

Session Command / Menu Command Equivalents

This appendix is intended for those who are familiar with Minitab and who want to find the menu equivalents for session commands. The session commands are listed on the left, and the locations of those commands are on the right.

The symbol ▶ indicates submenus; for example, Calc ▶ Set Base means "Choose Set Base from the Calc menu." The sequence Stat ▶ Time Series ▶ Autocorrelation means "Choose Time Series and then Autocorrelation from the Stat menu."

"Not available" means that there is no menu equivalent for the given session command. *"Not available in the Student Edition"* means that that command is available from the menus in the commercial version of Minitab, but is not available (either from the menus or from the Session window) in the Student Edition.

A

ABSOLUTE	Calc ▶ Functions and Statistics ▶ General Expressions...
	Calc ▶ Functions and Statistics ▶ Functions...
ACF	Stat ▶ Time Series ▶ Autocorrelation...
ACOS	Calc ▶ Functions and Statistics ▶ General Expressions...
	Calc ▶ Functions and Statistics ▶ Functions...
ADD	Calc ▶ Functions and Statistics ▶ General Expressions...
ANCOVA	*Not available in the Student Edition*
ANOM (macro)	*Not available in the Student Edition*

ANOVA	Stat ► ANOVA ► Balanced ANOVA...
ANTILOG	Calc ► Functions and Statistics ► General Expressions...
	Calc ► Functions and Statistics ► Functions...
AOVONEWAY	Stat ► ANOVA ► Oneway (Unstacked)...
ARIMA	Stat ► Time Series ► ARIMA...
ASIN	Calc ► Functions and Statistics ► General Expressions...
	Calc ► Functions and Statistics ► Functions...
ATAN	Calc ► Functions and Statistics ► General Expressions...
	Calc ► Functions and Statistics ► Functions...

B

BASE	Calc ► Set Base...
BOXPLOT	Graph ► Boxplot...
BREG	*Not available in the Student Edition*
BRIEF	*Not available*

C

CAPA (macro)	*Not available in the Student Edition*
CCF	Stat ► Time Series ► Cross Correlation...
CCHART	Stat ► SPC Charts ► C...
CDF	Calc ► Probability Distributions ► distribution
CENTER	Calc ► Standardize...
CHISQUARE	Stat ► Tables ► Chisquare Test...
CODE	Calc ► Code Data Values...
CONCATENATE	Calc ► Concatenate...
CONSTANT	Stat ► Fit Intercept
CONTOUR	*Not available in the Student Edition*
CONVERT	Calc ► Convert...
COPY	Calc ► Copy Columns...
CORRELATION	Stat ► Basic Statistics ► Correlation...
COS	Calc ► Functions and Statistics ► General Expressions...
	Calc ► Functions and Statistics ► Functions...
COUNT	Calc ► Functions and Statistics ► General Expressions...
	Calc ► Functions and Statistics ► Column Statistics...
COVARIANCE	Stat ► Basic Statistics ► Covariance...
CPLOT	*Not available in the Student Edition*
CTABLE	*Not available in the Student Edition*
CUSUM (macro)	*Not available in the Student Edition*

D

DEFINE	*Not available in the Student Edition*
DELETE	Calc ▶ Delete Rows...
DESCRIBE	Stat ▶ Basic Statistics ▶ Descriptive Statistics...
DIAGONAL	*Not available in the Student Edition*
DIFFERENCES	Stat ▶ Time Series ▶ Differences...
DISCRIMINANT	*Not available in the Student Edition*
DIVIDE	Calc ▶ Functions and Statistics ▶ General Expressions...
DOTPLOT	Graph ▶ Dotplot...

E

ECHO	*Not available*
EIGEN	*Not available in the Student Edition*
END	File ▶ Other Files ▶ Stop Storing Macro
ERASE	Calc ▶ Erase Variables...
EWMACHART	Stat ▶ SPC Charts ▶ EWMA...
EXECUTE	File ▶ Other Files ▶ Execute Macro...
EXPONENTIATE	Calc ▶ Functions and Statistics ▶ General Expressions...
	Calc ▶ Functions and Statistics ▶ Functions...

F

FFACTORIAL	*Not available in the Student Edition*
FFDESIGN	*Not available in the Student Edition*
FRIEDMAN	*Not available in the Student Edition*

G

GBOXPLOT	Graph ▶ Boxplot...
GCCHART	Stat ▶ SPC Charts ▶ C...
GEWMACHART	Stat ▶ SPC Charts ▶ EWMA...
GHISTOGRAM	Graph ▶ Histogram...
GICHART	Stat ▶ SPC Charts ▶ Individuals...
GLM	*Not available in the Student Edition*
GLPLOT	Graph ▶ Scatter Plot...
GMACHART	Stat ▶ SPC Charts ▶ Moving Average...
GMPLOT	Graph ▶ Multiple Scatter Plot...
GMRCHART	Stat ▶ SPC Charts ▶ Moving Range...
GNPCHART	Stat ▶ SPC Charts ▶ NP...

GOPTIONS	*Not available*
GPCHART	Stat ▶ SPC Charts ▶ P...
GPLOT	Graph ▶ Scatter Plot...
GRCHART	Stat ▶ SPC Charts ▶ R...
GRID	*Not available in the Student Edition*
GSCHART	Stat ▶ SPC Charts ▶ S...
GTPLOT	Graph ▶ Pseudo 3-D Plot...
GUCHART	Stat ▶ SPC Charts ▶ U...
GXBARCHART	Stat ▶ SPC Charts ▶ Xbar...

H

HEIGHT	Graph ▶ Set Options...
HELP	Data Screen Menu ▶ Help...
HISTOGRAM	Graph ▶ Histogram...

I

ICHART	Stat ▶ SPC Charts ▶ Individuals...
INDICATOR	Calc ▶ Make Indicator Variables...
INFO	Edit ▶ Get Worksheet Info...
INSERT	File ▶ Import ASCII data...
INVCDF	Calc ▶ Probability Distributions ▶ distribution
INVERT	*Not available in the Student Edition*
IW	*Not available*

J

JOURNAL	File ▶ Other Files ▶ Start Recording History...

K

KRUSKAL-WALLIS	Stat ▶ Nonparametrics ▶ Kruskal-Wallis...

L

LAG	Calc ▶ Functions and Statistics ▶ General Expressions...
	Stat ▶ Time Series ▶ Lag...
LET	Calc ▶ Functions and Statistics ▶ General Expressions...
LOGE	Calc ▶ Functions and Statistics ▶ General Expressions...
	Calc ▶ Functions and Statistics ▶ Functions...

LOGTEN	Calc ▶ Functions and Statistics ▶ General Expressions...
	Calc ▶ Functions and Statistics ▶ Functions...
LPLOT	Graph ▶ Scatter Plot...
LVALS	*Not available in the Student Edition*

M

MACHART	Stat ▶ SPC Charts ▶ Moving Average...
MANN-WHITNEY	Stat ▶ Nonparametrics ▶ Mann-Whitney...
MAXIMUM	Calc ▶ Functions and Statistics ▶ General Expressions...
	Calc ▶ Functions and Statistics ▶ Column Statistics...
MEAN	Calc ▶ Functions and Statistics ▶ General Expressions...
	Calc ▶ Functions and Statistics ▶ Column Statistics...
MEDIAN	Calc ▶ Functions and Statistics ▶ General Expressions...
	Calc ▶ Functions and Statistics ▶ Column Statistics...
MINIMUM	Calc ▶ Functions and Statistics ▶ General Expressions...
	Calc ▶ Functions and Statistics ▶ Column Statistics...
MOOD	*Not available in the Student Edition*
MPLOT	Graph ▶ Multiple Scatter Plot...
MPOLISH	*Not available in the Student Edition*
MRCHART	Stat ▶ SPC Charts ▶ Moving Range...
MTSPLOT	Stat ▶ Time Series ▶ Time Series Plot...
	Graph ▶ Time Series Plot...
MULTIPLY	Calc ▶ Functions and Statistics ▶ General Expressions...

N

N	Calc ▶ Functions and Statistics ▶ General Expressions...
	Calc ▶ Functions and Statistics ▶ Column Statistics...
NAME	*Not available*
NMISS	Calc ▶ Functions and Statistics ▶ General Expressions...
	Calc ▶ Functions and Statistics ▶ Column Statistics...
NOCONSTANT	Stat ▶ Fit Intercept...
NOECHO	*Not available*
NOJOURNAL	File ▶ Other Files ▶ Stop Recording History
NOOUTFILE	File ▶ Other Files ▶ Stop Recording Session
NOTE	*Not available*
NPCHART	Stat ▶ SPC Charts ▶ NP...
NSCORES	Calc ▶ Functions and Statistics ▶ General Expressions...
	Calc ▶ Functions and Statistics ▶ Functions...

O

ONEWAY	Stat ▶ ANOVA ▶ Oneway...
OUTFILE	File ▶ Other Files ▶ Start Recording Session...
OW	*Not available*

P

PACF	Stat ▶ Time Series ▶ Partial Autocorrelation...
PARETO (macro)	*Not available in the Student Edition*
PARPRODUCTS	Calc ▶ Functions and Statistics ▶ General Expressions...
	Calc ▶ Functions and Statistics ▶ Functions...
PARSUMS	Calc ▶ Functions and Statistics ▶ General Expressions...
	Calc ▶ Functions and Statistics ▶ Functions...
PBDESIGN	*Not available in the Student Edition*
PCA	*Not available in the Student Edition*
PCHART	Stat ▶ SPC Charts ▶ P...
PDF	Calc ▶ Probability Distributions ▶ distribution
PLOT	Graph ▶ Scatter Plot...
PRINT	Edit ▶ Display Data...

Q

QCMACROS	*Not available in the Student Edition*

R

RAISE	Calc ▶ Functions and Statistics ▶ General Expressions...
RANDOM	Calc ▶ Random Data ▶ distribution
RANK	Calc ▶ Rank...
	Calc ▶ Functions and Statistics ▶ General Expressions...
RCHART	Stat ▶ SPC Charts ▶ R...
RCOUNT	Calc ▶ Functions and Statistics ▶ Row Statistics...
READ	File ▶ Import ASCII data...
REGRESS	Stat ▶ Regression ▶ Regression...
RESTART	File ▶ Restart Minitab
RETRIEVE	File ▶ Open Worksheet...
RLINE	*Not available in the Student Edition*
RMAXIMUM	Calc ▶ Functions and Statistics ▶ Row Statistics...
RMEAN	Calc ▶ Functions and Statistics ▶ Row Statistics...
RMEDIAN	Calc ▶ Functions and Statistics ▶ Row Statistics...

RMINIMUM	Calc ▶ Functions and Statistics ▶ Row Statistics...
RN	Calc ▶ Functions and Statistics ▶ Row Statistics...
RNMISS	Calc ▶ Functions and Statistics ▶ Row Statistics...
ROOTOGRAM	*Not available in the Student Edition*
ROUND	Calc ▶ Functions and Statistics ▶ General Expressions...
RSMOOTH	*Not available in the Student Edition*
RSSQ	Calc ▶ Functions and Statistics ▶ Row Statistics...
RSTDEV	Calc ▶ Functions and Statistics ▶ Row Statistics...
RSUM	Calc ▶ Functions and Statistics ▶ Row Statistics...
RUNS	Stat ▶ Nonparametrics ▶ Runs Test...

S

SAMPLE	Calc ▶ Random Data ▶ Sample from Columns...
SAVE	File ▶ Save Worksheet As...
SCHART	Stat ▶ SPC Charts ▶ S...
SET	Edit ▶ Set Patterned Data...
SIGN	Calc ▶ Functions and Statistics ▶ General Expressions...
	Calc ▶ Functions and Statistics ▶ Functions...
SIN	Calc ▶ Functions and Statistics ▶ General Expressions...
	Calc ▶ Functions and Statistics ▶ Functions...
SINTERVAL	Stat ▶ Nonparametrics ▶ 1-Sample Sign...
SORT	Calc ▶ Sort...
SQRT	Calc ▶ Functions and Statistics ▶ General Expressions...
	Calc ▶ Functions and Statistics ▶ Functions...
SSQ	Calc ▶ Functions and Statistics ▶ General Expressions...
	Calc ▶ Functions and Statistics ▶ Column Statistics...
STACK	Calc ▶ Stack...
STDEV	Calc ▶ Functions and Statistics ▶ General Expressions...
	Calc ▶ Functions and Statistics ▶ Column Statistics...
STEM-AND-LEAF	Graph ▶ Stem-and-Leaf...
STEPWISE	Stat ▶ Regression ▶ Stepwise...
STEST	Stat ▶ Nonparametrics ▶ 1-Sample Sign...
STOP	File ▶ Exit
STORE	File ▶ Other Files ▶ Start Storing Macro...
SUBTRACT	Calc ▶ Functions and Statistics ▶ General Expressions...
SUM	Calc ▶ Functions and Statistics ▶ General Expressions...
	Calc ▶ Functions and Statistics ▶ Column Statistics...

T

TABLE	Stat ▶ Tables ▶ Cross Tabulation...
TALLY	Stat ▶ Tables ▶ Tally...
TAN	Calc ▶ Functions and Statistics ▶ General Expressions...
	Calc ▶ Functions and Statistics ▶ Functions...
TINTERVAL	Stat ▶ Basic Statistics ▶ 1-Sample t...
TPLOT	Graph ▶ Psuedo 3-D Plot...
TRANSPOSE	*Not available in the Student Edition*
TSPLOT	Stat ▶ Time Series ▶ Time Series Plot...
	Graph ▶ Time Series Plot...
TTEST	Stat ▶ Basic Statistics ▶ 1-Sample t...
TWOSAMPLE	Stat ▶ Basic Statistics ▶ 2-Sample t...
TWOT	Stat ▶ Basic Statistics ▶ 2-Sample t...
TWOWAY	Stat ▶ ANOVA ▶ Twoway...

U

UCHART	Stat ▶ SPC Charts ▶ U...
UNSTACK	Calc ▶ Unstack...

W

WALSH	Stat ▶ Nonparametrics ▶ Pairwise Averages...
WDIFF	Stat ▶ Nonparametrics ▶ Pairwise Differences...
WIDTH	Graph ▶ Set Options...
WINTERVAL	Stat ▶ Nonparametrics ▶ 1-Sample Wilcoxon...
WRITE	File ▶ Export ASCII data...
WSLOPE	Stat ▶ Nonparametrics ▶ Pairwise Slopes...
WTEST	Stat ▶ Nonparametrics ▶ 1-Sample Wilcoxon...

X

XBARCHART	Stat ▶ SPC Charts ▶ Xbar...

Y

YESNO	*Not available*

Z

ZINTERVAL	Stat ▶ Basic Statistics ▶ 1-Sample Z...
ZTEST	Stat ▶ Basic Statistics ▶ 1-Sample Z...

APPENDIX B

Additional Installation and System Notes

Optimizing Performance

There are many ways to manage memory on a PC, and you will need to determine precisely how you should set up your computer to optimize Minitab's performance. This section explains how Minitab uses memory. It also explains some of the options you have to control memory management on your PC.

How Minitab Uses Memory

Minitab is a large program that cannot fit within the 640Kb conventional memory provided in the MS-DOS (PC-DOS) operating environment. To work around this limitation, Minitab uses a virtual memory paging mechanism, where the program is divided into many smaller parts, called *pages,* that can be brought into the paging area and executed as needed.

Minitab needs about 470Kb of conventional memory to start with the full worksheet, plus at least 150Kb of memory to use for the paging area. Minitab can use the 150Kb of memory for paging from available conventional memory, extended memory, or expanded memory. If more than 150Kb of memory is available, Minitab will use it, and run faster as a result. (If you have less than 470Kb of conventional memory available when you start Minitab, your worksheet will be less than the full worksheet size of 3,500 cells.)

Making Minitab Run Faster

Minitab won't run properly if your computer is not set up to take advantage of the extended or expanded memory that is installed. You must first make sure you have an extended memory manager such as Microsoft's HIMEM.SYS or Quarterdeck's QEMM386.SYS installed on your hard disk and specified properly in your CONFIG.SYS file.

The section called Installation and Setup, early in this manual, explains how to do this. You receive the extended memory manager HIMEM.SYS with *The Student Edition of Minitab,* but you can use a different one if you wish. The only requirement is that the extended memory manager you have must conform to the XMS 2.0 or higher specification.

You can use a disk caching program, such as SMARTDRV.SYS, with Minitab, as long as you still have enough memory available for Minitab to use. There is no noticeable difference in Minitab's performance between having free extended memory, free expanded memory, or using a disk caching program.

Making Minitab's High-Resolution Graphics Run Faster

Each time you produce a high-resolution graph, Minitab writes two temporary files, named MTB$$$xx, to the disk. These files take about 600Kb of disk space. Minitab deletes these files as soon as the high-resolution graph clears from the screen. By default, Minitab writes these temporary files to the current directory. You can change this default by using the environment variable TMP.

If you have enough memory to set up a RAM disk with at least 600Kb of space, while still leaving sufficient memory available for regular Minitab operation, you can greatly speed up high-resolution graphics. Instructing Minitab to write these temporary graphics files to a RAM disk instead of to your hard disk will improve graphics performance.

First, set up the RAM disk according to the instructions in your DOS manual. Next, specify the RAM disk as the default location for the temporary graphics files. For example, if the RAM disk is drive E on your system, use this command:

```
SET TMP=E:\
```

Last, include the command to set up the RAM disk in your CONFIG.SYS file and the SET TMP command in your AUTOEXEC.BAT file.

Note: Windows users should not use a RAM disk.

Notes for Network Administrators

There are a few issues that you should be aware of when setting up Minitab to run on a network: file access, setup for temporary files, individual configuration files, and using a shared printer or plotter.

File Access

Make sure that all users can read all files in the Minitab directory and its subdirectories. The tutorials assume that students access sample files from the Sample Files disk, because many labs do not allow students to copy such files to a file server. The tutorials do not require that students save their changed data files, but for those who would like to, they can save them to the Sample Files disk.

Setup for Temporary Files

Make sure users can write temporary files to a disk that has 600Kb of available space. Minitab writes temporary files to disk in three different situations: 1) when the user executes a high-resolution graphics command, 2) when the user executes the DOS shell command, SYSTEM, and 3) when the user retrieves or saves a Lotus file.

When the user executes a high-resolution graphics command, Minitab writes two temporary files to disk. These are named MTB$$$xx, where xx is a one- or two-letter character string. When the high-resolution graph clears from the screen, Minitab deletes the files.

When a user executes the DOS shell command, SYSTEM, or retrieves or saves a Lotus file, Minitab writes a temporary file of about 500Kb in size to disk.

By default, Minitab writes these temporary files to the user's current directory. This will be a problem if that directory is write-protected on your system. You can change this default with the environment variable TMP. For example, if you want Minitab to write a user's temporary files to the G:\TEMP directory, put the line

```
SET TMP=G:\TEMP
```

in that user's AUTOEXEC.BAT file. Minitab assigns a unique name to each temporary file so that Minitab does not inadvertently overwrite one user's temporary file with another user's temporary file.

Deleting the Temporary Files

Normally, Minitab deletes the temporary files during the user session. However, if the user session aborts, those temporary files remain on the disk. If you do discover these files on your system, you should delete them.

Individual Configuration Files

Set users up so that their individual configuration files, MTB8_A.CFG and MINITAB.INI, are in their own directory, not in the main MINITAB directory.

When you execute MSETUP to specify screen and printer drivers and other setup parameters (see Getting Started [Part I] of this manual), Minitab saves those settings in a file named MTB8_A.CFG. Upon startup, Minitab looks in the user's current directory for this file before looking in the main MINITAB directory. To prevent each user from overwriting information set by the previous user, put a copy of the appropriate MTB8_A.CFG in each user's directory.

If a user changes screen colors by choosing Set Colors from the Edit menu from within Minitab, Minitab saves that information in a file named MINITAB.INI in the user's current directory. As long as the user has write privileges to the current directory, this should not require any action on the administrator's part.

Shared Printers

Minitab has two options for sending output directly to a printer: 1) The PAPER command, which sends output directly to the printer as it appears on the screen, and 2) "P to print or plot," which sends high-resolution output directly to the printer while a high-resolution graph is on the screen.

These options are designed for a stand-alone PC with a printer cabled directly to it. They may not work on a network with shared printers. If this is the case on your network, please instruct your users to use these alternatives:

Instead of using PAPER, use the OUTFILE command (choose Start Recording Session... from the Other Files submenu in the File menu). This stores a record of the Minitab session in an ASCII file, which the user can print out later from the DOS prompt.

Instead of pressing P to print high-resolution graphics, store the graph in a file by using the FILE subcommand or by checking "Store in file" in the Graph dialog box. Then print the graph by using the DOS command COPY to copy the file to the appropriate output port.

Notes for Windows Users

Minitab supplies a PIF file for your use of Minitab as a non-Windows application under Windows Version 3.0. Non-Windows applications do not need a PIF file to run unless the application has memory requirements different from Windows defaults. Since Minitab requires the use of extended memory, the supplied PIF file requests a minimum of 150Kb and a maximum of 1024Kb of extended memory from Windows. The PIF file has been set up for both the standard and the enhanced modes of Windows. You may want to edit the PIF file to suit your needs.

Windows suggests that all PIF files be stored in the WINDOWS subdirectory. We recommend that you move the file MINITAB.PIF from the MINITAB subdirectory to the WINDOWS subdirectory. The PIF file assumes that you have installed Minitab in C:\MINITAB. If Minitab is installed in a different location, edit the PIF file to reflect the correct drive and directory.

Neither Microsoft, Minitab, nor Addison-Wesley guarantee that non-Windows applications can coexist or be multi-tasked under Windows. Minitab has been tested by itself and with non-Windows applications. If you experience problems, you may need to terminate applications to determine the conflict. Refer to the troubleshooting section of the Windows manual.

PC Details

Worksheet size: 3,500
Number of columns: 100
Number of constants: 100
Number of matrices: Matrices are not supported in the Student Edition
Maximum width of alpha format variables: 80
Alpha data supported in the following commands: COPY, CONVERT, CONCATENATE, DELETE, ERASE, INFO, INSERT, PRINT, READ, SET, SORT, STACK, UNSTACK, WRITE.
Maximum number of characters per line for

READ free format: 512 (max. IW)
READ formatted: 2048
WRITE free format: 132
WRITE formatted: 512
Defaults for:
 OW: 78 (maximum 132)
 OH: 0
 IW: 160 (maximum 512)
 BRIEF: 2
 HEIGHT of plots: 17
 WIDTH of plots: 57

Maximum number of open files: 6 (5 nested macros plus an outfile)

Worksheet Size

When you start Minitab, the Session window displays the worksheet size, or the maximum number of cells that columns can occupy. Since Minitab also uses the worksheet for work space when executing your commands, it is generally advisable to limit your data to approximately half of this number.

The largest possible worksheet is 3,500 cells. If you have less than the required memory on your system, Minitab still runs but your worksheet size is reduced.

Data Screen

The Data screen provides a full-screen view of the Minitab worksheet and is useful for entering and editing data. Use [Alt]-D to enter the Data screen and [Alt]-M to leave it. For more information, press [F1] from within the Data screen.

PC/DOS-Specific Commands

The subcommand LOTUS can be used with SAVE and RETRIEVE to interface directly with Lotus 1-2-3 or Symphony spreadsheets. The DOS commands TYPE, CD, or CHDIR, and DIR work from within Minitab as they do from DOS.

DOS Shell Commands

To temporarily exit Minitab to DOS, type:

```
MTB> SYSTEM
```

Note: Do not change your DOS PATH during a Minitab session, or load a TSR, mouse driver, etc.

To return to your Minitab session type:

EXIT

See HELP SYSTEM for more information.

Break

To interrupt a running macro, press Ctrl-Break. Minitab finishes the command it is executing and then returns to the MTB > prompt. The macro file will be closed, but any other files, e.g. outfiles, journal files, etc. will remain open.

To interrupt high-resolution graphics or to interrupt display of output to the screen from the commands PRINT or TYPE, press Ctrl-Break.

At any other time, Minitab ignores Ctrl-Break and will not return you to the MTB > prompt until the command has been fully executed.

Color Selection

To change the colors on your screen, choose Set Colors from the Edit menu from within Minitab. After you choose OK, Minitab saves the new color settings in a file named MINITAB.INI in your current directory. The next time you start Minitab from that directory, Minitab reads MINITAB.INI and set screen colors accordingly.

Command Line Arguments

There are several optional arguments you can use when you start Minitab. The syntax for executing Minitab is:

MINITAB [-?] [-S nnnn] [-I MACRO_FILE]

-? Prints a usage message explaining the optional command line arguments to the screen without starting Minitab.

-S By default, 8,192 characters of your Minitab session are kept in a buffer. This means that while in Minitab, you can scroll back through the Session window as far back as 8,192 characters. If this buffer fills up, Minitab deletes the first half of the buffer to make room for new text.

If you have enough conventional memory, you can increase the size of this buffer. For example, typing:

MINITAB -S 10000

starts Minitab with a Session window buffer size of 10,000 characters.

If you are low on memory, you may want to decrease your buffer size, especially if you are not getting the full worksheet size of 3,500 cells. Decreasing the buffer size allows the worksheet to grow, up to the limit of 3,500 cells. The trade-off rate is one worksheet cell gained for every four characters of buffer size lost. The buffer size must be at least 2,000.

The -S argument does not affect an outfile, which stores all of your session no matter how long it is.

-I MACRO_FILE Specifies a macro file to execute upon startup. Use this argument to override STARTUP.MTB or to run Minitab in a batch program.

Upon startup, Minitab looks in your current directory for a file named STARTUP.MTB that Minitab executes automatically if it exists. If you start Minitab with the -I argument, however, Minitab ignores any file named STARTUP.MTB and executes the specified macro file instead.

For example, the command

MINITAB -I C:\TEST\RUNS

starts Minitab and automatically executes the file named RUNS.MTB in the C:\TEST directory.

Setup for Temporary Files

Minitab writes temporary files to disk in three different situations: 1) when you execute a high-resolution graphics command, 2) when you execute the DOS shell command, SYSTEM, and 3) when you retrieve or save a Lotus file.

When you execute a high-resolution graphics command, Minitab writes two temporary files to disk. These are named MTB$$$xx, where xx is a one- or two-letter character string. When the high-resolution graph clears from the screen, Minitab deletes the files.

When you execute the DOS shell command, SYSTEM, or retrieve or save a Lotus file, Minitab writes a temporary file of about 500Kb in size to disk.

By default, Minitab writes these temporary files to your current directory. You can change this default with the environment variable TMP. For example, if you want Minitab to write your temporary files to the C:\TEMP directory, put the line

SETTMP=C:\TEMP

in your AUTOEXEC.BAT file.

Deleting the Temporary Files

Normally, Minitab deletes the temporary files during your session. However, if the session aborts, those temporary files remain on the disk. If you do discover these files on your system, you should delete them.

Running Minitab as Part of a Batch Program

You may want to write a batch program that uses several different applications including Minitab. Here are some tips for doing that:

Start Minitab using the -I argument described above.

Insert the command BATCH at the top of your macro. This ensures that the macro executes without pausing for user input (except for cases where you have specifically programmed that in, such as with READ 'TERMINAL').

End the macro with the command STOP. This exits Minitab and passes control back to the batch program.

APPENDIX C

High-Resolution Graphics

Any word processing application that can do screen captures or import PostScript files can use Minitab graphs. *The Student Edition of Minitab* uses PostScript-compatible printers to display high-resolution graphics in word processed reports through the PostScript Device Plotter Driver. This appendix shows you how to implement Minitab graphics into documents produced by WordPerfect 5.1 and Microsoft Word 5.0. Both packages allow you to add a caption to the graphic, size and rotate it, put a border around it, and perform numerous additional layout tasks.

PostScript Printer Instructions

Minitab implements PostScript printers as plotters because of the smaller graphics file size and the higher resolution allowed through the plotter driver. To use your PostScript printer with Minitab, you must first select a PostScript device driver.

Setup for a PostScript Printer

- At the DOS prompt, open the MSETUP menu; change to the directory where Minitab is installed, then type **MSETUP**
- Choose the "Select Plotter Driver for Hi-Res Graphics" command from the MSETUP menu
- Select PostScript Device

A message tells you that you have chosen the file AHDPS.EXE as the PostScript device. (You may have to reinstall this driver if you removed it earlier; screen prompts will explain how to do this.) When you save Minitab graphics as plotter files, Minitab saves them in a format that can be interpreted by a PostScript printer.

Producing a PostScript Graph in Minitab

Before creating the Minitab graph, first set the hard copy device as a plotter:

- Choose **G**raph ► **S**et Options
- Press [Alt]-L to choose the third option, Hard-copy device is a plotter (this is the session command GOPTIONS; PLOTTER)
- Press [↵]

If you want to save the graph in a PostScript file:

- Press [Alt]-F for Store in **F**ile

Because you have selected a PostScript driver as your plotter device, Minitab saves the graph you make in a format that can be interpreted by a PostScript printer. Create the graph, and then indicate where it should be stored.

Minitab prompts you to give a filename; the graph appears on the screen. You can press Q for Quit or N for Next. When Minitab has displayed all the graphs you requested, it returns to the Session window. It has saved the graphics file in a format that can be imported into any word processing program that can interpret PostScript printer files.

Including High-Resolution Minitab Graphs in Reports

For the best resolution, use file import rather than screen capture to include graphics in your documents. With screen capture, the graphic's resolution is only as good as the resolution of your screen. For example, if you have a CGA monitor with 640 x 200 resolution, the graphic will not be as sharp as one stored in a PostScript file.

The next two sections explain how to include Minitab high-resolution graphs in both WordPerfect 5.1 and Microsoft Word 5.0 documents. For complete information on incorporating graphs into your reports, refer to your word processing documentation.

Minitab Graphics in WordPerfect 5.1 Documents

Use the following steps to import the stored graphic file into WordPerfect:

- Start WordPerfect

When you are ready to include the stored graphic file:

- Press [Alt]-[F9] to display the Graphics menu
- Select Figure
- Select Create
- Select Filename and enter the filename of the Minitab graphics file (you can also press [F5] to list your files)
- Select Edit
- Select Invert Off

WordPerfect imports the file into your document. You can use the Figure options to position the graphic on the page, and the Edit options to size, rotate, and invert it. When you edit the graphic, you will see a box indicating that this is a PostScript printer file. To see how the graphic looks on the page, print it on any PostScript-compatible printer.

You can also use the WordPerfect screen capture utility called GRAB to capture Minitab screen graphics so you can include them in your WordPerfect documents.

- Copy the WordPerfect file GRAB.COM into a directory in your path
- At the DOS prompt, type **GRAB** to start the screen capture utility; type **GRAB /H** for help using GRAB options
- Start Minitab
- Display the high-resolution graphic you want to capture
- Press [Alt]-[Shift]-[F9] simultaneously (a two-tone chime indicates that GRAB is working; a box appears on the screen)
- Use the arrow keys to move the box and [Shift] plus the arrow keys to size the box to include the part of the graphic you want to capture
- Press [↵]

This saves the selected part of the graphic as file GRAB.WPG. If GRAB.WPG already exists, then the file will be named GRAB1.WPG, GRAB2.WPG, and so on, up to GRAB9999.WPG.

Repeat the previous four steps to GRAB additional Minitab graphics.

- Exit Minitab
- Start WordPerfect

When you are ready to include the captured graphic, press [Alt]-[F9] to display the graphics menu. Perform the following steps:

- Select Figure
- Select Create
- Select Filename and enter the filename of the Minitab graphics file
- Select Edit
- Select Invert Off
- Press [↵]

Graphics captured using GRAB will not have resolution as high as graphics stored in PostScript files, but you can print them on any printer.

Minitab Graphics in Microsoft Word 5.0 Documents

Minitab high-resolution graphics can also be included in a Microsoft Word 5.0 document using either file import or screen capture. Again, file import usually gives you a better graphic than screen capture if you have a low-resolution monitor. Microsoft Word also supports import of PostScript files. To import these PostScript files into your Word document:

- Start Word
- In your document, move the highlight to where you want to insert the graphic
- Press [Esc] to put Word in command mode and choose Library Link Graphics

- Enter the filename of the graphics file you want to put into the document or press [F1] to display a list of files

If Word can't detect the correct format of the file, you may need to press [F1] and select the correct format (PostScript).

- In the "alignment in frame" field, press [F1] and select Left, Right, or Centered (Centered is the default)
- Change the "graphics width" field, if necessary
- Change the "graphics height" field, if necessary
- Press [↵] to import the graphic

As in WordPerfect, you will not be able to view the graphic until you have printed it.

You can also use Capture.COM, Microsoft Word's screen capture utility, to include Minitab screen graphics in Word documents. Here's how you use it to capture a Minitab screen graphic.

- Make sure the Capture.COM file is in the path
- At the DOS prompt, type **CAPTURE** to start the capture utility
- Start Minitab
- Display the high-resolution graphic you want to capture
- Press [Shift]-[PrintScrn]
- Use the filename supplied by Word or enter a filename of your choice (up to 8 characters); Word adds the .SCR file name extension
- Use the arrow keys to position the boundary lines around the part of the graphic you want to capture; use [Tab] to activate the bottom and right lines for clipping, or to reactivate the top and left lines
- Press [↵] to capture the graphic

  Repeat the last four steps to capture additional screen graphics.

- Exit Minitab

You can import the file created using screen capture into Microsoft Word using the procedure described in the beginning of this section.

APPENDIX D

Error Messages

Minitab catches most mistakes before placing the session commands in the Session window, reporting them in a message box, with suggestions for correcting the problems. When you press [↵] or click OK in the message box, Minitab places the text cursor in the text box containing the error. When appropriate, the portion of the text that is causing the problem is highlighted.

Minitab does not discover errors involving the data values in a column until it attempts to execute session commands. In this case, the Session window displays a message explaining the error. To return to the last dialog box to correct the mistake, choose Edit Last Command Dialog from the Edit menu. The keyboard shortcut [Alt]-L makes this easy.

Error Types

There are three types of error messages, listed below in increasing order of severity.

Notes

If you do something that Minitab thinks might be an error, Minitab prints a note, but still completes execution of the commands. For example, Minitab prints a note if you add two columns of unequal length, divide by zero, or take the square root of a negative number. When it is not possible to compute an answer, Minitab sets the result equal to the missing value code *.

Error (command skipped)

If an error is too serious for reasonable action to be taken, Minitab prints an error message describing the nature of the problem, and it does not execute the command. In a macro, if the command does not involve any storage of data (for example, plotting a graph or displaying a table), the remaining commands in the macro are executed.

Error (fatal)

In a macro, if an error is too serious for reasonable corrective action to be taken, and it occurs in a command that involves storage of data (for example, storing the sum of a column or storing fitted values), Minitab prints the error message. Minitab does not execute remaining commands in the macro; it just checks them for correct syntax and "echo prints" them.

The following tables discuss error messages and problematic situations that may occur when you use Minitab on DOS computers. Detecting and correcting these errors can help you avoid mistakes that produce incorrect answers or destroy valuable data.

Error Messages

If you see any of the following error messages, take the action described.

Error Message	Cause	Action
"Not ready error reading drive A Abort, Retry, Ignore?"	There is no disk in drive A (or B), the drive door/latch is not closed, or the disk drive is faulty.	Insert the correct disk in the specified drive and close the drive door/latch. Type I, for ignore, to return to Minitab. If necessary, retype the Minitab command. Use the Retry and Abort options with caution. Under certain conditions, Retry can destroy the files on the diskette by overwriting the directory. Abort will exit Minitab without giving you the chance to SAVE your worksheet.

"*ERROR* Requested file does not exist."	Minitab cannot locate the file requested by RETRIEVE, READ, SET, INSERT, or EXECUTE. Either the file is not in the directory you specified or the command you are using is not appropriate for the file type.	Include the location of the file (the path) within the single quotes with the file name. For example, enter: MTB> RETRIEVE 'C:\MINITAB\DATA\PROF' or MTB> EXECUTE 'A:MACRO1' If you still get the same error message, you may need to use a different command. Use the READ, SET, or INSERT commands with ASCII data (*.DAT) files. Use the RETRIEVE command with saved worksheet (*.MTW) files.
"*Check for filename with no quote" *ERROR* Missing or stray quote *Name or file may be ignored *Check for file-name with no quote Worksheet saved into file: MINITAB.MTW or Worksheet retrieved from file: MINITAB.MTW"	One of these messages is displayed when you forget to enclose the file name in single quotes, or you used the wrong type of quotes.	Enter the Minitab command with the file name correctly enclosed in single quotes. For example, enter MTB> RETRIEVE '\DATA\PROF' Note that the file may have been saved or retrieved under the default file name, MINITAB.MTW.
"Bad command or filename" (in response to typing MINITAB)	DOS cannot locate MINITAB.BAT, the command file used to start Minitab.	The directory that contains MINITAB.BAT is not in the path. Set up the path to include the MINITAB directory (or other directory that contains the Minitab files).
"*ERROR* Not enough memory - conversion not complete."	The LOTUS subcommand used with SAVE and RETRIEVE requires additional memory above the amount required to run Minitab.	Divide the worksheet into two parts and convert each part separately. Combine the two parts after each has been converted. Use the WRITE and READ commands to divide Minitab worksheets.

"Write fault error writing device COM1, Abort, Retry, Ignore, Fail" (and the printer stops)	May occur when you print a stored (with the FILE subcommand) plotter-style graphic.	Enter R (for Retry) one or more times to complete output at the printer.
"Font File Not Found: AHD106.FNT. Please make sure the file is in your path." The screen mode may also be altered, causing the cursor to disappear or stop flashing, the screen to go blank, or other abnormal screen behavior.	The AHD106.FNT file is missing from your hard disk.	First, correct the screen mode by entering MODE BW80 or MODE CO80 at the DOS prompt. Then, install the AHD106.FNT file from the original Minitab diskettes into the Minitab directory on your hard disk.
"Graphics Error Number 15 in Subroutine Number 304." Also, the screen mode is altered, causing the cursor to disappear or stop flashing, the screen to go blank, or other abnormal screen behavior.	The printer driver (*.PRT file) that you selected in MSETUP is corrupted.	First, correct the screen mode by entering MODE BW80 or MODE CO80 at the DOS prompt. Then install the printer driver file for your printer from the original Minitab diskettes into the Minitab directory on your hard disk.
"*ERROR* Unknown object in worksheet" encountered after a RETRIEVE of a Student Edition Release 8 worksheet in Release 1 of The Student Edition of Minitab.	The Student Edition Release 8 worksheets contain Data screen information that was not used in Release 1.	Ignore this message.

"You need 580K of disk space to run a plot" encountered when you try to create a high-resolution graph, even though before you started Minitab you had over 2 MB of disk space available.	You may be running Windows, which uses hard disk space for file swapping. Although it appeared as if you had enough space for Minitab, Windows used that space at the time you attempted the graph.	Create more available space on your hard disk. Increasing RAM will also help because Windows will then require less disk space for file swapping.

The following table discusses problems you may encounter that do not produce error messages.

Symptom	Cause	Action
High-resolution graphics output is distorted or unreadable.	The current screen, printer, or plotter graphics driver is not the correct driver or is not the best driver for your graphics device.	Use MSETUP to select a different screen, printer, or plotter driver. Try driver files for similar devices.
The Hercules Monochrome Graphics driver does not work with the Hercules Monochrome graphics board.	The Hercules Monochrome graphics board is in half-page mode while Minitab expects it to be in full-page mode.	Set the graphics board to full-page mode by entering HGC FULL at the DOS prompt.

Any of the following: 1) no blinking cursor on the screen; 2) bands or bars of reverse video on the screen; 3) larger or smaller than normal characters in the screen; 4) completely blank screen.	The activity that you were performing (often graphics-related) inadvertently put the screen in the wrong mode.	Return the screen to the normal mode. At the DOS prompt, enter: MODE C080 (for color monitors) or MODE BW80 (for monochrome monitors).
Either of the following: 1) Minitab exits to DOS, or 2) your computer locks up.	You may have an OUTFILE or JOURNAL file open to a floppy disk with no available space.	Make sure the floppy disk on which you want to write an OUTFILE or JOURNAL has enough space for the file.
When your Minitab directory is not on the PATH and you attempt to run Minitab from a directory other than your Minitab directory by typing \MINITAB\MINITAB, you get the DOS message: "Bad command or file name."	The batch file MINITAB.BAT calls the true Minitab executable file, MTB8_S.EXE, which cannot be found because it is not in the current directory or on the path.	Do one of the following: 1) modify the MINITAB.BAT file to read: C:\MINITAB\MTB8_S . . . and place MINITAB.BAT in a directory that is on your PATH, or 2) put the Minitab directory on your PATH.
Pressing the PrintScreen key causes the printer to do strange things.	Minitab's new menu interface uses the extended ASCII character set and some printers can't handle this extended set.	Don't use PrintScreen.

Minitab hangs the computer or aborts with a MATH error.	There are several potential causes for this behavior, all of them originating with inconsistencies or misconfigurations within the particular computer's hardware, BIOS and/or DOS. These are: 1) a math coprocessor is installed, but a dipswitch is set incorrectly, indicating that a coprocessor is NOT installed; 2) the operating speed of the math coprocessor is not compatible with the speed of the math processor. 3) there is a bug in MS-DOS 3.2 that manifests itself during certain floating point operations. 4) there is an incompatibility in your ROM-BIOS. 5) Your version of DOS is "mismatched."	For each of the above causes, try the following: 1) Check your hardware manual to see if there is a dipswitch that must be set for a coprocessor. 2) Check your hardware manual to make sure that the operating speed of your processor and coprocessor are compatible. Some machines also have switches that allow you to toggle between normal speed and "turbo" speed. Try this. 3) Either update your version of DOS or obtain a "patch" from Microsoft. 4) Update your ROM-BIOS. 5) Try booting your machine from your original DOS diskettes and if your machine doesn't crash during the same Minitab operations that caused it to crash before, then your DOS is probably "mismatched." Reinstall DOS, making sure that it is installed properly. Another test for coprocessor problems is to type at the DOS prompt: C:\>SET N087=8087 NOT USED then run Minitab again and try to make it crash. If it works now where it crashed before, then the problem is probably in your coprocessor hardware setup.
The mouse does not operate when you start Minitab.	Your mouse driver is not properly installed and/or loaded. Even if your mouse works correctly in Windows, the driver must also be loaded correctly for non-Windows applications.	Follow the directions that came with your mouse for correct installation and setup.

A displayed graphic behaves abnormally.	An illegal or unknown pathname used as an argument to the FILE subcommand produces a correct error message and another SUBC> prompt is displayed. If you respond to this SUBC> prompt with a '.' (which nullifies the FILE subcommand), the behavior of the subsequent plot may be problematic.	At the SUBC> prompt, retype the FILE subcommand with a valid pathname or type ABORT.
Minitab cannot print a graphic on a HP LaserJet Series II connected to a serial port, COM1.	The driver for the HP LaserJet Series II printer (AHDLJTP.PRN) requires that the printer be connected to the parallel port, LPT1.	Use the HP LaserJet Series II driver, connect the printer to a serial port, COM1, and use the DOS MODE command to redirect output from LPT1 to COM1. Enter the MODE command as follows: MODE LPT1:=COM1:

APPENDIX E

Student Edition Limits and Drivers

This appendix contains lists of the software features that are contained in the professional version of Minitab, but that are not included in this Student Edition package. It also lists the screen and printer drivers that are included in the Student Edition.

Student Edition Limits

The following is a summary of the Minitab Release 8 features that are not included in the Student Edition:

- CORR storage to matrix
- COVARIANCE storage or matrix
- The following REGRESS subcommands:
  - WEIGHTS
  - MSE
  - XPXINV
  - RMATRIX
  - HI
  - TRESIDUALS
  - COOKD
  - DFITS
  - VIF
  - PURE
  - XLOF
  - TOLERANCE
- BREG

The following ANOVA subcommands:
  RANDOM
  EMS
  TEST
  RESTRICT
ANCOVA
GRID
CONTOUR
FFDESIGN
FFACTORIAL
GLM
all multivariate commands
MOOD
FRIEDMAN
The following TABLE subcommand:
  LAYOUT
The following TALLY subcommand:
  STORE
LVALS
MPOLISH
PBDESIGN
RLINE
RSMOOTH
CPLOT
CTABLE
QCMACROS
RREG
ROOTOGRAM
The following subcommands for RANDOM, PDF, CDF, AND INVCDF:
  BETA
  CAUCHY
  LAPLACE
  LOGISTIC
  LOGNORMAL
  EXPONENTIAL
  GAMMA
  WEIBULL
Matrix commands, including READ, PRINT, ERASE, COPY, ADD, SUBTRACT, and MULTIPLY involving matrices.

Screen and Printer Drivers Supplied with The Student Edition of Minitab

Screen Drivers

Driver	File	
ATI VGA Wonder	AHDATIP.DSP	800 600
Generic IBM-compatible CGA	AHDIBMG.DSP	640 200
Generic IBM-compatible EGA	AHDIBME.DSP	640 350
Generic Monochrome VGA	AHDIBMP.DSP	640 480
Generic Color VGA	AHDIBMV.DSP	640 480
Hercules Monochrome Graphics	AHDHERC.DSP	720 348
IBM Color Graphics Adapter	AHDIBM.DSP	640 200
Everex Viewpoint VGA	AHDEVGP.DSP	800 600
Orchid Technology Designer VGA	AHDVPLN.DSP	800 600
Orchid Technology Designer 800	AHDVPLN.DSP	800 600
Paradise VGA Professional	AHDPARP.DSP	800 600
Prism Elan, Elite, and Eclipse VGA	AHDPSMP.DSP	800 600
Toshiba T3100	AHDTOSH.DSP	640 400
Tseng Labs ET-3000 Extended VGA	AHDVPLN.DSP	800 600
Tseng Labs ET-4000 Extended VGA	AHDTL4P.DSP	800 600

Printer Drivers

Driver	File
CalComp ColorView 5913	AHDCLVW.PRT
Canon LBP-8 and 8III	AHDCNA2.PRT
Epson-Compatible 8-pin Color	AHDCO8.PRT
Epson-Compatible 8-pin B/W	AHDBW8.PRT
Epson-Compatible 24-pin Color	AHDCO24.PRT
Epson-Compatible 24-pin B/W	AHDBW24.PRT
Epson GQ-3500	AHDEPGQ.PRT
HP DeskJet	AHDDJET.PRT
HP LaserJet+ and Series II	AHDLJTP.PRT
HP LaserJet Series III	AHDLJTP.PRT
HP Paint Jet	AHDPJET.PRT
HP PaintJet XL	AHDPJXL.PRT
IBM PC Graphics Printer	AHDBW8.PRT
IBM ProPrinter	AHDBW8.PRT
Kodak Diconix 150 Plus	AHDDCNX.PRT
Okidata Microline 192/193 Plus	AHDOKIP.PRT

Panasonic KXP4450	AHDPA44.PRT
PostScript Compatible	AHDPSCT.PRT
Ricoh PC Laser 6000	AHDRCPC.PRT
Seiko CH-5504	AHDSI04.PRT
Sharp JX-720	AHDSHRP.PRT
Sharp JX-730	AHDSH73.PRT
Tektronix 4693D/DX	AHDTK93.PRT
Tektronix 4696	AHDTK96.PRT
Tektronix ColorQuick (4697)	AHDTK97.PRT
Toshiba P1351 and P351	AHDTOSH.PRT
Xerox 4020	AHDXJET.PRT

Plotter Support

Driver	File
PostScript Device	AHDPS.EXE

APPENDIX F

Statistical Reference Texts and Companion Textbooks

Textbooks for General Statistics

Blaisdell, Ernest A. *Minitab Supplement for Introduction to Statistics.* Philadelphia: W. B. Saunders, 1992.

Bond, Kenneth M., and James P. Scott. *MINITAB Student Supplement to Accompany Elementary Statistics.* 5th ed. Boston: PWS-Kent Publishing, 1988.

Brase, Charles, and Corrine Brase. *Understandable Statistics: Concepts and Methods.* 4th ed. Lexington, MA: D.C. Heath, 1991.

Byrkit, Donald. *Statistics Today: A Comprehensive Introduction.* Menlo Park, CA: Benjamin/Cummings Publishing Company, 1987.

Devore, Jay, and Roxy Peck. *Introductory Statistics.* St. Paul, MN: West Publishing Company, 1990.

Dietrich, Frank, and Thomas Kearns. *Basic Statistics: An Inferential Approach.* 3rd ed. San Francisco: Dellen Publishing Company, 1989.

Freund, John. *Modern Elementary Statistics.* 7th ed. Englewood Cliffs, NJ: Prentice Hall, 1988.

Freund, John. *Statistics: A First Course.* Englewood Cliffs, NJ: Prentice Hall, 1986.

Gitlow, Howard S., and Rosa Oppenheim. *Stat City: Understanding Statistics Through Realistic Applications.* 2nd ed. Homewood, IL: Richard D. Irwin Publishing, 1986.

Goldman, Robert, and Joel Weinberg. *Statistics: An Introduction.* Englewood Cliffs, NJ: Prentice Hall, 1985.

Goldman, Robert, and John McKenzie. *Minitab Supplement to Statistics: An Introduction.* Englewood Cliffs, NJ: Prentice Hall, 1986.

Groeneveld, Richard. *Introductory Statistical Methods: An Integrated Approach Using MINITAB.* Boston: PWS-Kent Publishing, 1989.

Groves, John E. *Introductory Statistics (Solutions Manuals).* St. Paul, MN: West Publishing Company, 1990.

Hernon, Peter. *Statistics for Library Decision Making.* Norwood, NJ: Ablex Publishing Company, 1989.

Hoaglin, David, Frederick Mosteller, and John Tukey. *Exploring Data Table Trends and Shapes.* New York: John Wiley & Sons, Inc., 1985.

Johnson, Robert. *Elementary Statistics.* 5th ed. Boston: PWS-Kent Publishing, 1988.

Judd, Charles, and Gary McClelland. *Data Analysis: A Model-Comparison Approach.* Orlando, FL: Harcourt Brace Jovanovich, Inc., 1989.

Khazanie, Ramakant, and William Lennox. *Elementary Statistics in a World of Applications.* 3rd ed. Glenview, IL: Scott, Foresman and Company, 1990.

Kleinbaum, David, Lawrence Kupper, and Keith Muller. *Applied Regression Analysis and Other Multivariable Methods.* 2nd ed. Boston: PWS-Kent Publishing, 1988.

Knudsen, Jon. *Innforing I Minitab.* Norwegian University Press, 1990.

Koopmans, Lambert. *Introduction to Contemporary Statistical Methods.* 2nd ed. Boston: PWS-Kent Publishing, 1987.

Lillestrol, Jostein. *Sannsynlighetsregning og Statistikk.* 4th ed. Norwegian School of Economics & Bus. Ad., 1991.

Lillestrol, Jostein. *Statistisk Dataanalyse Med PC.* 2nd ed. Norwegian School of Economics & Bus. Ad., 1989.

Mansfield, Edwin. *Basic Statistics with Applications.* New York: W. W. Norton & Company, 1986.

Mendenhall, William. *Introduction to Probability and Statistics.* 8th ed. Boston: PWS-Kent Publishing, 1991.

Meyer, Ruth K., and David D. Krueger. *Minitab Computer Supplement to Accompany Statistics by Example.* San Francisco: Dellen Publishing Company, 1991.

Moore, David, and George McCabe. *Introduction to the Practice of Statistics.* New York: W. H. Freeman, 1989.

Morris, Clare. *Quantitative Approaches in Business Studies.* 2nd ed. Pitman, 1989.

Ott, R. Lyman, and William Mendenhall. *Understanding Statistics.* 5th ed. Boston: PWS-Kent Publishing, 1990.

Ott, R. Lyman. *An Introduction to Statistical Methods and Data Analysis.* 3rd ed. Boston: PWS-Kent Publishing, 1988.

Owen, William, and W. F. Cutlip. *Finite Mathematics.* Orlando, FL: Harcourt Brace Jovanovich, 1991.

Round, David. *Statistics Resource Book.* New York: John Wiley & Sons, Inc., 1988.

Ryan, Barbara, Brian Joiner, and Thomas Ryan. *Minitab Handbook.* 2nd ed. Boston: PWS-Kent Publishing, 1985.

Salvia, Anthony A. *Introduction to Statistics.* Philadelphia: W. B. Saunders, 1990.

Sanders, Donald H. *Statistics: A Fresh Approach.* 4th ed. New York: McGraw-Hill Publishing Company, 1990.

Scheaffer, Richard, and Lyman Ott. *Elementary Survey Sampling.* 4th ed. Boston: PWS-Kent Publishing, 1990.

Sincich, Terry. *Computer Supplement to Statistics by Example.* 3rd ed. San Francisco: Dellen Publishing Company, 1987.

Sincich, Terry. *Statistics by Example.* 4th ed. San Francisco: Dellen Publishing Company, 1990.

Statistics: An Inferential Approach. 3rd ed. San Francisco: Dellen Publishing Company, 1989.

Staudte, Robert G. *Seeing, Through Statistics.* Englewood Cliffs, NJ: Prentice Hall, 1990.

Tanner, Martin. *Investigations for a Course in Statistics.* New York: Macmillan Publishing Company, 1990.

Weiss, Neil A. *Elementary Statistics.* Reading, MA: Addison-Wesley Publishing Company, 1989.

Weiss, Neil A. *Minitab Supplement to Accompany Elementary Statistics.* Reading, MA: Addison-Wesley Publishing Company, 1989.

Weiss, Neil, and Matthew Hassett. *Introductory Statistics.* 3rd ed. Reading, MA: Addison-Wesley Publishing Company, 1991.

Weiss, Neil. *Minitab Supplement to Accompany Weiss/Hassett Introductory Statistics.* 2nd ed. Reading, MA: Addison-Wesley Publishing Company, 1987.

Williams, Thomas A., Dennis J. Sweeney, and David R. Anderson. *Statistics: Concepts and Applications.* St. Paul, MN: West Publishing Company, 1986.

Textbooks for Academic Disciplines

Behavioral Sciences

Couch, James V. *Fundamentals of Statistics for the Behavioral Sciences.* 2nd ed. St. Paul, MN: West Publishing Company, 1987.

Gravetter, Frederick, and Larry B. Wallnau. *Essentials of Statistics for the Behavioral Sciences.* St. Paul, MN: West Publishing Company, 1991.

Gravetter, Frederick J., and Larry B. Wallnau. *Statistics for the Behavioral Sciences.* 2nd ed. St. Paul, MN: West Publishing Company, 1988.

Gravetter, Frederick J. *Study Guide to Accompany Statistics for the Behavioral Sciences.* 2nd ed. St. Paul, MN: West Publishing Company, 1988.

Hildebrand, David. *Statistical Thinking for Behavioral Scientists.* Boston: PWS-Kent Publishing, 1986.

Howell, David. *Fundamental Statistics for the Behavioral Sciences.* Boston: PWS-Kent Publishing, 1989.

Howell, David. *Statistical Methods for Psychology.* 2nd ed. Boston: PWS-Kent Publishing, 1987.

Marascuilo, Leonard A., and Ronald Serlin. *Statistical Methods for the Social and Behavioral Sciences.* New York: W. H. Freeman, 1988.

Pagano, Robert. *Understanding Statistics in the Behavioral Sciences.* 2nd ed. St. Paul, MN: West Publishing Company, 1986.

Sax, Gilbert, and Robert Hess. *Principles of Educational and Psychological Measurement and Evaluation.* 3rd ed. Belmont, CA: Wadsworth Publishing Company, 1989.

Serlin, Ronald. *Minitab Manual to Accompany Statistical Methods for the Social and Behavioral Sciences.* New York: W. H. Freeman, 1989.

Wallnau, Larry B., and Frederick J. Gravetter. *Instructor's Manual with Test Bank and Solutions to Accompany Statistics for Behavioral Sciences.* 2nd ed. St. Paul, MN: West Publishing Company, 1988.

West, Robert. *Computing for Psychologists Statistical Analysis Using SPSS and MINITAB.* New York: Gordon and Breach Science Publishers, 1991.

Biological Sciences

Dawson-Saunders, Beth, and Robert Trapp. *Basic and Clinical Biostatistics.* East Norwalk, CN: Appleton & Lange Publishing Company, 1989.

Glantz, Stanton A., and Bryan K. Slinker. *Primer of Applied Regression and Analysis of Variance.* New York: McGraw-Hill Publishing Company, 1990.

Business

Aczel, Amir. *Complete Business Statistics.* Homewood, IL: Richard D. Irwin, Inc., 1989.

Allen, Andrew T., and Denise Dimon. *Using Minitab with Statistics: Principles and Applications.* Glenview, IL: Scott, Foresman and Company, 1989.

Bancroft, Gordon, and B. O'Sullivan. *Math and Statistics for Accounting and Business Studies.* 2nd ed. New York: McGraw-Hill Publishing Company, 1989.

Bechtold, Brigitte. *Statistics for Business and Economics.* Boston: PWS-Kent Publishing, 1989.

Bell, Peter C., and Peter Newson. *Statistics for Business with MINITAB Text and Cases.* Redwood City, CA: Scientific Press, 1987.

Berenson, Mark, and David Levine. *Statistics for Business and Economics.* Englewood Cliffs, NJ: Prentice Hall, 1989.

Bond, Kenneth M., and James P. Scott. *Essential Business Statistics: A Minitab Framework.* Boston: PWS-Kent Publishing, 1988.

Bond, Kenneth M,. and James Scott. *Minitab Student Supplement to Accompany Elementary Statistics for Business.* 2nd ed. Boston: PWS-Kent Publishing, 1985.

Bond, Kenneth M., and Lori Tanaka. *Instructor Manual for Essential Business Statistics: A Minitab Framework.* Boston: PWS-Kent Publishing, 1988.

Bridge, John. *Managerial Decisions with the Microcomputer.* Philip Allan Publisher Ltd., 1989.

Brown, William. *Introducing Econometrics.* St. Paul, MN: West Publishing Company, 1991.

Campbell, Stephen. *Applied Business Statistics: Text, Problems, and Cases.* New York: Harper & Row Publishers, 1987.

Chen, Shaw K. *Study Guide to Accompany Statistical Analysis for Decision Making.* Needham, MA: Allyn and Bacon, Inc., 1989.

Cooke, William. *Quantitative Methods for Management Decisions.* New York: McGraw-Hill Publishing Company, 1984.

Croucher, John S. *Introductory Mathematics and Statistics for Business.* New York: McGraw-Hill Publishing Company, 1989.

Cryer, Jonathan, and Robert Miller. *Statistics for Business: Data Analysis and Modeling.* Boston: PWS-Kent Publishing, 1991.

Cutshall, Rex R. *Business Statistics: Microcomputer Experiences Using Minitab.* Boston: PWS-Kent Publishing, 1989.

Dielman, Terry. *Applied Regression Analysis for Business and Economics.* Boston: PWS-Kent Publishing, 1991.

Hildebrand, David, and Lyman Ott. *Statistical Thinking for Managers.* 3rd ed. Boston: PWS-Kent Publishing, 1991.

Hirschey, Mark. *Managerial Economics, Computer Supplement.* 6th ed. Dryden Press, 1990.

Iman, Ronald, and W.J. Conover. *Minitab Manual: Modern Business Statistics.* 2nd ed. New York: John Wiley & Sons, Inc., 1989.

Iman, Ronald, and W.J. Conover. *Modern Business Statistics.* 2nd ed. New York: John Wiley & Sons, Inc., 1989.

Ingram, John, and Joseph Monks. *Introductory Statistics for Business.* Orlando, FL: Harcourt Brace Jovanovich, Inc., 1989.

Jarrell, Stephen. *Basic Business Statistics.* 2nd ed. Needham, MA: Allyn and Bacon, Inc., 1990.

Jarrett, Jeffrey, and Arthur Kraft. *Statistical Analysis for Decision Making.* Needham, MA: Allyn and Bacon, Inc., 1989.

Johnson, Aaron, Marvin B. Johnson, and Rueben C. Buse. *Econometrics: Basic and Applied.* New York: Macmillan Publishing Company, 1987.

Johnson, Robert. *Elementary Statistics for Business.* 2nd ed. Boston: PWS-Kent Publishing, 1985.

Kazmier, Leonard J., *Business Statistics (Schaums Outline Series).* 2nd ed. New York: McGraw-Hill Publishing Company, 1988.

Kenkel, James. *Introductory Statistics for Management and Economics.* 3rd ed. Boston: PWS-Kent Publishing, 1989.

Kvanli, Alan, and Wilke English. *Study Guide to Accompany Introduction to Business Statistics: A Computer Integrated Approach.* St. Paul, MN: West Publishing Company, 1986.

Kvanli, Alan, C. Stephen Guynes, and Robert Pavur. *Introduction to Business Statistics: A Computer Integrated Approach.* St. Paul, MN: West Publishing Company, 1989.

Lapin, Lawrence L. *Statistics for Modern Business Decisions.* 5th ed. Orlando, FL: Harcourt Brace Jovanovich, Inc., 1990.

Lerman, Zvi, Ben Horim, and H. Levy. *Statistics: Decisions and Applications in Business and Economics.* 2nd ed. New York: Random House, 1988.

Levine, David, and Mark Berenson. *Basic Business Statistics: Concepts and Applications.* 4th ed. Englewood Cliffs, NJ: Prentice-Hall, 1989.

Levine, David, Mark Berenson, and David Stephan. *Using Minitab for Business Statistics.* Englewood Cliffs, NJ: Prentice-Hall, 1989.

Mansfield, Edwin. *Statistics for Business and Economics: Methods and Applications.* 3rd ed. New York: W. W. Norton & Company, 1987.

Mason, Robert D. *Statistical Techniques in Business and Economics.* 7th ed. Homewood, IL: Richard D. Irwin Publishing, 1990.

McClave, James, and Frank Dietrich. *A First Course in Statistics.* 3rd ed. San Francisco: Dellen Publishing Company, 1989.

McClave, James, and Frank Dietrich. *Statistics.* 4th ed. San Francisco: Dellen Publishing Company, 1988.

McClave, James, and G. Benson. *A First Course in Business Statistics.* 4th ed. San Francisco: Dellen Publishing Company, 1989.

McClave, James, and G. Benson. *Statistics for Business and Economics.* 4th ed. San Francisco: Dellen Publishing Company, 1988.

Meek, Gary E., Howard L. Taylor, Kenneth A. Dunning, and Keith A. Klafehn. *Business Statistics.* Needham, MA: Allyn and Bacon, Inc., 1987.

Mendenhall, William, and Terry Sincich. *A Second Course in Business Statistics: Regression Analysis.* 3rd ed. San Francisco: Dellen Publishing Company, 1989.

Mendenhall, William, James Reinmuth, and Robert Beaver. *Statistics for Management and Economics.* 6th ed. Boston: PWS-Kent Publishing, 1989.

Mendenhall, William. *A Course in Business Statistics.* Boston: PWS-Kent Publishing, 1984.

Meyer, Ruth K. and David D. Krueger. *Minitab Computer Supplement to Accompany A First Course in Business Statistics.* 4th ed. San Francisco: Dellen Publishing Company, 1989.

Meyer, Ruth K., and David D. Krueger. *Minitab Computer Supplement to Accompany A First Course in Statistics.* 3rd ed. San Francisco: Dellen Publishing Company, 1989.

Meyer, Ruth K., and David D. Krueger. *Minitab Computer Supplement to Accompany Statistics for Business and Economics.* 4th ed. San Francisco: Dellen Publishing Company, 1988.

Meyer, Ruth K., and David D. Krueger. *Minitab Computer Supplement to Accompany Statistics.* 4th Ed. Dellen Publishing Company, 1988.

Meyer, Ruth K., and David D. Krueger. *Minitab Handbook for Business Statistics.* San Francisco: Dellen Publishing Company, 1988.

Miller, Robert B. *Minitab Handbook for Business and Economics.* Boston: PWS-Kent Publishing, 1988.

Monks, Joseph, and B Newton. *Statistics for Business.* 2nd ed. New York: Macmillan Publishing Company, 1987.

Nebebe, Fassil. *Statistics with Minitab.* Needham, MA: Ginn Press, 1990.

Neter, John, William Wasserman, and Michael H. Kutner. *Applied Linear Statistical Models.* 3rd ed. Homewood, IL: Richard D. Irwin Publishing, 1990.

Olson, Charles, and Mario Picconi. *Statistics for Business Decision Making.* Glenview, IL: Scott, Foresman and Company, 1984.

Oltman, Debra, and James Lackritz. *Statistics for Business and Economics.* Pacific Groves, CA: Brooks/Cole Publishing Company, 1991.

Pappas, J. L., and Mark Hirschey. *Managerial Economics.* 6th ed. Dryden Press, 1990.

Perles, Benjamin, John Freund, and Frank Williams. *Elementary Business Statistics: The Modern Approach.* 5th ed. Englewood Cliffs, NJ: Prentice Hall, 1988.

Pfaffenberger, Roger, and James Patterson. *Statistical Methods for Business and Economics.* 3rd ed. Homewood, IL: Richard D. Irwin Publishing, 1987.

Roberts, Harry. *Data Analysis for Managers with Minitab.* 2nd ed. Redwood City, MA: Scientific Press, 1991.

Romano, Albert, Mario Picconi, and Charles Olson. *Statistics: Principles and Applications.* Glenview, IL: Scott, Foresman and Company, 1983.

Shannon, Patrick, and David Groebner. *Business Statistics: A Decision-Making Approach.* 3rd ed. Columbus, OH: Merrill Publishing Company, 1989.

Siegel, Andrew F. *Practical Business Statistics with Statpad.* Homewood, IL: Richard D. Irwin Publishing, 1990.

Soskin, Mark D. *Using Minitab with Statistics for Business and Economics.* 3rd ed. New York: W. W. Norton & Company, 1987.

Toh, Rex, and Michael Hu. *Basic Business Statistics: An Intuitive Approach.* St. Paul, MN: West Publishing Company, 1991.

Trower, Jonathan K. *Introduction to Statistics on Minitab.* Columbus, OH: Merrill Publishing Company, 1988.

Trower, Jonathan K. *Using Minitab for Introductory Statistical Analysis.* Columbus, OH: Merrill Publishing Company, 1989.

Wells, Jane. *Using Minitab with Statistics for Business Decision Making.* Glenview, IL: Scott, Foresman and Company, 1984.

Wonnacott, Thomas, and Ronald Wonnacott. *Introductory Statistics for Business & Economics.* 4th ed. New York: John Wiley & Sons, Inc., 1990.

Engineering

Devore, Jay. *Probability and Statistics for Engineering and the Sciences.* 3rd ed. Pacific Groves, CA: Brooks/Cole Publishing Company, 1990.

Dougherty, Edward R. *Probability and Statistics for Engineers and Computer Scientists.* Englewood Cliffs, NJ: Prentice-Hall Publishing Inc., 1990.

Lochner, Robert, and Joseph Matar. *Designing for Quality the Best of Taguchi and Western Experimental Designs.* Quality Resources, 1991.

Mendenhall, William, and Terry Sincich. *Statistics for the Engineering and Computer Sciences.* 2nd ed. San Francisco: Dellen Publishing Company, 1984.

Miller, Irwin, John Freund, and Richard Johnson. *Probability and Statistics for Engineers.* 4th ed. Englewood Cliffs, NJ: Prentice-Hall, 1990.

Scheaffer, Richard, and James McClave. *Probability and Statistics for Engineers.* 3rd ed. Boston: PWS-Kent Publishing, 1990.

Health Sciences

Breckenridge, Mary B., and R.C. Like. *Community-Oriented Primary Care: From Principle to Practice.* Washington, DC: US Government Printing Offices, 1987.

Daniel, Wayne W. *Biostatistics: A Foundation for Analysis in the Health Sciences.* 5th ed. New York: John Wiley & Sons, Inc., 1991.

Mathematics

Allen, Arnold O. *Probability, Statistics and Queuing Theory with Computer Science Applications.* 2nd ed. New York: Academic Press, 1989.

Blaisdell, Ernest A. *Minitab Supplement for Statistics and Probability in Modern Life.* Philadelphia: W. B. Saunders, 1988.

Fox, William, Frank Giordano, Stephen Maddox, and Maurice Weir. *Mathematical Modeling With Minitab.* Pacific Groves, CA: Brooks/Cole Publishing Company, 1987.

Freund, John. *Mathematical Statistics.* 4th ed. Englewood Cliffs, NJ: Prentice Hall, 1987.

Giordano, Frank, and Maurice Weir. *A First Course in Mathematical Modeling.* Pacific Groves, CA: Brooks/Cole Publishing Company, 1990.

Kitchens, Larry. *Exploring Statistics: A Modern Introduction to Data Analysis & Inference.* St. Paul, MN: West Publishing Company, 1987.

Kvanli, Alan. *Statistics: A Computer Integrated Approach.* 2nd ed. St. Paul, MN: West Publishing Company, 1988.

Newmark, Joseph. *Statistics and Probability in Modern Life.* 4th ed. Philadelphia: W. B. Saunders, 1988.

Triola, Mario. *Elementary Statistics.* 4th ed. Menlo Park, CA: Benjamin/Cummings Publishing Company, 1989.

Triola, Mario. *Minitab Statistical Software Student Laboratory Manual and Workbook.* Menlo Park, CA: Benjamin/Cummings Publishing Company, 1989.

Social Sciences

Anderson, Ted, and Stanley Sclove. *Statistical Analysis of Data.* 2nd ed. Redwood City, CA: Scientific Press, 1986.

Anderson, Ted, and Barrett Eynon. *MINITAB Fundamental/RW Software for Students and MINITAB Guide to The Statistical Analysis of Data.* Redwood City, CA: Scientific Press, 1987.

Anderson, Ted, and Barrett Eynon. *Minitab Guide to the Statistical Analysis of Data.* Redwood City, CA: Scientific Press, 1986.

Anderson, Ted, and Stanley Sclove. *Solutions Manual for The Statistical Analysis of Data.* 2nd ed. Redwood City, CA: Scientific Press, 1986.

Monk, Andrew. *Exploring Statistics with Minitab: A Workbook for the Behavioral Sciences.* New York: John Wiley & Sons, Inc., 1991.

Ott, R. Lyman, Richard Larson, and William Mendenhall. *Statistics: A Tool for the Social Sciences.* 4th ed. Boston: PWS-Kent Publishing, 1983.

Pedhazur, Elazar, and Liora Pedhazur Schmelkin. *Measurement, Design, and Analysis: An Integrated Approach.* Hillsdale, NJ: Lawrence Erlbaum Associates, 1991.

Richardson, John, and Peter Hernon. *Microcomputer Software for Performing Statistical Analysis: A Handbook for Supporting Library Decision Making.* Norwood, NJ: Ablex Publishing Company, 1988.

Other

Staudte, Robert G. and Simon Sheather. *Robust Estimation and Testing.* New York: John Wiley & Sons, Inc., 1990.

Credits

MINITAB at Work acknowledgments:

Trees: Allegheny National Forest; photo courtesy of George Bellerose/Stock, Boston
Infant Mortality: From testimony presented to the Atomic Energy Commission, 1971; photo courtesy of Virginia L. Blaisdell/Stock, Boston
Pizza: Survival of Selected Indicator and Pathogenic Bacteria in Refrigerated Pizzas, Journal of Food Protection, Vol. 50, No. 10, October 1987, pp. 859–861; photo courtesy of Kristen M. Duerr, 1991
Supernovas: Roger Johnson, David Spenny, and Tony Forest, *The Distribution of Supernova Remnants in the Large Magellanic Cloud,* Publications of the Astronomical Society of the Pacific, 100:683–686, June 1988; photo courtesy of Elizabeth Hamlin/Stock, Boston
Rock Bass: Douglas Noltie, *A Method for Measuring Reproductive Success in the Rock Bass (Ambloplites rupestris), with Applicability to Other Substrate Brooding Fishes,* Journal of Freshwater Ecology, Vol. 3, No. 3, June 1986; photo courtesy of Douglas Noltie
Prescriptions: Allen Shaughnessy, Ronald O. Nickel, *Prescription-Writing Patterns and Errors in a Family Medicine Residency Program,* The Journal of Family Practice, Vol. 29, No. 3, 1989, pp. 290-295; photo courtesy of Tim Barnwell/Stock, Boston
Aortic Coarctation: Patrick Carey and P. Syamasundar Rao, *Remodeling of the Aorta After Successful Balloon Coarctation Angioplasty,* Journal of American College of Cardiology, Vol. 14, No. 5, Nov. 1, 1989, pp. 1312–1317; photo courtesy of N. R. Rowan/Stock, Boston
Wheat Futures and data set: Albert Parish, *Market Forcasting Models: ARIMA,* Technical Analysis of Stocks & Commodities, October 1990, pp. 88–96; photo courtesy of Jeff Albertson/Stock, Boston
Acid lakes data set courtesy of J. M. Eilers, G. E. Glass, A. K. Pollack, and J. A. Sorensen

INDEX

Special Offer Upgrade Card

You can upgrade to the professional version of MINITAB for only $250

As an exclusive to **Student Edition** users, Minitab offers you the opportunity to upgrade to a professional MINITAB product. Here is what you will get:

A worksheet of 1000 columns, plus as many data values as the memory on your computer will allow

Additional statistical capabilities:

- More regression options, such as best subsets and weighted regression
- More non-parametric procedures
- More quality control functions
- Matrix commands
- More powerful analysis of variance commands, such as general linear models
- Multivariate statistics
- Design of experiments
- More presentation-quality graphics

MINITAB Technical Support:

- MINITAB Technical Reports
- Reduced prices on upgrades to new releases of MINITAB
- Corporate newsletter announcing MINITAB developments
- Invitations to user group meetings
- Access to the MINITAB macro library
- Direct technical support by MINITAB staff
- Free membership in the MINITAB Users Group
- The MINITAB Users Group Newsletter

. . . . and much, much more.

The professional version of MINITAB is a statistical standard throughout business, finance, government, and industry. In virtually any aspect of statistical analysis, MINITAB has come to be differentiated by its ease of use and its simplicity. In no area has this adoption of MINITAB been more rapid than statistical problem solving in connection with quality control. In the manufacturing sector alone, three-quarters of the 50 largest manufacturing firms in America use MINITAB.

All major U.S. auto manufacturers
12 of the largest 15 chemical companies
8 of the largest 10 computer companies
10 of the largest 15 electronics companies
8 of the largest 10 forest product companies

Industry by industry, America's leading manufacturing firms are using MINITAB.

Order Instructions for Special Upgrade Offer for Student Edition Users

Conditions of the offer:

- Offer applies only to single-copy purchases of MINITAB
- Offer valid only on purchases made through MINITAB or an authorized distributor
- Void where prohibited
- This offer subject to change without notice

How to Upgrade Your Copy of MINITAB

1. Fill out the shipping information below.
2. Enclose payment. (Checks should be made out to Minitab Inc., or to the appropriate distributor.)
3. Send the order form, payment, and the original set of Student Edition disks to:

U.S. and Canada
Minitab Inc.
3081 Enterprise Drive
State College, PA 16801
1-800-448-3555

Worldwide
Minitab Inc.
Telephone: 1-814-238-3280
Fax: 1-814-238-4383

Note: Please **do not** write in shaded areas; type or print neatly.

CID ______ PERPETUAL ______

ICO# ______ LICENSE PERIOD ______

DATE ______ CLASS: A C G ______

Shipping Address

Name ______ Title ______
First *Last*

Dept. ______ Organization ______

Address ______ City ______

State/Province/Territory ______ ZIP/Postal Code ______

Country ______ Phone ______ Fax ______

Billing Information

Check: ❑ Payment Enclosed

Credit Card:

❑ Visa—Card No. ______ Exp. Date ______

❑ Mastercard—Card No. ______ Exp. Date ______

Signature ______

❑ WINDOWS (3.5" DISKS) ❑ MACINTOSH (3.5" DISKS) ❑ DOS (3.5" OR 5.25" DISKS)

ITEM	TYPE	DESCRIPTION	DISK SIZE	QUANTITY	UNIT PRICE	TOTAL PRICE	ACCT/SUBACCT
1.				1	$250	$250	
2.				1	$10	$10	

PRODUCT TOTAL	$250.00
SHIPPING & HANDLING	$10.00
IN PA, ADD 6% SALES TAX	
GRAND TOTAL	

ISBN 0-201-95373-0